Lordship and Society
in the March of Wales
1282–1400

Lordship and Society
in the March of Wales
1282–1400

R. R. DAVIES

1478
1978

CLARENDON PRESS · OXFORD

Oxford University Press, Walton Street, Oxford OX2 6DP

OXFORD LONDON GLASGOW NEW YORK
TORONTO MELBOURNE WELLINGTON CAPE TOWN
IBADAN NAIROBI DAR ES SALAAM LUSAKA ADDIS ABABA
KUALA LUMPUR SINGAPORE JAKARTA HONG KONG TOKYO
DELHI BOMBAY CALCUTTA MADRAS KARACHI

© Oxford University Press 1978

British Library Cataloguing in Publication Data

Davies, R R
    Lordship and society in the March of Wales,
    1282–1400.
    1. England — Social conditions.   2. Wales —
    Social conditions.
    I. Title
    309.1'424   HN383   77–30177

ISBN 0–19–822454–0

Printed in Great Britain by
Western Printing Services Ltd., Bristol

Preface

The March of Wales in the later middle ages is an exciting and challenging subject for the historian; but it is also one which, to borrow a famous phrase, can scarcely be approached without an effort. It is not difficult to see why. The uneven and inadequate character of the documentation imposes its own constraints on the historian. More seriously, the diversity of the March makes the subject an intractable one: the contrasts in geographical character and historical development between and within the forty or so lordships of the March are often more striking than any common pattern which the historian might detect within them. Indeed it can be argued that the history of the March is no more than the history of its constituent lordships and that what is called for is a series of monographs securely founded on detailed local knowledge and exemplifying the rich diversity of the March. This is certainly one of the most urgent needs of Marcher historiography. Yet it seems to me that there are also questions to be asked about the March and about Marcher lordships and society in general as well as about individual lordships in particular. It is to some of these questions that I have tried to address myself in this book.

Such a general approach runs its own risks and I am well aware that I have not escaped them. The history and individual characteristics of each lordship have been sacrificed in the search for those features which are common to the March as a whole. Some lordships in the March have been favoured at the expense of others in the measure of attention they have received, often inevitably so because of the unevenness of the documentation but sometimes more arbitrarily because of the constraints of time and patience. The plurality of Marcher lordships and the diversity of Marcher society must make the historian more than usually aware of how fragile and provisional are many of his generalizations and how schematic is the pattern which he imposes on the evidence. Nevertheless, I hope that this general approach has its compensations, more especially in directing attention to issues which might be lost sight of in more local studies and in posing questions which will be of interest to the historians of medieval society in general as well as to those of Wales and the March in particular. It will have amply fulfilled its purpose if it helps to place the March of Wales on the agenda of historical discussion and research within and without Wales and persuades other scholars to pose different questions to the Marcher evidence and to provide more satisfying answers.

The reader is entitled to a brief explanation of certain idiosyncracies of style and spelling. The personal and place names of Wales pose a problem for anyone writing in English. Like so many of the men of the medieval March I have chosen the road of compromise, preferring to observe the conventions of modern Welsh orthography where possible but adopting English forms where these (e.g. Abergavenny, Brecon) were and are in general use. This is not a course which recommends itself on grounds of consistency or linguistic purity; but I have assumed that comprehensibility should be the historian's prime concern in these matters. For much the same reason, I have deliberately forsworn the use of Welsh county units, whether of the old (post-1536) or new (post-1973) style, preferring to identify a place by referring to the Marcher lordships in which it was located in medieval times e.g. Wrexham (Bromfield and Yale), rather than Wrexham (formerly Denbighshire, now Clwyd). This may not make for ease of reference on a modern map; but I trust that it is the least cumbersome and most immediately useful course to adopt in terms of this book. In referring to medieval persons, I have taken the liberty of dispensing with 'de' since current practice, sometimes including it (e.g. Gilbert de Clare) or sometimes not (e.g. Roger Mortimer), seems arbitrary. Most seriously, the constraints of modern publishing have compelled me to dispense, especially in Part IV, with some of the supporting and confirmatory evidence on which conviction in a historical argument must often rest.

This book has been so long in the making that many of the debts contracted while writing it have become, in medieval accounting terminology, desperate. I only hope that the creditors will take some consolation that at last those debts are publicly acknowledged. Drs. R. A. Griffiths, D. H. Owen, J. B. Smith, Llinos Smith, and Jennifer Ward have all kindly allowed me to cite their unpublished theses. The secretaries of the Departments of History at University College, London, and University College of Wales, Aberystwyth, have always coped willingly and efficiently with various drafts of the book. Edmund Fryde kindly scrutinized the book in page proof. My greatest debt in respect of the book is to four friends—Ralph Griffiths, David Morgan, Brynmor Pugh, and Glanmor Williams. They all read the original draft of the book and gave generously, indeed extravagantly, of their time and advice. Whatever merits the book may have is largely due to their penetrating comments and that the book was ever completed owes much to their kindness and encouragement. The publication of the book has been made possible through the generosity of two bodies: the British Academy and the Isobel Thornley Bequest (University of London). I thank them both for their generosity and for the confidence they have shown in me and in this book.

Two other debts will, in their different ways, always be outstanding. The one is to the late Bruce McFarlane from whose guidance, friendship, and example I, in common with many of his pupils, still draw inspiration. The other is to my wife and family.

R. R. D.

Contents

List of Maps

NOTE

The medieval March is very well served in terms of maps. For the southern and eastern March there is the truly outstanding work of William Rees, *A Map of South Wales and the Border in the Fourteenth Century* (Southampton: Ordnance Survey. 1932. Four Sheets). For the northern March Melville Richards has provided valuable maps in 'Some Unpublished Source-Material for the History of the Lordships of Denbighshire', *Transactions of the Denbighshire Historical Society* 14 (1965), 197–208. For the lordships of Denbigh and Bromfield and Yale, there are excellent maps in D. H. Owen, 'Tenurial and Economic Developments in North Wales in the Twelfth and Thirteenth Centuries', *Welsh History Review* 6 (1972), 117–42 and A. N. Palmer and E. Owen, *Ancient Tenures of Land in North Wales and the Marches* (2nd edn., 1910) respectively. For more general maps of the March two works are outstandingly helpful: W. Rees, *An Historical Atlas of Wales* (1951 and subsequent editions) and M. Richards, *Welsh Administrative and Territorial Units, Medieval and Modern* (Cardiff, 1969).

Abbreviations

Arch. Camb.	*Archaeologia Cambrensis*
B.B.C.S.	*Bulletin of the Board of Celtic Studies*
B.L.	British Library
B.P.R.	*Register of Edward the Black Prince*
C.A.D.	*Catalogue of Ancient Deeds*
C.C.R.	*Calendar of Close Rolls*
C.Ch.R.	*Calendar of Charter Rolls*
C.F.R.	*Calendar of Fine Rolls*
C.I.P.M.	*Calendar of Inquisitions Post Mortem*
C. Inq. Misc.	*Calendar of Inquisitions Miscellaneous*
C.P.R.	*Calendar of Patent Rolls*
C.W.R.	'Calendar of Welsh Rolls 1277–95' in *Calendar of Chancery Rolls, Various, 1277–1326*
Cal. Anc. Corr. conc. Wales	*Calendar of Ancient Correspondence concerning Wales*
Cal. Chancery Warrants	*Calendar of Chancery Warrants, I, 1244–1326*
Cartae	*Cartae et alia munimenta quae ad dominium de Glamorgancia pertinent*
Cat. MSS. Wales in B.M.	*A Catalogue of the Manuscripts relating to Wales in the British Museum*
E.H.R.	*English Historical Review*
Ec.H.R.	*Economic History Review*
Glam. C.H., III	*Glamorgan County History. Vol. III. The Middle Ages*
Mont. Colls.	*Montgomeryshire Collections*
N.L.W.	National Library of Wales
N.L.W.J.	*National Library of Wales Journal*
Penbrokeshire	George Owen, *The Description of Penbrokeshire*
Rot. Parl.	*Rotuli Parliamentorum*
S.R.O.	Shropshire County Record Office, Shrewsbury
S.B.Y.	Unpublished survey of lordship of Bromfield and Yale, 1391 (together with extracts from fourteenth-century court rolls): B.L. Add. Ms. 10013
S.D.	*Survey of the Honour of Denbigh, 1334*

Staffs. R.O.	Staffordshire County Record Office, Stafford
T.C.S.	*Transactions of the Honourable Society of Cymmro-dorion*
T.D.H.S.	*Transactions of the Denbighshire Historical Society*
T.R.H.S.	*Transactions of the Royal Historical Society*
U.C.N.W.	University College of North Wales
V.C.H.	*The Victoria History of the Counties of England*
W.H.R.	*Welsh History Review*

PUBLIC RECORD OFFICE REFERENCE NUMBERS

(All references to unpublished material relate, unless otherwise specified, to documents at the Public Record Office, London.)

C. 47	Chancery Miscellanea
C. 133–5	Chancery Inquisitions Post Mortem
C.P. 25 (i)	Common Pleas, Feet of Fines
Chester 2	Palatinate of Chester, Enrolments
Chester 25	Palatinate of Chester, Indictment Rolls
D.L. 7	Duchy of Lancaster, Inquisitions Post Mortem
D.L. 10	Duchy of Lancaster, Royal Charters
D.L. 25	Duchy of Lancaster, Ancient Deeds
D.L. 28	Duchy of Lancaster, Accounts Various
D.L. 29	Duchy of Lancaster, Ministers' Accounts
D.L. 30	Duchy of Lancaster, Court Rolls
D.L. 36	Duchy of Lancaster, Cartae Miscellaneae
D.L. 37	Duchy of Lancaster, Chancery Rolls
D.L. 40	Duchy of Lancaster, Returns of Knights' Fees
D.L. 41	Duchy of Lancaster, Miscellanea
D.L. 42	Duchy of Lancaster, Miscellaneous Books
D.L. 43	Duchy of Lancaster, Rentals and Surveys
E. 28	Exchequer, Council and Privy Seal Records
E. 101	Exchequer (King's Remembrancer), Accounts Various
E. 159	Exchequer (King's Remembrancer), Memoranda Rolls
E. 163	Exchequer (King's Remembrancer), Miscellanea
E. 179	Exchequer, Lay Subsidy Rolls
E. 326	Exchequer (Augmentation Office), Ancient Deeds. Series B.
J.I. 1	Justices Itinerant, Assize Rolls
K.B. 27	King's Bench, Plea Rolls
L.R. 2	Exchequer, Auditors of the Land Revenue, Miscellaneous Books
S.C. 2	Special Collections, Court Rolls

S.C. 6   Special Collections, Ministers' Accounts
S.C. 8   Special Collections, Ancient Petitions
S.C. 11   Special Collections, Rentals and Surveys

Map I

The Marcher Lordships of Wales in the Fourteenth Century

Introduction

In January 1250 a royal messenger was dispatched with a letter to Walter Clifford, lord of Clifford, Glasbury and Cantrefselyf and one of the most redoubtable barons of the Welsh March. His journey ended in an extraordinary fashion when Clifford, offended by the tone of the letter, compelled him to swallow the royal message, seal and all.[1] Walter Clifford, it is true, paid heavily for his act of grotesque bravado; but his was not the first nor the last act of defiant impudence by a Marcher lord. A few years later John Fitzalan, lord of Oswestry and Clun, greeted a royal writ with the astounding declaration that 'in the parts of the March where he now resided, he was obliged to do nothing at the king's mandate and nothing would he do'.[2] Incidents such as these served to confirm in the minds of contemporaries the reputation of the March of Wales for extraordinary unruliness and of its lords for 'extreme arrogance and presumption'.[3]

That reputation had been shaped over a long period of time and it was, like all reputations, a compound of fact and fiction. The March was a military frontier and had been so for centuries; as such it became the focus both for the romantic tales and for the chilling fears associated with areas of constant warfare. It was a land fit for heroes, where dashing young knights such as Roger Clifford of Eardisley or John Giffard of Brimpsfield could carve a reputation for themselves and emerge as the prototype of the noble warrior in the *chansons* of the period.[4] The March was one of the few areas where Norman lords could

---

[1] Matthew Paris, *Chronica Majora*, ed. H. R. Luard (Rolls Series, 1872–83), v, 95.

[2] R. W. Eyton, *Antiquities of Shropshire* (1853–60), vii, 257.

[3] The phrase is used by Robert de Torigni of Hugh Mortimer of Wigmore (d. 1181), *Chronicles of the Reigns of Stephen, Henry II and Richard I*, ed. R. Howlett, iv (Rolls Series, 1889), 184.

[4] For Roger Clifford see *Anglo-Norman Political Songs*, ed. I. Aspley (1953), 16–19; and for John Giffard see F. M. Powicke, *King Henry III and the Lord Edward* (Oxford, 1947), 530.

wage private wars without royal reproach; it therefore provided an ideal setting for tales of private feuds and heroic bravery, such as the *Legend of Fulk fitz Warin*. But there was a darker side to the military reputation of the March. It was a country where warfare was so common that deeds were dated by memories of recent invasion[5] and where parishioners recalled with horror 'that the dead in time of war are buried in the fields because the church . . . is so near to Wales that part of the parish belongs to the Welsh and part to the English'.[6] It was a land of war where ruthless mercenaries, such as the merciless Fawkes de Breauté, could be let loose to learn their savage trade uninhibitedly.[7] It was as a land of violence, more particularly of the violence of war, that the March of Wales entered the consciousness of medieval Englishmen. That was part of its reputation.

But the March was more than a frontierland of armies; it was also a frontierland of peoples. It had that exotic quality— once more compounded of inquisitiveness and fear—that all border areas possess. Here peoples of different languages, different cultures, different laws, different customs met. A few men, it is true, could approach the differences with equanimity and with curiosity, as was the case with Gerald of Wales; but for the vast majority of Englishmen, these differences bred suspicion and tension. Wales began in the March; and the Welsh were uncomfortably different, even strange. They were not to be trusted; they were, like acts of God, beyond even the guarantees of law.[8] Englishmen wanted to keep at arm's length from them and nowhere more so than in the March. The men of Chirbury hundred, for example, were afraid of being treated 'as though they were Welshmen'; and the men of Huntington for the same reason insisted that their lordship was in the county

---

[5] See, for example, a deed of Alberbury Priory of 1263: 'regnante Henrico filio regis Johannis, et Lewelyno filio Griffini tunc existente cum Griffino filio Wenunven cum exercitu non modico ad destruendum Marchiam et maxime Rogerum de Mortuomari'. H. Owen and J. B. Blakeway, *History of Shrewsbury* (1825), I, 125–6, n. 4.

[6] This petition of *c.* 1300 is quoted in part in H. J. Hewitt, *Mediaeval Cheshire* (Chetham Society, 1929), 10, n. 3.

[7] Ralph Coggeshall, *Chronicon Anglicanum*, ed. J. Stevenson (Rolls Series, 1875), 204.

[8] Eyton, op. cit. x, 367 for a final concord with a clause of warranty 'versus omnes homines praeter Walenses'. Cf. warranty clause 'maxime contra Walenses' *Cartae*, IV, no. 814.

of Hereford and not in the March.[9] For the March was dis-
concertingly different, an area where one could credibly locate
tales of Gog and Magog[10] but not an area which an Englishman
would visit without trepidation. This fear of the unknown and
the different contributed in good measure to the evil reputation
of the March amongst Englishmen.

But by the fourteenth century that reputation had come above
all to be associated with one word—lawlessness. The king's writ
did not run in the March, and the area thereby lay beyond the
reach of royal justice and of the common law of England. It was
impossible to pursue an offender from England into the March
or to compel a man from the March to answer for an offence
committed in England or against an Englishman. In short, the
protection of the king's law ended at the March. So also did the
concepts of a common law and a single judicial authority, for
each lordship in the March was a self-contained judicial unit.
Each Marcher lord was the final arbiter of justice within his
own lordship, 'life and death, lands and goods', as one sixteenth-
century commentator put it, 'being subject to the pleasure of
peculiar lords'.[11] It was little wonder that the law-abiding
Englishman should regard the March with suspicion, even with
horror, for it clearly lacked the basic judicial safeguards to
which he was accustomed. For him it was a truly lawless
district, a land where criminals could flee with impunity and
whither men and women were abducted to be freed only on
payment of a ransom.[12] Here indeed were the ingredients of an
evil reputation. That reputation was inevitably most persistent
among the inhabitants of the English border counties, for it
was there that the consequences of Marcher lawlessness were
most frequently and immediately felt. The men of the March,
so it was alleged, raided these border counties, burning and
looting, killing or ransoming their victims and then retiring to
the sanctuary of their lordships, where English sheriffs were
powerless to act against them. Likewise, English merchants

[9] Eyton, op. cit. XI, 73; *C. Inq. Misc. 1219–1307*, no. 1870.
[10] 'The Legend of Fulk Fitzwarin' in Coggeshall, *Chronicon Anglicanum*, ed.
Stevenson, 280.
[11] Rice Merrick, *A Booke of Glamorganshire Antiquities*, ed. J. A. Corbett (1887), 88.
[12] For abduction and threats of abduction to the Welsh March see *Year Book 12
Edward II 1319*, ed. J. P. Collas (Selden Society, 1964), 130–2; *Year Book 11
Richard II*, ed. I. D. Thornley (Ames Foundation, 1937), 9; *C.P.R. 1327–30*, 73, 87.

travelling in the March were frequently attacked and their goods seized, but could find no redress for the offences as the area lay beyond the reach of the king's writ.[13] This chorus of protest at Marcher lawlessness increased in volume and attracted much wider support during the Glyn Dŵr rebellion, for that rebellion served to highlight the administrative and judicial anomalies of the March. The March of Wales was now in thoroughly bad odour with English politicians and it only remained for its reputation for lawlessness to be enshrined in parliamentary statute. That was finally achieved in 1536. 'And forasmoche' declared the so-called Act of Union of England and Wales (27 Henry VIII c. 26), 'as there be many and dyvers lordshippes marchers within the said countrey . . . of Wales lieng betwene the Shires of Englande and the Shires . . . of Wales and beyng noo parcelle of any other Shires where the lawes and due correction is used . . . by reason whereof hath . . . bene practised . . . within . . . the said lordshippes . . . dyvers detestable murders, brennyng of houses, robberies, theftes, trespasses, rowtes, riotes . . . And the said offenders theruppon making theyr refuge frome lordeshipp to lordshippe were and contynued without punysshement or correction. . . .' That was the reputation of the March of Wales and it is a reputation which has never been impugned.

Whether the reputation is well-deserved or not is not at issue, for the significance of a reputation is not circumscribed by the limits of its factual basis. What seems to be undeniable is that the reputation has too often stood between the March and serious historical study. Some devotees indeed there have been. The greatest amongst them was also the earliest, George Owen of Henllys (*c.* 1552–1613), whose *Treatise of Lordshipps Marchers in Wales* is one of the few sustained and scholarly books on the subject.[14] His work, for all its faults, was informed by a remarkably clear and cogent mind and supported by tireless research in the public records. His *Treatise* posed many of the vital questions about Marcher history and suggested some of the possible answers. There Marcher historiography stood for

---

[13] *Rot. Parl.*, ii, 397; iii, 81, 272–3, 295, 308, 352–3, 397.

[14] Edited with a superabundance of loving care by Henry Owen in *Penbrokshire*, iii, 127–286. For George Owen's career, see B. G. Charles, *George Owen of Henllys* (Aberystwyth, 1973).

three centuries, for most of the books which dealt with the subject thereafter rifled Owen's *Treatise* in a brazenly unacknowledging manner.[15] In our own century some very notable advances have been made in Marcher history, albeit at a considerable tangent to the questions that exercised George Owen's mind. In a pioneering study Professor William Rees did much to illuminate the social and agrarian history of the area in the fourteenth century,[16] and more recently Mr. T. B. Pugh has contributed very substantially to our understanding of the legal and financial structure of the Marcher lordships in the final century of their history.[17] Geographers, likewise, have been attracted to study the area by the multifarious problems posed by a frontier zone on such issues as settlement- and field-patterns.[18] Paradoxically Marcher studies are perhaps weakest where one would have expected them to be strongest, at the local level. Here again there are inevitably some major exceptions, such as the invaluable collections of source material for Glamorgan and Pembroke,[19] the remarkable studies contributed by local enthusiasts such as A. N. Palmer or Lord Rennell of Rodd,[20] the occasional study of seignorial estates which embraces a Marcher lordship,[21] and, most valuable of all, the recent co-operative history of Glamorgan and Gower in the Middle Ages.[22]

[15] *Penbrokshire*, III, 131–4 n. 1.

[16] *South Wales and the March 1284–1415: A Social and Agrarian Study* (Oxford, 1924). His magnificent *Map of South Wales and the Border in the Fourteenth Century* (4 sheets, 1932) is indispensable for the study of the March.

[17] *The Marcher Lordships of South Wales 1415–1536: Select Documents* (Cardiff, 1963).

[18] Especially Dorothy Sylvester, *The Rural Landscape of the Welsh Borderland: A Study in Historical Geography* (1969). Another valuable geographical introduction to the area is provided by Roy Millward and Adrian Robinson, *The Welsh Marches* (1971).

[19] *Cartae; A Calendar of the Public Records Relating to Pembrokeshire*, ed. H. Owen, 3 vols., Cymmrodorion Record Series 7 (1914–18).

[20] Especially A. N. Palmer and E. Owen, *A History of Ancient Tenures of Land in the Marches of North Wales*, 2nd edn. (Wrexham, 1910); Lord Rennell of Rodd, *Valley on the March: A History of a Group of Manors on the Herefordshire March of Wales* (Oxford, 1958).

[21] Notably the studies of the lordships of Denbigh and Usk which appear in G. A. Holmes, *The Estates of the Higher Nobility in Fourteenth-Century England* (Cambridge, 1957), 93–107.

[22] Edited by T. B. Pugh (Cardiff, 1971). Substantial contributions to the history of individual Marcher lordships have been made in a number of postgraduate theses, notably the following (in chronological order): B. P. Evans, 'The

But, broadly speaking, the March of Wales has not been well
served either by the local studies which are the necessary ground-
work for more general analyses nor by the general studies
which serve to inform local research with a framework of
necessary hypotheses. For Welsh historians the very terminology
of the medieval period has served to put the March at a disadvantage. For the English government, pre-Conquest Wales
was divided into 'pura Wallia', the independent areas of
Wales still ruled by native princes, and the 'marchia Wallie',
the Marchland which had been conquered by Anglo-Norman
lords; and after the Edwardian Conquest this contrast was
largely perpetuated in the distinction drawn between the
Principality (the five counties of Anglesey, Merioneth, Caernarfon, Carmarthen and Cardigan) and the March (the rest of
Wales, with the exception of Flintshire). It is perhaps inevitable
that the history of what is 'pure' and independent should occupy
pride of place in the studies of Welsh historians. The March was
of secondary interest in the evolution of an independent Welsh
political tradition and it has thereby occupied a back-seat in
Welsh historiography. Nor has the March fared much better
at the hands of English historians. Their interest in it is confined
to those periods, such as the years 1258–65 or the reign of
Edward II, when the March impinges directly on English
politics.[23] For the rest they tend to regard Marcher history as
an exercise in historical pathology, in the ills which would have
befallen the body politic of England had it succumbed to the
fragmentation of authority which prevailed in the March.

Beyond such general considerations, there are more particular
reasons for the relatively undeveloped state of historical studies
of the Welsh March. In the first place, the area is notoriously
poor in historical documents of the medieval period. It lay

Family of Mortimer' (University of Wales, Ph.D. thesis, 1934); J. B. Smith, 'The
Lordship of Glamorgan: A Study in Marcher Government' (Univ. of Wales M.A.
thesis, 1958); R. R. Davies, 'The Bohun and Lancaster Lordships in Wales in the
Fourteenth and early Fifteenth Centuries' (Univ. of Oxford D.Phil. thesis, 1965);
D. H. Owen, 'The Lordship of Denbigh 1282–1425' (Univ. of Wales Ph.D. thesis,
1967); Ll. O. W. Smith, 'The Lordships of Chirk and Oswestry, 1282–1415'
(Univ. of London Ph.D. thesis, 1971).

[23] See, in particular, T. F. Tout, 'Wales and the March during the Barons' War
1258–67,' *Collected Papers*, II (Manchester, 1934), 47–101 for the former period; and,
most recently and helpfully, J. R. Maddicott, *Thomas of Lancaster 1307–22* (1970),
for the latter period.

beyond the administrative and judicial ambit of the English government in normal circumstances and therefore its affairs have left little trace in the public records of the period. Such Marcher records as have survived in the government archives came there as a result of the political forfeiture of the lord or the minority of his heir or (as in the case of the Lancaster and Bohun documents) as a consequence of the accession of the lord to the throne of England. Their survival is, accordingly, spasmodic and highly selective. For much of the documentation of the March we must, therefore, turn from the government records to the archives of the great seignorial families who ruled the March. Here we are faced immediately with the fact that many of the seignorial archives of the later Middle Ages have either been totally or partially lost or dispersed. For example, in the case of the great Marcher family of Mortimer we have an interesting cartulary and a unique family chronicle, but the vast majority of the estate and household records no longer survive.[24] The archives of another leading Marcher family, the earls of Arundel, have fared much better, at least at a local level; but even they have been widely dispersed.[25] Such archival accidents inevitably mean that our documentation for the March is both patchy chronologically and uneven geographically. Some of the greatest lordships—such as Glamorgan, Pembroke, Abergavenny and Powys—are notably ill-served by the records, while none of the smaller Marcher families— such as the Brians of Laugharne or the Camvilles of Llanstephan —has left more than a few stray documents.

[24] For the Mortimer Cartulary see Holmes, op. cit. 11, n. 3. There is a further list of Mortimer archives in B.L. Egerton Roll 8723. Three short Mortimer chronicles survive: the longest and most interesting is printed in Sir William Dugdale, *Monasticon Anglicanum*, ed. J. Caley, H. Ellis and B. Bandinel (1817–30), vi, part i, 348–55; a second ending at 1306 is transcribed in B. P. Evans, 'The Family of Mortimer', 486–512; and the third has been edited by John Taylor, 'A Wigmore Chronicle, 1355–77', *Proceedings of the Leeds Philosophical and Literary Society (Literary and Historical Section)*, 11 (1964–6), 84–6. To them may be added the *Chronicon Laudanenses* (B.L. Cotton Nero A. IV) which is also largely focused on the Mortimer family. The most substantial collection of Mortimer accounts is to be found in the Thoresby Park Collection amongst B.L. Egerton Charters and Rolls; but many have strayed into other collections such as the N.L.W. Slebech Collection or U.C.N.W. Whitney Collection.

[25] The most substantial groups of Arundel accounts relating to the March are distributed amongst the following collections: N.L.W., Chirk Castle and Aston Hall; Shrewsbury Public Library, Craven; and S.R.O., Powis and Acton of Aldenham.

The embarrassing sparseness of sources is one of the major problems of Marcher history; the almost equally embarrassing diversity of the March is another. Wherever we touch Marcher history it seems to disintegrate into plurality and to defy the analytical categories of the historian. Geographically the March (or rather the historian's March) is not a compact or unified district; it straddles both the highland and lowland zones of Britain. These geographical contrasts within the March go a large part of the way to explain the historical diversity of the area. In 1300 the March included both lordships which had been under Norman control for over two centuries and districts which had known foreign rule for less than a generation. This contrast was no mere matter of chronology, for it had a profound impact on the pattern of authority and on the social configuration of medieval Wales. The March, for example, comprised districts such as lowland Glamorgan or southern Pembroke where the pattern of feudal tenure was as complex as anywhere in England; it also included lordships such as Maelienydd and Builth where the knight's fee was unknown. It comprised districts such as lowland Radnor or Usk where a heavy overlay of immigrant settlers had been established for centuries; it also embraced areas such as Denbigh or Dyffryn Clwyd where non-Welshmen were a small, recently-introduced minority still largely entrenched behind the walls of castles and boroughs. And so the contrasts within the March could be multiplied. Furthermore they were not merely the contrasts between one district and another, for broadly speaking they were contrasts which were to be found within every Marcher lordship—between upland and lowland Clun, between the Welshry and the Englishry of Radnor, between northern and southern Pembroke. Each lordship had its own march, its own particular variation on the theme of border diversity. Nor does the diversity of the March end there. It was reinforced by the 'constitutional' fragmentation of the March. Each Marcher lordship was an internally sovereign lordship, a law unto itself both literally and metaphorically. There was no common supervisory authority to give an overriding unity to the area. All the attributes of public life were here fragmented into private hands—politics, justice, taxation, law, even warfare. It was a fragmentation which was inherited from the pre-Marcher history of Wales, where authority was essentially decentralized and where *morcellement* was the keynote both of inheritance and of politics.[26] It is a fragmentation which means that, looked at from one angle, the March as such has no history; it is never more than the individual and highly diversified histories of its constituent lordships.

That may be so; but it is not the whole truth. Even the diversity of the March can be turned to the historian's advantage. To study Marcher history is in itself an exercise in comparative history, for the geographical diversity and the uneven pace of historical development within the March serve to highlight both the divergences and the similarities between and even within individual Marcher lordships. Furthermore the historian need not capitulate entirely to the fragmentation of the March, for beneath the infinite variations certain distinctive features are common to the historical development of the area as a whole. It is, in the first place, an area where the concept and content of lordship can be studied more clearly than in any part of England. The March was the sum of its lordships. As a historical category the March was created by its lords; its extent was coterminous with the range of their military power and seignorial authority. Within their lordships, each lord was free to display the power of his authority, his *dominium*, in a form inhibited only by the conventions of the period and by the practical limits on his power. The March is thereby an ideal area for an analysis of the range and character of lordship in medieval society and the more ideal in that the lordship was that of a foreign élite exercised over a native society.

Marcher society—or rather certain facets of it—forms another obvious unifying feature of Marcher history. Marcher society is by definition, a frontier society. 'The Welsh borderland', so the geographers assure us, 'is the hybrid zone *par excellence* in all Britain'.[27] It had been so for centuries before the advent of the Normans. Here the highland and lowland zones of Britain met; and so inevitably did the peoples of England and Wales. What the Normans did was to add a novel, if numerically small, element to the racial chemistry of the March and, above all, a

---

[26] The classic statement of this argument is, of course, provided by J. G. Edwards, 'The Normans and the Welsh March', *Proc. British Academy* 42 (1956), 155–77.

[27] Sylvester, *Rural Landscape of the Welsh Borderland*, 41.

new purposefulness and drive to the military campaigns of the frontier. By 1300 the March of Wales was a time-honoured frontierland indeed: the tides of Anglo-Saxon and Norman, of conqueror and settler had flowed and ebbed across it for at least six centuries. And in the process a distinctively Marcher society had been formed. To say so is not to deny the great contrasts within the social configuration of the March. Striking as these contrasts are, however, they are overridden by the fact that all the March was, in greater or lesser measure, a frontierland of peoples. Within each and every lordship, in varying degrees, there were two peoples—native and settler; the interaction between them—in terms of language, social relations, culture, law, *mores*, land practices and so forth—forms part of the abiding fascination of the March.

Lordship and society in the March form the themes of this book; the fourteenth century is the chronological setting. It is neither the most exciting nor the most formative period of Marcher history: the pioneering days of conquest and settlement, of initial confrontations and compromises lay in the past. But for the first time in centuries the March was at peace; no longer was its history dominated by accounts of military campaigns. With peace came archives. It is in the fourteenth century that the March finally emerges from the pre-scriptive phase of its history and that its documents become sufficiently plentiful, whatever their shortcomings, to allow us to study its governance and society in some measure of depth. Moreover it is a century of momentous importance in the history of the March. The conditions of peace transformed the barons of the March from a race of *conquistadores* who ruled by the sword into lords of men and of land and allowed them to display the range and character of their lordship more extensively than ever before. Marcher society likewise comes more closely within range of historical analysis, for the historian benefits by the anxiety of the Marcher lords to exploit their lordships to the full and to do so with the aid of written surveys, accounts and court-rolls. He is allowed, as it were, to look over the shoulder of the governors of the March and thereby to catch a glimpse of Marcher society. Furthermore the natural calamities of famine and plague in the fourteenth century quickened the tempo of social change and thereby served to highlight those economic and social movements which transformed Marcher society in the later Middle Ages. Lordship and society are our twin themes; but first the March of Wales must be defined and its lords clearly identified.

I

THE MARCH AND ITS LORDS

I   The March

To define the precise extent of the March of Wales in the Middle Ages is a more difficult problem than may at first appear. A measure of geographical imprecision is a characteristic of all marches, for a march is by definition a broad zone on or beyond the frontiers of a country or an ill-defined and contested district between two countries. Such frontier zones are unlikely to have clearly defined boundaries. The March of Wales was no exception: there was no well-defined boundary between England and Wales in the medieval period. If men looked for such a boundary, they could and did on occasion refer to a major landmark such as Offa's Dyke or the River Severn.[1] But even allowing for the hazy geographical knowledge of medieval men—a knowledge, or rather ignorance, which allowed them to refer to Eaton Tregose or Castle Goodrich, both of them well within the bounds of Herefordshire, as being 'in Wales' or 'in the March'[2]—it is clear that neither Offa's Dyke nor the Severn could be regarded as more than a metaphorical boundary. They were the figurative phrases for a boundary that did not in fact exist. Instead of a boundary there was a march. The contemporary phraseology exemplifies this clearly enough: Wigmore is 'on the borders of the county of Hereford' and so likewise is Radnor; Ellesmere is in 'the Welsh march adjoining Shropshire'; Oswestry is in 'the march between England and Wales'; Knighton and Norton are 'in Welshry' and so is Moldsdale.[3] It is the phraseology of imprecision: the March of Wales can only be described, at least by English administrators, in terms of its relationship to English counties.

[1] For references to Offa's Dyke as an administrative or geographical boundary see, for example, *C.P.R. 1232–47*, 18; *Rot. Parl.*, I, 2. In the early fifteenth century men 'born beyond Severn' were officially regarded as being 'in no way Welsh': D.L. 42/15, fol. 170ᵛ.; D.L. 42/16, fol. 40.

[2] D.L. 28/1/10, fol. 6ᵛ; *C.F.R. 1391–9*, 211–12.

[3] *C.I.P.M.*, IV, no. 183; *C.P.R. 1327–30*, 72; B.L. Harleian 1981, fol. 27; *C.I.P.M.*, II, no. 248; ibid. IV, no. 235.

More fundamental than such geographical imprecision, however, is the fact that for the historian the March of Wales is a term of art. It corresponds neither to the normal lay usage of the term nor to that of the geographer for whom the March is 'a narrow zone of transition between the lowlands of England and the uplands of Wales'.[4] The historian's March is both broader and narrower—broader because it trespasses far into the uplands (as in the lordships of Brecon, Glamorgan and Ceri) and even reaches the Irish Sea (in the county of Pembroke); narrower because it excludes certain districts (notably the county of Flint) which by any geographical definition must be characterized as a part of the March. For historical purposes the March is the area defined by the military enterprise and seignorial power of the Anglo-Norman lords in the two centuries or so between 1066 and 1284. The historian's March is coterminous with the extent of Marcher lordships. It thereby comprehends districts (such as the lordships of Chepstow, Usk, Monmouth and Radnor) which clearly straddle the borderland between England and Wales; but it also includes areas which for the geographer lie in the heart of upland Wales (such as the lordships of Maelienydd and Gwerthrynion) or at the confines of the country (notably in the case of the county palatine of Pembroke). The historian's March is also noteworthy for what it excludes or came to exclude. It excludes all those districts which came to form part and parcel of the king's lands in Wales in and after 1284. It clearly excludes the Principality of Wales (as it came to be known) in its post-1284 form, that is the five shires of north and west Wales (Anglesey, Caernarfon, Merioneth, Cardigan and Carmarthen); likewise it definitely excludes Flintshire, the three-piece administrative district of Engelfield, Hopedale and Maelor Saesneg which Edward I placed under a single sheriff responsible in turn to the exchequer at Chester; arguably, but less categorically, it excludes those royal lordships (notably Montgomery, Builth, Newcastle Emlyn and Haverford) which were not a part of the Principality proper. Finally the March excludes all lands which were clearly part and parcel of the shire-system of England, subject to the authority of the sheriff, to the visits of royal justices itinerant, to the national tax system of English kings.

[4] R. Millward and A. Robinson, *The Welsh Marches* (1971), 9.

For the historian, therefore, the March is an area defined by the accidents of history as much as—or even more than—it is shaped by geographical factors. As such its extent varied from one period to another according to the fortunes of war in the March and to the success of failure of the Marcher barons in asserting their lordship in the region. This elasticity of the March as a historical category helps to explain why the question of the precise extent of the March was already a vexed question in the medieval period. It was notably a vexed question in that area where shire ground and March overlapped. The barons of the Exchequer were asked more than once whether an area was in the March or not; they had recourse to Domesday Book and the Red Book of the Exchequer to answer such queries.[5] The position of Radnor, for example, was in question: it appeared in Domesday Book and in the 1250s it was regarded as being within the confines of Herefordshire;[6] but the Mortimer family vigorously and, eventually, successfully countered such a claim. Likewise the position of Glasbury was the subject of several inquiries in the 1270s: was it 'in Walecheria' and therefore in the March or was it part of the county of Hereford?[7] Significantly the jurors were asked whether Glasbury 'is now or ever was' within Herefordshire, with the clear assumption that the March of the present was not always the March of the past. It was, as we shall see, a fully justified assumption. Again the inhabitants of Archenfield in 1334 declared that it was in the March and thereby exempt from royal taxation. The barons of the Exchequer thought quite otherwise and so did the sheriff of Herefordshire; but in the late fifteenth century Archenfield was still regarded as an area where the king's writ could not be served.[8] Such uncertainty as to the extent of the March survived the so-called Act of Union of 1536 and indeed grew thereafter. George Owen tells us that by Elizabethan times 'it was now growne a doubte and question which are and were Lordships Marchers in Wales and which were not.'[9]

---

[5] *Select Cases in the Court of King's Bench*, ed. G. O. Sayles, v (Selden Society, 1958), 99–101.

[6] *Domesday Book*, 187; *C.C.R. 1251–3*, 220.

[7] *C.P.R. 1272–81*, 116–17; *C.C.R. 1272–9*, 54–5, 335.

[8] *Rot. Parl.*, ii, 82; B.L. Add. 4510, fols. 61–4. *Early Chancery Proceedings Concerning Wales*, ed. E. A. Lewis (Cardiff, 1937), 248.

[9] *Penbrokshire*, iii, 173.

For an antiquarian lawyer such as George Owen the question was a legalistic, constitutional one; he expended a great deal of ingenuity attempting to define the criteria—such as conquest from the Welsh, tenure in chief of the king and the exercise of *jura regalia*—of a true Marcher lordship.[10] Historically his ingenuity was misplaced, for whether a district was or was not part of the March was determined not by the application of static theoretical criteria but by the ebb and flow of historical events. Domesday Book, for example, makes it abundantly clear that districts which were later undeniably part of the March were in 1086, and probably for several decades earlier, equally undeniably part of the shire system of England. For example, Knighton and Norton—although waste—were regarded as part of the Shropshire hundred of Leintwardine in the time of William I; but by the reign of Edward I they were said to be 'in Welshry' and so they were to remain.[11] Likewise in the northern borderland, many villages with unmistakably Anglo-Saxon names—such as Sutton, Allington, Hoseley and Gresford—were at Domesday Book (1086) 'not formally merely, but actually and organically, a part of Cheshire', whereas by the fourteenth century they were equally organically part of the Marcher lordship of Bromfield and Yale.[12] Sometimes we can date this process of movement from county into March more narrowly. For example, Radnor, as we have seen, was still regarded as being in Herefordshire in 1250; by 1304 it had moved to 'the borders of the county' and we may well assume that it was the masterful and forceful Roger Mortimer (d. 1282) who moved it there; before long it moved out of the county altogether and became firmly ensconced in the March.[13]

But the major reason for the uncertain extent of the March in the two centuries before 1284 rests, of course, in the fluidity of the military situation and with it of seignorial control in the area. The Anglo-Norman penetration of Wales was a long-drawn-out affair, proceeding by fits and starts and suffering

[10] ibid. 173–84.

[11] *Domesday Book*, 260b; R. W. Eyton, *Antiquities of Shropshire* (1854–60), XI, 346–7.

[12] A. N. Palmer and E. Owen, *A History of Ancient Tenures of Land in the Marches of North Wales*, 2nd edn. (Wrexham, 1910), 144.

[13] *C.I.P.M.*, IV, no. 235.

prolonged and severe setbacks. Starting soon after the Norman conquest of England it was only finally completed in the wake and under the aegis of Edward I's final conquest of Gwynedd in 1282–3. We may take as an instance the great lordship of Brecon: it was first brought under Norman rule by Bernard of Neufmarché in the late eleventh century and Norman military control was never thereafter totally lost in the area; but it was only in the 1270s that this control was finally (as it proved) placed on a secure basis and that a military frontier zone was at last converted into an area for the exercise of firm seignorial control.[14] The uncertain character of Anglo-Norman penetration meant that the map of the March, both militarily and in terms of lordship, contracted and expanded from one generation to the next. Some lordships, it is true, were more militarily vulnerable than others; but the measure of vulnerability was not simply a factor either of the date of initial conquest (as the case of north-east Wales shows) or of distance from the English border (as is exemplified by the history of the county of Pembroke). It is the fortunes of war which explains, for example, why Kidwelly in the south-west became a Marcher lordship whereas Flint in the north-east did not. It is only when the fluidity of this military situation was finally removed in the late thirteenth century that the March took a definitive shape for the historian. In that process of definition politics as well as war played a prominent part. For example, the territorial generosity of Edward I to a few great English magnates added vast areas of north-east Wales to the category of Marchland in the 1280s;[15] whereas a few years earlier the politico-military designs of the same king terminated the short-lived history of the Marcher lordships of Carmarthen and Cardigan, held by Earl Edmund of Lancaster from 1265 to 1279.[16]

By 1300 the map of the March had, for the first time in centuries, acquired a measure of stability which, as it happens, was to continue virtually unchanged until the Henrician legislation of the 1530s. That stability was, of course, largely a byproduct of military events, above all of the conquest of

---

[14] W. Rees, 'The Medieval Lordship of Brecon', *T.C.S.* (1915–16), 165–224.

[15] See below, p. 27.

[16] *C.Ch.R. 1417–25*, 287; *C.P.R. 1258–66*, 513, 627–3. The full rights of other Marcher lords were extended to Earl Edmund's estates: *C.P.R. 1266–72*, 299.

Gwynedd in the royal campaigns of 1277 and 1282–3 and with
it of the removal of the threat to the military security of the
Marcher lordships. It was also largely a consequence of the
activities and policies of Edward I. But the map of the March in
1300 also bears heavily the imprint of the enterprise, military
and otherwise, of the Marcher lords themselves. That was true
of every Marcher lordship, but in terms of the definition of the
extent of the March in the late thirteenth century it was
particularly true of the peripheral lordships of the March,
notably of Clun, Oswestry, Caus and Wigmore. In these lordships which straddled March and shire-ground—much of
which were absorbed into English counties in 1536—the lords
had to defend their lands against the attacks of Welsh armies, to
uphold the Marcher status of their lordship against royal
lawyers, to usurp liberties and to expand their claims. The
historian benefits by this need for constant vigilance; nowhere
can he study more effectively the making of the map of the
medieval March.

Take the lordship of Clun. At Domesday Book most of it
belonged to the Shropshire hundred of Rinelau; and equally
after 1536 it became firmly and conclusively incorporated in
the county of Shropshire.[17] But for most of the intervening
period it was in effect more a Marcher lordship than part of an
English shire. In the extreme west of the lordship, beyond
Offa's Dyke, lay the hill district of Tempseter. Of its Welsh
character there could be no doubt. The lord's control there
until the late thirteenth century was occasional and unsure at
best;[18] and its tenantry was governed by Welsh law and custom
and paid its dues in kind.[19] It was, in the words of the escheator,
'multa Walecheria', one of the true frontier districts of England
and Wales. East of Offa's Dyke the lordship became more
English in character and population; but it also continued to

---

[17] This is so in spite of the confusing entry in the Act of Union which assigns
Clunesland to Montgomeryshire: W. Rees, *The Union of England and Wales* (Cardiff,
1948), 60, n. 18.

[18] This can be seen in the inquisition of 1267 quoted in Eyton, op. cit. XI, 231
n. 3: 'Preterea circa Forestam de Clun est multa Walecheria que multum solebit
valere domino tam in dominicis redditibus quam in aliis perquisitis et exitibus;
de qua non possumus ad presens facere extencionem propter disturbacionem
Walensium factam per Lewelinum filium Griffini et ballivos suos'.

[19] Note the references to payment of *cylch* (a circuit due) and *trethcanteidion* (a
render of 100 oxen) in the inquisition of 1302: *C.I.P.M.*, IV, no. 90.

retain its Marcher character. The *caput* of the lordship at Clun and the surrounding area were withdrawn from the jurisdiction of the sheriff of Shropshire and were formed into the new hundred of Clun, normally outside the ambit of the king's law, justice and taxation, a Marcher district in all respects.[20] Most of the remainder of the lordship fell within the hundred of Purslow and came more clearly within the ambit of the county jurisdiction of Shropshire and the taxation system of England. But even so, this part of the lordship was an Arundel franchise of the most fully-fledged variety: Purslow, the vill which gave its name to the hundred, was an Arundel manor and the Fitz-alans had held the custody of the hundred 'from time immemorial'.[21] The rest of the lordship lay within the hundred of Munslow and the further east one went the more English became the place-names and the population and the more securely did the officials of the king and of the county of Shropshire operate.[22] But even in these eastern districts the feudal and jurisdictional unity of the lordship prevailed, for over and above their obligations to the hundred and shire courts, the free tenants also owed suit to the lord's *curia* at Clun, the focal point of the lordship and the expression of its territorial integrity under the rule of the Fitzalans. The lordship of Clun was not an immunity of the same scale as, say, the lordships of Glamorgan and Brecon; but in most senses it was, and was regarded as, a Marcher lordship. Already in 1221, John Fitzalan as lord of Clun had stood up in court on behalf of one of his tenants and had asserted quite roundly that in his franchise the king could not lay his hand nor did the king's writ run there.[23] A century later much the same point was made by counsel on behalf of Edmund Fitzalan, earl of Arundel: Clun was in Welshry outside the body of the county; the earl was the keeper of the law there and had a chancery for the purpose; and therefore the king's writ did not run there nor did he have

[20] Eyton, op. cit. xi, 228–9. According to the tax returns of 1341 Clun, Obley and Hagley were said to be 'in Welshry': ibid. 248–9.

[21] *Placita Quo Warranto*, 681; *Rot. Parl.*, ii, 74. The hundred of Purslow was confiscated by Edward I in 1294 but restored by Edward II in 1308: E.159/67 m. 11; *C.P.R. 1307–13*, 52.

[22] For example in 1327 a commission was appointed to investigate offences at Edgton in the lordship of Clun in Shropshire: *C.P.R. 1327–30*, 78.

[23] Eyton, op. cit. xi, 247.

cognizance of cases arising there.[24] The earls of Arundel had no doubt that Clun was a Marcher lordship; and, though royal lawyers and officials might occasionally express doubts, they were effectively right. It was a feudal honor which had been converted into a Marcher lordship partly because of its territorial unity under a single lord, partly because of its military frontier position, partly because it straddled the border of English and Welsh, and partly because its lords exploited every opportunity to assert its immunity from royal writ and royal tax and thereby to increase the resemblances between it and the neighbouring lordships of the March. And once it had attained its Marcher status, it retained it. Leland had no doubt that 'Clune was a lordshipe marched by it selfe afore the new Acte [of 1536]' and in 1586 an old man of eighty could still recall vividly and dramatically the days when the lords of Clun 'had and held *jura regalia*'.[25]

What was true of the lordship of Clun was even more true of the lordship of Oswestry. Indeed, since both lordships were held by the house of Fitzalan from the early thirteenth century onwards, it is more than likely that the status of the one was made to approximate to that of the other.[26] And in this process of approximation Clun followed where Oswestry led. Oswestry, like Clun, was a border district which was gradually withdrawn from the county administration so that by the late thirteenth century it was conclusively regarded as being part of the March. Before the Norman Conquest of England, the hundred of Mersete (which more or less corresponded to the later lordship of Oswestry) was part of the lands of King Edward and at Domesday it was certainly considered to be within Shropshire. But its frontier character—subject as it was to raids until the end of the thirteenth century[27]—meant that powers of ad-

---

[24] K.B. 27/230, m. 93ᵛ; *Year Book 12 Edward II*, ed. J. P. Collas (Selden Society, 1964), 130–2.

[25] John Leland, *The Itinerary in Wales in or about the Years 1536–9*, ed. L. Toulmin-Smith (1906), 53; T. Salt, 'Ancient Documents Relating to the Honor, Forest and Borough of Clun', *Shropshire Archaeological and Natural History Society* 11 (1887–8), 244–72 at 258.

[26] For example, in 1302 the lordships of Clun and Oswestry were said to be outside the bounds of any county: *C.F.R. 1272–1307*, 448.

[27] See the interesting account of raids on Kinnerley given in an inquisition of 1277: *C. Inq. Misc. 1219–1307*, no. 1059.

ministration as well as of defence devolved into the hands of the local commander; and the Fitzalans, who were lords of Oswestry from the time of Henry I, availed themselves of every opportunity to assert the independence of their lordship (and its appurtenant manors)[28] both of county administration and of royal governance. By the thirteenth century the Marcher status of Oswestry was fully developed. It lay outside the purview of the sheriff, of the visiting justices itinerant, and of the king's writ; its lord granted rights and liberties to others but retained 'those things which pertained to regality' to himself.[29] The area was described as 'the liberty of Oswestry in the March of Wales out of the county'.[30] And so it remained, for the jurors of the sixteenth century, like the old man of Clun, recalled quite clearly that the lord of Oswestry had '*jura regalia*, treson onlie excepted, within this Lordship'.[31]

In between the two Fitzalan lordships of Clun and Oswestry, lay the Corbet barony of Caus whose history in terms of Marcher status was very similar. As in the case of Clun, its western part, Gorddwr, formed a Welshry which was certainly outside an English county and was a frontier military area until the Edwardian campaigns in Wales.[32] Beyond it lay an area known as the hundred of Caus which was technically part of Shropshire, as even the Corbets themselves would admit, but whose liberties were so extensive that they were tantamount to asserting that the area was a Marcher lordship. Peter Corbet, when challenged by the *quo warranto* commissioners of Edward I, claimed that no royal officer could enter the vills of Caus, that its tenants owed no suit of court to county or hundred, and that they were not bound to appear before royal justices or

[28] For example, Ruyton was detached from the hundred of Baschurch and annexed to the Arundel hundred of Oswestry. It thereby came to enjoy Oswestry's status as part of the March of Wales, Eyton, op. cit. x, 112; *C.Ch.R. 1300–26*, 183.

[29] Eyton, op. cit. x, 316; 343–4. The phrase about regality ('que pertinet ad regalitatem') appears in a Shrewsbury Abbey charter which Eyton dates *c.* 1262.

[30] *Rot. Parl.*, I, 206b–207 (1306).

[31] *The Lordship of Oswestry 1393–1607*, ed. W. J. Slack (Shrewsbury, 1951), 13–14. The Marcher status of the lordship of Oswestry has been fully discussed and documented in Llinos Smith's Ph.D. thesis 'The Lordships of Chirk and Oswestry, 1282–1415' (Univ. of London, 1971).

[32] For Gwyddgrug Castle in Gorddwr and for a useful map of the area, see C. J. Spurgeon, 'Gwyddgrug Castle, Forden and the Gorddwr Dispute', *Mont. Colls.* 57 (1961–2), 125–37.

ministers.[33] It was a catalogue of liberties of such daring comprehensiveness that it was little wonder that the Crown attorney was prompted to retort that such immunities were of the essence of kingship itself.[34] Caus had been virtually transformed into a Marcher lordship; and in its case we can date the transformation fairly closely. It did not go back to the pioneering days of the twelfth century when the Corbet lords were too concerned with problems of survival and conquest to attend to such matters as liberties and immunities. Rather does it appear that it was Thomas Corbet, lord of Caus 1222–74, who arrogated to himself powers of high justice and excluded the king's officers from his liberty. The process of usurpation was continued in similar fashion by his son Peter, lord of Caus 1274–1300, who was accused of withdrawing twenty-one vills from Shropshire into the Welshry and of holding pleas of the Crown.[35]

At much the same time that Thomas and Peter Corbet were shaping the Marcher lordship of Caus, their contemporary Roger Mortimer, lord of Wigmore 1246–82, was taking advantage of the political turmoil of the 1260s and the close personal friendship of Edward I to lay the foundations of what was to be the greatest of Marcher inheritances of the fourteenth century. The aspect of the achievement that concerns us here is the method and extent to which the Mortimers were able to assert the Marcher status of their border lands. It was a process which was compounded of royal impotence, permissiveness and even support on the one hand and of blatant grasping of every opportunity to extend their power and to usurp liberties by the Mortimers on the other hand. In the case of the great Shropshire manors of Cleobury Mortimer and Chelmarsh, for example, it was a generous royal grant which exempted the area from suit of county and hundred courts and from the visits of royal officers.[36] Cleobury thus became, in Eyton's words, 'an independent and autonomous liberty of the marcher

---

[33] *Placita Quo Warranto*, 677, 681; Eyton, op. cit. VII, 6–35; *V.C.H. Shropshire*, VIII (1968), 324–5.

[34] 'Predicte libertates faciunt coronam regis integram per quam qui est rex': *Placita Quo Warranto*, 686.

[35] *Rotuli Hundredorum*, II, 96; *Placita Quo Warranto*, 681–6; Eyton, op. cit. VII, 34–5.

[36] *C.Ch.R. 1257–1300*, 61 (1266). This grant was made by Henry III 'at the instance of Edward, the king's son'.

type'.[37] But Mortimer was not content with his good fortune; and he used the royal charter as a pretext to extend precisely the same liberties to a further twenty of his manors.[38] In Wigmore, the home of the Mortimers from the early days of the Norman Conquest, the position was less promising, for Wigmore was certainly within the ambit of county administration. But 'from the time of the siege of Kenilworth' (1266), so the record tells us, the stewards began to exclude royal officers from the liberty, and to claim exemption from the king's writ, the king's justices and the king's taxes.[39] Wigmore had been raised, surreptitiously and by default of royal vigilance, into 'a great franchise of independent status'.[40] At much the same time, as we have seen, Radnor, Knighton and Norton moved out of the radius of county administration and royal supervision and into the March. Roger Mortimer of Wigmore deserves to be remembered as one of the great architects of the late medieval March. His work was to some extent undone during the rule of his son Edmund (1282–1304) by the vigorous action of Edward I;[41] but it was resumed in an extraordinarily successful fashion by his grandson Roger (1304–30). The latter's assumption of the title of earl of March in 1328 was not merely an indication of the territorial base of his political power but was also a virtual declaration of the Marcher status of those lands.

We have looked at the lordships of Clun, Oswestry, Caus and Wigmore in some detail because their history shows clearly that the extent of the March was not constant or inelastic. Geography and race did a great deal to determine the extent of the historical March; but it was also to a considerable degree a man-made March in the sense that its extent was also determined by the ambition, drive and good fortune of the Marcher lords. It was they who pushed the military frontier of the March westwards at the expense of the Welsh princes; it was they also who pushed the frontier of the March eastwards at the expense of royal and county jurisdiction. We can identify some of these men such as John Fitzalan of Oswestry and Clun (1217–40),

---

[37] Eyton, op. cit. III, 40; IV, 221–2.

[38] *Placita Quo Warranto*, 675, 677, 681.

[39] *Rotuli Hundredorum*, ii, 90–1, 108; *Calendar of Ancient Correspondence Concerning Wales*, ed. J. G. Edwards (Cardiff, 1935), 101–2; E.159/67, m. 48 and m. 63.

[40] Eyton, op. cit. XI, 326, 349.

[41] See below, p. 260.

Thomas and Peter Corbet of Caus, and the two Roger Mortimers of Wigmore; and we can also pinpoint the most successful
periods in which they operated, particularly the middle years
of the thirteenth century. Their methods also are recognizable:
they extended the Welshry status of the extreme west of their
lordships eastwards; they usurped immunities through royal
indifference and political opportunity; and in the permissive
atmosphere of frontier areas they found it no great problem to
transform a collection of liberties into a claim to Marcher
status. Such claims to Marcher status were more assailable in
the eastern March than in the heartlands of the west, as the
quo warranto inquiries of Edward I quickly showed. Yet nowhere
was it more true than in the March that prescription could soon
elevate recent usurpation to the status of indefeasible and immemorial right.

The March of Wales in 1300 had been shaped by the activities
and ambitions of its lords. It had also been shaped by the kings
of England and by none more so than by Edward I. His
Welsh campaigns of 1276–7 and of 1282–3 and their consequences did more than any other sequence of events to
determine the final shape of the medieval March. Militarily
they effectively removed the *raison d'être* of the March as a
buffer zone between England and the independent principalities of Wales. Territorially they ensured that in the ranks
of the lords of Wales no man was now the peer of the king of
England. Terminologically they converted the old distinction
between the Wales of the native princes ('pura Wallia') and
the March ('marchia Wallie') into a new distinction between
'the king's lands in Wales' (later created into a principality for
Edward of Caernarfon 'and his heirs being kings of England')[42]
and the March. Those royal lands henceforth defined one clear
boundary for the March of Wales; and the definition of that
western boundary was one of Edward I's contributions to the
shaping of the historical March.

It was not his only contribution. Between 1279 and 1282 he
transformed the map of the March by a series of territorial
grants to his followers out of the lands forfeited by Llywelyn ap

[42] J. G. Edwards, *The Principality of Wales 1267–1967* (Caernarvon, 1969) provides a definitive study of the legal and constitutional position of the royal lands
in Wales after 1284.

Gruffudd, prince of Wales, and his supporters. In 1279 Roger Mortimer of Wigmore was granted Ceri and Cydewain; in 1282 during his campaign in north Wales Edward I distributed some of the spoils of his victory to his friends: the lordship of Denbigh was granted to Henry Lacy, earl of Lincoln; Dyffryn Clwyd to Reginald Grey; Bromfield and Yale to John Warenne, earl of Surrey; and Chirkland to Roger, the second surviving son of Roger Mortimer of Wigmore.[43] By this rare display of territorial munificence, Edward I had manifested the scope of royal largesse in determining the fortunes of his followers and the future of his dominions; he had also in three years done more than any single Marcher lord to extend the limits of the March. Only one doubt remained: could the lordships newly created by royal munificence be regarded as fully-fledged lordships of the March or not?

That their position was different from that of old-established lordships such as Glamorgan or Pembroke is undeniable. They were royal creations, the gifts of a man who was punctilious to a degree about the terms of his grants and about the obligations which his largesse entailed. Edward I was not a man to forget his own generosity: in 1292, for example, the earl of Surrey was reminded that he held Bromfield and Yale by the king's gift.[44] Furthermore, the relationship of each of these lords with the king was a personal one of friendship, obligation and respect; they were hardly in a position to be assertive of the Marcher status of their newly-acquired lands. Nor did the foundation charters of the lordships provide a secure basis for claims to full-blown Marcher status. They were, it is true, to be held 'as freely and wholly as other neighbouring *cantrefi*' or 'as fully and wholly as David son of Gruffudd [brother of Llywelyn ap Gruffudd, prince of Wales] held them'; but in the atmosphere of the 1280s (when Edward I's lawyers were applying the most rigorous of tests to claims to franchises) he would be a bold, even foolish, man who placed much trust in such vague and generalized clauses. Finally when Edward of Caernarfon was granted the Principality of Wales in 1301, it was made transparently clear that all the newly-created lordships of 1279–82 were to be

---

[43] *C.Ch.R. 1257–1300*, 211, 262; *C.W.R.*, 223, 240–1.
[44] *C.P.R. 1281–92*, 500. Cf. *Rot. Parl.*, I, 93b.

held in chief as of the Principality, not of the Crown.[45] All in all, there were many reasons for doubting the full Marcher status of these new lordships in the first generation of their existence.

A century later, and indeed well before then, such doubts would be misplaced, and that for several reasons. In the first place, Edward I's friendship ensured that the new lordships were in effect, whatever might be the theory, treated as if they were of Marcher status, just as much as his hostility served to call the independence of many of the old Marcher lordships in question. The newly-created lordships became lordships Marcher by reason of royal affection. Furthermore, by the mid fourteenth century they were all, with the exception of Dyffryn Clwyd, constituent parts of the two greatest Marcher in-heritances of the period—those of the earls of Arundel and March; and it was only natural that their lords should treat all their Marcher lands, however divergent their origins, on a par. And so they did. From the rather uncertain beginnings of 1282, therefore, these new lordships came to enjoy a fully-fledged Marcher status. To assert otherwise is to put constitutional theorems above historical facts.[46]

The military and political activities of Edward I in Wales had yet other repercussions on the question of the extent of the March. His definition of the extent and administration of 'the king's lands in Wales' (later called the Principality) in the Statute of Wales of 1284 automatically raises the issue of the status of those lordships which were regarded as tenurially dependent on the Principality. The status of the newly-created northern lordships of Denbigh, Dyffryn Clwyd, Chirkland and Bromfield and Yale has already been discussed and will pre-occupy us again in a later context. It is to a group of lordships along the southern borders of the Principality that we must refer here briefly. The doubt regarding their status need not detain us long for it is a question more of constitutional propriety than of fundamental importance in the history of the March. Along the borders of the county of Carmarthen lay a series of

---

[45] Edwards, *Principality of Wales*, 14–16, 31–4. It is particularly noteworthy that the earl of Lincoln was commanded to do homage and fealty to the prince for Denbigh 'by order of the king' in 1303.

[46] As A. J. Otway-Ruthven does in 'The Constitutional Position of the Great Lordships of South Wales', *T.R.H.S.*, 5th ser. 8 (1958), 15, n. 4.

Marcher lordships which were tenurially and jurisdictionally dependent on the Principality of Wales rather than on the Crown of England. Some of them—notably Kidwelly, Llanstephan, Laugharne, St. Clears, Narberth and the episcopal lordship of Llawhaden—were old Marcher districts long since conquered by baronial enterprise; others—especially Iscennen and Cantref Bychan (the two commotes of Hirfryn and Perfedd centred on Llandovery)—were more recent creations of the final Edwardian conquest of Wales.[47] To make them dependent on Carmarthen as the southern centre of the Principality was part of a deliberate royal policy aimed at preserving the tenurial integrity of old Welsh *cantrefi* (administrative divisions), at establishing the new Principality as the residuary legatee of the powers and jurisdiction of the native Welsh princes,[48] and at countering the expansionist ambitions of the Valence lords of Pembroke.[49]

It was a dependence which involved attendance at the county court and sessions at Carmarthen, but very little other intervention except during periods of seignorial minority.[50] It was not a dependence which can be said to have greatly compromised the Marcher status of these lordships (unless we stand by George Owen's criterion of tenure-in-chief of the Crown as a qualification for such status). Nor was it, on the whole, an issue which occasioned much friction. Some of these lordships were in the hands of minor Marcher families such as the Camvilles, Brians and Audleys who were unlikely to stage a constitutional confrontation on the question; whereas in the case of

[47] Another district as to whose position there was some dispute was the Mortimer lordship of Cwmwd Deuddwr, *C.I.P.M.*, VII, no. 387, p. 279. According to a petition of 1332, Edward I had recovered it from Edmund Mortimer and held it during his lifetime, S.C. 8/240, no. 11952.

[48] For this policy in north and east Wales, see Edwards, *Principality of Wales*.

[49] In 1282 the lordships of Haverford and Narberth, over both of which Valence attempted to claim superior jurisdiction, were said to be held of the king in chief and in 1288 it was specifically stated that Llawhaden was 'infra procinctum Comitatus de Kermerdyn et non infra procinctum comitatus Pembrochie': *C.I.P.M.*, II, no. 446; *Penbrokshire*, II, 379 n. 12. In 1292 Edward I brought an action for the recovery of the commote of Ystlwyf against William de Valence and his wife and claimed that it was within the county of Carmarthen: *Abbreviatio Placitorum* (1811), 286.

[50] R. A. Griffiths, *The Principality of Wales in the Later Middle Ages: The Structure and Personnel of Government I: South Wales, 1277–1536* (Cardiff, 1972), 14–17.

Kidwelly and Iscennen, their lords were so powerful that the jurisdictional dependence was either waived or ignored.[51]

Yet that this tenurial and jurisdictional dependence on Carmarthen was not altogether a non-issue is shown by the case of Gower.[52] Gower's vulnerability was compounded of several elements. It was regarded historically as part of Ystrad Tywi and thereby dependent on Carmarthen. Furthermore the breach in the history of the descent of the lordship in the late twelfth century meant that the lords of Gower—unlike those of Glamorgan, for example—could not claim to hold their land 'by ancient conquest' or 'from time immemorial'. Theirs was a title which was eventually dependent on a royal grant, that of King John to William Braose in 1203; and where a king could grant, he could also intervene. Nor was that all: the claim that Gower had been judicially dependent on Carmarthen in the thirteenth century provided another pretext for intervention as did the disputes between Braose and Beauchamp about their respective claims to the lordship. All in all, there was ample opportunity for the king of England or the prince of Wales to intervene in the affairs of Gower and to do so in a fashion which seemed to undermine its Marcher status. The king's court could act as an appellate tribunal to hear the grievances of the men of Gower against their lord; royal commissions were established to investigate the malpractices of seignorial officials; lands alienated there without royal licence were confiscated; and even the lordship itself was seized into royal hands for default of justice. It was a catalogue of royal intervention which must have sent shivers down the spine of any self-respecting Marcher lord. The history of Gower, particularly under its last Braose lord (1290–1326), was for the March a cautionary tale of how any weaknesses in the 'constitutional' position of a Marcher lordship could be devastatingly exploited by the kings of England. After such experience, it was only a grant of full Marcher rights by the Crown[53] and a declaration that the lordship was a barony held in chief of the king on the same

---

[51] *C.C.R. 1307–13*, 18, 359 (Henry of Lancaster); *C.P.R. 1321–4*, 245–6 (Iscennen was elevated to the full status of a Marcher lordship for the younger Despenser in 1323).

[52] For fuller details see W. Rees, 'Gower and the March of Wales', *Arch. Camb.* 110 (1961), 1–30 and *Glam. C.H.*, III, ch. v *passim*.

[53] *C.Ch.R. 1300–26*, 46–7; *C.Ch.R. 1341–1417*, 167–8.

conditions as other baronies of the March of Wales[54] which could restore credibility to Gower's claim to be regarded as a lordship Marcher.

There remains yet one other lordship whose Marcher status was effectively defined by Edward I, namely that of Powys, 'one of the most Royallest, greatest, lardgest and best seignories and Lordship Marcher of Wales', as George Owen enthusiastically described it.[55] And so it was; but its distinctiveness in this particular context was the uniqueness of its progression to Marcher status. Of all the Marcher lordships, it was the only one which graduated to that status without undergoing the intermediate stage of a military conquest. Instead it passed directly from the status of the independent Welsh principality of southern Powys to that of the barony of the Pool held in chief of the Crown of England. When precisely this change in status happened is not clear, nor whether it was accompanied by a formal resignation of 'the name and circlet of principality.'[56] In fact it was a change of status which was but a natural culmination of the prolonged dependence of the princes of southern Powys on the kings of England for their political survival; and there is little doubt that the directing hand of Edward I lay behind the move as well as behind the various territorial settlements of the family of Powys between 1277 and 1290.[57] By 1293 at latest the barony of Powys (or The Pool) had been constituted[58] and would henceforth be regarded as part of the March.[59]

This review of the extent of the March in 1300 has deliberately concentrated on those lordships which had been only recently

---

[54] *C. Chancery Warrants 1244–1326*, 238; *C. Inq. Misc.*, III, no. 489.

[55] *Penbrokshire*, III, 158.

[56] According to Nichols (*Collectanea Topographica et Genealogica*, VIII (1843), 183), Owen de la Pole in 1283 surrendered all his lands to Edward I and received them back 'sub nomine et tenura liberi Baronagii Anglie resignando Domino Regi heredibus suis er coronae Anglie, nomen et circulum principatus'; but he gives no source for his statement. The tradition of a separate crown of Mathrafal survived long, for it is mentioned in an inquisition of 1428 printed in full in *Mont. Colls.* 1 (1868), 254–6.

[57] See J. C. Davies, 'Lordships and Manors in the County of Montgomery' *Mont. Colls.* 49 (1946), 74–151; F. M. Powicke, *King Henry III and the Lord Edward* (Oxford, 1947), 666, 676; *C.W.R.*, 328–32.

[58] It was so called in the inquisition of that year, *Mont. Colls.* 1 (1868), 142–8.

[59] The inquisition *post mortem* of 1309 appears under the marginal title, 'Marchia Wallie comitatu Salopie adjacente'.

created or whose Marcher credentials (*vis à vis* either the counties of England or the Principality of Wales) were open to some measure of doubt. It has not concerned itself with what may be called the classical March, those lordships (such as Brecon, Abergavenny, Glamorgan, Usk, Newport, Chepstow, Monmouth and Pembroke) whose Marcher status was not open to doubt. But even this limited review should have served to underline the fact that the extent of the March was determined not by legal or constitutional criteria but by the flow of historical events. The major factors which determined its extent in 1300 stand out clearly enough and warrant re-emphasis. The extent of the March was in part, and in good part at that, a factor of the see-saw history of the Anglo-Norman conquest of Wales. It expanded and contracted with the success or failure of that conquest. The history of the lordship of Maelienydd is a case in point: the Welsh chronicler tells us that it was conquered for a second time by the Mortimers in 1144 but it was not until the reign of Edward I that it was finally and securely conquered.[60] And it was only then that its Marcher status was secure. The extent of the March was also in part a factor of English politics, for the rule of a weak king could be the occasion for extending Marcher status to lands which had hitherto been under English county administration. It was, for example, during the reign of Stephen that Clun was probably first withdrawn from the purview of the sheriff of Shropshire;[61] while the years of the Barons' War were in the March, as in England generally, one of the most fertile periods in the usurpation of liberties. Needless to say, the extent of the March was also determined by the forcefulness and ability of the Marcher lords themselves, by their military prowess, by their political adroitness and opportunism; and in none of these qualities were most of them lacking. Finally, and paradoxically, the extent of the March in 1300 owed more to one man than to any other, and that man was Edward I. His successful campaigns in Wales provided the Marcher lords at last with a basis of military security for the exercise of their lordship, and his grant of lands to his followers transformed and augmented the March in a dramatic fashion.

[60] J. B. Smith, 'The Middle March in the Thirteenth Century', *B.B.C.S.* 24 (1970), 77–93.
[61] Eyton, op. cit. XI, 228.

The March of 1300 was very different from the March of 1275; it bore heavily the mark of Edward I's personality and policies.

Furthermore this quarter century moulded the March of Wales into a shape that it was to preserve for the rest of its existence as a historical category. That is why the March of 1300 corresponds remarkably closely to the March of the Act Union of 1536. The correspondence is, however, more geographical than anything else, for the March of 1300 was much less monolithic and far more variegated historically than the March of 1536. For the March of 1300 was historically a recent amalgam and it still bore clearly the marks of amalgamation. It consisted of old lordships conquered over centuries by Anglo-Norman barons, of recent royal creations carved out of lands conquered during the campaigns of 1277–82, and of a Welsh principality only recently demoted to the ranks of a Marcher barony. It was during the fourteenth century that these marks of amalgamation were gradually eradicated and that all Marcher lordships, regardless of their differences in origin, came to share distinguishably common features and to appear as an unity to the outside world. Then could it be said that the March of Wales had finally taken shape.

'I AM a baron of the Welshry' asserted Richard Fitzalan, earl of Arundel in 1293 proudly, even defiantly.[1] He was thereby flaunting his membership of an exclusive group, that of the lords Marcher. Contemporaries were quite convinced that the lords of the Welsh March formed a self-consciously corporate group, united by self-interest and characterized by certain patterns of political behaviour. For example, the *barones de Marchia* who helped the royal cause at Rye in 1217 were apparently a well-defined group;[2] and, even more clearly, during the period of baronial rebellion in the early 1260s, the lords of the March appeared to outsiders as a relatively united and extremely powerful force in the political alignments of the period.[3] The same was true, if not more so, in the turbulent politics of Edward II's reign when the coherence of the Marchers as a group was strengthened by their opposition to the ambitions of the younger Despenser and by their equally united defence of the custom of the March.[4] And, to give a final example, when the revolt of Owain Glyn Dŵr in the early fifteenth century focused English attention on the problem of Wales once more, the Commons in Parliament placed the responsibility of defending the country squarely on the shoulders of the lords Marcher as a group and even expounded an historical explanation of that group-responsibility.[5]

To the outside world, therefore, the Marcher barons often appeared as a recognizable, even united, group; and this was an impression which they themselves periodically fostered. They might, as a group, take common action in defence of their judicial liberties, as they did in the Parliament of 1335;[6] and as individuals they stood proudly on the rights which they shared

---

[1] *Abbreviatio Placitorum*, 231.   [2] *C.P.R. 1216–25*, 109.
[3] See T. F. Tout, *Collected Papers*, II, 47–101; and F. M. Powicke, *Henry III and the Lord Edward*, esp. 431–4.
[4] Below, pp. 287–8.   [5] *Rot. Parl.*, III, 624–5.
[6] ibid. II, 91.

with their fellow-Marchers. [7] Likewise when the liberties of the March were threatened by political action, the Marcher lords closed their ranks speedily and effectively: against the pretensions of Edward I in the 1290s, of the younger Despenser in Edward II's reign, and of the Black Prince in the mid-fourteenth century. [8] In times of crisis the group-solidarity of the Marcher lords could be highly effective and impressive. That cannot conceal from us, however, that for the most part their unity was essentially negative; it was almost exclusively shaped by their reaction *against* any threat to the March and its liberties. It had few positive qualities about it. This is, indeed, what we would have expected, for in any group portrait of the Marchers it is the differences between them—in wealth, in their territorial interests outside the March, in the measure of their influence and participation in English politics—which are striking.

At no time was this more apparent than in 1284, on the morrow of the Edwardian Conquest. [9] Some of the Marcher barons in that year were of ancient stock. Pride of place in terms of seniority goes to the Mortimers of Wigmore and the Corbets of Caus, for both families had established themselves in the March in the first generation after the Norman conquest of England and had an unbroken record as Marcher families thereafter. Of an age with the Corbets and Mortimers was the house of Braose: it had secured a foothold in the March in the late eleventh century and had built a large empire for itself by 1200. But soon after it fell on evil days and by 1284 it was no more than a shadow of its old self, confined to the single lordship of Gower and Kilvey. Next in seniority came the Fitzalans of

---

[7] For example, in 1240 Gilbert Marshall claimed the same rights of custody of episcopal temporalities as were enjoyed by his fellow-Marchers and over a century later the earl of Arundel allowed a case to be heard in the king's council 'provided this does not prejudice him or his heirs or other lords of the March': *Abbreviatio Placitorum*, 109; *C.P.R. 1350-4*, 467-8. For a like case see *Select Cases in the Court of King's Bench under Edward I*, II, ed. G. O. Sayles (Selden Society, 1938), lvii–lviii.

[8] Below, pp. 265, 271-3.

[9] The genealogical and family details which form the backbone of this chapter are drawn from a variety of sources, notably G. E. C[okayne], *The Complete Peerage of England, Scotland, Ireland, Great Britain and the United Kingdom*, new edn. ed. V. Gibbs (1910-59); I. J. Sanders, *English Baronies. A Study of their Origin and Descent 1086-1327* (Oxford, 1960); and G. A. Holmes, *The Estates of the Higher Nobility in Fourteenth-Century England*.

Oswestry and Clun and the Clares of Glamorgan, Newport, Caerleon and Usk, both of whom had made their initial début in the March in the days of Henry I, though the history of the Clares had been a discontinuous one both chronologically and geographically. These were the five senior houses of the March in 1284; but some of the smaller Marcher houses could also boast a respectable degree of antiquity. The Fitzmartins of Cemais were in the ranks of the original Norman *conquistadores* of south-west Wales and ruled there until they failed in the male line in 1326; the Camvilles had been lords of the small but strategic lordship of Llanstephan since the late twelfth century and the Fitzherberts lords of Blaenllyfni from much the same period; while in the northern March the Montalt family, the hereditary stewards of the earls of Chester, first established a precarious foothold in Moldsdale in the early twelfth century and, in spite of the vagaries of warfare, survived as lords of the area until the fourteenth century. Alongside these long-standing families we could no doubt place several of their mesne-tenants whose families had likewise been prominent in the history of the March for centuries, families such as the Lestranges of Knockin (co. Salop), the Pichards of Ystradyw (Brecon) and the Someris of Dinas Powys (Glamorgan).[10] These older families were in some ways the Marcher barons *par excellence*. They were the ones whose very outlook and *mores* had been conditioned by centuries of frontier existence. They had helped to shape the March; and they in turn had been shaped by it.

But in 1284 they were in a minority; in that year only some eight of the twenty-four major barons of the March had a Marcher family history which extended beyond 1200. The rest were recent recruits; most of them belonged to families which had only been associated with the March since the 1240s. The explanation of this basic fact is twofold: death without

---

[10] The Lestranges are one of the few Marcher families to have been dignified with a full-length family history—Hamo Le Strange, *Le Strange Records A.D. 1100–1310* (1916). For the early history of the Pichards see D. G. Walker, 'Ralph son of Pichard', *Bulletin of the Institute of Historical Research* 33 (1960), 195–202; they were still tenants of the lords of Brecon in the fourteenth century: *C.I.P.M.*, XIII, no. 167. Likewise the Someris were lords of Dinas Powys from the days of Robert fitz Hamon until they failed in the male line in 1323, *Glam. C.H.*, III, 18; *Cartae*, I, no. 35; *C.I.P.M.*, VI, no. 428.

direct male heirs and royal policy. Death had played havoc with Marcher families on more than one occasion in the twelfth century; but never did it do so more drastically and dramatically than in the middle years of the thirteenth century. Among the families which failed in the male line were Braose (1230), Lacy (1241), Marshall (1245), fitz Baderon of Monmouth (1257), Clifford (1263), Chaworth (1283) and Cantilupe (1283) and in their stead new names appeared in the ranks of Marcher lords, notably Bohun, Bigod, Valence, Verdon, Geneville and Giffard. Premature death and, more crucially, the lack of direct male heirs had engineered a transformation in the personnel of the March in the half century before 1284.

And what death began, the royal will completed. For it was one of the most distinctive features of the March in 1284 that several of its most prominent lords were new men introduced into the area by the Crown. The pattern had been indeed established by Henry III when he bestowed several Marcher lordships on the Lord Edward in the 1250s and likewise endowed Edward's brother, Edmund, with the lordships of Carmarthen and Cardigan, later to be supplemented by the lordship of Monmouth and Threecastles. But it was to be the military campaigns of Edward I and his subsequent territorial endowments which, more than any other single event, served to transform the personnel of the Marcher lords. One family on which Edward I visited his generosity was, it is true, among the oldest in the March, namely the Mortimers of Wigmore: Edward's close friend, Roger Mortimer (d. 1282) was granted the lands of Ceri and Cydewain in 1279 and Roger's second surviving son, another Roger (d.1326), was rewarded with Chirkland in 1282. But on the whole Edward I's munificence was directed to men whose names were new to or at least recent in the March: Henry Lacy, earl of Lincoln (Denbigh); John Warenne, earl of Surrey (Bromfield and Yale); Reginald Grey (Dyffryn Clwyd); and John Giffard of Brimpsfield (Iscennen and later the lordship of Cantrefbychan centred on Llandovery). The Edwardian endowments of 1279–83 had transformed the March in terms both of its political geography and of the personnel of its lords.[11]

The majority of the lords Marcher in 1284, therefore, were

[11] Above, pp. 26–9.

new men or at least members of families recently promoted into the ranks of the Marcher baronage by the accidents of marriage, death and royal generosity. Most of them fitted easily, indeed enthusiastically, into their new role and became staunch upholders of the liberties of the March. But in the March they were *parvenus*. Their outlook had not been shaped, as had that of older Marcher families such as the Corbets, the Mortimers and the Fitzalans, by centuries of experience as frontiersmen, hardened by continual warfare and softened by the arts of co-existence. Furthermore, their coming served to undermine even further such cohesion as the Marcher lords had enjoyed in the early and even in the mid-thirteenth century. For they were almost without exception families whose fortunes had been made in England not in the March and whose preoccupations and political gravitation remained primarily English. That is why the Marchers, as a group, were a less identifiable and cohesive community in 1284 than they had been in 1250. The new blood which had been introduced amongst them had greatly diluted their Marcher outlook.

The difference in outlook was a very real one, but it was more a question of increased emphasis than of an entirely new departure in Marcher attitudes. For at no stage in their history had the lords of the March been a self-contained group whose interests, territorially or otherwise, were confined to the March. For almost without exception[12] they also held lands in England and often in Ireland as well; and their Marcher estates were only a part, and not necessarily the most important part, of their total inheritance. Most of them, it is true, had ambitions which were specifically Marcher in terms of territorial designs and even in the promotion of marriage ties which might further those designs; but in no sense was their outlook totally or exclusively Marcher. They were lords of the March; but they were also, and often more self-consciously, barons of England. That had always been true in some measure; but it was demonstrably more so after the profound changes in the personnel of the March from 1240 onwards. Furthermore, not only were the Marcher lords of 1284 also barons of England, many of them were also key figures in the English political

---

[12] The one major exception is, significantly, the native Welsh house of de la Pole of Powys which failed in the direct male line in 1309.

scene. This again was no totally new feature; but it was a more pronounced characteristic by the reign of Edward I than at any time previous. It can be expressed rather crudely and inadequately in figures: in 1200 only one English earl, the Earl Marshal, held large estates in the March;[13] by 1307 seven out of the ten earls of England were lords of the March. The March had become much more clearly the land of the top people, the top people of English politics.

In this group portrait of the Marcher lords in 1284 one final point, albeit a negative one, needs to be emphasized. The March was by and large a land of secular lordship; the Church's rôle as lord and landowner was a relatively minor one.[14] On the map of the March only three ecclesiastical lordships, Pebidiog and Llawhaden held by the bishop of St. Davids and Bishopcastle by the bishop of Hereford, could compare in size and compactness with the lay lordships of the area. The bishop of St. Davids indeed was far and away the richest of the Welsh bishops and he could claim, rightly and proudly, that his territorial endowment entitled him to the status and privileges of a Marcher lord.[15] So also could the bishop of Llandaff, the only other Welsh bishop whose cathedral lay in the March, in respect of his meagre and scattered estates;[16] and so could the heads of the monastic houses of the March when occasion required. The prior of Goldcliff, for example, declared in 1322 that he was 'a lord of the Marches and has his liberty there like other lords of the Marches'.[17] Even so and even making due allowances for the pockets of ecclesiastical estates to be found in every lordship and for the lavish gifts made to Cistercian houses, the pattern of territorial lordship in the March was far less affected by ecclesiastical endowment than it was in England. Above all, the March on the whole lacked those large and long-established Benedictine estates which were such an outstanding

[13] This figure is admittedly rather distorted by the fact that King John held the earldom of Gloucester's lands in Glamorgan.

[14] For an analysis of church possessions in Wales see Glanmor Williams, *The Welsh Church from Conquest to Reformation* (Cardiff, 1962), 269 ff., 345 ff.

[15] *C.Ch.R. 1341–1417*, 289–90; *Valor Ecclesiasticus* (London, 1810–34), IV, 379. The Marcher status of his lands also extended to his estates in the Principality: R. A. Griffiths, *The Principality of Wales*, I, 12.

[16] Already in 1250 he had asserted that he held his lands of the king in chief only: *Cartae*, II, no. 547.

[17] *C.P.R. 1321–4*, 163.

and influential feature of the tenurial and economic structure of medieval England. The lords of the March were pre-eminently lay lords.

Such then were the lords of the March in 1284—a group of men divers in origins, in their experience of the March and in their territorial interests outside it. Few of these families of 1284, however, survived unscathed during the next century, for the accidents of birth, marriage, death and politics continued to play havoc with them. On occasion the misfortune was only temporary: that was the hiatus of lordship caused by the premature death of the lord and the consequent prolonged widowhood of his wife and minority of his heir. It was almost unknown, indeed, for a Marcher family to have the great good fortune of an unbroken succession of male heirs of full age during the fourteenth century. Only the Greys of Dyffryn Clwyd managed such a remarkable feat for the century as a whole.[18] For the vast majority of Marcher lords a minority was a natural hazard whose consequences profoundly disrupted the effectiveness of their rule. For example, in the case of the Mortimers of Wigmore the periods of minority amounted to forty-six years in the fourteenth century as a whole;[19] and like-wise whereas the rule of the Hastings family in the March (Abergavenny, Cilgerran and later Pembroke) spanned over a century (1283–1389) the heirs were minors for almost half of that period. Under the normal rules of feudal tenure such pro-longed minorities entailed an equivalent period of royal custody; and in many cases this certainly happened.

Given that minorities were so common and their consequences so undesirable from the family's point of view, it is not surprising that ways were increasingly devised to mitigate, if not to avoid altogether, those consequences.[20] A lord might secure from the king a concession that his executors should hold and administer his estates for a period after his death and use the profits for the

---

[18] Dyffryn Clwyd, in fact, passed to a cadet branch of the Grey family in 1323 as a result of parental gift.

[19] But it is only fair to add that occasionally the heir received some of his estates before he came of age. For example, Roger Mortimer second earl of March (d. 1360) received some of his Welsh lands in 1341 whereas the rest of his estates were not granted to him until 1346: Holmes, op. cit. 14–15.

[20] My brief discussion of this topic is largely based on Holmes, ibid. ch. II and J. M. W. Bean, *The Decline of English Feudalism 1215–1540* (Manchester, 1968).

execution of his will.[21] The king might also award the custody of the estates to the widow and the minor;[22] he might grant the minor a part or even the whole of his inheritance before he came of age; he might exempt him from payment of relief.[23] All such grants, however, were arbitrary acts of royal munificence; they were much too insecure as a means of escaping the consequences of a minority. From the mid-fourteenth century a much more radical legal device became increasingly popular and one in which the initiative lay with the landlord himself, even if he had to secure a licence or confirmation from the king. This was the enfeoffment to use whereby a lord devised some of his estates to a group of persons (normally friends, relatives or retainers) with instructions to hold them to his use while he lived and to dispose of them after his death in accordance with his will. The history of the Mortimer estates in the March will show how these enfeoffments operated. On the eve of his departure overseas in 1359, Roger Mortimer, second earl of March, conveyed some of his estates, including the lordships of Narberth and Blaenllyfni, to a group of feoffees, and on his death in the following year these estates were exempted from the normal rules of custody and were instead administered by the feoffees or executors of the late earl.[24] His son, Earl Edmund (d. 1381), followed his father's example enthusiastically, enfeoffing most of his Marcher estates.[25]

Enfeoffments to use served in some degree to mitigate the consequences of prolonged minorities and to ensure a measure of continuity of purpose and administration during the nonage of the heir. But minority was not the only problem that ensued

[21] As happened in the case of Humphrey, earl of Hereford (d. 1373): *C.P.R. 1370–4*, 233, 291–2; *C.C.R. 1369–74*, 505. In spite of the promise, the executors had to give the king a gift of £100 for the privilege: S.C. 6/1156/22, m. 2.

[22] For example, this happened in the case of the Despenser lands in 1376 and 1390: *Glam. C.H.*, III, 183 and n. 126.

[23] The earl of March secured such an exemption in 1357: B.L. Harleian 1240, fol. 47ᵛ.

[24] For the arrangements see Holmes, op. cit. 45–6; and for accounts of the Marcher estates while they were in the hands of the executors B.L. Egerton Rolls 8704–5, 8709–10.

[25] For the arrangements Holmes, op. cit. 51–3. How they worked can be clearly grasped by comparing two account rolls of Mortimer lands in the 1380s—one for Clifford which was in the hands of the royal custodians of the estates (U.C.N.W. Whitney Collection 316) and the other for Radnor which was administered by the late earl's executors (N.L.W. Radnor account, 1384–5).

from the premature death of the lord. It was then also that the widow came into her own. She would receive as of right a third of her late husband's estates as dower; and to these she would add any lands which were hers by inheritance or by joint enfeoffment with her husband. It is not surprising, therefore, that dowager ladies loom large in the history of the late medieval March as indeed of English aristocratic society generally. For a few years in the early 1330s three successive widows held most of the Mortimer lands in the March.[26] The heir to the Mortimer estates, Roger second earl of March, had to wait until 1358 before he was able to reassemble the whole of his inheritance which had been so fragmented by the law of dower. The Mortimer widows might be difficult to match in numbers; but other Marcher dowagers were more powerful territorially. The thrice-widowed Elizabeth Burgh ruled as lady of Usk, Caerleon and Trelech for thirty-three years;[27] while her near neighbour, Agnes widow of Laurence Hastings earl of Pembroke (d. 1348), held Abergavenny as dower for twenty years and added to it the custody of the county of Pembroke.[28] Most extraordinary of all in this saga of widows was the history of the lordship of Chepstow which was ruled by or on behalf of women from 1338 to 1399, first as jointure of Mary, countess of Norfolk (d. 1362) after the death of her husband (d. 1338) and then as part of the inheritance of his daughter, Margaret, countess Marshal, who survived her two husbands and her son-in-law and ruled Chepstow as a widow from 1372 to 1399.[29]

[26] Margaret de Fiennes (d. 1334) widow of Edmund Mortimer (d. 1304) held Knighton, Norton, Presteigne, Gwerthrynion and Radnor as dower; Joan de Geneville (d. 1356) widow of Earl Roger (d. 1330) held Ceri and Cydewain as dower and Ewyas Lacy and a moiety of Ludlow in her own right; and Elizabeth Badlesmere (d. 1355) widow of Edmund Mortimer (d. 1331) held Maelienydd and Cwmwd Deuddwr as her dower and eventually took them to her second husband, William Bohun earl of Northampton (d. 1360).

[27] For Elizabeth Burgh and her estates see Holmes, op. cit. 35–8, 58–9, 86 ff.; and his, 'A Protest against the Despensers, 1326', *Speculum* 30 (1955), 207–12. She also had custody of the lordship of Pembroke 1331–9: *C.F.R. 1327–37*, 288–9; *C.C.R. 1339–41*, 209–10.

[28] She secured Abergavenny in 1348 and the custody of Pembroke from 1351 and, subsequently, her rights of custody were confirmed after the death of her second husband, John Hakelut, in 1357: *C.C.R. 1346–9*, 575; *C.P.R. 1350–4*, 199; *C.C.R. 1354–60*, 438. For her vigorous defence of her rights as lady of Abergavenny, see S.C. 8/159, no. 7948.

[29] *Complete Peerage*, IX, 598–600. She devised Chepstow to the earl of Pembroke and Anne, his wife and her daughter, for forty years in 1372; but four years later

The implications of minorities and widowhood, of enfeoffments to use, jointure arrangements and dower portions extend
far beyond the details of genealogy, marriage and family settlements. They could and did profoundly affect the pattern of
lordship and of political and territorial power in the March. A
prolonged widowhood could well damage the prospects of an
heir and substantially reduce his landed wealth and possibly
thereby his political power. For example, Edmund Mortimer,
third earl of March (d. 1381) was never such a powerful
Marcher lord as he could have been because his mother,
Countess Philippa, outlived him and kept a large share of the
Mortimer lordships in the March (including Denbigh, Narberth, Maelienydd, Ceri, Gwerthrynion and Knighton, worth
all told about £1,500 per annum) out of his control.[30] Countess
Philippa did not remarry; but other Marcher widows did so
and thereby affected even further the pattern of territorial
power in the March. For the second husband during his wife's
lifetime would enjoy both her inherited and dower lands; and
if he survived her, he could continue to hold her inherited
estates by the courtesy of England. In the fourteenth-century
March there was perhaps no more discriminating connoisseur
of wealthy widows than William Mortimer de la Zouche. A
man of very modest means himself, he married successively
Alice Tony (d. 1325), widow of Guy Beauchamp, earl of
Warwick (d. 1315), and Eleanor Clare (d. 1337), one of the
Clare coheiresses and widow of the younger Despenser (d. 1326).
In respect of his wives' properties he became lord of Elfael and
Glamorgan and was a considerable figure in the March until
his death in 1337.[31]

Minorities likewise could affect the pattern of territorial
power in a crucial fashion; that is why the granting of the
wardship and marriage of minors and of the custody of their
lands was one of the most important and delicate arts of king-

Anne, now a widow, leased all her estates in England and Wales for ten years to her
mother: *C.I.P.M.*, xiv, no. 148; *C.C.R. 1374–7*, 333, 448–9.

[30] For Philippa's complicated dower arrangements see *C.C.R. 1360–4*, 46–7, 80–8,
135; Holmes, *Estates of the Higher Nobility*, 46. Accounts of her estates are to be found
in S.C. 6/1206/4; 1209/12–13; N.L.W. Slebech Collection. The account of Earl
Edmund's receiver-general for 1374–5 shows what a truncated inheritance was left
for him in the March: B.L. Egerton Roll 8727.

[31] *Glam. C.H.*, iii, 173–6; *Complete Peerage*, xii, ii, 957–60.

ship in the middle ages. Once more a single example from the March must serve to bear out this general point. The premature death of Edmund Mortimer, third earl of March, in 1381 was of momentous importance in the territorial politics of the March in Richard II's reign. Some of his lands remained in the hands of feoffees but others did not, and the question of who was to have custody of them was a major political issue in the early 1380s. The fact that they were eventually granted in 1384 to a consortium headed by the Earl of Arundel (even though he did not secure the marriage of the heir) helped to determine the political complexion of the March for the rest of the decade and was to prove vitally significant in the struggle between Richard II and his opponents in 1387–8.[32] Nor were the consequences of minorities and widowhoods confined to the chessboard of territorial politics; they might also have repercussions within the estates themselves. Lordship like kingship was intensely personal; it was bound to change its character when it was exercised by commission or by women. Many of the avenues of service and patronage were made available to his men by the lord; without him, such avenues were closed. The estates might be well, even ruthlessly, administered during a minority or a widowhood; but that could not conceal the fact that an estate without a lord lacked 'good lordship' in the broadest and best sense of that phrase. It is no coincidence that the only major revolt in the March in the fourteenth century, that of Llywelyn Bren in Glamorgan in 1316, flared up while the lordship was in royal custody. Its leader was a man who felt that he had been unjustly deprived of those perquisites of 'good lordship' which he had enjoyed in the past.[33]

The 'good lordship' that Llywelyn Bren had lost was that of Gilbert Clare earl of Gloucester, killed at Bannockburn in 1314. On his death the house of Clare ceased to rule in the March, for his estates were eventually partitioned between his three sisters. The disappearance of the house of Clare is only the most spectacular example of a general feature of the March

---

[32] *C.P.R. 1381–5*, 377; B.L. Egerton Roll 8730 (roll of expenses of custodians of the Mortimer estates, 1387). For comment, see Holmes, *Estates of the Higher Nobility*, 18–19; K. B. McFarlane, *Lancastrian Kings and Lollard Knights* (Oxford, 1972), 189; A. Goodman, *The Loyal Conspiracy. The Lords Appellant under Richard II* (1971), 34–5.

[33] *Glam. C.H.*, III, 72–86.

in the fourteenth century, namely the extinction of many of its leading families. The routes to extinction were several. Some families, especially the smaller ones, sold out, either weighed down by debt or anticipating the consequences of childlessness as an opportunity to sell the reversion of their estates. Such was the story in the case of the Fitzherbert family. John fitz Reginald (d. 1308) had a son and heir; but cash he had none.[34] So it was that in 1307 he surrendered his Marcher estates—Blaenllyfni, Bwlchyddinas, Talgarth and Caldicot—to Edward II in return for their re-grant to him for life and exemption from military and parliamentary services.[35] It proved a poor bargain for him, for he died the following year and his estates were dispersed. Talgarth came by purchase and exchange into the hands of an ambitious Marcher cleric, Master Rees ap Hywel;[36] while Blaenllyfni and Bwlchyddinas were used by the king to augment the territorial endowment of Roger Mortimer of Chirk.[37] Penury also contributed to the extinction of a much older and more distinguished Marcher family, the Corbets of Caus. Already in his lifetime a combination of debt and childlessness made Peter Corbet (d. 1322) fair game for the ruthless ambitions of his neighbours in the March, Edmund Fitzalan earl of Arundel (d. 1326) and Roger Mortimer of Chirk (d. 1326).[38] Both, however, were outwitted in their attempts by political catastrophe and death; and Corbet's widow managed to cling onto Caus until her own death in 1347. But hers was simply a holding operation and on her death the name of Corbet, one of the oldest in the March, disappeared.[39] A few years earlier, yet another old Norman family which, like the Corbets, had stamped its name as well as its rule on the March—the Montalts of Mold—sold out the reversion of its estates in anticipation of childless death.[40]

---

[34] For indications of the extent of his debt, see K.B. 27/18, m. 14d.; *C.P.R. 1307–13*, 27.

[35] *C.P.R. 1307–13*, 22, 27, 62.

[36] *C.P.R. 1301–7*, 447; *1307–13*, 153; *C.I.P.M.*, v, no. 106; *C.Ch.R. 1300–26*, 125; *C.F.R. 1307–13*, 37–8; *C. Chancery Warrants 1244–1326*, 313; S.C. 8/218, no. 10895; I. H. Jeayes, *The Charters and Muniments at Berkeley Castle* (1892), no. 531 (final quitclaim of Talgarth, 1353).

[37] *C.F.R. 1307–13*, 58; *C.P.R. 1307–13*, 293.

[38] Below, pp. 56–7.

[39] *C.I.P.M.*, VI, no. 318; R. W. Eyton, *Antiquities of Shropshire*, VII, 38.

[40] *C.A.D.*, V, 68 A.10947–9; *C.P.R. 1327–30*, 96; *C.C.R. 1327–30*, 267.

Other Marcher families became extinct in the fourteenth century not through failure of heirs or even of money but of the Crown's goodwill. Political forfeiture was normally the occasion. For most families in the fourteenth century, such as the Mortimers, the Fitzalans and even the Despensers, political forfeiture was a temporary calamity from which they recovered, either completely or in part, by the swing of the political pendulum and by the goodwill of the Crown. But for some families political forfeiture was the end of the road. Thus, after the execution of John Giffard in 1322 his estates were officially declared to have escheated *per defectum heredis*, though two of his half-sisters survived him; and the commote of Iscennen which had been in family possession since 1283 was granted to a series of royal favourites.[41] Much more clear-cut and dramatic was the case of Roger Mortimer of Chirk, for rarely was a family so comprehensively and unjustly disinherited as his was. In a political career of over forty years, he had rarely put a foot wrong before 1322. He had grown rich and powerful in royal service: as a younger son he had no landed inheritance of his own, but the king's favour had added Chirkland (1282) and Blaenllyfni (1310) to his wife's patrimony of Pencelli and Tir Ralph and had bestowed on him the major official position in Wales, that of justiciar of the Principality (1308–15, 1317–22). In the autumn of 1321 Roger Mortimer of Chirk was one of the most powerful men in Wales and the March and seemed to have established the secure foundations of a new Marcher house. That, however, was not to be; for in his case his disloyalty in

---

[41] *Complete Peerage*, v, 647–9. The story of the descent of the Giffard lands in the March is a complex one. John Giffard (d. 1299) held two groups of estates in Wales: the commotes of Hirfryn, Perfedd and Iscennen by royal grants in 1282–3 and Bronllys, Cantrefselyf and Clifford as second husband of Maud, daughter and heir of Walter Clifford (d. 1263) and widow of William Longespee (d. 1257). Of these estates, Iscennen alone passed to his son John and was thus confiscated in 1322. Hirfryn and Perfedd were granted to his daughter Katherine who married Sir Nicholas Audley and they remained in the hands of the Audley family until 1490 (*History of Carmarthenshire*, i, ed. J. E. Lloyd (Cardiff, 1935), 234); Bronllys and Cantrefselyf appear as the portion of another daughter Maud (d. 1311) and were subsequently acquired by Master Rees ap Hywel (*C.F.R. 1272–1307*, 421–2; *1307–19*, 92; *1319–27*, 92; *C. Inq. Misc. 1219–1307*, no. 1870); while Clifford reverted to Margaret, daughter of Maud Clifford by her first husband William Longespee. Margaret married Henry Lacy earl of Lincoln; and their only surviving child, Alice, took Clifford to her husband Earl Thomas of Lancaster (d. 1322). For these reasons, the Giffard forfeiture of 1322 was not so profound in its impact on the March as it might have been.

1322 proved his own undoing and, what is more, that of his family. He died in prison in August 1326, a few weeks before the political revolution which might have restored him to his former position and estates. In fact, that revolution only served to annihilate the fortunes of his family, for the greed of his nephew, Roger Mortimer of Wigmore, rode roughshod over family ties and affection. All that the son of Mortimer of Chirk was able to salvage were the lands he had inherited from his mother—Pencelli and Tir Ralph in the lordship of Brecon and Tedstone Wafre in Herefordshire; the earl of March, in a brazenly cynical act of magnanimity, graciously granted him those estates for life at a token rent![42] The fall of the earl of March in 1330 might have been expected to herald a recovery in the fortunes of his cousin of Chirk; but it was not to be so. It was not for want of trying,[43] but for want of royal support. Royal indifference or royal opposition could keep a family down; equally, royal favour could re-establish a family. In 1354 the Mortimers of Wigmore made a complete comeback; at much the same time their cousins of Pencelli finally capitulated to their misfortunes. In August 1359 John Mortimer, grandson of the first Mortimer of Chirk, quitclaimed most of his grandfather's lands (Blaenllyfni, Bwlchyddinas, Narberth and a third of St. Clears) to the earl of March and the great lordship of Chirk to the earl of Arundel; and at much the same time he was done out of much of his land in Pencelli by the earl of Hereford.[44] The nobles of the fourteenth century were well versed in the art of kicking a man when he was down; they had now extracted the final submission from John Mortimer. They could now afford to indulge their consciences and they did so by granting legacies and annuities to the descendants of Mortimer of Chirk.[45]

[42] *C.P.R. 1327–30*, 141–3; B.L. Harleian 1240, fol. 43ᵛ.

[43] *Complete Peerage*, IX, 255, quoting S.C. 8/263, no. 13104.

[44] B.L. Harleian 1240, fol. 43ᵛ., fol. 50; Holmes, *Estates of the Higher Nobility*, 15 (Mortimer-Arundel deal re. Chirk); R. R. Davies, 'The Bohun and Lancaster Lordships in Wales in the fourteenth and early fifteenth centuries' (Univ. of Oxford D.Phil. thesis, 1965), 98–100 (Pencelli).

[45] Roger, second earl of March, granted John Mortimer an annuity of a hundred marks from Marden and Wynforton (both of them former manors of Mortimer of Chirk!); and Earl Humphrey of Hereford (d. 1361) left £100 in his will for the purchase of lands for John Mortimer and his heirs in perpetuity. Edmund, third earl of March, likewise felt obliged to leave £500 in his will for his

The Mortimers of Chirk had been eliminated; but their story is in fact the exception not the rule, for most of the families of the March showed remarkable resilience and powers of recovery in the face of political disaster. From the point of view of the continuity of the family and of the inheritance it was another kind of calamity, and one from which there was no recovery, which created the greatest havoc—the failure of direct male heirs. It was this 'natural wastage' which above all transformed the ranks of the Marcher lords in the fourteenth as in the thirteenth century. The list of Marcher houses which so failed between 1300 and 1399 is eloquently long and distinguished: Mortimer 1304 (Richards Castle and Bleddfa); Bigod 1306 (Chepstow); Tony 1309 (Elfael); Pole 1309 (Powys); Lacy 1311 (Denbigh); Clare 1314 (Glamorgan, Newport, Usk, Caerleon); Geneville and Verdon 1314–16 (Ludlow, Ewyas Lacy); Giffard 1322 (Iscennen); Valence 1324 (Pembroke); Braose 1326 (Gower); Fitzmartin 1326 (Cemais); Montalt 1329 (Mold, Hawarden); Camville 1338 (Llanstephan); Audley 1347 (Newport); Warenne 1347 (Bromfield and Yale); Corbet 1347 (Caus); Lancaster 1361 (Kidwelly, Monmouth); Burghersh 1369 (Ewyas Lacy); Bohun 1373 (Brecon, Hay, Huntington); Hastings 1389 (Pembroke, Abergavenny); Brian 1390 (Laugharne); Audley 1391 (Cantref Bychan, Cemais). The list is not in fact an exhaustive one, especially as far as one-generation Marcher families are concerned; but it is long enough to make its point. Out of the two dozen or so leading Marcher families of 1284 only three (Grey of Dyffryn Clwyd, Mortimer of Wigmore and the Fitzalan earls of Arundel) survived in the male line by 1390.

Whether it came suddenly or with an inexorable slowness, death without a direct male heir was a spectre which haunted every noble family. For it spelled the extinction of the house, the end of the landed inheritance as an entity, and either its amalgamation with another inheritance or its dispersal between co-heirs or co-heiresses. It is little wonder that attempts were occasionally made, such as those by the earl of Surrey (d. 1347) or the earl of Pembroke (d. 1375), to forestall or at least to

---

distant and disendowed relative of Chirk: *C.C.R. 1360–4*, 47; *A Collection of all the Wills of the Kings and Queens of England*, ed. J. Nichols (1780), 55, 104.

control the consequences of such a calamity.[46] Nor was the absence of direct male heirs merely a domestic misfortune; it was often a matter of momentous significance in many other directions. Politically its significance is obvious and nowhere more so than in the March: the extinction of a family and the fate of its estates could profoundly, even permanently, affect the distribution of territorial power and thereby of political influence. To give one obvious example: the extinction of the house of Clare in 1314 cast its shadow over Marcher, and indeed English, politics for almost a generation. The native Welsh chronicler showed a true sense of perspective when he recorded it as the most important consequence of the battle of Bannockburn, for such it was from the viewpoint of the March.[47] Nor was the extinction of a family merely a matter of high politics; it touched the lives of the people of the March themselves. It brought them within the ambit of a new inheritance in which the importance of their own lordship might well be greatly modified; it often opened new avenues of service and it often closed old ones; it might bring a new 'style' of lordship; it certainly brought a new corps of officials. Lordship was personal; it was also familial. And so were the bonds of loyalty.

As one family after another failed in the male line, new ones took their place in the ranks of Marcher lords. They arrived, as usual, along the twin routes of marriage and royal support; indeed the routes were closely linked for the grant of the hand of an heiress was often an act of royal munificence. Among the most important new families which so appeared in the March in the fourteenth century were the Charltons, Despensers, Beauchamps, Montagues, Staffords and (rather earlier) Hastings. The Charltons of Powys and the Despensers of Glamorgan were both of them families who owed their Marcher estates to royally-provided wives, though in neither case could the remarkable territorial fortune which both eventually gained have been foreseen at the time of their betrothal. John Charlton secured the title to the large lordship of Powys in 1309 on the death of his wife's nephew, Griffith de la Pole—and thereby inaugurated the line of the Charltons of Powys. The house survived in the male line until 1421, but its power was rather

[46] Holmes, op. cit. 41–2.
[47] *Brenhinedd y Saesson or The Kings of the Saxons*, ed. T. Jones (Cardiff, 1971), 264.

restricted by the fact that its estates were confined to Shrophire and the March. The entry of the Charltons into Marcher circles had been a stormy one and a politically explosive issue;[48] that of the younger Despenser was even more so. His claim to Glamorgan as husband of the eldest Clare coheiress was un-impugnable; but the way in which he and his father ruthlessly established an empire for themselves in the March convulsed the politics of the area and indeed of England also from 1318 to 1326.[49] The empire crashed in 1326; but that was not the end of the reign of the Despensers as a Marcher family. They continued to rule in Glamorgan until 1413, though the effectiveness of their rule was hampered by prolonged periods of minority.[50]

Both Charlton and the younger Despenser were favourites of Edward II; another new Marcher family, the Montagues, owed their promotion entirely to the affection of Edward III towards William Montague (d. 1344), the first earl of Salisbury of his line. The lordship of Denbigh was bestowed on Montague in 1331 as a token of gratitude for his services to the king in effecting the downfall of the earl of March, its previous lord, in 1330.[51] He had to pay heavily for the security of his title to the lordship;[52] but it was no doubt worth it, for Denbigh with its gross income of £1,000 per annum was one of the most desirable of Marcher lordships.[53] Montague enhanced his standing as a Marcher lord in 1337 when he secured the reversion of the Montalt inheritance, including Hawarden and Moldsdale, from the queen mother and in the meantime rented it for 600 marks a year.[54] When he died in 1344, William Montague could feel confident that he had established the power of his house, both in England and in the March. Such confidence proved to be misplaced, for even the royal favour of

[48] For the Pole-Charlton dispute over Powys, see J. R. Maddicott, *Thomas of Lancaster*, 140–7.

[49] Below, pp. 279–81.

[50] *Glam. C.H.*, III, 167–83.

[51] *C.Ch.R. 1327–41*, 210.

[52] He paid £200 to Alice Lacy (who had inherited the lordship from her father Henry de Lacy earl of Lincoln); £1,000 to the younger Despenser's son and heir (his grandfather had held the lordship 1322–6); and £233.6s.8d. to the younger Despenser's widow: B.L. Egerton Charters 8715.

[53] Its value was given as 1,000 marks in the grant of 1331, but in the *Survey* of 1334 it was estimated to be worth £1,100 gross and was again valued at £1,000 gross in 1344: *S.D.* 323; *C.I.P.M.*, VIII, no. 532.

[54] *C.Ch.R. 1327–41*, 432–3; B.L. Cotton Charters, XI, 61.

Edward III was a fickle basis for a family fortune. That favour was not extended to the second Montague earl of Salisbury (d. 1397)—not only was it withheld but, even more damagingly, it was bestowed on others who regarded themselves as hereditary claimants to the Montague lands. More especially was the royal favour extended to the young Roger Mortimer who recovered Denbigh from the Montagues in 1354.[55] The Montagues retained Mold and Hawarden, but their career as major Marcher lords had been as brusquely terminated as it had been suddenly initiated in 1331. And on both occasions it was the royal will which determined the issue.

The same was true in the case of another new Marcher family, the Beauchamps. Their original entry into the ranks of Marcher barons was made via the relatively secure route of marriage. Guy Beauchamp, earl of Warwick (d. 1315) took as his wife Alice, sister and heir of Robert de Tony (d. 1309), lord of Elfael; and when Alice's third husband, William de la Zouche, died in 1337 the Beauchamps at last made good their claim to the lordship.[56] Elfael was a worthwhile acquisition; but it was not by Marcher standards a very rich lordship[57] A much sweeter plum fell into the Beauchamp lap in 1354 when the family was awarded the lordship of Gower after prolonged litigation. The judgement was not necessarily an arbitrary royal decision; but the shadow of the king's influence and favour probably lay over it.[58] Before long the power of the Beauchamp family was further enhanced in the March. A younger son, Sir William Beauchamp (d. 1411) farmed the lordships of Pembroke and Cilgerran from 1377 to 1387; soon after he became a Marcher lord in his own right, for in the settlement which followed the death of the last Hastings earl of Pembroke in 1389 he secured the lordship of Abergavenny as his portion.[59] Between them the two brothers, Earl Thomas of Warwick (d. 1401) and Sir William Beauchamp, made the family into a considerable force in the March during the reign

---

[55] Holmes, op. cit. 16 and for the reversal of Montague fortunes generally, ibid. 28-9.

[56] *C.I.P.M.*, v, no. 198; VIII, no. 112.

[57] In 1397 it was valued at £194: *C. Inq. Misc. 1392-9*, no. 228.

[58] Holmes, op. cit. 39; *Glam. C.H.*, III, 249.

[59] *Complete Peerage*, I, 24-6; R. I. Jack, 'Entail and Descent: The Hastings Inheritance, 1370-1436', *B.I.H.R.* 38 (1965), 1-19.

of Richard II.[60] But it was not to last; for in 1396–7 Richard II engineered the reversion of the 1354 judgement in favour of the Beauchamps and Gower was restored to Mowbray. Yet again the fickleness of royal favour had undone the territorial fortune of a family.

Of all the new houses that made their first appearance in the March in the fourteenth century, none was to last longer than the house of Stafford. The year 1347 was the *annus mirabilis* for this family, for within a few months two Marcher lordships came the way of Ralph, lord Stafford. As great-grandson and coheir of Alice Corbet he inherited a share of Caus lordship on the death of Beatrice Corbet and by 1357 he had bought out the share of one of the other coheirs, Edmund Cornwall.[61] From his second wife, Margaret, daughter and heir of Hugh Audley, earl of Gloucester (d. 1347), he acquired an even greater territorial prize, the lordship of Newport and Gwynllwg. The Staffords had become a leading Marcher family at a stroke; and the elevation of Ralph Stafford to an earldom in 1351 set the seal on his new-found wealth and favour. Nor was that the end of their Marcher fortunes, for marriage brought them even more power with their acquisition of the lordship of Huntington in 1402 and those of Brecon and Hay in 1421. Precisely a century later the execution of Edward Stafford, duke of Buckingham, brought to an end the last of the great Marcher families.[62]

One of the new Marcher families, that of Hastings, did not survive the fourteenth century. It was, in fact, older as a Marcher house than any of those mentioned so far. John Hastings (d. 1313) had inherited Abergavenny, Cilgerran and a third of St. Clears from his mother, Joan Cantilupe, in 1283 and thereby launched his family on its Marcher career. The family's power was greatly augmented in 1324 when it inherited a claim to the lands and title of the Valence earls of Pembroke, even though the claim was not realized for another fifteen years. To this very considerable Marcher inheritance was added a forty-year lease of the lordship of Chepstow in 1372 to John

---

[60] From February 1387 Warwick and his brother were also two of the custodians of the Stafford lands: *C.F.R. 1383–91*, 173–4.

[61] *C.I.P.M.*, ix, no. 50; *C.C.R. 1346–9*, 331–2, 395, *C.P.R. 1354–8*, 544; B.L. Additional Charters, 20435–6; 20439–40; 28645.

[62] For the Staffords as Marcher lords, see generally *The Marcher Lordships of South Wales 1415–1536*, ed. T. B. Pugh.

Hastings earl of Pembroke (d. 1375) and Anne his wife.[63] Potentially the Hastings family was one of the most powerful in the March in the mid-fourteenth century; but in fact, as we have already seen, its rule was undermined by prolonged minorities and it was finally extinguished in 1389 when the heir, John Hastings, was killed in a tournament.

The extinction of old families and the appearance of new ones was certainly a feature of the March in the fourteenth century; but even more striking in some ways was the longevity and good fortune of two of the oldest houses of the March— those of Mortimer and Fitzalan. Of the two the house of Mortimer was the senior.[64] It had established its base at Wigmore by the time of Domesday Book and had already started on its career as a Marcher family, for the Welshry of Pilleth was among its possessions. For the next two centuries, indeed, a great deal of its time and prowess was to be spent on military campaigns in the difficult area of the middle March; and its enterprise was eventually rewarded with the final conquest of the lordships of Maelienydd and Gwerthrynion.[65] Conquest brought its rewards, but slowly and uncertainly. It was to be by more peaceful arts that the Mortimers emerged, from the mid-thirteenth century onwards, into the front rank of Marcher families. It was Roger Mortimer (d. 1282) who showed the way or rather ways, for the success of the Mortimers as of so many other families was paved along the twin paths of marriage and politics. His bride, Maud Braose, was an heiress twice over—through her father William Braose (d. 1230) and her mother Eva Marshall; and the landed endowment she brought to her husband included the lordships of Radnor and Narberth and a moiety of St. Clears. Roger Mortimer had chosen his bride well; he chose his patron with equal acumen. By the 1260s he was high in the favour of the Lord Edward and he retained that warm affection until his death.[66] With affection came favours: franchises and privileges, and above all the grant of the lordships of Ceri and Cydewain in 1279

---

[63] *C.I.P.M.*, xiv, no. 148.

[64] For the careers of the Mortimers the articles by T. F. Tout in *The Dictionary of National Biography*, vol. xxxix are outstandingly helpful.

[65] J. B. Smith, *B.B.C.S.* 24 (1970), 77–93.

[66] Note the letter that Edward I wrote on Roger's death in 1282, summarized in *C.W.R.*, 257.

followed by the conferment of Chirk on his second son, Roger, in 1282.

Roger's son, Edmund (d. 1304), it is true, showed few of his father's personal qualities or his judgement in affairs marital and political; but his grandson, Roger (d. 1330) most certainly did so and in ample measure. In his case also marriage was the beginning of good fortune. His bride, to whom he was betrothed in 1301, was Joan Geneville, heiress of the extensive Geneville estates in the March and Ireland. Those estates included the lordship of Ewyas Lacy and a moiety of Ludlow; and both were soon amalgamated into the Mortimer inheritance. Ludlow, indeed, by mid-century had replaced Wigmore as the capital of the Mortimer empire. And the word 'empire' is hardly an exaggeration for the power which the house of Mortimer came to exercise in Wales and the March between 1310 and 1330 in the persons of both Roger Mortimer of Wigmore and his namesake and uncle of Chirk. The story of the growth and consequences of that predominance is too well known to require detailed repetition here. It was until 1322 very much a joint success-story. It was compounded of grants of land (Cwmwd Deuddwr to the nephew 1309; Blaenllyfni to the uncle 1310), of offices (the justiciarships of Wales and Ireland) and of patronage (such as the lion's share in the marriage of the young earl of Warwick); and it was riveted by well-calculated marriages, notably those of the daughters of Mortimer of Wigmore to John Charlton, the heir of Powys and to Thomas Beauchamp, the heir to the earldom of Warwick and the lordship of Elfael. By 1321 the two Mortimers had built up in Wales and in Ireland what appeared to be an unchallengeable position in terms both of lands and offices. All, however, was lost in the débâcle of 1322; but the setback proved for Mortimer of Wigmore, unlike his uncle of Chirk,[67] to be only temporary. For in a period of almost four years as virtual regent of England from January 1327 to October 1330, Roger Mortimer of Wigmore established a truly unparalleled position for himself in the March and the Principality of Wales.[68] Mortimer's ambitions were boundless; but he never forgot in his few years of glory that his was a Marcher family and it was in the March that his success was most transparent. It was therefore peculiarly

[67] Above, p. 47.   [68] Below, p. 281.

appropriate that the earldom conferred on him in October 1328 should bear the novel title of the earldom of March and that the celebration tournament should be held at Wigmore in the presence of the king.[69]

Two years later Roger Mortimer was executed. But his political success outlived him, for when Edward III visited his favour on Roger's grandson, the second Earl of March (d. 1360), in the 1350s that favour extended not only to the family inheritance as it stood in 1322 but also to some of the acquisitions of the period 1327–30, including Denbigh, Blaenllyfni, Clifford and Glasbury, and Montgomery and Builth on lease.[70] The success story of the Mortimers had been resumed and their position as the premier family of the March was assured. One further marriage put the matter beyond doubt: that of Earl Edmund (d. 1381) to Philippa daughter of Lionel, duke of Clarence and through her mother sole heiress of the extensive estates of Elizabeth Burgh. Those estates came into Mortimer possession in 1368. They greatly extended the family's power in England and Ireland, and in the March the addition of the lordships of Usk, Trelech and Caerleon put the superiority of the house of Mortimer beyond question. By the end of the fourteenth century the Mortimers had ruled in the March for over 300 years. Merely in terms of survival that was an outstanding record compared with that of most baronial families. It was all the more impressive in that the family also managed to surmount a series of political disasters—from the moment of their misplaced support for the rebellion of 1088 to the great calamity of 1330. But they had done more than merely survive. They had prospered; more particularly and even spectacularly had they prospered in the century from 1270 to 1370. In 1270 Roger Mortimer held four major Marcher lordships; in 1373 Edmund Mortimer's inheritance included sixteen Marcher lordships of his inheritance and two more under his control.

[69] The novelty of the earl's title astounded the author of the *Annales Paulini* (*Chronicles of the Reigns of Edward I and Edward II*, ed. W. Stubbs (Rolls Series, 1882–3), I, 343). The tournament at Wigmore and the royal visits there are described in the Wigmore chronicle (*Monasticon Anglicanum*, VI, i. 352) and even more vividly in the Ludlow annals (B.L. Cotton Nero A. IV, fols. 59–60).

[70] The recovery of the Mortimer fortunes in the 1350s is admirably documented in Holmes, *Estates of the Higher Nobility*, 15–17. To the list of those who lost their lands as a result of the come-back should be added Richard Talbot who was ousted from the lordships of Blaenllyfni and Bwlchyddinas: *C.I.P.M.*, VIII, no. 714.

Such is the measure of the success of the house of Mortimer in the March.

Its only serious rival in the March was the house of Fitzalan, the earls of Arundel. It too was an old-established house. It had held the lordship of Oswestry since the reign of Henry I and Clun since the reign of John; and these frontier lordships were strengthened by the Fitzalan manors in Shropshire. It was, at least until the mid-thirteenth century, primarily a Marcher family for it was only then that it acquired a claim to the earldom of Arundel and to extensive lands in England. It was in the March that it had one of its favourite residences at the castle of Shrawardine.[71] The fourteenth century was the golden age of the Fitzalan family. Its rule from 1287 to 1397 was only interrupted by two brief periods of royal custody (1302–6), (1326–30), and its affairs were directed by three remarkably able earls: Edmund (1302–26), Richard (1330–76) and Richard (1376–97). The estates of the family were greatly extended during the century, both by extensive purchases and by inheritance (notably by the acquisition of the Warenne lands in 1347); and under Earl Richard (d. 1376) the liquid assets of the family became immense.[72]

The growth of the landed wealth and prestige of the Fitzalans in England during the fourteenth century was more than matched by the increase in their estates and status in the March. How important the March was in the territorial ambitions of the family was made evident enough by Earl Edmund in 1315. So anxious was he to secure the reversion of the lordship of Caus, strategically placed between his own lordships of Oswestry and Clun, that he was willing to entice its lord, Peter Corbet, with a life-grant of the manor of Chipping Norton and

[71] It was renamed Castle Philippa in the 1390s as a token of affection for the earl's new bride, Philippa Mortimer, widow of John Hastings (d. 1389). For its splendid fittings see *C. Inq. Misc. 1392–9* no. 237. It was being extensively repaired and rebuilt in the 1390s: Shrewsbury Public Library Craven Collection 9777 (account of receiver of Oswestry 1394–5).

[72] The wealth of Earl Richard (d. 1376) is well known, particularly from the inventory of his ready cash and of debts owed to him at his death (B.L. Harleian 4843, fol. 393). To it can be added a revealing list of his assets in the March in 1370, Shrewsbury Public Library Craven Collection 5923. It has been estimated that he spent £4,000 on acquiring land in West Sussex alone: *Fitzalan Surveys*, ed. M. Clough (Sussex Record Society, 67), xxvi, n. 1. For recent discussions of his wealth and of his loans, see K. B. McFarlane, *The Nobility of Later Medieval England*, 88–91 and G. A. Holmes, *The Good Parliament* (Oxford, 1975), 74–7.

£20 of rent and to buy out the claim of his rival, Roger Mortimer of Chirk, with a gift of land and £1,000 in cash.[73] As it happens the deal fell through because of a royal veto on it;[74] but Arundel had clearly shown that he was willing to sacrifice some of his manors in England in order to consolidate his position in the March.

The royal will had baulked Arundel's ambitions in 1315; it served to transform them in the 1320s and to do so where it mattered most for Arundel, in the March. He stood with the king in 1322 and soon reaped his rewards: Ceri, Cydewain, Gwerthrynion and Cwmwd Deuddwr out of the forfeited lands of Mortimer of Wigmore, Chirkland out of those of Mortimer of Chirk, and the posts of justiciar of Wales and warden of the March.[75] His success proved to be short-lived; but his execution in 1326 did not in the long run involve the ruin of the family nor even the loss of all its recent acquisitions. For when Richard Fitzalan was restored to the family lands and earldom in 1330–1, the lordship of Chirk (part of the political spoils of 1322) was added to them and henceforth remained a firm part of the family inheritance. It was a strategically important acquisition for it lay next to the family lordship of Oswestry. The Fitzalan estates in the March were neatly rounded off in 1347 when most of the Warenne estates were finally acquired by Earl Richard of Arundel on the death of his uncle, John Warenne, earl of Surrey. It was an acquisition which had long been anticipated but which was only secured (and not even then in its totality) by the constant watchfulness of the Fitzalans.[76] It brought them in the March the lordship of Bromfield and Yale, doubly attractive because of its wealth (it was worth close on £1,000 a year) and of its position contiguous to the existing Fitzalan lordships of Oswestry and Chirk.

The Fitzalans towered in the March of Wales; only the Mortimers could match them in wealth and power and they

---

[73] B.L. Harleian 1240, fol. 49ᵛ. (20 February 1315); Additional Charters 20438 (14 February 1315); *C.P.R. 1313–17*, 266 (14 March 1315).

[74] *C.C.R. 1313–18*, 226–7 (7 May 1315).

[75] *C.Ch.R. 1300–26*, 442; *C.F.R. 1319–27*, 86–7; *C.P.R. 1324–7*, 171.

[76] For this remarkable episode, see E. R. Fairbank, 'The Last Earl of Warenne and Surrey and the Distribution of his Possessions', *Yorkshire Archaeological Journal* 19 (1907), 193–267. It is one of the most instructive episodes in the territorial politics of the fourteenth century.

were beset by dowagers and minors. Never did this Fitzalan pre-eminence appear more outstanding than in the early 1390s. Richard Fitzalan, earl of Arundel, was then hereditary lord of Oswestry, Clun, Chirkland, Bromfield and Yale; he held a third of the lordship of Abergavenny in respect of his second wife; he headed the consortium which controlled the Mortimer estates during the heir's minority. His family links riveted his power in the March even more firmly: his son-in-law and former ward, John Charlton, was lord of Powys and briefly justiciar of north Wales; another son-in-law, Sir William Beauchamp, succeeded to the lordship of Abergavenny in the 1390s; while the young earl of March was Arundel's brother-in-law. Arundel's power in the March was made manifest in the political crises of the period: it was there that he helped to scotch Richard II's ambitions in 1387–8 and it was from his castle at Holt that he cocked a snook at John of Gaunt in 1393.[77] Perhaps the most remarkable demonstration of his power and arrogance was the document he caused to be included in the survey of his lordship of Bromfield and Yale in 1391; it took the form of a reissue of a royal statute, the Statute of Wales of 1284, in the earl of Arundel's own name, complete with additions and amendments. No one basked more ostentatiously in the regality of their Marcher position than did the earls of Arundel; no one had better reason to do so.[78]

The growth in the power of the houses of Mortimer and Fitzalan is only the most remarkable manifestation of a notable feature of Marcher (as indeed generally of English) aristocratic society in the fourteenth century—namely the concentration of more land in the hands of fewer families.[79] Numerically this can be expressed in the fact that the number of Marcher lords had been reduced from twenty-five to fifteen in the course of the century; in terms of landed estates it meant that more and more lordships were paired with others under the rule of a single family—Caus and Newport under Stafford; Elfael and Gower under Beauchamp; Abergavenny, Pembroke and

[77] R. R. Davies, 'Richard II and the Principality of Chester, 1397–9', *The Reign of Richard II*, ed. F. R. H. Du Boulay and C. M. Barron, 259.

[78] S.B.Y., fols. 2–8. His father before him had also stood on his Marcher dignity: *C.P.R. 1350–4*, 467–8.

[79] Cf. G. A. Holmes, *Estates of the Higher Nobility*, 40; K. B. McFarlane, *The Nobility of Later Medieval England*, 16, 59–60, 151–3.

Cilgerran under Hastings, as well as the Mortimer and Fitz-alan complexes. In terms of the group composition of the Marcher lords the most striking development of the fourteenth century was the elimination of many of the smaller families such as Fitzherbert, Tony, Braose, Montalt and Corbet and their replacement by more powerful baronial families such as Stafford, Beauchamp and Montague. This meant that the March was more than ever the preserve of the major aristocratic families of England: nine of the seventeen English earls and dukes in 1390 had a major stake in the March.[80] As a result the March had become in large measure a land of absentee lords, a land where the powers of lordship were exercised by deputy.

That notwithstanding, lordship was still personal in many respects. Some of the smaller lords of the March—such as the Greys of Ruthin, the Corbets of Caus or the Brians of Laugharne —were doubtless frequent visitors to their Welsh estates;[81] and even the great families were not altogether strangers to the March—Bohun at Caldicot and Huntington, Lancaster at Grosmont and Monmouth, Fitzalan at Clun, Chirk and Shrawardine, Hastings at Abergavenny and Despenser at Cardiff.[82] For the Mortimers, of course, Wigmore and, later, Ludlow were the normal base; and when the earl of March came of age in 1393 he signalled it with a forty-day progress around his Welsh estates.[83] Such a progress was, and was meant to be, a spectacle. When Henry, earl of Derby and recently created duke of Hereford visited his lordship of Brecon in 1397 his retinue rode on forty horses while his supplies (bought and

[80] They were as follows: the dukes of Lancaster and Gloucester, the earls of Arundel, Derby, March, Salisbury, Stafford and Warwick and the dowager countess of Norfolk (included in the list as she was countess and later duchess of Norfolk in her own right).

[81] *V.C.H. Shropshire*, VIII, 309 (Corbets); B.L. Egerton Roll 8732 (Sir William Brian resident at Laugharne, 1389); S.C. 2/216/13, m. 16; 217/8, m. 25; 220/1, m. 17ᵛ (Lords Grey of Ruthin resident at Ruthin or Maesmynan, 1333, 1336, 1384).

[82] For example, Earl Humphrey of Hereford (d. 1361) visited Brecon in 1337, 1344–5 and 1352 and Huntington in 1342 (D.L. 29/671/10810, m. 1–m. 20); Earl Henry of Lancaster (d. 1345) and his son frequently visited Grosmont and occasionally Kidwelly (E. 326/8707, 11045; *C.P.R. 1313–17*, 222; D.L. 41/9/1, m. 14; D.L. 40/1/11, fol. 52ᵛ); Earl Richard of Arundel was a frequent visitor to Clun and Chirk in the 1340s. (N.L.W. Chirk Castle Accounts, D. 10–12, 14; S.R.O., 218/2); the earl of Pembroke died on a visit to Abergavenny in 1348 and Edward Despenser on a visit to Glamorgan in 1375 (*C.I.P.M.*, IX, no. 118, *Glam. C.H.*, III, 179).

[83] B.L. Egerton Roll 8740, 8741.

commandeered as they went) and belongings were carried ahead in wagons drawn by fourteen horses. This was lordship in progress; and even if the tenants were not impressed they soon would be. For this was more than a social occasion. It was a visit with a purpose and that purpose was achieved when the tenants of Brecon and Hay granted their lord a massive gift of two thousand marks.[84]

That gift was given in a court over which the duke presided in person at Brecon on 6 November 1397. This is a reminder to us that in the last resort the exercise of lordship was still personal and that the will of the lord was an active constituent of his lordship. In most day-to-day affairs his lordship was exercised by deputy and through a hierarchy of officials; but his residual powers were great, especially in matters of justice and finance. Decisions in difficult cases were referred to him; petitions were addressed directly to him; cases were frequently deferred until his coming; he himself on his visits could preside at his court or at his exchequer; favours were his to give or to withhold; debts could be pardoned 'de sua gracia speciali ore proprio'; and so forth.[85] He often, indeed generally, took such decisions with the advice and in the presence of his council; but he was free to disregard or to override even that constraint if he so cared.[86] Herein lay the wilful element in lordship as in kingship, the element that lay beyond bureaucracy and delegation. It could be exercised magisterially as when the earl of Surrey reserved his position over his claims to the escheated lands of the men of Bromfield and Yale, or mercifully as when the earl of Hereford pardoned the huge communal debts owed to him by his tenants of Brecon, or pettily as in the case of the Earl of March who disseised his tenants 'by extortion', or greedily as in the case of the younger Despenser whose malevolence towards the men of Gower extended to a fine of two thousand sheep.[87] The fashion and frequency with which the lord chose to exercise this ultimate power could impress the stamp of his personality on his lordship

---

[84] D.L. 28/1/10, fol. 7ᵛ; S.C. 6/1157/4.

[85] Examples of such seignorial intervention are legion, notably in the court rolls of the lordships of Clun, Caus and Dyffryn Clwyd.

[86] For an excellent example, see *B.P.R.*, I, 96–7.

[87] This selection of examples is taken from the following sources: S.B.Y., fol. 171, fol. 178; D.L. 29/671/10810, m. 5 (1340); S.C. 6/1234/2 (1332); *Cartae*, III, no. 908 (1323).

and shape the reputation he left behind him. The men of Dyffryn Clwyd did not forget the extortionate character of the rule of Reginald Grey (d. 1308) nor those of Chirkland the mercilessly grasping lordship of the Mortimers; and in both cases it was the rule of an individual, their lord, that they had in mind.[88] The person of the lord lay at the very centre of lordship.

Furthermore, the character of the lord impressed itself on his lordship in ways other than those of his decisions of grace and will. His estates and his tenants were, of necessity, involved in one way or another in his activities and ambitions. His military and political career impinged sooner or later on them, in the form both of demands for more revenue and of opportunities for service and patronage. Take the case of Roger Mortimer, the fourth earl of March (d. 1398). His estates and his tenants were intimately involved in the fulfilment of his ambitions; their resources in men, money and materials were deployed for the promotion of his policies. His Irish campaigns in particular pressed in on them: revised assessments of old renders; accelerated payment of revenue to pay troops embarking at Chester; recruiting those troops from among his Welsh tenants, shipping millstones from Anglesey and lead from Flint to provide for his needs in Ireland and so forth.[89] This was lordship in action. And with the demands came opportunities: to serve as officials in the earl's far-flung estates as did Philip ap Morgan of Tredegar,[90] to enlist in his armies as the men of Ceri and Cydewain had enlisted in those of his father,[91] to share in the benefits of his ecclesiastical patronage and of his educational support.[92] The lordship of Roger Mortimer encompassed the lives of his Welsh tenants in a variety of ways; and it was without a doubt a personal lordship. Nowhere is this more clearly manifested than in an ode addressed to him by one of his tenants of Denbigh, Iolo Goch.[93] For the ode reveals, as no

---

[88] S.C. 8/108, no. 5359 (petition of the Welsh community of Dyffryn Clwyd); J. Y. W. Lloyd, *History of the Princes, the Lords Marcher and the Ancient Nobility of Powys Fadog* (1881–7), IV, 19; *C. Inq. Misc.*, II, no. 1203 (petition of men of Chirkland and subsequent inquisition).

[89] S.C. 6/1184/22 (account of receiver of Denbigh, 1396–97); *C.P.R. 1396–9*, 118.

[90] Below, p. 206.   [91] B.L. Egerton Roll 8751.   [92] Below, p. 224.

[93] *Cywyddau Iolo Goch ac Eraill*, ed. H. Lewis, T. Roberts and I. Williams, 2nd edn. (Cardiff, 1937), 45–8.

account roll can ever do, the dimensions of affection and involvement that were of the essence of good lordship. It was within the framework of lordship that the March of Wales lived in the fourteenth century, and it is to an analysis of the nature of that lordship that we must now turn.

II

MARCHER LORDSHIP

Introduction

LORDSHIP, *dominium*, was a word which was frequently on the lips of medieval men. It was a word which expanded and contracted in its meaning according to the context in which it was used. As an abstract concept it was central to the philosophical discussions of university scholars; as a social term it was deeply embedded in the feudal terminology of medieval society; as a term of convenience it could refer to the geographical basis of a lord's power. But, above all, lordship was the generic term which was used for the great variety of rights which men exercised over other men and over their lands. As such it was 'for more than a thousand years . . . one of the dominant institutions of Western civilization' and 'the main framework of the medieval economy'.[1]

These tributes to the power of lordship in medieval society come, significantly enough, from the writings of French historians. Their English colleagues have given far less attention to the theory and practice of lordship; indeed the word 'lordship' itself is a far less familiar item in English historical terminology than are *Herrschaft* and *seigneurie* in continental historical writings. It is not difficult to see the reasons why. On the one hand, the wealth of manorial documents has led English historians to concentrate on the landed aspects of lordship at the expense of its other features; on the other hand, the incursion of royal power into so many spheres of seignorial authority has meant that the lordship they study is, or appears to be, a restricted, even an emasculated, one.[2] It is only in areas such as Northumbria and Cumbria—where manors were few, where baronies still showed strong traces of Celtic influence, where private and public rights were completely merged—that we

---

[1] M. Bloch, 'The Rise of Dependent Cultivation and Seignorial Institutions', *Cambridge Economic History of Europe*, I, ed. M. M. Postan, 2nd edn. (1966), 236; G. Duby, *The Early Growth of the European Economy* (1973), 43.

[2] R. H. Hilton, *A Medieval Society* (1968), is a notable attempt to provide a rounded study of lordship in an English context.

can study in England a pattern of lordship closely akin to that of the Welsh March.[3] That is why the historian of the March may be better served by the studies of continental historians, for they have directed attention away from 'the state' to the analysis of 'lordship and what belonged to lordship' and have shown that the gulf between royal lordship and noble lordship was, generally speaking, far less significant than the English experience might suggest.[4] This latter point is particularly relevant to the Welsh situation for there likewise the distinction between lordship and kingship had never been clearly articulated; indeed it scarcely existed. And it is within this native Welsh mould that Marcher lordship was in good part shaped.

The March is therefore an ideal area for the study of lordship. Here lordship remained integral. It had not been too closely circumscribed within the formulae of feudal relationships; it had not been sabotaged by theories of *quo warranto* and by notions of king-centred liberties; it had not been unduly fragmented by the accidents of political geography; it had not been undermined by a co-existing pattern of royal justice and administration; it had not been greatly compromised by mediatization or subinfeudation; it had certainly not been reduced to the mere level of manorial authority. Lordship in the March breathed an altogether freer air than in England; here we can study it in all its facets. For the lord was much more than a lord of land or a collector of rents. He was also lord of men, captain of war, fountain of justice, focus of loyalty and source of governance. His dependants were not merely his tenants; they were, and they were called, his subjects. The lords of the March were clearly powerful men and it is a study of the lordship that they exercised which forms the theme of the following chapters.

[3] J. E. A. Jolliffe, 'Northumbrian Institutions', *E.H.R.* 41 (1926), 1–42; G. W. S. Barrow, 'The Pattern of Lordship and Feudal Settlement in Cumbria', *Journal of Medieval History* 1 (1975), 117–38.

[4] Walter Schlesinger in *Lordship and Community in Medieval Europe*, ed. F. L. Cheyette (1968), 78–9. I have found the essays in this volume and the two volumes of R. Boutruche, *Seigneurie et féodalité* (Paris, 1959–70), particularly helpful.

Military Lordship

MILITARY power was the original foundation and ultimate sanction of all lordship. Nowhere was this more transparently and immediately true than in the March of Wales, for there lordship was acquired—or in George Owen's picturesque phrase, 'purchased'[1]—by conquest and sustained by military strength. 'He has there', was the tart comment of the Hereford-shire Domesday on Osbern fitz Richard's Marcher lands, 'what he can take; and nothing else'.[2] That truism still applied in the thirteenth century. Lordship in the March was still lordship by conquest. The king of England acknowledged it to be so when he issued commissions to Marcher lords to conquer as much land as they could from the Welsh and to hold it free from all royal claims.[3] Here, if anywhere, the sword—and not a rusty one at that—was the only true title to lands and liberties; lordship was coterminous with the reach of that sword. It was, for example, 'by ancient conquest' that the great Clare lordships in the March were held of the king in chief; and it was a title whose truth no one could gainsay.[4] Indeed the earl of Gloucester himself considered such a title, based as it was exclusively on the enterprise of his ancestors, to be sufficient reason for him not to have to answer in the king's court for his conduct in the March.[5] But conquest in the March was neither so ancient nor so secure as to become merely a memory or a title to franchise. For until the end of the thirteenth century and even beyond, military vigilance was a continuing pre-condition of lordship in the March; military tenurial duties

---

[1] *Penbrokshire*, III, 139.

[2] *The Herefordshire Domesday* (Pipe Roll Society, new ser. 25, 1950), 65.

[3] For examples of such commissions, see *Rotuli Chartarum*, I, i (Record Commission, 1837), 66 (William de Braose, 1200); *C.P.R. 1258–66*, 72–4 (Edmund 'Crouchback'; Gilbert, earl of Gloucester, 1266).

[4] *C.I.P.M.*, v, no. 538 (1314).

[5] *Select Cases in the Court of King's Bench under Edward I*, II (Selden Society, 1935), ed. G. O. Sayles, lvii–lviii (1281).

retained a relevance there which they were fast losing in England.[6]

For until then the March was a land of war, interrupted on occasion by peace.[7] The ethos of its society, and particularly of its lords, was proudly militarist. That may have been true of English aristocratic society generally in the middle ages; but the conditions of the March meant that there the gap between ideal and reality barely existed. Prowess in arms was there a practical necessity as well as a conventional virtue; war was less a pastime and more a way of life. Gerald of Wales had been eloquent on that score in the late twelfth century and he spoke with the authority of family experience. This appetite for war and for the profits that came by war knew no bounds: it had secured for the Marchers a leading role in the Norman conquest of Ireland as well as of Wales.[8] The militarism of the March remained vigorous and strident in the thirteenth century; those who excelled in arms were still saluted as the paragons of society. It was, for example, as 'a warlike and vigorous man' that Ralph Mortimer of Wigmore (d. 1246) was proudly commemorated by the family chronicler; and it was as Reginald Grey, *primus et conquestor*, that the first English lord of Dyffryn Clwyd (d. 1308) was remembered.[9] They and their like were worthy companions of those 'most valiant knights of the host', to whom, as legend would have it, William I had committed 'the lands of the March'.[10]

War encompassed the lives of these men in all sorts of ways: a deed about land might recall a Welsh raid in its dating clause; a witness in court in 1307 might assert that he had received neither goods nor money 'before or after the war of Madog ap Llywelyn' (1294–5).[11] Wars were the framework of their memory. Robert Banastre declared in 1278 that he had known nothing but war since he became lord of Prestatyn. He recalled how his ancestors had been expelled from their lands by the

---

[6] *C.I.P.M.*, v, no. 412 (1313), for an example of the military service due from a Marcher lordship, that of Abergavenny.

[7] This is reflected in the tentative peace-time valuations given to Marcher property, e.g. Elfael Ismynydd is worth forty marks 'in time of peace': *C. Inq. Misc. 1219–1307*, no. 1060 (1277).

[8] *Giraldi Cambrensis Opera*, vi, ed. J. F. Dimmock (Rolls Series, 1865), 220.

[9] *Monasticon Anglicanum*, vi, i. 350 ('bellicosus vir et strenuus'); for Reginald de Grey, see S.C. 2/218/4, m. 21 (1354); 218/8 m. 4 (1360), 219/2, m. 29 (1365).

[10] 'The Legend of Fulk Fitzwarin', *Chronicon Anglicanum*, ed. J. Stevenson, 278.

[11] For the former case see above p. 2; for the latter, S.C. 2/215/69, m. 4.

Welsh in the time of Richard I, just as the Welsh lord of Afan in 1365 remembered bitterly how the land of his forbears had been conquered by Robert fitz Hamon in the late eleventh century.[12] Theirs was a violent society: even their churches—such as Ewyas Harold with its seven-foot thick walls or Ilston (Gower) with its massive tower, battlements and arrow-slit window-openings or Ewenni priory (Glamorgan) with its battlemented enceinte—betokened their war-dominated mentality, just as their prayers and benefactions commemorated those who had fallen in the conquest of the March.[13] Their heroes inevitably were men or even women who had excelled in arms; in the March, where life and legend so easily met, they found those heroes near to hand—men such as Fulk Fitzwarin whose legend was woven out of fact in the mid-thirteenth century and who thereby became the prototype of the valiant warrior in Anglo-Norman romance and Welsh poetry alike or Amazonian heroines such as Maud of St. Valéry who defended the remote fortress of Painscastle (Elfael) so bravely that it was renamed Maudcastle in her honour.[14] This was no society for the weak-stomached; to be tired of war in the March was tantamount to a resignation of lordship. It was because he was wearied with war, so the record has it, that William Hautenot surrendered the border manor of Lydham (Bishopcastle) to the king, just as Sampson Haleweia preferred land and security in England to the constant battling for his rights in Glamorgan or just as Thomas ap Madog transferred the manor of Kinnerley (Oswestry) to James Audley since he himself 'could not hold it peacefully against the Welsh because of his want of weight and power'.[15] He who ruled peacefully in the March ruled by the

[12] *Rot. Parl.*, I, 2; *Cartae*, IV, no. 1027 (1365).

[13] On Ewyas Harold, see N. Pevsner, *Herefordshire* (1963), 28, on Ilston and Ewenny, *Glam. C.H.*, III, 381–2, 404, 440. In 1199 Roger Mortimer gave lands in Maelienydd and Gwerthrynion to the abbey of Cwmhir for the souls of his family, his men and 'those who had died in the conquest of Maelienydd': *B.B.C.S.* 24 (1970), 81.

[14] For the date and background of *The Legend of Fulk Fitzwarin*, see E. A. Francis in *Studies in Medieval French presented to Alfred Ewert*, ed. E. A. Francis (Oxford, 1961), 322–7; and for Fulk's reputation in Welsh literature see the brief but suggestive note by R. T. Jenkins in *The Dictionary of Welsh Biography* (1959), 265. For Maud of St. Valéry and the legends about her, see J. E. Lloyd, *A History of Wales from the Earliest Times to the Edwardian Conquest* (1911), 585–6 and n. 56.

[15] *C.I.P.M.*, II, no. 747 (1290); Rice Merrick, *A Booke of Glamorganshire Antiquities*, 76; *C. Inq. Misc. 1219–1307*, no. 1059 (1277).

sword; his lordship was a military lordship or it was no lordship at all.

Nowhere was this more graphically demonstrated than in the castle, for the castle was and was meant to be a visible manifestation of lordship. Its very etymology proclaimed it to be so: the words *donjon* and *dominium* have a common parentage, that of lordly authority. Conquest and castle were inseparably associated—and so, inevitably, were lordship and castle.[16] For the castle in the March was in a real sense the head of the lordship, *caput honoris*. So much was this the case that the name of the castle was often adopted for the lordship as a whole—as happened in Elfael whose two commotes were renamed after the two castles of Colwyn and Painscastle[17] or in the case of the lordships of Caus or Radnor. Likewise when new lordships were added to the March in 1282, the first act of their new lords was to build castles, both as a military insurance and as a visible expression of their lordship. At Denbigh, for example, Henry Lacy began to construct his castle within a few days of being granted the district on 16 October 1282.[18] That district had hitherto been known as the *cantrefi* of Rhos and Rhufoniog and the commote of Dinmael; it was now constituted into a lordship or honor and henceforth took the name of its castle at Denbigh.[19] The change was more than a change of nomenclature; it was a token of a new kind of lordship based firmly on military authority. The castle's towering presence was a permanent reminder to the Welsh of the power and authority of their new lord: it was 'the tower of the bold conqueror'; within its sombre grey walls was 'the seat of his wrathful justice.'[20] So it was regarded; and so it was meant to be regarded. Above the castle gate, so tradition has it, Henry Lacy caused to be sculpted an image of himself in long, stately robes: the gaze of the lord was to be forever over the lordship.[21]

---

[16] For the correlation of castle and conquest, see J. G. Edwards, 'The Normans and the Welsh March', *Procs. British Academy*, 42 (1956), 167–8.

[17] Lloyd, op. cit. 585, n. 55.

[18] R. A. Brown, H. M. Colvin and A. J. Taylor, *The History of the King's Works* (1963), I, 333.   [19] *S.D.*, 1.

[20] I have borrowed these quotations from Rhys Goch Eryri's striking description of Caernarfon castle: *Cywyddau Iolo Goch ac Eraill*, 310 especially lines 6 ('Tŵr dewr gwncwerwr') and 22 ('Llidfainc . . . llwydfaen').

[21] John Leland, *The Itinerary in Wales*, 97–8.

Denbigh was but one of the castles of the March, for the March was the land of castles *par excellence* in the whole of Britain. It had long been so: among the earliest castles to be built in Britain was that at Richardscastle, built by Richard fitz Scrob the first Norman lord of the March in the days of Edward the Confessor. But it was in the twelfth and thirteenth centuries that the March came to bristle with castles; it was then that the lords of the March (to borrow a contemporary comment on Duke Frederick of Swabia)[22] seemed to drag a strong castle by the tail of their horses wherever they went. Many of these earth and wooden mottes were built hurriedly in the course of campaigns and they were often abandoned once they had fulfilled their original purpose. In the modern county of Montgomeryshire, for example, it has been calculated that only thirteen of the forty-two castles proceeded beyond the motte stage.[23] The castles of the March were fewer in number in the late thirteenth century than they had been; but even so they remained numerous. It is difficult to be precise, but we would not be far wrong to claim that there were still some ninety castles in the March in the fourteenth century; and even if we make a generous allowance for disrepair or for temporary disuse, the minimum number which were militarily defensible rarely fell short of sixty.[24] Nowhere was lordship in the British Isles so securely underpinned by military power as in the March of Wales. This feature is to be explained in good measure by the prolonged and uncertain character of the Anglo-Norman conquest of Wales and by the plurality of the conquerors, each of whom needed a military base for his authority. This proliferation of castles in the March is all the more striking when we recall that the Crown lands in the

---

[22] Quoted in R. Boutruche, *Seigneurie et féodalité*, ii, 31.

[23] C. J. Spurgeon, 'The Castles of Montgomeryshire', *Mont. Colls.* 59 (1965–6), 1–60 at p. 2.

[24] The study of castles in Wales and the March has been greatly advanced by the indispensable lists published by A. H. A. Hogg and D. J. C. King: 'Early Castles in Wales and the Marches', *Arch. Camb.* 112 (1963), 77–124; 'Masonry Castles in Wales and the March', ibid. 116 (1967), 71–132; 'Castles in Wales and the Marches: Additions and Corrections', ibid. 119 (1970), 119–24. Some of the castles—e.g. Clun, Dolforwyn and Llantrisant—which Hogg and King have classified as 'uncertain' for the fourteenth century can be shown to have been in use from documentary evidence. For individual castles the official Ministry guides are, of course, a major (if uneven) source of information.

Principality and Flintshire in the fourteenth century were defended by only fourteen castles in all. It was the March, not the Principality, which was the land of castles.

Not all these Marcher castles, of course, were equally important in terms of military strategy or architectural strength. Some such as Caerphilly (Glamorgan), Kidwelly or Whitecastle (Monmouth) compared favourably in their military architecture with the great Edwardian fortresses in Gwynedd; others such as Bronllys (Brecon) or Huntington were much more modest buildings; and yet others such as Weobley (Gower) or Candleston (Glamorgan) seem to have barely graduated beyond the stage of fortified residences. They varied in age as well as in architectural strength: some such as Chepstow or Cardiff (Glamorgan) had a history which went back unbroken to the earliest days of the Norman penetration of the March; a few such as Carregcennen (Iscennen) or Dolforwyn (Cydewain) occupied sites first fortified by native Welsh princes; several, notably Chirk, Ruthin (Dyffryn Clwyd), Holt (Bromfield and Yale) and Denbigh, were part of that great castle-building spree which followed the Edwardian conquest of Gwynedd; and a handful such as Picton (Pembroke), Benton (Walwynscastle) and Aberedw (Elfael) were possibly not begun until the fourteenth century. Most of them were strategically well-sited—at a crucial river crossing (such as Holt), overlooking an estuary (such as Newport) or commanding a vital route from upland to lowland (such as Caerphilly); but not all of them were equal in military significance. After all, their location and distribution had not been determined, as was the case with the Edwardian castles in Gwynedd, by a single coherent military strategy; rather were they built to suit the varying needs, resources and ambitions of each individual Marcher lord and at different stages in the history of the March. Finally, their distribution on the map of the March was very uneven: a few such as Cefnllys (Maelienydd) or Bwlchyddinas (Blaenllyfni) were distant mountain fortresses; but the great majority were concentrated either in the coastal plains of Pembroke, Gower, Gwent and Glamorgan or in the major river valleys of Usk, Wye and Severn. In Glamorgan, for example, it has been estimated that of twenty-three castles only six were located over 600 feet above sea level; and none of those six seems to have survived into the fourteenth century.[25] This distribution pattern was a matter both of geography and of history: it coincided with those districts which were easiest of penetration and which had therefore been most intensively settled by the Norman lords and their followers. The lords of the Welsh March ruled from the plains.

The castles of the March were less numerous in 1300 than they had been in the past; but architecturally and militarily they were much more impressive. For the thirteenth century as a whole, and the middle and later decades in particular, witnessed a massive investment on the part of the Marcher lords in their castles. It was an investment which converted them into highly defensible stone castles, comparable with those in any part of Britain or indeed Europe. This achievement has been largely overshadowed by the Edwardian castles built in Wales after 1277—largely because of the undoubted magnificence of those castles, the extraordinary speed and purposefulness with which they were constructed, and the unprecedented documentation for their building history. Indeed, this extraordinary burst of royal building was not confined in its impact to the Crown lands in Wales, for in some of the new Marcher castles of the late thirteenth century—notably Ruthin, Denbigh, Holt and Chirk—the hand of royal policy and the experience of royal masons (notably Master James of St. George) were evident in their early stages.[26] Even so, the capital outlay of the Marcher lords on their castles in the thirteenth century—though the documentation is almost totally lacking— would seem to compare well with that of the Crown and in terms of a proportion of their resources might well exceed it. Some built anew: Caerphilly begun in 1268 is, of course, apart from the four post-1282 castles just mentioned, the outstanding example; but for the great majority it was inevitably a case of refurbishing and rebuilding, often over a protracted period, and in the process many of the castles—such as Chepstow, Whitecastle, Swansea or Laugharne—were radically transformed. All the families of the March participated in this great process of reconstruction, both great lords such as the earls of Gloucester, who in the late thirteenth-early fourteenth century

[25] *Glam. C.H.*, III, 422.
[26] *The History of the King's Works*, I, 327–35.

invested a small fortune in building new castles at Caerphilly, Llanbleddian and Morlais and in repairing existing ones such as those at Neath and Llantrisant,[27] and smaller families such as the Chaworths of Kidwelly or the Camvilles of Llanstephan who built two equally impressive castles from much more restricted resources. They did so because no lord could militarily afford to 'opt out' in thirteenth-century Wales. Accordingly it was military considerations which were in the forefront of the minds of the Marcher castle builders. Nowhere indeed can the technological innovations of military architecture during the thirteenth century be better studied than in the castles of the March, whether in the adoption of the cylindrical stone keep as at Pembroke or Bronllys (Brecon), in the concentration on massive gatehouses as the focal defensive point of the castle as at Kidwelly or Llanstephan, in the addition of large new baileys to an original early-Norman keep as at Chepstow, in the use of an extensive barbican as an added defence to the gatehouse as at Castle Goodrich (co. Hereford) and indeed in providing in Caerphilly the prototype of an elaborately defended quadrangular concentric castle commenced almost ten years before the great Edwardian fortresses in the North. These Marcher castles are a permanent reminder to us that the lords of the March were lords of war before they were lords of men and lords of land.

They still remained so in some measure in the fourteenth century and to that extent the castle certainly retained its *raison d'être*. It could be put in a state of defence against a threatened invasion or native unrest;[28] and equally it could be garrisoned and provisioned during the frequent political crises of the period. Most of the Mortimer castles in the March, for example, were well stocked with arms and supplies in the 1320s[29] and so were those of the earl of Arundel in the

---

[27] For the castles of Morlais and Llanbleddian see, briefly, *Glam. C.H.*, III, 431–2, 442. Llantrisant castle was extensively reconstructed in the aftermath of the 1294–5 rebellion and hostages were taken from the men of Meisgyn until it was finished: S.C. 8/128, no. 6389.

[28] Two examples may be cited: Radnor castle was garrisoned by six men in August–September 1337 and Pembroke castle by a very large force of almost 150 men during the tense summer months of 1377 when an invasion by the Welsh pretender, Owain Lawgoch, supported by the French was expected: S.C. 6/1209/7; *Cal. Public Records re. Pembrokeshire*, III, 35–6.

[29] For a list of Roger Mortimer's effects at Wigmore in 1322, see *Archaeological*

1390s.[30] But on the whole the fourteenth century was for the March a century of peace. Accordingly the castle's functions, which even in the past had never been exclusively military, became more varied. A few of the Marcher castles became favoured residences of their lords and in the process shed some of their austerely military functionalism: Shrawardine was so favoured by the earls of Arundel and Monmouth by the house of Lancaster;[31] while the earls of Hereford and Thomas of Woodstock found Caldicot congenial and spent lavishly on it.[32] Only a few of the castles, however, were singled out for such distinction; for the majority their role was a more humble, but nevertheless crucial, one as the administrative and judicial headquarters of their respective lordships. There the lord's ministers had their chambers and official residences; there the rents and tributes of the lordship would be brought; there at the exchequer the accounts would be audited and the bailiffs examined; there the chief courts of the lordship would be assembled and there also would be the lord's gaol. The castle was the meeting point of lordship and community: it was there that the common assemblies of the lordship congregated;[33] it was there at the castle gate that the tenants would be arrayed for the selection of troops to serve in the lord's army.[34] The castle, so wrote the surveyor at Holt in 1391 in an almost rhapsodical passage, 'is the common focus for the whole lordship, for it is to this castle that the whole lordship is dependant, intendant and annexed as its principal seat'.[35] His rare moment of eloquence was not

Journal 15 (1858), 354–62, and for the arms and provisions in his castles in 1330, S.C. 6/1236/1. The arms at the earl of Hereford's castle of Huntington in 1322 included 33 basinets, 37 lances and 9 haubergeons: S.C. 6/1145/7.

[30] The arms included catapults, guns and gunpowder: *C. Inq. Misc. 1392–9*, nos. 229, 233, 235.

[31] For Shrawardine see above p. 56 n. 71. The future Henry V was born at Monmouth in September 1387 and a new hall and chamber were constructed there at considerable expense in the 1390s: D.L. 29/615/9839.

[32] Extensive building work was carried out at Caldicot in the 1340s and in the 1370s, and Thomas of Woodstock spent over £311 on the castle in the five years 1384–9: D.L. 29/671/10810, m. 9, m. 10; 680/11003, 11106–11010; S.C. 6/921/16–17.

[33] The great court of Bromfield and Yale met—much to the inconvenience of the tenants—at a *communis locus* near Holt castle and a great hall was eventually constructed there for the purpose: S.C. 2/226/19, m. 6 (1385); J. Y. W. Lloyd, *History of Powys Fadog*, II, 74, 164 (1467, 1529).

[34] As happened in Dyffryn Clwyd in 1360: S.C. 2/218/8, m. 5.

[35] S.B.Y., fol. 3.

misplaced, for in the March the castle was truly the *caput* of the lordship in peace as well as in war.

But military lordship was a matter of men as well as of castles; and of those men the most important were the lord's camp-followers, his *fideles*. They were his partners in war and conquest; they had been duly rewarded in the territorial share-out which followed conquest; now they were the prime defenders and upholders of his lordship. For in the March of Wales the bond between lord and vassal still remained close and meaningful in the late thirteenth century and beyond; the feudalism of the March was archaic but at least it was alive. The pattern of feudal tenure, it is true, was very unevenly distributed in the March, even more so than the pattern of castles. It more or less coincided, as one would expect, with the pattern of Anglo-Norman penetration. In many lordships, especially in the highland districts of the middle March, such as Elfael, Maelienydd, Builth, Iscennen and Llandovery[36], knight service was unknown. Elsewhere, in the lowlands, such as Pembroke, the Vale of Glamorgan, Gwent and the Englishries of Radnor, Clun, and Oswestry, the feudal pattern was as well-developed and as complex as anywhere in England. The barony of Carew, to give one example, was held of the county of Pembroke by the service of five knights' fees; but within the barony itself a prolonged process of subinfeudation had led to the creation of some fourteen fees, many of which in turn had been subdivided and each of these fractions was often held by several men.[37] In the lowlands even the Welsh had been brought within the ambit of feudal tenure, and a splendidly hybrid institution, the Welsh knight's fee,—partible among male coheirs and lacking the lords rights of wardship and marriage—had been created. Such Welsh fees coexisted with their more normal English partners in lordships as far apart as Cemais, Usk and Chepstow.[38] Feudal institutions had been extensively transplanted into the March. Indeed the process was not finished. For when new lordships Marcher were created in 1282, their lords set about vigorously endowing their followers with land to be held on

---

[36] This is specifically said to be so in the case of Llandovery: *C.I.P.M.*, VI, no. 56.
[37] *C.I.P.M.*, XI, no. 300.
[38] *C.I.P.M.*, III, no. 371; IV, no. 434; VI, no. 710.

feudal terms.[39] Anglo-Norman feudalism had its swan-song in
the March of Wales in the late thirteenth century.

It is appropriate that it should be so, for the military conditions of the March ensured that the obligations of the vassal
were not archaic tenurial conventions. In the March the lord's
feudal vassals still formed the core of his fighting force, particularly on his campaigns in Wales. At least sixteen of the men
in the retinue of twenty five which Thomas Corbet led in Wales
in 1263 held knights' fees or free tenancies of him in the barony
of Caus just as the six sergeants who served his son in the 1277
campaign were drawn from his own military tenants.[40] When
the campaigns in Wales were over, service elsewhere was
demanded of the vassals and on the whole they seem to have
served willingly. It is significant in this context that one of the
earliest surviving indentures for permanent military service
comes from the March. In it one of the major vassals of the earl
of Gloucester in Caerleon, Ralph Bluet, secured the service of
one of his fellow vassals of the lordship, William Martel, to
attend him as a valet in wars in England, France, Scotland or
elsewhere and in peace in tournaments. Both men served in the
retinue of the lord of Caerleon, for we know that Bluet was in
the earl of Gloucester's squadron in Scotland in 1303 and was
there again in 1314 when his lord fell at Bannockburn.[41] The
vassals of the March were still serving soldiers of their lord.
That service was required in the castle as well as in the host; for,
as in early-Norman England, castle guard was probably the
most regular and useful aspect of feudal military service. It was
so at the beginning of the thirteenth century: in 1208 King
John as lord of Glamorgan ordered the barons and knights of
his honor to repair his houses in Cardiff castle and to perform
castle guard.[42] It was, more surprisingly, still the case (if only
by default) in the fifteenth century: Grimbald Pauncefoot of

---

[39] For examples, see N.L.W. Roger Lloyd Collection, 1 (creation of one-sixth of a
knight's fee in Dyffryn Clwyd); D.L. 36/2, no. 248 (1286) and *Arch. Camb.* 6th ser.
12 (1912), 246–7 (creation of two fractional knights' fees in Denbigh); *C.P.R.
1307–13*, 405–6 (creation of a knight's fee in Bromfield, 1308). Cf. *C.Ch.R. 1257–
1300*, 246–7 for the creation of one and a half knights' fees in Monmouth in 1280.

[40] *V.C.H. Shropshire*, VIII, 325; R. W. Eyton, *Antiquities of Shropshire*, VII, 331. Cf.
the Glamorgan vassals in the Earl of Gloucester's retinue in 1245, M. Altschul,
A Baronial Family in Medieval England: The Clares 1217–1314 (Baltimore, 1965), 72.

[41] *Cat. MSS. Wales in B.M.*, III, 641–2 (1297); Altschul, op. cit. 279–80.

[42] *Cartae*, II, no. 321.

Crickhowell was hauled before the court of the duke of York in
1433 to explain why he had failed in his duty of guarding,
repairing and maintaining Grimbaldstower in his lord's castle
of Blaenllyfni.[43]

The vassal's service, however, was not exclusively military;
he was also expected to proffer advice to his lord and to attend
his court. Here again the March kept alive feudal traditions
which had almost completely faded in England. When the lord
paid a visit to his estates in the March, his local knights, his
fideles, attended on him to give him the benefit of their counsel
and company as good vassals ought.[44] Nor was the performance
of the duty of *consilium* restricted to such rare ceremonial
occasions; it was performed much more regularly in the court
of the lordship, whether the lord was present or not. For the
feudal vassals were the suitors *par excellence* of the lordship's
central court; that court indeed was essentially a feudal *curia*.[45]
At Clun, for example, the military tenants of the lordship were
the suitors of the court of Tempseter; at Pembroke, the 'full
court' consisted of the steward, the sheriff and the vassals
(*fideles*) of the lord; while in Gower, judgement was given by
the oath of twenty-four knights (*milites*).[46] Vassalage in the
March was clearly still in the fourteenth century a matter of
active obligations in peace as in war.

This was so because feudal institutions had a resilience and
purposefulness in the March which they lacked in England.
The explanations are not far to seek. In the first place, the unsettled conditions of the March meant, as we have seen, that
the military obligations of the feudal vassal still remained
practical and immediate. Secondly, the feudal geography of
the March meant that the honor there was a self-contained,
integral unit whose lord exercised a monopoly of fealty within
its boundaries. Lordship and honor were geographically
coterminous, or more or less so. That was the case, for example,
in Glamorgan and consequently county court (*comitatus*) and
honorial court (*curia*) were there one and the same. As a result

[43] B.L. Egerton Roll 8708.

[44] For an illuminating example, see the list of knights in attendance on Gilbert,
earl of Gloucester, on his visit to Usk in April 1289: *Cartae*, IV, no. 963.

[45] R. R. Davies, 'The Law of the March', *W.H.R.* 5 (1970), 13–14.

[46] S.R.O. 552/1/22, m. 1 (Clun, 1387); *C.A.D.*, III, D. 242; *Penbrokshire*, II, 469
(Pembroke, 1267, 1342); *Cartae*, IV, no. 961 (Gower, 1336).

the lord's vassals were a self-consciously coherent and active group whose loyalty (within the lordship) lay exclusively to their lord and was not compromised by alternative tenurial ties or by the demands of royal government. Their affairs were often ordered by a separate officer;[47] they might be assessed separately for taxation;[48] they regarded themselves jealously as the peers of their lordship;[49] they shared an ethos of military companionship and a pride in being a closed immigré caste, racially and militarily as well as socially superior. They were truly an élite. Nowhere does the coherence of this feudal community in terms of military action and even more markedly as an advisory body appear more vividly than in a letter dispatched by the vassals (*fideles*) of the earl of Pembroke in 1244.[50] The weight of their opinion was that of men who were the agents of lordship, military and otherwise, in the March of Wales. They were supported in a fashion by the burgesses of the Marcher towns. Towns, like castles, were instruments of conquest; and their burgesses were expected to fend for themselves and for their lord militarily as well as to prosper economically. Economic warfare has an almost literal meaning in the history of Marcher boroughs.[51]

Peace came to the March in the fourteenth century; but Marcher society was understandably cautious in its approach to such a novel experience. The investment in castles continued—at Kidwelly, for example, a massive new gatehouse was built at great cost in the 1390s[52]—and so did the building of town walls. The settler population was still equipped for the call to arms: when Griffith Verdon, a second generation settler holding by knight service in Dyffryn Clwyd, died in 1321 his goods included all the accoutrements of war: basinet, aketon,

---

[47] B.L. Egerton Rolls 8704–5: *bedellus militum* in Blaenllyfni, 1362–5.

[48] This was so, for example, in Brecon—'de dono hominum militum', 'de dono dato . . . per tenentes et residentes feodorum militum': S.C. 6/1156/18, m. 3 (1372); 1157/4 (1399).

[49] When Richard Siward was tried in the court of his feudal lord of Glamorgan and was confronted with the lord's champion, he challenged the right of the champion to fight him, because he (the champion) 'non est de comitatu nec par suus': *Cartae*, III, no. 805, p. 552.

[50] *Cal. Anc. Corr. conc. Wales*, 48, partly quoted below, p. 206.

[51] Below, pp. 321, 323–4.

[52] Some £350 was spent on it in the four years for which we have accounts between 1388 and 1400.

jupon, hauberk and gloves.[53] He and his like lived nervously, fearing the proverbial 'lightheadedness' of the Welsh. Their fears were amply fed by periodic rumours of native revolts or by threat of invasion from France or by tales of Messianic Welsh pretenders—notably in 1335, 1337, 1345, 1369–70, 1376–8 and 1385–6. But in fact none of the threats of revolt materialized and Wales and the March experienced (with the exception of the localized rebellion of Llywelyn Bren in Glamorgan in 1316) an unprecedented century of peace after 1300. And inevitably the soft habits of peace set in. The best animal replaced the best armour as the heriot due from military tenants.[54] Comfort began to assume its place side by side with defence in the construction of castles: Chirk, for example, was endowed with the luxury of glass windows in 1345.[55] Indeed many of the castles were allowed to fall into disrepair so that they became (in the words of the surveyor's report on Wigmore in 1325) more objects of honour than of profit.[56]

In another direction, however, the military aspect of lordship was fostered in the March in the fourteenth century. The Marcher lord was not only a lord of castles, of vassals and of burgesses; he was also a lord of Welshmen. He now learnt to harness the service of these Welshmen in the promotion of his military ambitions. This was not, of course, a new departure: the lords of the March had certainly recruited armies from their Welsh estates in the thirteenth century, not least the huge levies which they contributed towards Edward I's campaigns in Wales from 1277 to 1295.[57] But from the 1290s the direction of this military recruitment was turned outward—to Scotland, France and Ireland; Marcher contingents came to play a leading role in the armies of the king of England and of his captains, many of whom were also lords of the March. Each Marcher lord regarded his lordship jealously as his own recruiting area from which other recruiting officers were ex-

---

[53] S.C. 2/216/3, m. 3ᵛ; N.L.W. Roger Lloyd Collection, 1–4.

[54] This happened in Dyffryn Clwyd in the time of Hugh de Wimpton, steward *c.* 1314–16: S.C. 2/217/7, m. 9ᵛ.

[55] N.L.W. Chirk Castle Collection, D. 12.

[56] Quoted in B. P. Evans, 'The Family of Mortimer', Ph.D. thesis (Univ. of Wales, 1934), 398. Cf. *C.P.R. 1364–7*, 413 for like comments on the castles of Llanstephan and Penrice (Gower).

[57] J. E. Morris, *The Welsh Wars of Edward I* (Oxford, 1901); M. C. Prestwich, *War, Politics and Finance under Edward I* (1972), ch. IV.

cluded;[58] he had the first claim on the military service of all his tenants and enforced that right by proclamation.[59] The Welshmen so recruited were his troops, serving under his standard,[60] wearing clothes in colours that were probably distinctively his,[61] and drawing their pay from him. They were the lord's proprietary army. Here was a different dimension to his military lordship.

Service in the lord's army was not a new experience for Welshmen, for it was an obligation which all free Welshmen had owed to their native princes and from which even the most ample grant immunities could not exempt them. This was an obligation which the Marcher lords willingly inherited. The sole duty of the men of Cantref Tewdos (Brecon), for example, apart from suit of court, was service with their lord in time of war at their own expense within the lordship, at his without it; and likewise the men of Bromfield and Yale, who passed from the tutelage of native prince to Marcher lord overnight in 1282, were bound to serve with their lord in person and at his pleasure ('cum corpore domini et . . . pro voluntate sua') in England, Wales, Scotland and elsewhere for reasonable wages.[62] The theories of obligation, therefore, gave the lords of the March a large pool of military manpower in their lordship; the history and habits of the Welsh ensured that theory was matched by practice.

The foreign wars of the fourteenth century gave ample opportunities for their military prowess to be displayed and for the lords of the March to exploit the military manpower of their lordships.[63] They did so enthusiastically. Global figures of their

[58] In 1298 the earl of Surrey insisted that he alone had the right to recruit men in his lordship of Bromfield and Yale; and likewise in 1342 the earl of Hereford successfully claimed that he alone could array troops in his mesne lordships of Pencelli and Bronllys: E. 159/71, m. 35ᵛ; D.L. 29/671/10810, m. 6ᵛ; *Foedera, Conventiones, Litterae* etc., ed. T. Rymer revised edn. (1816–69), II, ii, 1192.

[59] Such a proclamation was issued in the case of the burgesses of Ruthin in 1359: S.C. 2/218/7, m. 6ᵛ.

[60] Three standards were bought for the lord of Brecon's Welshmen going on royal service in 1346: D.L. 29/671/10810, m. 13.

[61] Red and white cloth was bought for the earl of Arundel's Welsh troops: N.L.W. Chirk Castle Collection, D. 9 (1342).

[62] *C.I.P.M.*, III, no. 552; S.B.Y., fol. 68ᵛ.

[63] See, in general, D. L. Evans, 'Some Notes on the History of the Principality of Wales in the time of the Black Prince', *T.C.S.* (1925–6), 25–110, esp. 45–77; A. D. Carr, 'Welshmen and the Hundred Years' War', *W.H.R.* 4 (1968), 21–46.

military recruitment are certainly impressive—such as the astonishing figure of 6,200 men who were to be levied for service in Scotland in 1322 or the quota of 3,500 or so Marcher men summoned for the Crecy campaign;[64] but much more reliable and instructive from our point of view are the local figures of those who actually served. They show military lordship in action, persistently. Take the case of the lordship of Chirk in the 1340s when its lord, Richard Fitzalan earl of Arundel, was one of the leading war-captains of Edward III. As warden of the Scottish March he took fifty-two archers north in 1342; three years later a contingent of 100 archers accompanied him overseas; in 1347 fifty-five mounted and forty-six foot archers travelled from Oswestry to Dover and embarked for Calais; and finally in 1348 a further eighty-one archers were led by the constable of Chirk to join the earl at Sandwich.[65] The pressure on Chirkland in the 1340s—and it is well to remember that its taxable population in 1290 was just over six hundred and fifty[66]—may have been unusual because of its lord's prominent military role; but it was to Wales that the lords of the March generally looked for the rank and file of their armies.[67]

These Marcher troops were selected at special assemblies held at the castle gate.[68] They were often led by Welshmen of note from the lordship: the Dyffryn Clwyd contingent for the Scottish campaign of 1322 was to be led by Llywelyn ap Madoc, a wealthy local Welshman and the descendant of a family which had grown rich and privileged in the service of the native Welsh princes. It was appropriate that he held his extensive lands by military service and that when he died in 1343 among his goods were an ancient shield and a pair of gambesons, the mementoes of an old warrior.[69] The Marcher lords would never be short of

[64] *C.P.R. 1321–24*, 98, 136, 178–9; *B.P.R.*, I, 55 revised in the light of the figures from *Crecy and Calais (1346–7) from the Public Records*. ed. G. Wrottesley, William Salt Society, Transactions, 18 part 2 (1897), 69.

[65] N.L.W. Chirk Castle Collection, D. 9–D. 14. Not all the troops need have been recruits from Chirkland.

[66] E. 179/242/55.

[67] Cf. the list of ninety-two archers from his Marcher estates which Edmund, earl of March recruited for his expedition to Brittany in 1375: B. L. Egerton Roll, 8751; E. 101/34/6.

[68] See above p. 75, n. 34. The proclamation of the array on this occasion was made in Ruthin fair.

[69] For his commission, *C.P.R. 1321–4*, 74; for his lands, R. I. Jack, 'The Lordship of Dyffryn Clwyd in 1324'. *T.D.H.S.* 17 (1968), 40; for gifts by Welsh princes to

military talent and military leadership in their estates in Wales. But it would be mistaken to think that military service was regarded as an unmixed blessing even by Welshmen. Many absented themselves from the selection assemblies and were duly mulcted;[70] others opted for a fine as an alternative to service in the lord's army;[71] yet others purchased their freedom before their destination was reached, whether they were at Porchester or Pontefract.[72] Even those who stayed at home found that the military preoccupations of their lord bore down relentlessly on them: their horses were commandeered[73] and so was their money. The men of Chirkland not only contributed archers to their lord's campaigns but war subsidies also: forty marks in 1341; another twenty marks in 1345; while their neighbours of Bromfield and Yale were dunned by their lord (the earl of Surrey) in 200 marks towards his cost 'in defensione status regni Anglie' in 1339.[74] The military commitments of the lord clearly meant much to his Marcher tenants, sometimes too much. Even the lords themselves were driven on occasion to protest that saturation point had been reached in the military demands made of their lordships.[75]

The military resources of the Marcher lordships were exploited to further the king's campaigns overseas; they might also be deployed to serve the lord's ambitions nearer home. For a loyal tenantry, and militarily a well-trained one at that, was a considerable asset in the domestic crises of the fourteenth century. The retinue of the earl of Hereford in 1312, for ex-

his ancestors, *N.L.W.J.* 3 (1943), 29 32, 159; for his goods on his death, S.C. 2/217/8, m. 25. See also below p. 418.

[70] As happened in Bromfield in 1345 or in Dyffryn Clwyd in 1359: S.C. 2/226/18, m. 11; 218/7, m. 22.

[71] Examples are very common. In 1359 twenty-nine of the men of Dyffryn Clwyd paid their lord £12 8s. 4d. rather than accompany him to France: S.C. 2/218/7, m. 30.

[72] Two Welshmen paid a mark each to leave their lord's army at Porchester in 1325 and another gave a red ox to be permitted to leave the army at Pontefract in 1333: S.C. 2/216/6, m. 17ᵛ; 216/13, m. 1ᵛ.

[73] When Meuric ap Gruffudd of Clun refused to hand over his horse to the footsoldiers of the lord, he himself was ordered to go to Chipping Norton to join the lord's contingent: S.R.O. 552/1/11, m. 11 (1345).

[74] N.L.W. Chirk Castle Collection, D. 8, D. 12; S.C. 2/226/17. Likewise in 1333 the men of Dyffryn Clwyd granted £11 3s. 8d. towards the costs of their fellow-tenants serving the lord in Scotland: S.C. 2/216/13, m. 2. For military and other subsidies in Chirkland, see Llinos Smith in *B.B.C.S.* 23 (1969), esp. 159–60.

[75] *C.C.R. 1337–9*, 402.

ample, was augmented in the confrontation with the king, by 'a crowd of Welshmen, wild men from the woodlands', no doubt from his lordship of Brecon; just as Earl Thomas of Lancaster drew on the manpower of his newly-acquired lordship of Denbigh on the same occasion.[76] Wild Welshmen they might be, but they served their purpose brutally well. They did so again in 1321, when the pardons show how well the Marcher lords had deployed their political and military power in preparation for their showdown with the Despensers.[77] When Roger Mortimer of Wigmore, for example, paraded in London in July 1321 with his followers 'all clothed in green with their arms yellow', many of those followers were his Marcher tenants. Those same followers stood by him in his years of power after 1327: when a coup was planned against him in January 1329 it was nipped in the bud by a Mortimer army drawn from Wales and the March.[78]

Marcher lordships remained important military counters in the domestic politics of England throughout the fourteenth century: their geographical position on the periphery of the English political stage, their strength as large territorial blocs under the sole control of their lords, the prominence of those lords in English aristocratic circles, and the military potential of the lordships in terms of castles and manpower ensured them such a role. Nowhere, perhaps, does this military dimension of Marcher lordship figure more clearly than in the crucial events of July–August 1399. The success of Henry Bolingbroke's campaign in those months is to be explained in part—though not necessarily in major part—by the degree of prior organization on his estates; and of these estates none was more crucial than those in the March, both those he had acquired by marriage (Brecon, Hay) and those he claimed as his father's heir (Monmouth, Kidwelly, Iscennen), for they were strategically placed in relation to Richard II's concentration of power in the west. Their officers, like those of so many other Lancastrian estates,[79] showed exemplary zeal and foresight in their

---

[76] *Vita Edwardi Secundi*, ed. N. Denholm-Young (1957), 27, 32; *C.P.R. 1313–17*, 21–5.

[77] *C.P.R. 1321–4*, 15–20.

[78] *Monasticon Anglicanum*, VI, i. 352; *C.P.R. 1327–30*, 347; S.C. 6/1206/1 (Welshmen from Cydewain in attendance on Mortimer, 1329–30).

[79] R. Somerville, *History of the Duchy of Lancaster*, I, 136–7.

master's affairs: Monmouth castle was heavily guarded 'ad resistendum inimicos domini'; the gates of the great castle at Kidwelly—where Richard II had so recently lodged *en route* to Ireland—were stopped up with mortar and stones in anticipation of a return visit; the moats at Hay and Brecon were cleaned and a new drawbridge installed; and spies were dispatched throughout south Wales to check on the lord's enemies and the king's friends. Finally and most significant of all from our viewpoint, when Bolingbroke reached Gloucester he was met by an army of his loyal tenants from Cantrefselyf, Brecon and Llywel pledged to defend him against his enemies.[80] This is what lordship, good lordship, meant in military terms. Many a Marcher lord if questioned about the value of his lordship might have been prompted to answer curtly (in the words of the Highlander): 'five hundred men'.[81] That was good value indeed in the fourteenth century.

[80] D.L. 29/615/9840; 584/9240; S.C. 6/1157/4 (receivers' accounts for Monmouth, Kidwelly and Brecon, 1399).
[81] Quoted in M. Bloch, *French Rural Society* (1966), 72.

4   The Consolidation of Lordship

CONQUEST was only the beginning of lordship. It assured the conqueror no more than a fragile military superiority and the uncertain fruits of that superiority. The full-blown powers of Marcher lordship were neither automatically conferred by conquest nor were they—as is sometimes inferred—apostolically transmitted, at least in their entirety, from native prince to Marcher lord. It was only by the dint of unremitting effort by the lord and his officers that the vague overlordship which came in the wake of conquest could be converted into a precise and profitable authority over land and men, that is into a meaningful lordship. At the heart of the problem lay land. Contemporaries were fond of quoting the maxim that there was no land without a lord; the converse was equally true: there was, normally, no lordship without land, *nulle seigneurie sans terre*. For though lordship was more than a question of the control of land—it was also the right to control men and to exercise justice—lordship without a territorial basis was inconceivable. And the broader that territorial basis the more secure was the authority of lordship; the narrower it was, the more likely was it that lordship would degenerate into a bundle of insubstantial claims.

Nowhere was this more obvious than in the Clare lordship of Glamorgan; nowhere indeed is the hiatus between conquest and lordship more evident.[1] Glamorgan had been initially

---

[1] Glamorgan is far and away the best served of Marcher lordships in historical studies. Much of the original material for the study of the lordship is conveniently assembled in G. T. Clark's splendid *Cartae*. I am also heavily indebted to the following studies: *Glam. C.H.*, III; M. Altschul, *A Baronial Family in Medieval England: The Clares, 1217–1314* (Baltimore, 1965); J. B. Smith, 'The Lordship of Glamorgan: a Study in Marcher Government' (Univ. of Wales M.A. thesis, 1957); J. C. Ward, 'The Estates of the Clare Family, 1066–1317', Ph.D. thesis (Univ. of London, 1962). The article by J. B. Smith, 'The Lordship of Glamorgan', *Morgannwg* 2 (1958), 9–38 is outstandingly helpful.

conquered as far back as the 1090s by Robert fitz Hamon; and
that conquest had been sustained by the castles that he and his
followers built in the Vale of Glamorgan. The lord retained the
commote of Cibwr for himself, built a castle at Cardiff as the
caput of his lordship, and established manors such as those at
Roath and Leckwith. But even in lowland, Normanized,
Glamorgan much of the authority of the lord was no more than

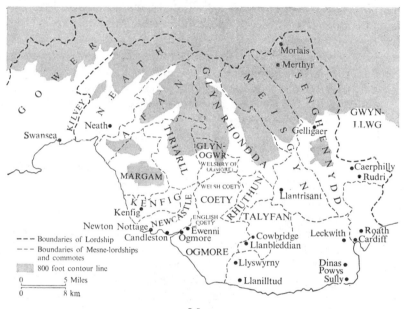

Map 2

The Lordship of Glamorgan

the supervisory feudal control of a feudal lord. The mesne
manors held of the lord were valued at almost £500; the lord
himself, however, had to be content with a castle-guard rent of
£12. 5s 0d. a year from them and the profits of his county
court.[2] If his lordship was no more than occasional in the mesne
manors of the Vale, it was barely noticeable elsewhere in the
lordship. This was true, for example, of some of the larger
sub-lordships, such as Coety held by the Turbervilles 'with

[2] These estimates come from the inquisition of 1262 published in *Cartae*, II,
no. 615.

royal liberty', by a token sergeanty of hunting and with the
sole proviso that the lord should have wardship and marriage.[3]
It was even more true of the Welsh commotes (i.e. administrative units) of the uplands—Senghennydd, Glynrhondda,
Meisgyn and Afan. They were in the hands of native Welsh
rulers whose ties of obligation to the lord were minimal. Their
independence in theory was matched by an independence of
fact: the lord of Afan, for example, was impudent enough to
confirm the grants of the earl of Gloucester himself,[4] and in the
turbulent politics of the thirteenth century these native Welsh
rulers did not refrain from allying with the lord's enemies and
waging open war on him. Lordship had many dimensions to it
within the land of Morgan: it ranged from the precise and
powerful authority which the lord exercised around Cardiff
to the almost meaningless *superioritas* which he claimed over
the commotes of the uplands.

It was the achievement of the thirteenth-century lords of
Glamorgan and more particularly of Earl Richard (1240–62)
and Earl Gilbert the Red (1262–95) that they transformed this
situation. They did so by converting a remote superiority into
a precise territorial authority. They were the architects of a
second conquest of Glamorgan, a conquest in depth which gave
a new meaning to their lordship and which deserves comparison
with Edward I's policies in Gwynedd. It was compounded of
conquest and eviction, purchase and pressure. It began about
1245; it was virtually complete by 1290. It was heralded by a
dramatic case in the county court at Cardiff in the 1240s when
Richard Siward, lord of Llanbleddian, Talyfan and Rhuthun,
one of the greatest mesne lords of Morgannwg, was accused of
felony against the earl and dispossessed of his lands.[5] The case
was a calculated trial of strength between the lord and one of
his major vassals. Its outcome not only vindicated the lord's
judicial superiority; it also extended the territorial basis of his
lordship very substantially. Even more dramatic and far-
reaching in its effects was the way the lords of the Welsh
commotes were either dispossessed or made subject to the over-

[3] *C.I.P.M.*, v, no. 538, p. 333.
[4] *Cartae*, iii, no. 814.
[5] The record of this vital case is published, rather inaccurately, in *Cartae*, ii, no.
535. For comment on it, see Altschul, op. cit. 70–5.

lord's authority in an undoubted fashion. The commotes of Glynrhondda and Meisgyn were seized from Hywel ap Maredudd, their native ruler, in 1246 and ruled henceforth from the new castle and town that the earl founded at Llantrisant; in 1247 the rulers of Afan, drawn from a line of native lords who had been outstanding in their opposition to Norman rule, acknowledged the jurisdictional superiority of the county court of the earl at Cardiff and soon capitulated to his authority in general, adopting the splendidly Normanized name of 'de Avene' as token of their new submissive status; finally in 1267 the earl of Gloucester completed his take-over of the independent Welsh commotes by seizing and imprisoning the ruler of Senghennydd and building the splendid castle at Caerphilly as a new military bulwark and administrative headquarters for the commote. In a series of swift, decisive strokes over twenty years the earls of Gloucester had made themselves immediate lords of the highlands of Glamorgan. The new castles that they built, whether on the edge of the highlands as at Llantrisant or Caerphilly or on high mountainous ridges as in the case of the remote fortress of Morlais, were and were meant to be manifestations of the new-found authority of the lords of Glamorgan. This process of deliberate consolidation was completed in 1289 when Earl Gilbert bought out most of the lands of Neath Abbey between the rivers Nedd and Tawe in exchange for £100 in annual rent. It was a high price to pay; but a price that was more than compensated by the accession of territorial power and by the augmentation of the authority of lordship. No one could now doubt the *dominium* of the lords of Glamorgan; even the figures of the lord's income speak eloquently of the transformation that had been achieved. Glamorgan was estimated in 1317 as being worth £1,276 to its lord; £917 (i.e. 72 per cent) of that sum, it has been calculated, came from lands where direct lordship had been asserted since 1245.[6]

The earls of Gloucester were also lords of Newport and (from 1247) of Usk and Trelech; and policies learnt in one lordship were soon applied to the others. The summary eviction of native Welsh rulers which had proved such an outstanding success in Glamorgan was copied in Gwent: in 1270, Maredudd ap Gruffudd was evicted from the commotes of Edlegan, Llefnydd

[6] Ward, op. cit. 262–3.

and Machen and his lands were amalgamated into the lordships of Caerleon and Newport.[7] On the whole, however, more
subtle methods had to be employed in the eastern lordships,
even though the ends were the same. In 1268–9, cash and lands
in England were used as successful baits to persuade the
coheiresses of the lordship of Caerleon to make it over to
Gilbert Clare; and in like fashion the earls deployed a combination of pressure and purchase to consolidate their lordship in
the area by acquiring the manors of Tregrug (Usk) and Tintern
Parva (Trelech) and lands in Magor (Caerleon).[8]

Between them Earl Richard and Earl Gilbert had transformed
the nature of lordship in the Clare estates in the March. They
had placed it on a firm territorial basis. Their achievement may
be measured in statistical terms: the income from their Marcher
lands in 1266 stood at about £850; by 1317 it had increased
almost threefold to £2,500.[9] And it had done so not through
the fortunes of marriage and inheritance, but by dint of a
consistent, even ruthless, policy of consolidation. 'Fuit dominus
et quasi rex' was the comment on the power of the lord of
Glamorgan in 1247;[10] it was even more true by the end of the
century. Edward I had occasion to know it: during his triumphal
progress through Wales in 1284 he was received by the earl of
Gloucester in Glamorgan 'with the greatest honour' and, as
Trevet remarks with barely-concealed surprise, 'conducted to
the boundary of his own lands by the earl at his own expense.'[11]
Earl Gilbert was at the peak of his power and all the world,
even the king, was to know it. He used the rare occasion of a
royal visit to preen his Marcher feathers, to 'treat the king of
England as if he were a brother potentate'.[12] The message could
hardly have been lost on a monarch so hypersensitive of his
regality as was Edward I. Nemesis came in the 1290s. The great
cause célèbre of 1290–2 represented the first frontal royal assault
on the liberties of the March by a king of England and it was

---

[7] *C.I.P.M.*, II, no. 289; *The Welsh Assize Roll 1277–84*, ed. J. Conway Davies
(Cardiff, 1940), 276; Altschul, op. cit. 129.

[8] Ibid. 126; B.L. Add. 6041, fol. 78.

[9] These are the figures tentatively suggested by Altschul, op. cit. 203–4. They
need to be treated with some caution, but at least they give an indication of the
dimensions of increase of Clare revenue in the March.

[10] *Cartae*, II, no. 535, p. 554.

[11] *Annales Sex Regum Angliae*, ed. T. Hog (English Historical Society, 1845), 309.

[12] J. E. Morris, *The Welsh Wars of Edward I* (Oxford, 1901), 202.

appropriate that its victim was the greatest exponent of those liberties, the lord of Glamorgan.[13] This great royal dressing-down was followed within a few years by another shattering experience for the lord of Glamorgan, the revolt of 1294–5. In Glamorgan that revolt was led by Morgan ap Maredudd, the son of the Welsh ruler of Machen, Edlegan and Llefnydd whom Earl Gilbert had disseised in 1270. It was largely concentrated in the upland commotes of Glamorgan where the earls had been so busily asserting their authority during the previous generation, and it was specifically aimed against Earl Gilbert and not against the king of England. It was a revolt of the community against its lord, and Edward I was never slow to make capital out of such revolts. He himself marched into Glamorgan to make good the shortcomings of Earl Gilbert's own military efforts; he received the Welsh rebels of the lordship into his own royal peace contrary to the earl's wishes; he pardoned Morgan ap Maredudd and soon showered favours and responsibilities on him; and, unkindest cut of all, he took Glamorgan into royal custody for four months.[14] In December 1295, Earl Gilbert the Red died at Monmouth. He had lost his prolonged duel with Edward I and nowhere was that more obvious than in the March of Wales. Yet, the very extent of the reaction of the 1290s, on the part of Welsh community and king alike, was, paradoxically, a tribute to the success of the policies of Earl Gilbert and his father. They were among the major architects of the late medieval March.

The Clare earls had consolidated their authority in the March under the turbulent conditions of the thirteenth century; they had indeed turned those very conditions to their advantage by interpreting political disaffection as ample pretext for territorial confiscation. But the enhancement of lordship went on in peace as well as in war; only the methods were different. It was so in Glamorgan itself: its Despenser lords in the fourteenth century incorporated some of the rich manors of the Vale, such as Sully, Dinas Powys and Newton Nottage, into their demesne and even succeeded in completing the work of the Clare earls by buying out the last of the native dynasties, the Avenes of Afan.[15] But it is Brecon which provides us with

---

[13] Below pp. 259–60.   [14] Below pp. 261, 263.

[15] *C.I.P.M.*, IX, no. 428, p. 333; Rice Merrick, *A Booke of Glamorganshire Antiqui-*

one of the finest examples of how lordship could be extended in conditions of peace. As a Marcher lordship its history was similar to that of Glamorgan: the Normans had initially established a foothold there in the late eleventh century but it was not to be for another two centuries that their lordship could be regarded as militarily secure.[16] Only then could the full potentialities of the lordship be exploited. They were amply and eagerly recognized by contemporaries.[17] 'There is a very fine and great lordship in those places,' wrote an excited royal commissioner to Edward I about Brecon in 1302, 'which will be worth at least two thousand marks a year if it is well managed.'[18] It was a sanguine, almost misleading, report, calculated to please an impecunious king; but its point was a fair one. Good management could indeed make a fine lordship of Brecon; and it was amply provided by Humphrey Bohun IV, earl of Hereford and lord of Brecon 1336–61. He was, in many ways, an unlikely exponent of the arts of lordship and good management—a life-long invalid, a pious bachelor given to the company of priests and Augustinian canons. Yet his achievement was, in its own undramatic way, quite as significant as that of the lords of Glamorgan.

The problem that faced him in Brecon was clear: within his 'very fine and great lordship' his authority was often no more than indirect and spasmodic. Most of the rich lowland manors of the valleys of Usk and Llynfi were held by the lord's feudal vassals by the service of some eighteen knights' fees;[19] and the territorial rights of these vassals had become more secure over the years. They called themselves 'lords' (*domini*) of their lands;[20] and so they were, for the rights of the earl over them were strictly circumscribed by the rules of feudal custom. This was particularly true of the great mesne lordships of Bronllys and

ties, ed. J. A. Corbett (1887), 74–5; J. B. Smith, unpublished thesis, op. cit. 222–3.

[16] For the early history of the lordship, see W. Rees, 'The Medieval Lordship of Brecon', *T.C.S.* (1915–16), 165–224.

[17] The following paragraphs are based on my unpublished D.Phil. thesis, 'The Bohun and Lancaster Lordships in Wales in the fourteenth and early fifteenth centuries' (Univ. of Oxorf, 1965), 95–115, where the arguments advanced here have been more amply documented. Only essential references are provided here.

[18] *C. Inq. Misc. 1219–1307*, no. 1870.

[19] *C.I.P.M.*, III, no. 552.

[20] For example, the Burghills called themselves lords of Y Fenni, John Mortimer was known as lord of Llanfilo and John Gunter as lord of Gunterston: *Arch. Camb.*, 4th ser. 14, 278–9; D.L. 25/1606; N.L.W. Badminton Deeds, 14868.

Pencelli: their lords were so powerful territorially and often politically that they regarded themselves and were regarded by others as virtually independent. They were taxed separately by royal commissioners;[21] their estates were treated as tenancies in

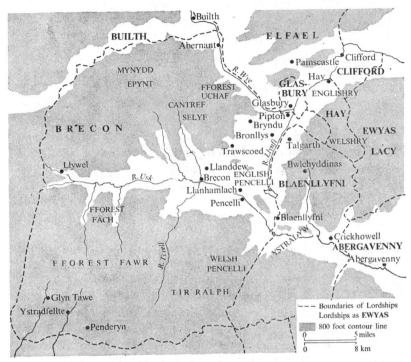

Map 3
The Lordships of Brecon, Hay and Blaenllyfni

chief by the king;[22] and they themselves challenged the over-lordship of the lord of Brecon over their lands.[23] Here was one clear threat to Marcher lordship in Brecon. Another came from a different direction, from the corporate communities of the lordship. In much of Brecon the lord exercised little direct territorial lordship; he did no more than collect fixed annual

[21] E. 179/242/48 (1292).

[22] Hence the inquisition *post mortem* on Bronllys in *C.I.P.M.*, III, no. 544.

[23] In 1290 Roger Mortimer of Pencelli appealed against his lord, the earl of Hereford, in the king's court: T. Madox, *Baronia Anglica: An History of Land-Honors and Baronies and of Tenure in Capite* (1736), 154–5.

renders or farms from virtually self-governing communities, whether the alien community of the chartered borough of Brecon or, much more significantly, the Welsh communities which effectively ruled most of upland Brecon. Finally, the pious generosity of the lord's ancestors and others had created within the lordship large enclaves of ecclesiastical authority which were effectively beyond the pale of seignorial finance and jurisdiction. They included the episcopal estates of the bishop of St. David's clustered around the castellated residence at Llanddew, the generous benefactions given to the Norman priory at Brecon, an occasional estate bestowed on an English abbey such as that at Llansbyddid given to Malvern priory, and most recently and munificently the vast tracts of pastureland in the Epynt hills which had been granted in an extravagance of wanton piety to the Cistercian abbey at Dore. Lordship in Brecon—as so often in the March—simply fitted into the interstices of alternative sources of authority; it often looked as if it might be smothered by them. The lords of Brecon certainly had their work cut out for them.

Earl Humphrey IV set about it purposefully.[24] In 1340 he stripped the borough of Brecon of all its privileges and reduced it to the status of a seignorial vill. His own officials took over the administration of the town and with spectacularly good results: over the next ten years the average annual yield was 40 per cent higher than it was in 1340 (£86. 13s. 4d.: £119). Direct lordship was clearly profitable. The Welsh community was treated in the same way as the burgesses. In 1340 the right to lease the Great Forest, the single most important source of revenue in the lordship, was resumed into the lord's hands and once more the results were impressive (£46. 13s. 4d.: £56. 5s. 0d.) The earl next turned his attention to his feudal vassals and initiated a single-minded policy of territorial consolidation, notably in Pencelli and Bronllys. His methods paid little regard to legality and exploited to the full his jurisdictional supremacy in his own lordship. Threats, confiscations, imprisonment and *quo warranto* inquiries were the weapons in his armoury. Between 1347 and 1357 he had secured, either permanently or temporarily, all or some of the lands of the

---

[24] Most of his achievement has been deduced from the accounts of the receiver of Brecon 1336–54 and 1356–8 in D.L. 29/671/10810.

families of Pichard, Devereux, Sowton and Mortimer (some-
time of Chirk) in Pencelli; to cater for this sudden augmentation
of his territorial wealth, eight new reeveships were created in the
area within the decade. Like results were achieved in Bronllys
and Cantrefselyf: its mesne lord, Sir Philip ap Rees, was hauled
before the court at Brecon (where Earl Humphrey was both
plaintiff and judge) on a trumped-up *quo warranto* charge and
his lands were finally confiscated in August 1351.[25] In this
process of territorial consolidation Earl Humphrey worked
hand in glove with his ambitious brother and heir presumptive,
William Bohun, earl of Northampton (1337–60).[26] Between
1351 and 1358, William Bohun invested a small fortune, quite
possibly from the profits of his military career, in the purchase
of lands in Bronllys and Cantrefselyf.[27] The purposefulness of
the policies of the Bohun brothers was not in doubt. Nor was
their success: the lordship of Brecon by 1361 was worth over
£1,500 gross and over half of that income came from territorial
acquisitions made by Earl Humphrey IV and his brother since
1336.[28] They had indeed made of Brecon 'a very fine and great
lordship'.

Other Marcher lords no doubt did the same, even if their
measure of success was neither so striking nor so well-documented. Their methods varied. Some had sufficient ready cash to
make outright purchases: Earl Edmund of Lancaster, for
example, expended considerable sums in the 1270s to consolidate his territorial authority within his lordship of Monmouth.[29] Some made it their policy to convert the mesne fees
of their lordships into demesne manors whenever and however
they could: this is how the earls of Arundel greatly strengthened
their lordship in Oswestry in the fourteenth century and brought
such rich manors as Kinnerley and Ruyton under their direct
control.[30] Others did not scruple to use force to achieve their

---

[25] R. R. Davies, D.Phil. thesis, 95–103, 108—11.

[26] For his career and for his purchases in England see G. A. Holmes, *The Estates of the Higher Nobility* (Cambridge, 1957), 22–3.

[27] For these purchases, see D.L. 25/1285, 1602, 1618–28; D.L. 36/1, nos. 217–19, 261; C.P. 25(1)/83/43, no. 158; *C.P.R. 1350–4*, 258, 261, 294.

[28] R. R. Davies, D.Phil. thesis, 114, 158 for these calculations.

[29] Many of his purchases are recorded in the Duchy Cowcher Book, D.L. 42/1, fol. 17ᵛ–fol. 24; those from Sir William Coleville alone cost him 118 marks and twenty acres of land.

[30] R. W. Eyton, *Antiquities of Shropshire*, x, 111, n. 5; xi, 28; *C.I.P.M.*, vi, no. 1

ends: it was, according to his own evidence, while he was imprisoned in Swansea castle in 1355 by Thomas Beauchamp, earl of Warwick and lord of Gower, that Thomas Avene was compelled to quitclaim his right to the important manor of Kilvey. No uniform pattern is to be detected in this story of the consolidation of the territorial authority of the Marcher lords. As so often in the March, variety not uniformity is the keynote; and that variety was shaped both by the social structure of each lordship and by the character of each lord. Yet in general it can hardly be doubted that the elbow room for the extension of seignorial authority was far greater in the March than in England; the mere size of each lordship and the almost uninhibited power of the lord ensured that it should be so. Several Marcher families seized the opportunity with both hands. Thus the proportion of the landed income of the Clare family that came from the March rose from 23 per cent in 1266 to 42 per cent in 1317 and that increase was substantially to be explained by an assertion of their lordship by the Clare earls. Such results were one compelling reason why lordship in the March was so attractive.[31]

Land was the basis of lordship; but it was not the only one. Justice was also an attribute of lordship, and nowhere more so than in the March. It was imperative that the lord should guard and foster his judicial rights not only because they were astonishingly profitable (as we shall see later) but also because judicial control was one of the most effective—and often the only—manifestations of the lord's authority throughout his lordship. The insistence of the lord that all his tenants, including the mightiest of them, should perform suit at his court or that he alone should have the right to hear certain offences did not merely arise out of a jealous officiousness; it was an integral part of his campaign to sustain his lordship over his lands.

Brecon once more provides us with a highly instructive case. We have already noticed the wide measure of authority claimed by the mesne lord of Bronllys; it was matched by the judicial liberties he exercised.[32] He claimed cognizance of

p. 73. The achievement of the earls of Arundel in this respect is analysed in Llinos Smith's unpublished Ph.D. thesis 'The Lordships of Chirk and Oswestry, 1282–1415' (Univ. of London, 1971), 56–63.

[31] *Glam. C.H.*, iii, 251 and n. 237 (Kilvey); Ward, op. cit., 262–3 (Clare income).

[32] This paragraph is based on the *quo warranto* proceedings against Sir Philip ap

almost all pleas, including pleas of the Crown, in his free court at Bronllys; he also claimed the right to pardon accused persons and to receive the chattels of his tenants even when they were convicted elsewhere. It was a comprehensive collection of judicial liberties which left the lord of Brecon with no more than a most tenuous jurisdictional superiority in Bronllys. It was not a situation which Earl Humphrey IV of Hereford was likely to tolerate. The arguments which he and his legal counsel advanced in their *quo warranto* inquiry into the rights of the mesne lord of Bronllys in 1349 articulate those judicial powers which a Marcher lord regarded as peculiarly his own. No one except the Marcher lord himself had the right to Crown pleas; he alone could have a chancery and writs and therefore he alone was able to deal with civil or appellate cases; only he had a court of record; and he had the sole right to grant pardons. It was an eloquent *exposé* of the judicial lordship of a Marcher lord. The result of the inquiry was a foregone conclusion: Sir Philip ap Rees, the mesne lord of Bronllys, was convicted in his absence and his lands were confiscated. Four other mesne lords were also hauled into court and were given a clear warning that the rights of the lord of Brecon were not lightly to be usurped by others. It was an exercise in the assertion of lordship.

At much the same time that Earl Humphrey Bohun was asserting his judicial superiority within the lordship of Brecon, Earl Roger of March was following his example in the neighbouring lordship of Blaenllyfni. In January 1356 Grimbald Pauncefoot of Crickhowell, the most important vassal in Blaenllyfni, was fined £100 for exceeding his judicial rights as a mesne tenant by executing a felon without judgement, by not handing him over to the court of his superior lord, and by detaining a man outlawed in the lord's court.[33] And, as we would expect, the Clare lords of Glamorgan had always been jealous guardians of their judicial rights as Marcher lords. They had upheld and extended the jurisdiction of their county-court (*comitatus*) at Cardiff so that its authority extended throughout the lordship;

Rees 1349–51. The original copy of this case is in Staffs. R.O. D. 641/1/5, no. 1; there is a later copy in D.L. 41/6/11. For fuller details and for the background to the case, see R. R. Davies, D.Phil. thesis, 125–30.

[33] B.L. Egerton Roll 8708.

and in a declaration in 1299 they had reasserted the power of that court and the right of their coroner to have jurisdiction throughout Glamorgan.[34]

Another lordship whose lords fought a prolonged battle to assert their judicial supremacy was that of Pembroke.[35] The lords of Pembroke claimed that their 'royal jurisdiction' (*totum regale*) extended not only to the lordship (*dominium*) of Pembroke itself but to 'the entire county' palatine (*integer comitatus*), with the exception of the episcopal lands. That is, it embraced the lordships of Cemais, Narberth, Cilgerran and Haverford and the barony of Walwynscastle. The lord of Pembroke claimed that all the knights and freemen of the whole county of Pembroke owed suit to his county-court;[36] that he alone, as lord of the honor, should have a chancery and a seal; that all Crown pleas were reserved to himself; and that his officers had the right to make summonses throughout the county.[37] This campaign to uphold the judicial integrity of the county of Pembroke in the wake of its territorial fragmentation after the death of the last Marshall earl of Pembroke in 1245 was vigorously pursued by the lords of Pembroke throughout the late-thirteenth and fourteenth centuries. Its success varied: in Haverford and Narberth, in the hands respectively of the Crown and of the Mortimers, it was largely ineffective; in Cilgerran the problem was resolved when its lords (the Hastings family) succeeded to the lordship of Pembroke in 1324; in Cemais and Walwynscastle (both held by relatively small Marcher families, fitz Martin and Brian respectively) the jurisdictional superiority of Pembroke was grudgingly but effectively acknowledged[38] and that in spite of the prolonged

---

[34] *Cartae*, III, no. 798; Altschul, op. cit. 261–5, 269.

[35] Much of the evidence for this struggle is conveniently assembled in *A Calendar of the Public Records relating to Pembrokeshire* (3 vols.) and in the text and overflowing footnotes of *Penbrokshire*.

[36] This point had been acknowledged by most of the co-parcenors in the 1250s: *C.P.R. 1367–70*, 91–2; *Cal. Anc. Corr. re. Wales*, 210–12.

[37] The essence of the case is best gathered from the statement of it made in 1290: *Rot. Parl.*, I, 30–2.

[38] For the agreements with the lords of Cemais see I. H. Jeayes, *Catalogue of Muniments at Berkeley Castle*, 142–6 (1277) and *C.C.R. 1288–96*, 188 (1290; confirmed in 1378, *C.P.R. 1377–81*, 261). J. H. Round commented at length on these agreements in 'The Lords of Kemes', *Family Origins and Other Studies*, 73–102. For the terms of the agreements with the lords of Walwynscastle see *C.I.P.M.*, IX, no. 118, pp. 218–29.

minorities of the Hastings family.[39] The story forms yet another significant chapter in the assertion of lordship in the March of Wales.

Map 4
The County of Pembroke and its Lordships

That same lordship had to be asserted over the lord's feudal vassals. Subinfeudation was, of course, originally an act of seignorial largesse calculated to redound to the honour and

[39] A great deal of the evidence (most of it now lost) for the effectiveness of Pembroke's judicial control of Cemais is gathered together in *Baronia de Kemeys* (*Arch. Camb.*, Supplement, 1861) and in *Penbrokshire*, II, 425 ff. For the withdrawal of suit of court during minorities, see *C.C.R. 1354–60*, 438; *C.P.R. 1374–77*, 194.

power of the lord by investing his dependants with a share in his lordship; but too often it proved to be, in the long run, a mortgaging of the powers of lordship and of the authority of the lord. Nowhere did the consequences of loss of control over mesne vassals appear more vividly than in the lordship of Gower under its last Braose lord, William (1290–1326). He and his father had frittered away their lands, driven to it no doubt by impecuniousness and improvidence;[40] he gave away or sold whole manors and even the castle of Loughor, which he bestowed on his factotum, John Iweyn;[41] he did not even stop short of mortgaging towers within the castle of Swansea itself. He was dissipating his lordship; his vassals saw their opportunity and seized it. After a prolonged campaign and with the active connivance of Edward I, they extracted from their lord a wide-ranging charter of liberties in 1306.[42] Its details do not concern us here; but its general intent is highly illuminating. It circumscribed the lord's power in many directions: it limited, for example, his rights of purveyance and his freedom of action in judicial matters. Even more significantly it entrenched the authority of the lord's major vassals: it granted them extensive jurisdictional rights over their own tenants; it confirmed their authority in the *comitatus*, the main court of the lordship; it secured for them, rather than for the lord, the confiscated lands of felons; and so forth. It was the victory of vassals over lordship, of subinfeudation over *dominium*. It was not a lesson that was lost on other Marcher lords.

Most of them—at least those in the southern and eastern March where subinfeudation was most extensive—were well aware that their mesne lords must be kept on a tight rein if they were not to get out of control. In the first place, the feudal rights of the lord had to be jealously guarded. He claimed primer seisin, that is the exclusive right of custody, of the estates of his vassals in the March, regardless of whether they

[40] The remarkable list of alienations is published in full in *Cartae*, III, no. 893. For Braose's improvidence, see J. C. Davies in *T.R.H.S.*, 3rd ser. 9 (1915), 33 ff.

[41] Loughor was granted to Iweyn in 1302 and was but one of many Braose grants to him: Hereford Cathedral Archives, nos. 1311–13, 1529, 1769. Iweyn was killed in 1322 and his lands were recovered by John Mowbray, the heir to Gower, in 1328: *Sir Christopher Hatton's Book of Seals*, no. 397. For Iweyn's career, see R. A. Griffiths, *The Principality of Wales*, I, 258.

[42] The charter is published in *Cartae*, III, no. 851. For the background to it, see *Glam. C.H.*, III, 232–41.

held in chief of the king in England: the lord of Brecon had successfully asserted that right in 1299.[43] He alone was to enjoy the custody and wardship of his vassals. They were well worth enjoying, as the Brecon evidence makes clear. The wardship of Rees ab Ieuan was sold for £40 in 1338 while the lands of the Devereux and Whitney heirs, which were retained in the lord's custody, brought in £20 annually.[44] Secondly there were certain rights (other than the jurisdictional ones) which Marcher lords regarded as peculiarly their prerogatives, notably the rights to levy troops at the king's command within their lordships;[45] to levy tolls and to determine the weights and measures within their lands;[46] to have exclusive claims to forest and free warren as did the king in the kingdom of England; to determine relations with other lordships by holding days of the March[47] and by receiving outsiders (*extranei*) into their protection.[48] These were the *prerogativa domini*, those rights which a Marcher lord regarded as the inalienable features of his lordship. They were to be jealously guarded even at the cost of confiscating the estates of recalcitrant vassals, as the lord of Glamorgan showed in the case of Richard Siward in 1245 and the lord of Brecon in the case of Sir Philip ap Rees in 1351. A Marcher lord had indeed to be masterful if he was to preserve his lordship intact.

That mastery needed to be demonstrated in yet another direction, that of the Welsh community of his lordship. The other problems of lordship—those of territorial consolidation, judicial superiority and the control of mesne tenants—were in their fashion, familiar enough on English estates; the problem of the Welsh was, however, altogether more unfamiliar and intractable. It was quite simply this: in many Marcher lordships—particularly those of the middle March—the lord's authority over his Welsh subjects (for 'tenants' would certainly be a misleading word) was remote and tenuous. Let us take the

---

[43] C. 133/91, no. 2, inquisition 13; *C.C.R. 1296–1302*, 254, 270. The earl of Gloucester had virtually made the same claim in 1290, *Cartae*, III, no. 769.

[44] D.L. 29/671/10810, m. 2–m. 3, m. 17, m. 19, m. 21; S.C. 6/1156/18.

[45] *Penbrokshire*, II, 461 (Cemais, 1320).

[46] B.L. Egerton Roll 8708 (Blaenllyfni, 1358).

[47] D.L. 37/10, no. 70 (Glamorgan, 1442).

[48] S.C. 2/219/3, m. 30 (Dyffryn Clwyd, 1360); S.R.O., 552/1/30, m. 1ᵛ (Clun, 1398).

case of the lordship of Brecon. When the royal commissioner visited it in 1302 he was thrilled by the sight of two thousand Welshmen swearing fealty to the king through an interpreter. It was indeed an impressive ceremony; but it concealed the realities of the situation. The Welsh community (or communities) of Brecon was a corporate body whose relationship with its lord was defined and confined by the charters of liberties it had secured from its lord.[49] It could appoint its own proctors to bargain with him; it collected its own farms; it assessed and answered for its own subsidies. It recognized the lord's *superioritas* in the lordship if only by paying him a recognitory gift on his first entry into it. Beyond that, however, its obligations were confined to monthly suit at the court of Brecon and military service with the person of the lord.[50] Its duties to the lord were as minimal as those of the proudest vassal. Furthermore the community and the kindred groups that composed it exercised allodial rights over their land; their lord was in no way their immediate *land*-lord. Outside the river valleys of Usk, Tarell and Llyfni, the Welsh owed no rents or specific services for individual tracts of land. Instead they gave the lord a biennial *commorth* (or subsidy) of cows and annual fixed farms for the forests and mills. Financially these various issues were highly remunerative; but they were common tributes to the lord not individual rents, and the internal arrangements for their distribution and collection lay entirely in the hands of the community. As a result the seignorial administrative structure over most of Brecon was skeletal to the point of being non-existent.[51]

This pattern of relationship between lord and Welsh community was not peculiar to Brecon. The Welshmen of Cibwr in Glamorgan, for example, did no service for their lands except suit of court once a month.[52] In the Mortimer lordship of Maelienydd, likewise, the direct landed control of the lord was largely restricted to the district around the seignorial castle and borough of Cefnllys. The rest of the lordship was still divided into Welsh *swyddi* (shires) and within them the lord's

---

[49] The Brecon charters of liberties do not survive; but they are mentioned in 1297: *Cal. Anc. Corr. re. Wales*, 101.
[50] *C.I.P.M.*, iii, no. 552.
[51] R. R. Davies, D.Phil. thesis, 130–2, 137–8.
[52] *C.I.P.M.*, iv, no. 235.

territorial authority was minimal: rents only contributed a paltry £15 out of a gross yield of over £215.[53] This picture of a largely autonomous Welsh community and of the restricted and even remote powers of lordship over that community does not, of course, apply to the whole March. Lordship in the March was most effective in the lowlands. It was also, it would seem, more effective in those districts where Marcher lords inherited from the native Welsh princes a well-established authority over land. Marcher lordship was, for example, more securely based in the newly-conquered lands of Denbigh or Bromfield and Yale—as their splendid surveys show—than in Brecon or Maelienydd where the Norman lords had been struggling for superiority for centuries. That this should be so is due, in some measure, to the achievement of the native Welsh princes in converting their lordship (*arglwyddiaeth*) into a precise authority over land.

The Marcher lords sought to follow their example. None more so than Earl Humphrey IV of Hereford as lord of Brecon. He bargained with the Welsh community; he cajoled them to recognize his authority; he bullied them to accept it. And he did so with some measure of success: in 1341, 186 men from Cwmwd Commos attorned to him for their services and presented him with a gift of £100 as a token of their new relationship; in 1345 a further group of Welshmen acknowledged his landlord-ship and became his 'new tenants' (*novi tenentes*).[54] Other Marcher lords were no doubt pursuing similar policies: John of Gaunt, for example, succeeded in persuading some of the Welshmen of Glynogwr in upland Glamorgan to enter into a closer tenurial relationship with him.[55] In this campaign to consolidate the lord's control over the native Welsh no device was more effective or far-reaching in its consequences than the custom of escheat.[56] It served as an entrée into a field which was otherwise closed to the lord by community charters and by the

[53] See the receiver's account for 1356–7 published by E. J. Cole in *Transactions of the Radnorshire Society* 34 (1964), 31–9.

[54] D.L. 29/671/10810, m. 5, m. 6ᵛ, m. 9, m. 10.

[55] D.L. 29/592/9445 (1381).

[56] The seminal article on this subject remains that of E. A. Lewis, 'The Decay of Tribalism in North Wales', *T.C.S.* (1902–3), 1–75. Further light is thrown on the subject by the articles of T. Jones Pierce, *Medieval Welsh Society*, ed. J. B. Smith (Cardiff, 1973).

masonic rules of Welsh kinship-inheritance. It was an opportunity for him to bring land out of the control of the community and its fixed renders and within the ambit of his own will and into a system of individual rent. The question of escheat was recognized by all parties for what it was—the crucial issue in the relationship of lord and community. The Welsh community strove hard to keep it under its control: its value may be gauged by the fact that the men of the southern Principality were willing to pay £1,000 to retain the right.[57] The lord, for his part, realized that the custom of escheat could be a thin—indeed a not so thin—end of a wedge for asserting a firmer control over land and the land market. That is why, for example, the earl of Surrey insisted that he should have utter freedom to dispose of escheated land within his lordship of Bromfield and Yale.[58] The point of his insistence comes out clearly from the abundant evidence of nearby Denbigh.[59] There the lord's rights of escheat, in good part inherited from the native rulers, were firmly established; they were applied ruthlessly to the lands of all who died against the lord's peace or who failed to pay their dues or to perform their services. The results were truly spectacular: in the four commotes of Ceinmeirch, Isdulas, Uwchaled and Isaled some 29,000 acres out of a total surveyed acreage of 68,000 were classified as escheated land; in Ceinmeirch the proportion was as high as a half. Financially the results were equally impressive: in 1334 out of a total income of over £1,000, some £533 (or 53 per cent) came from the rents of escheated land.[60] Even more significant in the present context is that escheat proved to be in Denbigh as elsewhere an excellent opportunity for the definition of lordship over land; Henry Lacy and his successors exploited this opportunity to the full. Escheated land was lavishly bestowed on English settlers—at least 4,000 acres was so bestowed; the rest was leased to Welshmen to be held for a fixed money rent per acre and at the will of the lord. It was, furthermore, by his

[57] *Rot. Parl.*, IV, 90–1; *C.P.R. 1413–16*, 380.

[58] S.B.Y., fol. 170.

[59] The rest of this paragraph is based on *S.D.* and on the introduction to it by P. Vinogradoff and F. Morgan. The Denbigh evidence has been carefully analysed in D. H. Owen's Ph.D. thesis 'The Lordship of Denbigh 1282–1485' (Univ. of Wales, 1967).

[60] See also Holmes, *Estates of the Higher Nobility*, 93–7, 158–60.

control of escheated land, associated with some compulsory exchange, that the lord was able to impose his will in the most dramatic and far-reaching fashion on the life of the lordship—by creating entirely English settler communities (as at Lleweni), by carving out new parks and manors for himself (as at Ystrad Cynon) and by the enforced resettlement of Welshmen in distant parts of the lordship (such as Prys and Gwytherin). Denbigh provides the most outstanding example of the role that the custom of escheat played in the shaping of lordship in the March, as indeed in the whole of Wales. It made the lord a *dominus terrae*; and in a rural society that was the most powerful lordship of all.

Escheat was one of the major routes to the assertion of lordship over the Welsh community; control of waste, pasture and forest was the other. This is a topic to which we must return[61]; but it must be briefly mentioned here. In a largely pastoral and forested country, the control of these resources was vital. Contemporaries knew it well. When a community had its lord in a corner, one of its prime ambitions was to extract concessions from him over forest and pasture. It was a measure of the plight of John fitz Reginald that he had to concede to his men of Talgarth, Ystradyw and Crickhowell the right to hunt throughout the lordship, to fish where they pleased, and to have common pasture. And all for a hundred marks.[62] A masterful lord, on the contrary, never relaxed his control over these assets: the lord of Bromfield and Yale, for example, never allowed his men to forget that their ancestors had, as an act of contrition after the revolt of 1294–5, surrendered their rights over the forests and wastes of the lordship.[63] The control of these rights is one of the most accurate barometers of the success of lordship in the Welsh March.

The dimensions of lordship, it should by now be clear, varied widely within the March and indeed within every lordship. Beyond the minimal acceptance of the lord's *superioritas*, there was no such thing as an uniform measure of lordship. On this basis each lord built or failed to do so. If he succeeded, not only did he reap the profits financially, but also in terms of his own authority. If he failed to do so, his lordship, like his castles,

---

[61] See below pp. 120–7.   [62] E. 326/B. 8812 (1299).
[63] S.B.Y., fol. 171, fol. 178 (1379).

could become 'more a source of honour than of profit'. That was precisely what happened in Gower in the early fourteenth century: lordship was dissipated. It happened even more dramatically in many a Marcher lordship in the fifteenth century: the value of Denbigh, for example, fell from almost £1,000 in 1400 to £50 in 1500.[64] That was a devaluation of authority. For in the March, even more than in England, the line between 'a great and fine lordship' (to borrow once more the words of the royal commissioner of 1302) and a collapse of seignorial authority was perilously thin. Eternal vigilance was the price of Marcher lordship.

[64] *Glam. C.H.*, III, 573 and n. 96.

Demesne Lordship

LORDSHIP had many dimensions to it in the Middle Ages; but nowhere was its authority more immediate or untrammelled than in the land which the lord himself controlled directly, his demesne. Elsewhere his lordship was limited in varying degrees by the rights and powers of others, be they vassals, tenants or communities; here, however, it knew no such restrictions. Even the vocabulary of the period proclaimed that lordship was different here; it graduated from *dominium* to the more possessive *dominicum*. The term demesne was applied to all the land and resources of the lordship which the lord regarded as peculiarly his own, whether exploited directly by him or leased to others for his profit. It included arable land, meadow, pasture, forest and waste; it also embraced the waters of the lordship, its fisheries, its mills, its ferries. The birds of the air and the beasts of the forest might also be part of the lord's demesne wealth: the lords of Ogmore specifically reserved to themselves the falcons and porpoises of the sea coast just as those of Haverford counted the rabbits and hawks of their offshore island as part of their demesne possessions.[1] In short, whatever the lord deemed his own, that was his demesne.

It is with his arable land that we must begin, for it was in many respects the demesne *par excellence*. Its exploitation was a visible token of the lord's direct participation in the economic life of the lordship. Indeed in the case of the March we dare go even further: there without an arable demesne, there would be no manor. That might not be true of England;[2] but the March, unlike England, was not a land full of manors. The lordship and existing Welsh divisions such as the commote served well enough as units of seignorial administration; there was no need to introduce the fiction of the manor into such a setting if it did

---

[1] D.L. 42/107, fol. 3; W. Rees, *South Wales and the March 1284–1415*, 138, n. 3.

[2] I have in mind in particular Maitland's discussion of the definition of a manor in *Domesday Book and Beyond* (1960 edition), 140–54 and in *The History of English Law* (1898) 594–605.

not fulfil a specific function.[3] The lordship of Dyffryn Clwyd may serve as an example: the lord's authority there was both precise and profitable, but the framework of that authority was not the manor but the three commotes of Llannerch, Dogfeilyn and Coelion. The lord, indeed, also enjoyed a manorial lordship within Dyffryn Clwyd, but only in a few specifically designated manors.[4] The manor as an unit of lordship was the exception not the norm in Dyffryn Clwyd; and that was so in most of the March.

What were these Marcher manors like? Dyffryn Clwyd may once more provide us with an example. The manor of Maesmynan, when it was leased in 1372, had sufficient arable to produce sixteen quarters of wheat and thirty quarters of oats annually; it also had a park, meadowland and pasture, a hall, chamber, kitchen, granary, grange, oxhouse, dairy, dovecote and orchard and a group of customary tenants.[5] Its manorial credentials were unimpugnable even by English standards. Manors such as Maesmynan were very unevenly distributed throughout the March. In some lowland lordships there might be several such seignorial manors: Usk and Caerleon had at least eleven between them; Abergavenny eight; in Monmouth in the mid-thirteenth century there were at least a thousand acres under the plough on its five manors; in Brecon a century later the lord's demesne arable must have totalled at least a thousand acres distributed in manors in the valleys of the Wye, Usk and Llynfi.[6] Elsewhere in the March, however, the manor scarcely figured in the economic landscape of the lordship or in the revenue of its lord: there were no manors in such lordships as Ceri, Gwerthrynion or Iscennen and even in lowland lordships such as Kidwelly or Llanstephan the seignorial manor was peripheral in importance.

[3] Cf. J. Conway Davies, 'Lordships and Manors in the county of Montgomery', *Mont. Colls.* 49 (1946), 74–151.
[4] These were Ruthin, Llysfasi, Bathafarn and Maesmynan and (possibly) Aberwheeler and Penbedw.
[5] S.C. 2/219/8, m. 11.
[6] G. A. Holmes, *Estates of the Higher Nobility* (Cambridge, 1957), 102–3; *C.I.P.M.*, vi, no. 612; 'Ministers Accounts for the lordships of Abergavenny, Grosmont, Skenfrith and Whitecastle', *South Wales and Monmouth Record Society*, II–IV; R. R. Davies, 'The Bohun and Lancaster Lordships . . .' D.Phil. thesis (Univ. of Oxford, 1965), 174–5. These figures, of course, only relate to seignorial manors; they do not include the manors of the lord's vassals, etc.

This uneven distribution of demesne arable (or of manors) in the March requires an explanation. The answer is obviously in good part a matter of geography. The manor was a lowland institution; a distribution map renders that immediately self-evident.[7] So also does the terminology of the medieval extent: in Glamorgan, for example, the surveyors spoke of castles and manors in the lowland but of countries (*patriae*) elsewhere.[8] The demesne arable was largely restricted to the coastal plains and river valleys; it was only rarely (as at Cefnllys in Maelienydd) that it was found elsewhere. Historical reasons also serve to explain the uneven distribution of Marcher manors. Most of them were obviously Norman creations, founded to cater for the needs of an immigré aristocracy and of the garrisons of its castles. The lordship of Denbigh provides a late example: there Henry Lacy, earl of Lincoln, created a brand-new manor at Kilford (itself a new name) for himself, partly out of forfeited land and partly by compulsory exchange.[9] It was in like fashion no doubt that many of the manors of the southern March—especially the abundant manors of Pembroke, Gower and the Vale of Glamorgan—were created as home farms for the Norman *conquistadores* and their followers. But it would be mistaken to assume that the manor was altogether a foreign intrusion in the March. Manorial organization was already well known on the borders of Wales even before the Norman Conquest. Indeed one of the most revealing documents of pre-conquest manorialism in England comes from the great manor of Tidenham on the lower reaches of the Wye, while the Domesday Book entry for Chepstow reveals that the economic structure of the south-eastern March was readily amenable to the imposition of manorial organization.[10] Furthermore, it is now increasingly recognized that many of the Marcher manors took over a pre-existing native Welsh organization with demesne land (*tir bwrdd*) being worked by labour drawn from a servile vill (*maerdref*) and catering for the food requirements of the prince's court (*llys*). The lords of Denbigh, for example, took over such

[7] W. Rees, *An Historical Atlas of Wales* (1959), plate 47.
[8] For example, 'The castle and manor of Llanbleddian ... with the *patria* of Talyfan': *Cartae*, III, no. 886.
[9] *S.D.*, 1–2.
[10] *English Historical Documents*, I, ed. D. C. Douglas and G. W. Greenaway (1953), 817–18; *Domesday Book*, I, 162.

native manors (and it would be pedantic to deny them the title) at Dinorben and Ystradowen and so did the lords of Dyffryn Clwyd at Llysfasi (the name itself is significant) and those of Yale at Llanarmon. Even in the older Marcher lordships of the south, Norman halls were often founded on the site of Welsh *llysoedd* as in Llyswyrny in Glamorgan[11] and Liswerry in Caerleon. In this respect, as in so many others, the Marcher lords entered fully into the inheritance of their Welsh *antecessores*.

The original function of the demesne arable was to produce supplies for the lord and his followers. The vocabulary of the period proclaims it to be so, whether in Latin with its references to *dominicum mense mee*, in French where *demesne* seems to derive from *mesnie* (household), or in Welsh whose *tir-bwrdd* (tableland) is explicit enough.[12] Demesne farming in the March in the later Middle Ages was still geared in some measure to the personal needs of the lord and his household. For example, when the household of the young Gilbert, son of the earl of Gloucester, stayed at Usk in 1293 for fourteen weeks, it consumed most of the cereals grown on the demesne.[13] Likewise at Denbigh in 1305 some of the produce of the demesne was used to feed the workmen and garrison of the castle; while in Dyffryn Clwyd (where the Greys were frequent visitors) even after the end of demesne farming, the lord insisted that the lease should be paid to him in corn and delivered by the customary tenants to his castle at Ruthin.[14] But, by and large, most Marcher lords visited their Welsh estates too rarely to justify demesne farming merely in terms of their personal needs. The demands of the lord's kitchen and the palate of the lord himself were, it is true, still a consideration even at a distance from the March: John of Gaunt was partial to the lampreys of Rodley on the Severn estuary and Elizabeth Burgh to the salmon of Usk; Joan Valence's kitchens at Goodrich Castle (co. Heref.) were supplied with white herrings from Tenby and those of Henry Lacy at Aldbourne (co. Wilts.) with cheeses from Clifford and stockfish

---

[11] *Glam. C.H.*, III, 15–16.

[12] For the Latin example *Cartae*, IV, no. 969; for the etymology of *demesne*, F. Pollock and F. W. Maitland, *History of English Law*, I, 363, n. 1; for *tir-bwrdd*, *Llyfr Colan*, ed. D. Jenkins (Cardiff, 1963), 173–4.

[13] S.C. 6/1247/25.

[14] D.L. 29/1/2; S.C. 2/219/8, m. 11 (1372); 219/11, m. 9ᵛ (1376); 220/10, m. 15 (1396).

from Denbigh.[15] These, however, were exotic dishes. The economic rationale of the demesne, particularly of the demesne arable, lay no longer in the needs of the lord's table. Rather it lay in production for the market. That may always have been so in some measure; but it was probably in the course of the thirteenth century with the coming of more settled conditions that the Marcher lords, particularly those of the eastern March, began to concentrate on the production and marketing of cereals in a big way. For example, the earliest detailed accounts for the March, those for the Lord Edward's estates for 1256–7, show demesne production in full swing in the lordships of Monmouth and Abergavenny; indeed it was far and away the most important single source of revenue. For the remainder of the history of arable demesne-farming in the March—that is until the close of the fourteenth century— production for the market was to be the major determinant and profit-making the major consideration. This businesslike preoccupation with market production is reflected in the sophisticated calculations of the profits or loss of agricultural production or wainage (such as are to be found on the Marcher accounts of Earl Roger Bigod and Elizabeth Burgh),[16] and in the appointment of a general overseer of agricultural policy (as happened on the Bohun estates in the March).[17] The profits of demesne farming could be considerable: on the Lacy manors of Glasbury and Clifford in 1304–5 the sale of corn accounted for £69 out of a gross income of £147; and likewise in many other manors of the south-eastern March demesne profits constituted a major source of profit.[18] So attractive indeed was demesne farming at the turn of the thirteenth century that it was even undertaken in the rather unpromising new Marcher lordships

[15] *John of Gaunt's Register, 1379–1383*, ed. E. C. Lodge and R. Somerville (Camden Society, 1937), II, no. 810; C. A. Musgrave, 'Household Administration in the Fourteenth Century with Special Reference to the Household of Elizabeth de Burgh, Lady of Clare', M.A. thesis (Univ. of London, 1923), 126, n. 8; *Sir Christopher Hatton's Book of Seals*, no. 115; D.L. 29/1/2, m. 2, m. 18. For cattle see below pp. 115–16.

[16] For such calculations see R. R. Davies in *Ec.H.R.*, 2nd ser. 21 (1968), 214–16.

[17] In 1372 the fee of the 'supervisor stauri et gaynagi' in Brecon was £3 6s. 8d.: S.C. 6/1156/18.

[18] D.L. 29/1/2, m. 18. On the Clare lordships of Usk and Caerleon in the early fourteenth century 'direct demesne enterprise, rather than rents, was the major feature of the economy': M. Altschul, *A Baronial Family in Medieval England* (Baltimore, 1965), 253.

of the north: thus in the lordship of Denbigh, only twenty years after the conquest, the two seignorial manors of Kilford and Dinorben between them yielded over 200 quarters of wheat and 480 quarters of oats. The lords of the March like their colleagues in England experimented considerably with cereal farming on their demesnes especially in the period 1280–1340; and on the whole they did fairly well from it.[19] Much of the produce no doubt was sold locally, especially in the towns of the southern March; but some of it was possibly dispatched to more distant markets. If the new lord of Denbigh could buy his seed corn and wine in Chester, bring new millstones from Caernarfon and dispatch oxen to the fairs at Bolton and the household at Altofts (Yorks.), there is no reason why he should not market his cereals equally far afield.[20]

Whether demesne arable production was profitable or not depended in good measure not only on the vagaries of the weather and of market prices but also on the availability of a cheap, even free, labour supply, that is on an ample pool of villein labour. In this respect the March presents certain distinctive features. It was not, for the most part, an area of large concentrations of unfree tenants nor an area of heavy labour services. To this generalization there are of course exceptions, more notably from the extreme south-east and south-west of the March.[21] In general, however, it is the lightness—or, looked at from another viewpoint, the inadequacy—of villein labour services in the March which stands out. This meant that demesne agriculture had to look elsewhere for its labour supply. It found it, in part, in the services of Welshmen who lived beyond the bounds of the seignorial manor. In late-medieval Wales there always existed a large pool of under-employed labour which could be directed either into the armies of the English king or into the gangs of seasonal workers who migrated to the lowlands annually especially at harvest time.[22] Some of the latter found employment on the demesne of the Marcher lords: in the Bohun manors of Brecon, Bronllys and Hay in 1372 much of the harvest

---

[19] The best run of accounts that survive, those for the manors of the lordships of Usk and Caerleon, have been analysed and tabulated by G. A. Holmes, op. cit. 102–7, 161–3.

[20] D.L. 29/1/2, m. 1–1ᵛ (1305).

[21] Below pp. 379–81.

[22] For such migration see *Rot. Parl.*, II, 234.

was reaped by Welshmen who came down to the valleys for the purpose; and in the manor of Bicton near Clun in 1355 sixty Welsh customary tenants were paid for their mowing services.[23] For the more regular work of the manor, however, the lords of the March relied heavily—indeed in terms of profits too heavily—on paid labour, either permanent or seasonal. The importance of these paid workers (*famuli*) in the labour market of the medieval manor is now adequately recognized by historians; nowhere was their contribution more significant than in the March. Let us instance the Bohun manor of Bronllys (Brecon) in 1372: it had a demesne of 146½ acres under the plough that year; its labour resources consisted of four customary tenants whose labour dues only totalled nine days each annually, the ploughing and reaping services of extra-manorial customary tenants, and a force of nine full-time workers and two temporary helpers. In money terms, the payments (both in cash and kind) to the paid workers in Bronllys were almost four times as much as the value of the customary labour services (£19. 8s. 4d.: £5. 4s. 2d).[24] This pattern is repeated, to a greater or lesser degree, in most of the manors of the March: there was a staff of eleven paid workers at Usk in 1292, thirteen at Clifford in 1305, seven at Roath (Glamorgan) for half a year in 1315, ten (including, it is true, four shepherds) at Bicton (Clun) in 1355.[25] This meant that demesne production in the March was generally not subsidized by low labour costs; its profitability—and thereby its continuing feasibility—depended on good crop yields and buoyant market prices.

This heavy reliance on paid labour meant that the profit margins in demesne farming in the March were often dangerously small. Thus, the scrupulous auditors of Elizabeth Burgh calculated the overall profits on her considerable cereal farming in Usk and Caerleon in 1339 as less than £30.[26] It was indeed a poor return, especially in relation to the total value of almost £1,000 for the twin lordships. Considerations such as these

[23] S.C. 6/1156/13, 15, 18; S.R.O. 552/1A/3.
[24] S.C. 6/1156/13; R. R. Davies, D.Phil. thesis, 175–7.
[25] S.C. 6/1247/25; D.L. 29/1/2, m. 18; *Cartae*, III, no. 743 (wrongly dated); S.R.O. 552/1A/3.
[26] Holmes, op. cit. 146. The figure may, admittedly, have been exceptionally low. In 1330 the 'profit de la gaynerie' stood at almost £65 from these lordships: S.C. 11/799.

must have played a major role in determining how long demesne farming continued in the March. In some lordships it was abandoned at an early date: in Kidwelly certainly by 1300; in Chirkland by 1324; in Denbigh probably by 1334; and in the Mortimer manors of Norton, Pembridge and Radnor by the 1330s.[27] Elsewhere it continued much later: on some of the granges of Usk until at least the 1360s; on the Brecon manors until 1373; on the earl of Stafford's manors both at Caus and at Newport until the 1380s; so also on some of the Grey manors in Dyffryn Clwyd; and on the Beauchamp manors in Elfael until the 1390s.[28] No single, simple formula will comprehend such a varied chronological pattern of demesne leasing; but in general terms much the same considerations seem to have prevailed in the March as in England. The strategic position of the demesne arable, both in relation to active market centres and to the remainder of the lord's inheritance, was doubtless one such consideration. Thus at Kidwelly the exploitation of the demesne arable in the shadow of the great castle was a worthwhile proposition for the Chaworth family for whom Kidwelly was a major estate;[29] it was far less so for the junior line of the house of Lancaster which succeeded to Kidwelly in 1296 and for whom Kidwelly was a rather distant outpost. The personal attitude of the lord and, above all, the unbroken continuity of estate policy and administration were also much more important considerations than is often realized. The final blow to the Lancaster demesnes in the March came with the death of Duke Henry in 1361 and the short-lived division of the inheritance between his two daughters; likewise in Brecon the ending of demesne farming in 1373 requires no other explanation than the death in that year of the Bohun earl of Hereford without a male heir. On most manors, however, it was the low profit margins, the high labour costs and the problems of marketing and administrative supervision which persuaded the Marcher lords to opt out of demesne exploitation and, by and large, these problems became much more acute in the March as in England

---

[27] Davies, D.Phil. thesis, 241; N.L.W. Chirk Castle D. 3; *S.D.*, 3–7; Holmes, op. cit. 97; B. P. Evans, 'The Family of Mortimer', 450.

[28] Holmes, op. cit. 106, n. 6; Davies, D.Phil. thesis, 185; *V.C.H. Shropshire*, VIII, 317; Rees, op. cit. 254; S.C. 2/220/5, m. 12; *C. Inq. Misc. 1392–9*, no. 228.

[29] An inventory of Patrick Chaworth's goods at Kidwelly in 1283 included 48 oxen, 43 steers and sown corn worth £30: C. 133/35, no. 10, m. 20.

in the second half of the fourteenth century. Caldicot may serve as an example: in 1361–2 the sale of wool, corn, cattle and services yielded £10. 7s. 3d. while the costs of labour and of the upkeep of the manor totalled £10. 7s. 5d. It was a situation which Mr. Micawber would have appreciated. The earl of Hereford certainly did so; demesne farming was promptly abandoned at Caldicot in Michaelmas 1362.[30]

The abandonment of demesne arable farming is more than a chapter in the economic history of the March; it has a bearing on the character of lordship itself. For the significance of the demesne arable was far greater than either its size or its profits might suggest. It was for the lord a direct stake in the economic life of the lordship; in its demand for labour, for supervision and for the marketing of its produce it impinged in a very real fashion on the tenants of that lordship. Hence leasing of the demesne cannot but have weakened in some measure the nature and impact of lordship. It hastened the process whereby the lord became little more than an absentee rent-collecting land-lord, 'a "stockholder" in the soil', in Marc Bloch's phrase.[31] It thereby removed much of the *raison d'être* of the manor.

Arable demesne farming may have faced special problems in the March in terms of labour supply and marketing oppor-tunities; pastoral agriculture, on the other hand, clearly enjoyed special advantages there. Contemporaries were not slow to notice them. Already in 1265 a jury commented that the lords of Elfael 'could have in pasture 1,000 oxen and cows, 2,000 sheep, 500 horses . . . and swine as many as they willed without number'.[32] The Marcher lords began to exploit the pastoral wealth of their lordships in the later middle ages, in terms both of cattle and of sheep. They already had dairy farms in their Marcher manors such as that at Roath (Glamorgan), and small herds of cattle and oxen to cater for their immediate needs as at Usk;[33] but it was not until the fourteenth century—or so at least the surviving evidence suggests—that they turned seriously towards beef production. Nowhere more so than in Brecon.

[30] D.L. 29/680/10999. Davies, D.Phil. thesis, 220–1. For a similar case at Ogmore see *Glam. C.H.*, iii, 229 and n. 106.

[31] *French Rural Society*, 101.

[32] Quoted in W. Rees, op. cit. 115, n. 1.

[33] *Cartae*, iii, no. 742 (1315); S.C. 6/1247/25 (1293).

Throughout most of the fourteenth century the lord of Brecon had a full-time stock-keeper in charge of a vaccary of some 300 cows and calves in Fforest Fach; and so profitable was the enterprise that three further vaccaries were established in Fforest Fawr, Trawscoed and Abernant. The herds were often replenished from the biennial render of cows which the tenants of Brecon owed to their lord and from the cattle distrained for the non-payment of debts. Much of this livestock went to cater for the needs of the lord's larder and for the restocking of his English herds: in 1349 twenty drovers accompanied over 400 head of cattle to the Bohun household in Essex and in the following year an almost equal number was driven to Kimbolton (co. Huntingdon) and Oaksey (co. Wilts.).[34] These long cross-country cattle journeys—for even as the crow flies Kimbolton is some 130 miles from Brecon—reveal vividly how closely tied a noble household was to its estates, however distant, for its meat provisions. And the Bohun household was certainly not unique in this respect: the households of Henry Lacy at Altofts (co. Yorks.), of Roger Mortimer at Wigmore (co. Heref.), of Elizabeth Burgh at Bardfield (co. Essex) and Clare (co. Suffolk), of the Black Prince at Berkhamsted (co. Herts.), of Nicholas Audley at Monnington (co. Heref.) and of the Fitzalans of Arundel all looked to their various Welsh estates for good and cheap supplies of cattle.[35]

As yet seignorial cattle-rearing in the March was mainly a factor of the household's demand for beef; its sheep-farming enterprises, on the other hand, were exclusively geared to the national and international markets in wool. On those markets the wool of the Welsh March ranked amongst the very best in Britain;[36] that, combined with the low labour-costs of sheep-rearing, made it a doubly attractive prospect to the Marcher lords. It was not an opportunity which they were likely to let pass. Already in 1185 we hear of Henry II buying 1,710 ewes

[34] D.L. 29/671/10810; S.C. 6/1157/2; S.C. 6/1156/18.

[35] See, respectively D.L. 29/1/2, m. 2 (Lacy); S.C. 6/1206/1; 1209/1 (Mortimer); S.C. 11/799 (£245 spent on cattle at Usk for Elizabeth Burgh's household); *B.P.R.*, I, 72; III, 279, 307, 393; D.L. 36/2, no. 107 (Black Prince); W. Rees, op. cit. 80, n. 1 (Audley); N.L.W. Chirk Castle D. 1, D. 15 (Arundel). For parallel examples in England, see J. M. W. Bean, *The Estates of the Percy Family 1416–1537* (1958), 14; and K. B. McFarlane, *The Nobility of Later Medieval England*, 194.

[36] T. H. Lloyd, *The Movement of Wool Prices in Medieval England*, Econ. H.R. Supplement 6 (1973), 10–11.

for stocking the estates of the honor of Gloucester including no doubt those in Glamorgan,[37] and certainly the earls of Gloucester and Norfolk had flocks in the south-eastern March by the late-thirteenth century. But once again the surviving evidence suggests that it was in the fourteenth century that the Marcher lords exploited the pasturelands of their lordships for sheep-rearing in a big way. In this respect they took over, literally and otherwise, the role that the Cistercian abbeys had played during the last two centuries: in Elfael the Beauchamps took over the land, the granges and quite probably the flocks of the Cistercian abbey of Cwmhir, and in Brecon the Bohuns did the same in the case of Dore Abbey. Brecon, in fact, provides us once more with the best-documented example of the scale and chronology of sheep farming in the March in the fourteenth century. The earls of Hereford certainly had flocks on their Brecon lands in the early years of the century;[38] but it was a deliberate policy of land purchase and stock-buying—especially the lease of the Dore Abbey pastures in the Epynt hills—in the 1350s by William Bohun, earl of Northampton which transformed the scale of the Bohun sheep-farming enterprise in the March.[39] By 1370 the seignorial flock there exceeded 3,000 distributed in eight centres, three of which were former Cistercian granges.[40] The Bohuns were taking their sheep farming very seriously.

So were many other Marcher lords. That is clear enough, even if the evidence is unsatisfactory. The earl of Pembroke had a flock at Kingswood (Pembroke); Elizabeth Burgh had 514 sheep at Trelech in 1330; the earl of Stafford had a flock of almost 900 sheep in Caus in the 1370s; the Brians of Laugharne and Walwynscastle had 1,859 sheep and 668 lambs on their estates in the late-fourteenth century; and the earl of Warwick still had a sizeable flock at Elfael in 1397.[41] How valuable these flocks were in the eyes of their owners is illustrated by the fact that when Reginald Grey leased his manor of Maesmynan

---

[37] *Pipe Roll, 31 Henry II*, Pipe Roll Society 34 (1913), 155.
[38] There were 290 sheep at Hay and a further 80 at Huntington in 1322: S.C. 6/1145/7.
[39] See above, p. 95.
[40] S.C. 6/1156/18, m. 1d; W. Rees, op. cit. 257; R. R. Davies, D.Phil thesis, 183.
[41] *Cal. Public Records re. Pembrokeshire*, III, 119; S.C. 11/799; *V.C.H. Shropshire*, VIII, 317; B.L. Egerton Roll 8714; *C. Inq. Misc. 1392–9*, no. 228.

(Dyffryn Clwyd) in 1372 he reserved the profit of sheep and wool to himself.[42] Not surprisingly the two greatest sheep farmers of all in the March were the earls of March and Arundel. We are singularly ill-informed about the Mortimer flocks; but their size may be gauged from the fact that in 1337 fourteen sacks of wool were sent from Radnor *en route* to Dordrecht and a further thirty sacks were ready for dispatch in 1340,[43] and sheep-farming certainly continued on some of the Mortimer estates until the end of the century.[44] The Fitzalan earls of Arundel were probably major sheep-farmers in the March from an early date;[45] but it is not until the mid-fourteenth century that the precise extent of their flocks can be determined.[46] In 1349 their flocks in Shropshire and the March totalled 5,385; and seem to have stayed around that figure for the rest of the century with, of course, some fluctuations. Clun was far and away the most important centre (there were well over 3,000 sheep there in 1372) with smaller flocks at Ruyton and Oswestry.

These Marcher flocks were only part of a more general seignorial investment in sheep-farming in England in the fourteenth century. Elizabeth Burgh switched from arable to sheep farming in the 1330s and by the end of the decade her flocks totalled 7,862 sheep;[47] those of the earl of Arundel in 1349 stood at about 15,000 and had probably increased by the end of the century.[48] It is not surprising to learn that the earl of

[42] S.C. 2/219/8, m. 11.

[43] S.C. 6/1209/7 published in *Transactions of the Radnorshire Society* 38 (1968) 39–43; *C.C.R. 1339–41*, 568.

[44] There were 231 sheep and 88 lambs at Clifford in 1389 and a further 300 were bought to increase the stock there in 1392: U.C.N.W., Whitney Collection 316; Rees, op. cit. 256.

[45] In a valuation of Clun over two years early in Edward II's reign, the sale of wool accounted for £395 out of a total of £1,145: S.R.O., Acton of Aldenham, 775.

[46] The major sources for Arundel sheep-farming in the March are as follows: S.R.O. (i) Acton of Aldenham, 1093 (valor of all Arundel estates, 1349); (ii) 552/1A/1 (valor, 1351); (iii) 552/1A/2–12 (various accounts for Clun, 1354–1413); Shrewsbury Public Library Craven Collection and N.L.W. Aston Hall (ministers accounts for various manors of the lordship of Oswestry). The demesne farming activities of the earls of Arundel in Chirkland and Oswestry are fully discussed in Llinos Smith, 'Lordships of Chirkland Oswestry', chap. III.

[47] For the expansion of sheep-farming on Elizabeth Burgh's estates in East Anglia, see Holmes, op. cit. 89–90; the total of her sheep is taken from S.C. 11/801.

[48] The former figure comes from the valor of 1349 (above, n. 46); for the size of the Arundel flocks in Sussex at the end of the century, see L. F. Salzman, 'The

Arundel's assets in 1376 included wool worth almost £2,042.[49] The attraction of sheep-farming to the nobility lay partly in its profits and partly in the fact that it was amenable to closer central supervision than arable farming. It certainly received such supervision. Professional stock-keepers were appointed on most estates;[50] there was an integrated system of sheep-rearing as between the various manors and a careful allocation of flocks;[51] the weighing and sorting of wool was undertaken by the lord's top officials;[52] and the profits were normally paid directly to the lord's coffers, not to local officials. Sheep-farming was conducted as a big business. It was aiming at an international market: the Mortimer fleeces in 1337 were destined for Dordrecht; the wool of Brecon was sent direct to London for sale; while it was to a London merchant, Richard Marlowe, that the Clun wool-yield was sold in 1395.[53] It is difficult to know accurately the degree of profit, since the local accounts rarely allow us to calculate the cost of sheep-farming and the price of wool-sales over a number of years. But there are a few stray indications: the fourteen sacks from Radnor in 1337 (not necessarily all from one year's yield) realized £123; the sale of wool from Brecon in the early 1370s yielded about £65 a year; while at Clun in the reign of Edward II the Fitzalans appear to have estimated the clear profit from wool (after the deduction of the expenses on sheep and the wages of shepherds) at over £170 a year. The figures such as they are all point in the direction of a high level of profitability, especially when compared with arable agriculture with all its attendant problems.

The ample pasturelands of the March could be put to yet other uses. They could be made to serve the lord's pleasure. One of the earliest acts of Henry Lacy as lord of Denbigh was to stock the parks of his new lordship with deer from the Delamere forest in Cheshire.[54] His three parks in Isaled alone

Property of the Earl of Arundel, 1397', *Sussex Archaeological Collections* 91 (1953), 32–53.

[49] B.L. Harleian 4840 fol. 393 ᵛ.

[50] There were certainly stock-keepers in charge of the Grey, Bohun and Fitzalan flocks.

[51] This is particularly clear on the Bohun and Fitzalan estates.

[52] At Clun in 1387 the steward and auditor spent three days at the task: S.R.O. 552/1A/8.

[53] S.C. 6/1209/7; S.C. 6/1157/4; Shrewsbury Public Library 9777 (account of the receiver of Oswestry 1394–5).   [54] *C.C.R. 1279–88*, 278.

covered almost 700 acres while his neighbour of Dyffryn Clwyd had six parks in his small lordship. Some of these parks, it is true, went back to the days of the native princes; but the majority of them were either created anew or much enlarged by the Marcher lords. Nothing was allowed to stand in the way of the park, neither the land of tenants (who were compulsorily expropriated) nor even a water mill (as at Postyn in Denbigh).[55] They were lovingly looked after, carefully and expensively enclosed with fences, guarded by keepers and lodges, and well stocked with deer. And little wonder. Good hunting was one of the few reasons, short of war, which could persuade the English nobility to visit their lands in Wales. It was the prospect of being able to take at least seventy deer which enticed the Fitzalans to visit their lordship at Clun;[56] it was a well-stocked park which made Grosmont into the favourite Marcher residence of the house of Lancaster; and likewise the Staffords came to Minsterley park (Caus) for its deer and the Bohuns to Huntington because of 'un bele park'.[57] Hunting called for horses and so the lords established studs for the purpose: already by 1295 Henry Lacy had two studs at Denbigh and the earls of Arundel, as ever the most enterprising of Marcher lords, had no fewer than four studs on their Marcher lands—at Chirk, Holt, Bromhurst park near Oswestry and above all at Clun.[58]

Good hunting was to be had in the March and good hawking too;[59] but the Marcher pasturelands were more than the playground of the medieval nobility. The demesne status of the seignorial parks was, of course, beyond question; but the Marcher lords also claimed, and did so with increasing success,

---

[55] For the parks of Isaled, see *S.D.*, 51; for those of Dyffryn Clwyd *T.D.H.S.* 18 (1969) 31 (Nantywrach should be added to this list); for lands enclosed in park, see *Extent of Chirkland 1391–93*, ed. G. P. Jones (Liverpool, 1933), 8; S.C. 2/217/11, m. 20ᵛ; 218/9, m. 30 (Bathafarn park); for the mill at Postyn S.C. 6/1182/5.

[56] *Fitzalan Surveys*, ed. M. Clough, Sussex Record Society 67 (1968), 52. The larder of Clun castle was certainly well-provisioned with venison and its parks with deer: S.R.O. 552/1A/1, 8. The earls of Arundel spent large sums on the repair of their parks in Chirkland.

[57] D.L. 43/15/3, m. 2 for Grosmont; *V.C.H. Shropshire*, viii, 298 for Minsterley; *C. Inq. Misc. 1219–1307*, no. 1870, D.L. 41/4/18 (*c.* 1412) for Huntington.

[58] For Denbigh D.L. 29/1/1, m. 1ᵛ; for the Arundel studs S.R.O. 552/1A/1 (1351); *C. Inq. Misc. 1392–9*, nos. 229, 234, 235. The stud at Clun included over 160 horses in 1397.

[59] For example, Roger Mortimer, first earl of March, had a falconry at Aber-

that the pasture, forest, waste and water of the lordship in general were also part of their demesne in the broadest sense. 'The forests and chaces' so it was asserted in Blaenllyfni, 'belong to the castle and have been in the hands of the lords, time out of mind'.[60] The cocksureness of the assertion barely conceals the novelty of the claim; that is betrayed by the reference to time immemorial, often a medieval euphemism for recent innovation. Recent or not, the claim that the non-arable resources were the lord's immediate property had immense consequences for the practice and profits of lordship. In a largely pastoral and forested country such as the March, it was a vital claim for lord and community alike. It was so, as we shall see, in terms of authority; it was equally so in terms of profit. Contemporaries were well aware of what was at issue. The hard-headed surveyor of the lordship of Denbigh spelt it out in £. *s. d.*: he pointed out, for example, that the community of Segrwyd paid only a nominal rent of 6*s*. 8*d*. for 366 acres of woodland and waste but that the lord could make a profit of £2. 14*s*. 5*d*. on top of that sum if only he were to lease the land at a minimum rate of twopence an acre.[61]

The pasture and forest of the March, as we have seen, could be appropriated to rear the lord's flocks and herds and to provide him with good hunting. That, however, was not the limit of their potential. The sale of timber, for fuel or for building, could be a major if rather erratic source of income. The lordships of the south-eastern March excelled in this respect: the sale of wood at Monmouth in 1257 realized almost £50; while at Trelech the sale of timber and charcoal averaged well over £100 per annum in the early fourteenth century and reached a peak of £200 annually (or some 20 per cent of the gross yields of the lordships of Caerleon and Usk) in the three years 1328–31.[62] Even elsewhere in the March the sale of wood could be a not altogether negligible item of seignorial revenue: in the bailwick of Marford (Bromfield) in 1383, for example, the sale of fuel yielded £17. 8*s*.[63] Alongside timber we might also

hafesp and kept sparrowhawks (for which Wales was famous) at Chirk: S.C. 6/1206/1; J. Y. W. Lloyd, *Powys Fadog*, IV, 44.

[60] Quoted in W. Rees, op. cit. 116, n. 3.   [61] *S.D.*, 11–12.

[62] *South Wales and Monmouth Record Society* 4 (1957), 13 for Monmouth; for Trelech J. C. Ward, op. cit. 262 and G. A. Holmes, op. cit. 107, n. 6.

[63] S.C. 6/1305/7.

include the profits of coal-mining which was beginning to assume substantial proportions, especially at Llansamlet in the lordship of Gower where the net profits by the end of the century were estimated at £90 annually.[64]

The profits of wood and coal could be substantial; but even greater were the indirect perquisites of the lord's claim to be lord of the waste and water, forest and pasture of his lordship. Such a claim implied that others would have to pay for the use— and abuse—of these resources; and a corps of seignorial officers was busily employed to assert that claim. In Dyffryn Clwyd, for example, ten foresters and seven parkers looked after the eleven forests and twenty-seven areas of reserved woodland which the lord claimed as his own;[65] and much of the work of the lord-ship's courts was concerned with the consequences of the diligence of these officers. The pasture was, with some exceptions, declared to be the lord's and the community had to lease it from him, either on an annual farm or by a payment pro-portionate to the number of animals grazing. The lordship of Brecon, rich in good grazing land, affords us examples of both methods: Fforest Fawr, the great mountain pastureland which rolled for miles south of the Usk valley, was leased annually to the Welsh community for a fixed render; whereas Fforest Uchaf in the foot-hills of the Epynt Mountains was controlled by a ranger whose duty it was to count the stock sent to pasture there and to assess a toll (*cyfrif*) of two capons and two hens for each animal.[66] Either way the lord did very well: the farm of Fforest Fawr rose from £46 13s. 4d. in 1340 to £109 13s. 4d. by 1400 and was one of the major sources of seignorial revenue, while the capons and hens of the 135 Welshmen who pastured their animals in Fforest Uchaf realized £16 16s. 2d. for the lord in 1372. Nor did the profits of pasture end there. Since the lord regarded uncultivated land as his own waste (*vastus domini*) any encroachment on it, be it for temporary or permanent culti-vation, had to be licensed. The lord of Bromfield and Yale

---

[64] *Glam. C.H.*, III, 250 and n. 236.
[65] R. I. Jack, 'Welsh and English in the Medieval Lordship of Ruthin', *T.D.H.S.* 18 (1969), 31.
[66] For his account, see S.C. 6/1156/16. The term *cyfrif* is illuminated by later documentation: *Records of the Court of Augmentations relating to Wales*, ed. E. A. Lewis and J. C. Davies (Cardiff, 1954), 203 and J. Lloyd, *The Great Forest of Brecknock* (1905), 7, 19–21.

appointed four bailiffs whose sole task was to answer for land assarted from the lord's waste and how profitable their business was may be gauged from the acccount of the bailiwick of Marford for 1383: out of a gross yield of some £290, £50 came in rent for land leased *de vasto domini*.[67] It is little wonder that the men of the lordship pleaded to have the right to hold all their vills 'with their wastes': their plea was understandable and their lord's refusal to grant it even more so.[68] Waste and pasture were valuable; to control them was to hold the community in the vice of lordship.

In the forest, the lord was an even more jealous upholder of his own rights. The forest lay under the lord's prohibition, his *defensio*; it was only by his express permission and normally after due payments made that any of his tenants could share with him the fruits of the forest. The trees were his, dead or alive. Indeed the lord's claim over the trees of his lordship was at once one of the most extensive and one of the most irksome manifestations of his authority. In Dyffryn Clwyd not only the trees of the forest but even those growing on the tenant's own land were regarded as the lord's own;[69] in Bromfield and Yale it was only by a self-vaunted act of seignorial magnanimity that the lord's tenants enjoyed the right to fell trees on their own land and then only during certain seasons, by view of the forester and for the sole purpose of constructing buildings.[70] No scignorial monopoly in the March was so comprehensive and, from the tenants' point of view, more irksome than this monopoly of wood. And it was a monopoly that was stringently upheld: the earl of Arundel in 1379 threatened a fine of £5 on anyone in his lordship of Bromfield and Yale cutting trees or underwood in his woods or wastes or on their own land;[71] that his threat was no empty one is made amply clear by the court rolls. The threat also extended to any unlicensed digging for turves or coals and to unlicensed assarting, for the land of the forest as well as its wood lay under the seignorial prohibition. The tenants of Brecon had good reason to know that: in 1353 they were fined £400 for acquiring lands in the forest without

---

[67] S.C. 6/1305/7.
[68] S.B.Y., fol. 170.
[69] This was laid down by the steward in 1360: S.C. 2/219/3, m. 25.
[70] S.B.Y., fol. 171.   [71] ibid. fol. 178.

the lord's licence.[72] The animals of the forest likewise enjoyed the lord's jealous protection; to hunt them without the lord's permission was to poach and for that the sentence was severe. Indeed the very possession of dogs or hounds was regarded as a presumption of an intent to poach: men who insisted on retaining their dogs in the face of a seignorial prohibition found themselves attendant on the lord's will and those who failed to comply with an order to kill their dogs were sent to gaol to contemplate their folly.[73] The rivers of the lordship as well as its forests were part of the lord's demesne. He might lease the fishery (as happened for example at Brecon or Monmouth) or he might exploit it directly himself (as was done to very good advantage with the rich salmon fishery at Usk). Whatever policy he adopted, he guarded his fishing rights jealously; anyone caught fishing without permission, especially if he fished with a net, ran the risk of heavy penalties.[74] Already to many men in his lordship the lord had assumed the menacing aspect of a giant gamekeeper, reserving to himself the God-given fruits of nature.

And here he was a wilful lord. In his demesne, particularly in his forest, he was uninhibited by the customs of the manor or by charters of liberties. Here men were truly at his mercy; they paid heavily for it. Whereas an amercement for an ordinary civil offence would be a few pence, those for forest offences were savagely punitive. They ran into shillings, marks, pounds: 6s. 8d. for taking timber; £3 for setting fire to the undergrowth; £5 for breaking into the park and hunting[75]. This ferocity of Marcher forest law is vividly evoked for us in Brecon, where the penalty for wandering within the forest of Cantrefselyf was the loss of the right foot or a fine of 20s. and the forfeiture of all goods.[76] Few men escaped. Even if they did so as individuals they would sooner or later be mulcted as members of their community: the men of Chirkland were fined £103. 5s. 4d. for

---

[72] D.L. 29/671/10810, m. 21.

[73] These instances, only two of many, come from the Dyffryn Clwyd court rolls: S.C. 2/218/4, m. 19ᵛ (1354); 218/5, m. 13 (1356).

[74] A seignorial injunction against fishing 'cum rethe vel alio ingenio' was issued in Dyffryn Clwyd in 1401: S.C. 2/221/4, m. 16ᵛ. Fines for unlicensed fishing are commonplace, e.g. S.C. 2/215/75, m. 7ᵛ (1316); 220/12, m. 32 (1389).

[75] These examples come from the same records—S.C. 2/216/3, m. 14; 219/3, m. 29ᵛ; 216/4, m. 2ᵛ (1320–66).

[76] D.L. 41/6/11 (1349).

breaking into the lord's park in 1350; three years later some of the communities of Brecon incurred a like fine.[77]

The lord's claim to be the immediate lord of pasture, waste, woodland and water forms one of the most crucial chapters in the history of lordship in the March as elsewhere in Europe. It is not a story which is well documented, for the lords (who were as yet the sole repositories of written evidence) suppressed any doubts as to their titles and construed them as immemorial rights. Nevertheless that much of this momentous claim to lordship over non-arable land was recent can scarcely be questioned. It is suggested by the existence of common forests where lordly authority was minimal, such as those of Pembroke and Gower;[78] it is reinforced by the occasional compromise as in Elfael where the lord's control of forest pastureland was restricted to the period from May to Michaelmas;[79] it is amplified by the complaints of the community, as in Glamorgan, against the afforestation policy of their lords[80] and by the occasional open conflict between lord and community over the title to woodland.[81] The evidence from the northern March is particularly illuminating. There the increase in seignorial power over woodland and waste took place against a background of recent conquest and in good part as a consequence of that conquest; as a result the struggle between lord and community was both foreshortened and highlighted. In Bromfield and Yale and in the western parts of Oswestry the lord's authority over woods, forests and waste was specifically founded on a recent quitclaim by the Welsh community, with the clear implication that such seignorial authority had not prevailed, at least to such a degree, in the time of the native princes. In Bromfield it was recalled bitterly in 1332 how the chief forester of the first Warenne lord of the lordship had brought the forest of Glyn, 'which hitherto was common, within the lord's prohibition' (*defensio*).[82] It was, one suspects, an act which had

[77] N.L.W. Chirk Castle, D. 15; D.L. 29/671/10810, m. 21.

[78] Rees, op. cit. 115.

[79] ibid. 116, n. 1.

[80] S.C. 8/128, no. 6839 for a petition about the activities of Earl Gilbert (d. 1295); *C.C.R. 1313–18*, 161 for a complaint about those of his son (d. 1314).

[81] In 1344 five men in Clun were amerced £4 16s. 0d. for daring to claim that a wood was theirs alone to the prejudice of the lord: S.R.O. 552/1/11, m. 1.

[82] S.B.Y., fols. 170, 171, 178; N.L.W. Aston Hall, 2776 (ii). Cf. the lord's share in the great waste of Prŷs in the Hiraethog mountains: *S.D.*, 107. There is an

ample precedents elsewhere in the March during the previous two centuries.

The lord's gain was the community's loss, and it was not a loss to which it resigned itself easily or without a struggle. How much it treasured its control of wood and pasture may be gauged by the fact that the community of Dyffryn Clwyd was prepared to pay the king 600 marks for the recovery of its rights as against its lord.[83] How much such aspirations preoccupied the communities of the March is admirably shown by the charters of liberties they secured from their lords.[84] Their demands are common to the whole March: the right to pasture their animals freely within the lordship (as they secured by the Talgarth charter of 1299 or the Chirk charter of 1324), the right to hunt outside the lord's park (as was assured to them in Clun in 1292 and Maelienydd in 1297), the right to free pannage for their pigs (as the men of Gower secured in 1306), the right to reasonable timber for the repair of their houses (as was granted allegedly in Dyffryn Clwyd and certainly in Chirk). These charters articulate the aspirations of the community and record the measure of their success in asserting their claim to forest and pasture *vis à vis* their lord.

This struggle between lord and community in the March in the fourteenth century is in fact only one brief chapter in a long story which reverberates down the centuries.[85] It occasionally erupted into open confrontation as in Dyffryn Clwyd in 1323 or in Chirkland in 1330, when the community celebrated the downfall of its lord with a great spree of hunting in his forests;[86] but for the most part it smouldered in a mass of individual incidents and fines. It is a struggle which explains in good part the role that the forest plays, in Wales as elsewhere, as an idyllic refuge from the harshness of lordship, in life and literature alike.[87] In the March the struggle had to it yet another dimension—that of native society against foreign authority. It

excellent discussion of the exploitation of forest resources on the Marcher estates of the earls of Arundel in Llinos Smith Ph.D. thesis, 149 ff.

[83] S.C. 8/108, no. 5359 (1323–24).

[84] For these charters, see below pp. 463–4.

[85] The case of the Great Forest of Brecon, which still remained in dispute until this century, is an excellent example. See the evidence collected in Lloyd, *Great Forest of Brecknock*.

[86] J. Y. W. Lloyd, *History of Powys Fadog*, IV, 17 ff.

[87] For the forest outlaw in life, see the remarkable letter of Gruffudd ap Dafydd

was to the indefeasible rights that it enjoyed under the Welsh princes that the community appealed; it even sought to uphold its claim by confounding the lord and his surveyors with abstruse Welsh terminology.[88] It may well have had a point; but the struggle over wood and pasture was certainly not peculiar to Wales. It was common throughout Europe and forms one of the stormiest and most long-drawn-out episodes in the relationship of lordship and community.[89]

In that relationship, one other item looms large—the seignorial mill. For along with woodland and waste it represented a deliberate attempt by the lord to extend his demesne lordship over his tenants, in this instance by the control of a crucial economic monopoly. To the community, and particularly to the Welsh community, such a monopoly represented an intrusion, and a recent and foreign one at that. The mill, as it saw things, was no part of the seignorial demesne; on the contrary, it was, in the picturesque phrase of Welsh law, one of the three indivisible gems of kindred (*tri thlws cenedl*).[90] The community asserted its right to take its corn to be ground whereever it chose and to build mills of its own without licence or payment. Its case was certainly not without an historical basis: in Bromfield and Yale the lord had only five mills and had to admit that in the rest he had no more claim than came his way by the escheat of the rights of parceners. Here is a clear indication that in the north-east March at least most mills were built by community or kin groups and for their own profit; the names of some of them—such as 'the mill of the sons and coparceners of Madoc of Crue'—amply bear this out.[91] Likewise in western Oswestry the lord conceded that his claim to suit of

---

ap Gruffudd now republished and redated in J. B. Smith. 'The Last Phase of the Glyndŵr Rebellion', *B.B.C.S.* 22 (1967), 250–60; and in literature see, for example, the delightful poem of Llywelyn ap y Moel, *Cywyddau Iolo Goch ac Eraill* (2nd edn,), 198–9.

[88] Note the peevish remark of the surveyor of Oswestry in 1602: 'They thinke they make no incrochments though they inclose all your Lordships wastes for they stand uppon a frivolous terme Kyttyr . . . for the word importeth comon in Welsh', *The Lordship of Oswestry 1393–1607*, ed. W. J. Slack (Shrewsbury, 1951), 59.

[89] The outlines of the story were brilliantly characterized in Marc Bloch, *French Rural Society*, 180–9.

[90] *Llyfr Colan*, ed. D. Jenkins, §617; *Llyfr Iorwerth*, ed. A. R. Wiliam (Cardiff, 1960), §88.

[91] S.B.Y., fol. 44. For the mills of the lordship, see D. Pratt in *T.D.H.S.* 13 (1964), 22–37. The lord's position with regard to mills was similar in Denbigh;

mill from his tenants had only come to him recently through surrender; while the men of Chirk and Dyffryn Clwyd alike asserted that the lord's claims over mills were a recent usurpation.[92]

They were undoubtedly right: in the March as in Europe generally the advance of lordship is nowhere more evident than in the growing seignorial control of the mill.[93] It was in part a matter of technology: the outlay involved in the erection and upkeep of a water mill often meant that the lord alone was in a position to invest in one. But capital investment was not enough in itself; to it was added the seignorial power of compulsion, the *ban*. A convenience was converted into a monopoly and a whole edifice of obligations was built around it: suit of mill became compulsory and so did the repair of the mill and the millpond and the carriage of millstones. These duties were officiously demanded and formed a major irritant in the relationship of lordship and community.[94] The lord for his part found his mills to be a vital source of profit and of seignorial power. He was quite prepared to invest heavily in them: in 1348 the lord of Chirk built four new mills (one of them a fulling mill); in 1391 his successor spent over £40 on the mills of the lordship.[95] It was all very well worth it for the returns were excellent: in Chirk the mills yielded over £67 in 1365; those of Haverford brought the lord more than a quarter of his income in 1327 (£44 : £167); the Mortimer mills in the middle March a decade later yielded £108 out of a gross yield of almost £600.[96] Mills were clearly big money. Furthermore they were visible expressions of the lord's economic authority in areas where that authority was often otherwise lacking: in Gelligynan in Yale,

e.g., in the mill of Barrog he held a thirtieth share by way of escheat: *S.D.*, 181. For the mills of kindred groups, see also T. Jones Pierce, *Medieval Welsh Society*, 211.

[92] N.L.W. Aston Hall, 2776 (ii); Llinos Smith, 'The Arundel Charters to the Lordship of Chirk in the Fourteenth Century', *B.B.C.S.* 23 (1968–70), 156; S.C. 8/108, no. 5359.

[93] The seminal, if rather outdated, essay is once more by Marc Bloch. It is published in translation in *Land and Work in Mediaeval Europe* (1967), 136–69.

[94] Thus the customary tenants of Bromfield and Yale were fined £5 for failing to perform their duty of carrying materials to the mill while those of Nanheudwy (Chirkland) bought off their obligation by payment of £8: S.B.Y., fol. 177; *Extent of Chirkland*, ed. Jones, 61.

[95] N.L.W., Chirk Castle, D. 14, 40.

[96] Ibid. D. 27; *Cal. Public Records re. Pembrokeshire*, 1, 62–5; S.C. 6/1209/6.

for example, the sole bond between the lord and his freeholders apart from fealty and homage was the obligation of his tenants to grind their corn at the mill of Llanarmon; in Kidwelly the earls and dukes of Lancaster held no demesne arable but they had twenty-one mills which brought them an annual income in excess of £60; in the Great Forest of Brecon where the lord's authority was otherwise so tenuous six mills stood as remote and profitable outposts of his rule, yielding 300 *summe* of oats worth £90 in the mid-fourteenth century.[97] No better tribute could be paid to the success of these mills than the fact that they, along with the boroughs, were the prime targets of any Welsh rebellion;[98] town and mill were symbols of economic exploitation as the castle was a symbol of military dominance.

Our definition of demesne lordship has purposely been a broad one. To have restricted the word to the sense that it is often given in discussions of the English manor—namely to the lord's arable with its appurtenant meadow and pasture—would have been to deny it much of its importance in the March. It was, as we have seen, in part a manorial demesne; but it was much more than that. The lord's arable, his herds, his flocks and his studs were important; but in the overall picture of lordship, of its profits and of its authority, it was his claim to include the forests and wastes, the pastures and mills within his *dominicum* which was the most significant dimension of demesne lordship in the March. Such a claim was certainly not entirely a new departure; but in the March, particularly in the northern March—for, as with so much else, the chronology of lordship varies greatly within the March—there is good reason to believe that the period from 1282 to 1400 was of notable importance in the successful assertion of such a claim. The borderline of demesne and allod, of the respective rights of lord and community were being redrawn. And by and large it was being redrawn in the interest of demesne lordship.

[97] *The First Extent of Bromfield and Yale A.D. 1315*, ed. T. P. Ellis, Cymmrodorion Record Series 11 (1924), 81; D.L. 41/9/8 no. 12; D.L. 29/573/9063; S.C. 6/1157/17.
[98] As happened during Llywelyn Bren's revolt in 1316: *Glam. C.H.*, III, 79.

6   Lordship of Men
and of Land

LORDSHIP in the March in the fourteenth century was already
at a fairly advanced stage of development; but beneath the
surface of the documents we can detect, or at least suspect, some
of the strands which had gone into its making and which still, in
good measure, shaped the nature of its authority. For lordship
was far from being a uniform institution; it comprehended a
vast range of differing powers, varied in their origin and
changing with the passage of time. Even within the March
itself, as we have already observed, lordship meant very
different things in different places and to different men. And
it is to lordship over men that we turn first, for it was in point
of time and importance the primary form of lordship. Maitland
had suspected that it was so. 'In origin' he wrote 'the rights of
the lord may be the rights of kings and ealdormen, rights over
subjects rather than rights over tenants'.[1] It is a suspicion which
has been amply confirmed by modern scholarship: it was in
village chieftainships and the powers exercised by them that
Marc Bloch saw one of the most rewarding avenues for the
study of the origins of the *seigneurie*;[2] it is in group-leadership,
whether of the family or of the retinue, that German historians
nowadays search for the origins of *Herrschaft*;[3] and likewise the
students of Anglo-Saxon society and etymology point out that
it is the bestowing of gifts and the providing of protection which
'are the essence of early medieval lordship'.[4] All are agreed that
in the history of lordship generally—as in that of its subsidiary

[1] *Domesday Book and Beyond* (1960 edition), 108.
[2] He developed this theme in particular in his chapter on, 'The Rise of Dependent Cultivation and Seignorial Institutions', *Cambridge Economic History of Europe*, I 2nd edn. (Cambridge, 1966), 235–90.
[3] See, especially Walter Schlesinger, 'Lord and Follower in Germanic Institutional History', *Lordship and Community in Medieval Europe*, ed. F. L. Cheyette, 64–99.
[4] T. M. Charles-Edwards, 'Kinship, Status and the Origins of the Hide', *Past and Present* 56 (1972), 12–13.

forms of feudalism and serfdom—it is the bond of lord to man rather than that of lord to land which is the anterior one.

This would also appear to be true of lordship in the March. Indeed we can go even further: in the March, as in Wales generally, the lord's control of men remained more central to the character of lordship than it did in most of England well into the later Middle Ages. The explanation appears to be as usual in part geographical, in part historical. The March was, by and large, a land of mountain and pasture. It was in that sort of environment that a well-founded territorial lordship developed most sluggishly; it was retarded by the power of the community over basic rights such as those of grazing and by the practical difficulties of asserting seignorial control over land which was only, at best, under temporary cultivation.[5] Furthermore in an area where population was thin in relation to land, the control of men was more important and almost certainly more profitable than the control of land. Land was abundant; men were scarce.[6] To these geographical reasons we may add historical ones. It can hardly be doubted that the Anglo-Norman lords of the March entered into a native Welsh inheritance where lordship was, or at least had been, more personal than territorial. Welsh society certainly knew lordship and that lordship no doubt had to it a territorial dimension— in terms both of the exploitation of a demesne for the upkeep of the court and of a growing claim on the part of the prince or lord to invest his men with land and to hear cases relating to land in his court. That may be so; but in the overall picture of early Welsh society, if we are not mistaken, it is not the lord's control over land which is striking but rather that of the community and particularly of the kin group. Land and law, those twin pillars of lordly authority in so much of medieval Europe, were in early Wales basically the spheres of the community. Its law was truly a *Volksrecht*, a customary law, both in substance and in administration; its land inheritance, at least for freemen, was firmly founded on a bedrock of kinship customs. Into both spheres, lordship could and did penetrate, deeply in places and

[5] Cf. J. E. A. Jolliffe, 'Northumbrian Institutions', *E.H.R.* 41 (1926), 40. See also G. W. S. Barrow, 'Northern English Society in the Twelfth and Thirteenth Centuries', *Northern History* 4 (1969), 1–28.

[6] Cf. G. Duby, *L'Économie rurale et la vie des campagnes dans l'occident médiéval* (Paris, 1962), II, 446–7.

increasingly so with the passage of time. Its original strength, however, seems to lie in other directions—in personal leadership in peace and especially in war and in the imposition of that leadership on the community. The dues owed to the Welsh princes, as they appear both in the native laws and in the post-Conquest extents, bear this out: they are more the tributes owed to the leaders of men than the rents paid to the lords of land. It was into such an inheritance of lordship that the Marcher barons entered. We can grasp the nature of that native inheritance most clearly in the Marcher lordships of the north-east where the transition from Welsh to Anglo-Norman rule was recent and sudden and we shall rely heavily on the evidence from those districts; but even in the older lordships of the March we catch glimpses of a pre-existing pattern of lordship. It was an inheritance which the Marcher lords could exploit and in time change; but it was also an inheritance which, in varying degrees, shaped the content of their authority.

The very first act of lordship, that of homage and fealty, proclaimed it to be a lordship of men. It was a dramatic affirmation of lordship, a great public-relations exercise in introducing the lord to his men and in placarding his authority over them. It was at its most spectacular when whole communities performed their homage *en masse*, as happened at Wrexham (Bromfield and Yale) in 1284 when twenty-nine leading men of the lordship did homage to their new lord individually, followed by a communal act of homage by the rest of the tenants 'with hands raised and joined unanimously'[7] or at Brecon in 1302 when two thousand Welshmen swore fealty to the royal commissioner through an interpreter.[8] But the ceremony was also performed weekly on an individual level in the courts of the lordship, for each new tenant on taking up his land swore fealty to his lord. He thus became his lord's 'man' and would thereafter be so described. To take a single example, when an affray happened in Knockin in 1303 and eight men were killed, each of the victims was described in the subsequent commission as the man of such and such a lord rather than as the inhabitant of a particular lordship.[9] The tie of locality was

[7] C. 133/47, no. 13 calendared in *C.I.P.M.*, II, no. 633.
[8] *C. Inq. Misc. 1219–1307*, no. 1870.
[9] *C.P.R. 1301–7*, 270.

assuredly not unimportant, but to it had been added the personal bond of lordship. And that bond, sealed by fealty and homage, was, at the very least, politically and judicially significant. It proclaimed the political loyalties of the man: when the men of Glamorgan in 1294–5 wanted to show that their quarrel was merely with the earl of Gloucester they did so by transferring their homage to Edward I; when the younger Despenser wanted to assert his overlordship of Gwynllwg he did so by pre-empting the homage of its tenants; or when Roger Mortimer seized the lordship of Clun in 1321 he immediately took the fealty and homage of its men, an act for which their lord subsequently pardoned them.[10] Judicially, homage and fealty were equally significant, for the lord's judicial power— both his protection and his mercy—extended only to those men who had acknowledged his lordship. The court rolls of Clun Welshry provide us with a sheaf of instructive examples: a man who lived in the lordship asserted that he was nevertheless the man of the lord of Maelienydd and need therefore not answer in the court at Clun; three others declared that they were not obliged to appear in his court because they had not sworn fealty to the lord; and likewise two brothers claimed successfully that the lord could not outlaw them for failing to appear in his court because they had not sworn fealty to him. Under these circumstances it comes as no surprise to find the lord of Clun initiating a case against a defendant to determine who his lord was (*quis est dominus eius*).[11] Neither residence in the lordship nor even possession of land within it were *per se* a sufficient answer to that question; fealty and homage were the litmus test of the bond of personal lordship.

This personal dimension of Marcher lordship emerges again in the renders that were paid to the lord. Those renders had little to do with land and much with respect. They are reminiscent of those traditional gifts which Tacitus tells us were given to lords as marks of reverence in early Germanic society. Such occasional gifts soon became customary (witness the Easter eggs and Christmas hens that English peasants frequently owed

---

[10] *Annales Monastici*, ed. H. R. Luard (Rolls Series), III, 387; *T.R.H.S.* 3rd ser. 9 (1915), 28; *Monasticon*, VI, i. 352; *Transactions of the Shropshire Archaeological and Natural History Society* 11 (1887–8), 251.

[11] S.R.O. 552/1/10–11 (1344–6).

to their lord), and in medieval societies the step from the customary to the obligatory was but a short one. In the March such renders retained their non-territorial character; they were still in the fourteenth century tributes paid to the lord and dues for various easements of the soil rather than rent for land. Nowhere is this more obvious than in the cow-renders which were such a distinctive feature of seignorial revenue in the March, as in Northumbria.[12] Their very terminology betokens their non-territorial character; they are 'subsidies' (*Commorth Calan Mai*), 'taxes' (*Trethcanteidion*), 'gelds' (horngeld). They were fixed tributes whose assessment and collection lay in the hands of the community. They were not related to the acreage of land nor, as far as the lord was concerned, to individuals. In Builth, a biennial *commorth* of forty cows was the sole payment made to the lord by the free Welsh community; likewise in neighbouring Brecon a tribute of 108 cows, later raised to 134, was the chief render of the Welshry; in Oswestry and Clun such cow-renders had been commuted into a money payment and in the latter lordship the commuted render paid biennially was known as the eight-pound tax (*Treth Wythbunt*).[13] The significance of these cow-renders in the pattern of lordship was fully grasped by a late-sixteenth-century commentator writing about the render of the men of Oswestry. 'Yt is not properely rent issueinge out of the land', he said, 'but only a some of money annexed as a Royaltie to my Lordes person beinge a Lord Marcher'.[14] That was precisely it.

His comment could equally have been applied to the host of other dues, especially the circuit renders, which the Marcher lords collected from their lordships. In the older March many of these dues had long since been consolidated into a single render and dressed in modern terminology under the name of rent of assize (*redditus assisae*); but even there a few lingered under their old names, such as the *gwestfa* (food-render) in Ewyas and

[12] For the distribution of these tributes in the March, see W. Rees, *South Wales and the March 1284–1415*, 229–34. For Northumbria, see Jolliffe and Barrow cited above p. 131, n. 5 and also W. Rees, 'Survival of Ancient Celtic Customs in Medieval England', *Angles and Britons*, 148–68.

[13] For Builth, Rees, *South Wales and the March*, 230; for Brecon, D.L. 29/671/10810; S.C. 6/1157/4; for Clun, S.R.O. 552/1A/6, 12 and W. Rees, op. cit. 230, n. 2; for Oswestry, *The Lordship of Oswestry*, ed. W. J. Slack, 151 ff.

[14] *The Lordship of Oswestry*, 15.

Threecastles or the *cylch* (circuit-due) in Elfael and Chepstow.[15]
In the newer lordships of the north-east, however, a whole
range of such tributes and circuit dues survived—we can count
at least seventeen varieties in the extent and accounts of Chirkland[16]—and they lay bare the nature of the lordship which
came the way of the Marcher lords. They are the remnants of a
bygone age when the lord and his court officers would tour
their lordships, consuming the food renders of their men as they
went and lodging in their homes. Those days were now past,
but they left a profound impression on the character of lordship and on the relationship of lord and community. In the
lordship of Denbigh for example, the great contrast within the
lord's revenue from his men was that between the *communes
consuetudines*, a term embracing all the old Welsh renders which
the Marcher lords had inherited from the Welsh princes, and
the new-fangled *firma*, the rents levied on all land which had
come into the lord's hands one way or another. The latter were
dues from land, the former dues from persons, at least in origin.
We may take our examples from some of the circuit-dues paid
by the freemen of the commote of Ceinmeirch in Denbigh.[17]
Among those circuit dues was an entertainment render (*pastus*)
of 8*s*. 1½*d*. for the upkeep of the court huntsman and his dogs
and of the chief page and other junior servants of the court
(*Pastus Lucrarii cum canibus, Penmacwy et Gweision Bychain*); it was
assessed—and this is for us the significant fact—at 1½*d*. a head
on the tenants of every freeman and on each houseowning
freeman without sub-tenants. That is, it was a poll tax which
varies, as the record puts it, 'according as to whether there were
more or less tenants of freemen and more or less freemen without
subtenants'. The same categories of freemen also paid another
circuit due, that of the prince's horse and an accompanying
servant (*Pastus stalonis et garcionis*).[18] This due was also a poll
tax but unlike the previous one it was assessed not at a flat rate
but in proportion to the goods of each contributor. It is an
assessment method which we can certainly trace elsewhere: in
Bromfield and Yale in 1376 it was adjudged that the circuit-due

[15] W. Rees, op. cit. 98, 228.
[16] For these various dues, see the introduction to *The Extent of Chirkland 1391–93*,
ed. G. P. Jones.
[17] *S.D.*, 46–7.
[18] For a comment on the history of this due, see *S.D.*, 148.

of sergeants (*cylch cais*) was levied from each tenant 'according to the value of his goods and chattels and not in proportion to his lands or tenements'.[19] Whatever the assessment methods, the 1376 judgement had seized on the essential fact about these circuit-dues: they were, in origin, a token of a personal not of a territorial lordship. English surveyors found such assessment methods strange; they wanted to relate the dues to land, but their attempts to do so represent no more than mathematical hypotheses. Furthermore, they serve to distort the nature of early lordship in the March, for it is the great virtue of the Welsh circuit-dues that their very archaism reveals to us a lordship which was truly personal and a lord who was more *dominus superior* than *dominus terrae*.

The same is true of the death duty (*ebediw*) which was payable to the lord on the death of one of his Welsh tenants. It too was a personal not a territorial obligation. It was a fixed sum and the variants in the tariff are to be explained either in terms of the status of the man (the *ebediw* payable by the son of a freeman was normally 10*s*., that of the son of an unfree man 5*s*.) or in terms of the degree of blood relationship to the deceased (whereas the son of a freeman paid 10*s*. any more distant relative, such as a brother, nephew or first cousin, was charged 20*s*.).[20] The personal character of *ebediw* is further exemplified in the dictum of the Welsh lawbooks that 'no man ought to pay more than one *ebediw* unless he holds different lands of two lords'.[21] In short, *ebediw* bore no relation to land; it was, as was the English heriot in its origin, the final discharge of the debt of personal obligation to the lord. The contrast between it and the relief (*relevium*) which was paid for succession to land held by English tenure in Wales is highly revealing. It is epitomized in the dues paid by scores of Welshmen on succession to their estates. Let us instance a single example: when Gruffudd Crach of Dogfeilyn (Dyffryn Clwyd) died in 1333 he held both Welsh free land (*more Wallensica*) and English measured land (*terra*

[19] S.B.Y., fol. 178. Likewise when the bishop of St. David's collected an aid from his tenants, it was assessed on the lands of Englishmen but on the stock of Welshmen: *Valor Ecclesiasticus* (Record Commission, 1821), IV, 379.

[20] The rules on *ebediw* (though not so called) are clearly set out in *S.D.*, 46–7 and were basically the same throughout the northern March. That they were observed is amply testified by the Dyffryn Clwyd court rolls.

[21] *Llyfr Colan*, ed. D. Jenkins (Cardiff, 1963), §27.

ad acras); his son and heir paid a fixed *ebediw* of 10s. for the former and a relief of 5s. 3d. for the latter rated according to its acreage.[22] The contrasts are manifold: between Welsh and English tenure, between hereditary land and measured land (the terms are contemporary), between a fixed and a variable inheritance due; but from our point of view even more significant is the echo of two kinds of lordship, one personal the other territorial, as reflected in the dues paid at death.

This lordship of men impinged on the tenants of the lord in life as well as in death. It was in respect of their persons, at least originally, that they owed service in the lord's army and suit at his court; it was the same personal bond which they acknowledged when they paid him a *mise* or gift of recognition on his first entry into the lordshp. Their marriages as well as their deaths, even their sexual delinquencies, were not beneath the lord's notice. Seignorial fines for marriage were a common burden of serfdom in England; but in the March, or at least in the lordship of Dyffryn Clwyd where the evidence is sufficiently abundant for one to speak without hesitation, such fines extended to free and unfree, Welsh and English alike. In particular the Marcher lords inherited from the native Welsh rulers the right to levy *amobr*, a virginity fine levied both for marriage and for sexual offences and raised at a fixed sum determined by the personal status of the woman—normally 10s. or 20s. if she were free; half that sum if she were unfree.[23] In origin *amobr* had been an almost honourable acknowledgement of the lord's role as protector of a woman's virginity; by the fourteenth century it had deteriorated into a sordid pretext for increasing the lord's revenue. Furthermore, whereas *amobr* according to Welsh law could only be levied once from a woman,[24] the Marcher lords extended its incidence to include every occasion of proven illegal sexual intercourse, until the woman was declared a common prostitute.[25] A profitable obligation it most certainly was: the surveyor of Denbigh in 1334 calculated the return on *amobr*

---

[22] S.C. 2/216/13, m. 20ᵛ.

[23] The former rate applied in Denbigh, the latter in much of Bromfield and Yale.

[24] *Llyfr Colan*, §27, §48.

[25] *S.D.*, 313–14 ('quousque communis meretrix devenit'). In Bromfield in 1336 three women were given white rods as recognition of their status as prostitutes (meretrices) 'so that their kinsfolk would not henceforth be troubled for *amobr*' ('ne amplius parentele eorum calumpnientur de amobr'): S.B.Y., fol. 175.

at £41 annually; in Kidwelly in 1395 it realized £21 6s. 8d.;
in Clun it was farmed for 15 marks a year; in Maelienydd,
where the lord's territorial income was negligible, it was a
substantial source of revenue.[26] Yet another Marcher custom
emphasized the personal control of lord over his men, namely
the practice (largely abandoned in England) whereby all or a
substantial share of the goods of a man who died intestate reverted to his lord. In Denbigh, for example, half the goods of a
married man who died intestate went to the lord, all of them if
he were unmarried.[27] It was a custom which incurred the dis-
approval of the church, which in England and elsewhere had
appropriated the right to distribute the goods of the intestate
for the good of his soul;[28] but it was too deeply entrenched and
too profitable for the Marcher lords to abandon it.[29]

Nowhere does the personal aspect of lordship appear more
vividly than in the case of one distinctive group of Marcher
inhabitants, the advowry tenants. These were men and women
who paid a tax, normally fourpence each, so that the lord would
avow them (Welsh, *arddel*, *arddelw*).[30]. Many of them, probably
a majority, were not born in the lordships in which they resided:
the Welsh term for them 'aliens' (*alltudion*) makes this clear and
is corroborated by post-Conquest references to them as 'immigrants and foreigners' and by knowledge of the provenance
of some of them.[31] Some were possibly seasonal workers; some
were squatters on marginal lands who graduated to the ranks of
small farmers; others were itinerant traders, and yet others were

[26] *S.D., passim*; D.L. 29/728/11986; S.R.O., 552/1/20, m. 2 (1380); S.C. 6/1209/
11 (1357).
[27] *S.D.*, 47; for the practice in Bromfield and Yale, see the extract published in
W.H.R. 5 (1970), 11, n. 38.
[28] F. Pollock and F. W. Maitland, *History of English Law*, II, 356–63. For an
unsuccessful petition by the bishop of Llandaff against the practice in the March,
see *Memoranda de Parliamento 1305*, ed. F. W. Maitland (Rolls Series, 1893), 73.
[29] Thus in Dyffryn Clwyd the goods of an intestate father were sold to his son
for 30s. while those of a murder victim realized £3 14s.: S.C. 2/219/2, m. 27
(1365); 219/5, m. 19 v (1368). On occasion the Marcher lords conceded that the
goods should be shared with the church after the payment of funeral expenses or
that half should go to the widow: S.C. 2/219/5, m. 18 v (1368); S.C. 2/218/8, m. 20 v
(1360).
[30] In Denbigh the officer in charge of the advowry tenants was called Rhaglaw
Arddelw (Rhaglou Arthlou): D.L. 29/1/2, m. 3.
[31] S.B.Y., fol. 19 ('adventicii et forinseci homines'). In Dyffryn Clwyd some of
them are specifically said to have come from the Principality and in Clun from
Ruthin and Merioneth: S.C. 2/218/1, m. 1v; S.R.O. 552/1/19, m. 2v.

craftsmen, as is indicated both by their names and by the fact that as many as 114 of them were recorded in the fast-growing town of Wrexham in 1391. They were strictly speaking outsiders or at best men of the periphery as far as seignorial extents and surveys are concerned; but such figures as we have suggest that they were by no means a negligible group in Marcher society: they range from forty-seven in the small lordship of Clifford to 112 in neighbouring Cantrefselyf, from sixty-five in Chirkland to an astonishing 857 listed by name in Bromfield and Yale in 1391.[32] They are obviously interesting as a social and economic group; but it is in respect of their position *vis à vis* the lord that they command our attention here. From the point of view of the lord's landlordship they did not exist. They held neither free nor unfree hereditary land; they paid none of the obligations usually associated with such land; indeed in Clun it was accepted that once a man took land he ceased to be in advowry and became a tenant.[33] Their tie to the lord was a personal one, pure and simple. His duty was to provide them with the basic benefit of lordship—his protection, his *mund*. He promised 'to maintain and defend them according to the law and custom of the lordship in all cases brought or to be brought against them in his court at the suit of any foreign parties' and to extend to them 'the privileges and liberties' of his lordship.[34] They for their part became his men: they were supervised by his officer, the *raglot advocariorum*; they were justiciable in his courts; the marriage of their daughters had to be licensed by him; their exit from the lordship had to be sanctioned by him; he would be compensated if they were killed; and when they died he seized their goods or at least a proportion of them and demanded an *ebediw* from their heirs. In short they paid him all the dues of personal lordship. They may have been landless; they were certainly not lordless.[35]

The case of the advowry tenants has highlighted for us the bond between man and lord as one of the constituent elements

[32] D.L. 29/1/2, m. 18; S.C. 6/1156/14; S.C. 6/1234/2; S.B.Y., fols. 97–104.

[33] S.R.O. 552/1/10, m. 16 (1344). In Dyffryn Clwyd, the effects of one advowry tenant included two goats, an ox, an affer and five acres of sown land: S.C. 2/217/14, m. 23ᵛ (1349).

[34] S.B.Y., fol. 19; S.C. 6/1157/5.

[35] The Dyffryn Clwyd and Clun court rolls are particularly rich in details on the status and obligations of advowry tenants.

in the make-up of Marcher lordship. But in a rural society lordship over men is soon transformed almost imperceptibly into lordship over land (and, for that matter, vice versa). That was already certainly if incompletely the case in the March by the fourteenth century. We would be hard put to it, and so would contemporaries no doubt have been, to draw a hard and fast line of distinction between the two lordships, that of the person and that of the land, for the two were inextricably intertwined. But we can at least catch an occasional glimpse of the borderland between the two lordships. We can note how the communal renders, those fossils of the personal lordship of the native princes, were being manipulated by the Marcher lords—how Roger Mortimer of Chirk raised *treth mud* from 5s. 7d. to £6 14s. 5d. and how the earl of Hereford more than doubled the value of the render of cows payable by his Welsh tenants of Brecon in a matter of eighteen years (£36 in 1340: £81 in 1358).[36] More significantly, many of these renders, communal and personal as they were in origin, were increasingly converted into individual rents due from specific plots of land. The process was already well advanced in Kidwelly by the fourteenth century. The free tenants of each *gwestfa* (the administrative unit of the area) were, it is true, grouped into units, each of which contibuted a cow towards the triennial *commorth* and to that extent the communal character of the render was maintained. But the acreage that each tenant held was also specifically recorded and so on occasion was the *commorth* contribution due from him.[37] To all intents, *commorth* in Kidwelly as elsewhere in the March had become a rent due from land; but the fact would be concealed for centuries by the conservatism of the extents.[38] Other dues likewise were being territorialized. *Ebediw* and *amobr*, which were in origin so clearly personal dues, came increasingly to be transferred to land. This territorialization of obligations was perhaps inevitable and all the more so as many men in the March already owed a land-

---

[36] *History of Powys Fadog*, IV, 19–20; D.L. 29/671/10810.

[37] D.L. 43/13/14 (an undated fourteenth-century rental of Carnwyllion).

[38] As can be seen by a comparison of the fourteenth-century rental with the early seventeenth-century ones published in *A Survey of the Duchy of Lancaster Lordships in Wales 1609–1613*, ed. W. Rees (Cardiff, 1953), 175 ff. The surveys of Oswestry of 1393 and 1702 transcribed in *The Lordship of Oswestry*, ed. W. J. Slack, also exemplify this extreme conservatism.

rent as well as a communal render to the lord. The lordship of
Hay provides us with an illuminating example.[39] The nine vills
of its Welshry owed a biennial *commorth* of twenty-four cows to
their lord and that the *commorth* was a personal render was made
manifest by the total absence of correlation between the acreage
of each vill and the number of cows owed. There was, on the
other hand, a precise and constant correlation between that
acreage and the rent that the 114 tenants owed for their land:
the rate was twopence an acre. The dues of the Welshmen of
Hay, and their case is in no way exceptional, represent a duality
of obligation: the one communal and personal, the other individual and territorial. It was inevitable that sooner or later the
two dues should coalesce and that both should eventually be
levied on land. That is certainly what the lords Marcher wanted.
The lord of Bromfield made his sentiments quite clear: in a
letter to his steward in 1346 he agreed to a grant of land for life
provided 'the services are commuted into cash and made
definite'; his successor likewise encouraged free tenants in the
lordship to surrender their Welsh hereditary lands and to
receive them back as tenants at will, paying a fixed rent per
acre.[40] Much the same sort of evidence of seignorial attitudes
comes from Brecon: the tenants of Rhydymaen were persuaded
to change over from a contribution of three-quarters of a cow to
the biennial *commorth* to an annual rent of 4s. 1d. and likewise
when the lands of Ieuan ap Maredudd, which had also contributed to the *commorth*, came into the lord's hands they were
re-let for an annual and individual rent.[41] Changes such as
these are not uncommon in the March; their significance lies
in the wish of the lord to establish an individual territorial bond
with his tenants, to be truly their landlord.

Landlordship was certainly not altogether a new feature in
the March. The authority of the Welsh prince over his men was,
we have suggested, originally a personal one but it was an
authority which became more and more insistent on its claims
over their lands also. The terse *dicta* of the lawbooks bear witness
to this: 'no land ought to be without a king' declared one of

[39] Cardiff Free Library, Brecon Documents no. 2 (Rental of 1340).
[40] S.B.Y., fol. 175ᵛ ('les ditz services soient mys en deniers et en certein');
fol. 177ᵛ (1376).
[41] D.L. 29/671/10810, m. 6, m. 17ᵛ (1342, 1350).

them echoing the current tag *nulle terre sans seigneur*; 'no man
ought to have possession of land except by judgement of law or
by the investiture of a lord' said another. Equally significant
was the new-fangled claim that the action of *dadannudd*, one
of the central actions in Welsh land-law, was restricted to those
who had been invested with their land by a lord.[42] The theory
of seignorial control over land was obviously already well-
developed in native Welsh society; so also were the practice and
terminology of that control. On succeeding to a kinsman's land,
a Welshman not only discharged to his lord the obligation of
ebediw on behalf of that kinsman but also gave the lord an
investiture fee (*gobrestyn*) for the land with which he was then
invested by rod in the lord's court. The whole ceremony, to
which was added the oath of fealty, manifested the lord's control
of man and land alike.[43] It was, therefore, into an inheritance
where lordship was already being riveted on land that the
Marcher lords entered. They accepted the distinctive features
of the Welsh tenurial scene—the custom of partibility, inheritance through membership of a kinship group (*gwely*),
circuit dues and other such renders; but they were left with
ample room to introduce and assert their own concepts of
landlordship. Nowhere does the minuteness of this landlordship
appear more clearly than in the splendid surveys which they
caused to be compiled in the fourteenth century and of which
the *Survey of Denbigh* (1334) and the unpublished survey of
Bromfield and Yale (1391) are the prize exhibits. It is little
wonder that the men of Dyffryn Clwyd recalled with awe the
time 'when Patrick de Crue last measured the lands' of the
lordship, for these definitive surveys cast their shadow over a
whole generation of rent-paying tenants.[44] They were in their
way as clear a demonstration of the masterfulness and thorough-

---

[42] *Llyfr Colan*, §§594, 609, 571. For comment see D. Jenkins, 'A Lawyer looks at
Welsh Land Law', *T.C.S.* (1967) (ii), 220–48.

[43] For details of the mechanics of seignorial control of land I have drawn heavily
on the Dyffryn Clwyd court rolls. The practice of *estyn* (investiture) is also recorded
in Caus (N.L.W. Peniarth, 280, fol. 71 [1401]) and Clun (S.R.O. 552/1/34, m. 1
[1400]); the practice of delivering land by rod, known also in England, survived
for centuries, e.g. *Survey of Duchy of Lancaster Lordships*, ed. Rees, 75; *Early Chancery
Proceedings concerning Wales*, ed. E. A. Lewis (Cardiff, 1937), 163.

[44] S.C. 2/215/69, m. 11 (1307). It is significant in this context that the extent of
Chirkland 1391–3 was known as 'the great extent' (*y stent fawr*) and was partly
translated into Welsh: B.L. Add. 46, 846, fol. 73 ff.

ness of the new lords of Wales as was Domesday Book of the new Norman lordship of England.

Above all they proclaim that Marcher lordship was assuredly a landlordship; that is evident enough from the care with which the name of each tenant and of each item of wasteland and assart is recorded. The account rolls bear out this impression, for they show that in the majority of Marcher lordships rents and renders for land formed the most important single item of seignorial revenue. Two examples from very different Marcher lordships may be cited: in Monmouth and Threecastles (excluding Monmouth town) in 1370 land-rents accounted for £187 out of a gross yield of £350 (to the nearest £);[45] in the thoroughly Welsh lordship of Chirkland in 1366 rents (many of them admittedly old Welsh renders in origin) accounted for £153 out of a gross yield of £513.[46] The proportion of revenue from land rents varied from lordship to lordship; it was at a maximum in a lowland lordship such as Usk or Chepstow, at a minimum in highland areas such as Ceri or Maelienydd.

Rents are the most obvious and regular token of lordship over land; but they do not exhaust the scope of that lordship. There were other occasions when the lord displayed his authority as *dominus terrae*. Death and succession were one such occasion, as we have seen; the sale or transfer of land was another. In the case of land held by English tenure, whether by charter or in fee, every sale, exchange or enfeoffment of land had to be enrolled in the court records, licensed by the lord, and a relief— either the annual rent of the land in question or a fixed rate fine such as 6*d*. or 1*s*. an acre—paid by the new tenant. In the case of land held by Welsh tenure, the method of land transfer was different but the lord's control was equally firm and profitable. Welsh law did not permit the outright alienation of hereditary Welsh land; the Welsh freeholder (*priodor*) was regarded as having no more than a life interest in his land and was accordingly prohibited from devising that land to the detriment of the kinsfolk who would succeed him. He was, however, permitted to demise his land to another for short

---

[45] D.L. 29/594/9506.
[46] N.L.W. Chirk Castle, D. 28. The gross yield includes £66 13*s*. 4*d*. from a communal subsidy while the total for rents incorporates the sale of corn paid by tenants.

periods, normally though not invariably four years at a time, for a sum of money and occasionally an annual rent, with the right of recovering the land at the end of the term on repayment of the sum in question. This device known as *prid* (or to later English lawyers as Welsh mortgage) is profoundly interesting for the student of Welsh medieval society as it provided a method of avoiding the straitjacket of Welsh inheritance custom;[47] but in the present context its significance rests in the role assigned to the lord. 'No man ought to sell or to demise (*prido*) land without the consent of the lord' was the dictum of Welsh law.[48] Herein lay the lord's opportunity, for it assured him a foothold in the sphere of Welsh land transactions, and it was a foothold which the Marcher lords jealously defended and exploited. The lord of Bromfield and Yale strictly enjoined that all *prid*-transactions required his licence under pain of forfeiture of the land and that all such transactions should be limited to a four-year term, while the lord of Dyffryn Clwyd in 1345 issued a self-styled statute on the question of *prid* which, among other clauses, insisted that all *prid*-arrangements must be registered in court and that the recovery clause (for the redemption of the land after four years) should be enforceable.[49] Their eye was focused on profit: the cost of the licence for registering a *prid*-deed was normally 8–10 per cent of the mortgage[50] and those who were convicted of evasion had to pay a sum equivalent to the whole mortgage.[51] Nor did the profits end there. The lord of Bromfield and Yale insisted that if the mortgagor died without heirs male or committed a felony, then the lord's rights of escheat included the land which he had mortgaged to others, and likewise if the mortgagee committed a felony or died intestate (for *prid*-lands like chattels could be passed by will) then the lands he had acquired by *prid* reverted to the lord.[52] On either score the lord was the beneficiary and that these were not theoretical claims is amply demonstrated by the court rolls.[53]

---

[47] On this aspect of *prid* see below pp. 407–10.

[48] *Llyfr Iorwerth* §88 .Cf. *Llyfr Colan* §629 where there appears to be a scribal error.

[49] S.B.Y., fol. 170; S.C. 2/217/11, m. 5.

[50] That at least was so in Dyffryn Clwyd. In the commote of Coelion 1390–9 sixteen *prid*-transactions involved mortgages totalling £21 1s. 2d. and brought the lord £1 12s. 11d. in licences: S.C. 2/220/12.

[51] For such a case see S.C. 2/219/1, m. 24ᵛ (1364).

[52] S.B.Y., fol. 170.

[53] S.C. 2/217/14, m. 22ᵛ (1349) for a case of *prid*-lands being taken into the lord's

The seignorial control of *prid*-transactions was clearly worth-while, sufficiently so for a commission to be issued in Bromfield in 1379 to inquire into evasions.[54] That is why, in the March and Principality alike, the English authorities were such zealous upholders of the Welsh custom of *prid* long after the native community had come to regard it as one of the most irksome shackles on its freedom.[55]

All in all, the lords of the March—or so at least the abundant evidence of the north-eastern March suggests—had established a fairly firm control of the land market and thereby enhanced the character of their landlordship. Evasion there no doubt was, and on a fairly substantial scale at that; but even so the profits for the lord were considerable. In Dyffryn Clwyd the lord's casual profits from land—by way of reliefs, entry fines, *ebediwau*, heriots and licences for *prid*-transactions—accounted for a third of the perquisites of court or some £20 per annum.[56] Land-lordship was clearly much more than merely the collection of rents; it was also the constant supervision—and exploitation—of succession to land and all activity on the land market.

Nor was that all. We have dwelt so far on landlordship in relation to tenant land, whether held by Welsh or English, free or unfree tenure. It was a sphere where the lord's oppor-tunities were circumscribed by custom, whether of the manor or of Welsh or English tenure. The inheritance customs of tenant land were in most cases beyond his intervention and the rents and renders due from the land were likewise established by custom. It was only in the case of his serfs and of their un-free land that the lord's powers were more ample, extending to coercion and compulsion.[57] But between tenant land on the one hand and demesne land on the other, there was an inter-mediate category of land where lordship was more direct and uninhibited. The survey of Bromfield and Yale provides us with our text: 'All lands . . . are annexed to *gafaelion* (i.e. Welsh

hands when the mortgagee was convicted of felony; S.C. 2/220/7, m. 23 (1390) for the lands of a mortgagor, who was killed feloniously, escheating to the lord. Cases such as these were sufficiently common and vexing for advice to be offered as to how they could best be circumvented: B.L. Add. 46846, fol. 151.

[54] S.B.Y., fol. 178ᵛ.

[55] For the Principality, see J. B. Smith, 'Crown and Community in the Princi-pality of North Wales in the Reign of Henry Tudor', *W.H.R.* 3 (1966), esp. 146–52.

[56] For example, the proportion in 1351 was £20 8s. 0d.: £62 12s. 6d. (less fines); in 1367, £23 12s. 2d.: £64 14s. 9d. (less fines).   [57] See below pp. 387–8.

tenure units), except escheated lands and land acquired from the waste'.[58] It was within these two exceptions—escheats and assarts—that landlordship was at its most effective. We have looked at both categories in a different context; but we must return to them briefly from the viewpoint of the landlordship of the Marcher lords.

The right of the lord to escheated land had already been asserted in the days of the native rulers, at least by the thirteenth century; that much is clear from the law texts and from the post-Conquest extents.[59] Furthermore, the occasions for the exercise of that right had been elaborated: failure or inability to pay renders or succession-dues (*ebediwau*), failure to perform services, failure of male heirs beyond the third degree, the capital offences of treason (*brad*) and ambush (*cynllwyn*).[60] The lords Marcher added one new major category to the list, that of a tenant dying while he was legally 'against the peace' of the lord or the king (*contra pacem*); and a most fruitful addition it proved to be. Welsh prince and Marcher lord had asserted their right; but the community did not bow to the claim without a struggle. It claimed, for its part, that all escheated land should revert to the community[61] and it realized clearly the threat to the whole basis of Welsh land tenure involved in the new law of escheat. The community fought a vigorous rearguard action, but there was too much at stake for the lords to surrender their claim. Escheat was profitable. It was so in individual cases: in Dyffryn Clwyd in 1367 the inheritance of a wealthy Welsh freeman which escheated to the lord through failure of male heirs was leased for an annual rent increased by 18*s*. 1½*d*. and an entry fine of £30.[62] It was even more spectacular in its overall effects both on the land market and on seignorial revenue in the March, as we have already seen in the case of Denbigh.[63] It was equally significant from the point of view of the lord's landed authority: escheated land was withdrawn from the control of kin-com-

[58] S.B.Y., fol. 65ᵛ.

[59] See especially *Llyfr Colan*, §288 and *S.D.*, 55 ('escaeta domini a tempore Principum').

[60] *S.D.*, 115, 130, 146 (*diffyg ardreth* and *diffyg ebediw*), 42 (*pro defectu servicii*), 47 *et passim* (failure of heirs); *Llyfr Colan*, §§283–5 (*brad* and *cynllwyn*).

[61] For example, the community of Ceri claimed that escheated land should revert to the *patria* not to the lord 'quia terra est Walensis': S.C. 6/1209/6 (1336).

[62] S.C. 2/219/5, m. 30ᵛ.   [63] See above p. 104.

munities and from the ambit of the archaic and static Welsh renders and was leased instead at an economic rent on an acreage basis and at the lord's will.[64] The advance in terms of landlordship was momentous.

Much the same was true of assarted land. Since the waste was the lord's waste, all land assarted from it was to be held directly of the lord and on his terms. The commote of Carnwyllion in the lordship of Kidwelly provides us with an illuminating example.[65] Most of the land there was held under Welsh tenure by kinship groups and for ancient fixed renders. In Llanedi, for instance, the eighty tenants who held 685 acres owed the lord a cow towards the triennial *commorth*, a contribution towards the entertainment render of the serjeants of the peace (*potura satellitum*) and various military and labour services. Outside this area of primary settlement, however, there lay a further 196 acres of land assarted from the waste (*terra affirmata de vasto*), and here each tenant—and all of them incidentally held in the area of primary settlement—paid the lord an individual rent of twopence an acre for his assarts.[66] In Carnwyllion as elsewhere in the March two patterns of rent co-existed; so did two patterns of lordship. For the lord, it can hardly be doubted that it was the latter form of lordship which was the more attractive. It was more truly a landlordship. It gave him scope to exploit his authority—to lease land for term of years, to let it at his will, to adjust the rent on competitive terms. It was in this direction that the future of lordship lay. In Allington (Bromfield and Yale) the earl of Arundel in 1391 received wheat and money renders totalling £5 3s. 1d. from the five units of Welsh tenure (*gafaelion*); his income from escheats, assarts and land leased at a fixed rate per acre, on the other hand, totalled £20 7s. 4d.[67] The moral was obvious: landlordship paid in terms both of revenue and of seignorial authority. It was not a moral that was lost on the Marcher lords. Their lordship became increasingly a lordship of land as well as a lordship of men.

[64] In 1318 the escheator of Dyffryn Clwyd was ordered to provide a written list of escheated lands and the names of men who could hold them best to the lord's profit: S.C. 2/216/1 m. 11.   [65] D.L. 43/13/14.
[66] This process of assarting proceeded apace during the fourteenth century; at least 144 acres were assarted in Carnwyllion 1340–90: D.L. 29/573 9063.
[67] S.B.Y., fol. 69ᵛ–fol. 76.

The distinction that we have drawn between these two aspects of lordship has, no doubt, a measure of artificiality about it. To the peasant of fourteenth-century Wales the distinction would no doubt be over-subtle; lordship, whether it touched the person or the land, was the power of coercion and exaction; to dissect it into its constituent parts is to conceal rather than to illuminate its all-embracing quality. Even so the distinction has its value. It serves to show once more that lordship was not a uniform institution, that its make-up varied from one country and one district to another. It was, by and large, within a native context where lordship over men was well-developed but where lordship over land was little more than what French historians call a *droit réel superieur* that Marcher lordship was shaped and slowly transformed. Furthermore, the distinction has, we believe, an undoubted contemporary validity: not all those who acknowledged the personal lordship of the Marcher lord were subject to his territorial lordship, witness the example of the advowry men; even in the case of those who were subject to both forms of lordship their obligations in terms of rent, of renders, and of personal obligations such as *ebediw* and *amobr* varied considerably according to the status both of their person and of their land. Finally, in the long-term evolution of lordship the distinction is an illuminating, indeed an essential, one. There had almost certainly been a time in the past when lordship in the March, was, primarily, a personal lordship; we have tried to identify some of the vestiges of that period which survived into the fourteenth century and beyond. There would be a time in the future when lordship would shed many of its personal aspects and become more exclusively a landlordship. We can trace part of that evolution in later centuries as the courts of the king and as the agencies of local government take over many of the functions of lordship and as many of the most obvious and objectionable features of personal lordship—such customs as the circuit-dues, *amobr*, *ebediw* and advowry—are abolished. In the fourteenth century we are still at the stage when both forms of lordship co-existed in varying degrees in different parts of the March. That is why the period is a particularly illuminating one for the study of lordship in the March.

Judicial Lordship

THE right to dispense justice lay at the very heart of lordship in the Middle Ages. That had not always been true in the past nor would it of necessity be so in the future; but in the period that is under study justice and lordship were closely interdependent. That held good of all forms of lordship, from the most exalted to the most humble. The lordship of God himself, the prototype of all human lordship, was conceived as essentially judicial in character; it was as the judge presiding at the last judgement that God was most frequently represented in the iconography of the period. The lordship of the king was likewise, at least in peacetime, regarded as primarily a judicial lordship. He was the fountain—and the lion—of justice; his crown existed, as Bracton put it, to do judgement and justice and to keep the peace. What was true of God and of king was true also of lords in general. Everyone who had pretensions to lordship claimed powers of justice over his men: 'by common law', as a lawyer said in the time of Edward II, 'every free man ought to have a court for his tenants'.[1] That judicial authority, however limited it might be, was in a real sense a *sine qua non* of lordship. Contemporaries were aware of that: when Richard Low of Brecon leased his lands to John Russell in 1329 for twelve years he also transferred to him his tenants along with their services; but he was careful to retain jurisdiction over those tenants for his own court.[2] He may have ceased to be their landlord for the duration of the lease; he had not, however, surrendered the residuary rights of lordship, those of justice over his men.

This judicial power of lordship was much more broadly conceived than the modern usage of the term might suggest.[3] It was more than the power of law-keeping *sensu stricto*; it was also the

---

[1] Quoted from the Year Book of 17 Edward II in *Select Pleas in Manorial and Other Seignorial Courts*, I, ed. F. W. Maitland (Selden Society, 1888), xli.

[2] D.L. 36/1, no. 215.

[3] Any study of judicial lordship in the March must, of course, rest largely on the court rolls not only on individual cases but also on the general character of court

power of governance. In the eyes of contemporaries the two powers were virtually inseparable.[4] For the lord's court was an assembly for the imposition of lordship over men and over land as well as for the maintenance of law and the punishment of crime. Parties in civil and criminal cases would obviously appear before it; but so also would those who had in any way offended the authority of the lord—by leaving the lordship without his permission, by failing to perform their services or to pay their rents, by contravening his ordinances and disobeying his commands. Lordship involved coercion and it was in his court that the lord coerced his men. It was there also that he communicated with them. It was there that he issued statutes and ordinances, on legal and non-legal matters alike—from the sale of shoes and the status of the concubines of priests to the proper procedure in cases of debt and the damages to be recovered for a false plea.[5] It was there that his charters were placarded.[6] It was there that he defined the services of his tenants and compelled them to pay their dues, supervised their land sales, registered their land-deeds, collected their death-duties and reliefs, and exacted fealty from them. In sum the court was *par excellence* an instrument of lordship. Our court-rolls

proceedings over a period of time. For the present chapter I have based my interpretation mainly on the court rolls of: (*i*) Dyffryn Clwyd: S.C. 2/215/64–221/2: 78 court rolls for the period 1294–1399 and far and away the most important collection; (*ii*) Clun: S.R.O. 552/1/1–32 for the period 1328–99; (*iii*) Bromfield and Yale: S.C. 2/226/17–22, isolated rolls for the period 1339–95. These are supplemented by the extremely important excerpts from the court rolls included in S.B.Y., fol. 171–fol. 178ᵛ and N.L.W. Peniarth 404 D., fol. 71–fol. 129; (*iv*) Ceri and Radnor: S.C. 2/227/40–57, isolated rolls for the mid-fourteenth century; (*v*) Chirk: N.L.W. Chirk Castle, 64–73 for the period 1349–86; (*vi*) Caus: N.L.W. Peniarth MS. 280 fol. 69; Staffs. R.O. D. 641/1/4T/1: 1398–1401. There are further court rolls for this lordship in the Marquess of Bath's archives at Longleat; (*vii*) Oswestry: B.L. Harleian 1970, fol. 78–fol. 82, transcript of court roll 1383–4.

The bias towards the northern and eastern March in such a selection is evident; it is largely dictated by the accidents of archive survival and is in some measure offset by the fact that both 'old' and 'new' Marcher lordships are represented.

[4] For example, the prince of Wales expresses his fear in a letter that his lordship (seignurie) would be destroyed 'pur defaut de bone governance et deue justificacioun': *Anglo-Norman Letters and Petitions*, ed. M. D. Legge (Oxford, 1941), no. 228 (*c.* 1401).

[5] These examples are taken from the following sources respectively: S.C. 2/215/72, m. 10ᵛ (1313); 222/5, m. 14ᵛ (1445); S.B.Y., fol. 170 (undated); S.R.O. 552/1/7, m. 8 (1337).

[6] The charter of 1401 to Oswestry town was proclaimed in full court in Oswestry, Chirk, Kinnerley, Melverley, Ruyton, Shrawardine and Holt: B. L. Harleian 1981, fol. 37ᵛ.

make that immediately clear and so do the perquisites of justice that the lord collected. Many of those perquisites had little to do with law as we know it; they had much to do with lordship. The profits of the courts of Dyffryn Clwyd for 1351 may serve as an example: their gross yield was almost £90 but over £20 of that sum came from succession- and conveyancing-dues for land, £10 from forest fines, £10 from a fine on the community, £6 13s. 4d. for the sale of marriage and wardship, and a further £4 or so from the lord's exercise of his economic monopolies. Judicial lordship clearly embraced a great deal.

Nowhere was it more ample than in the March, for there the lord's judicial powers were not limited or restricted by any competing or superior authority. All writs ran in the lord's name; they were issued by his chancery and under his seal; he could add to them at his discretion.[7] Offences were committed against the lord's peace or on occasion against the peace of king and lord alike;[8] it was the lord's peace that offenders had to purchase[9] and those who refused to abide by the lord's commands could be cast out of the protection of his peace.[10] His officers held all pleas, including the pleas of the Crown, in his name;[11] his courts had competence to deal with all offences short of treason against the king. He claimed the right to legislate for the men of his lordship, 'to declare, to add or to reduce the . . . laws, customs and services of their lordship whenever and howsoever it pleases them', as the earls of Arundel put it.[12] That this right did not go by default is amply proved by the court rolls. He also asserted the right to pardon all

---

[7] For the list of writs available in the chancery at Holt see S.B.Y., fol. 8v– fol. 9v; for writs *de cursu* in Pembroke in 1277 see *Catalogue of Charters and muniments at Berkeley Castle*, 145. The ready availability of writs and the lord's readiness to devise new ones were amongst the concessions in the Gower Charter of 1306: *Cartae*, III, no. 851.

[8] For examples of the former, S.B.Y., fol. 5 ('de quacumque transgressione pacem domini tangente'); S.C. 2/221/8, m. 5 ('felonice et contra pacem domini'), and of the latter S.C. 2/218/11, m. 10v ('contra pacem domini Regis et domini de Deffren Cloyt').

[9] S.C. 2/216/4, m. 1 ('pro pace domini habenda').

[10] The men on the estates of the bishop of Bangor were placed outside Lord Grey's protection by his command for refusing to contribute to a communal subsidy: S.C. 2/217/10, m. 13 (1345).

[11] For example, we have the record of the *placita corone* heard in Dyffryn Clwyd in 1316: S.C. 2/215/75, m. 16.

[12] S.B.Y., fol. 2: the quotation was borrowed from the Statute of Wales (1284).

offences, except treason against the king; and this was a right he frequently, indeed extravagantly, exercised.[13] The amplitude of Marcher judicial lordship was beyond all doubt. The king himself acknowledged it: when, for example, the king wished to confirm the Marcher status of the lands of the bishop of St. David's in 1383 he declared that the bishop should 'enjoy royal jurisdiction . . . as in the cognizance of all pleas, personal, real and of the crown', as was enjoyed by all other lords Marcher.[14]

This judicial lordship of the Marcher lords was already fully-fledged by the beginning of our period. It was already causing astonishment to royal lawyers and anger to the communities of the English border shires. We are not called upon here to trace the growth of this judicial lordship nor to enter into the discussions about its origins. It may not be amiss, however, to suggest that it was in the thirteenth century—no doubt in good part as a consequence of the greater measure of peace and of a more secure seignorial authority in the March on the one hand and the increasingly insistent advance of royal justice on the other—that the full extent of this judicial lordship was first articulated and realized. The Marcher lords did more, much more, than merely step into the shoes of their Welsh *antecessores*; they transformed the nature of lordship almost beyond recognition by a persistent policy of military, territorial and judicial control.

They took much pride in their judicial authority for it manifested clearly the masterfulness of their lordship and, one suspects, flattered their *amour propre*. They certainly did not consider it to be beneath their dignity to mete out justice to their own men. Henry of Bolingbroke presided in person at a court in Brecon in November 1397; the Greys of Dyffryn Clwyd not infrequently presided at their courts and exchequer in Ruthin.[15] Present or not, the lord's will was never more in evidence than in the affairs of his courts: fines would be cancelled at his command and others would be reassessed;[16] bills and petitions

---

[13] See below p. 173.   [14] *C.Ch.R. 1341–1417*, 289–90.

[15] For Bolingbroke, see above p. 60; for the Greys see, for example, S.C. 2/216/12, m. 19 ('preter j curiam nondum taxatur quia coram domino', 1331); 218/2, m. 18 ('coram nobis in scaccario nostro apud Ruthyn', 1351).

[16] S.C. 2/216/1, m. 12ᵛ ('dominus vult quod sint quieti', 1318); 218/8, m. 34 ('si predictus finis placuerit domino in adventu suo', 1360).

would be considered by him personally and proclamations made in his presence;[17] delicate issues such as those of status would be deferentially referred to his judgement and others would be suspended 'until he had spoken his will';[18] even the procedure to be followed in a case would await his decision.[19] Those who had been convicted were 'at his mercy' or 'in his will', and an expensive will it often proved to be.[20] Even those who had simply incurred his wrath had to pay heavily to buy back his favour.[21] Judicial lordship was most assuredly a personal lordship and that often meant an arbitrary lordship. Anyone who dared to question the lord's authority had to pay dearly for his impudence;[22] anyone pleading against the lord in his own court was peremptorily amerced;[23] anyone who interrupted the court's proceedings while the steward was sitting and who thereby detracted from the solemnity of the occasion was heavily punished;[24] anyone assaulting one of the lord's officers in the execution of his duties would be both amerced and gaoled for showing 'disrespect for the lord'.[25] Furthermore, law was a matter of grace as well as of justice; those who sought its protection had to pay for it—from £10 'to have the help of the court', or £2 for a jury or for the search of

[17] S.C. 2/218/9, m. 11ᵛ (a bill considered during lord's last stay in Ruthin, 1361); 220/1, m. 17ᵛ ('proclamacio facta in curia in presencia domini per dominum', 1384).

[18] S.C. 2/217/14, m. 33ᵛ ('aiornetur coram domino in adventu suo eo quod plura difficilia in dicto processu inveniuntur', 1349); 217/6, m. 22 ('quousque dominus dixerit voluntatem suam', 1341).

[19] 'Et sit in judicio domini utrum ponatur ad patriam vel in judicio suo proprio', S.C. 2/219/7, m. 25ᵛ (1371).

[20] For example, three of the lord of Clun's tenants, who were 'at his will' for failing to show distrained cattle to his bailiffs, were fined £7: S.R.O. 552/1/20, m. 6 (1381).

[21] For example, the burgesses of Monmouth in 1308 paid twenty marks to recover their lord's goodwill: D.L. 42/1 fol. 18.

[22] Such as the tenant of Overgorddwr in the lordship of Caus who was fined 20s. for daring to question his obligation to carry timber to the lord's mill at Forden: Staffs. R.O. D. 641/1/4T/1, m. 2 (1401).

[23] 'Alanus de Asphull in misericordia quia placitavit contra dominum', S.C. 2/218/4, m. 7ᵛ (1354). The theory that no action could lie against the lord in his own court also applied in seignorial courts in England: Pollock and Maitland, op. cit. I, 589.

[24] Thus Ralph ap Madoc of Brecon was fined 100 marks 'pro tumultu in curia' and a man of Dyffryn Clwyd £5 for striking another man 'in plena curia coram Senescallo': S.C. 6/1156/18, m. 1ᵛ (1372); S.C. 2/219/9, m. 5 (1373).

[25] S.B.Y., fol. 176 ('pro despectu domino').

the court rolls, to a mere 6*d.* to have the judgement of the court in a case of debt or the lord's protection over one's corn.[26] Even then we have not exhausted the lord's personal interest in the affairs of his court. Cases were, of course, often initiated in his name; but he also increasingly adopted the cases of other men, especially cases of felony, as his own and prosecuted them for his own profit. Even private actions were well within the ambit of his interests; in cases of felony (the concept was a new one to Wales) he insisted that his peace as well as that of the injured party must be satisfied,[27] while in successful civil actions, such as those of debt and contract, he would often claim a third of the damages awarded as his own.[28]

The courts were the instruments of judicial lordship. Their number and the range of their jurisdiction varied greatly from one lordship to another; uniformity was never a characteristic of lordship in the March. Some courts such as those of Chirkland, Denbigh or Dyffryn Clwyd, took the Welsh unit of the commote as the basis of their jurisdiction. Others approximated both in name and in function to local courts known in England: there were hallmoots to deal with the judicial business of demesne manors as at Hay, Monmouth, or Clun and in most places where there was an English settlement one would find a hundred court, as at Radnor, Kidwelly, Hadnock (Monmouth) or Castle Martin (Pembroke). Some courts catered for specialized aspects of seignorial jurisdiction, such as the forest courts or the piepowder or fair courts in the towns; others, in imitation of English example, dealt exclusively with criminal matters such as the assizes of gaol delivery or the twice-annual tourns where a local jury presented the names of suspected offenders to the lord's officers; yet other courts, such as the borough courts, were limited in their jurisdiction to specific groups in the community. Nor does the proliferation of courts end there. In many Marcher lordships there existed separate English and Welsh courts established on racial and tenurial

---

[26] S.C. 2/215/76, m. 13ᵛ (1317), 216/14, m. 13ᵛ (1334); 219/2, m. 4ᵛ (1365); Staffs. R.O. D. 641/1/4T/1, m. 2, m. 3 (1401).

[27] For example, in a plea of theft in 1314 the plaintiff paid a fine of 10*s.* for failing to proceed with the case while the defendant paid 100*s.* to buy off the lord's suit in the case: S.C. 2/215/73, m. 4.

[28] Thus when damages of £10 were awarded in a case of contract in 1363, a third went to the lord and the rest to the defendant: S.C. 2/218/11, m. 12ᵛ.

lines, served by different officers and different suitors, using different procedures and operating different laws. Across this racial divide there occasionally straddled a court with a splendidly Anglo-Welsh flavour to its name such as the 'Halimot Wallicorum' in Clun or the Welsh hundred court in Margam (Glamorgan).[29] Even then the jigsaw of jurisdiction in the March is not complete: within most lordships there were pockets of judicial franchises where mesne tenants and ecclesiastical corporations held their own courts for their own men. Some of these franchisal courts such as those at Bronllys (Brecon) or Coety (Glamorgan) claimed judicial rights hardly less than those of the lord himself; others claimed the status of a court baron along with the right to the forfeited goods of their tenants; yet others had barely more rights than an ordinary manorial court in England.[30] Such courts were very common indeed in the lowland districts of the older Marcher lordships of the south where foreign settlement and subinfeudation had been most pronounced. Indeed the lord of Gower had gone so far as to concede in 1306 that all his freemen of the English county of Gower should have jurisdiction over the minor assaults committed by their tenants.[31]

This proliferation of courts and especially of non-seignorial courts could easily have led to the fragmentation of the lord's judicial authority. That this did not happen on a large scale was due to the efforts of the Marcher lords in asserting the integrity and superiority of their judicial lordship.[32] In that task they were often well served by a central court (we use the term for want of a better one) where the unity of the lordship and the omnicompetence of the lord's judicial authority were more clearly manifested than in the myriad of subsidiary courts of a more local or specialized character. Such central courts may, on occasion, have had antecedents in the days of the native rulers: in Bromfield and Yale and in Chirkland the duty

<hr />

[29] S.R.O. 552/1/10; *Cartae*, I, no. 122.

[30] For Bronllys and Coety see above pp. 87–8, 96–7; the status of the court baron is well illustrated by the claims of the holders of such courts in Kidwelly in 1413 (J.I. 1/1154, m. 27, m. 33, m. 39); the court of Richard Low of Brecon (see above p. 149) provides an example of a minor manorial court of which there must have been scores in the March.

[31] *Cartae*, III, no. 851.

[32] For this theme see above pp. 96–9.

of correcting the judgements of the commotal courts lay with an *uchel lys* (superior court) whose Welsh ancestry is beyond doubt;[33] in Powys, where we would expect Welsh institutions to be particularly resilient, we hear of a 'great court of Powys';[34] in Maelienydd, another stronghold of Welsh customs, it was the site of the old Welsh court at Cymaron, not the new Mortimer castle and borough at Cefnllys, which was to serve as the judicial centre of the lordship.[35] Welsh precedents there may have been; but for the most part these central courts of the March, under the name of *comitatus* or *curia*, have a more distinctively feudal than Welsh origin. They are, significantly enough, to be traced most clearly in the older Marcher lordships—in Glamorgan (where the *comitatus* is first mentioned in 1126), Pembroke, Gower, Gwynllwg, Clun, Brecon, Blaenllyfni, Caus and Oswestry. Their composition, especially the role assigned in them to the lord's feudal vassals as suitors, and what we know of their business and procedure reflects their originally feudal character.[36] They still retained much of this feudal imprint in the fourteenth century: it was the suitors of the old knights' fees who gave judgements in the *comitatus* of Gower and it was the vassals (*fideles*) of the earl of Pembroke who sat beside the steward in the county court of Pembroke.[37] From the point of view of judicial authority the obvious service of these courts was their role as bastions of the lord's supremacy. The tenants of the lord of Gower had grasped that point well enough; that is why they demanded that the county court should not henceforth meet within the lord's castle at Swansea. Judicial lordship could easily become legalized oppression. For it was in this forum that the lord asserted his mastery over his mesne tenants: it was here that the earl of Gloucester had broken Richard Siward, that the earl of Hereford had dispossessed Sir Philip ap

---

[33] For the *uchel lys* see *Extent of Chirkland*, ed. G. P. Jones, 60 and S.B.Y., fol. 8 where it is glossed as 'duos proximos comotos adjacentes infra potestatem domini'. A disputed judgement was referred to precisely such a court (though not so called) in 1388: N.L.W. Peniarth 404 D., fol. 86. For a native Welsh reference see *Ancient Laws and Institutes of Wales*, ed. A. Owen (1841), II, 380.

[34] *Mont. Colls.* 10 (1877), 398–401.

[35] *C.P.R. 1292–1301*, 290.

[36] This argument is more amply advanced in *W.H.R.* 5 (1970), 13–15.

[37] *Cartae*, III, no. 851; *Penbrokshire*, II, 469 (1342), 485 (1427). For a late but helpful list of the suitors of the county court of Pembroke see *Cal. Public Records re. Pembrokeshire*, III, 61–2.

Rees and that the earl of March had cut Grimbald Pauncefoot down to size.[38] It was in this central court that the vassals performed their suit of court to the lord, just as they owed castle guard at the *caput honoris*; it was here that the lord exercised much the same jurisdiction over free land that the king in England exercised in the royal courts; it was here that final concords about such land were registered and assizes heard; it was here that he reserved for himself those cases that touched 'his estate and dignity as the lord of an honor' (the phrase is that of the lord of Brecon), such as the pleas of the crown and pleas initiated by writ from his chancery; it was here that he exercised a jurisdiction in error over the courts of his vassals (as was acknowledged in Gower in 1306) and over his own inferior courts (as seems to have happened in Glamorgan).[39] In short, this central court, in such lordships as it existed, exemplified more clearly than any other institution the judicial authority of the Marcher lord throughout his lordship.

The lord's courts, central and otherwise, brought his authority to bear on the life of the lordship in a multitude of ways. Most of them met every three or four weeks and thereby gave a frequency and regularity to lordship. In Dyffryn Clwyd, for example, it has been calculated that as many as 136 court sessions were held in the year 1322–3; the tenants of the lordship could have been left in little doubt that their affairs were closely supervised by the lord.[40] Few of them escaped the net of his courts: they appeared there as suitors, as pledges, as mainpernors, as litigants, as jurors; their shortcomings as tenants and inhabitants of the lordship as well as their offences came under the scrutiny of the courts. They were lucky if they escaped an amercement or a fine during the course of the year; even if they did so as individuals they would more likely than not be mulcted as members of the community. The lord's courts constituted, even more than the seignorial courts of England, 'a formidable element of control';[41] they more than any other

---

[38] See above pp. 88, 96–7.
[39] These central courts are notoriously ill-served by the surviving documentary evidence; but much can be learnt about the county courts of Pembroke, Glamorgan and Gower from the abstracts made from their records both by contemporaries and by later antiquaries.
[40] R. I. Jack in *T.D.H.S.* 18 (1969), 27.
[41] R. H. Hilton, *A Medieval Society*, 240.

institution brought the authority of lordship to bear on the life of the community.

Comprehensive the lord's judicial authority most certainly was; but it was not an exclusive authority. His word might often have appeared to be law; in reality it was not so. For the lord's judicial lordship operated, whether he liked it or not, within an established pattern of procedure and law.[42] Let us start with the composition of the courts. The lord's courts they most assuredly were: they were held in his name, presided over by his steward, and served by his officers. But neither the lord nor his officials were the judges of that court (except in minor cases often presented by his officers and touching the lord's interests); that function belonged either to the Welsh judge or to the suitors of the court. In the northern lordships of Denbigh and Dyffryn Clwyd the role of the Welsh judge was an important one: it was on his own word and in the light of his own knowledge and interpretation of the legal texts that he decided cases initiated by Welsh law. He may have been appointed and paid by the lord and the amercements that were due by Welsh law (such as the normal *camlwrw* (amercement) of three cows or 15*s*.)[43] were no doubt attractive to the lord; but the law that he declared and applied was not a seignorial ordinance but 'the law of Hywel', the law of Wales as it had been transmitted and glossed by lawyers over the centuries. In most of the March, however, the keepers and interpreters of law were not the Welsh judges but the suitors (*sectatores* or *iudicatores*, the latter term is particularly significant) of the court. In both the older lordships of the March such as Gower and the newer ones such as Bromfield and Yale the role of the suitors was firmly entrenched. Indeed they remained central in the courts of the March long after they had lost much of their significance as

---

[42] Much of what follows relies heavily in argument and documentation on articles published previously; see R. R. Davies, 'The Twilight of Welsh Law, 1284–1536', *History* 51 (1966), 143–64; 'The Survival of the Bloodfeud in Medieval Wales', *History* 54 (1969), 338–57; 'The Law of the March', *W.H.R.* 5 (1970), 1–30. The following footnotes are confined to some supplementary documentation touching the argument as it is developed here.

[43] Examples of such fines are common, e.g. S.C. 2/215/69, m. 13ᵛ ('in misericordia trium vaccarum secundum legem Wallensicam per iudicium Judicatoris', 1307); 215/71, m. 7ᵛ (1312), 216/1, m. 18 (1318). In Kidwelly, Welshmen won the concession that *camlwrw* should be fixed at the half-rate of 7*s*. 6*d*.: D.L. 42/16, fol. 43ᵛ (1356).

doomsmen, or law-finders, in England.[44] They remained so because the law of the March was by and large a customary, unwritten law and one which resided neither in lawbooks nor in the breast of the lord but in the memory of the suitors. Their duty was to declare that law and they did so frequently, as the evidence makes amply clear. They decided questions of substantive law: the suitors of the bailiwick of Marford in Bromfield and Yale, for example, gave it as their judgement in 1366 that the son of a free tenant retained his free status even though his father had sold all his hereditary lands.[45] They also decided procedural issues—whether an appeal of felony could or could not be terminated by duel, or the number of defaults that were permitted in response to an official summons.[46] These judgements were often called 'ordinances' or 'statutes'; and such in effect they were, for it was by their declarations that the law was made or found. Their function, we must insist, was to declare the law not to decide questions of fact in a particular case. They were doomsmen, not jurors.[47] Their judgements might be and indeed often were impugned by the steward; but their right to make such judgements was never called in question. 'The court passes judgement, not the lord': that tag from an old English law-book applied equally in the March.

What was true of the composition of the courts also applied to their procedure. It is clear that many cases especially those touching the lord's rights (such as forest offences or failure to perform services) or his unfree tenants were decided merely on the word of a seignorial officer. But in the great majority of civil and criminal pleas the litigant was swaddled by procedural rules which by their very formalism and conservatism stood between him and arbitrary justice. His action would be initiated either by plaint or by writ. Writs were an innovation in the March and were originally confined to English tenants

---

[44] For the decline in the importance of suitors in English courts see Pollock and Maitland, op. cit. i, 548–9, 594.

[45] S.B.Y., fol. 173 ᵛ.

[46] ibid. fol. 173 (1355); S.C. 2/219/7, m. 21 ᵛ (1371).

[47] A case held at Wrexham in 1361 illustrates the distinction clearly. The *suitors* were called to decide upon the issue of law viz., whether a defendant could collusively alienate his goods once an action against him had been initiated in court. But it was a *jury* which was asked to decide the guilt of the defendant in the case: N.L.W. Peniarth 404 D., fol. 111.

and to English tenure;[48] but like so much else in English law they were soon borrowed by Welshmen. Once the action had begun, there were certain procedural rules which had to be observed. That was true of all courts, of course; the distinctiveness of court procedure in the March lay in the coexistence of two traditions of procedure, the one English the other Welsh. On the one hand we hear of summonses, pledges, essoins, mainprise, presentment, vouching to warranty and so forth; on the other hand we still hear in the March in the fourteenth and fifteenth centuries of *cyfarch* (summons), *hawldisyfyd* (the sudden challenge), *tremyg* (the right to ignore a summons thrice) and *brwydrcyfaddef* (out-of-court arbitration in cases of assault). There was, of course, a good measure of similarity between the two procedural methods and above all an increasing adoption of English practices. This is again particularly obvious in the final stage of procedure, that of proof. Here again the degree of discretion allowed to the lord or his steward was minimal; proof was a matter for God or fellow-men, not normally for the lord. Many cases were, of course, terminated by the admission of the defendant or by his failure to appear or by the failure of the plaintiff to prosecute or by a licence to settle out of court. But there was also an ample variety of ways, well sanctioned in English practice and Welsh law alike, for deciding a case by proof: wager of law was popular in the March, all the more so as it corresponded closely to the Welsh *rhaith* (compurgation) and it was used frequently in civil and occasionally in criminal cases; in Welsh land pleas the use of aids and warrantors from amongst coheirs and relatives was a well-recognized feature of procedure; in civil cases the use of witnesses to the contract (*amodwyr*) to terminate a case was still in vogue in northern lordships, and so of course was the decision of the Welsh judge. Nevertheless, in both English and Welsh cases, proof came increasingly to rest with the verdict of the *patria*, the jury. The success of the jury had been as phenomenal in Wales as it had been in England; indeed it pre-dated the final Edwardian conquest of the country. Welshmen were prepared to pay heavily for this new boon, as was the man from Dyffryn Clwyd who considered 6s. 8d. not too high a price to pay to secure a

---

[48] 'Dictum est . . . de brevibus assisarum quorum usus et forma infra libertates et tenuras anglicanas sunt maxime': S.B.Y., fol. 6.

jury-verdict when he was accused of stealing corn worth 6*d.*;[49] they even grafted it onto cases—such as *sarhad*, (trespass), *amobr* (virginity-dues) and *galanas* (blood-feud compensation)— which in all other respects were deeply embedded in Welsh law. Jury was triumphant. Nowhere does this appear more clearly than in Clun where we learn of a successful proof by compurgation being quashed by the verdict of a jury and the compurgators amerced and where a series of juries of twelve, twenty-four and forty-eight formed a hierarchy of judicial appeal.[50]

The victory of the jury contributed to the strength of the community in judicial affairs, for the verdict of the jury is not, as Maitland pointed out, 'just the verdict of twelve men; it is the verdict of a *pays*, a 'country', a neighbourhood, a community'.[51] That, from the point of view of the present argument, is the vital point. The judicial lordship of the Marcher lords weighed heavily and frequently on the community; but the community also did a great deal to determine the nature of the justice that was ministered in the courts—as suitors, as pledges, as oath-helpers, as witnesses, as *amodwyr*, as assessors of damages, and above all as jurors, both grand and petty jurors. Justice (*justicia*) was the lord's justice; judgement (*judicium*) was the judgement of peers, of the community. That was one of the basic distinctions of medieval jurisprudence. It was generally observed in the March.

Judicial lordship was further confined by the law that operated in the courts of the March. The relationship of kingship and thereby of lordship to law was one of the most anxiously debated issues of medieval political theory. The Marcher lords knew little of theory and cared less for it; but of practice and of customs they knew a great deal. They—and for that matter the native Welsh princes—claimed the right to improve and to amend the law and to abolish parts of it; they also claimed and exercised the right to issue 'statutes' and ordinances.[52] They might even claim, as did the descendants of the earls of Warwick, that they had established laws in their conquered Welsh lands

[49] S.C. 2/216/3, m. 1 (1332).
[50] S.R.O. 552/1/33, m. 1; 3, m. 3; 30, m. 1 (1402, 1334, 1398).
[51] Pollock and Maitland, op. cit. II, 624.
[52] See above p. 151. For the Welsh attitude to the prince's rights *vis à vis* the law see *C.W.R.*, 198–9, 203, 206.

at their will.[53] But their memories served them ill. The law of the March—for such was the name given to the assemblage of discordant customs which prevailed in the Marcher lordships—bore but faintly the impression of the seignorial will. It was a compound of archaic practices, of feudal and local customs, of English writs and statutes and procedural methods and of a not inconsiderable corpus of Welsh law. It was not a uniform body of law. That should not surprise us: it grew out of the rich diversity of Marcher society and the fragmentation of judicial authority in the March where each lordship was a self-contained judicial and legal unit.[54] It was none the worse for that; even English local courts, it is now recognized, had on occasion a maturity of legal development especially in the field of civil actions (such as covenant, trespass and defamation) well in advance of that of the royal courts. And so it may well have been in the March; local justice and local law were not of necessity inferior in quality.[55] But they were likely to be archaic. There is much that is archaic about Marcher law: the feudal overtones of some of its substantive and procedural rules point in that direction as does the survival of outdated habits, such as the seizure of the goods of intestates.

Above all the complexity of the law of the March—it can be construed either as the richness of variety or as disorderliness—lay in the fact that it was a plural law, drawing on two (at least) legal traditions and catering for two peoples. It was a mixed law for a mixed population, administered often in different courts (English and Welsh), and often served by different officers and different procedures. Towards Welsh law and procedure the attitude of most Marcher lords was one of profiteering tolerance. Their attitude to Welsh law was of a piece with their attitude towards Welsh customs generally: strange they might be, but they were part of the established order which they had inherited and they were, therefore, by and large to be

---

[53] C. A. Seyler, 'The Early Charters of Swansea and Gower', *Arch. Camb.*, 7th ser. 4 (1924), 77.

[54] Thus in the bailiwick of Marford (Bromfield and Yale) in 1355 it was decreed that if 'foreign' parties should proceed in a case of felony, even though it was committed outside the lordship, the defendant should abide in his reply by the usage of the lordship: S.B.Y., fol. 172ᵛ.

[55] See in general S. F. C. Milsom's introduction to the 1968 edition of Pollock and Maitland. For defamation see ibid. II, 536–8; cases of defamation were common in Marcher courts.

upheld (even against the wishes of the Welsh themselves as in the case of the practice of *prid* or the denial of the English custom of dower)[56] and vigorously exploited. They even tolerated practices such as *galanas* (blood-feud compensation) which ran clean contrary to English legal theory and practice and even to Christian ethical teaching as it was interpreted in England. The habits of coexistence and the attractions of profit may explain their attitude; but it also sprang from an acceptance of the fact that Welsh law, especially land law and civil law, was too closely intertwined with the structure and customs of society for it to be dismantled or eradicated by seignorial edict.

But there was much more to the law of the March than a tolerated and attenuated inheritance of Welsh legal learning. It leaned heavily, increasingly so , on the law and legal practices of England and it did so in spite of the occasional act of bravado in declaring that the king's statutes did not apply in the March nor his writ run there. In fact his statutes were cited in the courts of the March and his register of writs formed the basis of the writs available in Marcher chanceries. Furthermore procedure in the courts of the March more and more resembled that of English seignorial courts (even if we concede that the clerks who wrote our court rolls may have followed their English formularies too slavishly); land-conveyancing methods came increasingly under English influence even in areas where Welsh tenure was most resilient; and proof by jury, as we have already seen, swept all before it. The terminology, the framework of procedure and the very substance of law in the March were becoming yearly more English. It was in part a victory of legal ideas and methods, in part a victory of men, both of the settler English population and of the alien administrators who presided at courts and organized their business.

Lordship certainly did not have it all its own way in the field of justice; its authority in the courts coexisted with and was supplemented by that of the community. The consequences of this partnership did much to shape the character of Marcher justice. The community, for example, generally propounded

---

[56] For *prid* see above pp. 143–5. Contrary to the rule laid down in the Statute of Wales, the privilege of dower was specifically withheld from Welsh women in the new lordships of the northern March unless their husbands held land by English tenure. The rule is given at length in S.B.Y., fol. 5 v–fol. 6.

the custom of the March; but it was the lord who promulgated it and gave it his assent. It was an *ordinacio patrie* but *ex assensu domini*.[57] Yet in this partnership, the role of the lord was an increasingly assertive one; Marcher lordship was on the offensive in the exercise of its judicial power as in so many other directions. The scope for such an offensive was ample enough. The private actions of his men became increasingly the public concern of the lord. This was most obviously true in the field of criminal actions. There English law and attitudes served the lord's interests well: the concept of felony as an offence against his peace, the notion of a coroner who must view every dead body and the practice of a jury of presentment declaring the names of suspected offenders gave the lord an immense power in criminal matters which Welsh law barely knew. The lord was now assuredly the keeper of the peace: he was a party in all cases of felony even if they were initiated as private appeals, for he alone had the right to pardon and to 'relax' his own suit against the offender. Even where Welsh law survived in criminal matters, as it did extensively in the northern and central March, the lord managed to ensure a substantial foothold for himself, not least in that most 'private' and family aspect of Welsh law, *galanas* or blood-feud compensation.[58] In civil actions, likewise, the lord was ever careful of his interests. Welsh legal practice had allowed and indeed encouraged extra-curial arbitration; but the lords of the March were anxious to make their courts the only forum for legal matters for, as one of them put it, 'the lord is party to the plaint'. A party he certainly was in the profits of the plaint, for in actions such as debt and contract he took a share of the damages awarded as well as the amercements for conviction and for false plea.[59] Even Welsh law could be manipulated to serve the interests of the lord, most notably and profitably by the employment of professional Welsh jurists (*dosbarthwyr*) to reverse decisions given according to Welsh law, for that law was notoriously harsh in its penalties on false

---

[57] *W.H.R.* 5 (1970), 10–11 and the examples cited there.

[58] See in general *History* 54 (1969), 353–7.

[59] S.B.Y., fol. 170ᵛ ('dominus est particeps in querela'). These petitions and the replies to them are revealing of the lord's attitude to civil cases. How well he did by such cases is amply illustrated by the court rolls. Thus in a successful plea of breach of contract of 1345 the lord took a third of the damages of 20*s.* as well as an amercement: S.C. 2/226/18, m. 3.

judgements.[60] In one way and another the lord was using his courts and the pleas of his men in them as an opportunity to assert his lordship and to do so profitably.

It was, however, in another direction that his lordship was being asserted most dangerously in judicial matters. To claim that he was a party to the pleas of his men was one thing; to claim that his word was superior or alternative to the judgement of the court was much more sinister. For that was to bestow on the lord's will an authority in judicial affairs which hitherto had rested with the community, as suitors and as jurors. We get an occasional echo of the conflict in those cases when the steward, or occasionally the lord himself, challenged a judgement given by the suitors in court.[61] It was a challenge which could only redound to the credit of the lord's authority over his courts, for in the last resort appeal lay to the lord's council and no further. We get an even sharper echo of the conflict in the complaint of the men of Gower, *parti-pris* as it no doubt is, that the lord 'was giving judgement in his courts there by a justice and sheriff . . . and does not permit judgements to be given by the suitors of those courts as has been accustomed'.[62] *Judicium curie* was giving way to *judicium domini*. Most telling of all the evidence are the charters of liberties, especially those of Maelienydd, Gower, Talgarth, Clun and Cemais, for they lay bare the anxieties of the community and by implication the ambitions of the lord in the field of justice. Their themes are recurrent. One is the right of accused persons to be mainperned provided they could find sufficient pledges and provided the offence was not too serious; another was the fear that men might be indicted merely on the word of a seignorial officer. Both arise out of an anxiety that the machinery of justice might be converted into an occasion for seignorial vindictiveness, unhampered by the customs of the country. That same anxiety was even more powerfully expressed on two central issues in most of these charters: the right to be tried by a jury of the country according

---

[60] In Kidwelly in 1410 the fine for false judgement was £10 but a note was added that it ought to have been £44 according to the law of Hywel Dda: D.L. 28/27/4. For this subject see briefly *History* 51 (1966), 160 and *T.C.S.*, 1963, I, 30–2

[61] Examples of such challenges may be cited from Clun (S.R.O. 552/1/20, m. 18 [1381]) and Bromfield and Yale (S.B.Y., fol. 177 [undated]; N.L.W. Peniarth 404D, fol. 86 [1388]; fol. 114 [1361]; fol. 129 [1391]).

[62] *C.P.R. 1301–1307*, 407.

to the established laws and customs of the district, and the right to have either a fixed tariff of amercements or at least amercements assessed, as the Talgarth charter of 1299 put it, 'according to the quality and quantity of the offence and the wealth (*potencia*) of the offender by the judgement of proved and sworn law-worthy men of the community'. It was over these issues, trial and amercement, that the arbitrariness of judical lordship could most powerfully and damagingly assert itself; it was here that the community took its stand. It was a conflict comparable to that over pasture, escheats and waste: the lord was attempting to make justice his 'demesne' affair; the community was struggling equally vigorously to keep it 'common'. It was a conflict which recalls Magna Carta, even in its very terms on occasion, as in the promise of the lord of Gower that 'to no one will we sell or deny justice'; it is appropriate that it should so remind us, for both conflicts revolved around the relationship of the will of the lord to the law of the land.

The lord's judicial authority was not limited to the pressure he could bring to bear on the courts of his lordship; his judicial power was increasingly manifested at its most masterful and majestic in courts which were not local in origin and where his authority was less inhibited by the customs of the community. His chief steward or other high-ranking officer could hold a tourn (to be distinguished from the twice-annual tourns or great courts where the grand jury made their presentments). There the affairs of his estates would be carefully scrutinized and heavy fines imposed on negligent officials and defaulting tenants.[63] The purpose of such tourns may strictly speaking have been administrative and financial rather than judicial; but the boundary between administration and justice was never well defined in the Middle Ages, least of all in the March where the lord was also justiciar and where his tenants were exclusively his justiciables. When, for example, a tourn was held by the deputy chief steward of the Duchy of Lancaster at Kidwelly in 1446 its business had little to do with administration

[63] For tourns on the Duchy of Lancaster estates see, R. Somerville, *History of the Duchy of Lancaster I: 1265–1603*, 114–15. The business transacted at such a tourn may be grasped from the tourn held by the earl of Stafford's auditor in 1386 (Staffs. R.O., D. 641/1/2/3) and from the instructions for a general circuit of the duke of Buckingham's estates in 1504 (published in *The Marcher Lordships of South Wales 1415–1536*, ed. T. B. Pugh, 281–6).

and much with the profits of justice. For profitable such tourns certainly could be: the tourn of the chief steward at Kidwelly in 1395 brought John of Gaunt £155 in communal subsidies, £153 in fines and £8 in confiscated goods.[64]

More frequent, more imposing and more obviously judicial than the tourn were the sessions in eyre which became a feature of justice in most Marcher lordships in the fourteenth century.[65] Here if anywhere the omnicompetence of the lord's judicial power was displayed in the lordship. The commission of the justices in eyre gave them the most ample powers: not only were they charged to hear all pleas, real, personal and of the Crown, but they were also authorized to inquire into the lord's rights, into the conduct of his officials, into liberties and jurisdictions, and in addition they were given powers to grant pardons, to assess fines and to reverse judgements given in all other courts of the lordship.[66] It is from about the mid-fourteenth century that we have record of such sessions in eyre in the March[67] and the very frequency with which they came to be held was a token of their success from the lord's viewpoint, if only in financial terms. In Denbigh, for example, we hear of at least four sessions being held in the eleven years 1359–70;[68] while in many Marcher lordships the habit of holding (and of redeeming)[69] the sessions every three years was well on the way to being established by the end of the century. The sessions as such bestowed no new judicial authority on the Marcher lords and their absence from some lordships, such as Chirkland and Dyffryn Clwyd, simply means that the lord considered the existing judicial machinery adequate in relation to the size of his lordship and to his authority within it. Nevertheless in terms of placarding judicial lordship in its most awesome form— to the accompaniment of solemn proclamations, the formal

[64] D.L. 30/132/2035 (1446); D.L. 29/728/11986 (1395).

[65] T. B. Pugh, op. cit. 3–141 provides a comprehensive and definitive account of sessions in eyre in the March. To the lordships in which such sessions can be traced (ibid. 36–40) we can add Clun (S.R.O. 552/1A/8 [1388]) and Bromfield and Yale (S.B.Y., fol. 175ᵛ [1346]).

[66] T. B. Pugh, op. cit. 9, 18.

[67] Thus the first recorded sessions in eyre in Brecon was held in 1349: D.L. 29/671/10810, m. 16.

[68] In 1359, 1362, 1364, 1370: N.L.W. Wynnstay 89/101; *B.P.R.*, III, 440, 461, 463; S.C. 6/1183/3.

[69] For this practice see below p. 174.

surrender of office by all the local officials, the suspension of local courts and the imposition of massive communal fines— the significance of the sessions in eyre extends far beyond the business they did or did not transact. It comes as no surprise that when the Black Prince leased the lordship of Builth in 1348 he reserved to himself the right to hold sessions there.[70] He was thereby retaining one of the most potent and profitable institutions of judicial lordship in the March.

The justices in eyre were almost always drawn from the lord's council: the sessions at Kidwelly in 1380, for example, were held by the chief steward, the receiver-general and the auditor.[71] The panel of justices was normally larger and more diverse than this; but the sessions never shed their conciliar character. They brought the justice of the lord's council to bear on the local lordship. That council was in fact the final repository of the lord's judicial power. Its authority knew no limits: pleas were frequently deferred until its coming, especially if they touched the lord's rights but also if a major criminal case arose;[72] bills would often be laid before it by individual tenants and endorsed with the council's decision;[73] cases would be referred from the courts of the lordship and even from the sessions to its scrutiny;[74] as the repository of the lord's equitable powers it could attend to petitions asking for his grace and mercy; it could lay down legal rules, as did the council of Lord Grey which decreed that the conquest of Wales was the limit in time for pleas concerning land;[75] finally it could and did act as an appeal court in pleas of false judgement.[76] Its competence was, of course, far wider than merely judicial; it had also the last, and often the first, word in matters financial and administrative. From its judgement there was no appeal; only the foolish would dare to

---

[70] S.C. 6/1156/6.

[71] *John of Gaunt's Register 1379–83*, II, no. 1066.

[72] Examples include a case relating to the services due from land and a case of felony being referred to the lord's council: S.C. 2/218/7, m. 13ᵛ (1359); S.R.O. 552/1/15 m. 15 (1357).

[73] For this procedure, see Somerville, op. cit. 124–5; for an example of such a petition, see G. A. Holmes, op. cit. 129.

[74] T. B. Pugh, op. cit. 14.

[75] S.C. 2/215/76, m. 13ᵛ (1317).

[76] For examples of its appellate jurisdiction from judgements given by a jury of 48 in Clun and from the 'superior court' (*uchel lys*) of two commotes in Bromfield see S.R.O. 552/1/30, m. 1 (1398) and N.L.W. Peniarth 404 D, fols. 86–7 (1383–95).

petition parliament as a final desperate act and thereby incur the lord's wrath.[77] The omnicompetence of his council and the finality of its judgements were the lord's trump cards in his attempt to assert his judicial lordship over his Marcher lands.

This judicial lordship was and has remained in retrospect the most distinctive feature of Marcher franchise. It was also the most abused aspect of Marcher lordship. That at least was the unanimous opinion of most observers in the sixteenth century and it has not been much questioned since. Their opinions have the advantage of recent experience and vivid recollection; they have the obvious disadvantage of having been written with a purpose—to highlight the disorder of the March in order to acclaim more loudly the need for reform and the achievement of the Tudor sovereigns. Their opinions deserve our attention, but only as opinions and then only as opinions for the last half-century of the history of the March. For the fourteenth century any assessment of the character of Marcher justice must rest on the study of the court rolls and an unsatisfying assessment it will inevitably be. Not only will it vary from one lordship to another; still more limiting, the court records themselves, where they do exist, have the same inbuilt bias as all administrative records. They are never more than the records of the lawkeepers.

Yet we need not surrender entirely to a counsel of despair. The records of the courts of the March are at least sufficient in bulk to allow us to advance certain comments, more impressions than conclusions. The first such comment arises directly out of the court rolls themselves. Justice may have been capricious and unsatisfactory in the March; but the courts themselves met with unfailing regularity (even during the Glyn Dŵr revolt), and operated on much the same principles and transacted much the same business as the local courts in England. That is not to claim much; but it is at least to assert that the machinery of justice, with the obvious exception of the royal dimension (and that dimension, as it is now increasingly recognized, has been too often allowed to blot all else out), was no different in essentials in the March from that of contemporary

---

[77] As did the tenants of Sir Philip ap Rees of Bronllys in 1348 against the earl of Hereford, their superior lord: *Rot. Parl.*, II, 218–19. Their action seems to have led directly to the downfall of Sir Philip ap Rees; see above pp. 95–7.

England. A truism maybe, but one which needs to be asserted. Nor was the treatment of criminals basically different; the March in the fourteenth century was not the criminals' paradise that it has sometimes been made out to be. Marcher lords, it is true, found in the Welsh legal tradition an attitude towards homicide which was diametrically opposed to that which had developed in England in the twelfth and thirteenth centuries; it was the contrast between homicide seen as a private, emendable offence against the peace of the slain man and of his kin, and homicide regarded as a capital crime, a felony committed against the king's peace.[78] Marcher law with its usual ambivalence leaned in both directions: it accepted and exploited the Welsh tradition but equally it subscribed to English practices. English penal methods were the rule not the exception in the March: executions were common; so were torture and the use of the pillory.[79] Marcher justice, as we see it in the rolls, was certainly not 'soft'. When an old man in Clun in the reign of Elizabeth was asked to recall the bad old days of Marcher rule he did so by recounting the occasion when two men were hanged on either side of the brook which divided the lordships of Ceri and Clun.[80] His story has many aspects to it; but his memory was not one of a Marcher justice which left crimes unpunished.

Even in the maintenance of law and order the Marcher lords were far from negligent. The practice of binding men over in recognizances to keep the peace, which became a major feature of royal policy towards the March in the late-fifteenth century,[81] was certainly no new departure. Such a practice was extensively and unremittingly applied in lordships such as Dyffryn Clwyd throughout the fourteenth century. Men who for any reason were likely to break the peace were bound over in recognizances which ranged from £20 to £300;[82] others were bound over to

[78] *History* 54 (1969), 350–51.
[79] Five men were hanged in Dyffryn Clwyd in 1316; two more and three women in 1323. Two men were tortured for refusing to plead in 1319, one unto death. We could add easily to this gruesome catalogue.
[80] *Transactions of the Shropshire Archaeological and Natural History Society* 11 (1887–8), 258.   [81] T. B. Pugh, op. cit. 29–31.
[82] Thus in 1394 eight men were bound over in recognizances of £40 each to keep the peace, while in 1399 Bleddyn ap Dafydd Goch found eight mainpernors for his recognizance of £300 to keep the peace towards all men in the lordships of Dyffryn Clwyd and Denbigh: S.C. 2/220/12, m. 13ᵛ; m. 34ᵛ. In Dyffryn Clwyd the use of such recognizances appears to have been adopted in the 1320s.

appear in courts whether as jurors or as defendants; yet others were bound over not to leave the lordship. It was a crude method of peace keeping; but for lack of a police force it was one of the few ways available. That it worked relatively well may be assumed from the occasional heavy fine on those who failed to abide by the terms of their recognizances.[83] Even contemporaries acknowledged on occasion that Marcher justice had its attractions. In 1331, for example, the community of the county of Pembroke pleaded for the appointment of a competent and suitable steward as the absence of such an officer had led to the ordinary people (*menez*) being oppressed by great evildoers (*grantz meffesours*).[84] The plea is a plea for lordship, for to the men of Pembroke as to many in the March the judicial protection of the lord, inadequate as it might be, alone stood between them and the oppression of more local tyrants.

Marcher justice in the fourteenth century was not without its merits; but its shortcomings were also abundant. Judicial lordship was too often a remote lordship; its power was frequently surrendered into the hands of local *potentes*—'strong men' would not be too inapt a rendering of the medieval term—who used the façade of judicial office as a countenance for social and economic oppression. 'What was important', it has so rightly been observed of medieval England, 'in an inevitably decentralized state was not so much what the law was, as who administered it, and in whose interests'.[85] What was true of England was even more true of the March. It was not the machinery of justice which was at fault, but rather its personnel and the relationship of that personnel to the distribution of social power in the community. The whole gamut of the abuse of judicial office—from forging court rolls through maintenance, embezzlement and bribery to attempted murder—can be illustrated adequately from Marcher documentation. The shortcomings were exacerbated by the distance from the supervision of the lord's council and by the habit of leasing office for a long term of years. The borderline between the

---

[83] When two brothers who had been bound over to appear in court under a recognizance of £40 failed to do so, they were subsequently fined £100: S.C. 2/222/5, m. 14.

[84] *Cal. Public Records re. Pembrokeshire*, III, 13–14.

[85] R. H. Hilton, *A Medieval Society*, 219.

officers of justice and the *grantz meffesours* seemed on occasion to be merely an academic one.

Grantz meffesours there certainly were in the March as in medieval society generally. The justice of the lady of Pembroke and his servant were killed by a gang of such men in 1359, while some decades later the peace of the same county was gravely threatened by William Wyriot and his accomplices.[86] In the Mortimer lordship of Clifford in the late 1380s, the steward was so afraid of the activities of a band of outlaws led by William Solers that he summoned tenants from four nearby lordships to attend him when he came to hold courts there.[87] Such cases are legion. They do no more than lift the corner of the veil on a violent society where the borderline between a semblance of justice and the rule of might was tenuous indeed. Indeed it was so tenuous because justice itself was scarcely to be distinguished from organized crime. It was often pettily arbitrary where the lord's rights were concerned; to assault his pigswain or to kill his falcon was to lay oneself open to his unremitting mercy.[88] Such arbitrariness could easily degenerate into tyranny; and that the March certainly knew. Take the case of William Haiworth: he fled from the wrath of the lord of Blaenllyfni to the nearby lordship of Glamorgan; his lord, Sir John fitz Reginald (d. 1308) bribed the sheriff of Glamorgan to hand Haiworth over to him; once inside the borders of Blaenllyfni he was tortured until he died, without a charge being laid against him or an opportunity being given for him to reply.[89] Exaggerated such cases no doubt are; but they are echoed by too many others for us to treat them with total unbelief. The lord of the March was often the greatest *meffesour* of all. It is little wonder that the *herwr* (bandit) was as romantically idealized a figure in the poetry of Wales as the outlaw was in the contemporary literature of England.

---

[86] *Penbrokshire*, II, 472–3; *Cal. Public Records re. Pembrokeshire*, III, 33–4, 37–8; D.L. 29/584/9237.   [87] U.C.N.W. Whitney Collection, 316.

[88] 30s. for the former offence; 26s. 8d. for the latter, whereas the normal amercement would be 6d. or 1s. Sentences were occasionally even more quixotically profiteering: Richard the Mason's sentence for rape in 1359 included the obligation to serve the lord free of charge for one year! S.C. 2/216/1, m. 17; 219/3, m. 42; 218/7, m. 5ᵛ.

[89] S.C. 8/50, no. 2496; *C.P.R. 1301–7*, 383. For a similar charge against Joan Beauchamp of Abergavenny and her steward, see *Early Chancery Proceedings conc. Wales*, 216.

Marcher justice was vitiated in two other directions according to sixteenth-century critics. One lay in the fragmentation of judicial authority in the March with each lordship as a self-contained judicial unit and lacking any common supervisory control so that, in the words of the so-called Act of Union of 1536, criminals made their refuge from lordship to lordship and so continued without punishment or correction. This judicial fragmentation was certainly a problem and one which was wide open to abuse; but the issue was far more complex than Tudor apologists suggested and will command our attention later.[90] The other charge was that justice in the March was debased and its whole purpose undone by the fact that the lords were more concerned with profits than with justice. It is a charge that it would be difficult to deny, for if the tag *justicia est magnum emolumentum* applied anywhere it did so in the March. That was so in civil cases. It was even more true—and this to the critics was the real abuse—in major criminal cases. Felony in England was a bootless crime; in the March on the other hand the felon could often avail himself of the custom that, having satisfied the appellor, he could also buy off the suit of the lord and thereby secure his life and limbs and often his goods and chattels. In Clun and Caus the price for such redemption (*redemptio vitae*) was fixed at £7; in Dyffryn Clwyd and elsewhere it varied according to the discretion of the lord and the gravity of the offence.[91] It was a practice which prevailed throughout the March—in Chepstow and Monmouth as well as in the more thoroughly Welsh lordships of the north; and remunerative it most certainly was.[92] The custom was a Welsh one[93] and had much to commend it: it alleviated much of the obvious barbarity of medieval penal practice; it gave the lord an opportunity to exercise his prerogative of mercy; it conformed with Welsh notions that compensation was morally preferable to execution and that any human soul was worth a pound of

---

[90] Below, pp. 238–48.

[91] N.L.W. Peniarth 280, fol. 71 (Caus, 1398); S.R.O. 552/1/2, m. 9 (Clun, 1332); Dyffryn Clwyd court rolls *passim*.

[92] T. B. Pugh, op. cit. 63 (Chepstow); D.L. 42/16, fol. 229[v] (Monmouth, 1408).

[93] 'Come la custume est en Gales', D.L. 41/16, fol. 229[v]. Cf. *History* 54 (1969), 353. For the restricted use of fines for homicide in England, see N. D. Hurnard, *The King's Pardon for Homicide before A.D. 1307* (Oxford, 1969), esp. 114–19.

gold.[94] But, to anyone trained in English law, it was a vicious practice which could easily deteriorate into a cynical selling of justice. And that is precisely what happened on occasion.[95]

Justice was sold not only to felons, convicted and otherwise, but to whole communities also. Already by the late-fourteenth century a practice had developed which was to become one of the most notorious features of Marcher justice for the rest of its history—that of proclaiming the sessions in eyre only to redeem them immediately the justices assembled by a huge communal fine, given generally in exchange for a communal pardon of various offences and of outlawries and often of any false judgements of which the community might have been convicted.[96] The sessions which were meant to be the most solemn demonstrations of judicial lordship had already become in the phrase of a Brecon account of 1373 occasions 'for the lord's profit' ('pro proficuo domini'). The men of Glamorgan in the mid-sixteenth century had the measure of such sessions: they seemed 'to have the face of an ernest admynistracion of justice', but they existed 'in effect to none other purpose but ungodly to exacte great sommes of monye on the said inhabitantes'.[97] It might be unfair to apply their censure to Marcher justice generally; but that a concern with profits was a major preoccupation of judicial lordship in the March is abundantly shown by the account rolls.

Rough Marcher justice certainly was and so was most medieval justice.[98] Whether it was rougher than contemporary English justice is not a comparison that is amenable to proof. What however is beyond doubt, what is made abundantly evident by court rolls and account rolls alike, is that in terms of the authority, the prestige and the finances of the lord, his judicial powers occupied a central position in the make-up of his Marcher lordship. Furthermore judicial lordship in the

---

[94] The phraseology is borrowed from Dafydd ab Edmwnd's famous elegy on the execution of Sion Eos: *Oxford Book of Welsh Verse*, ed. T. Parry (Oxford, 1962), 138–41.

[95] D.L. 29/671/10810, m. 6 (execution of a man who fails to pay a fine of 9s.).

[96] T. B. Pugh, op. cit. 36–43; below pp. 183–4.

[97] Ibid. 48.

[98] Cf. the remarks of K. B. McFarlane, *The Nobility of Later Medieval England*, 114–15.

March was more ample in its claims, more authoritative in its power and better endowed in its machinery by the end of the fourteenth century than at any previous point in its history. This was truly the heyday of Marcher lordship.

'THERE is a fair lordship there', remarked the council of the Black Prince in its report on Bromfield and Yale in 1347, 'well worth two thousand marks a year'.[1] The report was rather optimistic, but the equation that it assumed was unquestionably true: in the final analysis the attractions, the 'fairness', of a lordship were in direct proportion to its financial value. For the later medieval nobility and its advisers needed to be taught no lessons about the value of healthy finances; they recognized that status without means was an idle fiction, that lordship and wealth were closely dependent if not altogether synonymous,[2] and that therefore they must reap the maximum profit from their estates. This preoccupation with profit is evident wherever we look. It is manifest in the crabbed calculations of profit (*proficuum* or *valet*) which became increasingly fashionable in the margins of seignorial accounts; it is evident also in the evolution of a new financial document, the valor, whose express purpose was to give an overall view of the potential income of all the estates of a lord in a single year;[3] it appears again in the memoranda submitted to the lord's council especially by the auditors, for they abound with calculations of financial risks, with penny-pinching financial reforms and with a whole host of policies to maintain and to increase the lord's revenue;[4] it is written large in the pages of the seignorial surveys where the surveyors take an obvious pride in recording not only every

[1] *B.P.R.*, I, 96–7.

[2] G. A. Holmes, *The Estates of the Higher Nobility*, 4; K. B. McFarlane, *The Nobility of Later Medieval England*, 8–9.

[3] *Marcher Lordships of South Wales*, ed. T. B. Pugh, 154–7, 234–6; R. R. Davies *Ec.H.R.*, 2nd ser. 21 (1968), 214–18.

[4] A good example of such a memorandum is one on the affairs of the lordship of Narberth in the 1390s (B.L. Egerton Charters, 8718), submitted to the great council of the earl of March. It works out the profits to be made from a rearrangement of local offices and from the sale of timber over a number of years. Cf. Holmes, op. cit. 126–8.

item of the lord's revenue but also the ways, and the degree to which, it could be augmented.[5]

How profitable in fact were the Marcher lordships and what were the major sources of their revenue? For the answers to such questions we turn naturally to the account rolls of the lords and by and large they serve us well. They are, however, not without their shortcomings; to recognize these is to recognize the limitations of any answers we may provide. The distribution of the account rolls, both chronologically and geographically, is very uneven: Chirkland and Brecon, for example, are well provided and we shall draw heavily on their accounts; not so Glamorgan or Pembroke. Accounts for single years often survive but, valuable as they are, they have their own particular pitfalls: annual income fluctuated very considerably and deductions based on the yield (or the arrears) of a single year often distort the true picture of seignorial revenue. Even when the financial records are fairly abundant—and it is rare indeed for us to have the full range of accounts, local and central, for a single lordship for one year—they are not without their problems: to distinguish, and to do so consistently, between potential and actual income and between gross and clear yield is no mean feat for medieval auditor or modern historian.[6] Finally, though we shall argue that the income of most Marcher lordships shared certain general features, this should not be allowed to conceal from us the wide variations from one lordship to another and, indeed, from the rule of one lord to the next. As with all else that pertains to lordship, so with its finances: the personal attitude of the lord did much to determine the success of his policies.[7]

Beneath this individuality and diversity, however, it is possible to distinguish certain common features in the structure

[5] For example, *S.D.*, 323 calculates that the income of the lord could be increased by 10% (£110 : £1,100).

[6] T. B. Pugh, op. cit. 145–236 provides an excellent introduction to the nature and problems of the financial records of the Marcher lords.

[7] A notable example is the way in which Richard Fitzalan, earl of Arundel (d. 1397), applied his business acumen to husband the resources of the Mortimer estates while they were in the custody of a consortium headed by him, 1383–93. For Arundel's role in the consortium, see B.L. Egerton Roll, 8730; for his careful methods, see U.C.N.W. Whitney Collection, 316 (dilapidation costs extracted from Sir John Bromwich's executors); for a glowing tribute to the achievements of the consortium, see *Monasticon*, VI, i, 354.

of Marcher finances; it is to these common features rather than to the local variants—such as the importance of coal mining in the income of the lords of Gower or of the sale of wood and charcoal in that of the lords of Usk—that we must direct our attention. In the income of many Marcher lords, rents and farms formed the single most important and certainly the most stable category of revenue. A few selected figures may bear this out: in Chirkland in 1366 rents and farms accounted for £362 out of a gross income of £513; in the receivership of Monmouth for the three years 1386–8 for £1,351 out of £1,839 gross; in the Duchy of Lancaster estates in the March (Monmouth, Kidwelly, Ogmore and Brecon) in 1400 for £1,661 out of £2,576 gross; and in Newport in 1401 for £235 out of £537 gross.[8] If these figures are fairly representative, they indicate that it was from his role as a lord of land and of tenants and as a lord of demesne resources such as forests, mills, pastures and escheated lands that the lord of the March derived his most substantial and reliable income. That was often certainly the case; but it was not always so. In some lordships, often those with large Welshries racially and tenurially speaking, rents and farms do not play such a prominent role in the lord's revenue. The contrast is clear on the Lancaster estates in the March in 1386–8, for whereas rents and farms accounted for 73 per cent of the gross yield of the eastern lordship of Monmouth, that proportion fell to 41 per cent in the western lordship of Kidwelly.[9] Likewise in the Mortimer lordships of the middle March in the 1330s (then in royal custody) the rent roll brought in only some 19 per cent of the lord's revenue and most of that rent came from the English townships on the eastern border of the lordships.[10] These variations have more than a fiscal significance; they help to pinpoint the transition in the character of lordship from one district to another, often indeed within a single lordship. In other lordships of the March, particularly in the lowlands of the south-east, the profits of demesne production competed with rents and farms for primacy of place in the lord's revenue. But in general direct demesne production, whether

---

[8] N.L.W. Chirk Castle D. 28; D.L. 43/15/1–2; D.L. 29/728/11991; T. B. Pugh, op. cit. 150. All figures quoted in this chapter are to the nearest pound.

[9] D.L. 43/15/1–2.

[10] S.C. 6/1209/6 published by E. J. L. Cole in *Transactions of the Radnorshire Society* 23 (1963), 36–43.

arable or pastoral, did not occupy a leading place in the income of most Marcher lordships (as opposed to individual manors). Even in the Bohun complex of Marcher lordships (Brecon, Hay and Huntington), where the lord pursued arable farming on four manors and maintained very large herds of cows and sheep, demesne production (before the deduction of very high costs of £160) contributed but £273 out of a gross yield of £1,543.[11] Marcher revenue was never so heavily dependent on demesne profits that the decline of demesne farming would bring a financial crisis in its wake. Brecon again shows this well: by 1398 demesne farming had long since been entirely abandoned there, yet the gross yield of the lordship (less the lordship of Huntington and a third of Cantrefselyf worth between them *c.* £165 of the yield of 1372) still stood at the handsome figure of £1,405.[12] The strength of Marcher revenue, the 'fairness' of Marcher lordship, clearly lay elsewhere.

It lay in good part, as we have seen, in rents and in farms; in this respect it was not very different from the revenue of lordship in England.[13] It lay much more distinctively in court issues and extraordinary income, for it is with these two categories that the specifically Marcher features of the lord's revenue—and thereby of his lordship in general—stand out. The Brecon figures for 1398 just quoted illustrate the point forcibly: of the gross yield of £1,405, well over half (£778) came from court issues and extraordinary income. It is a situation common throughout the March, but largely unparalleled in England. Both categories of revenue deserve our close attention, for it is they above all which serve to explain the 'fairness' of Marcher lordship in the eyes of the medieval nobility.

Let us begin with court issues. Judicial lordship, as we have seen, was at its most ample in the March; nowhere is that more strikingly reflected than in the perquisites of justice. Here the records of the March speak with an unwonted uniformity: court issues were high in old lordships such as Caerleon, Usk and Newport as well as in more recent ones such as Maelienydd and Chirk.[14] Nor is this phenomenon of high court profits a one-

[11] S.C. 6/861/1; 1156/13–19 (1372).

[12] D.L. 29/633/10317; S.C. 6/1157/4. Huntington and a third of Cantrefselyf had been assigned to the duke of Gloucester in the partition of the Bohun estates.

[13] Cf. Holmes, op. cit. 112.

[14] In Caerleon and Usk in 1339 court issues accounted for £245 out of a gross

year wonder, as accounts for consecutive years amply show: in Chirkland in the decade 1340–50 (where only two receivers' accounts are wanting) they averaged £97 annually or 22.4 per cent of the gross yield; in the Lancaster lordships of Kidwelly and Brecon from 1412–20 (excluding 1419) they averaged £127 (19.8 per cent) and £232 (18.3 per cent) respectively.[15] Court issues, unlike rents and farms, inevitably fluctuated greatly from year to year; but in most Marcher lordships they normally contributed a significant proportion of the seignorial revenue. Indeed judicial lordship was not infrequently more profitable than landlordship. It was so, for example, in Maelienydd where in 1357 the profits of justice accounted for some 60 per cent of the lord's income (£129: £216); it was even more so in Lower Senghennydd (Glamorgan) in 1373 where 80 per cent of the revenue (£144: £179) came from this source.[16] Both these districts, it will be noticed, were Welsh upland areas; it is from such districts, not from the lowland manors, that the lord made his judicial fortune. This contrast in the geography of judicial profits in the March appears time and again: in Usk and Caerleon in 1339 £193 out of the total court issues of £245 came from the four Welsh bedelries; in Cantrefselyf (Brecon) 68 per cent of the Welsh bailiff's income in 1372 came from judicial profits but only 7 per cent of the income of the lowland manor of Bronllys; in nearby Hay in 1375 almost all the court issues (£31 10s. 4d. out of £32 10s. 2d.) were payable by the Welsh communities of the uplands;[17] in Clun likewise it was from the Welshry of Tempseter not from the lowland demesne manors around Clun that the bulk of the court income came.[18] The conclusion is fairly obvious: the lord's landlordship over the Welsh communities of his Marcher estates was, as we have

yield of £967, in Newport in 1401 for £244 out of £537: Holmes, op. cit. 146; T. B. Pugh, op. cit. 150. For Maelienydd and Chirk see below, p. 180.

[15] N.L.W. Chirk Castle D. 8–D. 15; R. R. Davies, 'The Bohun and Lancaster Lordships in Wales in the fourteenth and early fifteenth centuries' D.Phil. thesis (Univ. of Oxford, 1965), 372 based on D.L. 29/730/12016, 12018; 731/12019, 12021, 12023, 12026; 732/12030, 12031; 734/12047 (wrongly attributed to Henry VI in *P.R.O. Lists and Indexes*, V (i), 89).

[16] *Transactions of the Radnorshire Society* 24 (1964), 31–9; *Cartae*, IV, no. 1040.

[17] Holmes, op. cit. 146; S.C. 6/1156/13, 14; S.C. 6/1157/2.

[18] Thus in Clunton and Kempton court issues were only of minimal importance in 1372 (£1: £37), whereas in the Welshry of Tempseter they regularly formed the most important source of revenue—£51: £76 in 1383; £90: £108 in 1385 and £33: £58 in 1413: S.R.O. 552/1A/4, 6, 7, 12.

seen, often confined to a few fixed renders; but in financial terms this weakness of landlordship was more than amply compensated by the astonishing profitability of judicial lordship. Furthermore, the central role played by court issues in the structure of Marcher revenue immediately distinguished Marcher lordship from lordship in England. The contrast was plain to see: the Marcher courts of Elizabeth Burgh, for example, brought her more profit than did all her English courts put together, and likewise in 1401 the judicial income from the single Marcher lordship of Newport was well in excess of all that the earl of Stafford collected from the courts of his extensive English estates.[19] Nor was this importance of court issues, as far as we can see, a late development prompted in some way by an attempt to bolster seignorial incomes in an age of declining profits. The perquisites of justice were already a major constituent of Marcher income in the early fourteenth century: the Fitzalan surveyors in 1301 already expected them to account for £119 out of the yield of £317 for Clun; in the earliest receiver's account for Chirkland, that of 1323, they already contributed £119 or some 40 per cent of the gross yield: likewise by the 1320s the Dyffryn Clwyd courts yielded an average income of about £100 annually which they were to maintain for the rest of the century.[20]

The profits of justice came from a variety of sources, some of which were only peripherally judicial in character. The fees for the succession to and the transfer of land contributed a very substantial, often the major share, of such profits;[21] fines imposed on tenants more in respect of the coercive powers of lordship than of its judicial authority strictly speaking—fines for failure to perform services or to pay tolls, for forest offences, for disobedience pure and simple and so forth—also contributed handsomely towards these profits. Even within the more strictly judicial sphere, the lord's financial interests were prominent—in the exaction of amercements for failure to prosecute or to appear in court as well as for conviction, in the fees paid for the

[19] Holmes, op. cit. 145–7; Pugh, op. cit. 150.
[20] *Fitzalan Surveys*, ed. M. Clough, 52–65; N.L.W. Chirk Castle, D. 1; S.C. 2/216/3 (courts of Dyffryn Clwyd, 1322): £107; S.C. 2/216/5 (courts of same, 1325): £92.
[21] See above pp. 143–5; for the importance of entry fines and heriots in the manorial courts of Newport lordship see Pugh, op. cit. 172–5.

benefits of his justice, in a share of the damages awarded to parties in civil actions, in fines for settling out of court and, very profitably, in the forfeited chattels of felons and intestates.[22] Over and above these court profits were the fines, often separately itemized in the accounts in respect both of their financial importance and of their character: they were offered to the lord before or after conviction to bring the case to a premature end (*finis*) and in order to secure the lord's favour and thereby to avoid the prospect of a more dire punishment. They were a major source of judicial revenue, whether imposed on individuals—we hear of Madoc Llwyd of Chirkland making a fine of £100 with his lord[23]—or on communities. Their importance in the March was greatly enhanced by the widespread practice which we have already noticed of redeeming the lives and lands of convicted felons by payment of a fine to the lord. In many Marcher lordships fines augmented the profits of justice very considerably, even doubled them on occasion.[24] Of these fines one category deserves a special mention in the present context: these are the fines, often fixed in amount by Welsh custom, which were paid by the local communities for wrongful judgements subsequently reversed on appeal either by hired experts in Welsh law or by the lord's council.[25] Thus the *patria* of Oswestry was dunned in a sum of a hundred marks for such a wrongful judgement in the 1360s and the community of Bromfield and Yale was mulcted in a like sum in 1382.[26] Justice and profit were close accomplices in the March.

Nor have we in fact exhausted the emoluments of justice in the March, for they also figure prominently in the other distinctive category of Marcher income, that of casual revenue.[27] 'Casual' and 'extraordinary' were the contemporary terms for this category of revenue: they referred to the fact that such

[22] Above pp. 138, 164–5, 173–4.
[23] N.L.W. Chirk Castle, D. 11 (1344). He was doubtless Madoc Llwyd ab Iorwerth Foel of Bryncunallt. Cf. the fine of £200 on Almaric Weedon, later reduced by the lord of Dyffryn Clwyd to £60: S.C. 2/216/13, m. 1.
[24] The following examples of the proportion of fines to other court profits (less fines) may illustrate this point. Dyffryn Clwyd 1359, £53 : £68; 1360, £28 : £47; 1367, £16 : £65; 1368, £46 : £42; Kidwelly 1395, £70 : £135.
[25] See above p. 164 and, for fuller references, R. R. Davies in *History* 51 (1966), 160.   [26] N.L.W. Aston Hall, 6916; S.C. 6/1305/7.
[27] This whole question has been much illuminated, especially for the fifteenth century, by T. B. Pugh, op. cit. 145–9.

revenue was not part of the regular, annual income of the lord (as were rents, farms and profits of court) but, like parliamentary taxes in the king of England's income, was an occasional feature of his budgets. The pretexts for raising such casual revenue were many; and though there was much overlap between them we can for convenience divide them into several categories. Some, as we have suggested, arose out of the lord's judicial power in its most ample sense. Notable among these were the communal fines which Marcher communities were obliged to pay to their lord from time to time to placate his wrath for some dereliction of duty or for some offence in derogation of his authority. The men of Gower, for example, paid their lord a thousand marks in the late-thirteenth century for certain unspecified offences; the bondmen of Mochnant and Cynllaith in Chirkland were fined £40 in 1379 for their 'disobedience' and the community of Nanheudwy in the same lordship were likewise fined £135 for not carrying timber to their lord as was their duty.[28] The lord of Brecon likewise manufactured a host of varying reasons for mulcting his tenants: 100 marks for wrongful judgement; £400 for acquiring land without permission; £500 for evading the earl's tolls; £720 for attacking the men of the lordship of Builth—all of them within the space of five years, 1352–7.[29] The arbitrariness of lordship rarely weighed more heavily on the March than in these communal fines, imposed wilfully and exacted relentlessly. The earl of Arundel, that most masterful and resourceful of Marcher lords, even made such fines retroactive: in 1348 he levied a communal fine on Chirkland for forest offences committed 'in the time of his father' who had died a mere twenty-two years previously![30]

To this category of communal fines a new and, as it proved, invaluable item was added during the course of the fourteenth century—the fines offered for redeeming the sessions in eyre, either before they were held or in order to bring them to an early close, in return for a general pardon.[31] The men of Haverford we know for certain paid such a fine in 1392[32] and

---

[28] E. 159/66, m. 11 v (this fine was made before 1290); N.L.W. Chirk Castle, D. 35, D. 51.   [29] D.L. 29/671/10810, m. 20–m. 23.
[30] N.L.W. Chirk Castle, D. 14.
[31] For this practice see above p. 174.
[32] *Cal. Public Records re. Pembrokeshire*, I, 52; for the appointment of justices in Pembroke and Haverford, *C.P.R. 1377–81*, 133, 570.

by the early-fifteenth century the primarily fiscal purpose of such sessions was openly acknowledged. The council of the Duchy of Lancaster, for example, threatened either to hold the sessions in Wales 'or eles that ye King may be contended and answered of as good a fyne or betre as he has be at oyere sessions yere holde before yis tyme'.[33] 'Good' those fines certainly were. They formed a major item in the lord's casual revenue: the sessions of June 1375 in Brecon, for example, yielded £1,800 as a 'gift',[34] while those held in the Lancaster estates in the March in 1413 realized almost £3,000.[35] Already by the 1420s and possibly earlier many of these general fines for the redeeming of the sessions had been placed on a fixed basis and were to remain one of the most distinctive features of Marcher finances.[36] If we add these redemption fines to the already large profits of the local courts we begin to appreciate the dramatic significance of the judicial authority of the Marcher lords in the make-up of their finances.

The categories of casual revenue we have discussed so far have about them a judicial or quasi-judicial appearance; there remain other categories of casual income whose justification was different. They masquerade under a series of largely euphemistic names—'gifts', 'aids', 'tallages', 'mises', 'subsidies'. Some were gifts given on the lord's succession to or first entry into his lordship as tokens of 'his superiority and new lordship and regality' (the phrase is used in the Lancaster lordships): Earl Humphrey of Hereford, for example, took such aids from his men of Brecon between 1337 and 1341 while Earl Roger of March used the occasion of his progress through his Welsh estates in 1393 (on reaching his majority) to exact like gifts.[37]

[33] D.L. 42/18, f. 146 (1440).   [34] S.C. 6/1156/18.
[35] The records of these sessions are in J.I. 1/1152–3; the profits they yielded are recorded in D.L. 29/731/12019.
[36] See, in general Pugh, op. cit. 36–43 and for the fines for the redemption of sessions in the Principality, R. A. Griffiths, 'Royal Government in the Southern Counties of the Principality of Wales, 1422–85' (Ph.D. thesis, Univ. of Bristol, 1962), 57 ff. The practice of redeeming the sessions was also well-known in fourteenth-century England; see *The English Government at Work III: 1327–36*, ed. J. F. Willard, W. A. Morris and W. H. Dunham jnr. (Cambridge, Mass., 1950), 14–15 and J. G. Edwards, 'Taxation and Consent in the Court of Common Pleas, 1338', *E.H.R.* 57 (1942), 473–82.
[37] D.L. 29/671/10810, m. 1–m. 5; B.L. Egerton Rolls 8736, 8739–41. In the mesne lordship of Caldicot, the earl of Buckingham received three barrels of wine worth £16 on his first visit as lord in 1384: D.L. 29/680/11007.

Others took the form of gifts given either for the grant or for the confirmation of charters of liberties to Marcher communities: the charter of Maelienydd in 1297 cost the community £500, those of Kidwelly and Iscennen in 1356 £300, while the three charters granted to the men of Chirkland between 1324 and 1355 brought the Fitzalans the princely sum of £2,933 6s. 8d.[38] Nor does that by any means exhaust the occasions on which the lord of the March could call on the financial aid of his Welsh tenantry. He would do so when he led an expedition in the service of the king (as did the earl of Surrey from the men of Bromfield and Yale in 1339);[39] he would do so again when his daughter was married (as did the earl of Arundel from his tenants of Chirkland in 1325);[40] he would do so frequently without giving a reason, simply demanding a gift or a subsidy for the sake of his finances.[41]

Whatever the pretexts, casual revenue became an increasingly important and frequent item of Marcher income in the fourteenth century. Its frequency may occasionally be gauged from the accounts: in Brecon during the twenty years 1337–58 some item of casual revenue (totalling almost £4,000) was demanded by the lord on at least ten occasions and since many of these subsidies were paid in instalments rarely a year passed without the men of Brecon contributing towards such subsidies; in Chirkland, likewise, it has been calculated that the tenants paid almost without a break for forty years for their charters of liberties and in addition proffered several other gifts to the lord; in Dyffryn Clwyd we have record of at least seven extraordinary grants being given to the lord between 1338 and 1371.[42] What

[38] *C.P.R. 1292–1301*, 290; D.L. 42/16, fol. 43ᵛ–fol. 45ᵛ; Llinos Smith, 'The Arundel Charters to the Lordship of Chirk in the Fourteenth Century', *B.B.C.S.* 23 (1969), 153–66.

[39] S.C. 2/226/17, m. 1 (200 marks). For war-subsidies given by men of Chirkland see above p. 83. Cf. the gift requested by the Black Prince from the men of Flint in 1346 towards his forthcoming expedition: *B.P.R.*, I, 34.

[40] N.L.W. Chirk Castle D. 3. Cf. the subsidy of 20 marks granted by men of Dyffryn Clwyd towards the marriage of the lord's daughter: S.C. 2/221/13, m. 33 (1437). For other similar feudal aids see Pugh, op. cit. 147–8.

[41] For example, the men of Tempseter (Clun) gave a 'gift' of forty marks to their lord in 1334 and another one in 1399 (S.R.O. 552/1/3, m. 2; 1/30, m. 4); the men of Denbigh gave a 'subsidy' of 480 marks to the Black Prince in 1370 (S.C. 6/1183/3) and the men of Aberedw and Colwyn (Elfael) a 'common gift' of £8 in 1403 to the earl of Warwick (B.L. Egerton Roll 8770).

[42] For Brecon, see R. R. Davies, D.Phil. thesis, 150–2, 403 based on D.L.

had been occasional and extraordinary was becoming regular and ordinary. That is reflected in the fact that by the early fifteenth century some of these extraordinary dues—such as the mises paid on the entry of a new lord or the fines for redeeming the sessions—were becoming fixed in quantity and were standardized at a rate to be maintained until the sixteenth century.[43]

They were certainly heavy in their incidence. Accounts for consecutive years are difficult to come by but such as we have point in the same direction: in Brecon in the decade 1337–46 casual revenue accounted for 25 per cent of the money collected by the receiver; in Chirkland in a comparable period, 1340–50, it constituted on an annual average £87 or 20 per cent of the gross receipts; in Kidwelly and Brecon in the years 1412–20 the proportion reached the astonishing figure of 39 per cent. Such figures, exaggerated as these examples may possibly be, call for comment, for they draw attention to a category of seignorial income which was unparalleled, at least in its magnitude, outside the March. The lords in England might tallage their serfs and might on occasion call for an aid from their feudal tenants; but the income they derived from these sources was paltry compared with the extraordinary revenue which they could levy in the March. Figures once more speak louder than words: in the years 1412–20 (excluding 1419) the southern English estates of the Duchy of Lancaster yielded £1,477 in casual revenue to Henry V compared with a massive £6,393 from his Marcher estates. Nor does the contrast end there, for whereas most of the English casual income came by way of the profits of feudal wardship and marriage and was thus largely payable by well-to-do individuals, the Marcher casual revenue was truly communal in its incidence. It weighed on all the inhabitants alike and may indeed, as in the case of court issues, have discriminated unfairly as between Welshries

---

29/671/10810; for Chirk, Llinos Smith in *B.B.C.S.* 23 (1969), 159. The Dyffryn Clwyd grants (variously called mise, subsidy, common fine and gift) were made in 1338, 1345, 1351, 1361, 1365, 1369, 1371.

[43] Thus by 1400 the mises payable on the Lancaster estates had been established at £241 13s. 4d. for Kidwelly; £513 6s. 8d. for Brecon and Hay and £66 13s. 4d. for Monmouth: see R. R. Davies, D.Phil. thesis, 366. For the standardizing of the rates for redeeming the sessions see Pugh, op. cit. 37–8.

and English districts.[44] It was in fact a virtual form of taxation. Indeed it was levied at a rate comparable to or even higher than English parliamentary taxation in the fourteenth century: in Chirkland, for example, a fifteenth on moveables levied by Edward I in 1292 realized £67;[45] for much of the fourteenth century the men of the lordship paid more than that to their lord annually in casual revenue. It is little wonder that they should refer to their contribution as 'the great tax' (*y dreth fawr*); nor does it come as a surprise to learn that Henry V should claim that the March's exemption from parliamentary subsidies was in itself a reason for demanding from the Duchy of Lancaster lordships there a grant towards his wars.[46] In fact, from the incomplete evidence at our disposal we can hardly doubt that the March in the fourteenth century was taxed at least as heavily and as regularly as was England. But with this difference: it was taxed in the interests of its lords not of the king.

Here was a major reason why Marcher lordship was such an attractive prospect to English lords. Financially, Marcher lordship *was* different: the profits of justice and casual revenue assured that it was so. Let us return to our overworked accounts: 46.4 per cent of the receiver of Brecon's charge 1337–46, 42.5 per cent of the gross yield of Chirk 1340–50, and 58 per cent of the gross yield of Brecon and Kidwelly 1412–20 came from these twin sources. We may have laboured the point but we do so in the belief that we are here at the very heart of the distinctiveness of Marcher lordship. The financial lordship of the lords Marcher had to it dimensions—notably in judicial affairs and in taxative powers—which in England had largely, if not exclusively, been appropriated by the king. It is here that we grasp most forcibly the character of Marcher lordship; it is here that we realize what made the Marcher lords 'lords royal'.

We may grasp it yet more clearly if we seek to gauge how much wealth flowed from the March into the coffers of the English nobility in the fourteenth century. It is an exercise

---

[44] Thus in the Duchy of Lancaster lordships 1412–20, 39% of the gross income of Brecon and Kidwelly came from casuals but only 7·1% of that of Monmouth: R. R. Davies, D.Phil. thesis, 372.

[45] E. 179/242/55.

[46] D.L. 42/17, fol. 238ᵛ–fol. 239 (1420). He had in fact obtained a war subsidy totalling £1,173 6s. 8d. from these Marcher lordships in 1417: D.L. 29/731/12026.

fraught with problems, but well worth undertaking at least in general terms in order to show the profitability of Marcher lordship. Several Marcher lordships were worth near £1,000 gross or more per annum—Glamorgan, Brecon, Denbigh and Bromfield and Yale most notably; several others, including Newport, Monmouth, Abergavenny, Kidwelly, and Usk and Caerleon came into the £500 plus bracket; others we can place fairly confidently in the £250 plus category, including Oswestry, Dyffryn Clwyd, Clun, Chirkland, Ceri and Cydewain, Gower and Pembroke.[47] Reservations we may certainly have about these figures; even so they remain impressive, the more so if we recall that £1,000 of landed revenue was regarded as ample competence for an earl in the fourteenth century.[48] In fact several noble families drew more than that amount from their Marcher estates alone: such was the case with the houses of Lancaster, Hastings,[49] Bohun and Despenser, while those of Fitzalan and Mortimer, like that of Clare in an earlier generation,[50] belonged to the £2,000 plus group in respect of their Marcher lands. The political importance of the Marcher lordships to the English nobility has long been appreciated; their financial contribution has not so often been duly recognized. The case of the earls of March is not surprising in view of their title: in 1398 it was estimated that £2,409 out of a clear yield of almost £3,400 came from their Marcher lands.[51] But other instances are more surprising: almost 38 per cent of the landed income of the rich dowager, Lady Elizabeth Burgh, came from her Marcher estates, a third of the earl of Hereford's income by the 1370s, two-thirds of that of the Lords Despenser, between a

[47] See Appendix below pp. 196–8.

[48] Holmes, op. cit. 4, 23 and McFarlane, op. cit. 159–60, taking the higher endowment of the earl of Northampton in 1337 as a guideline.

[49] I have found no reliable valuations for Cilgerran and Ystlwyf, but as Abergavenny was worth, conservatively, £550–£600 gross and Pembroke £320 the Hastings family's estates in the March must have been worth £1,000+ gross. The remarks in the text do not make allowance for minorities or dower-portions.

[50] The value of the Clare estates in the March was given in the partition of 1317 as £2,523. The estimate is possibly on the high side: *Glam. C.H.*, III, 603.

[51] These figures are based on the valuations of the Mortimer estates made after the death of Earl Roger (d. 1398) in preparation for the assignment of dower to his widow: S.C. 11/23; B.L. Egerton Charters 8753. The value of the Marcher estates includes Wigmore (£120) and the excess realized on Builth and Montgomery (£38 6s. 8d.) both held at farm; but no value is given for some Mortimer lordships in the March such as Ewyas Lacy.

third and a quarter of the earl of Stafford's landed revenue, and some 15 per cent of the huge territorial fortune of John of Gaunt,[52] while the great wealth of the house of Fitzalan was based in good part on the annual landed income of its Marcher estates, estimated in 1351 at £1,732 (on the low side) and by 1397 at £2,154.[53] In the light of these figures the gloating over the 'very fine and great' and 'fair' lordships of the March is understandable as is the striving for an estate there.

Most of this Marcher income appears to have been collected vigorously and successfully by the lord's officials in the fourteenth century. The problem of arrears, it is true, appears to have been more acute on the Marcher estates of a lord than on English ones and understandably so in view of the financial pressure on them; but it does not seem to have made major inroads into the lord's revenue as yet. Take the case of the earl of Arundel. His income from the March was near if not over £2,000 annually by mid-century and his officials there handed £2,428 to him in the financial year 1370.[54] In the light of these figures the arrears of his officers in the March in 1376 amounting to £437 (excluding allowances and instalment payments) were modest indeed. Those arrears almost certainly had accumulated over a number of years but only £61 of them did his auditors place in the category of 'ancient desperate debts'.[55] They were clearly hopeful about the rest; we have no reason to doubt their judgement. For what we know of other Marcher lords in the fourteenth century suggests that they coped ably and on the whole highly successfully with the problem of arrears. They meant to exact the last penny of their profits from the March.[56]

Little enough of that profit was spent in the March itself. Local expenditure naturally varied considerably from one year to the next and from one lordship to another. Among the most important determining factors were the costs of demesne farming—they accounted for half of the local expenses on the Bohun estates in 1372 (£161 : £320)—or of the personal visits of the

[52] See S.C. 11/799, 801 (Burgh); R. R. Davies, D.Phil. thesis, 157–8 (Bohun); 74–5 (Lancaster); *Glam. C.H.*, III, 608, n. 102 (Despenser); Pugh, op. cit. 149 (Stafford).
[53] S.R.O. 552/1A/1; *C. Inq. Misc. 1392–9*, 227, 229, 233–5.
[54] Shrewsbury Public Library 5923 (List of Arundel assets in the March 1370–1).
[55] B.L. Harleian 4840, fol. 393ᵛ.
[56] See R. R. Davies, *Ec.H.R.* 2nd ser. 21 (1968), 211–29.

lord (hence the relatively high local expenses in Chirkland in the early 1340s); but as neither factor was a significant feature of Marcher life, local expenditure was generally kept low. The construction of a mill or of a weir or extensive repairs to castles might occasionally augment local expenses; but on the whole administrative overheads—such as the fees of officials or the costs of holding courts—were the major items in such expenses. By and large, the lord could expect that somewhere between 70 and 90 per cent of the gross revenue of his Marcher estates would be at his disposal. Some of it might be assigned in annuities or as payments to his creditors; some might be earmarked for the expenses of his household or for items of personal expenditure; most of it would be delivered to one of his central financial officers such as the wardrober or the receiver-general or to the lord in person. There was little thought of capital formation, of investing the profits of lordship in the local estates, with the exception of some purchase of stock or of the occasional loan to a local merchant. The income was the personal fortune of the lord to be spent as he wished, largely on his personal magnificence and pleasures, in building, on conspicuous consumption and even more conspicuous waste, on maintaining the status of lordship in peace and in war, and in a minor degree on investment in land or in loans to others.[57] Wealth flowed from the March to the English nobility; very little of it returned there. 'Good' lordship was not unknown in the March; but for the most part lordship there was more than usually parasitic.

The Marcher lords waxed rich; many of them waxed even richer during the course of the fourteenth century. They did so mainly by acquiring more estates in the March, normally through the accidents of marriage or the munificence of the Crown. The profits of individual lordships may occasionally have declined; but as there were fewer Marcher families by the end of the century than at the beginning there was more of the Marcher cake to be divided among those that survived.[58] None did better than the house of Fitzalan: its Marcher income was estimated fairly reliably at £545 in 1301; by 1397 that sum had

[57] On noble expenditure see K. B. McFarlane, *The Nobility of Later Medieval England*, 83–101, and R. H. Hilton, 'Rent and Capital Formation in Feudal Society', *Proceedings of the Second International Conference of Economic History, Aix-en-Provence* (1962), II, 33–68.
[58] Cf. above pp. 58–9.

almost quadrupled to £2,154.[59] In terms of personal fortunes—
and those were the only terms which mattered to the family—
such a large increase reduced any fluctuations in the income of
individual lordships to the insignificant. The Fitzalans are the
outstanding example, closely paralleled by the Mortimers;
but the point applies equally to all families to some degree. It
was along the lines of marriage and politics (and war profits)
that noble fortunes were made and unmade, not in terms of the
yield of individual manors. That is as true of the March as it is of
England.[60]

Even in terms of the yield of individual lordships, some
Marcher lords certainly grew wealthier during the course of the
fourteenth century. There are some *prima facie* reasons why this
should be so. Few Marcher lords were by mid-century arable
demesne farmers on a large scale—at least in proportion to the
rest of their Marcher revenue—so that their income was not
likely to be affected in a major fashion by the agrarian problems,
notably the rising cost of labour, which beset many English
landlords. The Marcher lords, it is true, continued and even
intensified their interest in pastoral farming throughout the
century, but that remained a profitable enterprise. Most
Marcher income, as we have seen, came from other sources.
Much of it came from fixed renders paid by the community
regardless of fluctuations in its numbers; such renders were far
less likely than individual rents to respond to a decline in
population or to an economic recession. A great deal of the
remainder of Marcher income came from court issues and
casual income, both of them items which fluctuated more in
response to the whim of the seignorial will than to that of any
economic movement. On a negative level, local costs in the
March in the fourteenth century were at a minimum: neither
the heavy military expenses which consumed so much of
Marcher income in the thirteenth century nor the lavish fees
which often undermined Marcher revenue in the fifteenth
century made heavy inroads into the gross income. *Ex hypothesi*,
the fourteenth century was the heyday of Marcher finance.

That hypothesis is not without factual support. The Bohun

---

[59] *Fitzalan Surveys*, ed. M. Clough, 51–74; *C. Inq. Misc. 1392–9*, 227, 229, 233-5.
For the growth of the Arundel estates, see above pp. 56–8.

[60] The point has been forcefully made by K. B. McFarlane, *Nobility*, esp. 186, 212.

complex of Marcher estates (Brecon, Hay and Huntington) affords once more some of the most telling evidence.[61] The value of these estates increased by at least 40 per cent between 1337 and 1372 and the increase continued to the end of the century. Part of that increase was achieved by a process of territorial consolidation within the lordship which we have already traced;[62] about a sixth of the gross yield of 1372 (£1,543) came from the fruits of the careful estate-building of Earl Humphrey of Hereford (d. 1361) and his brother Earl William of Northampton (d. 1360). Even more significant in the present context was the increase in the yield of the lordship achieved by a deliberate and sustained policy of raising rents and leases. The figures are an impressive tribute to the estate management of the Bohun family. The major render paid by the Welshmen of Brecon to their lord, a biennial cow-tribute (*commorth*), was more than doubled in eighteen years (1340–58) from £36 to £81, both by increasing the number of cows payable from 108 to 134 and more significantly by raising the commuted value of each cow gradually from 6s. 8d. to 12s. 0d.[63] Equally spectacular results were achieved in the major leases of the lordship (those of Brecon town, the Great and Little Forests and the *leyrwyt*); they rose by 117 per cent between 1340 and 1399 (£142 : £308). If to these increases we add the court issues and the casual income we can hardly doubt that the value of Brecon lordship overall doubled during the fourteenth century. The rate of increase of seignorial income may have been exceptional in the case of Brecon; but the increase itself was certainly not unique. The value of the estates of the house of Lancaster in Wales improved by 25 per cent between the 1330s and the 1380s partly by the acquisition of more land (especially the commote of Iscennen in 1340) but also in good part by the relentless exploitation of court issues and casual income.[64] Again in the Fitzalan lordship of Chirk the gross yield rose steadily from just under £400 in the early 1340s to well over £500 by the mid-1360s, though later it was to fall off

[61] For documentation see R. R. Davies, D.Phil. thesis, 152–8.
[62] Above pp. 92–5.
[63] In Hay in 1374 the tenants challenged the lord's right to exact more than 7s. per cow as *commorth* rate: S.C. 6/1156/21, m. 1ᵛ.
[64] Based on a comparison of the valors of 1331–2 and those of 1386–8 and 1391: D.L. 40/1/11, fol. 45v, fol. 50; D.L. 43/15/1–3.

somewhat. In this case, as in that of Brecon, the increase came as much from pressure on rents and farms as from the exploitation of court and casual revenue.[65] If these three examples (selected because the graph of income can be traced over a number of years) are at all representative, they suggest that Marcher lordship was not only profitable, but continuously and increasingly so for much of the fourteenth century.

Such a high level of seignorial income could only be achieved by unremitting financial pressure on the tenantry of the March. 'Ad maximum detrimentum possidentium' (the phrase is that of the Earl of Gloucester, himself a prominent Marcher magnate)[66] could well have been the motto of many Marcher lords. Their policy is written large in the accounts: defaulting officials were fined and imprisoned; tenants in arrears with their rents had their goods distrained; rentals were commissioned with the express purpose of increasing the lord's profit;[67] commands were frequently issued for the speedy collection and dispatch of local revenue; special commissioners were dispatched to supervise local administration and to expedite the collection of the lord's revenue.[68] Once more figures speak more eloquently than words of the consequences of such pressure: in 1349 at least 568 head of livestock were impounded from the earl of Hereford's debtors in Brecon and a further 167 oxen and steers were purchased from the sale of their goods; in the decade 1337–46 the receiver of the lordship collected well over £7,000 for his lord and only some 2 per cent of his 'charge' was outstanding at the end of the period.[69] Like figures could be quoted from other lordships. They point in the direction of a harsh, almost merciless, efficiency of the financial administration of the Marcher lords. Occasionally they went too far: the 1315–16

[65] The gross yield of the lordship less court and casual revenue rose from an annual average of £260 in the mid 1340s to almost £400 in the mid 1360s: N.L.W. Chirk Castle D. 11–D. 13, D. 25–D. 28; Llinos Smith, Ph.D. thesis, 'The Lordships of Chirk and Oswestry 1282–1415', Ph.D. thesis (Univ. of London, 1971), 183–7.

[66] Quoted in R. H. Hilton, *A Medieval Society*, 132.

[67] Note, for example, the entry on a Lancaster account of 1378—'memorandum ad faciendum unum novum rentalem quia dicitur quod multum proficiet domino': D.L. 29/594/9507.

[68] William Bagot and John Bromwich were given such a commission in Kidwelly in 1389 and to startlingly good effect, as the payment of arrears in the next few years shows: D.L. 29/584/9239.

[69] D.L. 29/671/10810, m. 16; R. R. Davies, D.Phil. thesis, 154.

revolt in Glamorgan was probably prompted in good part by the ruthless financial regime of the custodians of the lordship;[70] even the hard-pressed receiver of Brecon was driven to protest in 1340 that he could not collect £618 of his charge 'because of poverty, as the tenants had nothing';[71] the lord of Dyffryn Clwyd was compelled in the late fourteenth century to reduce some rents because of protests from his tenants and the difficulty of letting land;[72] the growing arrears figures, difficult as they are to interpret, suggest that as the century drew on the gap between income claimed and income collected was greater than most lords were prepared to concede. Already there were indications that all was not well with Marcher income: the profits from Usk and Caerleon seem to have fallen sharply during the course of the century;[73] in large lordships such as Denbigh and Chirk the high level of income of mid-century was not always maintained thereafter and the same was true of smaller mesne lordships such as Ogmore or Caldicot.[74]

Yet it would be quite misleading to end on a sombre note. The fourteenth century was, on the whole, an era of high and even increasing profits for most Marcher lords; it was a period when new sources of finance were exploited and when the distinctiveness of Marcher revenue stood out more clearly than ever before or after. The great crisis of Marcher revenue, in which the income of many of the major lordships would collapse dramatically, lay as yet in the future.[75] In the meantime Marcher lordship was at its most profitable. Convoys of bullion left the March throughout the year bearing its wealth to the

[70] *Glam. C.H.*, III, 75–6.

[71] D.L. 29/671/10810 m. 4.

[72] Between 1379 and 1383 he remitted at least £3 1s. 2d. of the annual rent of his bond tenants because of the sharp fall in their numbers: S.C. 2/219/13, m. 13, m. 28; 220/1, m. 26; 220/3, m. 8.

[73] The gross value of Usk and Caerleon in 1330 was £1,191, in 1339 £967; by 1398 their valuation stood at £467: S.C. 11/799, 801, 23. Such a sharp fall suggests that the figures are in some way not comparable.

[74] For Denbigh, see Holmes, op. cit. 98–100; in Chirk a change in the accounting methods makes comparisons difficult but contemporary notes of profit suggest that average income fell from £500+ in the 1360s to £400+ in the 1380s and 1390s; for Ogmore *Glam. C.H.*, III, 300; for Caldicot, R. R. Davies, D.Phil. thesis, 227–9.

[75] The crisis which undermined the revenue of many Marcher lordships in the fifteenth century has not been fully studied; but its dimensions have been amply suggested in the studies of T. B. Pugh in *Glam. C.H.*, III, 190 (Glamorgan); 256–8 (Gower); 683, n. 96 (Denbigh); and in *The Marcher Lordships of South Wales*, 160, 175–7 (Newport and Brecon).

noble residences of England: in December 1387 it required an escort of eleven archers to accompany the treasure-carts laden with £1,400 of the yield of the Mortimer estates from Wigmore to London.[76] Alternatively the fruits of lordship could be hoarded in the castles of the March to be spent or lent as occasion required: the auditors of the earl of Arundel could gloatingly report that his coffers in the March, probably at Holt and Clun, contained over £19,000 in ready cash at Michaelmas 1370.[77] Either way Marcher lordship paid handsomely; the Marcher lords made sure of that. Never was a Marcher lordship a more 'fair' prospect for an English lord than in the fourteenth century. But that 'fairness' was bought at the price of mounting financial pressure on Marcher society, particularly native society, at the very time when the population of the area was drastically reduced. The financial success of Marcher lordship thereby contributed substantially to the discontent which erupted into rebellion under Owain Glyn Dŵr's leadership in 1400.

[76] B.L. Egerton Roll, 8730.
[77] Shrewsbury Public Library 5923. By Michaelmas 1371 £6,649 remained in the coffers at Holt, £3,267 in those at Clun and £11,193 was outstanding as loans advanced to various persons. On 13 July 1375 his Marcher hoard stood at £10,981: B.L. Harleian 4840, fol. 393.

APPENDIX

Valuations of Marcher Lordships

1 ABERGAVENNY (H): £667 (1348); £505 clear (1386); £529 clear (1387)
2 BRECON, HAY, HUNTINGTON (B): £1,543 (1372); £1,313 (1374); £1,187 (1375); £1,405 (1398)
3 BROMFIELD AND YALE (F): £831 (1351); £967 clear (1397)
4 BUILTH (M): £200 (1398)
5 CAERLEON AND USK (M): £746 (1317); £1,191 (1330); £967 (1339); £467 (1398)
6 CAUS (S): £264 (1401)
7 CERI AND CYDEWAIN (M): £294 (1360); £320 ? clear (1398)
8 CHIRK (F): See text, p. 000; £414 clear (1397)
9 CLUN (F): £398 (1351); £251 clear (1397); £256 (1404)
10 DENBIGH (M): £1,100 (1334); £1,000 (1344); £1,199 (1397); £904 ? clear (1398)
11 DYFFRYN CLWYD: £545 (1308); £492 (1323)
12 ELFAEL (W): £?194 clear (1397)
13 GLAMORGAN (D): £1,276 (1317); £1,201 (1349); £1,037 (1375)
14 GOWER (W): £300 (1316); £386 (1400)
15 HAVERFORD: £161 (1325); £153 (1355)
16 KIDWELLY (L): £333 (1331); £291 (1332); £517 (1386–91); £522 (1395)
17 ISCENNEN (L): £138 (1386–91); £158 (1395)
18 MAELIENYDD (M): £216 (1357); £160 (1360); £334 ? clear (1398)
19 MONMOUTH (L): £514 (1331); £619 (1332); £527 (1386–91); £509 (1395)
20 NARBERTH (M): £47 (1360); £94 (1366)
21 NEWPORT (S): £459 (1317); £537 (1401)
22 OSWESTRY (F): £233 (1351); £376 clear (1397)
23 PEMBROKE (H): £247 (1324); £320 (1349)
24 RADNOR AND GWERTHRYNION (M): £314 (1339)
25 WIGMORE (M): £120 ? clear (1398)

This appendix has the very limited purpose of indicating in very broad terms the relative value of some, but not all, of the major Marcher lordships at certain points in the fourteenth century. Its shortcomings are compounded of the deficiencies of the documentation and of my own patchy knowledge of it. The reliance to be placed on individual figures varies considerably according to the nature of the source and it would be hazardous, even foolish, to draw any deductions from a comparison of the valuations of individual years. Nevertheless the appendix will have served its purpose if it suggests the dimensions of the yield (gross unless otherwise stated) of some of the Marcher lordships and the scale of the income that major English families might draw from them.

The following abbreviations have been used to designate the ownership of the lordships in 1370.

B = Bohun   D = Despenser F = Fitzalan H = Hastings
L = Lancaster M = Mortimer   S = Stafford W = Beauchamp

For the two largest Marcher inheritances of the late-fourteenth century, those of Fitzalan and Mortimer, two sources have been used recurrently in the following tables, viz. the royal inquisitions into the Fitzalan estates in 1397 (*C. Inq. Misc. 1392–9* nos. 228–35) and the dower valuation of the Mortimer lands in 1398–9 (S.C. 11/23; also B. L. Egerton Roll, 8753). Both sources appear to be fairly accurate where we can compare them with local accounts.

Notes to Appendix to Chapter 8
(these refer to each numbered lordship)

1 W. Rees, *South Wales and the March*, 242; D.L. 43/15/1.
2 R. R. Davies, D.Phil. thesis (Univ. of Oxford, 1965), 404–8.
3 S.R.O. 552/1A/1; *C. Inq. Misc. 1392–99*, no. 229.
4 S.C. 11/23 (Builth yielded £66 13s. 4d. beyond its lease-rate of £113 6s. 8d.).
5 *Glam. C.H.*, III, 603; S.C. 11/799, 801, 23.
6 Staffs. R.O. D. 641/2/6, m. 3ᵛ–m. 4.
7 *C.C.R. 1360–64*, 46–7; S.C. 11/23.
8 *C. Inq. Misc. 1392–9*, no. 233. The finances of Chirkland have been exhaustively and ably analysed in Dr. Llinos Smith's thesis (Univ. of London, 1971).
9 S.R.O. 552/1A/1; *C. Inq. Misc. 1392–9*, no. 234; S.R.O. 552/1A/2.
10 *S.D.*, 323; *C.I.P.M.*, VIII, no. 532; S.C. 6/1184/22; S.C. 11/23. The finances of the lordship of Denbigh are fully discussed in Dr. D. H. Owen's unpublished thesis (Univ. of Wales, 1967).
11 C. 134/3, no. 5, m. 6 (This estimate includes the 'easements' of the castle of Ruthin declared to be worth £100 for a king or an earl but less for an ordinary man [pro alio simplici homine]); C. 134/82, no. 9.
12 *C. Inq. Misc. 1392–99*, no. 228.
13 *Cartae*, III, no. 886; J. B. Smith, unpublished thesis (above p. 86, n. 1), 396.
14 *Cartae*, III, no. 877; *Glam. C.H.*, III, 250.
15 *Cal. Public Records re. Pembrokeshire*, i, 61–6, 118–20.

16–17 D.L. 40/1/11, fol. 45ᵛ, fol. 50; D.L. 43/15/1–3; D.L. 29/728/11986. The figure for 1386–91 is based on the average yield of the four years 1386, 1387, 1388 and 1391.

18 S.C. 6/1209/11; *C.C.R. 1360–64*, 46–7; S.C. 11/23.

19 As for 16–17.

20. *C.C.R. 1360–64*, 46–7; N.L.W. Slebech Collection, 9.

21 *Glam. C.H.*, III, 603; *The Marcher Lordships of South Wales, 1415–1536*, ed. T. B. Pugh, 49.

22 S.R.O. 552/1A/1; *C. Inq. Misc. 1392–9*, no. 235.

23 *Cal. Public Records re. Pembrokeshire*, III, 83–6, 24.

24 S.C. 6/1209/8.

25 S.C. 11/23.

9   The Management of Lordship

'THERE is a very fine and great lordship in those places which, if it were well managed, would be worth not less than two thousand marks a year'.[1] The conditional clause in the commissioner's report on the Bohun estates in the March in 1302 spelt out a basic truth: great lordship required good management. It was a truth of which contemporaries were well aware.[2] The nature of the problem of management varied considerably from one estate to another, most obviously according to the total size of the lord's landed inheritance. Marcher lordships were almost without exception part and parcel of wider inheritances and shared thereby the problems of management posed by such territorial complexes. Indeed in the March those problems were even more acute. That was partly because an English lord's Marcher lands were geographically at the farthest remove (unless he had Irish estates) from the centre of his territorial interests and power and from the normal radius of his itineration; lordship was always likely to prove most difficult at its peripheries. This problem of distance was compounded by the obvious fact that a lord's Marcher estates were in Wales: at best that meant an alien, conquered population, an unfamiliar social framework and an incomprehensible language; at worst it meant the threat of rebellion and the need for a military presence. Such a situation called for sensitivity as well as efficiency in the conduct of the lordship. Lordship in the March was extraordinarily ample and unusually rewarding; it was also exceptionally demanding of the skills of management.

Management was in part a question of adequate institutions, of an efficient framework of offices and officers in the service of

[1] C. Inq. Misc., 1219–1307, no. 1870.
[2] See in general T. F. T. Plucknett, The Medieval Bailiff (Creighton Lecture in History, 1953); N. Denholm-Young, Seignorial Administration in England (1937) esp. chap. IV; D. Oschinsky, Walter of Henley and other Treatises on Estate Management and Accounting (Oxford, 1971); K. B. McFarlane, The Nobility of Later Medieval England, 47–53.

lordship. That framework inevitably varied in many of its particulars from one Marcher lordship to another; but in its general outlines it was broadly similar in all lordships. Each lordship had a two-tiered framework of institutions, one local and the other central.[3] The central institutions were focused on the major castle of the lordship, the centre of governance, justice and finance as well as of military power. At this central level the lordship itself—whether it was called a county, an honor, a barony or simply a lordship—was the unit of governance.[4] Within it the lord's authority was complete; his lordship was, administratively speaking, a kingdom in miniature. Accordingly there developed within it a framework of institutions comparable, on a vastly smaller scale, with those of the kingdom of England itself. Some of the greater lordships—Glamorgan, Pembroke, Haverford, Gower and Abergavenny amongst them—had their own chanceries and no doubt their own registers of writs.[5] Many of them had their own exchequers, which in some lordships was a financial office but which in others, such as Bromfield and Yale, combined the functions of secretarial department and accounting office.[6] Within the lordship the lord's written commands were authenticated either by his personal seal or more frequently by a special seal deputed for the affairs of his Marcher estates. Indeed the possession of such a seal came to be regarded as one of the more obvious manifestations of the independence of Marcher status: when a Marcher lordship was taken into royal custody its affairs were still conducted under its own seal and when Raglan

---

[3] For Marcher government in general, see W. Rees, *South Wales and the March 1284–1415*, 68–109 and A. J. Otway-Ruthven, 'The Constitutional Position of the Great Lordships of South Wales', *T.R.H.S.*, 5th ser. 8 (1958), 1–20.

[4] Glamorgan and Pembroke were normally called counties, while Gower was divided into two counties, one English and one Welsh. Other lordships were occasionally so designated, e.g. Newport (*C.I.P.M.*, v, no. 538) and Haverford (*C.P.R. 1292–1301*, 116); even in Kidwelly there was a building called the Shire Hall (D.L. 29/584/9242). Other Marcher lordships were called honors (e.g. Brecon, Monmouth, Haverford) or baronies (e.g. Llanstephan, Brecon, Walwynscastle) or quite simply lordships (*dominia*) or lands (*terrae, patriae*).

[5] Otway-Ruthven, art. cit. 7–8. For the chanceries of Haverford and Abergavenny see *C.P.R. 1292–1301*, 496 (1300) and N.L.W. Badminton Deeds, 1684 (1393) respectively.

[6] Otway-Ruthven, art. cit. 8–9. Dyffryn Clwyd also had its own exchequer which was the administrative centre of the lordship and at which private debts could also be acknowledged (e.g. S.C. 2/216/1, m. 18ᵛ [1318]).

was elevated to the status of a Marcher lordship in 1465 'an authentic seal for commissions, writs and warrants' was regarded as a prerequisite of its Marcher governance.[7] These quasi-royal institutions of government in the March were served by a small staff of central officers comparable with those to be found on any major lay estate in England—a steward who was the lord's deputy and had general oversight of the governance of the lordship, a receiver who was in charge of financial and secretarial affairs, and a constable who looked to the military security of the lordship. These three key officers (occasionally reduced to two) were frequently but not invariably complemented by a handful of other officers with authority throughout the lordship: a coroner to hear pleas of the Crown, a sheriff or a bailiff itinerant to execute the orders of the court, an interpreter and a Welsh judge to reveal the secrets of the Welsh language and of Welsh law, an escheator and a forester to supervise two of the major demesne resources of the lord, and a stock-keeper (*instaurator*) to co-ordinate agricultural policy on the lord's manors. The central organization of Marcher lordship was, on the whole, one of neat simplicity and of fair efficiency in its division of responsibilities. It was also highly economical in terms of manpower and fees: the salaries of the four men who were charged with the central administration of a large lordship such as Brecon barely exceeded £40 out of a gross yield of £1,500 and even when the costs of all the local officers and of the expensive visits of the auditors are included the administrative bill for the lordship was less than £100.[8]

At the local level Marcher governance presents a more complex and in many ways a less imposing appearance. Each lordship was divided into a puzzling variety of local units—in the lowlands into Englishries, baronies, knights' fees, manors, boroughs, bailiwicks and so forth; in the highlands and more distinctively Welsh areas into native Welsh divisions of *cantref*, *cwmwd*, *swydd*, *gwestfa*, and *maenor*. This diversity of units was matched by a diversity of officers: bailiff, reeve, beadle and

[7] For the engraving of seals for Marcher lordships in royal custody, see F. Palgrave, *Issues of the Exchequer, Henry III–Henry VI* (Record Commission, 1837), 201, 242, 246; for Raglan see *C.P.R. 1461–7*, 425–6. Among the Marcher lordships which had their own seals were Glamorgan, Pembroke, Usk, Haverford, Abergavenny, and Bromfield and Yale.
[8] These figures are based on the accounts for 1371–2: S.C. 6/861/1; 1156/13–19.

forester operated side by side with *rhaglaw, rhingyll, cais* and *amobrwr*. Nor does the complexity end there; alongside these seignorial units and officers we must place such other units as the parish, the vill and the *gwely* (the Welsh tenurial unit) which were also occasionally called into service by the lord and his officers. Clearly the machinery of local governance in the March had about it little of the neat efficiency of the structure of central institutions in the lordship. It was an amalgam of English and Welsh units and officers, of offices which served specific areas (bailiwicks, manors, commotes etc.) or particular groups of tenants (Welsh, English, free, unfree, advowry-men) or special categories of land (escheats, forests). It luxuriated with anomalies and sinecures. In some lordships, such as Brecon, the local administration was extremely skeletal; elsewhere, as in Clun, a superfluity of officers battened on the lordship and its tenants.[9] At the central level the lord could shape institutions to meet his needs; at the local level, on the other hand, he took over a pre-existing framework of offices and officers, many of them of native Welsh origin and most of them encumbered with a fixed tariff of fees.[10] It was at this level that office became hopelessly entangled in a web of social relationships and customs which steadily reduced its efficiency *vis à vis* the lord and proportionately increased its profitability to its holder. Reforms, indeed, were attempted—*commortha* (the right of local officials to levy subsidies) might be abolished by decree, new officials (such as the bailiff itinerant) might be provided, commissioners with wide-ranging powers could be appointed (as happened in Kidwelly in 1388); but the impact of such reforms was rarely more than marginal. The Marcher lords by and large had to live with a cumbersome if not altogether inadequate machinery of local governance.

Good management was in part a question of efficient and effective institutions; it was more, much more, a question of

---

[9] For Brecon see above p. 102; for Clun see the charter of 1317 published in *Transactions of the Shropshire Archaeological and Natural History Society* 11 (1887–8), 249–50. By the terms of his charter the lord promised to limit the number of officers in Tempseter, but even so the complaints about an excess of officers continued, e.g. S.R.O. 552/1/20, m. 18 (1380)—4 grooms and 2 foresters too many in the forest.

[10] A comprehensive list of the various fees claimed by the local officers in Bromfield and Yale is given in S.B.Y. fol. 18ᵛ–fol. 20.

efficient personnel. The commissioner of 1302 had no doubt about it: the Bohun estates in the March could be worth two thousand marks a year 'but there have been bad and disloyal stewards and bailiffs'. What then constituted 'suitability' for office in the March? We may arrive at an answer partly by a prosopographical study of the agents of lordship and partly by a consideration of the attitudes, declared and otherwise, of Marcher lords and their councils towards local appointments. Among the criteria for office, local ties and local knowledge occupied a prominent place; indeed in the case of the basic local offices such as those of bailiff, reeve and *rhingyll* these were the overwhelming considerations. That was inevitable. These were offices which demanded local knowledge and a fairly regular local presence. Many of them also required the services of men who already carried weight in the locality in respect of their wealth and social standing, for without such qualities an amateur officialdom (for such it was) was unlikely to be obeyed. In the March, as in medieval England, local administration was largely possible only by a surrender of power into the hands of men who were already the economic and social leaders of their community. That is why dynasties of such local officers are not unusual;[11] that is also why several of them figure prominently in Welsh genealogical collections.[12] 'If they are removed' said a Welsh justiciar pleading on behalf of two of his bailiffs, 'the peace will be worse kept in those parts'.[13] What was true of the Principality applied equally in the March: good management could not dispense with local influence.

In the central posts of Marcher governance local influence and knowledge were by no means so overwhelmingly important; but even so they had their attractions. Local gentry, who, had they lived in England, would have served the king as justices of the peace, commissioners, tax-collectors, and knights of the shire figure fairly prominently in the higher ranks of

[11] Such as the family of Hywel Gam which administered Pencelli for the lords of Brecon for much of the fourteenth century or the family of Einion Sais discussed below, pp. 225–6.

[12] A case in point is Meredydd Bwl ap Dafydd Ddu, twice beadle of Iscennen and collector of a communal fine in the early fifteenth century. His genealogy is given in Lewys Dwnn, *Heraldic Visitations of Wales*, ed. S. R. Meyrick (Llandovery, 1846), I, 26 and his considerable territorial wealth is suggested by a late rental: D.L. 43/12/14, fol. 28ᵛ.

[13] *C. Inq. Misc. 1307–49*, no. 68.

Marcher administration. Many of them were drawn from the lord's feudal tenants—men such as Sir Matthew le Sore of St. Fagan, Sir Edward Stradling of St. Donats or Sir John St. John of Fonmon who served as sheriffs of Glamorgan[14]—or from more recent immigré families such as the Pulestons and Egertons in Bromfield, the Swynmores in Denbigh, the Thelwalls and the Salesburys in Dyffryn Clwyd.[15] For their receivers the lords turned naturally to the burgesses of the Marcher towns; there they found men of unimpugnable loyalty and often of considerable experience in civic and business affairs. Thomas Pontefract came from Yorkshire to Denbigh in the train of his lord, Henry Lacy, and served him and his son-in-law, Thomas of Lancaster, as receiver of Denbigh for at least twenty years;[16] Adam Skolle and Henry Churchesdon were both leading burgesses of Brecon town who were placed in charge of the administration of Brecon lordship by the earl of Hereford; John of Gaunt likewise looked to some of the burgesses of Kidwelly such as Thomas Hervy and Roger Aylward for his local receivers, while the earls of Gloucester relied on the services of the burgesses of Usk.[17] All these men brought local knowledge and standing to their management of the lord's affairs; some of them showed considerable administrative skill and thereby came to serve several Marcher lords simultaneously. Such a one was John Sergeant of Monmouth. A man of modest territorial means and good administrative stock (his father had been a steward of Earl Henry of Lancaster in the 1320s and 1330s) he himself was receiver and deputy steward of the Lancaster lordship of Monmouth for over thirty years, steward of the Hastings lordship of Abergavenny and feoffee of Richard Talbot of Archenfield.[18] John ap Gwilym, receiver of Mon-

---

[14] *Glam. C.H.*, III, 689–91.

[15] Members of these families served as stewards in their respective lordships in the fourteenth and early-fifteenth centuries.

[16] D.L. 29/1/1, m. 1 (1297); Nottinghamshire Record Office, D.D. 325/1, m. 10 (1317); *S.D.*, 65, 86.

[17] For Bohun and Lancaster officials in the March, see R. R. Davies, 'The Bohun and Lancaster Lordships in Wales in the Fourteenth and Fifteenth Centuries', D.Phil. thesis (Univ. of Oxford, 1965), 387–97; for Clare officials, J. C. Ward, Ph.D. thesis (cited above p. 86, n. 1), 356–52; for Fitzalan officials, Llinos Smith, 'The Lordship of Chirk and Oswestry, 1282–1415', Ph.D. thesis (Univ. of London, 1971), 77–87, 440–3.

[18] For his offices, D.L. 29/615/9836–39; *Cat. MSS. re. Wales in B.M..*, III, 582;

mouth 1399–1413 and 1418–24, had many of the same qualities; he was a man of modest territorial wealth and local standing and clearly a man of no mean administrative abilities for he was also receiver of Chepstow and later receiver and deputy steward of the Mortimer lordship of Usk.[19]

With John ap Gwilym we have in fact passed from the ranks of Anglo-Norman and English settler families into those of the native Welsh gentry as stewards and receivers of the Marcher lords. They were certainly not excluded from office; their standing in the local community and often their family tradition of loyalty to Marcher houses were assets which could not be overlooked. It was Madog ap Llywelyn, scion of an old Welsh family, whom Thomas of Lancaster chose for the delicate post of receiver of Bromfield and Yale in 1318 (the lordship had only recently been extorted from the Earl of Surrey). He was among the wealthiest men of his lordship; 'the best man who ever lived in Maelor Gymraeg' according to the Welsh *Brut*, and a man whose social eminence is still witnessed for us in the splendid effigy of him which rests in Gresford church.[20] There were many men like him in the service of the Marcher lords: Philip ap Hywel, member of a remarkable border family whose service to the Marcher lords dated from the early thirteenth century and himself steward and close confidant of both Bohun and Mortimer lords, royal commissioner and constable of royal castles in the March; Adam ab Ifor, 'lord of Llanfair Cilgedin' and steward of Monmouth for Earl Henry of Lancaster and his son; Gruffudd of Glyndyfrdwy, Welsh 'baron', descendant of the native princes of Powys, grandfather of Owain Glyndŵr and steward of the Fitzalan lordship of Oswestry in the mid-1340s; Meurig ap Rees constable of Brecon and faithful supporter of the Bohun family; and Philip ap Morgan, steward of

---

C.P.R. 1396–9, 38; for his lands, Monmouth Record Office, Llanarth Court 26; D.L. 42/17 fol. 165; N.L.W. Badminton MSS., 1508.

[19] For his offices *C.P.R. 1405–8*, 34; N.L.W. Badminton MSS., 924–5. His lands are listed in his *inquisition post mortem*, D.L. 7/1 no. 46, while his purchases and leases of land are well recorded in the documentation of the period.

[20] For his official position, see J. R. Maddicott, *Thomas of Lancaster*, 339; for his obituary *Brut y Tywysogyon*, Peniarth MS. 20, 237; for his effigy, C. A. Gresham, *Medieval Stone Carving in North Wales* (Cardiff, 1968), 185–6; for his lands, *The First Extent of Bromfield and Yale A.D. 1315*, 40, 46, 61, 65. According to a note in N.L.W. Peniarth MS. 404 D. fol. 111, the rent due from his lands was over £11 annually.

several of the Mortimer lordships in the March and an active and important councillor of the earl of March (d. 1398).[21]

With these Welshmen we touch upon another consideration which weighed with the Marcher lords in deciding the appointments they made to local office: how far was it wise or desirable to appoint Welshmen to key offices in the March. At the local level there was little alternative, but in the case of the central officials—steward, receiver and constable—different, and even conflicting, considerations competed with each other. On the one hand was the openly acknowledged belief that local men, and Welshmen at that, were essential for the effective governance of the March. The vassals of the earl of Pembroke had propounded such a view in 1244: 'it is not easy', they declared, 'in our part of Wales to control Welshmen except by one of their own race'.[22] The same sentiment was echoed by one of the earl of March's officials a century and a half later: reporting to the earl's great council on the affairs of the lordship of Narberth he suggested that a steward ought to be appointed who could arbitrate in the disputes between the Welshmen and Englishmen of the area and the name of a local Welshman, Maurice Wyn, was proposed. The memorandum provides us with a rare insight into decision-making in the field of local appointments.[23] On the other hand, the March like the rest of Wales was a conquered country, exploited as a colony by an alien nobility. It was but natural that this nobility should prefer to rely on loyal and experienced Englishmen for the key posts in the management of its Marcher lordships. On the whole and in spite of the examples we have quoted, this consideration weighed more heavily than the first in Marcher appointments. If we take the most important office of all, that of steward or head of the administration (occasionally termed constable as in Brecon or Dyffryn Clwyd or sheriff as in Glamorgan), Welshmen are very much the exceptions in such lists as we can compile: not a single one in Bromfield and Yale or in Dyffryn Clwyd (in the

---

[21] He was steward of Usk 1385-6, of Clifford and Glasbury 1388-9 and of Denbigh 1394-7: *Cat. MSS. Wales in B.M.*, IV, 912; U.C.N.W. Whitney 316; N.L.W. Wynnstay 100/202. His importance as a member of Mortimer's council can be gauged from the account of the receiver of Denbigh 1396-7 (S.C. 6/1184/22); during that year he visited Ireland three times on the lord's business.

[22] *Cal. Anc. Corr. conc. Wales*, 48.

[23] B.L. Egerton Roll, 8718 (1395-7).

latter case our list is fairly complete); one in Denbigh (Philip ap Morgan); two in Brecon out of thirteen known constables or stewards (Meurig ap Rees and Hywel Fychan ap Hywel ab Einion); one sheriff in Glamorgan out of twenty-three (Hywel ap Hywel); four stewards in Kidwelly out of a list of thirteen (John ap Hicdon, Henry ap Philip, Henry Don, William Gwyn ap Rhys); one in Monmouth out of fifteen (Adam ab Ifor); one in Clun (Adda ab Owen); three in Oswestry (Master Gruffudd Trefor, Gruffudd of Glyndyfrdwy, Adda ab Owen). We should not lean too heavily on lists which are often incomplete; but we cannot ignore the evidence where it speaks so clearly and unanimously. Welshmen were not totally excluded from the top posts of Marcher administration, but their appointment was very much an exception. The issue was a politically-loaded one and probably became increasingly so during the course of the century. The feeling that they were 'outsiders' in the governance of their own country was a not insignificant cause of disaffection on the part of Welshmen. It was acknowledged even by contemporaries as one of the principal reasons behind the revolt of Llywelyn Bren in Glamorgan in 1316; it almost certainly played a prominent part in the build-up to the Glyn Dŵr revolt.

Local men, whether English or Welsh, had much to recommend them as agents of Marcher lordship; but their possible shortcomings were also self-evident. Their ties with the locality and with the community might compromise both their efficiency and their loyalty to the lord. That is why he might often prefer to rely on men from outside the March in the governance of his Marcher estates. He might draw the personnel from his estates in England: men from the Grey manors in Bedfordshire and Buckinghamshire administered the Grey Marcher lordship of Dyffryn Clwyd for much of the fourteenth century.[24] Equally the lord could second men who were on his central staff or in close personal attendance on him to manage his estates in the March: Richard Rivers, confidant, retainer and auditor of Earl Henry of Lancaster was also his steward of Kidwelly for twenty-five years (1308–33); in Brecon likewise the earl of

---

[24] Among the constables were William Brickhill (pre-1308), Henry Walton (1329–34) and Nicholas Bletchley (1351, 1364–7), all of them men bearing the names of Grey manors.

Hereford appointed one of his auditors, John Stanes, to act as constable of the lordship in the 1340s; while on the Mortimer estates a trusted servant and feoffee such as John Gour could also serve his lord as steward of one of his Marcher lordships. But it was above all—or such at least is the impression—from the English border counties, especially Herefordshire, Gloucestershire and Shropshire, that the Marcher lords recruited men for the key posts in their lordships. Their names abound in lists of the top Marcher administrators: Roger Cheney 'steward of the earl of Arundel and at that time (1316) sheriff of Shropshire'; Walter Shockenhurst likewise sheriff of Worcester and constable of Brecon; William Banastre of Hadnall, eight times knight of the shire for his native Shropshire but also in his time steward of three Marcher lordships and a frequent justice in eyre in others;[25] Roger Partrich of Dorstone (co. Hereford) faithful servant of the Mortimers and steward and receiver of many of their lordships in the middle March;[26] the Oldcastles of Herefordshire who served the Hastings earl of Pembroke and the Beauchamp earls of Warwick on their Marcher estates.[27] And so the examples could be multiplied. Wales was to be ruled from Ludlow in the sixteenth century; the March was already much governed by the squires of the English border counties two centuries earlier. It was men such as these who introduced the habits of English local government and of English legal practice into the March.

They were, however, busy men, attending to their own affairs and serving in county administration in England as well as occupying important posts in one or even several Marcher lordships. Their services needed to be complemented by those of men who could give a more continuous and possibly more informed attention to the affairs, particularly the financial affairs, of lordship. That is why the good management of the March, as of English seignorial affairs generally, leaned heavily

[25] R. W. Eyton, *Antiquities of Shropshire*, x, 159 (Cheney); R. R. Davies, D.Phil. thesis, 141 (Shockenhurst); R. A. Griffiths, *The Principality of Wales*, I, 111 (Banastre).

[26] He was at various times steward of Dinas, Ewyas, Clifford, Glasbury, Radnor, Gwerthrynion and Wigmore, receiver of Wigmore, and deputy receiver-general of all Mortimer estates in Wales and the March.

[27] John Oldcastle was steward of Abergavenny 1370–5 (Monmouth Record Office, Llanarth D. 2, 27; Capel Hanbury 0132); Thomas Oldcastle was probably steward of Elfael in 1397 (B.L. Egerton Roll, 8769).

on a small body of clerks. Some were of high standing such as Richard Brugge, abbot of Haughmond who was a key figure in the administration of the Fitzalan estates in the March in the mid-fourteenth century or the abbots of Wigmore who, naturally enough, likewise acted as receivers-general of the Marcher estates of their founding family, the house of Mortimer; but most of them were ordinary beneficed clerks such as David the Clerk, John Joie and John Becot, successive receivers of Kidwelly in the 1320s and 1330s, Nicholas Bletchley receiver of Dyffryn Clwyd 1348–54, Robert Eggerley receiver of Oswestry 1391–4 and author of the magnificent Fitzalan extents of the 1390s, or Andrew Hore receiver of Brecon 1390–5. Several of them were university-trained men such as Master John Fairford, graduate of Oxford, canon of Abergwili and receiver of three Marcher lordships;[28] others gained their experience in seignorial households, as did John Waltham clerk of the earl of Hereford's wardrobe and later receiver of Brecon; most of them had probably received an elementary training in estate accountancy and administration. They brought to seignorial governance qualities which often complemented those of the stewards: professional expertise, an independence of local connections and secular preoccupations, and a measure of geographical and professional mobility. If good management was to be measured in terms of profitability, as it often was, then these clerk-receivers occupied a crucial role in determining the success or failure of lordship.

Profit, in fact, played an important role in determining appointment to office in the March, for many of the local offices were sold to the highest bidder and formed a substantial source of revenue for the lord. Large sums were realized from such sales: £40 for a life-grant of the reeveship of Tempseter (Clun); £40 for a like grant of the post of *rhaglaw* of the courts of Dyffryn Clwyd; £45 for that of forester of Coelion also in Dyffryn Clwyd; £5 a year to be *rhingyll* of Iscennen.[29] In the annual revenue of a Marcher lord the income from such sales could be substantial: £31 out of £135 in the commote of

[28] A. B. Emden, *A Biographical Register at the University of Oxford to A.D. 1500* (Oxford, 1957–9), II, 663–4; R. A. Griffiths, op. cit. 181–2.
[29] S.R.O. 552/1/1 (1329); S.C. 2/217/4, m. 9 (1349); S.C. 2/218/1, m. 21ᵛ (1350); D.L. 29/573/9063 (1399).

Ceinmeirch (Denbigh) in 1305; £32 from the Mortimer estates
in the middle March in 1336; £9 out of £29 of the income of
Welsh Talgarth in 1365.[30] Most impressive of all are the figures
from the Chirk accounts where the value of the sale of offices
rose steadily from £15 in 1341 to £68 in 1364 and where the
steward was especially rewarded for his zeal in the leasing of
offices.[31] From the lord's point of view the system certainly had
its attractions: it assured him a fixed revenue with no administrative overheads and, given the often intense competition
for local office, it could well serve to increase the profits of his
lordship. The drawbacks of the system are, perhaps, more
obvious to us than they were to contemporary lords: to treat
office as a vendible commodity was to adopt the line of least
resistance to the problem of governance and to surrender power
into local hands in return for a steady profit. It was in effect an
opting out of the duties of lordship. Local communities, understandably, distrusted the system: the men of Iscennen, for
example, preferred to pay their lord an annual fine rather than
face up to the prospect of profiteering local officials.[32] Even the
lords on occasion doubted the wisdom of the policy of leasing
offices: in the 1370s the Mortimer council was advised by a
senior Mortimer official to dismiss all the farmers of offices in its
mid-Wales lordships as they served the lord ill and oppressed
the people.[33]

Office might be sold at profit; equally and increasingly it
might be bestowed as a reward on one of the lord's faithful
retainers; in other words it came to be regarded as an item on
the lord's patronage roll. The retainer would regard the post
either as demanding no more than his minimal attention or
even entirely as a sinecure. In such cases the management
requirements of the local estate were subordinated to the overall
demands of the lord's patronage. It is an understandable and,
within certain bounds, unexceptionable development. It
served well one of the major preoccupations of lordship at all
times, that of providing an ample stock of patronage for its
retainers. It was no different from the well-acknowledged

[30] D.L. 29/1/2, m. 3; S.C. 6/1209/6; B.L. Egerton Roll, 8709.
[31] N.L.W. Chirk Castle D. 8–D. 30. The special reward was given in 1350.
[32] They paid £5 6s. 8d. annually to be exempt from the office of *ceisiad* (serjeant
of the peace): D.L. 29/573/9063. Cf. also W. Rees, op. cit. 107–9.
[33] B.L. Egerton Roll 8757.

practice of using canonries and other non-residentiary posts as rewards for deserving ecclesiastics; but, as with the church, it was important in terms both of public relations and of administrative efficiency that the practice should not be extended to those offices which (to adapt the language of the church) had 'the cure of lordship' attached to them. That, however, was already beginning to happen before the end of the fourteenth century. On some estates important posts such as that of steward were coming to be regarded as honorary offices, if not entirely as sinecures; they were granted for life or in reversion or to be held jointly by two men. Such practices, as we would expect, are most noticeable in the larger inheritances where the demands of patronage were most insistent as a consideration in the lord's policy.

We have dwelt at some length on appointment to office because it reveals the problems of management encountered by medieval lords. Appointment was a delicate task for, as we have tried to indicate, different and often conflicting considerations— those of social and even of racial status, of local and community interests, and of seignorial patronage as well as of efficiency— weighed with the Marcher lords and their councils in making their appointments. They certainly took the task seriously: senior officers made the recommendations; the lord's council considered and decided on them; the lord's attorney-general drafted the commission.[34] Even so, appointment was only the first, if crucial, step in the process of management. For kings and lords alike, management was also in the Middle Ages a struggle to prevent office from being converted too patently and brazenly into an occasion for private profit and power. The problem is one which is relatively common in medieval societies, that of an amateur officialdom, inadequately and irregularly paid, recouping itself by abuse of its office and itself drastically punished from time to time for its misdemeanours. In the March such an attitude to office was greatly reinforced by the native Welsh traditions that officials were not salaried but were rewarded by the lord with gifts of horses, robes and so forth,[35]

---

[34] Such at least was the procedure on the Mortimer estates even for relatively minor offices: B.L. Egerton Rolls 8718, 8757. The auditor might make recommendations for dismissal from office in the course of his reports as is shown by the letters appended to the view of accounts of the Lancaster estates in 1317: Nottinghamshire Record Office D.D. 325/1, m. 17.   [35] *C. Inq. Misc. 1307–49*, no. 68.

were able to draw on an acknowledged tariff of fees (*gobrau*) associated with their office,[36] and were permitted to go on circuit (*cylch*) among the lord's tenants and to exact a personal subsidy (*commorth*) from them.[37] This habit of treating office as a pretext for personal profit was compounded by the fact that few officials especially at the local level cared to or could draw a distinction between their official position and their local standing as landowners and leaders of the community. Office was an occasion to bolster their existing position in society and to bestow an aura of authority around their actions. The line between official power and social status, between administration and oppression was hopelessly unclear. Take the case of Sir John Skidmore, one of the most long-serving and distinguished of Marcher administrators. Among the charges laid against him in 1413 were those of levying a personal subsidy of £20 from the men of Kidwelly (where he was steward), of extorting gifts of animals under threats from other tenants, of selling offices and pocketing the bribes, and of using the labour services of his lord's tenants for his own land.[38] His is a by no means exceptional or particularly bad case.

The lords may have tolerated much of this abuse of office; but good management demanded that they should at least attempt to keep their officials on a fairly tight rein. And on the whole they did so. Most local officials (i.e. bailiffs, reeves, etc.) were rarely kept in office for more than a year at a time (unless they farmed their offices) and on assuming office they were required to take an oath and to find sureties for their good behaviour.[39] Likewise higher officials such as receivers were bound over in recognizances to perform their duties satis-

---

[36] Most local officials took a fee from everyone convicted in the lord's court. In Bromfield and Yale the rate was 4*d*. from every amercement of 1*s*. or more: S.B.Y., fol. 19. Cf. *Extent of Chirkland 1391–3*, ed. G. P. Jones, 5. In Dyffryn Clwyd the perquisites attached to the office of forester included a penny a day, a share of *cylchmarch* (circuit of the horse), *gobrau* (fees) and amercements: S.C. 2/219/6, m. 23ᵛ.

[37] When the officials of Carnwyllion (Kidwelly) were charged with levying *commorthau* (subsidies) they replied with a sense of hurt innocence that the right to do so was appended to their offices: J.I. 1/1153, m. 43.

[38] J.I. 1/1153, m. 2.

[39] See, for example, the instructions issued for the conduct of local officials in Kidwelly in 1374: *John of Gaunt's Register, 1372–76*, ed. S. Armitage-Smith (Camden Society, 3rd ser. 21 (1911)), II, no. 1587.

factorily and to answer for a fixed sum from their bailiwicks.[40] Furthermore the lord encouraged local communities to lodge complaints against the misconduct of his officials and such complaints were either considered by the lord's central officers or adjudged by a local jury.[41] Indeed in many respects the best guarantee of good management for the lord was to strike a happy medium between the zeal of his officials and the contentment of the community. He would be the beneficiary from the vigilance of both parties: a zealous official could augment his profits; a watchful community (often through interested third parties) could limit the peculation and misgovernance of his officials. The lord for his part was not slow to punish his officials for any failure to collect the revenue due from them or for any misconduct of which they were found guilty: distraint of chattels, large fines ($£20–£40$ were not unusual in the March) and imprisonment were among his penalties.

This interplay of local interest and central direction was one of the most constant themes of medieval administration, both royal and seignorial. For in the final analysis good management depended considerably on the measure and effectiveness of central supervision over local institutions and officials. Nowhere was this more obviously so than in the March, for in the virtual absence of royal authority it was the lord alone who could provide through his central officials any measure of control over local officials. That supervision was certainly provided in the March. Much of it came by way of personal visits of the lord's top officials, whether as individuals or as groups. The auditor came twice annually to examine the accounts and to submit reports thereupon to the lord; the chief steward came less frequently on a tourn, an inquisitorial visitation into the affairs of the local estates and into the conduct of local officials; the receiver-general likewise toured the estates. These same officials also figured prominently in the lord's council on its visits to the local estates 'to supervise the lordship, to

---

[40] Examples of such practices in the March are quoted in R. R. Davies, 'Baronial Accounts, Incomes and Arrears in the Later Middle Ages', *Ec.H.R.*, 2nd ser. 21 (1968), 221–2, 227.

[41] For examples of both procedures in Dyffryn Clwyd, see S.C. 2/217/11, m. 1ᵛ (*rhingyll* of Aberwheeler fined £5 by constable for various offences laid against him by community, 1346) and S.C. 2/218/9, m. 14ᵛ (jury of Welsh and English find *rhingyll* of Aberwheeler guilty of various misdemeanors, 1361).

examine the conduct of the officials and to raise money' and in general to attend to the 'well-being, governance and rule' of the lord's estates.[42] In the March, furthermore, these same men might appear yet again in a judicial guise as justices in eyre to hold the sessions but using the occasion to attend to administrative as well as judicial business. The results of all these visits are written large in the seignorial records of the time—in the expenses of the officials, in their detailed emendations on the local accounts, in their decisions and ordinances on local affairs, and in the written reports they submitted to the lord and his council.

The detailed supervision provided by these central officers and the crucial role they played in the management of seignorial estates may, perhaps, be most vividly grasped from the expense account of one of them, Walter Brugge receiver-general of the Mortimer estates, for the month of April 1389.[43] On 2 April he left Ludlow for Wigmore; three days later he travelled to the Mortimer estates in Usk where he spent nine days before travelling north to Clifford-on-Wye. There again he attended to his lord's affairs—and the celebration of Easter— before journeying to Builth, a lordship held at farm by the Mortimer executors. From Builth he embarked on the difficult journey across the mountains to the Tywi valley reaching Carmarthen by nightfall on 22 April. His destination was the distant Mortimer lordship of Narberth which he reached next day. He spent two days there on estate business and then slipped in a private visit, possibly a pilgrimage, to St. David's. On his return from Narberth he spent the day with Sir William Brian and his household at Laugharne before facing the homeward journey to Builth which he reached on 30 April. By then Walter Brugge must have been both saddle-sore and work-weary. In twenty-six days he had travelled well over 300 miles from one end of Wales to the other. A hard-riding cleric he must indeed have been for he had covered that mileage, often in rough country, in about ten days and had devoted the rest of his time to his lord's business. Kingship, we are often reminded, was in

---

[42] The phrases come, respectively, from the accounts of the visits of the council of the custodians of the Mortimer estates to Denbigh in 1387 and of the Fitzalan council to Clun in 1386: B.L. Egerton Roll 8730; S.R.O. 552/1A/8.

[43] B.L. Egerton Roll 8732.

the Middle Ages a matter of itineration. So was lordship, either in person or by deputy. Walter Brugge's ceaseless activity brought the expertise of a professional administrator and the authority of a high-ranking official to bear upon the local officialdom of the Mortimer lands in the March. It would be easy to overrate his success, though not his effort; but for absentee lords, as the Marcher lords by and large were, it was only through the progresses of men such as Walter Brugge (and his journeyings were by no means exceptional) [44] that a widely scattered inheritance could be administered and supervised with some semblance of efficiency and some measure of respect for the lord's commands.

Nor was central direction and supervision of local estates confined to the personal visits of the council and of senior officers. In the March, as on seignorial estates generally, many of the major and even minor decisions on local policy were increasingly reserved for the lord's council. These decisions were communicated in a fairly constant flow of directives to local officials and these directives, if they concerned financial matters, would be their authority for allowances at the audit. It is on the estates of John of Gaunt that the registers of such estate-correspondence first survive: the impression they convey is that of a central supervision which allowed little freedom of action to local officials in other than routine affairs and which unremittingly harassed any officials who defaulted on their accounts until their arrears were finally paid or pardoned. [45] Nor was the process of communication exclusively one-way: petitions and bills were regularly dispatched from the locality to the lord and his council in search of favours, mitigation of rents and so forth, while ministers and tenants were not infrequently summoned to appear before the council in person. [46] It was only by such incessant supervision—and John of Gaunt's

---

[44] There is another detailed account of a tour of the Mortimer Marcher estates by Brugge and Thomas Hildeburgh (the auditor) which took two months in B.L. Egerton Roll 8744. In 1358, to give one more example out of many, Nicholas Newton, chief steward of the earl of Hereford, travelled from Pleshy (co. Essex) to Brecon—not far short of 200 miles each way—thrice (February, June and August) to supervise the lord's affairs and to collect his revenue.

[45] See in general R. R. Davies, *Ec.H.R.*, 2nd ser. 21 (1968), 211–29.

[46] For the role of the council see in particular R. Somerville, *The Duchy o Lancaster*, I, 120–30 and the illustrative documents published in G. A. Holmes, *Estates of the Higher Nobility*, 128–31.

methods were in no way exceptional—that the lord of a large inheritance could retain direct control of the affairs of his local estates and prevent himself, in the words of the surveyor of Denbigh, from 'being greatly deceived'.[47]

Good management depended much on sound institutions and faithful officials; it also depended ultimately on the lord himself. It was so with kingship and lordship alike. The final comment of the royal commissioner of 1302 on the management of the Bohun lordships in Wales was eloquently brief: 'And the Earl was lax.' For on all seignorial estates the lord's will, as it has so rightly been observed, 'was the source of decision, . . . the mainspring of his vast administration'.[48] Without sure guidance from the lord, management soon faltered. That guidance need not, normally would not, take the form of detailed attention to the day-to-day running of the estates; but it did mean an informed appreciation of the problems of estate-management and a directing hand in the making and implementing of all major decisions. Most of the Marcher lords of the fourteenth century—or rather such of them as have left a fair measure of accounts behind them—seem to have displayed these managerial qualities in fair measure; some of them—Earl Humphrey of Hereford (d. 1361), Earl Richard of Arundel (d. 1376) and his son (d. 1397) among them—displayed them in very ample measure indeed. It was essential that they should do so, for nowhere was it more self-evidently true than in the March of Wales that the price of fine lordship was good management. Without it, lordship would eventually be undermined in terms both of its profits and, more crucially, of its authority. When that happened, other men, most of them local men, would begin literally to lord it in the March.

[47] *S.D.*, 235.
[48] K. B. McFarlane, *The Nobility of Later Medieval England*, 47.

LORDSHIP was at its most expansive in the March of Wales. Nowhere indeed did the powers of lordship and of kingship approximate more closely than they did there. Even in the correspondence of more sober observers, indeed in the official letters of the kings of England themselves, the phrases of majesty tumble out in reference to the March and its lords. They are 'lords royal' who enjoy a 'royal lordship' 'with royal liberty' and exercise a 'regal jurisdiction'.[1] The Marcher lords themselves were understandably even less diffident about proclaiming the majesty of their lordship: they vaunted their 'full regality' and their 'regal jurisdiction'; they jealously and punctiliously listed 'the prerogatives of the lord's sword'; they proudly asserted the regal quality of their lordship—*totum regale, regale suum*.[2] There was much pleasure and pomp in the sound of such majestic phrases; but neither kings nor lords nor lawyers could dwell long in the rarefied atmosphere of such abstractions. They preferred to talk of regalities rather than of regality, of multiple *iura regalia* rather than of a singular *regale*. These liberties were not comprehensively listed in the Middle Ages, for the March was never the subject of a royal *quo warranto* inquiry; but we can deduce fairly accurately from contemporary evidence what these liberties were and our deductions may be amplified and confirmed by the catalogue of Marcher liberties grandly and lovingly compiled by George Owen of Henllys in the sixteenth century.[3]

A long and impressive catalogue it certainly was. It began

[1] For these phrases as used in royal documents with reference to the Marcher lords, see respectively T. B. Pugh, ' "The Indenture for the Marches" between Henry VII and Edward Stafford (1477–1521), Duke of Buckingham', *E.H.R.* 71 (1956), 436–41 at 441; *C.I.P.M.*, XIV, no. 209, p. 220; *C.I.P.M.*, V, no. 538; *C.P.R. 1266–72*, 299.

[2] See respectively S.B.Y., fol. 4, fol. 170 (Fitzalan, 1391); *Rot. Parl.* I, 148 (William Braose, 1300); *Cartae*, III, no. 741 (Clare, 1281); *Rot. Parl.*, I, 30-2 (Valence, 1290).   [3] *Penbrokshire*, I, 10–13.

with the judicial omnicompetence of the Marcher lord's
authority. To English lawyers here lay the uniqueness of the
Marcher position: in the March, as they put it, the king's writ
did not run.[4] Negatively this meant that there the king of
England and his courts normally exercised no jurisdiction.
That point had already been forcibly argued by William
Braose, the greatest Marcher lord of his day, in 1199 when he
asserted bluntly that 'neither the king nor the justiciar nor the
sheriff ought to interfere in his liberty';[5] it was reiterated by the
Marcher jurymen in 1278 who refused to append their seals
to any inquisition which might be transmitted out of the March
and it was yet again proclaimed by the men of Montgomery in
1337 when they declared that they were not bound to answer
or obey the sheriff of Shropshire or any of the king's ministers.[6]
In positive terms this exemption from royal jurisdiction meant
that within the Marcher lordship the lord's writ ran rather
than that of the king[7] and that the lord of the March had
cognizance of all pleas (except treason) in his lordship. In short
the lord was the judicial master of his lordship with power of
life and death, limbs and chattels; his courts knew no limit
(with very few exceptions) to their competence; any judicial
franchises within his lordship derived from him and were
scrutinized by him.[8]

The lord's judicial omnicompetence was matched by a
territorial and seignorial competence within his lordship. He
was there the universal landlord; all land (with the exception
of church estates) was held mediately or immediately of him.[9]
He enjoyed within the lordship the same prerogatives that the
king enjoyed elsewhere: the right of primer seisin and prerogative wardship of all land held of him;[10] the right to create

---

[4] See, for example, the legal texts of the fifteenth century quoted by Professor
A. J. Otway-Ruthven in *T.R.H.S.*, 5th ser. 8 (1958), 10–11.

[5] Quoted in J. C. Holt, *The Northerners* (Oxford, 1961), 185.

[6] *C.I.P.M.*, ii, no. 289; *Select Cases in the Court of King's Bench*, ed. G. O. Sayles, v
(Selden Society, 1957), 97.

[7] As was expressly asserted to be the case by Henry III in 1268: *C.P.R. 1266–72*,
299; D.L. 10/111.

[8] For a contemporary exegesis of the 'regal jurisdiction' of the March see *Rot.
Parl.*, i, 148–9.

[9] As the lord of Glamorgan declared in 1290—'Omnes terrae et tenementa infra
patriam de Glamorgan existentia sunt de dominio suo': *Rot. Parl.*, i, 43.

[10] See above pp. 100–1.

boroughs, markets and fairs;[11] the right to grant free warren and to create forests;[12] the right to wreck, treasure trove and mines;[13] the right to royal fish such as porpoises and sturgeons;[14] the right to impose tolls within his lordship and to exempt men from paying them.[15] Furthermore Marcher lordships were normally exempt from the fiscal demands of the kings of England: only once during our period, in 1292, did the Marcher lords agree to pay a tax to the king and even then they hedged about the grant with a qualification that it was not to be used as a precedent.[16] And it was not.

Finally and in some ways most remarkably the lords of the March claimed and exercised the right to settle their disputes with each other and (before 1282) with the native princes and lords of Wales by their own treaties and if need be by waging war. Whether this right of making peace and war was part of a custom which the Marcher lords had acquired as the successors of the Welsh princes whom they had displaced (as Sir Goronwy Edwards has argued)[17] or whether it was a reflection of the practical necessities of a frontier situation[18] and of the well-recognized feudal customs of 'private' treaties and 'private' wars[19] is not an issue which we are called upon to decide here.

---

[11] For a claim that the right to establish markets and fairs was within the power of a lord of the Welshry, see *Select Cases concerning the Law Merchant, 1251–1779*, ed. H. Hall, III (Selden Society, 1932), 140–2 (1279).

[12] See, for example, *Cartae*, III, no. 878 (1316); IV, no. 991 (1344).

[13] ibid. III, no. 861 (1313) for a Marcher lord granting out the right of wreck.

[14] The earl of Warwick reserved these fish to himself in his charter to Swansea, ibid. I, no. 138. For further references, see Otway-Ruthven, art. cit. 14, n. 1.

[15] *Cartae*, III, no. 898; IV, no. 969. The earl of Hereford as lord of Brecon jealously upheld his right to demand tolls throughout his lordship from all his mesne tenants and from anyone passing through the lordship: D.L. 41/6/11 (Sir Philip ap Rees); *B.P.R.*, I, 31 (protest from the Black Prince).

[16] For this tax see J. E. Morris, *The Welsh Wars of Edward I*, 239. The article by J. R. Strayer and G. Rudisill, jnr., 'Taxation and Community in Wales and Ireland, 1272–1307', *Speculum* 29 (1954), 410–16 is vitiated in its references to Wales by a failure to recognize the distinction between Principality and March.

[17] 'The Normans and the Welsh March', *Procs. of the British Academy* 42 (1956), 170–4.

[18] As in Durham, for example, where the Bishop and his men on occasion concluded alliances and treaties with the Scots: G. T. Lapsley, *The County Palatine of Durham* (New York, 1900), 36–40.

[19] For 'private' warfare and treaties in feudal society see C. W. Hollister, *The Military Organization of Norman England* (Oxford, 1965), 7 and the literature cited there, and M. H. Keen, *The Laws of War in the Later Middle Ages* (1965), 72–81 209, 212.

What is beyond doubt is that the lords of the March did conclude treaties both with each other and with native Welsh princes: the *cydfodau* (border agreements) between various Marcher lordships are examples of the former[20] while the remarkable treaty of peace and concord ('fedus pacis et insolubilis concordie') between Llywelyn ap Gruffydd, prince of Wales, and Roger Mortimer, lord of Wigmore, in the autumn of 1281 provides the most significant instance of the latter.[21] It is equally clear that the use of war to decide disputes both between Marcher lords and between Marcher lords and Welsh princes was a well-recognized custom whose validity was not even directly questioned by Edward I.[22] Indeed, as Sir Goronwy Edwards has pointed out,[23] we have clear instances of the king of England himself acknowledging that men whom he had accepted as his faithful subjects might yet wage war in the March on their own account. Outside the strictly legal sphere, this custom was the most crucial, and most extraordinary, feature of Marcher franchise. Testimony comes from an unlikely and therefore all the more significant source—the register of the Irish manor of Gormanston, compiled in the late-fourteenth century.[24] The author was writing an *apologia* for the lords of the franchises of Ireland; but it was from the March of Wales that he culled his theory and his examples. Marcher lordship was the exemplar of the most powerful and integral lordship known within the realms of the king of England in the later Middle Ages.

The liberties of the March were clearly ample. In theory—and it is in the realm of theory that we are now dwelling—they left but a minimal scope for the authority of the king of England. It could have been said more truly of a Marcher lord in his lordship than it was said of the bishop of Durham in his

[20] See below pp. 246–7.

[21] *Littere Wallie*, ed. J. G. Edwards (Cardiff, 1940), 99–100.

[22] Edward I's action against the earls of Gloucester and Hereford in 1290–2 was not based on any condemnation of private war in the March but on Gloucester's disregard of a specific royal injunction issued for a particular occasion, the king's absence overseas. See below pp. 262–3.

[23] Art. cit. 171–2.

[24] *Calendar of the Gormanston Register c. 1157–1397*, ed. J. Mills and M. J. McEnery (Dublin, 1916), 7 (translation), 181 (text). The entries in the first few folios, including the one under discussion here, seem to have been copied into the manuscript in the early-fifteenth century.

palatinate that 'he may do as he will, for he is as King there'.[25] Indeed it is in comparison with the great English palatinates that the full extent of Marcher liberties stands out most precisely.[26] The lawyers of the fifteenth century grasped that point: the franchise of the March was more ample than that of a palatinate because the March was never a parcel of the realm of England, whereas the county palatine was such a parcel which had subsequently been elevated to the status of an immunity. In the palatinates no court was final in its jurisdiction for in cases of default or denial of justice, appeal lay to the court of the King's Bench; not so in the March, except in a few abnormal cases, for there the lord and his council exercised a final jurisdiction. Again, as Chief Justice Fortescue pointed out, one of the distinctions between Marcher and palatinate franchise was that if a man in the March were vouched to warranty (that is, called to testify on a point of fact by a litigant) he could not be summoned by royal officers whereas he could be so summoned in a palatinate.[27] Such legal distinctions could be multiplied; they illustrate that in the scale of liberties as seen by medieval lawyers the March stood at the apex. Indeed it would be more correct to say that it stood outside the scale, for the very notion of liberties as defined by lawyers such as Henry Bracton—that is, as powers which immemorially or otherwise had been delegated by the Crown—did not apply in the March.

By the late-thirteenth century Marcher liberties had assumed a fairly definitive form; henceforth they would be regarded by the outside world as the distinctive hallmark of Marcher lordship. Distinctive they certainly were; so distinctive indeed that we may, paradoxically, easily overrate their significance. We may, in the first place, be too easily dazzled by the theories and *dicta* of the lawyers. 'Marcher liberties' in the final analysis is but lawyer's language for Marcher independence, and Marcher independence rested ultimately neither on constitutional nor on

---

[25] Lapsley, op. cit. 31.

[26] For the English palatinates I have relied heavily on the following: H. M. Cam, 'The Medieval English Franchise', *Speculum* 32 (1957), 427–44; Lapsley, op. cit.; C. M. Fraser, 'Prerogative and the Bishops of Durham 1267–1376', *E.H.R.* 81 (1966), 449–73; G. Barraclough, *The Earldom and County Palatine of Chester* (Oxford, 1953).

[27] Lapsley, op. cit. 232–4.

judicial definitions but on what jurists themselves call 'the normative power of fact'. It rested on the military ability of the Marcher lords to maintain their power in the March; it rested on their capacity to assert their lordship over the community of their Marcher estates; it rested on the fortunes of English politics and above all on the attitude of the kings of England. Marcher liberties did not exist in a juridical or constitutional vacuum.[28]

Furthermore while these liberties were truly impressive in terms of prestige and potentially in terms of power, they were but a minor part, albeit the distinctive and even flamboyant part, of Marcher lordship. Lordship, in the March as elsewhere, was much more than the sum of its liberties; those liberties were no more, as it were, than the judicial or quasi-judicial external shell of lordship. For lordship encompassed the lives of medieval men in a whole variety of ways not envisaged in a catalogue of such liberties. The peasants of Roussillon came nearer than did the exponents of Marcher franchise to a rounded definition of the role of lordship in medieval society: 'a lord' so they declared, 'can and should compel his subjects'.[29] Their definition is echoed by that of a modern French historian: 'lordship is the power to command, to compel and to exploit; it is also the right to exercise this power'.[30] This lordly power of constraint and command—*zwing und bann* as the German phrase had it—bore down on medieval men in many ways: it impinged on their persons and controlled their land; it claimed their money in rents and taxes; it administered justice and governance to them; it commanded their service and their loyalty. What we get in the March, what we have tried to re-capture in the foregoing chapters, is an uninterrupted view of such lordship in action. For in the March the powers of constraint, which in England were often fragmented into several hands, were here ultimately concentrated in the hands of one man—the lord of the March. This was lordship as integral as it could be. That is why George Owen's description of the Marcher lords as the 'soveraigne governors of their tenantes and people' remains so apt.[31]

[28] See below Part III.   [29] Quoted in M. Bloch, *French Rural Society*, 79.
[30] R. Boutruche, *Seigneurie et féodalité*, II, 83.
[31] *Penbrokshire*, III, 140.

Lordship was the power to command, to compel and to exploit; by that criterion Marcher lordship was supremely effective. But there was more to medieval lordship than that. Lordship had its obligations towards all its men—from the meanest advowry-man via the ordinary land-holding peasant to the retainer bound to the lord by indenture for life. All of them had acknowledged his lordship; all of them had promised him service—be it personal, manual or military; all of them were in different ways his 'men'. All of them expected well of his lordship. To spell out what precisely they expected of lordship and indeed received from it is not easy, as the benefits of lordship for the majority of men were far less tangible and in every sense far less substantial than its demands. They may be comprehended by such generalized terms as protection and patronage. Protection is indeed a vague quality and can easily degenerate from a blessing into a racket; but it was a benefit which medieval men did not underestimate, either in military or in judicial terms. It was the lord's protection, as we have seen, which the men of Pembroke believed alone stood between them and the tyranny of the *grantz mefessours*.[32] It was the lord's peace, his protection, which stood guard over his lordship; that peace was extended to all his men and enforced by his officers. It was in his role as protector that he frequently took over the private appeals of his men and prosecuted them in his own name.[33] His protection extended to his men whenever a case was 'brought against them . . . at the suit of foreign parties';[34] it also accompanied them whenever they travelled outside the lordship in the form of letters of March exempting them from prosecution other than in his courts.[35] His protection elicited pardons for them at the hands of other men; it jealously and vigorously upheld their rights when they were threatened by neighbouring lords and communities.[36]

[32] See above, p. 171
[33] For example, a plaintiff in a case of felony in Dyffryn Clwyd in 1360 transferred his case to the lord and so did another plaintiff in a case of theft in 1366: S.C. 2/218/7, m. 7ᵛ; 219/3, m. 1.
[34] This was the promise the lord made to his advowry men: S.B.Y., fol. 19.
[35] See below, p. 245.
[36] Thus in 1400 the council of the earl of Arundel supported the claim of the men of Clun to secure compensation from the men of Stapleton for two Clun men killed in Stapleton. The councils of the two lords eventually agreed on a compensation fine of £24 payable to the men of Clun: S.R.O. 552/1/34, m. 4.

Patronage was another function of lordship. Indeed after a fashion protection itself was but one form of patronage; but whereas the lord's protection extended to many, his patronage in the narrow sense of the word was reserved for the few, in the March for the very few. It took a variety of forms: a deserving local cleric might be supported in his university training by his lord (as was Adam of Usk by Earl Edmund of March);[37] another might be presented to a benefice in the lord's gift (as was Edward ap Gwilym to the Grey living of Llanbedr Dyffryn Clwyd); a local merchant might be given a handsome loan as an incentive by the lord on the understanding that it was returned with profit in due course (two of the burgesses of Kidwelly were so patronized to the tune of £100 each by the earl of Derby in 1341);[38] more normally local leases and offices formed, as we have seen, a major channel of seignorial patronage to the men of the lordship; finally, a few men (such as Henry ap Philip of Kidwelly)[39] could aspire to the ultimate token of the lord's patronage—the grant of his livery and an annual retaining fee, either for a term of years or for life.

How important seignorial patronage was in the fabric of lordship and of local society we may best illustrate by example. Iorwerth ap Llywarch of Denbigh and his brother, Cynwrig, were men of considerable stature in local society under the rule of the native Welsh princes;[40] but they flourished even more successfully under the new English lords of Denbigh, Henry Lacy and his son-in-law, Thomas of Lancaster. Iorwerth brought to his new lords his knowledge of and power in the local community; he also brought them his unwavering loyalty—he was with Henry Lacy in Paris in 1286; he was at the side of Thomas of Lancaster in the crisis over Gaveston in 1311–12 and was again active in his support in 1321–2.[41] He paid the price of such loyalty—his lands were confiscated in

---

[37] *Chronicon Adae de Usk*, ed. E. M. Thompson, 22.

[38] D.L. 25/3578–80 (Walter and Adam Aylward).

[39] He is mentioned in Gaunt's retinue: *John of Gaunt's Register 1379–83*, ed. E. C. Lodge and R. Somerville (Camden Society, 3rd ser. 56–7, 1937), I, 12. For his career, see R. A. Griffiths, *The Principality of Wales*, I, 280–1.

[40] Cynwrig ap Llywarch's heraldic slab is in the church at Yspyty Ifan: C. A. Gresham, *Medieval Stone Carving in North Wales*, 153–5. He was the ancestor of the famous Plas Iolyn family: E. P. Roberts, 'Teulu Plas Iolyn', *T.D.H.S.* 13 (1964), 39–110.

[41] D.L. 36/2, no. 248; *C.P.R. 1313–17*, 21; *C. Inq. Misc. 1307–49*, no. 507.

1322 and only restored to him in 1330;[42] but he also reaped handsomely the profits of patronage. Negatively, he was given the virtual status of an honorary Englishman as he was exempted from the racial resettlement policy of the new Marcher lords and allowed to retain his ancestral estates at Lleweni. Positively, the fruits of patronage were lavished upon him: over 1,000 acres of land worth over £28 per annum and two water mills in his native lordship; lucrative local sinecures; and, not least, an entrée into the inner circles of his new lord, for by 1313 he was one of the earl of Lancaster's chamberlains.[43] Iorwerth ap Llywarch knew very well what good lordship meant.

So also did Einion Sais and his descendants in Brecon. The family of Einion Sais, alias Einion ap Rhys, came according to the genealogies of the stock of the independent Welsh princes of Brycheiniog (Brecon); but by the mid-thirteenth century it had adjusted itself fully to the rule of the Marcher lords. Einion Sais himself stood by the Bohun family in the difficult years of the mid-thirteenth century in the March and it was only reluctantly and under military pressure that he accepted the overlordship of Llywelyn ap Gruffydd, prince of Gwynedd and conqueror of Brecon.[44] Einion's descendants displayed the same loyalty: his son Hywel actively supported Humphrey Bohun (d. 1298);[45] his grandson Hywel Fychan stood by Humphrey's son in the calamity of 1322 and was fined £500 by the king for his loyalty to his lord;[46] his great-grandson, Llywelyn, served the last Bohun earl of Hereford (d. 1373) and his successor, Henry Bolingbroke, equally faithfully.[47] It was in the next

[42] *C.C.R. 1330–33*, 84.

[43] *S.D.*, 62, G. A. Holmes, *Estates of the Higher Nobility*, 135, 137, 140; *C. Inq. Misc. 1307–49*, no. 507. J. R. Maddicott, *Thomas of Lancaster*, 12.

[44] *Littere Wallie*, 28, 33–4; J. B. Smith in *B.B.C.S.* 24 (1970), 86.

[45] For Hywel's lands and for his co-parcenors see *C.I.P.M.*, III, no. 552; for his support of Humphrey Bohun see *C.P.R. 1292–1301*, 564. He was still alive in 1313: D.L. 36/1 no. 93.

[46] He was almost certainly the Hywel ap Hywel of Wales: *C.F.R. 1319–27*, 156. He was sheriff of Brecon 1332–44 and farmer of the lands of Mortimer of Pencelli (D.L. 25/1627). He appears frequently in the Bohun accounts of Brecon and was appointed one of the custodians of the lordship in 1361: *C.F.R. 1356–68*, 173.

[47] He received annuities from Bohun and Bolingbroke alike and was master-sergeant of the lordship: S.C. 6/1156/15; D.L. 42/15 fol. 159; *C.P.R. 1370–4*, 382. For the inscription on his tomb (no longer extant) at Brecon priory, see B.L. Harleian 3325, fol. 89.

generation, that of Llywelyn's sons, that the great test of loyalty came for the family during the Glyn Dŵr rebellion; but their loyalty to the lord of Brecon triumphed over any sympathy they may have had for the Welsh cause. That loyalty once more cost them dearly: Llywelyn ap Hywel was harassed by his enemies, the houses of his sons were burnt to the ground, and the most famous and redoubtable of those sons, Dafydd Gam, was captured and ransomed by the Welsh rebels.[48] Yet the family's loyalty remained as unflinching as ever. When the new lord of Brecon, Henry V, went on campaign in 1415 Dafydd Gam accompanied him with three men-at-arms and fell at Agincourt. It was a highly appropriate martyrdom for one whom a sixteenth-century antiquary so aptly characterized as 'a great stickler for the Duke of Lancaster'.[49]

He and his forebears had indeed been great sticklers for the lord of Brecon for over a century and a half and had enhanced the stature of his lordship both within and without the boundaries of Brecon. Their rewards were duly forthcoming: occasional gifts, such as the saddle given to Hywel Fychan by Earl Humphrey (d. 1361); key posts in the lordship such as those of constable, master-sergeant and sheriff (virtually a family preserve); lucrative farms and custodies; seignorial favours in abundance from timber for the repair of houses to pardons for felonies and trespasses, from permission to collect a personal subsidy to a handsome share of confiscated lands; annuities such as the five marks paid to Llywelyn ap Hywel by the earl of Hereford or the forty marks paid to his son by Henry IV; and quite possibly even the final accolade of knighthood which, according to legend, Henry V bestowed on Dafydd Gam at Agincourt. Good lordship was the due and proper return on good service; the family of Einion Sais had come to appreciate that equation well enough over the generations.

Men such as Iorwerth ap Llywarch or Einion Sais and his family were not only the recipients of seignorial bounty and office; they were also in their turn the focus of more local loyalties, services and rewards. They exercised, as it were, a mediate lordship on behalf of their lord; the co-operation of

---

[48] I hope to trace the history of the family during the Glyn Dŵr revolt in detail elsewhere. It provides the best-documented example of a loyalist family during the revolt.　　　[49] David Powel, *The Historie of Cambria*, ed. W. Wynne (1784), 320.

men such as they was essential to the functioning of Marcher governance and to the equilibrium of Marcher society. That is why the distribution of patronage to them was such a crucial feature of lordship. Nowhere more so than in the March, for there the Marcher lord provided the only major focus of service and reward; there was no alternative ladder of royal service and patronage. Furthermore it was vital that the benefits of the lord's patronage and the avenues of the lord's service should be open to local men and Welshmen at that, and should not be restricted to a foreign, colonial personnel. Without such a prospect, service and loyalty would turn sour; without it local men would be alienated from lordship and in the March such alienation could exacerbate the distinctions between conquered and conqueror and between native and alien into a dangerously explosive issue.

Even for the ordinary men of the March we should not too readily assume that lordship appeared only as an institution of financial and judicial exploitation. The lord was in some measure a focus of service for all his men: it was under his banner that they fought both at home and abroad; it was in his pay that they often served as labourers, masons, drovers and couriers. He was also a focus of loyalty: for the inhabitants of the March. even more than for those of England, their tie with their lord described their status *vis à vis* the outside world. They were, for example, not merely the men of Brecon but the men of the lord of Brecon. Such a tie assumed, and on the whole correctly, a total commitment to their lord and to his cause.[50] Such loyalty, it is true, sprang from a social ethos of deference rather than from any deep act of personal commitment; it was a reflex loyalty and as such could be very fickle indeed. Even Marcher lordship could not afford to be merely an institution of coercion and exploitation. If it failed in the duties of good lordship, if others within Marcher society began to provide those qualities of protection and patronage expected of a lord, then Marcher lordship itself would be the loser, in terms of profit and of authority.

'The great magnates' it has been said 'ruled the England of their day'.[51] The dictum could be applied even more appropriately to the March in the fourteenth century. There were, it is

[50] Below pp. 289–93.   [51] G. A. Holmes, *Estates of the Higher Nobility*, 1.

true, within each Marcher lordship other men and institutions who exercised lordship vigorously and successfully—bishops, monasteries, mesne lords and squires. These men also exercised powers of coercion and protection; they also dispensed protection and patronage; they called themselves 'lords' and were so regarded. At the local level Marcher society was often polarized around these men. Their lordship might be jurisdictionally and otherwise less complete than that of the Marcher lord; but what it may have lacked in authority was in good measure compensated by the fact that it was generally exercised in person at the local level. These men came increasingly during the course of the fifteenth and sixteenth centuries to dominate Marcher politics and Marcher society. If we are not mistaken, there was in that period a marked shift of social and economic power and of political leadership, in short of lordship, from the great Marcher lords into the hands of these mesne lords, squires, gentry or whatever we may prefer to call them.[52] We may detect signs of this shift of power and of lordship in the fourteenth century but as yet the great lords, the *barones de Marchia*, still dominate the social and political horizon of the March. The fourteenth century was indeed their century *par excellence*. It was a century of peace, when the resources of lordship were no longer heavily mortgaged in military affairs, at least in comparison with the twelfth and thirteenth centuries. It was a century when the Marcher lords were able to concentrate on giving a more precise and powerful content to their lordship. They did so vigorously and successfully, asserting their power over men and land alike, consolidating their estates and laying new claims to demesne resources, elaborating the machinery of their judicial control and devising new methods of augmenting the profits of lordship. Never was Marcher lordship more masterful. It was, more effectively than before or later, the source of authority and jurisdiction, the focus of worship and of patronage. The Marcher lord was indeed the 'soveraigne governor' of his lordship; its inhabitants were not only his tenants; they were also his subjects.

[52] Cf. M. E. James, 'The Concept of Order and the Northern Rising of 1569', *Past and Present* 60 (1973), 49–83; idem. *Family, Lineage and Civil Society: A Study of Society, Politics and Mentality in the Durham Region 1500–1640* (1974); R. B. Smith, *Land and Politics in the England of Henry VIII: the West Riding of Yorkshire, 1530–46* (1970).

III

THE MARCHER LORDSHIP AND THE WORLD BEYOND

11

Relations between Marcher
Lordships

THE character of Marcher lordship and its impact on Marcher
society has hitherto been our theme. That lordship, as has been
seen time and again, was exceptionally comprehensive. It was
comprehensive in terms of its authority over the men of the
March; and it was extensive also in its almost complete independence of any external control. Each Marcher lordship
was a self-contained and self-sufficient unit of governance. The
March was a collection of such lordships; it knew no unity.
Particularism here reigned supreme.

That particularism was compounded of several elements. It
was in part a question of geography. Marcher society partook
of the intense localism of most medieval communities. Localism
in its turn bred a sense of intense loyalty towards the native
community and a corresponding suspicion of the outsider. In
Dyffryn Clwyd, for example, the men of the neighbouring
lordships of Denbigh, Englefield, Mold and Yale were officially
designated as aliens (*extranei*) and were treated as such.[1] They
could not be expected to know or to respect the customs and
usages of the lordship nor to have a sense of loyalty towards it.
In the March this geography of particularism was strongly reinforced by a native Welsh tradition of the fragmentation of
authority. Neither Wales nor the March had known political
unity other than the short-lived military superiority of the
conqueror. The Marcher tradition of authority and loyalty
assumed particularism, *morcellement*, as the natural order of
affairs. So also did the political language of the March: it
spoke of countries (*gwledydd, patriae*) and assumed that each
would be autonomous and enjoy its own distinctive customs;[2]

---

[1] For such references to *extranei*, see S.C. 2/218/9, m. 2 (1361); 219/2, m. 12,
m. 12ᵛ (1365); 222/5, m. 3 (1441).
[2] Thus a fifteenth-century legal memorandum distinguishes the practice 'within
the lordship of Oswestry' from that 'within other countries' ('o vewn swydd

it spoke of aliens or 'other-country men' (*alltudion, extranei*) and devised special rules and obligations for them.[3] It was into this native tradition of separatism that the Marcher lords entered and they soon exulted in it. Their tenants were their subjects amenable only to their authority and answerable to no one else. The lords held their lordships with full regality and with the same uninhibited independence which the native Welsh princes had enjoyed in their kingdoms.[4] They introduced notions of 'the well-being of the lord and country' into their apologetics[5] and issued statutes and ordinances in defence of the interests of the lordship (*statuta patrie, ordinaciones patrie*).[6] They fostered the indigenous sentiments of local loyalty and harnessed them to their purpose; they equated service to the lord with the convenience of the country; they even introduced notions of 'treason to the lord' and 'sedition against the men of the country' into the language of the courts.[7] That is, they institutionalized the particularism of Marcher society and brought it under the umbrella of the lord's convenience. Local and personal loyalties were strong in England; but there the fragmented geography of lordship and the existence of an alternative pattern of loyalty to the king and of the institutions of a common polity—hundred, shire, royal justice and royal taxes—inhibited the development of a powerful particularism. In the March, on the other hand, these local and personal loyalties had a free hand; there was no competing focus of loyalty and authority.

groesoswallt . . . mewn gwledydd eraill') and makes it clear that these other countries are in fact neighbouring lordships: B.L. Add. 46, 846, fol. 151.

[3] It is true that the word *alltud* in the Welsh law-texts often refers to a non-Welshman; but in late-medieval Marcher records it is amply clear that the term alien (*extraneus*) refers to a man from another lordship.

[4] Thus the lords of Bromfield and Yale claimed that they were granted their lordships 'cum regalitate . . . adeo **integre sicut** dominus Wallensis eadem dominia tenuit': S.B.Y., fol. 170.

[5] For example, the sale of a tenement to an alien was said to be contrary to the lord's interest ('commodum domini') while the sale of goods to an alien was likewise condemned as being 'to the grave damage of the lord and the whole country' (ad grave dampnum domini et tocius patrie'): S.C. 2/217/6, m. 33 (1341); 218/3, m. 6 (1352).   [6] For such statutes see below p. 235.

[7] One of the charges against Richard Siward in 1245 was that of treachery to the lord of Glamorgan—'qui de consilio comitis fuit sicut seductor et felonus' (*Cartae*, II, no. 534, p. 551). In 1414 the charge against one of the tenants of Dyffryn Clwyd was that of being 'insidiatrix et receptrix hominum de Bromfield et Yale ad insidiandos homines et tenentes domini de Grey . . . ad grave dampnum domini . . . et tenentium suorum': S.C. 2/221/8, m. 14.

Ties of locality here coincided easily with ties of lordship. The March was a congeries of autonomous lordships. But how far and how effectively was this autonomy maintained and how far was it compromised in actual practice? We may best answer that question by considering two spheres of policy, those of economic and judicial affairs, where the problems raised by Marcher autonomy were most acute. In economic affairs the Marcher lord indeed treated his lordship as if it were a kingdom. He insisted on the distinctiveness of his lordship as an economic unit, expressed in the most elementary fashion in its own scale of weights and measures—the measures of Denbigh or of Ruthin, for example. Nor was this merely an unimportant local idiosyncracy: the right to determine his own scale of weights and measures throughout his lordship was one of the privileges of Marcher status, not to be lightly usurped by any mesne tenant.[8] Within the lordship, the lord sought to impose a measure of economic regulation and control (or so at least the abundant evidence from Dyffryn Clwyd suggests). Wages were fixed at 'statutory' levels long before the Statute of Labourers and those who offered or received excess wages were penalized.[9] The movement of labour out of the lordship, particularly during the peak harvesting period in the autumn, was likewise regulated from an early date and those who were convicted of leaving the lordship to sell their labour elsewhere were severely punished.[10] It was an attempt in part to ensure an adequate pool of labour within the lordship; but it was much more—in view of the relatively minor labour demands of most Marcher lords—an attempt to assert a strict control over movement into and out of the lordship. Such a rigid view of labour-mobility was difficult enough to enforce on a small manor; it presented

[8] This was one of the charges levelled in 1433 by the lord of Blaenllyfni against his mesne-tenant, Sir John Pauncefoot of Crickhowell: B.L. Egerton Roll, 8708.

[9] For an early example of fines for taking excessive wages contrary to the local statute (*statutum patrie*), see S.C. 2/215/69, m. 8 (Dyffryn Clwyd, 1307). The practice was also common in the Principality: *T.C.S.* (1925–6), 81–2.

[10] Such fines are common on the court-rolls of Dyffryn Clwyd, Bromfield and Yale and Clun. The fines could be as high as 6s. 8d. and were specifically imposed for breach of local statutes. Much of this illicit movement of labour was no doubt voluntary; but some of it was organized by professional recruiting agents (for such a one see S.C. 2/218/8, m. 1ᵛ [1360]—'communis conciliator servientium . . . ad eundum extra patriam ad deserviendum'). The rigid control of labour was seen by contemporaries as one of the distinctive customs of Wales: *C.P.R. 1422–9*, 265.

insuperable problems in a large Marcher lordship. Yet its interest remains: as universal landlord and sovereign governor of his lordship the Marcher lord could propound a wage and labour policy applicable throughout that lordship.

The Marcher lord could also shape or attempt to shape a commercial policy which applied throughout his lordship and which served to bolster both his authority and his profits. Marcher lords took no active part in trade, except possibly in the marketing of their own demesne produce and, indirectly, by an occasional loan of money to a local merchant.[11] But they could use their authority fairly effectively within their lordships both to direct trade and to profit by it. They could found boroughs and grant them charters of liberties; they could and generally did give those towns a monopoly of trade within their lordship; they could bestow extensive privileges on the burgesses and letters of protection on 'foreign' merchants. Their motives were not altogether altruistic for by concentrating trade in certain centres they could the more easily control and profit by it. Protection as so often was but the genial face of profit. The major instrument of seignorial commercial control and profit was, of course, the toll system. The March abounded with seignorial tolls; they were indeed one of the status symbols of Marcher lordship. The Marcher lord claimed the right to levy his tolls on all commerical transactions within his lordship, within and without franchise.[12] He entered a tariff of those tolls into his rentals amongst the items of his revenue.[13] He was right to do so, for the profits from tolls—normally levied on all goods worth fourpence or more and payable by the seller—could be substantial: £28 from Bromfield and Yale in 1345; £37 from Chirkland in 1365; £54 from Monmouth town in 1378.[14] The Monmouth figure in fact also contains the income from the prise of ale, another profitable and irksome item in the lord's commercial control. That control could be yet more profitable if the lordship had a coastline, for then the lord would levy a

[11] For such a loan by Henry of Grosmont see above p. 224. Among the money owed to Edmund Fitzalan, earl of Arundel (d. 1326) was a loan of £484 advanced to a Shrewsbury merchant, John Walsh: E. 163/2/22.

[12] As was vigorously asserted by the earl of Hereford in 1349: D.L. 41/6/11.

[13] For such tariffs, see *Extent of Chirkland*, 3–4, and *T.D.H.S.* 14 (1965) 53–73.

[14] S.C. 2/226/18, m. 11ᵛ; N.L.W. Chirk Castle D. 27; D.L. 29/594/9508.

toll on each ship that called in port and exact a prisage on cargoes of ale: the prise of wine in Milford, one of the premier ports of Wales, was expected to yield over £80 in the 1370s.[15] It is in the light of these figures that we should interpret the fierce fines that were both ordained and exacted for the evasion of the lord's tolls: a fine in Chirk equivalent to 240 times the value of the original tariff; elsewhere savage individual and communal fines (such as one of £500 laid on the community of Brecon in 1352).

Tolls were not only profitable; they were also a clear sign of the lord's mastery of his lordship. Not only were his tollbooths to be found in his boroughs (as was the Booth Hall at Cardiff where goods were examined and taxed); his tollgates were often to be found at the boundaries of his lordship, often indeed on remote mountain roads as in Brecon where the lord's tollgates were sited at Ystradfellte, Penderyn, Tir Ralph, Glyn Tawe, Penpont and 'Maenorydd Bychain'.[16] These were the outposts of the lord's commercial authority. There the lord would tax traffic passing in and out or even through his lordship. There he would show for the first time his discrimination against the alien, for if both parties in a commercial transaction were aliens both had to pay toll; not so if they were natives.[17] That discrimination against aliens was manifested in many other ways. The lord could regulate and even forbid trade with aliens in certain commodities. In Dyffryn Clwyd two statutes were issued on the subject: one in 1346 forbade tenants of the lordship to sell turves, wood, hay or straw outside the lordship under pain of a fine of 40s.; another of 1395 prohibited anyone from leaving the lordship with vendible goods before first offering them for sale in Ruthin market under pain of a penalty of 100s.[18] The lord might also veto sales of land or property to aliens as being 'contrary to the interests of the lord' or in contravention of a local statute;[19] he might prohibit his tenants from taking their corn out of the lordship to be ground and aliens from bringing

---

[15] *Cal. Public Records re. Pembs.*, I, 69. See also ibid. III, 222 for the reservation by the lord of his right to prisage of wine in his charter to Tenby.

[16] *Glam. C.H.*, III, 348; D.L. 29/730/12015, m. 15.

[17] *Extent of Chirkland*, 3.

[18] S.C. 2/217/11, m. 18 (1346); 221/1, m. 18ᵛ (1395).

[19] S.C. 2/217/6, m. 33 (1341: 'non esset ad commodum domini'); 215/72, m. 14 (1313: 'dimisit terram suam contra statutum patrie cuidam extraneo').

in their cattle to graze on his waste.[20] Such regulations indicate
an attitude of regarding the lordship in so far as possible as a
closed society and its tenants as favoured men. It was an
attitude compounded of paternalism and protectionism; it was
also proto-mercantilist in its jealous regard for the economic
well-being of the lordship.

Such policies, for such in effect they were, did not altogether
lack success. Many a Marcher lordship formed a fairly coherent
and relatively self-contained unit of economic geography and
marketing so that the lord's desire to exploit and protect its
economic activities was not imposed on an altogether artificial
unit. Furthermore his policies were actively supported by local
interest groups within his lordship—by the burgesses whose
privileges he maintained, by the employers of labour who shared
his desire to fix wages and to restrict the free movement of
labour, and by the community as a whole which was as
vigorously loyal to the interests of the lordship against exploitation by aliens as he was.[21] Furthermore, however exclusive
and inward-looking the economic attitude of the Marcher
lords may appear to be, it nevertheless had to it an inbuilt
external dimension. For each Marcher lordship was part and
parcel of a wider estates-complex and it developed close bonds,
economic and otherwise, with the lord's other estates. We have
already noticed the active cattle trade which had developed
between many Marcher lordships and the English estates and
households of their owners.[22] Nor was the trade a one-way affair:
the earl of Lincoln's stud at Ichtenhil (co. Lancs.) was supplied
with horses from Moelywig park in Denbigh but equally the
parks at Denbigh were stocked with deer from the great
Cheshire forest of Delamere.[23] Nor was the trade merely in
livestock: the new bridge over the river Bann at Coleraine was
built of timber shipped from the Mortimer estates in Usk,
while the mills of the Mortimer manors in Ireland were fitted
out with millstones transported from Anglesey.[24] The roads of

[20] S.C. 2/218/8, m. 13 (1360); *S.D.*, 107.
[21] For example, the men of Talgarth insisted that the lord should not accept
foreign animals into the common pasture except with the consent of the community
E. 326/B. 8812.
[22] See above, p. 116.
[23] D.L. 29/1/2, m. 1ᵛ (1305); *C.C.R. 1279–88*, 278.
[24] *Monasticon Anglicanum*, VI, i, 353; S.C. 6/1184/22 (1397).

the March were the arteries of lordship; the traffic on them was often from one estate centre to another—from Ludlow to Denbigh, for example.[25] That is why the Marcher economy has to it an almost colonial dimension: trade was often discouraged with neighbouring lordships but encouraged with distant centres of the lord's inheritance.

But we must not exaggerate. Seignorial control was firm of intent; but less impressive of achievement than the documentation might suggest. It often relied heavily on sectional and even racial elements in the community, most notably on the English communities of the chartered boroughs. Such an attitude made for fission rather than fusion in the economic life of the lordship and of its community. The fact that the Marcher boroughs were the first target of the Glyn Dŵr rebels in 1400 is comment enough on the consequences of that policy. Furthermore, while seignorial action could inhibit new developments in the March, it could not altogether control or stifle them. It might plead and cajole over the issue of keeping Marcher boroughs and Marcher trade within the framework of the original town-walls, but it could not prevent the development of large extra-mural suburbs as at Denbigh or Kidwelly;[26] it might stubbornly defend the trading privileges and monopolies of its own favoured borough as happened at Holt but it could not prevent the development of a more convenient and more popular centre of local trade such as Wrexham;[27] it might compile long lists of offenders against its wage-regulations but it was no more capable than the English government of enforcing a thoroughgoing policy of the control of wages and the movement of labour. If the lord's control of the economic affairs of his own lordship was less than complete, he could hardly expect to be able to insulate his lordship from outside contacts economically. Towns such as Ludlow, Shrewsbury and Carmarthen were already developing as major centres of exchange quite independent of any framework of a lordship-centred economy.

[25] B.L. Egerton Roll 8729 is an interesting undated account of a journey by one hack, twelve cart-horses and seven men from Ludlow to Denbigh. The round journey took just over a week. [26] Below pp. 335-7.
[27] D. Pratt, 'The Medieval Borough of Holt', *T.D.H.S.* 14 (1965), 9-74; *History of Wrexham*, ed. A. H. Dodd (Wrexham, 1957), 14-33, and B. Evans, 'Grant of Privileges to Wrexham (1380)', *B.B.C.S.* 19 (1960), 42-7.

The Marcher lordship was far more clearly and effectively a self-contained and self-sufficient unit in judicial and administrative matters than in economic and commercial affairs. Each lordship had its own laws—'the laws of the land of Maelienydd', 'the law and custom of the land of Brecon', 'the custom and usage of the land of Glamorgan'.[28] Each lordship also had its own hierarchy of courts. Within the lordship the lord's word in judicial matters was normally final; but his judicial arm reached no farther than the boundaries of his lordship. When men were outlawed, they could only be outlawed within his lordship; when they were sentenced to abjure his lands, that sentence was only effective within his boundaries. When, for example, 27 men were outlawed in the commote of Dogfeilyn (Dyffryn Clwyd) in 1382 the futility of the exercise was revealed in the marginal comment of the clerk of the court: 'they have no goods because they are aliens'.[29] For over the alien the lord exercised in theory little judicial authority or none at all. Since the alien was not his 'man' he was not normally justiciable in his court;[30] since he was foreign to the lordship he could not be expected to know its laws and customs.[31] Judicial lordship in the March was a combination of autonomy within the lordship and impotence outside it. In such a situation it is not altogether surprising that the alien should be treated with suspicion and that the lords Marcher should demand the unwavering judicial loyalty of their tenants. Heavy fines were decreed for men who dared to implead or vex fellow-tenants in the courts of other lordships; in Bromfield and Yale the penalty was as high as a hundred marks, for the offence was regarded as peculiarly heinous, 'contrary to the customs of the lordship and in derogation of the royal liberties and franchises of the lord of Bromfield'.[32] The judicial jealousy which in the case of the kings of England was largely directed against ecclesiastical and especially papal jurisdiction was in the March directed against the alien. In 1382 the lord of Dyffryn Clwyd issued a proclamation that no one from his lordship was henceforth to aid and counsel an alien at law with

---

[28] *C.P.R. 1292–1301*, 290; D.L. 41/6/11; *Cartae*, III, no. 534, p. 553.

[29] S.C. 2/220/1, m. 20ᵛ.

[30] See above p. 133.

[31] Thus in Dyffryn Clwyd it was recognized that aliens could not be expected to know the customs of Ruthin: S.C. 2/218/9, m. 9ᵛ (1362).

[32] N.L.W. Peniarth, 404 D., fol. 103 (1379). For similar penalties in Dyffryn

a tenant of the lordship under pain of a penalty of £2.[33] The tone of such an edict—and it is amply paralleled elsewhere in the March[34]—is that of a lord who regards his lordship as a virtual kingdom and who expects his men to share his jealous defence of the interests of that kingdom.

The March was a collection of such kingdoms. The problems posed by this judicial fragmentation of the March and by the vigorously defended judicial autonomy of each of its lordships are immediately obvious and were so to contemporaries. Indeed they have become one of the most notorious features of the March. We need not rely on the *parti-pris* statements of later publicists; the records themselves are eloquent enough of the abuses inherent in the situation. Men accused of felony fled from one lordship to another and even from England into a Marcher lordship; there they could fine with the lord and receive sanctuary from him.[35] It was not unusual for men to be abducted from one lordship to another and there compelled to pay a large ransom for their release.[36] Men outlawed in one lordship might find refuge in a neighbouring one and use their new home as a base from which to launch raids on their enemies.[37] Men threatened with legal action in their native lordship could transfer their goods to a nearby lordship and thereby place themselves outside the reach of the lord's power of distraint.[38] Marcher tenants committing offences in the English border counties went unpunished as there was no legal

Clwyd for impleading fellow-tenants in the court of another lordship see S.C. 2/219/1, m. 11, m. 31ᵛ (Caerwys, 1364); 219/6, m. 24 (Edeirnion, 1369); m. 31 (Denbigh, 1369); 220/1, m. 5 (Principality, 1382).

[33] S.C. 2/220/1, m. 17ᵛ.

[34] For example, in 1344 a man from Clun was accused of standing with the men of Maelienydd against the men of his own lordship: S.R.O. 552/1/11, m. 1.

[35] Three examples from the Dyffryn Clwyd court rolls may serve as illustrations: a felon flees from England into the March and fines with the lord (S.C. 2/216/12, m. 35 [1332]); a tenant from Dyffryn Clwyd flees to Glyndyfrdwy (S.C. 2/218/4, m. 13 [1354]); a man committing homicide in the lordship attempts to flee to Denbigh (S.C. 2/219/2, m. 29ᵛ [1365]).

[36] *C.P.R. 1327–30*, 80, 82 (a man and his wife abducted to Clun and held to ransom); S.C. 2/219/2, m. 16ᵛ, m. 19 (tenants of Dyffryn Clwyd abducted to Yale and Ystrad Alun). The practice was particularly rife during and after the Glyn Dŵr revolt.

[37] See, for example, *C.P.R. 1272–81*, 56.

[38] For example, the son of a Dyffryn Clwyd tenant whose father died suddenly (probably intestate) immediately drove his stock to Englefield: S.C. 2/220/1, m. 16 (1382).

sanction to compel them to appear to answer a charge outside
their native lordship, whereas English merchants on business
in the March were frequently arrested and had their goods
distrained for the debts of others and without any hope of redress.[39]

This catalogue of abuses could easily be lengthened; but it
is already long enough to show that most of the abuses arose
directly from the judicial fragmentation of the March. Such
abuses were not, of course, peculiar to the March: in some
degree the medieval notion of liberties and franchises, of
sanctuary and of protection meant that problems of overlapping
and competing jurisdictions were common enough. But in the
March the problem was altogether larger in its dimensions than
in England, for in the March there was in practice no overall
judicial authority with power 'within and without franchise'.
The problems of the March were in effect (and with the
necessary qualifications) those of the relations between judicially
sovereign lordships; that is, they were in their own fashion the
problems of 'international' relations.

When international relations break down, when the problems
of co-existence become so acute as to be intolerable, the result
is war. That alternative (as we have seen) was accepted, indeed
was jealously asserted as a rightful custom, in the March. In a
society where warfare was endemic and where native tradition
sanctioned war as a normal feature of relationships between
princes, it was but natural that the Marcher lords should
accept war as a method of settling their differences. A succession
dispute to a lordship was more likely in the March than in
England to take the form of raids and sieges, as well as the more
conventional routes of legal action: it was so, for example, in
the prolonged and bitter dispute over Powys between John
Charlton and Gruffudd de la Pole in the early fourteenth
century.[40] Likewise in the March territorial disputes between
neighbouring lords, which in England might have been contained within the political or judicial arena, readily escalated
into confrontations of force, as the younger Despenser found to
his cost in 1321. Even in the more normal course of relationships between Marcher lordships the occasions for open conflict

---

[39] For these complaints, see *Rot. Parl.*, ii, 352, 397; iii, 272–3, 295, 308.
[40] J. R. Maddicott, *Thomas of Lancaster*, 139–41, 147.

were near enough to hand. Disputes over the boundaries of lordships were one obvious *casus belli*. The most famous boundary dispute was, of course, the one between the lords of Glamorgan and Brecon: it simmered from one truce to the next during the thirteenth century before it boiled over into a series of raids and counter-raids in the late 1280s. But it was paralleled by others such as the prolonged disputes between the lords of Powys and Caus or those of Brecon and Llandovery.[41] The character of these frontier wars is admirably evoked by *The Legend of Fulk Fitzwarin*; its author spoke of a past age but 'private' wars were no distant memories for the Fitzwarins, for as lords of Whittington they still waged an occasional war against their neighbours, the Fitzalans of Oswestry, well into the late thirteenth century and even beyond.[42] According to one contemporary account it was a boundary dispute which was the immediate cause of the outbreak of the Glyn Dŵr revolt in September 1400.[43]

Another fertile source of friction in the March was the disputes which arose directly out of the judicial fragmentation of the area—from cattle rustling between lordships, from anger at sanctuary afforded to felons, from the murder of a local man in a neighbouring lordship, from attempts to avenge abductions. Thus, to give a late example, the border raids between Elfael on the one hand and Hay and neighbouring lordships on the other in 1450 were triggered off by the murder of a certain Gruffudd ap Meuric.[44] It had the character of a communal vendetta, as indeed did much of the warfare of the March. Some of it was occasioned by a fairly minor incident; much of it fed on a prolonged tradition of rivalry and hostility between neighbouring communities—between the men of Brecon and Builth or between the men of Kidwelly and Gower.[45] When we hear, for example, of discord between the men of Clun and Powys in 1363, or of a raid by the men of Glynbwch (Hay) on

---

[41] For the former see C. J. Spurgeon in *Mont. Colls.* 57 (1961–2), 125–37; for the latter J. E. Morris, *The Welsh Wars of Edward I*, 223–4.

[42] R. W. Eyton, *Antiquities of Shropshire*, XI, 40; *C.C.R. 1296–1302*, 495.

[43] J. E. Lloyd, *Owen Glendower* (Oxford, 1931), 30.

[44] N.L.W. Kentchurch Court, 1027.

[45] For disputes between Brecon and Builth see *C.P.R. 1281–92*, 317 (1289) and D.L. 29/671/10810, m. 23 (1357), and between Kidwelly and Iscennen and Gower see *Glam. C.H.*, III, 248 and *C. Inq. Misc. 1307–49*, no. 1417.

the town of Clifford in 1368 when 200 houses were burned, or
of the men of Montgomery raiding the lordship of Caus in
1398 and abducting four of its men, we need not assume that
we are describing more than communal violence.[46] The lord
could certainly disown his men in such cases: the men of
Brecon, for example, were fined £720 by their lord in 1357 for
their foray against their neighbours of Builth, just as a century
later the steward of Hay commanded his men to make resti-
tution to the men of Eardisley for offences committed against
them.[47] Yet given the jealously protective attitude of a lord
towards his lordship and his declared role of avowing and
maintaining the quarrels of his men, and given also the political
rivalries that often prevailed between Marcher lords, such
communal quarrels and raids were often either condoned or
even officially sanctioned by the lord. The lord of Bromfield and
Yale, for example, could hardly turn a blind eye when 500
men (allegedly) from his lordship raided Dyffryn Clwyd and
paraded outside the castle and town of Ruthin, terrifying the
Lady Grey who was then in the castle with child.[48] Such a
massive raid appeared too daring and too contrived to be
merely an outburst of communal violence. The lord might
indeed instigate such a raid: when the younger Despenser
authorized his men of Cantrefmawr to take distress on John
Giffard's men of Cantrefbychan in 1320 he was virtually issuing
a licence for Marcher warfare.[49] Violence was near the surface
in all medieval societies; local vendettas and punitive raids
were common; lords frequently maintained the quarrels of
their men, if need be with force. Yet even by medieval standards
the March was peculiarly violent. That this should be so is in
good part to be explained both by the judicial fragmentation
of the March and by the acknowledged right of Marcher lords
to wage war 'with banners displayed'.

Yet that is not the whole story. The fragmentation of judicial
authority certainly posed problems; but those problems were
not beyond solution. We must bear in mind in the first place

[46] N.L.W. Aston Hall, 6916; J. Taylor, 'A Wigmore Chronicle 1355–77',
Proceedings of the Leeds Philosophical and Literary Society (Literary and Historical Section) 11
(1964–6), 81–94 at p. 90; N.L.W. Peniarth 280D. fol. 70.
[47] D.L. 29/671/10810, m. 23; N.L.W. Peniarth 280D., fol. 50.
[48] S.C. 2/221/8, m. 20 (1413).
[49] *Cal. Anc. Corr. conc. Wales*, 184.

that several groups of Marcher lordships were owned by a single family, most notably the Marcher estates of the Clare family in the early fourteenth century and those of Mortimer and Fitzalan subsequently; the custom of each lordship might be different, but within the family complex of lands no man could be regarded as an alien in the eyes of the lord. Much more important, however, is the fact that the court rolls show fairly unequivocally that the judicial situation in the March was more complex than theory or later propaganda might suggest. It is clear, for example, that a man committing an offence outside his lordship could nonetheless be prosecuted, convicted and punished for that offence within his own lordship: thus a man abducting an ox from the county of Shropshire into the liberty of Clun did not go unpunished nor was a Bromfield man exempt from prosecution by his lord because his offence had been committed in Dyffryn Clwyd.[50] Furthermore the March was not necessarily a safe retreat for the alien or for the refugee from justice. He did not, as is often asserted, enjoy an automatic right of sanctuary. Thus when Madoc Goch crossed over from Ceri into Clun he found no joy in his new home; he was seized by the lord's officials and charged with being a common thief and an outlaw from Ceri.[51] Such a refugee if charged in court might refuse to reply to the charge and stand on his rights as an alien; even that, however, was no automatic visa to freedom, for more likely than not he would be imprisoned.[52] If an alien committed an offence in a Marcher lordship his status as an alien could prove a very fragile defence indeed, as the Dyffryn Clwyd records show. If caught redhanded, he could claim no exemption whatsoever;[53] in other cases he might be required to find pledges within the lordship who were bound to answer for him if he failed to appear;[54] he could be outlawed.[55] Even more significant are those cases where an alien is convicted in court

[50] S.R.O. 552/1/2, m. 5 (1333); S.C. 2/226/18, m. 11 (1345).
[51] S.R.O. 552/1/7, m. 10 (1336).
[52] Thus a man charged with homicide in Clun found that his pleas that he was an alien and that he was not caught red-handed could not save him from prison: S.R.O. 552/1/10, m. 12 (1344).
[53] For such a case see S.C. 2/213/10, m. 33ᵛ (a thief from Edeirnion caught red-handed fined £4 10s.)
[54] S.C. 2/218/11, m. 10ᵛ (1363).
[55] Ibid. m. 5. (In this case the goods of the outlawed alien were successfully claimed by his lord's officer, the *rhaglaw* of Yale.)

for an offence committed in the lordship and subsequently amerced or even hanged for it.[56] Nor was that all. There are cases in the court rolls of men from one lordship who had committed an offence in another Marcher lordship being tried and convicted for the offence in a third Marcher lordship. In Dyffryn Clwyd we have record of a man from Merionethshire being convicted of a theft in Yale and another from Denbigh being hanged for offences committed in Denbigh and Englefield.[57] Men such as these had good reason to know that theories of Marcher franchise and of the immunity of the alien meant, or rather could mean, little in actual practice. Indeed those theories themselves as they were on occasion propounded by contemporaries afforded little comfort to the alien criminal and little support for the opinion of Tudor writers that the fragmentation of justice in the March made for a criminals' paradise. Thus the custom of Bromfield as it was laid down in a ruling of 1355 declared that when foreign parties (*partes extranei*) were at law in the lordship in an appeal of felony, regardless of whether that felony was committed outside the lordship of Bromfield and Yale, then the defendant had to answer the appeal of the appellor.[58] The assumption behind the ruling is noteworthy: it is that aliens might well litigate in a Marcher lordship and that they might even do so about an offence committed elsewhere.

The practice of the courts, therefore, suggests a far greater flexibility in tackling the problems occasioned by the judicial particularism of the March than theory or later propaganda might indicate. Nor is that all. Marcher lords, like all possessors of franchise and privilege at all time, could be stubbornly jealous as defenders of their liberties and as protectors of the judicial immunity of their men at the expense of all else; but the problems that arose out of the judicial fragmentation of March touched them all and it was therefore but good sense for them to work out mutual agreements and common solutions.

[56] Thus a man from Edeirnion convicted of homicide in Dyffryn Clwyd made a fine of £8 to secure 'relaxation' of the lord's suit and had to find eighty pledges; another man from Edeirnion was hanged for offences in Dyffryn Clwyd: S.C. 2/216/1, m. 3 (1318); 210/14, m. 17 (1334). For a like case in Yale see S.C. 2/218/10, m. 16[v] (1362).

[57] S.C. 2/216/3, m. 17 (1321); 216/4, m. 33[v] (1323).

[58] S.B.Y., fol. 172[v].

They did so; and in the process they evolved what might be called an international law of the March.

One major item in that law was the letter of the march, *littera marchie*. This was a virtual official passport or safe-conduct issued by a lord to one of his tenants, normally (it would seem) for a specific journey. In it the lord acknowledged the tenant as his own and asked for his judicial immunity to be respected in other lordships.[59] If the tenant were arrested in another lordship he could produce his letter in court and ask to be extradited to the jurisdiction of his own lord.[60] It was a system which was clearly open to abuse; but in its essentials and provided that it was rigidly controlled by responsible officials it was a sensible way of establishing the credentials of *bona-fide* travellers in the March and of according to them the benefit of their judicial immunity.

Cases arising from the production of letters of the March were frequently referred to 'days of the march' or 'love days' held on the boundaries between neighbouring lordships. Such days of the march were a fairly common feature of most medieval frontier areas and were a recognized method of defusing and settling disputes between neighbouring lordships and neighbouring kingdoms. They were also an acknowledged feature of feudal practice where peers (*pares*) were encouraged to hold pleas on the boundaries of their fiefs instead of resorting to arms.[61] The lords of the March may, as usual, have drawn both on native Welsh tradition and on feudal practice in establishing days of the march as a recognized feature of relationships between their lordships. By the thirteenth century they were defending the institution vigorously as the accepted and sensible method of ironing out their mutual problems[62] and insisting that days of the march were one of the prerogatives of their lordship which no mesne tenant was allowed

[59] For a draft copy of a letter of the march in a contemporary formulary see B.L. Royal, 11 A. XI, fol. 11. For an example of a safe-conduct, granted by the steward of Denbigh to two men to go to Merioneth in search for cattle stolen by men from Powys, see Northumberland Record Office, Swinburne (Capheaton) Collection 1/99. (I owe this reference to Mr. D. A. L. Morgan.)

[60] See, for example, *The Marcher Lordships of South Wales*, ed. T. B. Pugh, 59, 65.

[61] See the passage from the *Leges Henrici Primi* quoted in F. M. Stenton, *The First Century of English Feudalism*, 2nd edn (Oxford, 1961), 89.

[62] *Glam. C.H.*, III, 592, n. 40 (earl of Gloucester, 1290); *Abbreviatio Placitorum*, 231 (earl of Arundel, 1293); *Rot. Parl.*, I, 397 (John Grey, 1322).

to usurp.[63] The fourteenth-century evidence allows us to catch a closer view of the day of the march and of the role it occupied in the 'international' law of the March. Such days of the march were normally held with all neighbouring lordships—in Dyffryn Clwyd with Denbigh, Yale, Flint and Edeirnion, and in Brecon with Abergavenny, Glamorgan and Ewyas Lacy. Their suspension was regarded as a virtual breakdown of relations between Marcher lordships and a prelude to war.[64] The day of the march was a meeting both of neighbouring officials and of the representatives of neighbouring communities. The deputation was normally led by the steward or his deputy and completed by a number of tenants who would serve on the joint-juries which decided issues at the court of the march.[65] For the day of the march was a solemn and formal occasion: cases could only be referred there by the steward or his deputy; arrested men would be exchanged and distrained goods handed over; due compensation would be fixed for offences committed in either lordship by the other's tenants. Side by side with such days of the march we must obviously place the more informal but equally important procedures of communication between the officials of neighbouring lordships: frequent exchanges of letters especially those asking for a case to be deferred or a fine to be pardoned, meetings of stewards where mutual problems could be ironed out,[66] and even local conferences between the councils of two lords.[67]

Letters of the march and days of the march betoken an attempt to establish a working arrangement between Marcher

[63] The earl of Hereford claimed it to be such in 1349 'propter occisionem et guerram que possunt evenire in tali casu': D.L. 41/6/11.

[64] In March 1321 the younger Despenser as lord of Glamorgan suspended the holding of days of the march with the lordship of Brecon: *Cal. Anc. Corr. conc. Wales*, 260.

[65] David Holbache, the steward, his fellow officers and some tenants led the Oswestry and Chirk deputation to a march-day with Powys in 1394: Shrewsbury Public Library, 9777. Attendance at days of the march was one of the tenurial obligations of the burgesses of Hay: Cardiff Free Library, Brecon Documents, 2. For a joint-jury of six men from each lordship acting at a day of the march see S.C. 2/218/5, m. 16 (1356).

[66] For example, a case concerning attachments made by the bailiffs of Denbigh within the lordship of Dyffryn Clwyd was referred to the joint judgement of the two stewards: S.C. 2/217/10, m. 5ᵛ (1345).

[67] Such as the meeting of the councils of John of Gaunt and Lord Despenser in 1368 (D.L. 29/615/9836) or of the councils of the earl of Arundel and the lord of Stapleton in 1400 (S.R.O. 552/1/34, m. 4).

lordships. It is little wonder, therefore, that Marcher lords often wished to go even further by establishing a written code of agreement (*composicio, cydfod*) for regulating their relations with their neighbours. No copy of such an agreement has to our knowledge survived for the fourteenth century; but that they were fairly common is beyond doubt. In Dyffryn Clwyd, to take the best-documented example, such agreements are mentioned with the neighbouring lordships of Denbigh, Flint, Yale and Dinmael; while it is clear that the Black Prince concluded like agreements, often of short duration it is true, with neighbouring lordships.[68] We may reconstruct the content of these agreements partly from copies of later agreements made by Tudor antiquaries[69] and partly from contemporary references in the court rolls They dealt with such issues as the mutual extradition of criminals, the exchange of lists of wanted men between stewards, the right to pursue suspects from one lordship to another, the extradition of refugee serfs, the process of disclaimer whereby a man who refused to stand to justice in one Marcher lordship would be delivered to the officials of his acknowledged lord, the enforcement of contracts made in other lordships, and the acceptance of an authenticated copy of the court proceedings of another lordship as lawful evidence in a Marcher court.[70] In short these agreements dealt with precisely the sort of problems which were bound to arise between judicially autonomous lordships and with the mechanics for their solution.

These agreements indicate once more that coexistence not confrontation is the normal theme of relations between Marcher lordships and between Marcher communities in the fourteenth century. Generally speaking neither lord nor community was

[68] Dyffryn Clwyd court rolls, *passim*; *B.P.R.* III, 149, 490.

[69] For these agreements (*cydfodau*) and the textual problems posed by the copies, see J. B. Smith 'Cydfodau or Bymthegfed Ganrif', *B.B.C.S.* 21 (1966), 309–24; 25 (1973), 128–34.

[70] For examples of these practices see respectively S.C. 2/216/13, m. 5ᵛ (extradition of criminals, 1333); 218/7, m. 22 (exchange of lists of wanted men, 1359); 218/6, m. 23ᵛ (right of pursuit, 1358); 218/10, m. 28 (extradition of serf, 1362); N.L.W. Peniarth 280 D, fol. 71 (disclaimer of a Mortimer tenant arrested in Stafford lordship of Caus, 1398); S.C. 2/218/11, m. 12ᵛ (enforcement of 'external' contracts, 1363); 218/8, m. 3 (cases in Ruthin determined on basis of record of a court at Denbigh, 1360). Many similar cases could be quoted from the Dyffryn Clwyd court rolls.

interested in erecting Marcher particularism into a pretext for the promotion of crime or in fostering a continued state of tension between Marcher lordships. The lords—no doubt often out of self-interest[71]—were willing to compromise the judicial integrity of their lordships for the sake of good order. The communities likewise curbed their own localism and assumed an increasingly important role in concluding treaties with their neighbours for the solution of their problems.[72] Those treaties spoke the language of good sense—of the need to punish evildoers and of the acceptance that no compensation was due for the death of a raider. Their search is for a *modus vivendi* not for a *casus belli*. That search was not a new one. Wales and the March had always been a land of many kingdoms where the relations with other countries (*gorwledydd*) and the status of the alien were questions which had exercised men of affairs for centuries. Wars and raids were an easy solution to the problems raised by such a situation; but there are hints in the native law texts that both the language and the methods of peaceful settlement had also been developing.[73] The Marcher lords inherited the particularism of the Welsh political situation and defended it jealously. But they also inherited and refined the solutions for the problems occasioned by such particularism.

[71] The tit-for-tat character of Marcher relationships is well illustrated by a case from Clun involving pledges from Knighton. It was postponed until it was learnt how the men of Clun were treated in Knighton courts: S.R.O. 552/1/19, m. 1 (1377).

[72] Thus both the Hay-Elfael treaty of 1451 (above p. 241, n. 44) and the *cydfodau* recorded by later antiquaries (above p. 247, n. 69) were concluded by the communities of the respective lordships, not by their lords. The phrases in the next sentence are taken from these sources.

[73] J. B. Smith in *B.B.C.S.* 21 (1966), 315.

12

The King and the Marcher Lords

HITHERTO in this analysis of Marcher lordship the Marcher lords have been conceded the full regality of their position. The kings of England have been barely mentioned except in observing the minimal degree of control that they normally exercised over Marcher lordship and the peripheral fashion in which their administration impinged on the March. In the internal history of the March, of its lords and of its inhabitants such an emphasis, we believe, is not misplaced; but in other respects it is most certainly an incomplete view. The March of Wales was insulated neither from the ambit of royal influence nor from the orbit of English politics. It is to the former that we will direct our attention in this chapter.

The king of England certainly occupied an important role in the affairs of the March; not even the proudest of Marcher lords could gainsay that elementary truth. In the first place, all Marcher lordships were held of the king of England (or, in a few cases, of his eldest son, the prince of Wales). On the death of a Marcher lord, his lordship would be taken into royal hands, normally by the escheator of one of the English border counties whose commission also included the March; if the heir were a minor, the custody of the lordship and the administration of its affairs remained with the Crown; if the descent of the lordship were in dispute, the issue would be settled in the court of the king, as that of the feudal superior; if the lordship were forfeited or escheated, it was for the king to grant it to whom he willed; if the lord alienated some of the land of the lordship or granted it to the church, a licence was at least technically required from the king;[1] if the lord wished to grant his lands to feoffees, royal permission was again necessary.[2] In short, the Marcher lordship

---

[1] See, for example, *C.P.R. 1301–7*, 447—licence for John fitz Reginald to enfeoff Rees ap Hywel with land in Talgarth, held in chief.

[2] For an example, see the enfeoffment of the Mortimer estates in the March in 1374: *C.P.R. 1374–7*, 33–4.

was encumbered with most of the incidents and obligations of feudal tenure; in a society where land was at the centre of politics such a tenurial connection was a formidable weapon in the armoury of royal control.

Yet it was a weapon whose edge was in some respects blunted. The feudal bond in normal circumstances assured the king no more than an occasional and haphazard measure of control over his tenants-in-chief; it was circumscribed by the accidents of death, minority and childlessness. Furthermore, in the later Middle Ages, as we have seen, even this measure of control was eroded by various legal devices, most notably the enfeoffment to use.[3] That was true of feudal tenure in England; but in the March the bond of king and tenant-in-chief was even more tenuous than in England. It often extended no further than the obligation of fealty and homage with the attendant incidents of marriage and wardship, but without any specific military obligation. The county of Pembroke, for example, was said to be held of the king in chief but either by an unknown service or by the honorary duty of carrying the king's sword at the coronation; likewise the great Clare estates in the March were held 'by ancient conquest'—with the firm implication that it was not tenure by royal grant—and 'by service unknown'.[4] The same was true of other Marcher lordships: Blaenllyfni was held in chief by doing homage and no other service, while Thomas Corbet (d. 1274), lord of Caus, defiantly claimed before the barons of the Exchequer that neither he nor his five ancestors since the conquest had rendered any relief for their Marcher lordship.[5] In general, the Marcher lords seem to have escaped many of the normal fiscal incidents of feudal tenure such as aids and scutages and to have made little if any contribution to the feudal levy of the realm.[6] Their military function was different from that of English feudal tenants: it was that of defending their own lordships and thereby of guarding the Welsh frontier for the king.[7] Where the military obligation, so

---

[3] Above, pp. 40–1.
[4] *C.I.P.M.*, v, no. 56; vi, no. 518 p. 323 (Pembroke); iv, no. 435, p. 322; v, no. 538, p. 332 (Glamorgan).
[5] *C.I.P.M.*, ii, no. 606, p. 365; R. W. Eyton, *Antiquities of Shropshire*, vii, 24.
[6] S. Painter, *Studies in the History of the English Feudal Barony* (Baltimore, 1943), 124–5; Eyton, op. cit. iv, 203–4.
[7] Thus the obligation of the lord of Abergavenny was 'to guard the country of

central to the feudal tie, was so weak it is little wonder that some of the other features of royal feudal control in the March were more honoured in the breach than in the observance. Even the royal right of prerogative wardship, one of the distinctive features of the king's feudal lordship, was not acknowledged in the March; even the royal escheators might be denied entry to execute their office in a Marcher lordship.[8] All in all, the feudal position of the Marcher lords was anomalous in many respects. Yet, anomalous or not, the feudal bond was one of the major links whereby the authority of the king of England in the March was both acknowledged and exercised.

The other major bond between the king and the Marcher lordships was a judicial one. Lawyers never tired of quoting the dictum that 'the king's writ runs not in the March'; the Marcher lords asserted with equal regularity that they had the right to hear virtually all cases in their courts; they might even venture in anger the opinion that royal statutes had no place in their land. Such claims seemed to shut the door fairly firmly and securely in the face of any royal attempt to exercise jurisdiction in the March. But the king had his answer. Edward I, as one would expect, expressed it most magisterially and most solemnly in the first statute of Westminster, 1275. 'This is to be understood', so declared one of the clauses of the statute, 'in all places where the king's writ runs; and if it be in the Marches of Wales, or in any other place where the king's writ runs not, then the king who is sovereign lord shall do right therein to all such as will complain'.[9] Likewise Edward II could invoke his 'superior lordship' and his duty 'to show justice to his subjects' as ample reason for hearing cases from the March.[10]

That superior lordship was not merely a matter of fine words; it operated along certain acknowledged channels and did so fairly effectively. As the ultimate source of justice for all his men, the king could certainly lend his ear to any complaint that came to him about an offence committed in the March.

Overwent at his own charges in the best manner he can for his own convenience and for the service of the king and the defence of the realm': *C.I.P.M.*, v, no. 412, p. 232.

[8] For example, in 1317 the steward of Chepstow refused to allow the royal escheator to execute his office: *C.I.P.M.*, vi, no. 16.

[9] 3 Edward I, c. 17.

[10] *C.P.R. 1321–4*, 163.

He could listen to the petition of the merchants of Hereford against the men of Brecon; he could attend to a plaint about an offence committed against his peace on the royal highway in the March; he could receive the petition of a mesne lord of the March against the actions of his overlord as in the case of Roger Mortimer of Pencelli against Humphrey Bohun, lord of Brecon; he could lend a sympathetic ear to the grievances of a Marcher community as did Edward I in the case of the men of Mae-lienydd.[11] He might, it is true, refer some of these petitions back to the appropriate Marcher court, for the king was on the whole a great respecter of franchises. But he could also show on occasion that his claim to superior lordship in the judicial affairs of the March was no mere bombast: if the earl of Hereford failed to appear to answer a complaint brought against him in respect of his Marcher authority, then he was to be distrained on his chattels in England and attached by his English lands; likewise the sheriff of Shropshire could be commanded to go in person into 'the liberty of Oswestry in the March of Wales and out of the county' to deliver a petitioner from the earl of Arundel's prison.[12]

As superior lord the king also exercised a supervisory authority, a jurisdiction in error, over the judicial decisions of the courts of the March. His claim to such a jurisdiction was generally accepted even by the greatest of the Marcher lords[13] and the procedure for enforcing it was fairly well established. Royal commissioners were appointed to go to the Marcher court to request a copy of the record of the case in question; it was then scrutinized by the justices of the court of King's Bench to determine whether there was any error in it. It was a procedure which no doubt annoyed the Marcher lords and certainly produced the occasional dramatic protest: the steward and suitors of the court of Talgarth promptly left the court when royal commissioners came there to demand the record of a case for scrutiny in 1290 and in the same year the sheriff of

---

[11] See respectively *Select Cases in the Court of King's Bench under Edward I*, i, ed. G. O. Sayles, 93–4 (1281); *Cartae*, iii, no. 741 (1281); *C.P.R. 1292–1301*, 108 (1293); *C.C.R. 1296–1302*, 107 (1297).

[12] *Select Cases in Court of King's Bench*, i, 94 (1281); *Rot. Parl.*, i, 207 (1306).

[13] Richard Clare had complied with the procedure in the Siward case in 1247 (*Cartae*, ii, no. 535) and his son also accepted it in a case of 1281 (*Select Cases in Court of King's Bench.* ii, vii).

Hereford and his party on a like mission to the Marcher court of Theobald Verdon at Ewyas Lacy were chased away by an angry steward and a crowd of 600 Welshmen.[14] Yet in spite of such hot-tempered opposition, the king never surrendered his claim to exercise such judicial scrutiny.

We must also recall that the king on occasion intervened in the judicial affairs of the March at the invitation of the Marcher lords themselves, for a Marcher lord would not stand on his Marcher dignity if he thought that royal justice would help him win his case. The list of Marcher barons who took their cases before the king would indeed be a long and distinguished one. In earlier days, such as those recalled in *The Legend of Fulk Fitzwarin*, such disputes might have been decided by force of arms; but it was some indication of a change of attitudes and of the growing respect even in the March for the judgement of the king's court as the indefeasible title to land that such disputes were increasingly referred to his arbitration. It was to him also that they appealed if they wanted a grant or confirmation of Marcher status: William Braose did so in 1304, the younger Despenser in 1318, the prior of Goldcliff in 1321, the earl of Warwick in 1360, the bishop of St. David's in 1383 and so forth.[15] A king who could confirm and even grant Marcher liberties was clearly not a peripheral figure in the politics of the March.

The king's judicial superiority in the March had to it yet other aspects. It reserved to itself all cases concerning treason. The right to pardon traitors was the king's alone; it was into his peace that they were admitted; it was with him that they fined for their lives, even though their lords normally received their lands and chattels.[16] Cases relating to advowson were likewise reserved for the king's court: this claim had already certainly been established by the late thirteenth century and developed into the one major exception to the judicial omnicompetence of

[14] *Select Cases in Court of King's Bench*, II, 5–6 (Talgarth); K.B. 27/129, m. 53 (Ewyas Lacy). For a similar reaction in Blaenllyfni in 1254 see *Abbreviatio Placitorum*, 138.

[15] *C.Ch.R. 1300–26*, 46–7 (Braose); 398–9 (Despenser); *C.P.R. 1321–4*, 163–4 (prior of Goldcliff); *C. Ch. R. 1341–1417*, 167–8 (earl of Warwick); 289–90 (bishop of St. David's).

[16] Thus in 1295 Edward I admitted the Marcher tenants of John Hastings into the king's peace; he granted their forfeitures to Hastings but reserved to the Welsh their lives, limbs and lands and to himself the right to mitigate grievous fines *C.P.R. 1292–1310*, 144.

Marcher courts in pleas of first instance.[17] Judicial superiority spilt over easily into other claims of superiority. No such claim was more far-reaching in its effects and more bitterly contested than that of the Crown to be the sole guardian of temporalities and collator to benefices in the March during an episcopal vacancy. The claim was gradually elaborated during the course of the thirteenth century and was undoubtedly, at least in the case of the bishopric of Llandaff, a departure from established practice. Edward I, however, was not a man to allow historical evidence to stand in his way; he appealed instead to the superior and inscrutable authority of 'the dignity of the Crown' and of 'the law and custom of the kingdom'. In a series of decisive cases in the 1290s, especially those against the lords of Gower and Glamorgan in 1290 and the lord of Bromfield and Yale in 1293, he unequivocally established the royal right on this issue.[18] This royal superiority could assume yet other forms: it could lay claim to many of the roads of the March as royal highways and as such under the protection of the king's peace;[19] it could assert the coastline to be its own and under the jurisdiction of the king's admiral;[20] it could and often did grant charters for the founding of fairs, for the collection of murage, and for the right of free warren in Marcher lordships, often at the request of the Marcher lords themselves.[21] Such claims and such practices could easily have been articulated into a catalogue of the king's *regalia* in the March. They were not, and the relations between the king and the Marcher lords were the better for it.

For, truth to tell, the king's authority in the March was not circumscribed by the ties of tenure and of judicial superiority nor by any theoretical framework of relationships with the

[17] See A. J. Otway-Ruthven in *T.R.H.S.*, 5th ser. 8 (1958), 11; *Cal. Anc. Corr· conc. Wales,* 181–2.

[18] A. J. Otway-Ruthven, art. cit. 17–18; Glanmor Williams, *The Welsh Church from Conquest to Reformation* (Cardiff, 1962), 46–55; *Glam. C.H.*, III, 70–1, 107–14; Margaret Howell, 'Regalian Right in Wales and the March: The Relation of Theory to Practice', *W.H.R.* 7 (1975), 269–88.

[19] For references to *viae regales* in the March see, for example, *Cartae*, III, nos. 741 (1281), 853 (1307).

[20] W. Rees, *South Wales and the March 1284–1415*, 48–9.

[21] See, for example, grants of fairs in *C.Ch.R. 1300–26*, 68 (Radnor), 123 (Llanfair), 183 (Ruyton), of free warren ibid. 165 (Roger Mortimer of Chirk's Marcher estates), and of murage *C.P.R. 1292–1301*, 144 (Abergavenny).

Marcher lords. In the normal run of affairs the king was well content with the place in Marcher affairs assured him by his position as feudal lord and as judicial sovereign; but circumstances often afforded him a more ample and more positive role than theory might suggest. Of those circumstances none was more common or more far-reaching in its effects than war, for the military facts of life paid little heed to 'constitutional' proprieties. Much of the conquest and the defence of the March had undoubtedly been undertaken by the Marcher lords themselves and at their own expense; their claim to hold their lordships by 'ancient conquest' was in good measure true and from it, as they saw it, flowed much of their title to Marcher liberties.[22] But even these 'private' conquests were either allowed or sanctioned by the king and on occasion actively supported by him. Furthermore, when the threat from the Welsh assumed truly menacing proportions and could not be countered by the piecemeal and localized efforts of the Marcher lords then the king of England would step in. Royal commanders with authority throughout the March would be appointed and the Marcher lords instructed to be attendant on them. John Grey, for example, was so appointed in 1255.[23] National security was no great respecter of franchise, Marcher or otherwise. Edward I drove home that point with characteristic vigour, little short of spleen, during the Welsh revolt of 1294–5. That the revolt was a national emergency endangering the king's plans at a vital and delicate stage and requiring a massive and coordinated military response was not in doubt; nor was the contribution of the Marcher lords—Clare, Bohun, Lacy and Giffard among them—in containing and suppressing the revolt. But after dealing with the revolt in north Wales, Edward I used the occasion of his military presence in Wales to display his authority in no uncertain terms towards the most powerful and recalcitrant, if already chastened, Marcher lord, Gilbert Clare. The king marched into Glamorgan in June 1295; he received the local rebel leader, Morgan ap Maredudd, and his followers into his own peace 'against the earl's wishes'; he took the homage of the major men of the lordship to himself and his heirs as kings of England; he exploited their enmity towards the

---

[22] *Cartae*, iii, no. 741 (1281)
[23] *C.P.R. 1247–58*, 553.

earl to his own advantage; he finally took the lordship into his own hands and appointed a royal custodian to be in charge of it. [24] Just as he had used the *cause célèbre* of 1290–2 to show that in a trial of strength the prerogative of the Crown was more powerful than the liberties of the March, so he used the occasion of the 1294–5 revolt to communicate a more basic, even crude, truth that military might was stronger than Marcher right.

The military mastery of the king of England in the March was demonstrated in another direction: his armies were full of men from the March, serving in the king's name and for his pay. It is true that the king's requests for troops were generally communicated to the Marcher lords, who thereby retained their power over the process of recruiting within their lordships. It is also true that the Marcher lords jealously and successfully safeguarded their right to be the sole recruiting agents within their lordships and withstood any attempts by the king to summon troops directly from Marcher mesne tenants. [25] Even these claims, however, were not always respected. The king on occasion appointed his own commissioners to levy troops for him in the Marcher lordships: Edward I, for example, did so for his campaigns in Flanders in 1297 and in Scotland in 1298. [26]

Even the liberties of the March were themselves not outside the range of royal action. There must be no misunderstanding on this score. The kings of England had in general no wish to question, let alone to subvert, the liberties of the March any more than they had a wish to undermine the authority and franchises of the English nobility. The liberties of the March deserved and were accorded the respect extended to all rightful title to property and franchise; indeed that respect was even more unquestioning because those liberties lay embedded in tradition and ancient usage, not in royal charters. Respect they certainly received. Even Edward I, no great respecter of franchises, refused in 1303 to interfere with the custom of the March; [27] his successors likewise turned deaf ears to the com-

---

[24] The most important texts for this episode are *Annales Monastici*, ed. H. R. Luard (Rolls Series, 1864–9), III, 387; IV, 526; *Cal. Anc. Corr. conc. Wales*, 280; *The Chronicle of Pierre de Langtoft*, ed. T. Wright (Rolls Series, 1868), II, 218; *C.P.R. 1292–1301*, 154.

[25] See above pp. 80–1.

[26] *C.P.R. 1291–1302*, 249–50; *C.C.R. 1296–1302*, 202.

[27] *Memoranda de Parliamento, 1305*, ed. F. W. Maitland (Rolls Series, 1893), 73–4.

plaints of the English border communities against the abuses arising out of Marcher liberties.[28] The reply of Edward III to a petition addressed to him by the countess of Pembroke reflects the tone of quiescent conservatism that normally characterized the royal attitude to Marcher franchises: 'The king wills that the lords [of the March] of Wales may use their franchises in Wales as they and their ancestors had used them in his time and in the time of his predecessors and that there shall be no new departure to the contrary' ('et qe nule chose soit fait de nouveau au contraire').[29]

Acquiescence and respect certainly describe the normal attitude of the kings of England to the liberties of the March. Yet kings on occasion did act differently. They could invoke their superior lordship, as did Edward III with respect to the affairs of Gower in the 1330s;[30] political motives might prompt them to adopt a tough line on Marcher issues, as in the case of Edward II in 1319–20 when he broached the sensitive question of the freedom to alienate lands held in chief in the March without royal licence in his support of the younger Despenser's territorial ambitions there;[31] they might almost officiously insist on their royal rights in the March as did Richard II in 1384 when he confiscated an advowson granted by the lord of Glamorgan because it had been alienated without royal permission.[32] Such incidents were normally few and far between; but they serve to remind us, as they reminded contemporaries, that the royal attitude towards Marcher liberties could well be a different and more aggressive one. 'Royal sufferance' it has been aptly observed in the case of the palatinate of Durham, 'was the basis of autonomy'; such also was the case in the March.[33]

Some kings were prepared—or obliged—to suffer much; others to suffer less. To this latter category Edward I certainly belonged. His attitude towards the March, its lords and its liberties, must command attention in some detail, not only in respect of its intrinsic interest but also because it reveals more

[28] *Rot. Parl.*, II, 352–3; III, 272–3, 308.
[29] S.C. 8/159, no. 7948 dorse. Cf. *C.C.R. 1348–53*, 532.
[30] *C.P.R. 1330–4*, 125, 128.
[31] Below pp. 279, 285.
[32] *C.P.R. 1381–5*, 483–4.
[33] C. M. Fraser in *E.H.R.* 74 (1959), 474.

forcibly than the attitude of any other king in our period that the liberties of the March were ultimately dependent on the good will of the king. There was much in the character and attitudes of Edward I to suggest that he might indeed adopt a forceful approach to Marcher liberties. He took an exalted view of the role and responsibilities of the Crown; he made much of the concept of 'the common utility' and of his own position as guardian and interpreter of that utility;[34] he elaborated the contemporary theoretical notion of 'necessity' (*necessitas*) into a virtual doctrine of reason of state which could be adduced to explain and justify any of his actions;[35] he matched it with an increasingly sophisticated distinction between the person of the king and the office of the Crown.[36] He and his lawyers had already subjected the franchises of England to a prolonged and searching inquiry; there was no reason why they should not apply the same Bractonian logic to the liberties of the March and apply it equally relentlessly. For Edward I was not a man to be cowed by precedent or by the lords of the March. Towards his English earls he displayed a quality of 'masterfulness' little short of a 'wilful abuse of his power'.[37] Many of those same earls—Gloucester, Hereford, Lincoln and Norfolk in particular —were also leading Marcher barons; Edward was unlikely to make much of the distinction between their roles as English earls and as Marcher lords. In either capacity they were his subjects.

Furthermore, Edward I's position in Wales and the March was one of unique power. He was the conqueror of Gwynedd. That conquest transformed the relation of Crown and Marcher lords, especially in Edward I's own reign. The king's military presence now dominated Wales in a permanent and un-precedented manner; the role of the Marcher lords as con-querors and defenders of the country was thereby palpably diminished. Territorially, the king of England came to tower in the affairs of Wales as never before; not a single Marcher

[34] For this concept, see T. F. T. Plucknett, *The Legislation of Edward I* (Oxford, 1949), 4–5.

[35] F. M. Powicke, *The Thirteenth Century 1216–1307* (Oxford, 1953), 520–8.

[36] F. M. Powicke, *Henry III and the Lord Edward* (Oxford, 1947), 725 and n. 1.

[37] The seminal article on this subject is that of K. B. McFarlane, 'Had Edward I a "Policy" towards the Earls?' reprinted in *The Nobility of Later Medieval England*, 248–67. The quotations come from pp. 266–7.

lord, not even the Clare family, could now match the king's territorial stake in Wales. Several of the Marcher lordships, and some of the largest at that, were Edward I's own creations. Still more profound in its repercussions as far as the Marcher lords were concerned was the change in attitude which was bound to flow from the military conquest and territorial annexation. A king who could declare majestically in 1284 that 'the land of Wales' had been 'annexed and united . . . to the crown of the . . . realm [of England] as a part of the body of the same' was in an altogether more commanding position *vis à vis* the Marcher lords than any of his predecessors.

Edward I returned to the March in 1291 when he presided at Abergavenny at the court which sat in judgement on the famous dispute between the earls of Gloucester and Hereford, lords of Glamorgan and Brecon respectively.[38] The case soon developed into a direct confrontation between the royal prerogative and Marcher liberty; and, as it turned out, it was but one of a sequence of incidents in the 1290s in which Edward I displayed his masterfulness in the March. There had already been several hints of the position he would adopt. We have already quoted his statutory dictum of 1275 that as sovereign lord he had the duty and right to attend to all complaints, even if they came from the March of Wales;[39] in 1281 he had marvelled at the way the earl of Hereford had used his Marcher status as a pretext for spurning a royal command and had ordered the earl and his bailiff to be summoned for contempt;[40] in 1285 he reminded his uncle William Valence, lord of Pembroke, that 'since all lands in the kingdom were held of the king in chief, the king was entitled to send justices to hear pleas wherever he wished' and so dismissed Valence's attempt to exempt Haverford from a visit by royal judges.[41] Such incidents indicated Edward I's intent clearly enough; after 1290 that intent was converted into action. The timing was surely not accidental: the conquest of Wales had been com-

---

[38] The proceedings are calendared in *Calendar of Chancery Rolls Various 1277–1326* (henceforth *C.W.R.*), 334–49. The most extended discussion of it is in J. E. Morris, *The Welsh Wars of Edward I*, 220–39.

[39] Above p. 251.

[40] *Select Cases in Court of King's Bench*, i, 93–4.

[41] J. R. S. Phillips, *Aymer de Valence, Earl of Pembroke 1307–1324* (Oxford, 1972), 251.

pleted and further secured by the suppression of the revolt of
1287; Gascon affairs had been put in order by the prolonged
royal visit of 1286–9; the Scottish and French problems which
were to preoccupy the king's attention for the rest of the reign
had as yet barely appeared on the horizon.

It is undeniable that the tempo of royal action in the March
quickens from 1290. The record speaks for itself: in 1290
Edmund Mortimer's liberty of Wigmore was twice confiscated
for his contravention of the liberties of the king as lord of
Montgomery;[42] again in 1290 the lords of Talgarth and Ewyas
Lacy had to submit the records of their courts to royal scrutiny;[43] in the same year Edward majestically and successfully
asserted his right to be sole keeper of temporalities and collator
to benefices in the March during episcopal vacancies and extracted a written acknowledgement on the issue from Gilbert
Clare;[44] during 1291–2 the great case between the earls of
Hereford and Gloucester was transformed into a platform for
the assertion of royal prerogative *vis à vis* Marcher custom; it
was concluded in January 1292 with the imprisonment of the
two earls and the confiscation of their Marcher lordships for
their lifetime; in the same session of parliament Theobald
Verdon, lord of Ewyas Lacy, was likewise imprisoned and his
lands and liberties forfeited for his contempt to the king's
officers;[45] the king also recovered Ystlwyf from William
Valence in that year and brought it within the jurisdiction of
the county of Carmarthen;[46] in November 1292 he warned
William Braose that if the latter failed to pay him an outstanding
debt of 800 marks the liberty of the March would not inhibit
the royal commissioners from entering Gower to collect the
money by distraint;[47] it was in 1292 also that Edward I, flushed
with recent success, requested and received the first and last
tax, a fifteenth on moveables, granted by the lords of the
March to the king of England;[48] it was during these years that

[42] *Rot. Parl.*, 1, 45.
[43] See above, pp. 252–3.
[44] *Rot. Parl.*, 1, 42–3; cf. above p. 254.
[45] The records of this important case are in K.B. 27/126, m. 38; K.B. 27/129,
m. 53–53ᵛ. The judgement against Verdon is in *Rot. Parl.*, 1, 81–2.
[46] *C. Inq. Misc. 1219–1307*, no. 1443; *Rot. Parl.*, 1, 50; *Abbreviatio Placitorum*, 286;
C.Ch.R. 1257–1300, 427.
[47] E. 159/66, m. 8ᵛ. For this case see also ibid. m. 9–m. 11ᵛ, m. 42–42ᵛ.
[48] J. E. Morris, *Welsh Wars of Edward I*, 239.

he supervised the arrangements for the division of the great inheritance of Gruffudd ap Gwenwynwyn and arranged for the demotion of Powys from the status of a Welsh principality to that of an English barony;[49] in 1293 the king's claim to the temporalities of vacant bishoprics was again asserted in the case of the bishoprics of St. David's and St. Asaph;[50] a commission was issued to investigate the grievances of the lord of Pencelli (Roger Mortimer of Chirk) against the lord of Brecon (the earl of Hereford), in spite of the normal custom that a mesne lord should first seek justice in his lord's court;[51] in 1293 again the king intervened in the private war between the lords of Oswestry and Whittington (the earl of Arundel and Fulk Fitzwarin);[52] he seized the lordship of Elfael into royal custody because of the failure of its lord, Ralph Tony, to appear before the royal justices;[53] he also recovered Cwmwd Deuddwr from Edmund Mortimer of Wigmore;[54] in 1294 he seized the earl of Arundel's private hundred of Purslow, part of the lordship of Clun, into royal custody and there it remained until the end of the reign;[55] in 1295, as we have seen, he used the occasion of a Welsh revolt as a pretext for seizing Glamorgan into royal hands for four months; in 1297 he encouraged the complaints of the men of Maelienydd and put pressure on their lord, Edmund Mortimer, to grant them a charter of liberties;[56] he acted very much in the same fashion towards the men of Gower and their lord, William Braose, from 1300 until 1306;[57] in 1299 the lordship of Oswestry was briefly taken into royal control because of the failure of the earl of Arundel to appear before the king's justices.[58]

It is a long catalogue and one which could easily be length-

[49] J. Conway Davies in *Mont. Colls.* 49 (1946), 94–102.

[50] Glanmor Williams, *The Welsh Church*, 49–50.

[51] *C.P.R. 1292–1301*, 108.

[52] R. W. Eyton, *Antiquities of Shropshire*, XI, 40; *Abbreviatio Placitorum*, 231. Cf. *C.C.R. 1296–1302*, 495.

[53] *C.C.R. 1288–96*, 313.

[54] This was so according to a petition of 1332: S.C. 8/240, no. 11952.

[55] E. 159/67, m. 11; *C.P.R. 1307–13*, 52. In 1293 Arundel and Edmund Mortimer were accused of withdrawing their Shropshire lands into their Marcher liberties and of refusing to allow royal tax-collectors to enter those lands: E. 159/66, m. 38; 67, m. 63.

[56] *C.C.R. 1296–1302*, 107; *C.P.R. 1292–1301*, 290.

[57] *Glam. C.H.*, III, 231–41.

[58] *C.C.R. 1296–1302*, 270.

ened. Clearly not all the cases mentioned were of equal importance: some were no more than technical judicial procedures; many of the harsh sentences imposed were soon reversed
by the king. Each case obviously needs to be considered in its
own context, personal, political, judicial and otherwise. Yet
the incidents are sufficient in number and sufficiently close to
one another in point of time, being largely concentrated in the
period 1290–7, for us to be able to analyse them as a group.
Edward I's tactics first command attention. There was—and it
is important to emphasize this—no general confrontation with
the Marcher lords as a group (even assuming that were possible)
nor any intention to contrive such a confrontation. Furthermore the liberties of the March were not the primary issue in
any of the cases. After their experience with the *quo warranto*
inquiries, Edward I and his advisers may have felt that a frontal
assault on liberties was not necessarily a prudent tactic. Their
approach to the liberties of the March was an oblique one.
Several avenues of approach were open to them. The king could
take over a private suit and insist that it should be heard regardless of whether the parties would subsequently have preferred
to settle out of court. This was his tactic in the Hereford–
Gloucester case: the case was begun at the suit of the earl of
Hereford, but at an early stage the king stepped in and commanded that the case should proceed regardless of the earl's
wishes, 'because this matter touches the king and his crown and
dignity'.[59] In fact the case already touched the king in another
respect, for Edward I had deployed one of his most effective
methods of bringing Marcher suits within his jurisdiction, that
of issuing a specific royal injunction to one of the parties in
question. The earl of Gloucester's offence in 1290 was *not* that
he had waged private war in the March but that he had done
so after a specific royal injunction; significantly enough the
inquiry into the facts was confined to the period after the
promulgation of that injunction.[60] Likewise the nemesis that
befell Theobald Verdon in 1291–2 was occasioned not by his
defence of Marcher custom but by his disrespect for a royal
injunction (not to vex the prior of Llanthony while the case
was *sub judice*) and by his contempt towards a royal officer,

[59] *C.W.R.*, 335; *C.P.R. 1281–92*, 452.
[60] *C.W.R.*, 334.

the sheriff of Hereford. Procedurally, the use of such injunctions enabled the king to assert his power without proceeding to the more delicate issue of Marcher liberties. Another *entrée* for the king into Marcher affairs was that of succouring the disaffection of local communities against their lord, thereby forging direct ties of obligation between crown and community: it was thus that he took the men of Glamorgan into his peace against their lord's wishes in 1295, that he supported the men of Maelienydd in their protests against Edmund Mortimer in 1297, and that he lent a sympathetic ear to the complaints of the men of Gower against William Braose from 1300 onwards. Edward enjoyed his role as the defender of the aggrieved; he exploited it well to his own advantage in the March as he was to do in the palatinate of Durham in 1302–3.[61]

He also exploited any weakness in the title or position of a Marcher lord to turn the screw of royal pressure. The uncertain claim of Valence to the commote of Ystlwyf and the fact that the Braose tenure of Gower was founded on a royal charter and an uncertain succession were soon seized upon by Edward's lawyers. The financial vulnerability of several of the Marcher lords was likewise exploited to ensure their political compliance. William Braose's debts to the king and growing insolvency made him an easy target for royal pressure. More remarkable is the way that Edward I compelled the obedience of some of his magnates, among them several Marcher lords including the earls of Arundel and Norfolk and Edmund Mortimer of Wigmore, by demanding the payment of their debts whenever they proved recalcitrant. Magnates who had pawned their lands to pay their debts to the king were unlikely to be too strident in their defence of the liberties of the March.[62]

Edward I may have approached the liberties of the March obliquely, varying his tactics according to each individual case. Yet he and his lawyers could not altogether keep their campaign in a low key; they were compelled, possibly unwillingly, to articulate general principles to explain and to justify the king's role in the affairs of the March. They might resort to Brac-

---

[61] See. G. T. Lapsley, *The County Palatine of Durham*, 128 ff.; C. M. Fraser, *A History of Antony Bek, Bishop of Durham 1283–1311*. (Oxford, 1957), 175–210.

[62] Michael Prestwich, *War, Politics and Finance under Edward I* (1972), 236–7. The earl of Arundel was forced to pawn some of his lands to Robert Burnell: *C.C.R. 1296–1302*, 70–1.

tonian arguments on the relationship of Crown and franchises.[63] But such an argument clearly had limited application in the March. Instead the royal lawyers propounded a series of more fundamental and far-reaching arguments in defence of the king's actions in the March. In the first place the jurisdictional immunity of the Marcher lords was effectively undermined: their belief that they could escape punishment by invoking the liberty of the March was directly called into question by the royal lawyers[64] and was disposed of by the use of royal injunctions which made no exception for Marcher privilege. On a more positive level, the king's judicial supremacy throughout his realms, already adumbrated in the Statute of Westminster of 1275, was articulated into a theory which overrode all franchises, Marcher or not. The king was 'debtor of justice to all'; he was the 'superlative record', superior to all his ministers and to the record of their courts. The argument was beginning to escalate into the dizzy realms of political theory: 'by his inner judgement' the king determined what was 'for the common benefit'; his 'conscience' was the guardian of what was 'useful and necessary for the realm and people'.[65] From that level it was but a short step to the ultimate argument that 'the king for the common good is by his prerogative in many cases above the laws and customs used in his realm'.[66] The liberties of the March had evoked from Edward I one of the most unequivocal declarations of his prerogative. Such arguments launched his lawyers into the dangerous seas of the relationship of the king to law. They drew back. Instead they relied on the phraseology of majesty: an offence was 'to the contempt of the king and to the prejudice of his royal dignity'; another usurped 'the king's right to the derogation of the Crown'; a claim to episcopal temporalities could not be allowed 'because of the royal privileges and the dignity of the Crown'.[67] Vague phrases indeed; but Edward I was deadly serious about the dignity of his office and hypersensitive to any slighting of it. William Braose, lord of Gower, had good reason to know that. In 1290 he had wisely decided

[63] As they did in the case of Gower: *Rot. Parl.*, I, 150a.

[64] *C.W.R.*, 343.

[65] These phrases are taken from counsel's argument in the Gloucester-Hereford case: *C.W.R.*, 342–4.

[66] Ibid. 336; J. E. Morris, op. cit. 229, n. 1.

[67] *Cartae*, III, no. 741 (1281); *Rot. Parl.*, I, 43a (1290), 94a (1293).

not to dispute the royal wish;[68] in 1305 he foolishly did so. When judgement was given against him in a family financial squabble in the Exchequer he railed against the judge and impugned the impartiality of his judgement. He was promptly summoned before the king and his council and told that such an offence was in contempt and dishonour of the king. He was sentenced to walk, ungirt and with his bare head bowed, from the bench at Westminster (while it was in full session) to the Exchequer to apologize to the judge; he was then to be imprisoned in the Tower at the king's pleasure.[69] So were those punished who in any way transgressed against the dignity of the Crown. It was that royal dignity (*dignitas Corone*) which was Edward I's ultimate and unanswerable response to the liberty of the March (*libertas Marchie*).

Edward I and his lawyers in the course of the various cases of the early 1290s had in fact elaborated a clear-cut theory of the relationship of the Crown to the Marcher lords and lordships. Did it amount to a 'policy' towards the March? The pointers in favour of a positive answer are considerable. In the first place, those Marcher lords who were reminded of the king's power in the March form a formidable list: Clare, Bohun, Warenne, Fitzalan, Valence, Braose, Mortimer, Verdon and Fitzreginald. Secondly, though the approach to each case was individual and oblique in terms of Marcher liberties, yet the campaign developed a momentum of its own. In 1291, for example, the Marcher lords summoned to serve as jurors in the Clare-Bohun case soon grasped that this was no ordinary judicial proceeding and they closed their ranks defiantly, albeit unsuccessfully, against what they regarded as a royal attack on the liberties of the March.[70] Consequently the king's lawyers who might have wished originally to keep the case on the level of ascertaining the facts and of punishing contraventions of royal commands (as they did in the case of Theobald Verdon) were compelled to raise issues of first principle, such as the relation of prerogative to law and of the dignity of the Crown to Marcher liberty. Furthermore, such legal declarations were accompanied,

---

[68] *Rot. Parl.*, I, 43a ('Dicit quod de jure illius custodie erga Dominum Regem non vult contendere').

[69] *Abbreviatio Placitorum*, 256-7.

[70] *C.W.R.*, 336-7.

as we have seen, by other manifestations of the king's master-fulness in the March—the levying of a subsidy there in his name, the taking of Glamorgan into royal custody during its lord's lifetime, the pressure on Marcher lords to issue charters of liberties to their tenants. Finally, this masterfulness in the March is much of a piece with the masterfulness which Edward I showed elsewhere in his attitude towards franchise—in his rigorous *quo warranto* inquiries, in his confiscation of the liberties of London and several other cities, in the way he secured the surrender of two of the great Anglo-Norman liberties of Leinster and reduced half of the liberty of Meath to county status, above all perhaps in the peremptory fashion in which he twice confiscated the great palatinate of Durham and compelled its bishop to grant a charter of liberties to his tenants.

We may speak of his 'policy' towards the March if we wish; but we would be mistaken if we believed that Edward I was in some way an enemy of the March or of its franchises. He could be a great stickler for his own Marcher franchises, even to the point of the ridiculous: when Edmund Mortimer of Wigmore tried and executed one of the men of Edward's lordship of Montgomery, the king was beside himself with anger, not at any injustice committed—the man was a felon—but from a deeply-felt affront to his liberties as lord of Montgomery. Mortimer's liberty was confiscated and only restored on pay-ment of 100 marks; he was also commanded to provide an effigy of the man he had so misguidedly executed so that it could be hung on the royal gallows at Montgomery![71] More-over, Edward had to his credit the creation of a number of large new Marcher lordships out of his conquests in Wales in 1282–3. Such a king surely cannot be regarded as an enemy of Marcher franchise as such. Indeed he was willing to confer and confirm Marcher status, as he did to William Braose in 1304, granting him and his heirs the same jurisdiction, royal liberties and free customs in Gower as the earl of Gloucester enjoyed in Glamorgan.[72] That grant takes us near to the heart of Edward I's attitude. He approved of franchises so long as their title was clearly founded on royal charter and thereby subject to his grace, favour and control. Likewise with the March: Marcher

[71] *Rot. Parl.*, I, 45 (1290).   [72] *C.Ch.R. 1300–26*, 46–7.

liberties were not, with a few exceptions such as the case of Gower, founded on royal charter; but the judicial cases of the early 1290s Edward I had shown that those liberties even so were within his power. Once he had established that point and established it sufficiently often and clearly, he was quite content to accept the status quo; once Gilbert Clare had acknowledged that episcopal temporalities in the March belonged during a vacancy to the Crown as of right, Edward granted Clare and his wife the right to such temporalities during their lives; once Clare and Bohun had been taught their lesson in January 1292 Edward soon restored their lands and liberties in the March to them; likewise in the case of Theobald Verdon, though as the most arrogant of Marcher sinners and a smaller political fish his Marcher liberties were withheld from him during his lifetime. Edward I was a master who was content with the acknowledgement of his mastery; he was not bent on the destruction of the Marchers and their liberties.

We may readily concede his mastery to Edward I and yet doubt whether the price he paid for it in political terms was not too high. The Marcher lords could not keep the March outside the range of the king's political and judicial activity; but neither could the king expect his Marcher activities to be without repercussions on the politics of England. The men who smarted under Edward's dressing-down in the March were the greatest magnates of England—the earls of Gloucester, Hereford and Arundel amongst them; their indignation, fanned by other grievances, spilt over into English politics. The earl of Gloucester, the most intransigent of Edward's opponents, died in 1295; that was just as well for Edward for he would have been a formidable enemy in the crisis months of 1297. But others remained: it was Richard Fitzalan, lord of Clun and Oswestry, who led the opposition to serving the king in Gascony in 1295; in the more critical confrontation of 1297 Edward's opponents were led by the earl of Hereford, lord of Brecon and the earl of Norfolk, lord of Chepstow, while among the few other men known to be involved were Fulk Fitzwarin of Whittington and Edmund Mortimer of Wigmore.[73] It is in fact the crisis of 1297 which highlights the possible consequences of Edward I's vigorous activity in the March in the early 1290s. His critics in

[73] M. Prestwich, op. cit. 76, 236, 249–50.

1297 had many other and more substantial grievances against him; but the Marcher dimension in their opposition must not be discounted. Edmund Mortimer one of the most powerful lords of the middle March may serve as an example. His relations with Edward (a great friend of his father's) had been soured in several directions—by his loss of Cwmwd Deuddwr, by the firm order to distrain his lands for the repayment of debts owed to the king in 1295 when he refused to serve overseas, by the almost unseemly readiness of Edward I to listen to the grievances of the Mortimer tenants of Maelienydd in 1297. It is little wonder that Edmund Mortimer was present at a baronial conference at Wyre in March 1297 or that he should be one of the men mentioned as in opposition to the king in September 1297. It is significant that the baronial 'parliament' which discussed the grievances against Edward met 'in the forest of Wyre in the March' in 1297;[74] it was equally significant that few Marcher lords accompanied Edward to Flanders later in the year.[75] Edward I was himself well aware of the significance of the March in the political scene of these crisis months. He had once more taken Glamorgan into royal hands in January 1297 because of the failure of the Countess Joan to comply with his wishes over her remarriage. That move helped to secure one key lordship and the king further sought to win the support of the men of Glamorgan by remitting their communal fines.[76] Even more sinister moves were afoot. In July 1297 Walter Hakeluyt, keeper of the lordship of Glamorgan, and Morgan ap Maredudd, one-time enemy of the late earl of Gloucester and leader of the revolt of 1295 in Glamorgan but now an active royal agent in the March, were given two important commissions—one to communicate the king's personal wishes to the men of the Principality and Glamorgan and the other to hear the complaints of the men of Brecon against their lord, the earl of Hereford, to defend them and to admit them into the king's peace.[77] The Welsh rebel leader of 1295 was being used as the king's *agent provocateur* to subvert the earl of Hereford's

[74] For this meeting see Powicke, *The Thirteenth Century*, 679–80. Wyre Forest is not in fact in the March; but it is near enough to explain the chronicler's statement. It was part of the Mortimer liberty of Cleobury Mortimer.
[75] M. Prestwich, op. cit. 234.
[76] *C.C.R. 1296–1302*, 34, 39.
[77] *C.P.R. 1292–1301*, 293.

authority in the March. His mission was unsuccessful, for he was outwitted by the earl who confirmed the lordship's charters of liberties, stocked his castles and generally won the support of his tenants.[78] Yet the significance of these events remains: they show how desperately close to civil war was the kingdom in the summer months of 1297,[79] how important the March was in the political alignments of those months, and how far Edward I was prepared to go to subvert the authority of his critics. They also show that by 1297, in the March as elsewhere, Edward I was reaping the consequences of his own masterfulness. When the political climate changed, the magnates whom he had cowed into submission struck back at a man who appeared to them less as the English Justinian, more as *le roy coveytous*, a man whose actions in the March earned the condemnation of that mildest of historians, R. W. Eyton, as 'greedy and too politic'.[80] Or rather not politic enough, for the weakness of Edward's attitude to the March was that his masterfulness blinded him to the political consequences of his actions.

The March in the 1290s had felt the impact of the royal will as never before, at least in peacetime. No other king attempted to imitate Edward I's masterfulness during our period. Occasional incidents there were, it is true; but nothing of a sustained character. We may pass over Edward II's challenge to the Marcher lords over the question of the need for royal licence for alienations of land held in chief in the March, for it was patently prompted by his desire to further the political and territorial ambitions of the younger Despenser. The next major challenge to Marcher status came not from a king of England but from a prince of Wales, from the Black Prince and his councillors. Edward was created prince of Wales by his father on 12 May 1343.[81] By the terms of his charter he was granted not only the Principality of Wales but also all the other Crown possessions in Wales and all rights there, including wardships and advowsons,

[78] *Cal. Anc. Corr. conc. Wales*, 101. This important letter is wrongly ascribed by the editor to 1321–2.

[79] According to the letter cited in n. 78 the earl of Hereford was telling the men of Brecon that he was against the king's peace.

[80] *Antiquities of Shropshire*, XI, 99.

[81] The whole question of the Black Prince's 'constitutional' position and policies in Wales has been discussed in two classic articles: D. L. Evans, 'Some Notes on the History of the Principality of Wales in the Time of the Black Prince (1343–76)',

belonging both to the Crown and to the Principality. It was an exceptionally generous grant for its terms clearly embraced much more than the Principality as such. The Prince's lawyers soon put it to the test. They claimed that Marcher lordships which had once been under the authority of Llywelyn ap Gruffudd, the first and last officially-recognized native prince of Wales, were tenurially dependent on the Principality, not on the Crown. The point was more than a legal quibble; on it depended the lucrative rights of custody and wardship of some of the major lordships of the March. The Prince's councillors advanced their claim vigorously, even impetuously: in 1347 they prepared a draft letter concerning the custody of the lordship of Bromfield and Yale well before the death of the earl of Surrey and in 1360 the prince commanded that the question of the custody of the lordship of Denbigh was to 'be hastened day and night until it be completed'.[82] Success attended their efforts: among the lordships whose custody the Prince secured were Denbigh (1344, 1360), Bromfield and Yale (1347), Laugharne (1349), Dyffryn Clwyd (1353) and Ceri and Cydewain (1360). The Prince also claimed that by the terms of his charter he had been given the temporalities of vacant bishoprics and the collations of cathedral churches throughout Wales.[83] Here again he was largely successful: the bishops of St. Asaph and Bangor swore fealty to him; he secured the custody of the temporalities of the bishoprics of Bangor, St. Asaph and Llandaff while they were vacant; he nominated to vacant benefices and assigned the most valuable dignities to his own servants; it was to him that the bishop of St. Asaph renounced any prejudicial words in his papal bull of provision; it was to his exchequer that the insignia of the bishop of Llandaff were sent for safe-keeping.[84]

So far the Black Prince and his councillors had done no more than assert the Prince's rights vigorously in the light of the 1343

T.C.S. (1925–6), 25–111 esp. 84–99 and J. Goronwy Edwards, *The Principality of Wales 1267–1967. A Study in Constitutional History* (Caernarvon, 1969), esp. 31–4. The present discussion attempts to do no more than to supplement these two studies from a Marcher point of view.

[82] *B.P.R.*, I, 31; III, 351.

[83] His ecclesiastical claims are discussed in D. L. Evans, op. cit. 94–9 and Glanmor Williams, *The Welsh Church*, 121–9, 138–9.

[84] For these last two incidents, see *B.P.R.*, I, 19, 91.

charter. The Marcher lords, who had only once before known the régime of an English prince of Wales, might well have been annoyed, especially by the aggressive tone of the Prince's claims; but constitutionally and legally they could hardly object. The Prince, however, did not leave matters there. His ambitions comprehended the whole of the March, not only those lordships which could be construed as tenurially dependent on the Principality; his letters to the lords of the March were imperious and peremptory. In 1347 on the death of Hugh Audley he seized the lordship of Newport, by no stretch of the imagination a part of the Principality, into his hands; his officers held an inquisition *post mortem* there and gave seisin of it to its new lord.[85] In the same year, acting on an order from the king, he commanded the Marcher lords to levy troops for the royal army; it was a disturbing departure from the normal etiquette of military summonses, for never previously had the Marcher lords been summoned to recruit troops other than by the king of England himself.[86] It is little wonder that some of them took the command ill. For Humphrey Bohun, earl of Hereford and lord of Brecon, this command was but one of a series of provocative letters he received from the Prince. In 1346 the Prince claimed exemption from paying toll to the earl's officials; in 1347 he prohibited the earl from entering into any of the temporalities of the bishopric of St. David's within the lordship of Brecon; in an undated letter, the most arrogant of them all, he forbade the earl from holding an eyre in his lordship on the grounds that it would be 'openly to the prejudice of the prince, to the diminution of his lordship of Wales and against the dignity of his coronet'.[87] The tone of this last letter and its phraseology of majesty were indeed reminiscent of Edward I at his most masterful.

The Marcher lords reacted. John Charlton, lord of Powys, refused to accept the Prince's writ and 'sent it back just as it was, sealed with prince's seal of the exchequer of Caernarvon';[88] the earl of Hereford ignored the grandiloquent language of the Prince's letter and proceeded to hold sessions in eyre at Brecon

[85] ibid. 1, 144, 147.

[86] ibid. 1, 52, 55.

[87] ibid. 1, 31, 77; *Cal. Anc. Corr. conc. Wales*, 225–6. Cf. the threatening tone of his letter to John Charlton of Powys: *B.P.R.*, 1, 35.

[88] *Cal. Anc. Corr. conc. Wales*, 246.

in 1350;[89] the bishop of St. David's, when commanded to do fealty to the Prince, prevaricated.[90] Above all, the Marcher lords knew they could appeal to Edward III over the head of the Black Prince and his power-hungry councillors. They did not do so in vain. On 24 October 1353 two of the Marcher lords whose lands had earlier been taken into the Prince's hands, the lords of Denbigh (the earl of Salisbury) and Bromfield and Yale (the earl of Arundel) did homage to the king 'in the presence and with the consent of the prince of Wales' for their lordships 'as immediately subject to the Crown of England'.[91] It was an exercise in legal definition; it was also an exercise in good public relations with the earls and a gentle but firm lesson to the Prince and his advisers. That lesson was incorporated in statute form in April 1354 when it was declared that 'all of the lords of the March of Wales be perpetually intendant and annexed to the Crown of England as they and their ancestors have been at all times heretofore and not to the principality of Wales'.[92] This statute, we may believe, was enacted very much under pressure from the Marcher lords who had been alarmed by the claims and commands of the Black Prince over the last eleven years. It set their minds at rest, although it was not always observed to the letter.[93] It also made clear that the king, not the prince, was the master of the March. As if to underscore that point, Edward III in a series of politically-motivated, quasi-judicial actions asserted his mastery in the March more decisively in 1354 than in any other year of his reign. He quashed the judgements which clouded the history of the two most powerful Marcher families, those on Edmund Fitzalan, earl of Arundel (d. 1326) and Roger Mortimer, earl of March (d. 1330); in a sequence of arbitrary decisions he restored the vast Mortimer estates as they stood at their fullest extent in 1330 to the young earl of March; he confirmed the earl of Arundel in his possession of the lordship of Chirk; he upheld the earl of Warwick in his successful claim to Gower. In a series

---

[89] D.L. 29/671/10810, m. 17.

[90] Glanmor Williams, op. cit. 121–2.

[91] *C.C.R. 1360–4*, 33.   [92] 28 Edward III, c. 2.

[93] J. G. Edwards, op. cit. 33–4. It is only fair to add that in 1373 the Black Prince conceded that his claims to the overlordship of Ceri and Cydewain was still disputed and allowed Edmund Mortimer seisin of the lordships without securing his homage and fealty: B.L. Harleian 1240, fol. 68.

of bold strokes, Edward III had profoundly influenced the politico-territorial complexion of the March; the Black Prince merely looked on. The Prince's ambitions in the March were baulked in two other directions by his father: in 1357 the king decreed that the bishopric of St. David's should pertain to the Crown for ever and the Prince and his officers were commanded not to meddle with it;[94] in 1360 when the Black Prince successfully claimed in a judicial case that Gower was part of the Principality of Wales, his father promptly conferred upon the lord of Gower the status and rights of a Marcher lord.[95] Thomas Beauchamp, earl of Warwick and lord of Gower (d. 1369) was one of Edward III's leading war-captains.

In several directions, therefore, the Black Prince's ambitions in the March were rebuffed. Nor was the defeat an ephemeral one. When Richard of Bordeaux was created prince of Wales in 1376 the status of the Marcher lords 'who of old were tenants of the Crown' and of the see of St. David's was specifically protected.[96] But the importance of the episode does not rest solely or mainly in the constitutional issues it raised. It was a reminder, if reminder were necessary, that the liberties of the March were no defence against the ambitions of an English king or, possibly, of a prince of Wales. It was also a reminder that the fate of Marcher lords and Marcher lordships was very much part and parcel of the politics of England. That is what Edward III, that master of political management, realized. In terms of his own political control the March was too important and too delicate an area to be abandoned to the insensitive expansionist designs of the Black Prince and his councillors; in terms of their political weight in the kingdom, the Marcher lords were too important to be left to foster a sense of grievance. Edward III could be as masterful and as arbitrary as Edward I; but in his dealings with the Marcher lords, more especially in relation to the ambitions of his son, he showed an acute awareness of the political repercussions of his actions. Edward I may have 'preferred masterfulness to the arts of political management';[97] Edward III's preference was otherwise.

[94] *C.C.R. 1354–60*, 382.
[95] *C.Ch.R. 1341–1417*, 107.
[96] *C.C.R. 1374–7*, 420.
[97] K. B. McFarlane. *The Nobility of Later Medieval England*, 267.

13 The March in English Politics

THE March, so we have tried to show in the previous chapter, was within the ambit of the king of England's authority and power; it followed, therefore, that it was within the orbit of English politics. For English historians, indeed, the main interest of the March and of its lords lies in the part they played from time to time in English politics. It was often a not unimportant role, as a few examples will soon serve to show: it was in the March that William Braose waxed rich and powerful in the late-twelfth and early-thirteenth centuries; it was there also, in Powicke's words, that Hubert de Burgh 'built up a kind of palatinate' for himself between 1228 and 1232;[1] it was from his vast estates in the March that Earl Richard Marshall opposed Henry III in 1233;[2] the lords of the March played a crucial and well-acknowledged role in the turbulent politics and campaigns of the years 1263–5;[3] it was to the forest of Wyre on the edge of the March, as we have seen, that the barons retired in 1297 to discuss their grievances against Edward I;[4] it was in the March that the younger Despenser first tasted defeat in the summer of 1321; it was there that he and later Roger Mortimer of Wigmore converted their political power into vast territorial fortunes in the decade 1320–30; it was to the March that Edward II and his favourite fled in vain in 1326. In the political history and geography of medieval England the March and its lords indeed occupy a prominent place.

It is a prominence which should not be underestimated; but it is a prominence which is often misunderstood and even exaggerated. In the first place, it is well to remember that the

---

[1] F. M. Powicke, *King Henry III and the Lord Edward*, 70; R. F. Walker, 'Hubert de Burgh and Wales, 1218–1232', *E.H.R.* 87 (1972), 465–94.

[2] Powicke, op. cit. 129–44; J. E. Lloyd, *History of Wales*, II, 678–82.

[3] T. F. Tout, 'Wales and the Marches in the Barons' War', *Collected Papers of Thomas Frederick Tout*, II, 47–100.

[4] See above p. 268.

March as such was not an issue in English politics; it was a datum in the political scene of the period. The attitudes of individual Marcher lords and the future of individual Marcher lordships might well be the subject of political discussion; but there was not, as far as we know, any attempt to place the March as such on the political agenda of the period. Nor was there any serious attempt to make a legal or constitutional issue out of the liberties of the March. The March only became an issue if a major revolt in Wales focused an unfavourable light on the military and other problems of the March (as happened briefly during the Glyn Dŵr revolt) or if the king and his advisers deliberately chose to place the question of the March as such on their political agenda (as did Henry VIII).

The March was not normally an issue in English politics; neither did the Marcher lords form a distinct political group in English political life. Their political behaviour was obviously a matter of interest and concern to English kings, especially before the final conquest of Wales in 1282–3. They ruled a militarily sensitive and important area; as frontiersmen accustomed to war as a way of life, they were possibly more ready to resort to arms than most English barons; as men with lands on the periphery of England, they might well ally with each other and even with the native Welsh princes in pursuit of their political ambitions. To that extent their political behaviour may have been more crucial, at least in politically unsettled periods, than that of any comparable group of barons in England; in these terms perhaps the closest parallel to the position of the Marcher lords was that provided on occasion by the Scottish border magnates, such as the Nevilles and the Percys. But even such special importance as the Marcher lords may have enjoyed in this respect was much reduced after the Edwardian conquest of Wales. Furthermore, the Marcher lords were not and never had been a cohesive political group acting with an unanimity of purpose on any political issue; not even in those periods such as 1263–5 or 1320–1, when historians speak confidently of 'the Marchers' and of 'a Marcher attitude', did all the Marcher lords adopt a common political line. Not only were they not united politically as a group, they were also not as individuals primarily Marcher in their interest, preoccupations or attitudes. The great majority of them were primarily

English barons with some Marcher and often Irish estates; they lived in England most of the time and their political orientation was firmly English. Sir Maurice Powicke has already protested that even in the context of the mid-thirteenth century 'both the importance and the isolation of the Marchers' as a group 'can be exaggerated';[5] his stricture has even more force in terms of the fourteenth-century political situation.

Marcher politics are not *sui generis*; at no point can they be divorced from English politics in general. That is not to deny that there were distinctive qualities about Marcher politics; but such qualities need to be considered within a more general framework of political activity. Foremost among these distinctive qualities we must place the geographical consideration, the obvious fact that the March lay on the periphery of the English political arena. It was peopled by an alien race and only recently had it been finally (as it proved) conquered. Much of it was mountainous and inaccessible; none of it had been brought directly under the control of the king's administration in the normal course of affairs. On occasion such distance lent a measure of enchantment to the political view of the March. 'For it was there', observed one well-informed contemporary chronicler with reference to the March, 'that the barons had their safest refuge; it was difficult for the king to penetrate it without a strong force'.[6] Political dissidents might well feel safer there: Richard Marshall, earl of Pembroke, certainly felt so in 1233–4; so also did the barons who assembled in Wyre forest in 1297. It was there likewise that assemblies were being convened in March–April 1321 aimed at the overthrow of the Despensers. The March was also an area where political disputes might be militarily determined without necessarily escalating into civil war in the kingdom as a whole. The conspiracies of March–April 1321 were followed by raids on the Despenser and Arundel estates in the March in May 1321.[7] These raids were so effective and so widely supported as to dissuade the king from attempting a broader military confrontation in England and thereby eventually brought about

[5] F. M. Powicke, op. cit. 433.

[6] *Vita Edwardi Secundi*, ed. N. Denholm-Young, 117.

[7] There is an exhaustive study of the Despenser war in Glamorgan by J. Conway Davies in *T.R.H.S.* 3rd ser. 9 (1915), 21–64. It can be supplemented on points of detail by the account in J. R. Maddicott, *Thomas of Lancaster 1307–1322*, 258–68.

the exile of the Despensers. In this respect the March could act as an apron-stage for English political disputes.

It could do so in respect not only of its geographical position but also of its strongly militarist traditions. In a land where warfare was endemic the resort to arms was less noticeable than it would have been in contemporary England. The transition from wars of conquest against the Welsh into 'civil' wars against English political enemies was an easy one in the March. It was all the easier since native and Marcher convention sanctioned the resort to war as a means of settling 'private 'differences. When during the tumultuous months of 1321 a royal official was prompted to remark that the March was a land at war (*terra erat de guerra*),[8] his report pinpointed one of the distinctive features of the Marcher political scene.

But perhaps the most distinctive quality of the March in fourteenth-century English politics lies neither in its peripheral position nor in its strongly militarist habits but rather in what we may call its political geography. The contrast with England in this respect is quite striking. In England, as has often been pointed out, the wide geographical dispersion of baronial estates, often in the form of a few isolated manors in several counties, profoundly affected the pattern of political life and on the whole militated against the growth of strong regional bases of baronial power. Furthermore, this 'tenurial mosaic . . . contributed powerfully, if indirectly, to the triumph of royal over feudal and franchisal jurisdiction'.[9] In the March the situation was quite otherwise. There each lordship formed a self-contained unit; the lord exercised a territorial and juris-dictional overlordship throughout it. Let us instance a single example, the estates of Henry Lacy, earl of Lincoln (d. 1311). His great English honours of Pontefract, Bolingbroke, Halton and Clitheroe comprised a congeries of properties and liberties, geographically scattered and interspersed with the properties and liberties of other men. Furthermore they were encompassed, to a greater or lesser degree, by a pattern of royal administration and justice. Over and above these four honours, Lacy also

---

[8] J. R. Maddicott, op. cit. 265.
[9] See in general F. M. Stenton, *Anglo-Saxon England*, 3rd edn. (Oxford, 1971), 27–9 and R. Lennard, *Rural England 1086–1135* (Oxford, 1959), 29–39. The quotations are taken from Lennard, pp. 35–9.

owned isolated manors in nine other counties of England. Compared with his English lands, his Marcher estates had the neatness of simplicity: they consisted of the single large lordship of Denbigh (comprising much of the modern county of that name). Within the lordship his authority was jurisdictionally and territorially unchallenged; he was there 'virtually king and justiciar'. It is true that Lacy's authority and direct control varied from one part of the lordship to another; but, apart from a few ecclesiastical pockets, all the land of the lordship was held of him. This contrast in tenurial geography had, or rather could have, its political implications. The simplicity of the tenurial situation (at the lordship level) in the March could be expected to lead to a closer alignment of territorial lordship and political loyalty than in the complex situation prevailing in England.

Other consequences flowed from the political geography of the March. Since the March was in these terms a land of large lordships—some forty-five at most controlled by less than two dozen English families—it was relatively easy to change its political complexion, in terms of its lords, by a few bold strokes. Edward II's victory over his baronial opponents at Borough-bridge in 1322, for example, changed the political map of the March even more dramatically and drastically than it did that of England. The forfeiture of the lands of the earls of Lancaster and Hereford, of the two Mortimers of Wigmore and Chirk, of John Giffard and Roger Amory meant that more than half of the lordships of the March and far more than that in terms of area and of wealth reverted to the king, most of them to be granted to his supporters. Likewise the fall of the two Despensers and of the earl of Arundel in 1326 changed the political configuration of the March in an almost equally drastic fashion. Again the confiscations of Richard II in 1397 left their imprint more decisively on the map of the March than on that of England. Nowhere, in short, can one appreciate more vividly the territorial impact of political revolution than in the March of Wales.

Nowhere, by way of corollary, was it easier for the political favourite to accumulate a territorial fortune for himself. It was a simple question of arithmetic: the number of counters on the Marcher territorial board was small and a man with the king's support could corner many of them for himself. William Braose had done so in the early years of John's reign;[10] Hubert de Burgh did so in some measure in the years 1228–32. But the empires of these two men were modest compared with those which the younger Despenser and Roger Mortimer assembled for themselves successively in the period 1318–30. Both men, it is true, already had a major foothold in the March—Despenser in respect of his marriage to the eldest of the Clare co-heiresses and Roger Mortimer in respect of both his paternal and his maternal inheritances; but their careers demonstrate admirably both the speed and the methods whereby a Marcher empire was pieced together. The younger Despenser's ambitions were clear enough: 'that Despenser may be rich and may attain his ends'.[11] He pursued those ambitions with an unscrupulous tenacity which marked him out in the eyes of contemporaries as the greediest of men (*homo cupidissimus*).[12] In territorial terms much of that greed was directed towards the southern March. As husband of Eleanor Clare, Despenser was awarded the lordship of Glamorgan in the partition of 1317 and thereby immediately rose to the front rank of Marcher lords. Such a position only whetted his territorial appetite and that appetite was soon being satisfied at an alarming speed. In November 1317 he was given a life grant of Dryslwyn and Cantrefmawr;[13] in 1317–18, almost immediately after the Clare partition, he began a process of unscrupulous harassment of his brother-in-law, Hugh Audley, and only ceased when Audley surrendered to him the lordship of Gwynllwg with its castle and borough of Newport;[14] in November 1318 he secured a solemn grant of all royal liberties in his lordship of Glamorgan in full parliament at York;[15] in July 1319 his nominee was placed in control of the lordship of Newcastle Emlyn;[16] and in the same year he had already initiated plans to try to secure the Braose lordship of Gower for

[10] The extent of Braose's territorial power can be vividly grasped from the map in W. Rees, *An Historical Atlas of Wales* (London, 1959), plate 38.

[11] The phrase is Despenser's own: *Cal. Anc. Corr. conc. Wales*, ed. J. G. Edwards, 219–20.

[12] The phrase is quoted from the Lanercost Chronicle in J. Conway Davies op. cit. 27, n. 4.

[13] *C.P.R. 1317–21*, 56; J. Conway Davies, op. cit. 31–2.

[14] J. Conway Davies, op. cit. 29–31.

[15] *C.Ch.R. 1300–26*, 398–9.

[16] *C.P.R. 1317–21*, 338.

himself. His letters to John Inge, his sheriff of Glamorgan, in these years lay bare, as does no other Marcher correspondence in the fourteenth century, his aims and his tactics and above all his single-minded determination that his Marcher plans should not be foiled.[17] Foiled they temporarily were in 1321 by the devastation of his estates and by his subsequent exile; but after the victory of Boroughbridge, he could fulfil his Marcher ambitions to his heart's content. Out of the spoils of the contrariants he secured the Bohun lordships of Brecon, Hay and Huntington, the Giffard lordship of Iscennen, and the Mortimer (of Chirk) lordship of Blaenllyfni for himself;[18] he compelled Elizabeth Burgh by threats and virtual imprisonment, to exchange the lordship of Usk for that of Gower and then proceeded by legal chicanery to recover the lordship of Gower also;[19] in 1323 he persuaded—and persuasion for the younger Despenser was no gentle art—the earl of Norfolk to part with the lordships of Chepstow and Tidenham for his life in return for an annual rent of 300 marks and soon after he compelled Elizabeth Comyn (women were an easy target for him) to surrender Castle Goodrich 'in the March of Wales';[20] he also acquired a reversionary interest in many of Alice Lacy's estates, including the border lordship of Clifford and Glasbury;[21] and in 1325 the king granted him the custody of the lands and the marriage of Laurence Hastings, heir not only to the Hastings lordships of Abergavenny and Cilgerran but also to the Valence earldom and county of Pembroke and the commote of Ystlwyf.[22] Behind a quasi-legal façade he had built an empire which

---

[17] The letters are published as follows: 18 January 1321 (*Cal. Anc. Corr. conc. Wales*, 219); 16 February 1321 (ibid. 220); 27 February 1321 (ibid. 180); 6 March 1321 (ibid. 259); 21 March 1321 (*E.H.R.* 12 (1897), 755–61 and also in *Cartae*, III, no. 894).

[18] *C.F.R. 1319–27*, 143; *C.C.R. 1318–23*, 617–18; *C.P.R. 1321–4*, 191, 222. Despenser paid an annual farm of £600 for the Bohun and Giffard lordships. In February 1323 Iscennen was given the virtual status of a Marcher lordship: *C.P.R. 1321–4*, 245–6; *C.A.D.*, III, A. 4886.

[19] G. A. Holmes, 'A Protest against the Despensers', *Speculum* 30 (1955), 207–12.

[20] *C.A.D.*, III, A. 4880; *C.P.R. 1324–7*, 116.

[21] *C.P.R. 1324–7*, 103. Alice Lacy was treated in much the same way by the Despensers as was Elizabeth Burgh; for the lands they secured from her see R. Somerville, *History of the Duchy of Lancaster*, I, 33–4.

[22] *C.P.R. 1324–7*, 95. Despenser was alleged to have postponed the division of the Valence estates and then to have weighted it in his own favour as guardian of Laurence Hastings: *C.I.P.M.*, VII, no. 391, p. 287.

stretched without a break from the banks of the Teifi to those of the Wye. His Marcher estates alone must have yielded him the huge landed income of about £4,000 a year by 1325–6, and if to these we add the income from estates in his custody the figure would be nearer £5,000 a year. His methods were the same elsewhere; but nowhere could they be employed to such dramatically good use in establishing a vast territorial complex as in the March of Wales. This was the land of the empire-builders of medieval English politics.

Despenser's empire was replaced by that of Roger Mortimer of Wigmore. His was not such a compact territorial complex as that of Despenser but it was assembled with equal speed and unscrupulousness. Mortimer already enjoyed by inheritance a large bloc of family estates in the middle March. To these he now added lands which he expropriated from his disinherited cousin of Chirk (Chirkland, Blaenllyfni, Narberth and a share of St. Clears),[23] major lordships forfeited by his political opponents (notably Denbigh from the elder Despenser and Oswestry and Clun along with all Fitzalan estates in Shropshire from the earl of Arundel)[24] and the reversion of several royal lordships (notably Montgomery and Builth).[25] These territorial spoils were further augmented by the grant of the custody of the estates of the most important minors in the March—those of James Audley, heir to Cemais and Cantref Bychan and of Laurence Hastings, heir to Pembroke, Abergavenny and Cilgerran, and also of the marriage of the dowager-countess of Pembroke.[26] Finally, his control of Wales and the March was placed on an official basis by the grant of key offices—those of justiciar of north and south Wales for life, of justiciar of the bishoprics of Llandaff and St. David's, and of chief keeper of the peace in Herefordshire, Worcestershire and Staffordshire.[27] Roger Mortimer virtually ruled England from 1327 to 1330 but the territorial base of his power was securely Marcher; it was therefore highly appropriate that when he was raised to comital rank in October 1328 he should assume the novel title of earl of March.

---

[23] Above, p. 47. [24] *C.P.R. 1327–30*, 328–9 (September 1327).
[25] ibid. 566 (Montgomery and Chirbury: April 1330); *C.F.R. 1327–37*, 147 (Builth: September 1328).
[26] *C.P.R. 1327–30*, 22, 108, 166, 311, 326 (February–October 1327).
[27] *C.F.R. 1327–37*, 19, 317; *C.P.R. 1327–30*, 152, 327.

The speed with which the younger Despenser and Roger Mortimer of Wigmore assembled their empires has served to pinpoint for us one of the distinctive features of the politico-territorial structure of the March; but it should not be allowed to conceal the even more basic truth that Marcher politics were English politics. To say so is not in any way to deny the local peculiarities of the Marcher situation nor is it to gainsay the unusual character of Marcher lordship; less still is it to deny that there could be a distinctively Welsh dimension to the political and military life of the March, particularly in terms of periodic war-scares and threats of native rebellion. Yet in terms of fourteenth-century political activity, the fate of Marcher lords and Marcher lordships—we are not speaking here of the responses of the native population or even of those of the native or settler gentry—was determined by the fortunes of English politics.

This interaction of 'national' political alignments and the local Marcher situation can best be appreciated by looking rather more closely at one particular period, the years 1310–21. We have selected this period for two obvious reasons: it was a period of unusual tensions in English political life and the impact of political alignments is thereby highlighted; it was also one of the most volatile periods in the history of the medieval March. It is to this latter aspect that we will first turn our attention. The period would have been a momentous one in the history of the March even had it been the most quiescent decade in English politics, for death wreaked havoc in the ranks of the Marcher lords in that period to a degree unparalleled since the 1230s and the 1240s. In 1308 John Fitzreginald, lord of Blaenllyfni and Bwlchyddinas, died and his lordship reverted to the king by arrangement; in 1309 the Tony lords of Elfael failed in the direct male line and so also did the ancient Welsh princely line of Powys; in 1311 Henry Lacy, earl of Lincoln and first English lord of Denbigh, died leaving his daughter Alice as his heiress; in 1314 the Genevilles, lords of Ewyas Lacy and a moiety of Ludlow, failed in the male line; in the same year, much more catastrophically and unexpectedly, the earl of Gloucester, greatest of the Marcher lords, was killed in battle leaving (after the alleged pregnancy of his widow was eventually proved false) three sisters as co-heiresses; in 1315 Peter

Corbet, anticipating his own lack of children and probably also prompted by impecuniousness, offered to sell the reversion of his lordship of Caus; in the same year, Guy Beauchamp earl of Warwick and in right of his wife lord of Elfael, died leaving a child of two as his heir; in 1316 Theobald Verdon, lord of a moiety of Ludlow and husband of one of the Clare coheiresses, died without a male heir of his body; in the same year Nicholas Audley, lord of Cantref Bychan, died leaving an heir who was to be in wardship for thirteen years; in 1318 the earl of Surrey was compelled to surrender the lordship of Bromfield and Yale to the earl of Lancaster; and finally there was much speculation about the future of the lordship of Gower with several Marcher lords waiting eagerly to clinch deals which they thought they had provisionally concluded with its spendthrift lord, William Braose. These were indeed momentous years in the March: in a matter of ten years a third or so of the lordships of the March either descended to a new family or were offered for sale or, most common of all, augmented the stock of lands in royal custody.

Succession to and control of land was much more than a matter of family interest and of domestic dispute; it was of the very stuff of medieval politics. At the centre of the political processes stood the king. He dominated the territorial politics of his kingdom, the March included. How effectively and how wisely he exercised that control in good measure determined his success as a king. This control was exercised in several ways. Marcher lordships reverted to the king on the death of their lords. It was for him to determine who should have the wardship and marriage of the heir and the custody of his lands, if he were a minor; it was for him also to grant the marriage of the daughters, if they were the heiresses, and of the widow. All such grants were, or could be, politically-loaded acts. When, for example, Edward II granted the hands of the two widowed sisters of the earl of Gloucester (and with them the prospect of a third each of the great Clare inheritance) to Hugh Audley and Roger Amory he thereby raised two of his household knights to the front rank of the English baronage: it was simultaneously an act of territorial munificence and of political engineering. Likewise when Edward II disposed of the custody and wardship of the lands and heir of the earl of Warwick he confirmed the fears of his political opponents (for he had previously promised that the earl's executors should have custody of the lands) and bestowed his largesse on his political favourites, granting the custody of the lands to the elder Despenser and the marriage of the heir to Roger Mortimer of Wigmore.[28]

The windfalls of feudal tenure were one major item of royal patronage; Crown estates were another. In the March a grant of one of the royal lordships (notably Builth, Montgomery and Haverford) was one of the surest indications of political favouritism. When the earl of Hereford, for example, was granted the lordship of Builth in 1317 it was by way of reward for his political loyalty or 'good service' as the contemporary phraseology had it; a particularly welcome reward it was, as it lay next to the Bohun lordship of Brecon.[29] When, however, the earl began to falter in his loyalty, his title to the lordship was called in question and finally revoked in 1321 (on the specious, but convenient, ground that it was contrary to the Ordinances of 1311) because of his open hostility to the younger Despenser.[30] The king's patronage extended to offices as well as to lands. In the March, it is true, he only had the right of appointment to office while a lordship was in his custody; but he could show his favour to a Marcher lord by granting him one of the major offices of the Principality. The ascendancy of the Mortimers, for example, was much enhanced by the tenure of the key office of justiciar of Wales by Roger Mortimer of Chirk from 1308 to 1322 with one brief break and likewise after 1322 the earl of Arundel's authority in north Wales and the March was assured by the grant of the justiciarship of the Principality.

Offices and land were the staple items of royal patronage; but the king's power was not exhausted thereby. As the fountain of justice and much the most powerful focus of influence in the kingdom, his support was the most valuable asset which a man

[28] For the king's promise to Warwick that his executors would have the wardship of all his lands south of Trent see *C.F.R. 1307–19*, 255. For the grant of the wardship ibid. 331 and of the marriage for a fine of 1,600 marks ibid. 369.

[29] *C.Ch.R. 1300–26*, 367.

[30] In the parliament of May 1319 it was alleged that the earl of Hereford was claiming a right to Builth prior to the royal charter and that the lordship had been granted to him for a farm below its actual value: *Documents illustrative of English History in the Thirteenth and Fourteenth Centuries*, ed. H. Cole (1844), 10. For the final resumption of Builth into royal hands see *C.F.R. 1319–27*, 50; *C. Chancery Warrants 1244–1326*, 519.

could have in the pursuit of his political and territorial ambitions. It was with his support, tacit or otherwise, that the younger Despenser began his empire-building in the March in 1318; it was his support which enabled Despenser to disguise his greedy ambition for Gower under the cloak of a high-sounding constitutional wrangle over Marcher custom. After 1322 that support lent a thin veil of quasi-legality to Despenser's activities as he bullied Elizabeth Burgh to surrender Usk to him and then disseised her of Gower. Rarely, indeed, was royal support so blatantly and so triumphantly harnessed to private ambition in the March as it was in the decade 1320–30. Times were unusual; but even when they were more normal, royal patronage and influence profoundly and continuously determined the distribution of political power in the March. The royal will withheld favours from some: it turned a deaf ear to the pleas of the heirs of Roger Mortimer of Chirk in the 1340s and 1350s and thereby consigned the family to the obscurity of local Herefordshire society;[31] it equally ignored the pleas of successive earls of Hereford for the restoration of the lordship of Builth.[32] It lavished favours on others: it rebuilt the fortunes of the Mortimers of Wigmore in the 1350s at the expense of an earlier generation of royal beneficiaries;[33] it responded to the plea of the earl of Arundel in 1347 that he should succeed to the Warenne inheritance, even though Edward III had been sorely, and for a brief while successfully, tempted by the prospect of using the Warenne lands as an endowment for one of his sons;[34] it granted custodies and leases in the March to its protégés on highly favourable terms, as did Edward III to Henry of Grosmont, earl of Derby and later earl and duke of Lancaster.[35] Not all acts of royal patronage in the March or

[31] Above pp. 46–7.

[32] Such pleas were made in 1327, 1335, 1345, 1360 and probably on other occasions. The story of these attempts is given in detail in my D.Phil. thesis, 'The Bohun and Lancaster Lordships in Wales in the Fourteenth and Early Fifteenth Centuries' (Univ. of Oxford, 1965), 105–7.

[33] G. A. Holmes, *Estates of the Higher Nobility*, 15–17.

[34] This fascinating episode can be reconstructed from an indenture of June 1345 printed in W. Dugdale, *The Baronage of England* (1675), i, 81–2 and from Edward III's subsequent revocation of it at the instigation of the earl of Arundel: *C.P.R. 1345–8*, 221, 480.

[35] In 1334 Henry was granted the custody of the lordship of Abergavenny, which he held until 1341, for a farm of 500 marks annually whereas the lordship must have been worth nearer 800 marks a year: *C.F.R. 1327–37*, 401. In 1342

elsewhere were politically motivated or politically significant; not all of them brought a financial bonanza to the recipient. But in general terms the king's patronage and influence were the single major determinant in deciding the political complexion of the March; they brought the power of central political life to bear on the affairs of the locality.

We can study this interaction of local Marcher affairs and national politics from yet another angle, that of local disputes. Such disputes and rivalries would have been easily contained and settled in a politically quiescent period; but in Edward II's reign they soon assumed a national significance as they were sucked into the cross-currents of national politics. The case of the succession dispute to Powys on the death of Gruffudd de la Pole in 1309 provides an excellent example.[36] It was on the face of it an ordinary family quarrel between two rival claimants—Gruffudd's uncle, another Gruffudd de la Pole, and Gruffudd's brother-in-law, John Charlton. But the dispute soon became noteworthy for two reasons. In the first place, it involved at the legal level an issue of principle of some importance, namely that of the respective role of Welsh and English inheritance customs in the March; for while de la Pole's claim was founded on the Welsh principle that there was no succession to land through the female, Charlton's claim, upheld by inquest, was based on English inheritance practice. That in itself made the dispute a delicate one and persuaded Edward II to declare that the issue closely touched the dignity of his Crown.[37] But the political implications of the case were in the context of the time far more explosive than the legal ones. John Charlton was a close confidant of the king, a member of his household from his days as a prince and later his chamberlain; it was from the king that he received in 1309 the hand of Hawise de la Pole and thereby his claim to Powys. As a result of this close personal liaison, Edward II's commitment to

he acquired the lease of Carmarthen and Cantrefmawr for ten years at £190 per annum and here he again made a very handsome profit: *C.F.R. 1337–47*, 263, 335. For the general pattern of royal patronage to Earl Henry see K. A. Fowler, *The King's Lieutenant. Henry of Grosmont, First Duke of Lancaster 1310–1361*, (1969) 28.

[36] Much the best account of this dispute is that in J. R. Maddicott, op. cit. 140–1, 147, 151, 184. There is a valuable biography of Charlton in J. Conway Davies, *The Baronial Opposition to Edward II* (Cambridge, 1918), 215–17.

[37] See the letter printed in J. Conway Davies, op. cit. 571, no. 56.

Charlton's claim was bound to be strong. Charlton was a king's man and the king maintained him with the stubborness of a good lord. Almost as a corollary, Charlton was a marked man in the eyes of the dissident barons and his removal from office was one of the items on the baronial agenda in 1311. Likewise, just as Charlton's claim to Powys was supported by the king, so Gruffudd de la Pole's counter-claim was upheld by Thomas of Lancaster. Gruffudd indeed became Lancaster's retainer and annuitant.[38] Nor was it merely Edward II and the earl of Lancaster who became involved in the case. Other Marcher lords also took up sides in the dispute, largely in terms of their current political alignments. Edmund Fitzalan, earl of Arundel and lord of Oswestry (which bordered on Powys), identified himself with Pole's claim by giving succour to his men;[39] that alliance created a lifelong enmity between Fitzalan and Charlton and helps to explain why Charlton executed Fitzalan in the revolution of 1326 without waiting for a formal judgement. Roger Mortimer of Wigmore, whose lands also bordered on Powys, took a different line: he supported Charlton's cause and so welcome was his support that he was rewarded by the grant of some land in Powys and by the gift of Charlton's son in marriage to his own daughter.[40] The dispute over the succession to Powys was essentially a domestic and local squabble. It was as such that it began and as such that it ended, for it outlived the reign of Edward II. But for a time in the 1310s it became an item on the agenda of English politics, not so much in respect of its own importance as because in a situation of political friction local causes soon found national champions.

This interplay of local issues and of national political alignments is illustrated again by the story of Gower in the same period. It is too well-known a case to need detailed discussion here. The prospect of a Marcher lordship being offered for sale was an exciting one and was bound to arouse a good measure of competition between prospective buyers. Several leading magnates had high expectations of securing the lordship for themselves: John Mowbray, the son-in-law of William Braose, lord

[38] J. R. Maddicott, op. cit. 54–5. Another Marcher lord who became Lancaster's retainer and whose cause the earl avowed was Fulk Lestrange.

[39] *C.C.R. 1307–13*, 555–6.

[40] *Monasticon Anglicanum*, VI, i, 351–2.

of Gower; Humphrey Bohun, earl of Hereford and lord of Brecon, who probably had put down a deposit on the lordship and who had certainly been promised a reversionary claim to it; the two Roger Mortimers of Chirk and Wigmore who had also apparently concluded a bargain with Braose; and the younger Despenser, the newly-arrived lord of Glamorgan. William Braose's sustained campaign of deception (for he was alleged to have made arrangements with all four parties!) made the issue a delicate one, but not one beyond solution in ordinary circumstances. What did transform the Gower issue into a major political crisis was the degree of support that Edward II extended to the younger Despenser in pursuit of his ambition and the legal tactic—that of the need for royal licence for all alienations of land held in chief in the March—which he employed to promote that ambition. The issue led to a war in the March in May 1321 and thereby contributed to the exile of the Despensers. But what needs to be emphasized here—as indeed it has been emphasized by historians elsewhere[41]—is that the dispute over Gower simply crystallized the opposition to the Despensers and gave their opponents both a cause and a place to stage a showdown. It was once more a case of the tensions of national politics being projected onto a local plane and focusing on a local issue.

The same is true again, albeit from a rather different angle, with regard to the acquisition of the lordship of Bromfield and Yale in 1318 by Earl Thomas of Lancaster. No incident indeed reveals more starkly than this one how far the Marcher lordships were territorial counters in the political struggles of this decade.[42] The year 1318 was one of a *détente* between the earl of Lancaster and his political opponents; and part of that *détente* was a territorial settlement that Lancaster concluded with John Warenne, earl of Surrey and lord of Bromfield and Yale. It was a settlement which was imposed under duress on Warenne, with the qualified approval of the king. Warenne, who had incurred Lancaster's deep personal enmity by abducting his wife in 1317, was regarded as a political lightweight and, not for the last

---

[41] J. Conway Davies, *T.R.H.S.*, 3rd ser. 9 (1915), 41–4; J. R. Maddicott, op. cit. 261.

[42] This incident has been reconstructed in detail for the first time by J. R. Maddicott, op. cit. 234–7.

time, both the king and his opponents sacrificed his territorial fortunes in the interests of political expediency. He was compelled to surrender all his Yorkshire, Welsh and Norfolk lands to Lancaster in return for lands and rents worth 1,000 marks annually in Somerset, Dorset and Wiltshire. Financially it was an outrageously poor bargain for Warenne—the lordship of Bromfield and Yale alone was worth over 1,000 marks a year; politically its aim was clear: to consolidate Lancaster's territorial and thereby his political power in areas where he was already in a strong position. Lancaster was already lord of Denbigh; the addition of Bromfield and Yale made him far and away the most powerful lord in the northern March. The final settlement between Lancaster and Warenne in November 1318 was preceded by a campaign of threats and harassment;[43] it was followed by a deliberate effort on Lancaster's part to cultivate local support for himself in his newly-acquired Marcher lordship: Hwfa ab Iorwerth, one of the leading Welshmen of Bromfield, was appointed to be his ewerer and another distinguished and highly-regarded local squire, Madog ap Llywelyn, was appointed as his receiver in Bromfield and Yale.[44]

This search for local support serves to remind us that there was more to fourteenth-century politics than the machinations of the king and his greater magnates; they certainly occupied the centre of the stage but their success or otherwise in politics depended on the degree of support they could command. Our view of Marcher politics hitherto has been deliberately one-dimensional. We have assumed for the sake of clarity of argument that the possession or custody of a Marcher lordship implied the total commitment of its inhabitants to the political ambitions of its lord. It is an assumption which enables us to align the territorial and political affiliations of the March clearly and neatly on a map; but it is not an assumption which is always sustained by the facts. Lordship did not imply, in the March or elsewhere, the unquestioning loyalty of the com-

---

[43] As is clear from the petition sent by the men of Bromfield and Yale to Warenne early in 1318: S.C. 8/177 no. 8830.

[44] In September 1321 Earl Thomas granted Hwfa ab Iorwerth, his ewerer, lands in Ruabon: D.L. 25/2234. The tomb of Hwfa's father is in Ruabon church: C. A. Gresham, *Medieval Stone Carving in North Wales*, no. 171. For Madog ap Llywelyn see above p. 205.

munity to the lord's political ambitions. It gave a strong presumption in its favour; but in the eyes of the gentry and squires, the leaders of local society, other considerations also weighed: the lord's 'affability, however rough'[45] or, in other words, his local reputation; the credibility of his political and military enterprises; the opportunities of service and reward he offered; and the prospect of an alternative focus of service. Marcher society was in some ways more politically naive and more politically insulated (in terms of an alternative focus of service) than English local society; it was also more powerfully dominated by the great Marcher lords. Even so, loyalty to a lord in a political crisis was no reflex action; it had to be carefully and sensitively fostered over a period of years.

Our examples come once more from the critical years of Edward II's reign, for it was in a crisis that the ties of loyalty were put to the test and it is only then that we can begin to penetrate beneath the surface of Marcher politics. During these years the contrast in the responses of the communities of Brecon and of Glamorgan to their respective lords is highly instructive. By the early fourteenth century the Bohun earls of Hereford had been lords of Brecon for three generations and during that period they had forged ties of service, loyalty and affection with many of the leading families of the lordship. Earl Humphrey (d. 1298) and his son, another Humphrey (d. 1322) had in particular shown a sensitive appreciation of the nature of good lordship as it was understood by Marcher communities. Two incidents in particular highlight that good lordship. When Edward I tried to undermine Earl Humphrey's authority in Brecon in 1297, the earl promptly sent commissioners to summon the men of the lordship, to confirm their laws and usages and their rights of pasture, and to remit many of their fines.[46] It was an exercise in good public relations; and it was successful. His son followed his example in 1316 during the revolt of Llywelyn Bren. It was at Ystradfellte in the lordship of Brecon that Llywelyn surrendered to the earl of Hereford; the earl and the two Mortimers dispatched a letter to the king pleading for mercy for Llywelyn and promising to vouchsafe him.[47]

---

[45] K. B. McFarlane in 'The Wars of the Roses', *Procs. British Academy* 50 (1964), III.   [46] *Cal. Anc. Corr. conc. Wales*, 101.
[47] *Vita Edwardi Secundi*, 67–8; *Cal. Anc. Corr. conc. Wales*, 68.

Llywelyn, however, fell into the clutches of the younger Despenser and was executed by him at Cardiff.[48] That incident served not only to fan Bohun's hatred for Despenser but also to forge new bonds of loyalty between him and his Welshmen: Llywelyn Bren's widow, Lleucu, was given a pension by the Bohuns and her seven sons fought for the lord of Brecon in 1321–2.[49] The reward for this careful cultivation of local support was the loyalty of the community in a political crisis. When Earl Humphrey went to parliament in 1312 he was accompanied by a crowd of 'wild Welshmen' from his Marcher estates;[50] and during the campaigns of 1321–2 most of the major figures of the lordship—both members of the old Anglo-Norman families of the lordship such as the Waldeboefs, Parpoynts, Havards, Pichards and Baskervilles and the leading Welsh squires such as Meurig ap Rees, Hywel ab Einion, Philip ap Hywel, and his redoubtable brother Master Rees—stood with him both in victory and in defeat.[51] His was a support in depth, founded on bonds of affection and obligation between the community, and especially its leaders, and the lord. 'They were all at one with their lord': the phrase of the commissioner of 1297 expressed the ideal equation in the relationship of lord and community.

It could, however, be otherwise. Just as the bonds between the lord and his feed retainers could be fickle (Earl Thomas of Lancaster found that to his cost in 1321–2 when amongst his retainers who deserted him were two leading Marcher men, Fulk Fitzwarin and Fulk Lestrange), so likewise could those between lord and community. Loyalty and support were not automatic reponses by the community towards its lord; indeed familiarity with a lord could be the source of hatred rather than of affection. The younger Despenser found that out to his cost in the March. He was lord of Glamorgan from 1317; but he certainly did not command the political loyalty of its tenantry. 'The Welshmen hated the rule of Hugh' was the tart comment of

---

[48] This was one of the charges brought against the Despensers in 1321: *Rot. Parl.*, III, 364.

[49] *C.P.R. 1321–4*, 77; D.L. 29/671/10810, m. 13–m. 16. Lleucu continued to draw the pension until 1346.

[50] *Vita Edwardi Secundi*, 32.

[51] For lists of the Welsh supporters of the earl of Hereford in 1321–2 see *C.P.R. 1321–4*, 18, 77, 167; *C.C.R. 1318–23*, 428, 458; *C.F.R. 1319–27*, 156.

a well-informed chronicler.[52] That hatred was by no means confined to the native Welsh; it extended into the higher echelons of Glamorgan society as the lists of his local opponents in 1321–2 show.[53] Despenser was well aware of his own unpopularity, of the morose attitude of his tenants, and of rumours that his Welshmen were allying with those of Brecon; but his only response was to send blustering letters to his sheriff of Glamorgan and to demand that hostages be sent to him from each commote as security for its good behaviour.[54] Such a crude insurance policy was no substitute for good lordship. Despenser found little support for his cause in the March in 1321 and he was afforded no refuge there in 1326.[55] This contrast between the response of the communities of Brecon and Glamorgan to their respective lords—and it is a contrast which can be studied elsewhere in the March—serves to remind us that there is more to the politics of the March than the machinations of its lords; politics was also in part the art of persuasion and the men who needed to be persuaded above all, in the March as elsewhere, were the gentry, the leaders of the local community.

For the community was involved in the political fortunes of its lord. If he were successful, if he won royal favour, then his men could be expected to partake in some measure of his success. If his political career ended in disaster, then the local community would most certainly feel the repercussions. The men of Brecon, to take one example, paid dearly for the fall of their lord in 1322. Some of them, most notably Master Rees ap Hywel, suffered prolonged imprisonment; others lost their lands, at least temporarily; yet others had to pay heavy ransoms to the king, as did Hywel Fychan ap Hywel whose loyalty to his lord cost him £500.[56] The impact of defeat, moreover, touched the lordship as a whole: royal troops invaded it in

---

[52] *Vita Edwardi Secundi*, 110.

[53] *C.P.R. 1317–21*, 581; *C.R.F. 1319–27*, 100.

[54] In one letter Despenser complained that his tenants in Glamorgan acted sourly and morosely towards him and in another that his Welshmen were allied with the men of Brecon: *Cartae*, iii, no. 894; *Cal. Anc. Corr. conc. Wales*, 260.

[55] It is rather significant in this context that Caerphilly castle, Despenser's last outpost in 1326, was manned almost exclusively by non-Marcher men: *C.P.R. 1324–7*, 344; *1327–30*, 10.

[56] For Master Rhys ap Hywel see *C.C.R. 1318–23*, 427; *C.Ch.R. 1300–26*, 451; *C.A.D.*, iii, A. 4883. For Hywel Fychan ap Hywel see *C.F.R. 1319–27*, 156 and for his family see above, pp. 225–6.

1322 creating havoc wherever they went; the livestock and produce of the demesne manors were sold; and then in July 1322 the lordship was turned over to the greed of the younger Despenser.[57] He imposed a fine of 3,000 sheep on the community for the support it had given to its lord; he stripped the lordship of its timber; and even as late as 1324 he raked the ashes of the past with a commission of inquiry into those who had supported the rebels in 1321–2.[58] It is no wonder that when John Bohun recovered the lordship in November 1326 he would report that it was 'in divers ways destroyed and wasted'.[59] In Brecon as elsewhere, the sins of the lord had been visited upon his lordship. Marcher communities were caught up in the political ambitions of their lords, whether it was in supporting those ambitions or attempting to frustrate them. Thereby the March and its communities were, from yet another angle, within the ambit of English politics and, in the words of a contemporary lawyer, 'within the power of the king of England'.[60]

[57] For Sir Gruffydd Llwyd's commission (23 January 1322) to seize the lordship see *C.F.R. 1319–27*, 91; for the effects of his raids and for the sale of demesne stock see the account-roll for Hay and Huntington, S.C. 6/1145/7; for the lease of the lordship to Despenser see *C.F.R. 1319–27*, 143.

[58] *Cartae*, III, no. 908 (*c.* 1322–3); *C.F.R. 1319–27*, 262 (March 1324); *C.P.R. 1321–4*, 449 (April 1324).

[59] *C.P.R. 1324–7*, 345.

[60] *Year Book 12 Edward II 1319* (Selden Society, 1964), 130. (The argument was advanced with respect to Clun.)

IV

MARCHER SOCIETY

Introduction

MARCHER lordship operated within the context of Marcher society; it also helped to shape the character of that society. It is to an analysis of this Marcher society that we now turn, albeit with reluctance, for the problems of Marcher history are nowhere more daunting than at the level of social analysis. That this should be so is in good measure a factor of the documentation at the historian's command. It is not merely a question of the uneven distribution of the sources, both chronologically and geographically; it is the more basic issue of their character and provenance. They are by and large the archives of lordship. It is through the eyes of the Marcher lord and of his officials that we are allowed to study Marcher society; that is a restricting, even a distorting, viewpoint. It is, of course, not a problem that is peculiar to the historian of the March; English social historians of the medieval period likewise have to work within the confines of seignorial documentation. In the March, however, the problem is more acute: manors there were few in number and manorial documents are proportionately less valuable for the historian; lordship exercised there only a tenuous and remote control over many aspects of local society and its records are accordingly formalized and reticent; it was furthermore an alien lordship which accepted a framework of native institutions and customs which it rarely understood.

Seignorial documents, moreover, were never meant to be quarries for sociological data. Their sole purpose was to attend to the lord's interest—to account for his revenue, to determine the obligations and dues of tenants, to record his administration of justice, to keep a check on his officials; such light as they may cast on contemporary society is incidental to their primary purpose. This is notably true of those great land surveys of late medieval Wales in which historians have placed such confidence, surveys such as the *Record of Caernarvon* of 1352 or the *Survey of Denbigh* of 1334. Their appeal is obvious: they apparently survey the territorial structure of native society comprehensively and definitively; they are as invaluable to the Welsh historian as is Domesday Book to the English historian for they provide concrete evidence for the study of pre-Conquest as well as of post-Conquest Welsh society. They help us, in Maitland's phrase, to accustom 'our eyes to the twilight before we go into the night'.[1] But our enthusiasm needs to be tempered with much caution. The purpose of such surveys, it cannot too frequently be emphasized, was *not* to analyse contemporary society but to determine the liability for renders and dues owed to the lord, to define the tenant's duties and the lord's rights. All social arrangements that did not bear on this primary purpose were beyond the surveyor's purview and thereby beyond the historian's reach. Let us instance a single minor example: according to the rental of the lordship of Dyffryn Clwyd of 1324 Iorwerth ap Llywelyn held forty-two acres of land in Dogfeilyn commote for a rent of 35*s*.; it was only because his heriot was not forthcoming that we learn that the land was in fact held during his lifetime by three other men.[2] It was the function of the survey to determine the rent for the land and the liability for it, no less and no more; but, as this example shows, the gap between fiscal liabilities and social realities might be very considerable. This draws attention to another shortcoming of the documents and particularly of the rentals, their intense conservatism. They belong to that category of documents 'which, for governmental and fiscal purposes, endeavour to preserve fictitious continuity and uniformity in the midst of change and variety'.[3] In the case of the lordship of Bromfield and Yale, for example, three rentals of 1315, 1391 and 1445[4] suggest in their format and contents a measure of conservatism in the social and economic structure of the area which is belied by other documents. What these rentals and like seignorial documents (such as the ministers' accounts) which were based upon them show, in fact, is the

---

[1] *Domesday Book and Beyond* (1960 paperback edn.), 415.
[2] *T.D.H.S.* 17 (1968), 26; S.C. 2/217/8, m. 15ᵛ (1342).
[3] F. W. Maitland, *Domesday Book and Beyond*, 428.
[4] *The First Extent of Bromfield and Yale, 1315*, ed. T. P. Ellis; B.L. Add. Ms. 10,013; L.R. 2/251. Excerpts from the latter are printed in A. N. Palmer and E. Owen, *History of Ancient Tenures of Land in North Wales and the Marches*, 217–31; but they are wrongly attributed to 1508.

conservatism of approach of the estate-officials; their attempts to preserve an antiquated structure of renders and of rent-assessment serve to conceal rather than to reveal the realities of the social structure.

Nor can the social historian look for salvation to other categories of historical documentation. Some indeed there are. Petitions and charters of liberties form one important category. They are invaluable in that they do not emanate from the lord or his officials; they serve to articulate the anxieties and problems of individuals and communities and thereby they bring us nearer to social realities. But even they deal only with those anxieties and problems to which the lord was a party or which were regarded in some way as within the ambit of his authority. The other major category of documents are the collections of deeds which, in the case of Wales, only begin to become common from the fourteenth century onwards. Once again they have the advantage of being non-seignorial in character; they serve to correct the imbalance and particularly the social conservatism of seignorial sources. But their limitations are equally clear: they are normally the archives of one family and rarely one that can be regarded as representative; they are the archives of success but rarely can that success be adequately related either to the other affairs of the family or to the general social context of the period.

With the shortcomings of the documentation we must learn to live but to live in the clear knowledge of the limitations that they impose on our analysis. The very terminology of social analysis, for example, is largely determined by the sources. They divide Marcher society into certain broad groups, defined largely in terms of tenure and law—Welsh and English, free and unfree, feudal tenants and advowry men, and such like. These categories are clearly often inadequate and even artificial in terms of social analysis; but we must, at least in the first instance, adopt them as our own. The nature of the sources also means that this analysis concentrates on the twin fields of land and law; it was precisely on these two features of contemporary society that lordship impinged most forcefully and frequently and that the documentation is most revealing. In a society where land was the major basis of wealth and where the judicial powers of the lord were so far-reaching, the study of land and law clearly occupies an important place in social analysis. Yet it is an analysis which rarely succeeds in describing society except on the lord's terms. It only catches rare glimpses of the mechanics of social relationships and of the tactics of social pressure; it can only very inadequately define those ties of respect, obligation and affection which bound social groups together. Too often the historian only glimpses the social nexus *via* the distorting mirror of judicial documents. The court rolls, for example, speak of riots and confederacies and of the collection of unofficial subsidies (*cymorthau*); they conceal the social fabric which was the background of such incidents and practices. They call it a crime which native society often took for custom.

The exigencies of the documentation pose one problem for the historian; the variegated character of Marcher society poses another. The varieties of the March and of Marcher society were manifold: those of highland and lowland zones; of mainly arable and of predominantly pastoral communities; of areas of nucleated villages and those of dispersed settlements; of quilleted open fields and of *bocage* landscape; of districts such as Maelienydd and Iscennen where the non-Welsh element in the population was minimal and of other districts such as Radnor or southern Pembroke where the immigrant population was by the fourteenth century numerically superior; of areas such as lowland Gwent where the unfree population preponderated and of other areas such as Builth or upland Brecon where there survived but few traces of serfdom; of lordships such as Monmouth which had known foreign rule and alien settlement for centuries and of other lordships such as Denbigh and Dyffryn Clwyd which came to that knowledge suddenly in the thirteenth century. 'Sitting astride both a physical and a cultural boundary', the March is for the geographer 'one of the critical areas in Britain in relation to rural landscape features';[5] it is also for the historian a fascinating area in terms of the complexity of its social features, a complexity explained by the diversities of geographical setting and of historical development and a complexity which is amenable to detailed historical investigation for the first time in the fourteenth century. The danger in the study of such a variegated society is that of straitjacketing its individual features and divergences within a

[5] D. Sylvester, *The Rural Landscape of the Welsh Borderland*, 38.

simplistic framework of social analysis. The society of each and every region of the March deserves to be studied in detail if the nuances of its structure and of its development are not to be overlooked. We are back once again with the plurality of the March.

To admit that this is so, however, is not to surrender to a counsel of despair but to admit that in describing Marcher society in the fourteenth century in general terms we are attempting no more than to establish a broad framework of social analysis. It is a framework whose accuracy and completeness will no doubt vary greatly from one part of the March to another; but it will at least be a working hypothesis which others may use, modify or dismiss. It is a framework which will concentrate on certain specific issues—on the frontier character of Marcher society in terms of the relations between natives and alien settlers, on the nature of Welsh social institutions and customs and the impact of English influences on them, on the features and extent of unfreedom, on the distribution of landed wealth in Marcher society, and on the crucial changes in that society within the fourteenth century. Such a broad approach will of necessity dwell very unequally on the social structure and development of various parts of the March. In particular it will draw very heavily—and disproportionately so—on the evidence for the lordship of Dyffryn Clwyd, where an unparalleled series of court rolls allows as an insight into certain aspects of Marcher society for the century as a whole. Our analysis will also omit any systematic study of many cardinal topics in the field of social history—such as the distribution of population, the pattern of rural settlement, the extent of commercial activity, and so forth. Even so our subject is ample enough; Marcher society is no mean theme. It is with its 'Marcher' character, as a society where two or more races met, that we must begin.

MARCHER society was a frontier society. The facts of geography
dictated that it should be so. The March of Wales straddles the
area where the highland and lowland zones of Britain, in terms
both of relief and of geology, meet. Furthermore this frontier
quality of Marcher geography characterizes, in greater or lesser
degree, the physical features of almost every Marcher lordship;
each of them displays its own variation on the theme of a
geographical frontier. Such a frontier is most marked in Gwent
and Glamorgan where the antithesis between the uplands
(*Blaenau*) and the plains (*Bro*) is the most fundamental feature
in the geographical, and hence to a considerable degree in the
social, configuration of the area; but, it is no less striking in
inland lordships such as Clun and Brecon where the contrast
between the broad river-valleys and the great mountain massifs
provides much of the key to social development.

This frontier quality of its geography dominated the history
of the March in many obvious directions. It did so in military
terms: invasion along the coastal plains and river-valleys of
the March presented few problems as the first bands of Norman
conquistadores soon showed; but anything like a sustained military
control of the mountainous interior was an infinitely more
difficult task. So it was that conquerors and settlers alike were
generally content to dominate the plains of the March and
to exercise no more than a loose *superioritas*, both militarily and
governmentally, over the uplands. The geography of the March
equally clearly determined the chronology of foreign conquest:
it explains why lowland Pembroke was already firmly in
Norman control by the early twelfth century, whereas upland
border districts such as western Caus or the lordship of Builth
were still in dispute generations later; it explains likewise why
lowland Glamorgan fell to Robert Fitzhamon and his followers

in the reign of Rufus, whereas the upland commotes remained under native control until the reign of Henry III. Above all, for present purposes, the frontier character of its geography was the mould within which Marcher society was shaped; the contrast between upland and lowland communities—a contrast which comprehends race, agriculture, settlement patterns, social customs and much else—is one of the most abiding themes of the social history of the March. We can see it, to take but one example, in the lordship of Newport where to pass from the largely Anglicized and nucleated settlements of the plains such as the manors of Pencarn and Rumney to the dispersed forest settlements and Welsh upland hamlets of Machen was to cross as distinct a geographical, economic and agricultural frontier as anywhere in Britain.[1]

It was also to cross a racial frontier.[2] For it is one of the distinctive features of the March of Wales by the fourteenth century that the geographical frontier within it coincided, in very broad terms, with the racial frontier between settler and native or, as contemporary terminology had it, between English and Welsh. It was a racial frontier which had been many centuries in the making. The colonization of Wales by alien settlers had begun in the seventh and eighth centuries, at that very period which saw 'the emergence of Wales'; it continued thereafter in fits and starts, the tide of colonization flowing strongly at some periods, ebbing markedly at others; by 1300 the medieval phase of this prolonged process of alien colonization was more or less complete. It was inevitable that it should be the March, both along its eastern border with England and along its broad southern coastline, which should absorb almost all of these settlers. The settlers themselves were drawn from many races—from the English above all, but also from the Irish, Scandinavians, Normans, Bretons, Flemings and others. By the fourteenth century the great days of alien colonization in the March were virtually at an end; the movement had its swan-song in the hectic but short-lived bout of alien immigration into Wales which followed the final Edwardian Conquest of 1282–3. By then the racial contours of Marcher population were more firmly-drawn than they had been for centuries.

---

[1] *The Marcher Lordships of South Wales*, ed. T. B. Pugh, 184–236.
[2] I have given some preliminary consideration to the themes discussed in this

Those racial contours varied greatly from one part of the March to another. All we can attempt here by way of a few examples is to show how varied was the racial pattern both within the March as a whole and within individual Marcher lordships. Some lordships had but a negligible proportion of alien settlers: Chirkland was such a lordship, according to the subsidy roll of 1292.[3] There were other lordships with scarcely an Englishman in sight in their records; Gwerthrynion, Cwmwd Deuddwr and Iscennen were among them. Their remoteness and unattractive terrain proved too daunting for settlers. In other lordships, however, the immigrant population was already numerically dominant by the fourteenth century and probably much earlier. This was patently true of the lordship of Pembroke, where the population of manors such as Castle Martin and St. Florence was overwhelmingly English.[4] More usually the ratio of the races (according to the rather inadequate test of personal names) varied greatly from one part of a Marcher lordship to another. Many of the place-names of lowland Radnor are pedigree Anglo-Saxon and are attested by Domesday Book; the personal names of most of the taxpayers in 1292 are likewise unmistakeably English. But the population of the western half of the lordship was Welsh in name and in customs and so was that of the small neighbouring lordship of Bleddfa.[5] Much the same contrast, though not always of the same dimensions, is noticeable elsewhere in the March: in the lordship of Monmouth and Threecastles in 1292, 87 per cent of the taxpaying population around Monmouth itself bore English surnames, but the proportion declined sharply in the western parts of the lordship around Whitecastle;[6] in the lordship of Chepstow or Strigoil, one of the earliest to be conquered by the Normans, the villages in the immediate hinterland of the castle were populated almost exclusively by free and unfree Englishmen, but even in the later Middle Ages the interior upland

chapter in 'Colonial Wales', *Past and Present* 65 (1974), 3–23 and 'Race Relations in Post-Conquest Wales: Confrontation and Coexistence', *T.C.S.* (1974–5), 32–56.

[3] E. 179/242/55.

[4] *Cal. Public Records re. Pembrokeshire*, III, 88, 107–9.

[5] E. 179/242/57; W. Rees, *South Wales and the March 1284–1415*, 28; Lord Rennell of Rodd, *Valley on the March*, 127.

[6] E. 179/242/59. This impression is confirmed by a detailed rental of Whitecastle for 1386, D.L. 43/13/8. Cf. also D. Sylvester, *The Rural Landscape of the Welsh Borderland*, 387–93.

vills of the lordship, such as Wernhalen and Talgarth were still by and large Welsh in their population;[7] likewise in the large mesne lordship of Caldicot the nucleated villages on the Severn estuary levels were almost exclusively English, but the detached upland township of Shirenewton had a racially mixed population and the small hamlet of Woodseaves, in spite of its English name, was inhabited entirely by Welshmen.[8] In each of these three cases the contours of geography more or less coincided with those of race. They did so again in the final example, that of the large mesne lordship of Ogmore in western Glamorgan, where the tenant population comes into full view in a detailed rental of 1428.[9] Lowland Ogmore was already fairly securely in Norman control by the early twelfth century; its boundaries, indeed, possibly marked the limits of the first Norman invasion of Glamorgan. In the wake of the Norman conquerors—and possibly indeed ahead of them[10]—came the alien settlers. They came in large numbers; the predominantly English form of the personal, place- and field-names of lowland Ogmore bears witness to that. The Welsh population was by no means totally displaced: many of the inhabitants of Ogmore vill were still Welsh and, in common with much of the Vale of Glamorgan, lowland Ogmore was to be extensively re-colonized by a Welsh-speaking peasantry from the fifteenth century onwards. But in 1428 the plains of Ogmore still bore much of the English imprint which earlier generations of alien settlers had given them—family names such as Hyott and Stevenes, place-names such as Broughton and Southerndown, and field-names such as 'Langelande', and 'Westonfurlong'. To move from lowland Ogmore to the detached upland half of the lordship was to cross a sharp geographical frontier, from the fertile soils and limestone downlands of the Vale of Glamorgan to the narrow, steep-sided valleys and bleak uplands of *Blaenau Morgannwg*.

---

[7] W. Rees, op. cit. 144.

[8] C. 133/92, no. 8 (1298).

[9] D.L. 42/107. For a fuller discussion of the social structure of Ogmore and for full references to the documentation upon which the next few sentences are based *Glam. C.H.*, III, 285–311.

[10] There may well have been considerable Scandinavian colonization in lowland Glamorgan; see D. R. Patterson in *Arch. Camb.*, 6th ser. 20 (1920), 31–89; 7th ser. i (1921), 53–83; ii (1922), 37–60. Some of the twelfth-century inhabitants of Ogmore bore good Saxon names, e.g. Hugh son of Elfric, Godric 'fuller', Godwyn 'presbyter', Geoffrey son of Safrid, Edric 'sheriff'.

One of the alternative names for upland Ogmore, that of Ogmore in the Wood, bore witness to the geographical and agricultural contrast with the lowland half of the lordship: its alternative names, Ogmore Welshry and Glyn Ogwr, declared that the contrast was also one of race. Ogmore Welshry lived up to its name: its population was exclusively Welsh and so were the social customs of the tenants.

The racial contrast which was so clear-cut in Ogmore characterized, in greater or lesser degree, almost the whole of Marcher society by the fourteenth century. Administration and law, as we shall see, assumed the distinction of race as one of the most elemental lines of division in Marcher society. Furthermore this distinction of race had already by the thirteenth century become reduced from the multiple to the dual, for it had been simplified into a distinction between Welsh and English. Not only was that to simplify and even to distort the complex racial pattern of the March, it was also to sharpen the focus of the racial division and to lend it overtones of a distinction between superior and inferior. This English-Welsh dichotomy varied considerably in its importance and in its application from one part of the March to another. It varied in part in proportion to the degree of alien colonization and to the need to define the status and to protect the privileges of the settler population. It varied also in relation to the chronology of foreign conquest and settlement: the racial dichotomy appears to have been more sharply defined in those lordships where alien colonists had been most recently established and where their position as a settler élite, introduced in the wake of military conquest, was more obviously in evidence. Varied as it certainly was in its importance, the dichotomy of English and Welsh is, nevertheless, one of the few broad classifications—and a contemporary one at that—which may be applied to the analysis of Marcher society as a whole.

This preoccupation with race appears in its most stark form in the way that Marcher men were classified on occasion into Welshmen and Englishmen 'by blood' (*de sanguine*). It is a classification which in some respects has a very modern flavour to it; but it also corresponds with the assumption of medieval social theory that status-classifications (such as serfdom) were transmitted by blood and by birth. It was, of course, the most fundamental and most uncompromising of all racial distinctions, for classification by blood could not be waived by reference to legal or tenurial status. Welshness by this token was ineradicable: a Welshman could not escape from it by taking bond land or by leasing land by English tenure;[11] his racial status debarred him from any legal claim to land which his own brother had held 'to him and his English heirs';[12] and since a wife's status during her marriage depended on her husband's 'condition', an English-woman wed to a Welshman forfeited her English status, though not necessarily her English lands.[13] Had such a test of race by birth and by blood been rigidly applied it would have effectively made for racial apartheid in the March. In the wake of the reaction to the Glyn Dŵr rebellion, the racial divide was indeed for a time more sharply drawn along the lines of birth and of marriage. High office in Wales was henceforth closed not only to Welshmen but also to Englishmen married to Welsh women, with the clear implication that purity of stock and racial endogamy might henceforth be the tests of true English-ness;[14] the same strident racial note is struck in the formula that only Englishmen 'by birth and by blood' should be allowed to try fellow Englishmen in Wales.[15] Yet in spite of such occasional raising of the racial temperature, the Marcher lords of Wales by and large had neither the will nor the means, in the ordinary conduct of the affairs of their estates, to enforce a racial distinction exclusively on the basis of birth and of blood.

Indeed, the fact that they occasionally resorted to such a distinction suggests that for practical purposes they normally adopted rather different categories of racial classification, categories prompted less by a desire to ascertain purity of blood

---

[11] S.C. 2/218/6, m. 16 (three Welshmen are challenged to pay the forester's render (*arianfforestwr*) as the due pertains to their bodies as Welshmen and they cannot be exempted in respect of English lands they hold, 1358); S.C. 2/218/7, m. 5ᵛ (defendant admits that he is Welsh by blood (*de sanguine*) and so loses his claim to hold his wife's English land, 1359); ibid. m. 22 (a Welshman holding bond land is not exempt from Welsh services as those services pertain to his body as a Welshman).

[12] S.C. 2/218/10, m. 3 ('dictus Blethin . . . est Wallicus et nullomodo privilegia-tus', 1362).

[13] S.C. 2/218/7, m. 17 (1359). Cf. also S.C. 2/219/6, m. 19 (1369), 220/5, m. 12 (1385).

[14] *Rot. Parl.*, III, 509; *Statutes of the Realm*, II, 141.

[15] The phrase ('homines Anglicos de sanguine natos') is used in a privilege granted to Simon Thelwall of Denbigh in 1433: N.L.W. Wynnstay 101/121.

and more by the practical problems of administration and law. Perhaps the most common of such categories was that whereby Marcher society was classified on racial lines for the purposes of administration. Marcher tenants were not infrequently classified into Welsh and English for the purposes of collecting rent and of exacting labour services;[16] much the same racial classification might be employed by the lord when he wished to collect a subsidy or an aid from his lordship[17] or when he was prompted to grant a charter of liberties to his tenants.[18] Separate officers were often appointed for the Welsh and the English within a Marcher lordship. The Welshmen of the Mortimer lordships of Knighton and Bwlchyddinas had their own Welsh reeve; while in the new Marcher lordships of north Wales an English bailiff, or 'a bailiff among the English' as he was occasionally termed, was appointed to attend to the affairs of the alien settlers.[19] This administrative contrast is particularly clear in the mesne lordship of Bronllys (Brecon): there the lowland manor of Bronllys with its free and unfree population was under the care of a bailiff, whereas the extensive pasturelands and forests of Cantrefselyf were controlled by foresters and by a Welsh reeve (*Wallicus prepositus*) and his serjeant (*rhingyll*).[20]

What we have, in effect if not in name, in Bronllys is the administrative division of the lordship into a Welshry and an Englishry. It is an administrative division conceived in racial terms and it is one that pertains throughout the March. It may be found, for example, in Clun, Narberth, Radnor, Blaenllyfni, Hay, Talgarth, Kidwelly and Gower (where there was a Welsh and English county); it also prevailed in many mesne lordships of the March such as Afan, Coety, Ogmore (Glamorgan) and

---

[16] S.R.O. 552/1A/3 (wages of ninety-nine English and sixty Welsh customary tenants: Clun, 1355); B.L. Egerton 8708–9 (tenants of Blaenllyfni, Crickhowell and Talgarth divided into English and Welsh, 1365–1433).

[17] D.L. 42/1, fol. 29–fol. 29ᵛ; S.C. 6/1183/3 (Denbigh, 1310, 1370); S.C. 2/219/6, m. 23 (Dyffryn Clwyd, 1369).

[18] In the lordship of Clun a separate charter of liberties was granted to the Welshmen of Tempseter: *Transaction of the Shropshire Archaeological and Natural History Society* 11 (1887–8), 248–9. In Dyffryn Clwyd a common charter was granted to all English tenants holding measured acres: S.C. 2/217/10, m. 23ᵛ (pre-1308).

[19] B. P. Evans, 'The Family of Mortimer', Ph.D. thesis (Univ. of Wales, 1934), 416, n. 8; *S.D.*, liv (Denbigh); S.C. 2/215/69, m. 7 (Dyffryn Clwyd, 1307).

[20] S.C. 6/1156/13, 14, 16 (1372).

Pencelli (Brecon).[21] In the lordship of Bromfield and Yale we can see such an Englishry (or such in effect it was) being created in the late thirteenth century when the newly-established knights' fees were granted their own bailiffs and their own court (with the same laws as those of Holt town) and were totally exempted from 'the tenures, laws and customs of the Welsh tenants'.[22] In the case of Bromfield and Yale as in that of most Marcher lordships, Welshry and Englishry were well-defined territorial districts; indeed in some lordships, such as Huntington and Ogmore, Welshry and Englishry were geographically detached portions of one and the same lordships. Elsewhere, however, the Englishry did not exist as a geographical district; rather was it a collective term in administrative and legal parlance for the English tenants wherever they may have lived in the lordship. That seems to have been so in Dyffryn Clwyd; it was also the case in the lordship of Kidwelly where the jurors in the early seventeenth century could not 'make any perfecte boundaryes of the fforrenry (i.e. the Englishry) in respecte that diverse lands of the Welshry are intermyngled among the lands of the fforenry'.[23]

In very general terms the administrative division between Englishry and Welshry coincided both with the geographical division between lowland and upland and with the distribution of Welshmen and Englishmen within a Marcher lordship, although as with all administrative categories the coincidence was never more than very approximate. How close the co-incidence could be may be illustrated by the lordship of Hay.[24] Historically, Hay was one of the earliest areas in the March to succumb to Norman rule; Bernard of Neufmarché and his followers had seized control of it by the late eleventh century. Geographically, it conformed to the normal pattern of the March in that it was a lordship of contrasts, ranging from the rich soils of the broad valley-bottom of the Wye to the peaks of

[21] All these are well attested by contemporary evidence. Others could no doubt be added to them. Cf. W. Rees, op. cit. 29–31.

[22] S.B.Y., fol. 20–fol. 21 v.

[23] *T.D.H.S.* 8 (1968), 7–53; *A Survey of the Duchy of Lancaster Lordships in Wales, 1609–13*, ed. W. Rees, 210.

[24] This paragraph is based on an incomplete extent of Hay lordship of 1340 (Cardiff Free Library, Brecon Documents, no. 1) and on ministers' accounts for the lordship for the late fourteenth century (S.C. 6/1156/18, 21; D.L. 29/633/10317).

the Black Mountains, well over 2,000 feet high. This geographical pattern effectively determined the boundary between Welshry and Englishry; it generally coincided with the 650 feet contour line. The Englishry comprised the castle of Hay and its hinterland—the small market town at Hay, a settlement of customary tenants at Weston who worked on the lord's demesne, the farms of the free English tenants of the 'foreignry', and the districts such as Llanthomas (generally known under its English name of Thomaschurch) which had been sub-infeudated to the lord's vassals. The Welshry was much more extensive, but the agricultural opportunities of the tenants of its small scattered vills were largely pastoral. The contrasts between the Englishry and Welshry of Hay stand out clearly enough in the documents: they were separately administered—by the bailiffs of the castle and town on the one hand, by a Welsh reeve and serjeant (*rhingyll*) on the other. The tenurial obligations of their tenants contrasted sharply—the men of the Englishry paid rents and services for their lands, those of the Welshry gave the lord a render of twenty-four cows every other year according to the old Welsh custom known as *commorth Calan Mai*; the customary services due from the men of the two districts were separately itemized; even the pigs of Welshry and Englishry were separately assessed for pannage. Furthermore, in the case of Hay, the division between Welshry and Englishry fairly accurately coincided with the distribution of the races in the lordship: of the 114 tenants of the Welshry listed in the extent of 1340, every single one bore a Welsh name, while the personal- and place-names of the Englishry by the fourteenth century were overwhelmingly English.

Administration was one field in which the racial dichotomy of Marcher society manifested itself; law was another. To define a man's legal status in terms of race was a common feature of medieval societies, particularly of the multi-racial societies of early medieval Europe. Law, looked at in these terms, was part of a man's personal status; he was bound to that law in respect of his birth into a particular social group, be it a status or a racial group.[25] By this token Welshmen should live under Welsh law; it was a consequence of their Welsh 'condition', of their being Welsh. That argument had been propounded in the

[25] F. Pollock and F. W. Maitland, *History of English Law*, I, 13.

highest quarters; it was repeated time and again to Edward I's commissioners during their enquiry into the status of Welsh law.[26] The argument was reiterated in the court of King's Bench in 1331 by Hywel ap Gruffudd ab Iorwerth: since he was an alien, born in the parts of Wales, his case ought to be concluded by the law and custom of Wales.[27] Welshmen had no monopoly of the argument; it could equally be employed by English settlers in Wales. Since they were of English 'condition' they had the right to enjoy the law that pertained to that condition, the common law of England. The equation had the attractions, and the pitfalls, of simplicity: racial status determined legal usage and, increasingly and conversely, legal usage helped to determine racial status.[28]

This racial dichotomy was apparent in many aspects of Marcher law and justice. It was at its most obvious in the existence of separate Welsh and English courts such as may be found in Cantrefselyf (Brecon), Clun, Denbigh, Dyffryn Clwyd, Kidwelly, Coety (Glamorgan), Llanilltud (Glamorgan), Rhuthun (Glamorgan) and Narberth.[29] They were, as their titles proclaimed them to be, in origin courts for different racial groups where different laws and procedures would be observed; it was important that the distinction between them should be upheld. That is why the Englishmen of Narberth felt badly done by in the 1390s when cases were removed from the English to the Welsh court; that is why to secure the conviction of a Welshman for not appearing in the court of the Englishry of Kidwelly was a particularly disreputable piece of legal sharp practice.[30] Even where separate courts for Welsh and English tenants did not exist, the racial distinction was nevertheless observed in one and the same court by dispensing Welsh law to Welsh litigants and English law to English litigants.[31] Above

---

[26] *The Welsh Assize Roll 1277–84*, ed. J. Conway Davies (Cardiff, 1940), *passim*, esp. 265.

[27] *Select Cases in the Court of King's Bench under Edward III*, I, ed. G. O. Sayles (Selden Society, 1957), 62.

[28] This argument is more amply documented in *History* 51 (1966), 151–3.

[29] Welsh and English courts are recorded in all these lordships at some point in the fourteenth century. This does not mean, however, that such an arrangement was permanent; it seems not to have been so, for example, in Denbigh and Dyffryn Clwyd. In many cases the Welsh and English courts were the district courts for the Welshry and the Englishry respectively.

[30] B.L. Egerton Charter 8718; D.L. 37/9, m. 5 (1442).   [31] Above pp. 161–3.

all it was at the procedural level that the racial dichotomy figured most prominently at law. It did so in alternative methods for initiating pleas according as to whether the land was held by English or Welsh tenure;[32] it did so again in different legal rules which English and Welsh litigants observed;[33] it did so also in the different legal terms when cases relating to Welsh and English land could be pleaded;[34] it did so in the person of the officer—whether an English bailiff or a Welsh serjeant (*rhingyll*) who had the right to summon a defendant;[35] it did so finally in the method of determining a plea—whether, as it was put in one case, 'by the custom of the court and the law of England' or 'by the verdict of the Welsh judge (*judicator*)'.[36] Such differences of procedure and indeed of law are, of course, not unknown within a single country and between one and the same people; but in the March it was obvious enough that the duality of procedure and law coincided with and arose out of the dichotomy of race. The practice of Marcher courts recognized that fact openly enough. It recognized it in the common practice of empanelling separate presenting and petty juries for the English and Welsh communities;[37] it recognized it again in the common privilege extended to English settlers in Wales of being tried only by their fellow-Englishmen[38] and in the contrary claim of Welshmen to place themselves on the verdict of the Welsh *patria*;[39] it recognized it also in the common rule that in cases between Welsh and English parties a mixed jury, drawn equally from both races, should be empanelled.[40]

Welshmen were distinguished from Englishmen in the March

[32] This contrast is clearly spelt out in the lordships of Bronllys and of Bromfield and Yale: D.L. 41/6/11 (1349); S.B.Y. fol. 5–fol. 6 (1391).

[33] *W.H.R.* 5 (1970), 17–18.

[34] For references to the Welsh legal terms for land actions in Dyffryn Clwyd see S.C. 2/219/3, m. 31 (1366); 219/7, m. 29ᵛ (1371).

[35] Thus in 1314 a defendant in Dyffryn Clwyd who held his land by 'the law of the English' claimed that he ought not to be summoned or distrained by any Welsh bailiff: S.C. 2/215/73, m. 14.

[36] S.C. 2/219/9, m. 26 (1373).

[37] For examples see S.C. 2/216/1, m. 19 (Dyffryn Clwyd, 1318); J.I. 1/1153, no. 11 (Kidwelly, 1413).

[38] This was a very common provision in the charters of Marcher boroughs, e.g. those of Laugharne (1386) and St. Clears (1393); *C.Ch.R. 1341–1417*, 307, 335.

[39] As in a case in Clun in 1338: S.R.O. 552/1/8, m. 2.

[40] See, for example, S.C. 2/215/76, m. 5 (Dyffryn Clwyd, 1317); 226/18, m. 10 (Bromfield and Yale, 1345).

by law and by administration; they were also distinguished by different land tenures. 'The lordship of Narberth', so declares an early Stuart rental, 'is held in two tenures, namely the English and the Welsh'[41] This division was expressed in the differing dues for land held by English and Welsh tenure. 'And as they [English and Welsh tenure] are distinguished in names', remarked the surveyor of Kidwelly lordship, 'soe they are allsoe in the nature of their rents and services'.[42] Here we need speak only in very general terms: lands held by Welsh tenure contributed a fixed proportion towards old-established communal renders, whereas land held by English tenure paid an individual rent directly to the lord; the Welsh communal renders were more in the nature of tributes than of an economic rent, whereas the payment due from English land, often significantly called 'measured land' (*terra mensurata* or *terra ad acras*), was often a rent at a fixed rate per acre; likewise tenants by Welsh tenure paid a fixed personal death duty (*ebediw*), whereas those holding by English tenure gave either a heriot of the best animal or a relief directly proportionate to their rent and thereby to the acreage of their lands. By the sixteenth and seventeenth centuries many of these differences in dues had become fossilized and artificial; but in the fourteenth century they still served to highlight the distinction between native custom and settler practice.

The tenurial distinction applied equally to the central issues of the inheritance and alienation of land. Here again we need only speak of these differences in very broad terms. English law generally sanctioned primogeniture, Welsh law partibility among male heirs;[43] English custom permitted female succession to land in the event of the absence of direct male heirs whereas Welsh custom normally prohibited any claim to land based on descent through females;[44] English law permitted, indeed

---

[41] *Cal. Public Records re. Pembrokeshire*, II, 145.

[42] *Duchy of Lancaster Lordships in Wales 1609–13*, ed. W. Rees, 176.

[43] The contrast is neatly highlighted in a case of 1343 in Dyffryn Clwyd. Three brothers succeeded to their father's Welsh land; the eldest, however, claimed that all the land was his as it was held by English tenure: S.C. 2/217/9, m. 18ᵛ.

[44] The first (undated) petition of the Welsh community of Bromfield and Yale was for the right of female succession to land in the event of the failure of male heirs of the body; it was not granted (S.B.Y. fol. 170). Marcher lords even confiscated Welsh lands acquired by female succession (e.g. S.C. 2/221/9 m. 35); but the prohibition on female succession does not appear to have been universally applied (W. Rees; *South Wales and the March*, 210–11).

compelled, a husband to dower his wife with at least a third of his land whereas 'by Welsh tenure . . . no wife is to be dowered of the land and inheritance of her husband';[45] English law had firmly closed the door in the face of the claims of illegitimate children to land, but Welsh law and custom freely admitted the claims of bastard sons to a share in the paternal inheritance if they had been formally recognized by their father; English custom permitted the free alienation of free land whereas Welsh custom, as it was rigidly maintained by Marcher lords, prohibited the outright alienation of Welsh free land and allowed only renewable four-year mortgages and that only by the lord's licence. Now these tenurial differences, to which others could no doubt be added, were not merely of technical interest; they related to the major source of wealth and livelihood in the March. Furthermore, attempts were made from time to time to enforce these tenurial differences as an effective test of racial status, to insist that Welshmen should hold their land by Welsh tenure, Englishmen by English tenure. The court rolls of Dyffryn Clwyd provide ample evidence for such a policy: no Welshman, especially if he were unfree, was to acquire English land without the lord's licence; if that licence were forthcoming, then the English land in question might henceforth have to be held by Welsh tenure; Welshmen by blood could be debarred from succeeding to land held by their relatives by English tenure, while Englishmen for their part were prohibited by statute from employing Welsh methods for demising their lands.[46] The motive behind such a policy was clearly articulated in a statute of 1361 which prohibited unlicensed purchases or leases of land by Englishmen and burgesses from Welshmen and vice versa.[47] The boundary of race was to coincide in so far as possible with the boundary of land tenure; no one was to cross that boundary without the lord's permission.[48]

English and Welsh: the duality figures time and again in the

---

[45] S.B.Y. fol. 5ᵛ. This was the rule in other Marcher lordships (such as Dyffryn Clwyd), but not in all of them. In the Principality Welshmen were allowed to dower their wives with land by the terms of the Statute of Rhuddlan, 1284.

[46] See respectively S.C. 2/219/7, m. 14, m. 26 (1371); 218/10, m. 3 (1362); 217/11, m. 5 (1346). Many similar cases could be quoted.

[47] S.C. 2/218/9, m. 29ᵛ.

[48] It was not unknown for the lord to grant English status on condition that he could revoke the grant within the year at his will: S.C. 2/218/4, m. 15ᵛ (1354).

terminology of the March in the fourteenth century. It was a duality which had many dimensions to it—those of blood and birth, of administration, of law and of tenure among them. Here, indeed, lay part of its weakness, for the overlap between the various racial distinctions was never complete. Most Welshmen by blood lived in Welshries, used Welsh law and held their land by Welsh tenure. Most, but by no means all. And so some of the inner contradictions of the racial division become apparent. It was not at all unusual to find Welshmen living in Englishries, holding land by English tenure and pleading their cases in court by English law. It was less usual, but by no means unknown, to come across English settlers living in Welshries, purchasing a claim to Welsh land by Welsh mortgage and even, if it so suited them, claiming the right to plead by Welsh law. In these circumstances, the various definitions of race proved at best confusing, at worst contradictory. The conundrums that were posed for contemporary officials show that clearly enough. Did a Welshman acquire English status by securing English lands on lease? Did a Welshman forfeit his English status by alienating all his English lands? What was the racial status of an Englishwoman by birth, blood and land tenure who took a Welshman as her husband? How could one most equitably decide the claims of three sisters to an inheritance of English land when two of them were of 'Welsh condition' and the third of 'English condition'—presumably in respect of their respective marriages?[49] Well might the steward of Dyffryn Clwyd throw up his hands in despair and ask whether 'the law of nations' or the tenure of land determined the racial status of his tenants.[50] His despair was directed in part at the inadequacies and contradictions of contemporary definitions of race, in part at the anomalies which are bound to arise in applying such definitions in a multi-racial society.

Those anomalies were abundantly evident in the March. Social facts simply did not fit into the straitjacket of racial theory. We realize that this was so when we note, by way of example, that John ab Ithel was bailiff of the English town of Hay in 1375 and Heilyn ap Madoc English bailiff of the com-

[49] S.C. 2/219/4, m. 13 (1367); 218/9, m. 19^v (1361); 218/3, m. 14 (1352); 220/10, m. 29^v (1398) respectively.
[50] S.C. 2/217/7, m. 17^v (1342).

mote of Coelion (Dyffryn Clwyd) in 1398; that a fair proportion of the population of Coety Englishry in 1412 bore undeniably Welsh names; that Robert Castleford, a recent English settler in the lordship of Denbigh, held both English and Welsh land; that William Braose's charter of liberties of 1306 to his English county of Gower was in fact addressed to both his English and his Welsh men there; that whereas Dafydd ap Maredudd ap Llywelyn Chwith was 'Welsh and a Welsh freeman' (*uchelwr*) his brother Ieuan held by English tenure and claimed the benefits of English law.[51] Inconsistencies such as these meet us everywhere in our Marcher records; they make a mockery of any claim that the various methods of classifying Marcher society on racial lines were strictly observed in practice or that they exactly coincided with the actual distribution of the races.

That may be so; such inconsistencies and exceptions are a normal feature of any simple social classification. They do not, however, invalidate that classification; they only serve to qualify it. The racial cleavage was a fundamental line of division in Marcher society. It was also one of the boundary-lines of privilege. The English, however they were defined, were a privileged group. They were privileged in respect of office: they alone were entitled to hold most of the key posts in Marcher administration. They were also privileged at law: they jealously reserved to themselves such common law practices as essoining or granting land in dower; they claimed the right to be convicted only by their fellow-Englishmen; they denied the right of a Welshman to wager his law against an Englishman; they might even arrogantly assert that no Englishman ought to demean himself by being at law with a Welshman.[52] They were also privileged in other ways: they alone had the right to be burgesses without the lord's licence; they often secured exemption from tolls throughout the lordship; they claimed the right to brew their own ale without paying toll 'because they were English'.[53] A racial classification which extended such consider-

---

[51] S.C. 6/1156/21; S.C. 2/220/12, m. 31ᵛ; C. 47/9/32; *S.D.*, 254–5; *Cartae*, III, no. 891; S.C. 2/222/5, m. 2ᵛ (Dyffryn Clwyd, 1440).

[52] *History*, 51 (1966), 152–3. Cf. S.C. 2/216/14, m. 6: 'Et mos est patrie istius quod Anglicus non debet esse ad legem contra Wallicum' (Dyffryn Clwyd 1334).

[53] Thus the tenants of Wrexham claimed that they should not pay tolls 'like Welshmen because they were English': S.C. 2/226/18, m. 11ᵛ (1345); S.B.Y., fol. 175ᵛ (1346).

able privileges to one social group and withheld them from the other was of no mean social significance.

Nor was it merely a classification ordained from on high. Welshmen and Englishmen in the March were well aware of their identity as racial groups and of the consequences of the racial division within their society. That is obvious enough in the way in which the English communities of Glamorgan, of Pembroke or of the foreignry of Kidwelly petition as corporate groups;[54] it is obvious again in the way that the Welshmen of Englefield (co. Flints.) organized a subsidy amongst themselves in order to petition for the abrogation of the privileges of the English boroughs or in the way that the Welshmen of Narberth organized a campaign of judicial harassment against their English neighbours in the 1390s;[55] it is evident in the occasional revealing nickname such as that of *Drwgwrthgymro* (*Saxon-lover*) attached to two persons in Dyffryn Clwyd or in the argument advanced in court that it was tantamount to defamation to call someone a Welshman when he was not so.[56] The tensions of racial sentiment— tensions compounded of bitter memories, of resentment of privileges, of settler fears and of the problems of coexistence—were rooted in Marcher society itself; they were not artificially contrived by Marcher lord. 'They all as far as possible', as one contemporary aptly observed with respect to the Welsh and English of Overton (co. Flints.), 'maintain the state of each other'.[57] Nor were these racial differences merely matters of sentiment and prejudice; they were reinforced by differences in *mores* and outlook, in those features of everyday living which often distinguish one status-group from another but which in this case separated two races. Those differences included differences in language, in dress, in food; they also comprehended differences in moral standards and attitudes on such issues as marriage, legitimacy, and penal practice. Differences of this nature were still obvious in the sixteenth century: George Owen of Henllys late in Elizabeth's reign could remark how profoundly different the English and Welsh of Pembrokeshire were in 'maners, diete, buildinges and tyllinge of the

[54] S.C. 8/159, no. 7935; 165, no. 8242 (Glamorgan, *c.* 1322); *Rot. Parl.*, III, 518 (Pembroke, 1401); D.L. 7/1, no. 25B. (Kidwelly, 1430).
[55] Chester 25/24, m. 17 (1378); B.L. Egerton Roll, 8718.
[56] S.C. 2/215/75, m. 3ᵛ; 217/12, m. 19; 218/7, m. 4ᵛ (1316, 1348, 1359).
[57] *C. Inq. Misc. 1307–49*, no. 56 (1309).

land'.[58] Such differences were vitally important, far more so than the exiguous contemporary evidence would suggest. They were the very stuff from which racial suspicion and racial prejudice were manufactured. Approximate and often inaccurate the racial classification in Marcher society certainly was; artificial it was not. It would become increasingly more unreal as the differences in law, in land tenure, in social customs and even in sentiment were eroded or diluted; thereafter it would be retained to uphold privileges and monopolies and for reasons of administrative convenience and conservatism. In the fourteenth century, however, the racial classification was still a central and meaningful one for much of Marcher society. That is why it must occupy a central place in this social analysis.

[58] *Penbrokshire*, I, 39, 59–61.

The English

THE BURGESSES

THE most distinctive group of Englishmen in Marcher society were the burgesses of the Marcher towns. They were distinctive in respect of their corporate status and of their commercial and judicial privileges; they were distinctive in their occupations as merchants, traders and artisans in an overwhelmingly agrarian society; most obviously were they distinctive in that they lived in towns. For the towns of Wales were, almost without exception, alien plantations largely inhabited, at least originally, by immigrant settlers.[1] The great majority of them had been founded in the twelfth and thirteenth centuries by the Anglo-Norman conquerors of Wales. That the towns should be alien plantations was in part a chronological coincidence: the conquest of Wales coincided with the peak period of urban foundations and expansion in medieval Europe. Even in the native Welsh principalities, small urban centres—such as those at Pwllheli, Nefyn and Llanfaes—were emerging[2] at much the same time that the Norman lords were establishing new boroughs in other parts of Wales. But the new town foundations of Wales were not merely a local manifestation of a general European movement; they were also part of a deliberate policy. The town, along with the castle and the priory, was the visible token of the new, foreign regime that now ruled in the March. In this respect, the Marcher boroughs were true frontier towns, the agents of foreign domination, of economic colonization and of cultural diffusion in an alien environment.

[1] For the towns of medieval Wales in general, see E. A. Lewis, *The Medieval Boroughs of Snowdonia* (1912); H. Carter, *The Towns of Wales. A Study in Urban Geography* (Cardiff, 1965); M. W. Beresford, *New Towns of the Middle Ages* (1967). For a bibliographical guide to earlier work on individual boroughs, see W. Rees in *B.B.C.S.* 2 (1923–5), 321–82. For the charters of the Marcher boroughs the three volumes by Adolphus Ballard, James Tait and Martin Weinbaum on *British Borough Charters* (Cambridge, 1913–43) are invaluable; so also are the articles of Mary Bateson on 'The Laws of Breteuil', *E.H.R.* 15–16 (1900–1).

[2] T. Jones Pierce, *Medieval Welsh Society* (Cardiff, 1972), 120 ff.

Their plantation character was obvious enough. It was declared by the names they bore, names which occasionally proclaimed their alien origin as in the case of Grosmont (Monmouth) or Caus (so called probably in affectionate memory of the Corbet homeland in the *pays de Caux*) or which dwelt on their novelty as at Newport (one each in the lordships of Cemais and Gwynllwg), Newtown (Cydewain), New Moat (in the bishop of St. David's lordship of Llawhaden), the *nova villa* at Neath or the other *nova villa* which, appropriately enough, grew in the shadow of Newcastle (Glamorgan). The hesitant beginnings of these new boroughs was also manifested in the way that several of them were replanted within a few generations of their original foundation, as the primary site proved inappropriate or inconvenient. Such was the case at New Montgomery or New Radnor where 'new' was not only a token of recent establishment but also a declaration of contrast with earlier foundations which bore the same name. The plantation character of the Marcher boroughs is even more vividly expressed in the neat patterns of their street plans, for they are the patterns of foundations *de novo* rather than the untidy arrangements which so often characterize organic urban growth. The exigencies of the terrain and the priority given to military considerations in choosing the site of a town have meant that few of the Welsh boroughs—with the notable exception of Flint—can display in their street layout the geometrical, chequer-board patterns of some of the Gascon *bastides* or even of the English 'new towns' (such as Ludlow). Yet so many of the Marcher boroughs were stunted in their economic growth that their neat, if asymmetrical, street plans still display today their plantation character and the misplaced ambitions of their founders. Llanidloes (Powys), New Radnor, Newport (Cemais), New Montgomery and Holt (Bromfield and Yale) are instances which immediately spring to mind.

All Marcher boroughs, regardless of whether they were founded in the late eleventh or late thirteenth century, were seignorial foundations and seignorial rather than commercial considerations thereby dictated their location and much of their development. Their position more often than not was primarily selected in terms of the requirements of military strategy. In the south-west March, for example, the location of boroughs such as Laugharne, Llanstephan and Kidwelly was determined—as was that of the Edwardian boroughs of north Wales—not so much by the economic consideration of convenience for regional or even external markets but rather by the proximity to seignorial castles (whose needs they were meant to satisfy) and by easy access to the sea in terms both of opportunities for escape and of the provision of supplies. Likewise the location of many of the inland boroughs of the March, such as Painscastle in Elfael or Cefnllys in Maelienydd, was patently not determined by economic or marketing considerations but rather by the more immediate advantages of militarily defensible sites and by a commanding strategic position in the surrounding countryside. Military and economic considerations were, of course, by no means always incompatible. River crossings and road junctions were obvious points where the demands of military strategy and the opportunities for commercial exchange overlapped: hence it is that Monmouth and Brecon, to give but two examples, appear at an early date on the map of Norman Wales as the sites both of castles and of flourishing urban centres. Yet the point that needs to be emphasized in the present context is that it was the will of the Anglo-Norman *conquistadores* and their military preoccupations which were the original and primary considerations in the location and distribution of Marcher boroughs as we find them in the late thirteenth century.

Nor was the seignorial will merely the *primum mobile* in the history of Marcher towns; it continued to shape the character of those towns throughout the later Middle Ages. It could hardly be otherwise. The towns of the March were small—Cardiff with its 423 burgages was almost certainly the largest of them[3]— and too dependent on the lord for their military protection and commercial well-being for them to show any great measure of municipal independence. The relationship between burgesses and lord was a close and mutual one: the burgesses expected protection and favours, financial aid (for the building of town walls and bridges, for example) and commercial privileges from the lord; he in turn regarded them as the most trustworthy group of his Marcher tenants, men on whom he could draw for home-guard service in the defence of his lordship and for

[3] *C.I.P.M.*, IV, no. 435, p. 322.

administrative expertise and support in its governance[4] and occasionally even for financial aid.[5] Generally the relationship was a happy one; it was bound to be so given the considerable identity of interests between the two parties. Friction was, of course, inevitable on occasions. When William Valence rode roughshod over the liberties of Haverford, the townsmen appealed successfully to Edward I,[6] while in 1306 the burgesses of Swansea extracted one of the most ample charters from their lord, William Braose.[7] Both cases, however, were unusual: Haverford was the premier port of south-west Wales and its judicial position *vis-à-vis* the earldom of Pembroke was an issue of long-standing; Swansea was also an important port but its charter of 1306 was less a comment on its importance than on the abject position of its lord. In general, seignorial control and supervision of Marcher towns was firm if gentle; the town charters should not be allowed to conceal that truth. Few of the boroughs had their own mayors; even in Cardiff it was the lord's constable who presided over the borough courts.[8] The town charters were certainly no guarantee against seignorial intervention: the borough of Brecon, one of the oldest in the March, had its liberties confiscated by the earl of Hereford in 1340 and when they were restored some twenty years later it was in return for an increase of 40 per cent in the annual farm.[9] In general, however, relations between lords and towns were good in the March. The lords did all in their power to foster the economic life and opportunities of their boroughs—exempting them from tolls throughout their estates, conferring on them a monopoly of trade within the lordship, securing exemptions and franchises for them at the hands of the king of England, extending free gifts of money to shore up their finances[10] and

[4] For burgesses as estate officials, see above p. 204. Cf. the career of William Fort of Llanstephan as described by R. A. Griffiths in *B.B.C.S.* 24 (1971), 326–7.

[5] Thomas ap David and Walter Bace, both burgesses of Brecon, lent Henry V £53 6s. 8d. in 1417 towards his French campaign: D.L. 42/17 fol. 127ᵛ.

[6] *Annales Cambriae*, ed. John Williams ab Ithel (Rolls Series, 1860), 108; *Cal. Public Records re. Pembrokeshire*, 1, 35–7.

[7] For the text of the charter, see *Charters granted to the Chief Borough of Swansea*, ed. G. G. Francis (1867); for discussion, see *Glam. C.H.*, III, 365–69.

[8] *Glam. C.H.*, III, 347.

[9] The Brecon charters are printed in *B.B.C.S.* 2 (1923–5), 245–52; for the confiscation of the town's liberties in 1340, see D.L. 29/671/10810, m. 4.

[10] Earl Richard of Arundel (d. 1376) left £100 in his will for the aid and relief of the merchants of Oswestry and for the town's coffers: B.L. Harleian 1981, fol. 27.

even investing some of their money with local merchants in an attempt to encourage trade.

The obvious visible token of the seignorial character of the Marcher boroughs was that most of them were situated in the shadow of their lords' castles. An impregnable position (whether on a hilltop as in the original site of Denbigh or on a promontory as at Tenby) and ready access to water supplies and external provisions, by sea or down an estuary: these were the major determinants in choosing the site of a Marcher borough. Best of all was for the town itself to be included within a defence complex which embraced both town and castle. Such a unitary defence complex was most perfectly realized in the Edwardian castle-boroughs of the north; but it was also a notable feature of many Marcher boroughs such as Kidwelly, Chepstow, Monmouth, Tenby and Denbigh. The great majority of Marcher boroughs were in fact defended in some way or another, whether by a castle or town walls or ramparts or ditches or by a combination of such defences. Professor Beresford has calculated that 86 per cent of the 'new towns' of Wales were so defended as compared with only 38 per cent of those of England: it is a statistical contrast which serves to highlight the insecurity of the Marcher towns.[11] The mementoes of this age of insecurity are still with us, whether in the massive town walls of Tenby[12] or the surviving eight towers of the Chepstow walls, in the handsome bridge-gate at Monmouth or the single remaining gateway at Kidwelly.[13]

This same militarism coloured the obligations of the burgesses themselves. The burgesses of the March were warrior burgesses. Service in the lord's army figures as an obligation of burgess status in Wales from the twelfth century onwards;[14] indeed it is only in Wales that it can be traced as a duty incumbent on townsmen.[15] The needs of defence still remained in the forefront

---

[11] *New Town of the Middle Ages*, 183.

[12] For the famous town walls at Tenby see *Archaeological Journal* 119 (1962), 316–18. The walls were probably originally erected in the thirteenth century; but they were extensively repaired and rebuilt in the following two centuries at a stipulated width of six feet. Cf. *C.P.R. 1327–30*, 245; *Cal. Public Records re. Pembs.*, III, 234, n. 1.

[13] John Leland, *Itinerary of Wales*, provides much interesting information on the walls and gates of Marcher towns.

[14] As in the earliest Swansea charter (1153–84): *Glam. C.H.*, III, 362.

[15] A. Ballard and J. Tait, *British Borough Charters 1216–1307*, 114–15.

of the town-founders' minds in the thirteenth century: the lord of Holt insisted that each burgess should find a fencible man to guard the castle in time of war, while at Denbigh the primary obligation on the new burgesses was to find a fencible man ready at all times to serve 'for the defence and custody' of the borough, with the threat that failure to fulfil the obligation involved the automatic confiscation of burghal property.[16] 'And that they shall not go to the army', said the charter of Laugharne (1278–82), 'but guard the town as burgesses':[17] the phrase summed up the role of the Marcher burgesses as a militia force and explained thereby the basis of their claim to be exempt from service in the king's army.[18] Nor was their obligation an idle one. During most of the fourteenth century, it is true, it went by default; but the revolt of Owain Glyn Dŵr was to show what a vital role they could play in upholding English rule in Wales. It was they often, as at Kidwelly,[19] who were called upon to man the castles at the height of the emergency; it was from their funds that the town walls were extensively repaired as happened at Brecon, Hay and Monmouth;[20] it was they who lent money to the local commanders in order to pay the troops;[21] it was they who plied their boats to Bristol and Chester to provide much-needed supplies for the beleaguered garrisons.[22]

At Oswestry one of the consequences of the revolt was a provision in the charter of 1401 that henceforth the Welshmen of the hundred of Oswestry, who had hitherto owed the service of guarding the four gates of the town for three days and nights at the time of the fairs, should provide money instead, in order that Englishmen could perform the guard duty.[23] That

---

[16] S.B.Y., fol. 10 (1391); D.L. 42/1, fol. 30ᵛ–fol. 31ᵛ (1285).

[17] Ballard and Tait, op. cit. 114.

[18] For this claim see *Rot. Parl.*, II, 92a (1309). Cf. *B.P.R.*, I, 52 (1347).

[19] The garrison of one man-at-arms and six archers was augmented during the critical summer months of 1403 by an emergency force of fourteen burgesses, serving for nominal wages: D.L. 29/584/9242.

[20] The burgesses of Monmouth were ordered to contribute £50 for the repair of the town walls in 1402; those of Brecon 100 marks in 1404; those of Hay £40 in 1405. These sums were supplemented in varying degrees by the king: D.L. 42/15, fol. 170, fol. 179ᵛ, fol. 196. The 'foreign English' repaired the town walls at Kidwelly: *C.P.R. 1401–5*, 319.

[21] Two of the burgesses of Carmarthen lent £400 to Prince Henry for the defence of the town: D.L. 42/18, fol. 11.

[22] *C.P.R. 1401–5*, 297, 486, D.L. 29/584/9242; D.L. 42/17, fol. 155.

[23] B.L. Harleian 1981, fol. 36–fol. 36ᵛ (1401).

is but an instance in miniature of the way that the revolt of
Owain Glyn Dŵr had served to remind Welshmen and
burgesses alike that the boroughs of Wales were originally
founded as bastions of English rule and settlement. 'Our town
was established', so the burgesses of Newborough (co.
Anglesey) reminded the Black Prince rather obsequiously in 1347 'for the
habitation of Englishmen'.[24] This statement re-iterated the
current theoretical orthodoxy with regard to the original
purpose and present character of the plantation boroughs of
Wales, in Principality and March alike. The corollaries of that
theory were twofold: burgesses should by definition be Englishmen, and Welshmen were *per contra* 'foreigners', as far as towns
were concerned. Those twin equations were the touchstones of
urban policy and privilege in fourteenth-century Wales. It was
as 'the English burgesses of the English boroughs' in Wales that
the townsmen saw themselves; even in a native urban foundation such as Aberafan (Glamorgan), whose burgesses were
overwhelmingly Welsh by blood, it was as the lord's 'Englishmen' that the townsmen were designated; even as late as the
1390s, the burgesses of Hope (co. Flints.) could make much
play of their 'exiled status' and use it as a lever to secure a
comprehensive charter.[25] The decisions of Marcher courts and
officials served to remind Welshmen that in theory the status of
a burgess was denied to them: it could be pointedly emphasized
that they could only become burgesses by the lord's special
permission; they might find themselves faced with the need to
prove their Englishry before qualifying for burghal status; even
if they had lived in a Marcher town and enjoyed the privileges
of burgesses they might still face arbitrary expulsion simply
because they were Welshmen.[26] Indeed clauses in town charters
and ordinances specifically excluding Welshmen from the
right to become burgesses became more common in the late
fourteenth and early fifteenth centuries, especially so after the
outbreak of the Glyn Dŵr revolt. It was in 1401 that a Duchy

[24] E. A. Lewis, *Medieval Boroughs of Snowdonia*, 42. Cf. *Cal. Anc. Corr. conc. Wales*,
232.
[25] *Cartae*, III, no. 811 (1288–1313); IV, no. 1001 (1350); Chester 2/73, m. 3ᵛ
('in relevamen exilis status', 1399).
[26] For examples, see respectively J. A. Bradney, *A History of Monmouthshire*
(1904–33), III, i, 14–15 (Usk, 1397); S.C. 2/219/11, m. 4ᵛ (Ruthin, 1376); S.C.
2/218/7, m. 5ᵛ; 219/2, m. 7 (Ruthin, 1359, 1365).

of Lancaster ordinance insisted that the burgesses of Kidwelly must be 'suitable and faithful Englishmen'; in the same year the earl of Arundel made it clear that his charter to Oswestry was confined to 'the English burgesses' of the town; in 1408 Welshmen were forbidden to be burgesses of Brecon and the charter granted to the town in 1411 was specifically restricted to Englishmen born to English parents.[27] This racial orthodoxy was to survive for many generations yet: in the early sixteenth century the old Edwardian boroughs of north Wales flaunted their Englishness proudly and a borough such as Neath could still issue an ordinance in 1521 forbidding Welshmen from becoming burgesses.[28]

Moreover, it was a racial orthodoxy which had other aspects to it, some of them even more crucial in their consequences than exclusion from the ranks of burgesses. One of the most common privileges of Marcher burgesses was that which declared that they could not be 'convicted or adjudged by any Welshman . . . but only by English burgesses and true Englishmen'.[29] Much the same spirit of racial privilege informed the principle that no Welshman ought to wager his law against a burgess.[30] More important in their impact were the commercial privileges which were reserved for English burgesses. No Welshman, so ran one of Edward I's ordinances, was to reside within a walled borough or to trade outside the mercatorial boroughs.[31] That was to put the issue clearly, if rather too bluntly. The twin prohibition of the ordinance highlights the colonial character of the plantation boroughs of Wales: racial privilege and commercial monopoly went hand in hand. It was because they were Englishmen that the men of Wrexham claimed exemption from toll; it was because they were Welshmen that forty-three inhabitants of Dyffryn Clwyd were challenged to explain how they claimed the right to trade in Ruthin town and to enjoy its burghal privileges.[32]

[27] D.L. 41/10/49; B.L. Harleian 1891, fol. 36; D.L. 42/16, fol. 252^v; *B.B.C.S.* 2 (1923–5), 251.

[28] Lewis, op. cit. 259 ff.; *Glam, C.H.*, III, 354.

[29] As in the case of the charters of Laugharne (1386) and St. Clears (1393): *C.Ch.R. 1341–1417*, 307, 335. For the full texts see *Arch. Camb.* 4th ser. 10 (1879), Supplement, xliii–xlv.

[30] S.C. 2/218/1, m. 7^v (Ruthin, 1350).

[31] *The Record of Caernarvon*, ed. H. Ellis (Record Commission, 1838), 132.

[32] S.B.Y., fol. 175^v (1346); S.C. 2/219/1, m. 5, m. 27 (1364).

The fact that these Welshmen had obviously lived in Ruthin for a number of years—and the town indeed had its own separate Welsh community[33]—indicates that the racial orthodoxy was by no means rigidly observed in practice. That was most certainly the case. Most of the towns of the March had a fair proportion, and sometimes a majority, of Welshmen among their burgesses by the late fourteenth century.[34] Yet this did not serve to remove the impression that Marcher boroughs were centres of English settlement and privilege. In old Marcher boroughs, such as Swansea and Brecon, the burgess population remained predominantly English.[35] The newer boroughs were, if anything, even more self-consciously and exclusively English: there was not a single Welshman among the 63 original burgesses of Denbigh while the names of the burgesses of Ruthin reveal adequately enough their overwhelmingly English provenance.[36] Where Welshmen did form a significant proportion of the urban population, the two communities of Welsh and English burgesses might well keep themselves to themselves, as they apparently did at Laugharne.[37] So, however diluted in practice it may have been, the racial orthodoxy remained the framework for burgess status and burgess privilege throughout the March in the fourteenth century. It is in this context that the role of the boroughs as the prime targets for Owain Glyn Dŵr's first raids in September 1400 and of the burgesses as the staunch upholders of English rule in Wales is explicable. It is against this background of fear and envy also that we must place an incident at Denbigh in 1537 (but one which no doubt had many precedents throughout the March in the previous two centuries) when Welsh countrymen came in arms on market day and proclaimed at the cross 'that Welshmen were as free as Englishmen and that they should pay no stallage there'.[38]

---

[33] Thus in 1325 'the Welshmen of the town of Ruthin' were separately assessed for agistment dues; their English colleagues were presumably exempted: S.C. 2/216/5, m. 16.　　　　[34] See below, p. 447.

[35] *Glam. C.H.*, III, 373; *B.B.C.S.* 2 (1923–4), 253–4.

[36] For the provenance of early burgesses of Ruthin see R. I. Jack in *T.D.H.S.* 18 (1969), 50–83. Among the burgesses were men from Wigmore, Leicester, Wirral, Runcorn, Blackburn, Malpas, Basingwerk and Mold. One burgess, Hugh of Smethington, was the great-grandson of Thomas the carpenter of Rothwell, Yorks.

[37] *A History of Carmarthenshire*, I, ed. J. E. Lloyd (Cardiff, 1935), 324.

[38] Quoted in *The Agrarian History of England and Wales 1500–1640*, ed. J. Thirsk (Cambridge, 1967), 487.

The alien status of towns in the March meant that the prime concern of the burgesses was with survival, economically as well as militarily; as immigré settlers it was imperative that they should control their own food supplies. The burgesses of Harlech expounded the argument with admirable clarity: their capacity to defend the castle was directly related to their ability to provide themselves with food.[39] That is why so many of the original foundation charters of boroughs endowed each burgess with land as well as with a burgage and granted extensive rights of pasture and common to the burghal community: each of the new burgesses of Denbigh, for example, was granted at least a bovate of land in the fertile Vale of Clwyd while in the neighbouring borough of Ruthin the new English lord expelled the native tenants at Garthlegfa in order to create ample pasture and common for his burgesses.[40] That is also why so many of the early Marcher town charters, such as those of Newport (Cemais, *c.* 1241, 1273–81), Tenby, (Pembroke, 1265–94) or Kidwelly (1308), are more concerned with agrarian than with commercial privileges, with access to woods and with rights of pasture and common; their hinterland was for them primarily a source of food and only secondarily of commercial opportunity. It is in the light of such priorities that we must also explain why so many Welsh boroughs were surrounded by unusually extensive rural enclaves. The boundaries of the borough of Kidwelly, for example, extended far beyond the tiny settlement on the river Gwendraeth in the shadow of the massive castle; they were demarcated by four ancient crosses and the land within them was held in burgage tenure 'without any payment of rent or service otherwyse then the free Burgesses of the sayd towne weare wonte . . . to paye'.[41] At Denbigh, likewise, the area of the free borough encompassed all the land within half a league of the town itself.[42]

In such circumstances it is not surprising that many of the burgesses of the March were more farmers than traders or

[39] *Rot. Parl.*, I, 276 b.
[40] D.L. 42/1, f. 30ᵛ–fol. 31ᵛ (Denbigh); *T.D.H.S.* 18 (1969), 55; S.C. 2/218/4, m. 20 (Ruthin).
[41] *A Survey of the Duchy of Lancaster Lordships in Wales, 1609–13*, ed. W. Rees, 192. For the boundaries of the borough see the charters published in *Arch. Camb.* 3rd ser. 2 (1856), 274–81. For this subject in general see Beresford, op. cit. 219–25.
[42] *C.P.R. 1399–1401*, 440.

craftsmen. John Parker at Ruthin held in addition to his three burgages, six and a half acres in the town fields, eight acres in Rhoslyfeirion and nineteen acres in Efnechtyd; John Wilde, one of the most prominent burgesses of Holt in the late fourteenth century, owned fifty-two acres of rich land along the river Dee as well as seven burgages; while the goods of one of the early Welsh burgesses of Ruthin included 180 sheep, forty lambs and corn worth ten marks.[43] Survival may have originally prompted the burgesses' reliance on agriculture, but what was originally a necessity could soon be converted into an opportunity. The burgesses figured as among the most enterprising of the agricultural entrepreneurs in Marcher society. They often had more ready capital than others to invest in the market in land. One opportunity for their enterprise came with the leasing of the demesne of the Marcher lords: it was the townsmen of Brecon who took over the lease of the manor of Brecon in 1375, and it was likewise the burgesses of Hay who took the lord's demesne there on lease.[44] Even greater opportunities came with the unusually active market in native Welsh land in the later Middle Ages, a market which called for ready capital and for painstaking persistence in consolidating a landed estate by the piecemeal acquisition of individual plots. The Welsh burgesses certainly distinguished themselves in this respect: the enterprise of the Boldes of Conway—who built for themselves an estate of almost 2,000 acres in the Conway valley[45]—was matched on a smaller scale by that of other burgess families such as the Forts of Llanstephan, the Woodhalls of Holt or the Hollands of Abergele or by the purchases of individual townsmen such as Richard Ireland of Oswestry.[46]

Burgesses invested in land partly no doubt in order to ensure a regular income from rent for themselves and partly because in such a commercially underdeveloped society opportunities for

---

[43] S.C. 2/216/1, m. 7 (1319); S.B.Y., fol. 11ᵛ ff. (1391); S.C. 2/216 13, m. 1ᵛ (1333).

[44] S.C. 6/1157/2 (1375); D.L. 29/633/10317 (1398).

[45] T. Jones Pierce, *Medieval Welsh Society*, 195–7; C. A. Gresham, 'The Bolde Rental (Bangor MS. 1939)', *Transactions of the Caernarvonshire Historical Society* 26 (1965), 31–49.

[46] For the Forts see R. A. Griffiths, 'The Cartulary and Muniments of the Fort Family of Llanstephan', *B.B.C.S.* 24 (1970–2), 311–84; for the Woodhalls and the Hollands there is much material in the Flintshire Record Office (Trevor-Roper

investment were few. But the burgesses could also exploit the land directly themselves for market production. Some of them certainly did so. It was no doubt with an eye on the buoyant market in Marcher wool that the burgesses of Brecon sent their flocks to pasture in the foothills of the Brecon Beacons.[47] Likewise it was his eye for commercial opportunities which gave John Owen such a prominent role in both the urban and rural life of medieval Kidwelly. He was a notable burgess and reeve of his town; but he also held the lease of two local mills and of the rich grazing pasturelands of the Gwendraeth basin. Nor did his enterprise end there: he was a wool-merchant as well as a sheep-farmer and rose to the rank of major exporter of wool in south-west Wales in the 1390s, shipping as much as fifty sacks annually (worth some £450) through the Carmarthen staple[48] Exceptional John Owen no doubt was; but the range of his interests and activities may serve to show both the opportunities open to the enterprising burgess and the impact of such men on rural society in the March, in terms of marketing skills, capital investment and the incentive and example of agricultural production for regional, national and even international markets.

The affairs of men such as John Owen remind us that, however agrarian may have been the aspect of Marcher boroughs and the preoccupations of their burgesses, it is in other directions that we must look for the distinguishing features of urban life— in 'the separation from the rural hinterland, the specialization in non-agricultural occupations, the presence of merchants and artisans and, above all, in the existence of a market'.[49] The towns of the March were, indeed, primarily market towns, serving the needs and controlling the trade of an overwhelmingly agrarian society. Once their military function receded into the background, their future, indeed their very existence, as urban centres would depend on how adequately they fulfilled their

Collection) and U.C.N.W. (Kinmel Mss.) respectively; for Ireland see *The Lordship of Oswestry 1393–1607*, ed. W. J. Slack, 142–3, 165, and Llinos Smith, 'The Lordships of Chirk and Oswestry, 1282–1415', Ph.D. thesis (Univ. of London, 1971), 315–17.

[47] D.L. 42/17, fol. 79 (1414).

[48] For his career, see D.L. 42/15, fol. 194ᵛ, D.L. 42/16, fol. 26ᵛ, fol. 72, fol. 254ᵛ; D.L. 29/584/9242; *C.P.R. 1396–9*, 158; *Y Cymmrodor* 24 (1913), 143.

[49] R. H. Hilton, *A Medieval Society*, 169.

role as market centres. It was the control, indeed the monopoly, of local and regional trade which was the prime ambition of these market towns. The ambitions of the burgesses and the aspirations of the Marcher lords for their boroughs are clearly articulated in the town charters. That of Cardiff in 1340 is particularly revealing: all those who live by buying and selling in the lordship of Glamorgan ought to live 'in villis de Bourgh et non upland'; such men were to conduct their business in fairs, markets and towns and not elsewhere; they were to travel by the royal highways between towns so that they did not evade paying tolls.[50] Such commercial monopolies were, of course, of the essence of burghal privilege in medieval society generally. Yet rarely were such monopolies so exclusive in their character and so extensive in their geographical range as they were in the March. That was in part so because trading monopolies tend to be more common and more complete in colonized lands[51]; it was also in part to be explained by the territorial geography of the March. Marcher lordships were large units, much larger than the trading districts within which the commercial monopolies of most English boroughs operated; within each lordship the lord was free to bestow exclusive commercial privileges on his burgesses.[52] 'No merchant', said the lord of Haverford in an early charter (1219–31) to his burgesses, 'shall be in our land except he be resident in our borough'.[53] Such a statement may have been a pious hope; but the readiness of non-burgesses to pay in order to have the right to trade[54] or to enrol as chensers[55] and thereby to enjoy urban privileges shows that the burgesses' monopoly of trade was no empty claim. The March indeed was divided into market districts determined less by economic realities than by political geography and the will of the lord; its trade pattern was more akin in this respect, at least in terms of borough charters, to that of Scotland than of England.[56]

---

[50] *Cartae*, IV, no. 982.

[51] *Cambridge Economic History of Europe*, I, 2nd edn. (Cambridge, 1966), 473–4. Cf. ibid. III (Cambridge, 1963), 161–72.   [52] Cf. above pp. 234–6.

[53] Ballard and Tait, op. cit. 243. Cf. ibid. 289 (Swansea).

[54] One man paid £3 6s. 8d. for the right to trade in Ruthin for life: S.C. 2/219/1, m. 32 (1364).

[55] Chensers contributed substantially towards the revenue of some Marcher towns, e.g. Newport (*The Marcher Lordships of South Wales 1415–1536*, ed. T. B. Pugh, 171, n. 7).

[56] Cf. Ballard and Tait, op. cit. lxvi–lxvii.

None of these Marcher towns was large; rarely did their population exceed three or four hundred, huddled, as were the townsmen of Ruthin and Newport (Cemais) in four or five major streets.[57] Beyond the town houses and often in between them lay large tracts of open space and unoccupied burgages. Yet in some ways there was by Marcher standards a distinctive intimacy about borough life. In part it was the intimacy of a small closely-knit community in an alien and even hostile environment; in part it was the intimacy of a nucleus of population in a country of predominantly dispersed settlement; in part it was the intimacy of a focal point in the economic and social life of the surrounding *pays*. For however small these Marcher boroughs and however restricted their economic horizons, most of them served in greater or lesser measure as the obvious focus for the community life of their hinterland, not only commercially but also administratively, judicially and even socially and religiously. Some had famous churches (e.g. Tenby), venerated roods (e.g. Brecon), or schools (e.g. Haverford, Oswestry); many of them housed religious corporations— monasteries, priories, friaries, or collegiate churches; most of them were the obvious administrative centres for their hinterland, in both secular and religious affairs. Above all their weekly or twice-weekly markets and their twice-annual fairs were the natural focus for much local and even regional trade and for the sale of wares brought from England and beyond. Wales and the March could hardly lay claim to the knowledge of an urban society; but it had at least become a land of small market towns.

Few Marcher burgesses had aspirations in the direction of long-distance or wholesale trade on any considerable scale. Beyond the immediate needs of their native boroughs and their hinterland, the ambit of their trading activities probably rarely extended farther than a line of English towns just beyond the March—Chester, Shrewsbury, Ludlow, Hereford, Leominster and Bristol. Indeed it was much more likely that the merchants of these border towns were already beginning to exploit and

---

[57] The four streets of Ruthin are referred to in ordinances issued in 1365: S.C. 2/219/2, m. 2ᵛ. A rental of 1434 provides an interesting view of the town of Newport: B. G. Charles, 'The Records of the Borough of Newport in Pembrokeshire', *N.L.W.J.* 8 (1951–2), 33–45, 120–37.

corner such export trade as the March could offer, notably in cattle and wool.[58] It was, for example, to a Shrewsbury merchant that the prior of Ruthin sold his wool-stock in 1343 for £15, while the cloth trade of the town was at least in some measure controlled by the Dalbys, a family of Chester merchants.[59] In south-west Wales in the mid-fourteenth century the considerable export trade in wool was dominated from even further afield, by a number of Italian, German and Flemish merchants and their agents.[60] The pattern is a familiar one in many parts of Europe: the local merchant community had largely to be content with the profits of local retail trade. It was to counteract such a situation by a sudden injection of capital that Henry, earl of Derby and lord of Kidwelly, invested £100 each with two Kidwelly merchants, Walter and Adam Aylward, 'ad mercandizandum'—to be returned with profits at the end of the year.[61]

Earl Henry was supporting one of the more enterprising merchant families of the March: the Aylwards figure prominently in the meagre commercial records of the fourteenth century and Walter Aylward, we know, had been exporting hides to Gascony. They were not unique: other Marcher merchants—especially from Chepstow, Newport, Cardiff, Swansea, Kidwelly, Haverford and Tenby—also ventured into foreign trade. They plied their boats—bearing such names as *The George of Tenby* or *Le Spaynnol of Haverford*—along the coasts of south Wales and especially to Bristol; they doubtless took a hand in the active cereal trade with England and Ireland; some of them, such as John Owen of Kidwelly, were active wool-traders; yet others travelled farther afield to Brittany, Gascony, Flanders and Spain bringing home cargoes of wine, salt, iron and other commodities; some of them, such as the Wisemans of Tenby, were foreign traders of several generations standing.[62]

[58] For some early evidence of the Welsh cattle trade see H. P. R. Finberg, 'An Early Reference to the Welsh Cattle Trade', *Agricultural History Review* 2 (1954), 12–14 and R. H. Hilton, *A Medieval Society*, 13.

[59] S.C. 2/217/8, m. 9; 219/3, m. 1 (1366).

[60] *Y Cymmrodor* 24 (1913), 135–9.

[61] D.L. 25/3578/80 (1341).

[62] For Welsh foreign trade in the later Middle Ages two articles by E. A. Lewis still remain fundamental: 'The Development of Industry and Commerce in Wales during the Middle Ages', *T.R.H.S.* new ser. 17 (1903), 121–75, and 'A Contribution to the Commercial History of Medieval Wales', *Y Cymmrodor* 24 (1913), 86–159.

Such men, however, were exceptions. It was as market towns
that the vast majority of boroughs thrived or stagnated or
declined, and as such it was market forces which determined
their fortunes. Statistics of borough rents and profits, it is true,
are by no means always a faithful guide to the state of burghal
economy; but in many of the towns of the March the decay is
too obvious to be missed. Some decayed from natural causes:
the borough of Kenfig (Glamorgan) had had a tumultuous
history from its earliest days but it was the encroaching sand-
dunes and the shift in the sea-shore which eventually suffocated
its urban life so that Leland found it 'in ruine and almost
shokid and devoured with the sandes'. Other boroughs faltered
because their commercial opportunities were too limited, either
in terms of their relation to their hinterland—as happened in
the coastal boroughs of Laugharne and Llanstephan—or in
terms of the distribution of markets in any particular rural
area—hence the early decline of such centres as New Montgomery, Huntington and Grosmont. Others failed because the
artificiality of their commercial setting was too obvious once
the military opportunities which had called them into being
had been removed. Cefnllys and Caus are two obvious examples.[63] Not even the status of being the judicial and administrative capital of a lordship was an insurance against
decline. Such was the case of Holt, the *caput* of the lordship of
Bromfield and Yale: its burgess numbers (not necessarily an
accurate barometer of actual population) fell from 152 in 1315
to 78 in 1391; its commercial importance was steadily eclipsed
by that of the neighbouring unchartered 'mercatorial vill' at
Wrexham; it was even the 'measure of Wrexham', not that of
Holt, which was the commercial norm in the lordship; even
its position as the administrative centre of the lordship was
under challenge. Already by the 1390s, within a century of its
foundation, Holt had already assumed the aspect of a sleepy
country village which it has never subsequently lost.[64] Few

For trade between Bristol and south Wales, see also E. M. Carus-Wilson, *Medieval
Merchant Venturers*, 2nd edn. (1967), 4–13.
    [63] For the decline of Caus, see *V.C.H. Shropshire*, III, 310. For Cefnllys, see R.
Millward and A. Robertson, *The Welsh Marches*, 54–5; there were only twenty
burgesses there in 1332 (*C.I.P.M.*, VII, no. 387, p. 280).
    [64] *A History of Wrexham*, ed. A. H. Dodd (Wrexham, 1957), 23–33; B. Evans,
'Grant of Privileges to Wrexham (1380)', *B.B.C.S.* 19 (1960), 42–7, idem, The

other areas can match the Welsh March in the number of its failed or stunted boroughs, conceived in a spate of enthusiasm for the civilizing and Anglicizing influences of urban life but unrealistic in their location in terms of commercial opportunities.

Not all the Marcher boroughs, however, were failures. By 1400 several of them had outgrown their original strategic straitjackets and wore the aspect of flourishing market centres rather than that of garrison towns huddled behind the safety of their walls. At Ruthin, for example, less than thirty years after the final English conquest of the area and the establishment of an English borough, the lord justified the establishment there in 1310 of a collegiate church, to be served by a rector and seven priests, because 'the number of inhabitants and sojourners there has greatly increased'. The neighbouring small borough of Denbigh, built on a steep hillside and in the shadow of its massive castle, soon spilt over its original town walls: already by 1305 the fifty-two burgages *infra muros* were well outnumbered by 193 burgages *extra muros*.[65] Much the same story was repeated elsewhere—at Kidwelly, Cowbridge and Brecon, for example. Such extra-mural growth by no means always met with the lord's approval. At Kidwelly in 1401 the Duchy of Lancaster commissioners were appalled by the ruin of the old town within the walls and by the unbridled growth of an extra-mural settlement; they firmly enjoined the burgesses to take up residence within the walls before Michaelmas on pain of forfeiting their houses there.[66] But not even the fulminations of the Duchy commissioners or the threats posed by the Glyn Dŵr revolt could give the old walled town of Kidwelly more than a brief new lease of life; when Leland came there in the 1530s he found it 'nere al desolatid'.

The fate of the old walled town of Kidwelly is, indeed, an apt comment on the limits of seignorial control and policy in determining the urban development of the medieval March. The lords of the March could found boroughs and confer the most ample commercial and judicial privileges on their bur-

Medieval Liberty of Wrexham', *T.D.H.S.* 10 (1961), 236–8; D. Pratt, 'The Medieval Borough of Holt', ibid. 14 (1965), 9–74.

[65] *Arch. Camb.*, 3rd ser. 3 (1857), 96–9; D.L. 29/1/2, m. 3.

[66] D.L. 41/10/49.

gesses; but once the conditions of a military emergency had been removed, no end of charters or monopolies could ensure the economic success of a town. That depended on factors largely beyond the control of the lord—on the ebb and flow of trade, on the position of a town in relation to its local and regional markets, on the enterprise and opportunities of its burgesses, on the measure of competition from neighbouring towns and markets. That is why it is dangerous to assume that a decline in urban rents and farms necessarily indicated an adverse economic climate; it may be equally interpreted in terms of the collapse of seignorial economic control and of the evolution of alternative centres of marketing and exchange. Thus at the very time that many of the boroughs of Glamorgan were declining into the ranks of slumbering country villages, fairs and markets were multiplying in the countryside, contrary to the lord's prohibitions and the burgesses's privileges.[67] Likewise while the chartered borough of Chirk showed few signs of commercial vigour, older Welsh marketing centres such as Llanrhaeadr ym Mochnant and Llansilin flourished and so also did the village which grew up at the river crossing at Llangollen. Much the same story is repeated in Bromfield and Yale: the chartered borough of Holt continued to decline while rural markets such as Llanarmon still flourished and while the commercial significance of Wrexham—its tolls increasing from £17 in 1315 to £46 in 1391—earned it not only the title of *villa mercatoria* but also the grant of administrative and judicial privileges in 1380.[68]

By the late fourteenth century the urban pattern of the March as it had been originally established by the Anglo-Norman lords was changing fairly rapidly and the lord's authority over urban development and marketing was visibly declining. That is obvious enough in the failure of many of the town plantations of the thirteenth century, in the growth of extra-mural suburbs, in the development of country fairs and markets often unsupervised by the lord's officers, in the increasing number of Welshmen who were enrolled as burgesses

[67] *Glam. C.H.*, iii, ch. VII *passim*, esp. pp. 358–9.

[68] Its importance as a commercial centre is further shown by the fact that 114 advowry tenants are recorded as living there in 1391, many of whom were craftsmen: S.B.Y., fol. 100ᵛ.

or who traded in the towns. The seignorial response was predictable; it took the form of an attempt to shore up the privileges of the burgesses and to remind them of their original function. The Duchy commissioners at Kidwelly in 1401 made the point very forcefully: the burgesses were to take up residence within the walls of the old town; they were forbidden to sell any of their goods, either gross or retail, outside the town walls; they were prohibited from holding markets outside the town walls and from enrolling as burgesses other than faithful and suitable Englishmen. Such ordinances were an attempt to return to the colonial days of Marcher boroughs, when towns had been founded 'for the habitation of Englishmen' and when trade had been controlled and supervised by the lord's officers. The revolt of Owain Glyn Dŵr gave a brief new lease of life to such colonial notions; but in spite of ordinances and charters, the change in the character of urban life in the March would proceed apace in the fifteenth century.

THE ENGLISH RURAL SETTLERS

The alien colonization of the March was by no means restricted to the boroughs; it had also penetrated in varying degrees into the countryside around the towns. Between the rural and the urban settlers one cannot, of course, draw a rigid distinction, for the overlap between them was very considerable.[69] Many of the burgesses held an estate in the country nearby. Furthermore town and country settlers were bound by bonds of blood and privilege, by their role as an alien group in a colonial society. Together they formed the English community. Yet the 'foreign English' or 'the English outside the town', as they were occasionally called, deserve our attention in their own right.[70] In many parts of the March they were a much more numerous group than the burgesses and in an overwhelmingly rural society their influence was in some respects more far-reaching than that of the townsmen.

By the end of the thirteenth century, the chronology and

[69] Much of the evidence for this section is based either on the court rolls of Dyffryn Clwyd or on *S.D.* Detailed references have been kept to a minimum.

[70] Both phrases appear in the Denbigh evidence: *Records of Denbigh and its Lordship*, ed. J. Williams (Wrexham, 1860), 99–100 (inquisition of 1311); Nottinghamshire Record Office, D.D. 325/1, m. 24 (1317).

pattern of alien colonization had left widely differing imprints on the social and racial configuration of different areas of the March. By then the main contours of the alien settlement of the Marcher countryside were already fairly firmly drawn.[71] This means that in the present context we can do no more than study rather cursorily the tail-end of the story of Marcher colonization; the truly heroic age of that movement lay in the past. Heroic maybe, but also in some respects pre-historic, for the saga of the colonization of the south and eastern March in the twelfth and thirteenth centuries—let alone in earlier periods— is singularly ill-served in terms of contemporary documents. From 1282 onwards, however, the story is different: it was then, in the wake of the Edwardian conquest, that the lordships of Denbigh, Dyffryn Clwyd, Bromfield and Yale, and Chirkland were added to the map of the March and the story of their colonization—and that largely an alien colonization *ab initio*—is relatively well-recorded. We would not presume to claim that the evidence for this post-1282 phase of colonization necessarily serves as a reliable guide to the character of the earlier colonization of the March. The line from the particular example to the general argument in the March is always a most uncertain one and there is reason to believe, as we shall see, that this late phase of Marcher colonization was indeed unusual in several respects. Nevertheless, the constraints of our chronological framework apart, it is obviously sensible to proceed from the relatively well-documented to the less well-documented.

The first question to which we must direct our attention is that of the provenance of the settlers. Here the evidence—in so far as it is amenable to interpretation—speaks with a fair measure of unanimity for the post-1282 period. Many of the settlers were recruited from within the March and from the neighbouring English border counties. Among the rural settlers of Dyffryn Clwyd, for example, we find men from Ewloe (co. Flints), Montgomery and Clun in the March, from Chester, Frodsham and the Wirral in Cheshire and from Pitchford, Ludlow, Wenlock, Whitchurch and Pontesbury in Shropshire. This pattern of recruitment from the English border counties must have been repeated elsewhere in the March: it was from

[71] Cf. above pp. 302–6.

Herefordshire that many of the immigré families of Brecon and Talgarth—such as the Gunters, Devereux, Pichards, Baskervilles and Sowtons—were drawn; while many of the settlers of Gower and lowland Gwent and Glamorgan probably emigrated there from Gloucestershire and across the Bristol Channel from Somerset. Another major source of colonists were the English estates of the Marcher lords. Some of the new English tenants in Dyffryn Clwyd were recruited from Reginald Grey's manors in Wilton (co. Hereford), Dingestow (Monmouth), Eton (co. Bucks.), Weedon (co. Northants) and Bletchley (co. Bucks.). In Denbigh the majority of the immigré farmers were drawn from Henry Lacy's northern estates: their surnames proclaim their provenance unmistakeably and so also do the placenames whereby many of them were still distinguished—Pontefract, Peak, Sunderland, Skipton, Blackburn, Runcorn, Halton, Rochdale, Bridlington, Simonstone, Rossendale, Clitheroe and Castleford. Many of the earlier settlers of the March were likewise probably recruited on the English estates of their Anglo-Norman lords; some of them, indeed, in Glamorgan, Gower and southern Pembroke may have followed their Flemish lords overseas in search of adventure and good land. For some of them the March did not mark the end of their travels: among the colonists who sailed to the newly-conquered lordship of Ireland in the later twelfth century a not insignificant proportion was drawn from the recently-colonized districts of south-west Wales.[72] This fact reminds us that in the story of alien settlement in Wales we must allow a place not only for lord-directed immigration and recruitment but also for an influx of men attracted by the prospect of good land at cheap rents and by the favoured status often accorded to such colonists. When we find, for example, that among the settlers in Dyffryn Clwyd were men whose names proclaimed them to come originally from Lancaster, Westmorland, Carlisle, Kendal, York and Coventry it is probably of such a category of colonists that we should think. The colonization of the March in this respect was not merely an attempt to underpin a military conquest; it was also an aspect of the search for new lands to meet the needs of an increasing population. It was such a movement which had taken Anglo-Saxon colonists into the borderlands

[72] A. J. Otway-Ruthven, *A History of Medieval Ireland*, 115.

of Wales—notably in the present-day counties of Clwyd, Powys and Gwent—well before the Norman conquest of England. It was the same movement which accounted for the most momentous single phase of alien colonization in the history of the March, the transplantation of the Flemings into southern Pembroke—'since', as the native *Chronicle of the Princes* explained, 'there was no place for them to live on the coast (of Flanders), because (of the incursions) of the sea, or in the hinterland because of the great numbers of the people living in it'.[73]

Socially and vocationally the colonists of the March were a very mixed group. The men who gained most were the military retainers of the Marcher *conquistadores*. That had been true from the earliest days of Norman rule in Wales: in Glamorgan little is known about the process and chronology of subinfeudation but many of the gentry families of the Vale in the fourteenth century could plausibly trace their family fortunes to endowments received there in the first or second generation of Norman rule; in Gower the great charter of liberties of 1306 recognized twelve of the knights' fees as 'ancient' and accorded their holders a special position within the English community of the county of Gower; in Pembroke many of the villages of the southern half of the county—such as Wiston, Letterston and Walterston—still bear the names of Flemish knights to whom they were originally given in the early twelfth century.[74] This pattern was renewed in the lordships of north-east Wales in the late thirteenth century. Among the beneficiaries of Reginald Grey's largesse was his 'well-beloved squire', Adam Verdon, who received a share of the vill of Rhiwiau (Dyffryn Clwyd) by the service of a sixth of a knight's fee;[75] while in Bromfield and Yale in 1311 the earl of Surrey bestowed 400 acres on one of his retainers, John Wysham, for an annual rent of £10 and the service of a knight's fee.[76] Military retainers were members of the lord's household; other members of the lord's *familia*

---

[73] *Brut y Tywysogyon, Peniarth MS. 20 version*, ed. and translated by T. Jones (Cardiff, 1952), 27–8.

[74] *Glam. C.H.*, III, 71–18, 286–7; *Cartae*, III, no. 851; B. E. Howells, 'Pembrokeshire Farming, circa 1580–1620', *N.L.W.J.* 9 (1955–6), 239–50, 313–33, 413–39 esp. 316 ff.

[75] N.L.W. Roger Lloyd Collection, 1 (pre-1308). The family failed in the male line after two generations in Wales: S.C. 2/216/3, m. 3ᵛ.

[76] *C.P.R. 1307–13*, 405–6.

could likewise expect to partake of the benefits of his territorial munificence. Henry Lacy, earl of Lincoln (d. 1311) was outstandingly lavish in this respect: his chamberlain was given a handsome estate in Lleweni in some of the best farming land in north Wales; one of his cooks was rewarded with a life-grant of eighty-eight acres in Galltfaenan and another with fifty acres in Llewesog; his steward, Sir William le Vavassour, was also given an estate in Denbigh and he in turn bestowed part of it on his own squire.[77] Such a pattern of endowment must have been familiar enough in the earlier history of the March: service and reward alike were centred on the lord's household, military and domestic, and on the household of his major followers.

In the wake of the lord's household and of his military followers came a much more numerous and motley band of settlers: ordinary soldiers who settled down to enjoy the fruits of conquest but who, like the Flemings of Pembroke, remained 'equally fitted for the plough or the sword';[78] stonemasons and other skilled craftsmen drafted into the March to build castles and town walls, such as the Helpstons, who acquired an estate at Efnechtyd in Dyffryn Clwyd, or Adam Swynemore who first figures in the records of Denbigh as a mason (*cementarius*);[79] or ordinary peasants, such as Hugh Lackland (*Saunz Terre*) of Denbigh, in search of a territorial competence in the March denied them in their native English villages. It is here, perhaps, that the post-1282 records may be least representative: they relate chronologically to the tail-end of the colonizing process, geographically to areas which were often isolated and militarily insecure, and numerically to a rather restricted movement of immigrants. As such they probably refer to a colonizing movement which was but a pale reflection of that of earlier generations. In other parts of the March—in lowland Gwent and Glamorgan, in southern Gower and southern Pembroke—the

---

[77] *Arch. Camb.* 6th ser. 12 (1912), 246–7; D.L. 36/2, no. 248; D.L. 42/1, fol. 33–fol. 33ᵛ.

[78] *Giraldi Cambrensis Opera*, ed. J. F. Dimock, vi (Rolls Series), 83.

[79] For the Helpstons, see R. A. Brown, H. M. Colvin and A. J. Taylor, *History of the King's Works* (London, 1965), i, 254–6, 329, 388, 469; ii, 1056–7; for their professional and territorial fortunes in Dyffryn Clwyd see especially S.C. 2/215/70, m. 1; 215/72, m. 12ᵛ; 216/4, m. 7, m. 28; 216/9, m. 16 (1307–29). For Adam Swynemore, see D.L. 42/1, fol. 29ᵛ (1310).

evidence of personal place- and field-names, suggests a far greater measure of alien immigration and a much more drastic degree of social re-organization. In these areas entire districts were taken over by the colonists; and those colonists included considerable numbers—in terms of current population—of peasant settlers, unfree as well as free. It is only on such terms that we can begin to explain the high proportion of English customary tenants in the manors of the southern coastal lowlands from Chepstow to Gower, or the large numbers of English *gabulares* (customary tenants) on the rent-rolls of Pembroke manors such as Castle Martin or St. Florence, or the neat virgated customary tenures of the English tenants of the manors of the Vale of Glamorgan or the distribution in the southern March of a customary acre based upon the pole of nine feet, which seems to have been introduced into the area from south-western England and which was confined to areas intensively colonized by immigrant settlers.[80]

The post-1282 evidence may well mislead in another respect, that of the pace of the colonization movement. The colonization of the new lordships of the north-eastern March was effected with great speed; in its main outlines it was already complete within twenty years or so of their conquest. It was a process which ran parallel in point of time as well as in strategic purpose with the construction of the castles and the founding of boroughs. In Dyffryn Clwyd Alexander Sywell and Hugh Sprotton were granted their fees 'immediately after the Conquest';[81] in Denbigh the earl of Lincoln had made extensive grants of land in the countryside around the new borough by 1290, and by his death in 1311 the influx of English immigrants into the lordship had already virtually ceased. There were, of course, a few late arrivals; but on the whole, the Edwardian phase of Marcher colonization, if we may call it such, was sharp, short and purposeful. In many of the older lordships of the March alien immigration into the countryside was a much more protracted and spasmodic process, partly because of the uneven and often

[80] W. Rees, *South Wales and the March, 1284–1415*, 142–4; *Glam. C.H.*, III, 19–21 (Glamorgan), 210–13 (Gower); B. E. Howells, 'The Distribution of Customary Acres in South Wales', *N.L.W.J.* 15 (1967–8), 226–33; F. V. Emery, 'West Glamorgan Farming circa 1580–1620', ibid. 9 (1955–6), 392–400; 10 (1957–8), 17–32.
[81] S.C. 2/216/1, m. 13ᵛ ('statim post conquestum').

uncertain pattern of military conquest and partly because the number of colonists was, at least eventually, far greater. In Pembroke, the area of Anglo-Flemish colonization appears to have expanded southwards and westwards from the original colonial base in Castle Martin and the successive stages of this colonization—extending probably over a century and a half or more—appear to be reflected in three different customary acres in southern Pembrokeshire; in Gower, likewise, it is not fanciful to posit a primary area of Norman settlement in a group of southern manors and knights' fees and a secondary area in the north and north-west of 'the English county' of Gower, marked by the creation of new fees and by a later influx of new settlers.[82] Such chronological diversities serve to remind us once more how much the fabric of Marcher society has been determined by the variegated geographical character of the March and by the uneven chronology of its historical development. They also remind us forcefully that in the making of Marcher society in the pre-industrial age no period was more momentous than the twelfth and thirteenth centuries.

We may agree on the significance of the colonization movement; but we are singularly ignorant of the mechanics of colonization itself. The documentation for the post-1282 period makes it clear that the process of territorial partition and settlement was firmly controlled by the Marcher lords; it was never allowed to degenerate into a scramble for land. One of the initial steps of Reginald Grey, the new English lord of Dyffryn Clwyd, was apparently to dispatch a land surveyor, Patrick Crue, to his new lordship; it was a token of a firmness of purpose in asserting a precise territorial control over his newly-conquered estates.[83] In Denbigh, likewise, the great *Survey* of 1334 as well as earlier charter evidence makes it evident that the process of territorial endowment was directed by the lord and his officials and that all major beneficiaries were granted their lands by charter on specific terms. In Bromfield and Yale also the estates which were created for the lord's retainers in the eastern district of the lordship were instituted by charter and their extent carefully assessed.[84] Even in the literally pre-

---

[82] B. E. Howells in *N.L.W.J.* 9 (1955–6), 318–19; *Glam. C.H.*, III, 212–13.
[83] For references to this survey see S.C. 2/215/69, m. 11; 217/9, m. 4.
[84] S.B.Y., fol. 20–fol. 21 v; S.C. 6/1305/7.

scriptive era of Marcher colonization the control of Marcher lords over the processes of settlement appears to have been equally firm. This is suggested by the common equation throughout the March from the twelfth century onwards that a knight's fee should be equivalent to a carucate or 120 acres of land;[85] it is suggested again in the way that customary tenants of the lowland March were often allotted neat 'full' or 'half tenures', based on a unit of either twelve or twenty-four acres.[86] The neatness of the equations of later rentals should not, of course, be allowed to impress us unduly: beneath the symmetrical and even artificial formulae we must allow much room for the untidiness of human activities especially in such a turbulent period, for 'the fear and terror' (to borrow a contemporary phrase)[87] whereby many a local warlord imposed his will and called it right and for the individual and largely unrecorded enterprise of individual peasant settlers. To admit so much is to admit the obvious. Yet in the story of the colonization of the March as in that of the Norman settlement of England, the overriding impression is that of the measure of control—often in general but not infrequently in particulars— retained by the great lords themselves, the king included. This was colonization and settlement firmly enclosed within a framework of lordship.

The alien immigrants were accommodated in the March in a variety of ways. In certain districts the alien settlement was no more than the imposition of a new aristocracy on a native population; beneath the surface of foreign institutions such as the manor and the knight's fee often lay an indigenous tenantry. Such appears to have been the case in the lordship of Brecon, where territorial lordship, at least in the lowlands, was bestowed on an Anglo-Norman aristocracy in the twelfth and thirteenth centuries, but where there is little evidence of peasant immigration from England. Such also was the case in the lordship of Bromfield and Yale after 1282 where a foreign aristocracy was artificially and, as it proved, largely unsuccessfully imposed

---

[85] For examples of this equation, see *Episcopal Acts relating to Welsh Dioceses, 1066–1272*, ed. J. Conway Davies, I (Cardiff, 1946), 269 (late twelfth century); D.L. 36/2, no. 248 (Denbigh, 1286); *Cal. Public Records re. Pembs.*, III, 79–81 (Walwynscastle, 1307).

[86] *Glam. C.H.*, III, 20–1, 296.

[87] *Episcopal Acts*, op. cit. 237.

on a Welsh tenantry in the eastern half of the lordship.[88] Elsewhere, the colonists established new settlements of their own in
a countryside which was, even by medieval standards, thinly
populated. Few of them have left a direct record of their
activity. It is only in a rare moment of eloquence that a
Glamorgan charter records the achievement of Geoffrey
Sturmy who 'built his township in the wilderness which no one
had previously ploughed'.[89] It is rather the landscape itself
and the map which speak most eloquently of the enterprise of
these men: many of the secondary, if not the primary, settlements of southern Gower and southern Pembroke (to name but
the two most obvious districts) must have been founded on
virgin lands in the twelfth and thirteenth centuries; and place-
names such as Carew Newton, Newton near Manorbier (both
in Pembroke), New House in Narberth and Newton Nottage
(Glamorgan) likewise proclaim the role of English settlers in
extending the map of human settlement in the March. These
men were colonists in more than one sense.

Yet an immigration movement on the scale that we have
posited could hardly be effected without at least some displace-
ment of the native population. This is indeed precisely what
we would have expected in the case of an immigration movement which followed in the wake of a military conquest. It is
the post-1282 lordships which here again provide the most
telling evidence. In Dyffryn Clwyd the Welsh tenants of
Garthlegfa were expelled in order to accommodate the wishes
of the lord for a park and of his burgesses for common pasture.[90]
In Bromfield and Yale the Welsh freemen of Hewlington and
Eyton—both of them, significantly, Anglo-Saxon names which
bear witness to an earlier alien colonization of this district—
were compelled to exchange their lands in order to make room
for new English settlers.[91] Most remarkable of all were the
territorial policies undertaken in Denbigh to provide for the
new colonists.[92] Several vills were deliberately converted into
exclusively English settlements and the lands partitioned among

---

[88] S.B.Y., fol. 20–fol. 33.   [89] *Cartae*, I, no. 152.
[90] S.C. 2/218/4, m. 20, m. 21 (1354, but referring to the time of Reginald Grey,
d. 1308).
[91] S.B.Y., fol. 37–fol. 39.
[92] This subject is now definitively analysed in D. Huw Owen, 'The Englishry of
Denbigh: An English Colony in Medieval Wales', *T.C.S.* (1974–5), 57–76.

the colonists. Among such vills were Brynbagl, Berain, Gweny-
nog, Ystrad Cynon and Lleweni, all of them occupying some of
the richest arable lands in North Wales. The character of the
English takeover is vividly illustrated in the large vill of
Lleweni, the most extensive English preserve in the lordship.
Only one favoured Welshman, Iorwerth ap Llywarch, was

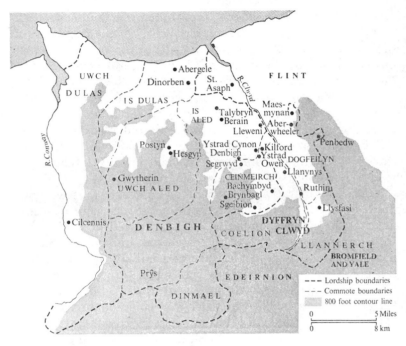

Map 5
The Lordships of Denbigh and Dyffryn Clwyd

allowed to retain his lands in the vill; the remainder of its rich
agricultural land was divided among 120 or so colonists, in
holdings ranging from a few to several hundred acres. Even in
some other vills where Welshmen were not expelled, English
farmers took over a significant share of the land: in Segrwyd
they held some 1,150 acres, in Bachymbyd 450 acres. All in all
in the two commotes of Ceinmeirch and Isaled, the major focus
of their settlement, English immigrants by 1334 held at least
10,000 acres of land.

The *Survey of Denbigh* of 1334 is revealingly frank about the way that this territorial takeover had been effected. Much of the land so granted to English settlers had been declared escheat for one of two reasons, either because the native tenants had died in revolt against the English regime (*contra pacem*) or through failure to perform the services due from the land (*pro defectu serviciorum*). Where the law of escheat failed, the lord invoked his right of compulsory exchange in order to effect his policy of territorial resettlement. Lleweni may serve again by way of example: such of its native freeholders as survived the rigorous scrutiny of their titles by the law of escheat were nevertheless required to surrender their lands and accept instead escheated lands in nearby vills such as Ereifiad, Taldrach, Llechryd and Tywysog. The fate of the unfree native tenantry was far worse: such of them as had escaped the confiscation of their tenements had their lands arbitrarily seized. They were, it is true, compensated for the lands so seized; but in exchange for fertile acres in Lleweni they were allotted an equal acreage in Prŷs—some fifteen miles away, over 1,500 feet above sea level, in the bleak mountain pasturelands of Hiraethog. It was an exchange whose scrupulous precision in terms of mathematical equivalents makes its transparent injustice in terms of the quality of the land exchanged more outrageous, even calculated.

The process of alien settlement in Denbigh after 1282 may have been more purposefully and thoroughly effected than in many other Marcher lordships; but it does give us a measure of insight into the ways an immigrant population was introduced into many areas of the Welsh March. It was a process which must often have been accompanied by arbitrary expulsion and which even lacked the pretence of compensation as at Denbigh. In the case of southern Pembroke, the native chronicler remarked that the Flemish settlers 'drove thence the rightful inhabitants who have lost their rightful land and their rightful place from that day to this'.[93] In Kidwelly, likewise, the establishment of an 'Englishry' or a 'foreignry', as it was alternatively called, was made possible only by the dispossession of the native inhabitants: when the area comes within

---

[93] *Brut y Tywysogyon* (*Red Book of Hergest Version*), ed. T. Jones (Cardiff, 1955), 52–5.

the purview of the documents in the late thirteenth century the names of its tenants—Colman, Russell, Aylward, Hogge—and of its local landmarks—Langelande, Revehulle, Fursdoune, Brodeford, Markway—reveal the thoroughness of the English colonization of the district.[94] It was a colonization prompted both by military and strategic considerations and by the attractions of good arable land. The rationale behind it was expressed clearly, if rather brutally, in the authorization granted to Payn Turberville, lord of Coety (Glamorgan), in 1316, immediately after the revolt of Llywelyn Bren, to remove the Welsh to the mountains and to inhabit the plains with Englishmen for the greater safety of the lands.[95] That same purpose could be achieved by rather less drastic means but once again with a clear eye on the problem of security: in north Wales Englishmen were encouraged by the king to secure the leases of escheated Welsh lands 'in order to intermingle (*enterlarder*) with the Welsh so . . . that the peace will be better assured and security improved by Englishmen so placed (*intermedlez*)'.[96] This was no administrative pipe-dream, for the evidence from Denbigh shows how the English position within the lordship was, no doubt deliberately, consolidated by granting the majority of escheated lands in key areas to English settlers.[97] The Welsh, for their part, were well aware that foreign colonization was often but an euphemism for dispossession at swordpoint: a Glamorgan Welshman could still recall bitterly in 1365 how Robert Fitzhamon had conquered the lands of his ancestors some 270 years previously, while in 1379 Welshmen of north-east Wales sought redress in Parliament for the wrongful expulsion of their ancestors by Reginald Grey almost a century earlier.[98] The March of Wales must have been full of such bitter memories. Conquest and colonization had left their usual political bequest: a group of disinherited and a mythology of disinheritance.

The impact of the settlers in the March obviously varied from place to place and from one period to another. In some areas they had come to form the great majority of the popula-

---

[94] N.L.W. Muddlescombe Deeds, *passim*; D.L. 42/1, fol. 36ᵛ (pre-1274).
[95] *C. Chancery Warrants 1244–1326*, 448.
[96] *C.C.R. 1339–41*, 251.
[97] *S.D.*, cxv.
[98] *Cartae*, IV, no. 1027; *Rot. Parl.*, III, 70a. (Cf. S.C. 8/113, no. 5628).

tion; elsewhere their settlements were but small islands in predominantly Welsh areas. Some of them by 1300 belonged to families which had settled in the March for two centuries or more; others were only hesitant first or second generation immigrants. Some of them came as individual pioneers prospecting for a fortune; others came in small local bands, as probably did the Flemings of Pembroke, or in family groups, as may have been the case with the Pigots or Swynemores in Denbigh or the Pulestons in Bromfield and Yale. In terms of social position and territorial wealth the settlers ranged over a wide spectrum, from customary tenants with but a few acres of land to gentry families who turned easily in the circles of English county society. The immigré tenants of the new lordship of Denbigh, for example, included both rich colonists such as Henry of Clitheroe and William Swynemore with estates of several hundred acres each and small peasant settlers such as the sixty Englishmen in Lleweni whose territorial endowment was less than ten acres each. Some settlers found the prospect of life in Wales less than attractive: Sir William le Vavassour had sold his estates in Denbigh by 1290, while John the son of Thomas del Peek who surrendered his holding in Efnechtyd (Dyffryn Clwyd) in 1332 'because of poverty' was not the first or last immigrant to discover that Wales was not a land of easy fortunes.[99]

On these wide divergences and even contradictions in the history of the 'foreign English' of the March we must insist; they are cardinal to an understanding of the evolution of Marcher society within and beyond the fourteenth century. Yet, in spite of such divergences, the validity of the contemporary classification of the rural inhabitants of the March into English and Welsh still stands. That the 'foreign English' regarded themselves as a distinct group we have already emphasized. Their cohesion as a group arose out of the obvious bonds of status, blood and language, out of the shared ambitions and common fears of a settler people. Their separate status— in spite of all social and economic differences—was officially recognized by the Marcher lords in the form of separate taxes, separate courts, separate laws, exemption from Welsh dues and the enjoyment of racial privileges.[100] They along with the

[99] D.L. 42/1, fol. 33; S.C. 2/216/12, m. 27.   [100] See above pp. 306–18.

burgesses were the men whom the lord turned to most readily for support in maintaining his authority. They formed an obvious home-guard force for the lord in the event of a native rebellion. Military obligation was a prominent feature of the tenurial obligations of English colonists in Wales. That was as true of ordinary peasants as it was of feudal landholders; in Radnor the 'free foreign tenants' each had to find a footman with a lance in time of war; the tenants of the Englishry of Bromfield and Yale were obliged to go to war at their own expense with the lord for the defence of the lordship; the small freehold estates of southern Pembroke 'were almost invariably held in return for military service'.[101] It was upon their shoulders as much as upon those of professional soldiers that the maintenance of English rule in Wales fell in the dark days of Glyn Dŵr's rebellion. The resistance to the Welsh rebels in Kidwelly was organized by Walter Morton, in Hay by John Bedell, in Brecon by John Havard; all three were members of well-established settler families who farmed in the vicinity of their respective towns and who stood to lose all if the revolt succeeded.[102] While the English position in the March remained precarious it was inevitable that the English community should in some measure keep itself to itself. The substantial estate granted to Alexander Sywell, one of the first English settlers in Dyffryn Clwyd, passed by a series of settler marriages to the Sprottons, the Crevequers, the Curteys and eventually to the Thelwalls; or, to take an example from among the lower ranks of immigrant families, Hugh Staleworthman, a first or second generation settler farmer holding twenty acres of land in Dyffryn Clwyd, married his daughter Alice to Roger Hoper (the English bailiff of Coelion commote) and his son Nicholas to Margery daughter of Howell Lytham. A few examples, easily as they could be multiplied, do not add up to statistical proof; but the court-rolls of Dyffryn Clwyd at least leave the impression that the colonial community was a community of inter-marriage for two or three generations after the original settlement. That impression is sustained by the observation of

[101] *C.I.P.M.*, iv, no. 41; S.B.Y., fol. 21 ᵛ; B. E. Howells in *N.L.W.J.* 9 (1955–6), 320.

[102] R. R. Davies, 'The Bohun and Lancaster Lordships in Wales in the Fourteenth and Early Fifteenth Centuries', D.Phil. thesis (Univ. of Oxford, 1965), 288–9.

George Owen on the English and Welsh communities of his native Pembrokeshire in Elizabethan times: 'these two nacions keepe eche from dealinges with the other, as mere strangers, so that the meaner sorte of people will not nor doth not usuallye joyne together in mariage'.[103]

The differences which George Owen so clearly observed between English and Welsh, settler and native, must have been far sharper two or three centuries earlier. To some of those differences—in laws, in tenure and in customs—we have already referred. Even as farmers the English settlers may have been distinctive in several respects. Most of the differences in farming methods which may be detected in later periods between the predominantly Welsh and predominantly English areas of Wales are, it is true, most immediately and plausibly to be explained in terms of the geographical and climatic differences between the regions in question. As far as we know, there was little in the agricultural skills or the technological methods of the immigrant settlers of Wales to set them firmly apart from native farmers. Yet in medieval society, the movement of men was the most potent agency of cultural diffusion, in agriculture as in other aspects of life. We have already referred to the introduction of customary acres, some of which were similar to those current in the English regions whence the Marcher colonists may have emigrated; in Denbigh we are indeed expressly told that its first English lord, Henry Lacy, earl of Lincoln, formally declared the perch of the lordship to be of 21 feet, as measured by his own feet.[104] We have also referred briefly to the role played by the settlers in the expansion of human settlement in south Wales. The evidence from Denbigh is once more particularly valuable, for there the late date of foreign immigration and the precise detail provided by the great *Survey* of 1334 help to pinpoint the achievement of the colonists. What the *Survey* reveals is that the English newcomers did well not only through the lord's generosity but also by dint of their own enterprise. In Brynbagl, eight English tenants settled there by Earl Thomas of Lancaster (d. 1322) proceeded to assart 160 acres from the waste; their neighbours in Cerneny-fed likewise won over 400 acres of arable from the waste in twenty years; in Ereifiad two-thirds of the land reclaimed from

[103] *Penbrokshire*, I, 39.   [104] *S.D.*, 2.

the waste was in the hands of English farmers in 1334.[105] Where
the explanation for such enterprise lies is impossible to know;
but it may not be altogether idle to speculate that it may partly
lie in the readiness of immigrant tenants, more accustomed to
permanent cultivation and perhaps to greater pressure on
arable resources, to win lands from the waste. It is in such
differences of attitudes and traditions that the English settlers
probably made their most substantial contribution to the
agrarian life of the March. The Flemings who settled in Pembroke, so Gerald of Wales tells us, were well versed in 'commerce
and the woollen industry'.[106] In view of their provenance there
is no reason to doubt his claim; it may indeed help to explain
in some measure the importance of the ports of Pembroke in the
commercial life of Wales in the Middle Ages. In more general
terms the alien settlers of the March may have been more
alive, as the Cistercians were, to the commercial potential of
Wales's pastoral resources than were the native Welsh themselves. We have already remarked on the enterprise of the
Marcher lords themselves in this respect and it may be significant that some of the largest tenant flocks of which record
survives were those of English settlers. Alan Sutton, a modest
English tenant in Dyffryn Clwyd, had a flock of almost 100
sheep, John Helpston the mason 152 sheep; the prior of Ruthin
we know sold a fair amount of wool to Chester merchants;[107]
while in the Englishry of Kidwelly men such as Morys Nicol
had over 360 sheep producing what Leland regarded as 'the
best woolle of Hye Walys'.[108] It is to George Owen that we
turn once more for a final example of the possibly divergent
agricultural practices of native and settler in the March. In his
Description of Penbrokshire he observed that the farmers in the
Welsh half of the county grew far more oats than those in the
English half. Keen farmer and social observer that he was, he
searched for an explanation: he found it in part in the different
quality of the land in the two districts but also (since this
explanation was by no means adequate) in the intense conservatism of Welsh agricultural practice—'the use thereof of

---

[105] ibid. 21–5, 109–16.   [106] *Opera*, vi, 83.
[107] S.C. 2/216/4, m. 28 (1323); 219/5, m. 19ᵛ (1368).
[108] J.I. 1/1152, m. 6ᵛ; J.I. 1/1153, m. 26; John Leland, *Itinerary of Wales*, ed.
L. T. Smith, 60.

auncient tyme and beinge brought upp therein [they] are hardlie drawn to alter their Custome'.[109]

George Owen's explanation may or may not convince us; but it is surely significant that an acute social commentator such as he should still seek to explain some of the contrasts within Marcher society in late-Elizabethan days in terms of the impact of the alien colonization of the twelfth and thirteenth centuries. We may have drawn unduly on George Owen's evidence. We have done so in part because he sheds light on areas of social analysis where our own documentation—concerned as it is with law, institutions and tenure—is unhelpful; but we have done so also because his pages remind us how strong the contrasts between the two communities, the English and the Welsh, remained even in the Pembrokeshire of his day. Those contrasts must, perforce, have been even more marked in the March two or three centuries earlier. Such contrasts, it is true, varied immensely from one part of the March to another; they were contrasts, as we shall see, which were already being reduced by the processes of co-existence.[110] We may be in danger of exaggerating them; but, in view of the gradual fusion of English and Welsh, we are in greater danger of under-estimating them. The March in the fourteenth century—in a sense more so than ever before and certainly more so than ever after—was a land of two races.

[109] *Penbrokshire*, I, 61.
[110] See below pp. 443–56.

THE FREEMEN

NATIVE society in the March of Wales in the fourteenth century was preponderantly a society of freemen. Such a bald statement requires immediate qualification. It needs, as usual, to be qualified geographically: there were parts of the March, notably the coastal lowlands of Gwent, Glamorgan and Pembroke, where bond and customary tenants, both English and Welsh, appear to have been in a clear numerical majority.[1] It also needs to be qualified chronologically: there is much to be said for the view, vigorously advanced in recent years by some historians, that prior to the twelfth century the population of Wales was predominantly bond and that this bond population supported a small ruling caste of warrior freemen. It also needs to be qualified by reference to the character of our documentation: seignorial evidence is no sure guide to the actual composition of the population (as opposed to the rent-paying tenantry) and in particular it may lead us to overestimate the number of freemen by its disregard of other important social groups, especially bond under-tenants, landless labourers, cottagers and craftsmen. We recognize fully the force of these qualifications; yet, within the limits of the evidence, it can hardly be denied that by the fourteenth century native Welsh society in the March was preponderantly a society of freemen. Even a brief glimpse at the evidence sustains such a contention: there were some lordships, such as Clifford and Builth, where the absence of villeinage was specifically commented upon by contemporary officials; in certain upland districts such as the Welshry of Hay lordship the lord had no bond tenants; in some lowland lordships, such as Whitecastle, which had long since been subjected to Anglo-Norman rule, the acreage of free land exceeded that of bond land and the number of free tenants that of customary tenants; in a thoroughly Welsh lordship such as Denbigh well

[1] W. Rees, *South Wales and the March 1284–1415*, 144.

over half of the townships in the lay lord's rental were exclusively in the hands of free tenants and another quarter were shared by free and bond communities;[2] in neighbouring Dyffryn Clwyd contributions towards a communal subsidy indicate that the free Welsh tenantry, in wealth though not necessarily in numbers, represented sixty per cent of the tenants of the lordship.[3] English historians as they pursue their studies towards the Welsh borderland have noted a sharp increase in the proportion of free tenants in the population and an equally sharp contrast with the social structure of the manorialized districts of England.[4] Even the most vigorous exponents of the view that the number of bondmen in Wales had been 'far more numerous in earlier centuries' are driven to concede that by the thirteenth century, in the lands under the control of the native princes of Gwynedd, they can posit a bond population of only 'approximately one-third the size of the total population'.[5] By the fourteenth century in many parts of the March such an estimate would probably err on the side of generosity.

Welsh freemen were neither a distinguishable economic class nor an identifiable social group. Yet they shared certain basic features in greater or lesser degree throughout the March and indeed throughout Wales as a whole. In the first place they were united by a pride in their status. In a legally hierarchical society such as that of medieval Wales no distinction was more elemental than the distinction of status. It was by reference to this distinction that a man's obligations and privileges, the value of his oath and of his life and his legal standing were determined.[6] Furthermore this bond of status in good measure over-rode the many regional differences within Wales. 'Every

---

[2] Ibid. 143 (Clifford and Builth); Cardiff Central Library, Brecon Documents, 2; D.L. 29/633/10317 (Hay, 1340, 1398); D.L. 43/13/8 (Whitecastle, 1386); D. H. Owen, 'Tenurial and Economic Developments in North Wales in the Twelfth and Thirteenth Centuries', *W.H.R.* 6 (1972), 118 (Denbigh, 1334).

[3] S.C. 2/219/6, m. 23 (1369). According to the incomplete rental of 1324 the composition of the tenant population of Dyffryn Clwyd, excluding the entirely bond districts of Aberwheeler and Penbedw, was as follows: free Welsh: 268; English: 100; customary and bond: 184.

[4] R. H. Hilton, *The Decline of Serfdom in Medieval England* (1969), 23–4.

[5] G. R. J. Jones, 'The Tribal System in Wales: A Re-assessment in the Light of Settlement Studies', *W.H.R.* 1 (1961), 125.

[6] D. Jenkins, *Cyfraith Hywel* (Llandysul, 1970), ch. II. In Dyffryn Clwyd in 1317 damages of £24 were awarded for the maiming of a free Welshman 'on account of the respect due to him and his kinsfolk': S.C. 2/215/76, m. 5.

Welshman born to Welsh parents (*Kymro vamtat*)', so declared the native law texts, 'will be an innate gentleman (*bonheddig cynhwynawl*), without taint of servility . . .'[7] At a basic level, Welsh free society was one.

Likewise the dues and obligations of Welsh freemen were, in spite of local variations, broadly similar in character throughout the March—notably suit of court, military service and contributions towards various communal renders. These renders display a bewildering range of local differences in terminology, incidence and method of collection; but beneath such differences it is not difficult to detect a common pattern in their character. In the first place, the terminology of the renders at a generic level was very much the same from one end of the March to another; it drew heavily on such Welsh words as *arian* (money), *cylch* (circuit), *porthiant* (food render), *gwestfa* (hospitality due), *commorth* (aid), *treth* (tax) and *twnc* (a commuted food-render). Such terms indicate clearly enough the original character of these dues: they were renders given towards the upkeep of the lord, his court, his officers and his horses. The Marcher lords, like their Welsh *antecessores*, received renders of cattle, corn and eggs from the free kindreds of their lordships.[8] Furthermore even with the transition from native to foreign lordship, these renders continued to preserve some of their original character. They were, as we have insisted earlier, basically recognitions of lordship not rents for land; they were, to borrow a contemporary phrase, 'live services' (*viva servicia*)[9] and were clearly distinguishable from land rents (*redditus ad acras*). Since they were tributes rather than land rents, their amount was in no way regulated by acreage. If they were individually assessed by the lord's officers that assessment was likely to be based on the individual's goods rather than on his land.[10] In fact, such individual assessments were late developments, for in origin the renders owed by Welsh freemen were communal dues, assessed either on the free community of the lordship as a whole (as was the case with the *commorth* of

---

[7] *Llyfr Blegywryd*, 58. Cf. *Llyfr Iorwerth*, §98.

[8] As in Cydewain (S.C. 6/1206/1; 1209/1), Brecon (D.L. 29/671/10810, m. 4), Chirk (N.L.W. Chirk Castle Accounts, D. 27) and Dyffryn Clwyd (S.C. 2/219/2, m. 10).

[9] The phrase is frequently used in *S.D.*, e.g. pp. 219, 224, 227, 278.

[10] See above pp. 133–6.

cows in Brecon, Builth, Clun, Oswestry and elsewhere) or on its constituent descent-groups (*gwelyau, gafaelion, progenies*). We are given a glimpse of the communal character of these renders in the records of meetings of the local communities of the March in their parish churches to apportion a share of the puture-dues on each individual 'according to his portion'.[11] It is true that by the fourteenth century many of these renders had lost their original *raison d'être* and were retained for the purpose of fiscal convenience and administrative conservatism. Some of these communal renders, it is also true, were shared by free and bond tenants alike; but others—such as the food render of the prince (*pastus principis*) in Denbigh or the aid of cows (*commorth*) in Builth—were confined to freemen. Indeed, payment of such distinctively free dues came to be regarded as one of the proofs of free Welsh status. Not only were they distinctively free dues; they were also distinctively Welsh dues. It was specifically from the dues of Welsh freemen that English settlers in the March claimed exemption when they leased former Welsh land.[12]

Free Welshmen were united in the legal status which they claimed and in the dues which they paid; but they were even more profoundly united in their belief that their freedom was a function of their nobility of blood. In the social terminology of medieval Wales the concepts of nobility, freedom and descent were inextricably interwoven. The common Welsh word for a freeman, *uchelwr*, was rendered in Latin texts as *optimas* or *nobilis*;[13] it is a translation which makes evident that in early Welsh society, as in that of much of medieval Europe, nobility and freedom were interdependent concepts.[14] Nobility and freedom alike in turn depended on descent, on blood. Here we come to the heart of the medieval Welsh notion of freedom.

[11] See, for example, S.C. 2/218/10, m. 13ᵛ (three vills fined for not coming to Llangynhafal church to divide the puture of foresters, 1362); 219/4, m. 23ᵛ (community of Coelion appoint five apportioners of puture who are to meet at Efnechtyd church, 1367).

[12] S.B.Y., fol. 20 (1391, communal exemption); N.L.W. Peniarth 404 D. fol. 105, (early fifteenth century, individual exemptions).

[13] *The Latin Texts of the Welsh Laws*, ed. H. D. Emanuel (Cardiff, 1967), *passim*; cf. Giraldus Cambrensis, *Opera*, VI, 166 ('nobiles qui Kambrice Hucheilwer quasi superiores viri vocantur'). In later documents *uchelwyr* was occasionally translated as 'franklins' or 'free tenants': N.L.W. Peniarth MS. 404 D., fol. 96 (1450); B.L. Add. 46546, fol. 73 (late fifteenth century).

[14] L. Genicot, 'La noblesse au moyen-âge dans l'ancienne Francie', *Annales* 17 (1961), 1–22.

Status was dependent neither on wealth nor on land. On that issue Welsh jurists and Marcher doomsmen were agreed: the jurists gave it as their opinion that even a landless man did not forfeit his innate gentility of blood; the doomsmen of Bromfield and Yale likewise declared that the son of a free tenant whose father had disposed of all his land nevertheless retained his status (*condicio*) as a free tenant.[15] It could hardly be otherwise, for status was a function of birth and of descent. Nowhere is this more evident, as we shall see, than in the sphere of the tenure and inheritance of land. Here suffice it to say that no Welshman could aspire to the position of a proprietor (Welsh, *priodor*; Latin, *proprietarius*)[16] until his male ancestors had occupied the land for three generations before him and that the title of his descendants to that land would be based on membership of an agnatic descent-group, the *gwely* or the *gafael*.[17] The *gwely* is indeed the immediate badge of identity of Welsh free tenure in most parts of the March—not only in Denbigh, and Bromfield and Yale but equally in Caus, Radnor, Blaenllyfni, Talgarth and the lands of the bishop of St. David's.[18]

Since free status was a function of blood and birth, kinship was the other side of the coin to status in medieval Wales. It is, of course, this obvious relationship between kinship and status which explains why observers from at least the time of Gerald of Wales onwards were struck by Welshmen's preoccupation, indeed obsession, with genealogy and their 'overmuch boastying of the Nobilitie of their stocke'.[19] It is true that within the period of historical evidence the ties of kinship were but one of the several relationships which formed the social cement of medieval Welsh society. It is also as well to recognize that the 'public' documents will allow at best but brief and partial glimpses of the essentially 'private' world of kinship ties. Yet such evidence as we have leaves us in no doubt that kin obligations still played a major role in Marcher society in the fourteenth century. The

[15] *Llyfr Iorwerth*, §87; S.B.Y., fol. 173ᵛ (1366).
[16] The terms *proprietarius* and *uchelwr* were used interchangeably, e.g. S.C. 2/222/5, m. 15, m. 26ᵛ (Dyffryn Clwyd, 1446–8).
[17] Below pp. 359–62.
[18] See briefly B.L. Add. Charter 20,403 (Caus Welshry, 1370); *C.I.P.M.*, IV, no. 41 (Radnor, 1301); *C.C.R. 1330–3*, 404 (Blaenllyfni, 1332); B.L. Egerton Roll 8709 (Talgarth, 1356); *The Black Book of St. David's*, ed. J. W. Willis-Bund (Cymmrodorion Record Series 5, 1902) *passim*; *Valor Ecclesiasticus*, IV, 379.
[19] Quoted in F. Jones, 'An Approach to Welsh Genealogy', *T.C.S.* (1948), 392.

paternal and maternal kindred up to the fourth degree (second cousins), at the very least, still received and paid monetary compensation (*galanas*) for homicide in certain parts of the March.[20] It was not unknown for the 'lineage and affinity' of a man to be bound over with him to maintain the peace, while the policy of holding men in custody as a guarantee of the good behaviour of their kinsmen was a recognized procedure for keeping the peace in March and Principality alike.[21] Kinsmen might be called upon to appoint a guardian for a minor of their blood or to determine the precise relationship (if any) between a plaintiff and defendant allegedly of the same stock;[22] they might be called upon to warrant a grant of land made by one of their kinsmen or to disclaim any title that they might have to the land in respect of blood relationship;[23] likewise they might receive a grant of land as a corporate group of kinsmen;[24] they might even apparently choose a man to act on behalf of the kindred in the lord's army.[25] These examples, to which many others could be added, serve to remind us that in fourteenth-century Marcher society, kinship obligations were not merely a matter of family affection and social conventions; they were, at least in certain directions, precisely specified and legally binding. In no direction were kinship ties more precisely specified or more obviously fundamental than in the field of land tenure and land inheritance. In a rural society, where the means of livelihood and the acquisition of wealth are largely determined by the distribution of land, few subjects are so central to social analysis as the impact of kinship customs on the inheritance and division of land.

'All the above-named tenants of the stock of Rhys Sais (*de progenie Rees*) . . . hold lands in the vills of Ruabon, Marchwiel, Gwersyllt, Bersham, Acton, Erlas and Sutton, as co-parceners (*tanquam participes*), of the Earl of Surrey by homage and

---

[20] R. R. Davies, 'The Survival of the Bloodfeud in Medieval Wales', *History* 54 (1966), 338–57.

[21] *The Court Rolls of the Lordship of Ruthin*, ed. R. A. Roberts, 42; R. R. Davies, art. cit. 349.

[22] S.R.O. 552/1/2, m. 9; 30, m. 4 (Clun, 1333, 1399).

[23] *Cartae*, I, nos. 126, 130; I, no. 561; III, no. 731 (twelfth–thirteenth centuries).

[24] See, for example, the grant of land to the heirs of Llywelyn and Gwrared ap Cuheilyn of *c.* 1270: *Penbrokshire*, II, 447–8.

[25] G. Roberts, *Aspects of Welsh History* (Cardiff, 1969), 183.

fealty'.[26] This entry from the Extent of Bromfield and Yale of 1391, an entry which could be readily paralleled from other Marcher surveys, focuses attention on one of the cardinal features of free, and in some measure unfree, landholding in medieval Wales. Title to land and its appurtenances was dependent on membership of a patrilineal descent-group. That descent-group or lineage was normally known as a *gwely* (L. *lectus*, E. bed) or *gafael* (L. *gavella*, E. holding).[27] This descent-group normally, but not invariably, took its name from the ancestor, eponymous or not, from whom all members of the group claimed descent in the male line. It was in respect of membership of such a descent-group that an individual free Welshman was entitled to a share of 'hereditary' or 'old' land as it was sometimes called (*terra de hereditate, terra antiqua*); the ultimate action for claiming such land according to Welsh law was appropriately enough termed an action 'of kin and descent' (*ach ac edryf*). It was by virtue of his membership of the descent-group that the freeman likewise laid claim to his share of the meadowland, pasture, waste and rights in mills and churches appurtenant to his descent-group. It was in respect of his membership of his descent-group likewise that he was expected to make his contribution towards the communal dues and renders owed by that descent group. Since the individual's claim to a share in the arable and its appurtenances was his by descent, he had no absolute right in the land; he held it as it were on trust as a member of the descent group, *de progenie*. This meant that he had no right to effect an outright alienation of the land; his power of alienation was restricted to a temporary lease of the land. If he died without an heir within the prescribed degrees, it was a bundle of rights and inheritance (*jus et hereditas*), rather than the land as such, which would be sold;[28] should his patrimony escheat through felony or by failure to perform services, it was his stake in the claims of his descent-group which reverted to the lord.[29] In such a society to be born

---

[26] S.B.Y., fol. 131.

[27] I am well aware that the original meaning of the word *gwely* may have been different; but in fourteenth-century surveys its usage appears to correspond to the anthropological term 'descent-group'.

[28] S.R.O. 552/1/1, m. 6 (Clun, 1329); N.L.W. Wynnstay 100/202; Plas yn Cefn 1562, 1583 (Denbigh, 1394–1444).

[29] As is evident from *S.D.*, *passim*.

into a descent-group was the key to gentility and land alike; that is why the contrast between those who were 'of the stock' (*de progenie*) and 'outside' of it (*extra progeniem*)—a contrast used in a survey of Ewyas Lacy—was such a profound one.[30]

We can grasp the role of the descent-group in relation to land tenure and to the assessment of tributes most securely if we proceed by example. It is chosen from the rich evidence of the lordship of Bromfield, alias Maelor Gymraeg. Most of the freemen of the area claimed descent, in their more modest moments and specifically for the purpose of land inheritance, from lineage-founders of the early twelfth century. Whether the genealogical claims were or were not historically accurate is in some measure beside the point; societies in which such lineages occupy a prominent position are adept at genealogical fictions and manipulations.[31] The importance of such genealogical records is to provide a quasi-historical explanation and validation of kinship ties and thereby of title to land. No better example can be chosen by way of illustration than that of the lineage of Madog ap Llywelyn ap Gruffudd, a leading *uchelwr* of Bromfield who died in 1331.[32] He was of the lineage of Elidir (*de progenie Elidir*); that is, he was descended in the male line from Elidir ap Rhys Sais who probably lived in the early twelfth century and from whom, correctly or not, many of the Welsh free men of Bromfield traced their descent.[33] In the case of Madog ap Llywelyn historical evidence enables us to trace his own descendants over the generations. Madog's great-great-grandson, John Eyton, lived in the late fifteenth century: his name reveals that, like so many of his social equals, he had succumbed to the English habit of adopting a surname in place of a patronymic but this in no way diminished his pride at being a member of the stock of Elidir. When Gutun Owain, one of the best-informed of all Welsh poet-genealogists, came to write John Eyton's elegy he referred to him as 'the deer of Elidir' and

[30] Quoted in B. P. Evans, 'The Family of Mortimer', Ph.D. thesis (Univ. of Wales, 1934), 463, n. 3.

[31] Cf. I. M. Lewis, 'Force and Fission in Northern Somali Lineage Structure', *American Anthropologist* 63 (1961), 94–112.

[32] See above pp. 205, 289.

[33] A. N. Palmer and E. Owen, *History of Ancient Tenure of Land in Wales and the Marches*, 44–52, 145–8; *Early Welsh Genealogical Tracts*, ed. P. C. Bartrum (Cardiff, 1966), 119.

as 'the head of the landed inheritance and retinue of the stock of Elidir'.[34] The poet was not thereby indulging in poetic extravaganza nor was he merely pandering to a nostalgic taste for genealogy; he was drawing attention to John Eyton's lineage and thereby to his claim to nobility of blood. Furthermore John Eyton's lineage was also his title deed to land. It was as a descendant of Elidir ap Rhys Sais and of Elidir's son, Meilir, that John Eyton and his forebears throughout the fourteenth and fifteenth centuries laid claim to their lands in Maelor Gymraeg. It was also in respect of their membership of the descent-group that they paid a fixed render to the new English lords of Bromfield and Yale.[35] The social organism of the descent-group, the *gwely*, was employed as the unit for the assessment of seignorial dues and it was as a unit of seignorial convenience that the *gwely*—rather like the hide in Anglo-Saxon England and the *mansus* on the Continent—was fossilized for centuries in the surveys of Wales and the March.[36]

Welsh free society, in March and Principality, was organized into patrilineal descent-groups (*progenies*): that is our first proposition. Our second proposition is as follows: for purposes of land-inheritance and land-alienation the Welsh freeman's kindred was a four-generation agnatic group (*parentela*). This is a proposition which we may make most immediately clear by example. Madog ap Llywelyn ap Gruffudd ap Cadwgan, we have just seen, was of the stock of Elidir; he shared that distinction with scores of other freemen of Bromfield and it was the basis of his claim to nobility of blood and to a share of the land of his descent-group. But for more immediate purposes, notably those of succession to and alienation of land, he belonged to a much more restricted kin-group, composed of all the male descendants of his great-grandfather (Cadwgan) and extending thereby as far as his agnatic second cousins male. Now the distinction between these two groups—the descent-group

---

[34] *L'Oeuvre poétique de Gutun Owain*, ed. E. Bachéllery (Paris, 1951), II, no. xlviii.

[35] *The First Extent of Bromfield and Yale, A.D. 1315*, T. P. Ellis, 127 (Madog ap Llywelyn); S.B.Y., fol. 81ᵛ (Madog and Jenkin ab Ieuan ap Madog, 1391); L.R. 2/251, fol. 17ᵛ (John Eyton, 1445).

[36] Cf. M. Bloch, *French Rural Society*, 150–67; G. Duby, *The Early Growth of the European Economy* (1974), 33–6; T. M. Charles-Edwards, 'Kinship, Status and the Origins of the Hide', *Past and Present* 56 (1972), 3–33, D. Jenkins; 'A Lawyer looks at Welsh Land Law', *T.C.S.* (1967), II, 220–47.

(*progenies*) and the kindred (*parentela*)—is twofold. First, all the members of the kindred are also members of the descent-group, since both are agnatically constituted; but obviously not all the members of the descent-group are members of the kindred, since the latter is restricted to common agnatic descendants within four generations. Secondly, the focus of the two groups is different: the focus of the descent group is the ancestor (Elidir), the focus of the kindred is a living individual, *ego* (Madog ap Llywelyn). The former has a fixed point of reference in the past; the latter has a fixed point of reference in the present and one that is confined to *ego* and his brothers.[37] It is only by appreciating the differences between these two groups that we can properly understand the kinship-system and with it the land inheritance customs of medieval Wales.

The four-generation agnatic kindred, so we are assured, is of great antiquity in Celtic society.[38] Its practical importance in relation to land is vouched for in several ways in the Welsh law-texts.[39] This emphasis in the law-texts on the four-generation agnatic kindred is amply supported by evidence from the March in the fourteenth century. It was from this kindred that a man's co-parceners (*comporcionarii*) were drawn; they were his co-heirs (*co-heredes, comporcionarii de consanguinitate*) who could be summoned to defend the title to the land or to shoulder inheritance dues with him.[40] If a man died without a male heir of his body, it was his agnatic relatives within the third degree (that is, up to and including his second cousins) alone who could lay claim to his inheritance as of right: that seems to have been the rule in the March generally.[41] How the rule operated may be demonstrated by one example from the Dyffryn Clwyd evi-

[37] For this distinction see R. Fox, *Kinship and Marriage* (1967), 163–74.

[38] Charles-Edwards, art. cit. 25 ff., *idem*, 'Some Celtic Kinship Terms', *B.B.C.S.* 24 (1970–2), 107–12; D. A. Binchy, *Celtic and Anglo-Saxon Kingship* (Oxford, 1970), 25.

[39] Note especially *Llyfr Colan*, §589; *Welsh Medieval Law*, ed. A. W. Wade-Evans (Oxford, 1909), 51 quoted in *T.C.S.* (1967), II, 238, n. 70.

[40] For typical cases see S.C. 2/218/9, m. 22ᵛ (co-parceners to appear in case relating to land, 1361); 218/10, m. 18 (right of co-heirs to recover share of inheritance on payment of proportion of *ebediw*, 1362); for the phrase *comporcionarii de consanguinitate*, see *Black Book of St. David's*, 164.

[41] It is firmly stated in *S.D.*, 47. In Dyffryn Clwyd the kindred of a man extended to the fourth degree (e.g. S.C. 2/219/1, m. 23, 'de parentela sua infra quartum gradum'); but in this context the relatives in the fourth degree (i.e. the third cousins according to the canonical method of computation) appear to have

dence, an example unique only in that the genealogical evidence (here simplified) is complete and reliable:[42]

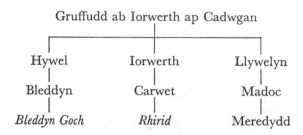

Gruffudd ab Iorwerth ap Cadwgan

Hywel	Iorwerth	Llywelyn
Bleddyn	Carwet	Madoc
Bleddyn Goch	*Rhirid*	Meredydd

When Meredydd ap Madoc ap Llywelyn died without a male heir of his body in 1332 his inheritance was divided between his second cousins, Bleddyn Goch ap Bleddyn and Rhirid ap Carwet. They were members of Meredydd's four-generation agnatic kindred; any male relative more distantly agnatically-related would not have been members of that kindred and would thereby be excluded from a claim to the land. Should a proprietor die without an heir within his kindred so defined, the land would escheat to the lord, to be sold[43] or to be offered to the nearest kinsman beyond the kindred on preferential terms.[44] Likewise Welsh law strictly decreed that no proprietor was to alienate land without the permission of the members of his kindred group. On that basis was built the policy of English kings and lords in Wales of prohibiting the outright buying and selling of Welsh land and forbidding unlicensed grants in fee or in mortgage except to a man's male co-heirs, that is his kindred.[45] Just as the *gwely* was fossilized for the sake of the administrative and fiscal convenience of the English lords, so likewise the kindred unit and its obligations were employed by them to control the market in Welsh land.

So far we have reviewed cursorily two cardinal features of the

been excluded by the definition. In both Denbigh and Dyffryn Clwyd, the four-generation agnatic kindred was the effective group for inheritance purposes.

[42] S.C. 2/215/72, m. 13; 216/12, m. 24ᵛ (1313, 1332).

[43] E.g., S.C. 2/219/5, m. 30ᵛ. (Inheritance of man dying without an heir of his kindred sold for £30: 1368.)

[44] As provided for in Denbigh (*S.D.*, 47) and Oswestry (B.L. Harleian 1970, fol. 82).

[45] S.B.Y., fol. 170; J. B. Smith in *W.H.R.* III (1966), 145–71; below pp. 407–10.

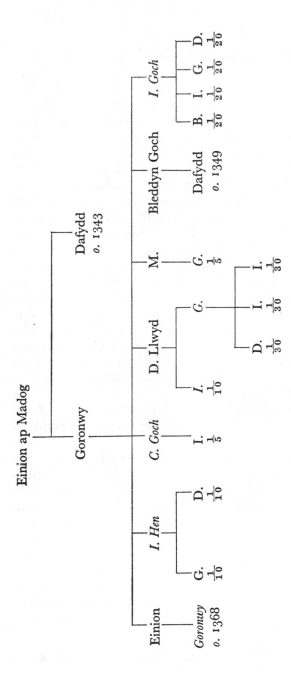

Einion ap Madog

o = died without surviving male heir of his body.
The seven heirs of Dafydd ap Bleddyn Goch (o. 1349) are indi-
    cated in italics.
The fractions represent the proportionate claims of the twelve
    heirs of Goronwy ab Einion (o. 1368).

kin system of medieval Wales as applied to land: title to land was determined by membership of descent-groups; inheritance of land was restricted within a four-generation agnatic kindred. Both these features of land tenure were profoundly affected by a third factor, the law of descent. That law was curtly defined in a contemporary extent as follows: 'land is to be divided among male coheirs'.[46] Such a brief statement requires to be amplified. In the first place sons born in and out of wedlock had an equal claim to a share of the inheritance, provided that the 'illegitimate 'sons had been avowed by their father. If direct male progeny (sons, grandsons etc.) survived, the patrimony (W. *treftadaeth*) was to be divided between them; failing such offspring, the land was divisible among male heirs up to the third degree. Division, *cyfran*, is the keystone of the Welsh law of descent. In one respect only was that principle compromised: beyond the first degree of relationship division was *per stirpes*, not *per capita*. That is, in the simplest of cases, if a man (A) were survived by two sons (B, C) and three grandsons (X, Y, Z) who were the children of another son (D) (who had predeceased him) his patrimony would theoretically be divided into thirds, one each for the two sons (B, C) and the third to be further divided between the three grandsons (X, Y, Z). It may be best once more to proceed by example from the Dyffryn Clwyd records, if only to reveal both the consequences and complications of *cyfran*.[47]

The seven sons of Goronwy ab Einion ap Madog were the victims of their parents' fertility; each had to be content with a seventh share of his patrimony. The impoverishment which such a division entailed was countered in some degree by the death of their uncle, Dafydd, without surviving male progeny in 1343 and likewise that of their nephew, Dafydd ap Bleddyn Goch, in 1349. It is, however, with the death of another member of the kindred, Goronwy ab Einion, in 1368 that we can best illustrate both the operation of the rule of partibility and the implementation of division *per stirpes*. His lands were divided between twelve persons: nine first cousins and three first cousins once

[46] *Extent of Chirkland, 1391–3*, 62.
[47] The major sources for this table are S.C. 2/217/8, m. 14ᵛ; 217/14, m. 25; 219/5, m. 17 (1343–68). For reasons of space I have referred to the majority of the kindred merely by the initial letters of their names.

removed (his farthest relations within the four-generation agnatic kindred). What is more they were, or should have been, divided unequally between the individual heirs in proportions which varied from 1/5th to 1/30th of Goronwy's inheritance. Whether land could be divided with such mathematical exactitude for practical purposes is, of course, another matter.

The case provides us with what is almost a *reductio ad absurdum* of the Welsh law of descent; it also compels us to consider very briefly the impact of such a law of descent and kinship principles on the economic structure and rural settlement pattern of the medieval March. In the eyes of Tudor observers, writing two or three generations after the statutory introduction of primogeniture with respect to land-succession in the so-called Act of Union 1536, *cyfran* or gavelkind was the prime explanation of the economic backwardness of Wales. Sir John Wynn in Denbighshire characterized it as 'the destruction of Wales' since it 'mangled' estates 'with division and subdivision'; his near-contemporary in Pembrokeshire, George Owen of Henllys, likewise remarked on the dread consequences of *cyfran*: 'the whole countrie was brought into smale peeces of ground and intermingled upp and downe with another, so as in every five or six acres you shall have ten or twelve owners'.[48] The litigants of the lordship of Elfael were even more alarmist and more mathematically precise in their calculations of the consequences of the custom: one small tenement, so they averred, became in three or four generations subdivided into thirty, forty or sometimes more parcels.[49] Their claim was no doubt prompted by the needs of special pleading; but both particular and general evidence from the March, notably from Dyffryn Clwyd, suggests that their case was exceptional rather than impossible. No individual instance is more telling than that of Iorwerth ap Cadwgan who probably lived *c.* 1220 and of whose male descendants we have a complete genealogical record in a court roll of 1313. Iorwerth had four sons, seven grandsons and nineteen great-grandsons. Such a replacement rate suggests that

---

[48] *History of the Gwydir Family*, ed. J. Ballinger (Cardiff, 1927), 14–16; *Penbrokshire*, I, 61. For a study of the impact of partibility on English medieval rural society see B. Dodwell, 'Holdings and Inheritance in Medieval East Anglia', *Ec.H.R.* 2nd ser. 20 (1967), 53–66.

[49] *Exchequer Proceedings (Equity) concerning Wales, Henry VIII—Elizabeth*, ed. E. G. Jones (Cardiff, 1939), 313.

within four generations he would, at a conservative estimate, have forty male descendants. Already in fact by 1313 the land which he had once claimed individually was divided between twenty-seven of his direct descendants. Overall figures of succession over a short period are not so impressive as individual examples over three or four generations; but they likewise confirm the impression of the consequences of *cyfran*. Table 1,

TABLE I

Succession to free Welsh holdings, Coelion commote
(Dyffryn Clwyd), 1341–50

| | Number of individuals succeeding | | | | | TOTAL |
	1	2	3	4	5	
Succession of son(s)	14	5	5	1	—	25
Succession of brother(s)	6	3	—	1	1	11
Succession of kinsman or kinsmen	9	2	2	3	2	18
Total of successions	29	10	7	5	3	54
Total of individuals succeeding	29	20	21	20	15	105

admittedly based on incomplete evidence, attempts to provide such overall figures of succession to land for a single commote in Dyffryn Clwyd over ten years. It reveals that in that period the land of fifty-four Welsh freemen passed to a total of 105 male heirs and that in twenty-five cases there was a multiple succession. It hardly confirms the worst fears of Tudor writers; but at least it indicates that the average number of male heirs succeeding to a free Welsh holding was almost exactly two, a figure supported from the evidence of the neighbouring commote of Llannerch (1329–49: deaths of forty-three free Welsh tenants; eighty-seven male heirs succeeding; twenty-two cases of multiple succession). If such an average rate of succession were maintained over four generations—and such a hypothesis assumes a steady population growth and a fixed male replacement ratio as well as the Welsh law of partibility—then by the end of that period a freeman's tenement and with it his claim to meadow, pasture, mills and churches could be divided between sixteen coheirs.

In a country where arable resources were in short supply, one of the likely results of such a law of partibility was to produce a countryside of open quilleted fields. George Owen, one of the most acute agrarian and social observers that Wales has produced, explained the relationship directly in such terms: 'this', he remarked *à propos* the practice of gavelkind, 'made the Countrie to remayne champion and without enclosures and hedging'.[50] It was of his native Pembrokeshire that he spoke, but his description could be applied, in greater or lesser measure, to many other districts of the March.[51] Evidence of open fields abounds, it is true, in those lowland areas of the March where foreign colonization had been considerable—in districts such as the foreignry of Kidwelly, where the documentary evidence of open-field husbandry is particularly good, or the Severn levels at Caldicot where open fields survived into modern times. Equally, however, the evidence of open-field husbandry in native Welsh districts is considerable. Many of the provisions of Welsh land law with regard to such issues as joint-ploughing (*cyfar*) and damages to crops are hardly comprehensible other than in terms of the prevalence of open-field agriculture, while detailed local studies of land-settlement and land-usage patterns in thoroughly Welsh districts such as Llysdulas in Anglesey, Llwydfaen in the Conway valley and Llanynys in Dyffryn Clwyd have amply confirmed the importance of open-field farming in Welsh society.[52] Contemporary title-deeds abound with details of Welsh quillets—*erwau* (acres), *drylliau* (fragments), *tiroedd* (lands), *clytiau* (pieces) and *lleiniau* (quillets), as they are variously called; and the names given to some of these quillets—such as *erw dwylath* (the two-yard acre), *erw dalar* (the headland acre) or *erw wythfed* (the eighth acre)—confirm the impression of small quillets distributed in open fields. So also do the detailed descriptions of those lands. When Iorwerth ap Hywel ap Gwyn, for example, wished to mortgage his land in

[50] *Penbrokshire*, I, 61. Cf. ibid. 178–80, 193–4 on the practice of 'rodvale' or 'rudvalle' in Pembrokeshire.

[51] On the subject of open fields in the March, see in particular Palmer and Owen, op. cit.; D. Sylvester, *The Rural Landscape of the Welsh Borderland*; and chapters by M. Davies and G. R. J. Jones in *Studies of Field Systems in the British Isles*, ed. A. R. H. Baker and R. A. Butlin (Cambridge, 1973).

[52] See especially T. Jones Pierce, *Medieval Welsh Society*, 87–101, 195–228 and G. R. J. Jones, 'The Llanynys Quillets: A Measure of Landscape Transformation in North Wales', *T.D.H.S.* 13 (1964), 133–58.

the 1340s he described it as twenty-four quillets (*landae*) in Acton Fawr (Bromfield) or when Ieuan ap Cynwrig ap Meurig sold out his land in the Dee valley in 1344 he was obliged to describe in detail twenty-seven quillets (*seliones, placeae, landae*).[53] Such a complex pattern of quillets may have been more obviously evident in the rich arable of the lowlands; in other parts of the March a *bocage* countryside and a pattern of temporary cultivation may well have been more common.

The consequences of gavelkind and of quilleted open fields often produced widely scattered holdings of land. Medieval farmers were acutely aware of variations in soil quality and in agricultural yield. Hence the concern to abide by the Welsh custom of partibility was tempered and refined by the need to give fairly comparable shares of lands of differing quality to each co-parcener. That need was satisfied in part by assigning to each proprietor, in addition to his stake in the arable, a share, in respect of his membership of a descent-group, in the common, wasteland, pasture and meadow. It was also satisfied in part by assigning to each freeholder a share in the various and often widely-dispersed lands of his descent group, much in the same way that the allocation of strips in open fields in parts of England appears to have been determined by the quality of the soil and the location of the land.[54] In Wales, however, such distribution was not confined to the open fields of a single village. The landed fortune of one Dafydd ab Einion, for example, was catalogued as follows in 1342: one messuage, one acre in Royton; one butt in Marchwiel; one messuage, sixteen selions in Gwersyllt; one acre in Trefydd Bychain.[55] Such an entry immediately focuses attention on the morcellated character of a small freeholder's estate, dispersed in minute parts in four townships. But that is not all: whereas Dafydd's lands in Royton and Marchwiel lay in the rich Dee valley, his main concentration of arable was some eight miles away in the open fields of Gwersyllt while another solitary acre lay some twelve miles away in the upland vill of Trefydd Bychain (much of which is over a thousand feet above

[53] East Sussex Record Office, Glynde Place Collection, no. 2613; Flintshire Record Office, Trevor-Roper Collection, no. 18.

[54] G. C. Homans, *English Villagers of the Thirteenth Century* (New York, 1941), 90–101; R. A. Dodgshon, 'The Landholding Foundations of the Open-Field System', *Past and Present* 67 (1975), 3–29.

[55] S.B.Y., fol. 175.

sea level). Nor is this an untypical example: it is a pattern which can be amply paralleled from most of the lordships of north-east Wales. There is *prima facie* every reason for believing that such a wide distribution and morcellation of inheritances was not an uncommon feature of free Welsh tenure elsewhere in the March.

It is a distribution pattern which may be explained in part in terms of land usage. There is much to suggest that a balance between the distribution of arable and pasture and also between permanent and temporary cultivation was taken fully into consideration in the division of lands between free Welshmen.[56] But in a kin-centred society the distribution of lands must also have an explanation, historically or mythologically, in the claims of the descent-groups in whose name the individual proprietor held the land. This is indeed what we find. Within the primary settlement of the descent-group, the morcellation of the land by the law of partibility produced an intricate pattern whereby the members of each kindred group held but a fractional share in the soil: when Ieuan ap Cynwrig ap Meurig's quillets in the open fields of Bromfield were listed we find that in thirteen out of twenty-one cases they bordered on one side at least with those of his brother; likewise the share of Madog ap Bleddyn Sais in the common meadow of Llanynys (Dyffryn Clwyd) was contiguous on three sides with the shares of his first cousins once removed.[57]

Just as morcellation led to the intermingling of the landed shares of members of the kindred, so likewise the expansion of the descent-group's claims into neighbouring districts or even farther afield was explained genealogically by asserting that the founder of the group or his immediate descendants had established their right to the land in question. No more perfect example of the application of this genealogical device can be instanced than the descent-group of Rhys ab Edryd (itself a segment of a larger descent-group, that of Edryd ap Marchudd) in the lordship of Denbigh.[58] Its lands were scattered in five

---

[56] G. R. J. Jones in Baker and Butler, op. cit. 442–5. There are occasional references in court rolls to holdings divided between valley and mountain, e.g. S.C. 2/221/8, m. 13ᵛ (one tenement 'in valle', one 'in montibus').

[57] Flints. R.O., Trevor-Roper Collection, no. 18 (1344); S.C. 2/221/2, m. 4ᵛ (1400).

[58] *S.D.*, xxxii–xxxv, 195–9, 245–61, 299–306; Table II. For excellent discussion

townships and two hamlets, widely separated from each other in distance and in the quality of their land. Most of the thirty-three members of the descent-group (or lineage) held land in at least two of the townships, often at a distance of at least seven miles from each other. Whether the explanation of this distribution of land in terms of the property of the lineage-founder and its division between his descendants is historically valid or not either in general outline or in all its details is in some respects of secondary importance: in terms of a kin-centred society it has the obvious virtue of providing a meaningful validation of land title and in terms of the fourteenth-century situation it provided an explanation of the pattern of land-distribution.

So far we have tried to explain very briefly and no doubt inadequately how some of the kinship- and descent-customs of medieval Wales still determined the inheritance, division and distribution of land in the March, or at least in parts of it, in the fourteenth century. Those customs, however, in their turn were affected by other factors which serve to compromise any theories we may wish to base on the laws of descent and inheritance. Nowhere was this more obviously so than with respect to the rule of partibility of inheritances among male co-heirs.

One obvious fashion in which the consequences of partibility might be countered was by the acquisition of more land. Just as in the descent-group itself the problem of growing numbers is catered for by lineage-segmentation, so in the territorial stake of the descent-group the problem is solved in some measure by the establishment of secondary settlements, either by the descent-group as a whole or by some of its lineage-segments.[59] It may well be, for example, that it was by some such process that the lineage of Rhys ab Edryd expanded its territorial claims from a restricted and fairly densely-populated coastal settlement at Abergele to the upland vills of Postyn and Hesgyn.[60] Furthermore, in addition to the development of secondary settlements for a lineage or part of it, we must also cater in our analysis for the considerable role of individual

of this case see G. R. J. Jones in *W.H.R.* 1 (1961), 114–16; and D. H. Owen, ibid. 6 (1972), 123–5.

[59] The classic study is that of Jones Pierce (op. cit. 87–101) on Llysddulas in Anglesey.

[60] Above p. 371.

assarting by enterprising peasants in the process of territorial expansion.[61] Within the lineage itself, the rate of growth of the population was clearly also a key factor in determining whether the law of partibility did or did not lead to the uneconomic morcellation of inheritances. Such evidence as we have suggests that in the March in the fourteenth century multiple successions, though common, were not of such proportions as has often been assumed in past and present discussions of partibility. Individual exceptions to such a statement are not difficult to find; but we have already suggested that in the early fourteenth century, during a period of probable population growth, the average number of male heirs succeeding to free Welsh holdings in Dyffryn Clwyd was almost exactly two. With the drastic impact of successive plagues on the population, the pressure on land eased: not only was there a growing proportion of vacant tenements, the average number of male heirs succeeding fell significantly to 1·5 in Coelion commote in the period 1370–90 (forty-one deaths of free Welsh tenants with heirs: sixty-nine heirs: twenty-two unitary successions: nineteen multiple successions). Even where excessive fertility might appear damaging in one generation, the accidents of birth and death could well reverse the trend in another, as the following example (once more from Dyffryn Clwyd) may serve to show (see diagram p. 374). In the normal course of events Dafydd ap Dafydd could only expect in theory a fifteenth share of his grandfather's inheritance. But events were rarely normal in the mid-fourteenth century. Three visitations of plague in 1349, 1362 and 1366 left Dafydd as either the sole heir or one of the coheirs of two uncles, his father, two brothers and his nephew (who died under age). By 1366 he should have secured, if the law of descent were strictly observed, a third of his grandfather's inheritance. Death as well as birth is a factor in the calculus of partibility. When Sir John Wynn tried to explain how his ancestors had escaped 'the division and subdivision of gavell kynde' whereas so many of his collateral relatives had not, he could only do so in terms of 'Gods mercie and goodness'.[62] That mercy was pre-eminently displayed in a selective process of mortality.

What God's grace could not fulfil, man's devices made good.

[61] Below pp. 403–4.
[62] *History of the Gwydir Family*, 14.

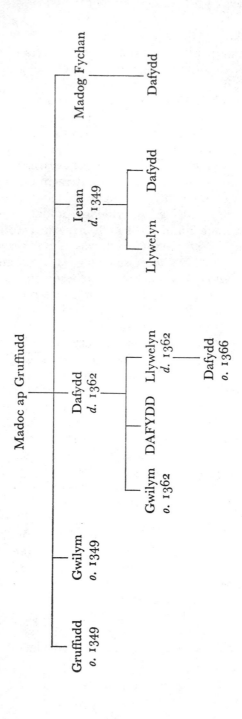

Madoc ap Gruffudd

Gruffudd
o. 1349

Gwilym
o. 1349

Dafydd
d. 1362

Gwilym
o. 1362

DAFYDD

Llywelyn
d. 1362

Dafydd
o. 1366

Ieuan
d. 1349

Llywelyn

Dafydd

Madog Fychan

Dafydd

d = died; *o* = died without surviving male heir of his body.

Welsh freeholders were fully alive to the problems posed by the rule of partibility. Brothers might choose to opt for consolidated blocs of their father's scattered estates rather than insist on a strict geographical application of the rule of partibility;[63] kinsmen might for a variety of reasons forego their share of a claim to an inheritance;[64] coheirs not infrequently preferred to hold their inheritance in common rather than allow it to be reduced into minute fractions by actual division;[65] co-parceners might well act as a group not only on their own inherited lands but also in the land market generally.[66] By such means and by informal family arrangements which by their very nature are unlikely to be recorded in seignorial documents, some of the effects of partibility were no doubt undone. Above all were they undone by the opportunities of the market in Welsh land. This is a topic to which we must return later;[67] but it may be as well to indicate briefly here by a single example how the constraints of kin inheritance and of the rule of partibility might be overcome by the enterprising Welsh freeman. Iorwerth ap Llywelyn ap Gruffudd was the brother of Madog ap Llywelyn ap Gruffudd (d. 1331), the Welsh *uchelwr* of Bromfield whose lineage and descendants we have discussed above.[68] Both were therefore drawn from the same stock; as such they would claim shares in the same lineage-lands and their descendants for two generations after them would continue to be members of the same four-generation agnatic kindred.[69] It is in that capacity that we meet Iorwerth, his grandson and great-grandsons in the rentals of Bromfield and Yale between 1315 and 1445.[70] By the rule of partibility the lands of Iorwerth ap Llywelyn's descendants should have been progressively 'mangled' over the genera-

[63] S.C. 2/215/73, m. 22ᵛ (one brother takes his father's land in Dyffryn Clwyd, the other his father's land in Edeyrnion, 1314).

[64] For examples see S.C. 2/216/6, m. 9 (two brothers surrender claim to a third); 219/8, m. 15 (one co-heir surrenders his claim to four others).

[65] *Extent of Chirkland*, 25–6; D.L. 43/12/14, fol. 8ᵛ (Kidwelly: X 'et coheredes sui tenent certas terras ibidem de eorum hereditate pro indivisivo'). Variations on this latter formula are very common.

[66] Examples of this practice are manifold in the Bromfield survey of 1391 (S.B.Y.).

[67] Below pp. 402–13.

[68] Above pp. 361–3.

[69] For a very interesting case of 1391 about a dispute within this kindred over the division of Madog ap Llywelyn's land see N.L.W. Peniarth 404 D., fol. 86ᵛ–fol. 87.

[70] *The First Extent of Bromfield and Yale*, 61; S.B.Y., fol. 80; L.R. 2/251, fol. 15ᵛ

tions. So, indeed, their hereditary lands may have been; but at the same time the family, notably Iorwerth Fychan (*fl.* 1332–77) ab Iorwerth ap Llywelyn, was piecing together individual parcels of land and thereby putting together an estate which was later to swell the territorial fortunes of the Trevor family.

Of this estate-building we would have known nothing had it not been for the chance survival of two small collections of title deeds.[71] This fact should serve to remind us, if reminder were necessary, how much we are the prisoners of our documentation in the study of native Welsh society. In particular it should serve to remind us that however valuable the surveys and extents may be in directing our attention towards descent-groups, their conservatism and even their archaism may distort our picture. That distortion may be corrected in good measure by supplementing the evidence of the surveys by that of the court rolls and title deeds. These classes of documents lead us away from a world of patrilineages to a world of sturdy individualism; in describing a holding they relate its geographical and occasionally its tenurial position, but very rarely its *gwely* affiliation. There is here no contradiction in the evidence; rather is it that the two varieties of documentation are complementary and need to be studied as such. That a Welsh free man of the fourteenth century had close ties of obligation with his kinsfolk in territorial, economic and other spheres is not in doubt; but those ties were not exclusive of other bonds nor were they necessarily the prime ones in his hierarchy of obligations. In terms of his economic and social life his ties with his neighbours were at least equally important. In some vills, it is true, kinsmen and neighbours were one and the same;[72] but more often than not the lands of kinsmen of one lineage would lie pêle-mêle among the lands of members of other lineages. 'And the whole *gafael* (i.e. the holding of a lineage) is intermingled with the other three *gafaelion*'. So runs an entry in *The Survey of Denbigh*:[73] in such a situation—and it is one which has

[71] Flints. R.O. Trevor-Roper Collection; East Sussex R.O., Glynde Place Collection.

[72] As is suggested, for example, in an entry concerning 'convicinos suos de consanguinitate Oyrionaldurth' (= Wyrion Aldurth = grandsons of Aldurth): S.C. 2/218/8, m. 13 (Dyffryn Clwyd, 1360). Cf. reference to 'the *parantela* of Map Heffryn in the township of Larkenhope' (Clun): S.R.O. 552/1/27, m. 4ᵛ (1397).

[73] *S.D.*, 176.

been admirably illustrated from one area of North Wales[74]—
the corporate character of the patrilineage and the effective
relations between kinsmen in the day-to-day affairs of life,
particularly agricultural life, would at best be tenuous, at worst
almost non-existent.

In such a situation it was the bond of vicinity which was often
the most effective of social bonds. That was true often in terms
of economic co-operation. The Welsh law-texts themselves had
set out detailed provisions for the co-operation of neighbours in
common ploughing schemes; it was the vill, the local grouping,
which was normally the unit for the payment of puture dues
and pannage rents to the lord; it was the community of the vill
which decreed when the animals should be moved up to the
common pasture and which appointed a common herdsman to
look after them. The vill as a unit of neighbours might hold land
in its own name as did 'the community of the vill of Llanynys';
it could lease land from the lord as at Denbigh; it could take
over a vacant kin holding as in Chirkland.[75] It was in such
practical economic co-operation with his neighbours and in
corporate action as a member of a local community—be it that
of men of his own race or status or men of his vill, parish,
commote or lordship—that the Welsh freeholder of the March
often appears in the documents.

Furthermore, it was as a member of a local unit, the vill (W.
tref), that the lord's demands in administrative and fiscal
matters were made upon the freeholder. It is true that most of
the Welsh renders were assessed—and continued to be assessed
for centuries—on the descent-group, the *gwely*, and then a proportion levied on each individual member of it; but it was the
vill which was for the lord and his officers the unit of attribution
and collection for such renders. In a fiscal pattern which is so
firmly based on the locality it was not the head of the patrilineage (*pencenedl*) but the proctors of the community and the lord's
officers who were the key men in local administration. Even
more obviously in judicial affairs it was either the individual or
the local community which was the focus of responsibility and
action. Kinsmen, it is true, might be called upon to testify as
compurgators or to contribute to a wergild-payment; co-

---

[74] Jones-Pierce, op. cit. 195–228.
[75] S.C. 2/217/1, m. 9ᵛ (1336); S.C. 6/1184/22 (1397); *Extent of Chirkland*, 10.

parceners might be summoned as warrantors in the land transactions of their kinsmen. But by and large it was as an individual,
supported by pledges drawn from among his neighbours and
affeered for his amercement by those same neighbours, that the
free Welshman of the March appears in the court rolls. Beyond
the individual it was the *patria*, not the *parentela* or the *progenies*,
which was the unit in judicial affairs. It was the vill which
would be expected to present offences in the lord's court and
which was held responsible for shortcomings in the administration of justice; it was by a verdict of the *patria* that most cases
would be decided. Even in the field of inheritance of land, the
very area in which the rights of kinsmen might be expected to be
dominant, the men of the vill could be summoned to supervise
the division of land.

The growing importance of locality ties was in part a factor of
the weakness and dispersed character of patrilineages in Wales
and the March; as such, the evidence from the March in the
fourteenth century is but an episode, and that a terminal
episode, in the long history of kinship institutions in Welsh
society. More immediately, the growth of locality ties was
almost certainly accelerated by the common demands—
financial, judicial, administrative and much else—made by
lordship, secular and ecclesiastical, of Welsh free society. Ties
of locality and ties of kinship are not, of course, mutually
exclusive; in many respects they are complementary. Yet the
relative strength or weakness of the one to the other is a key
feature in the evolution of medieval societies. Not the least of the
attractions of the study of free Welsh society in the March in the
fourteenth century is that we are allowed a glimpse of a society
in which kin ties are still elemental but in which the obligations
and bonds between the individual on the one hand and his
local community and his lord on the other are growing visibly
stronger. Out of this shift in emphasis in social bonds, modern
Welsh rural society was to emerge.

THE UNFREE

The March may have been preponderantly a land of freemen;
but the numbers of unfree and customary tenants there were by
no means negligible.[76] We are as yet very inadequately informed

---

[76] See in general Rees, op. cit. 149–83.

about the geographical pattern of unfreedom in the March;
but that there were major regional variations in that pattern
hardly admits of doubt. One region that immediately stands out
is the south-east, notably the lowlands of the lordships of Chepstow, Newport, Usk and Caerleon: there we find an unfree
tenant population comparable, both in numbers and in the
nature of the labour services, with that of the intensively
manorialized districts of southern England. Another distinctive
region appears to be the southern lowlands of the March—
notably in Glamorgan, Gower and Pembroke—where customary tenants were numerous but where their labour services
were generally very light; while in the eastern March a pro-
gressive increase in the number of customary tenants is noticeable in several lordships, such as Clun and Caus, as we move
eastwards into the Anglicized and manorialized lowlands. On
this map of unfreedom we would also find several upland lordships—such as Builth, Ceri and Cydewain—where the number
of unfree tenants was apparently negligible and some lowland
lordships—such as Kidwelly—where customary tenure was
restricted to a few isolated centres. This uneven distribution of
the unfree population and of customary tenure coincides in good
measure with the geographical relief of the March; but not
entirely so, for it is not unusual to come across bond vills in the
uplands, such as Llanarmon in the lordship of Bromfield and
Yale. Nor does it coincide neatly with the areas of intense alien
colonization and the early introduction of foreign lordship.
Clifford and Glasbury were said in 1325 to have no tenants
holding in villeinage while in the neighbouring lordship of Hay
there were but a few customary tenants and even they owed no
agricultural labour services: all three districts lay on the edge
of the March and had been within the ambit of Anglo-Norman
lordship and influence for generations.[77] In the lordships of
Denbigh and Dyffryn Clwyd, on the other hand, the new
English lords in 1282 found a substantial bond population and
one which may have been considerably greater at an earlier
period. A like contrast has been traced in the geographically
contiguous Fitzalan lordships of Oswestry and Chirk: it is not
in the eastern lowland lordship of Oswestry but in the upland
Welsh lordship of Chirk that we find the most extensive and

[77] *C. Inq. Misc. 1307–49*, no. 1014; S.C. 6/1156/18.

persistent traces of unfreedom.[78] Clearly no single formula, whether geographical or racial, will by itself explain the regional variations of Marcher unfreedom.

Within this regional pattern there were further local variations in the distribution of bond tenants and bond land within each lordship. Most Welsh bond townships were concentrated in the lowlands, with appurtenant pasture rights and occasionally with subsidiary settlements in the uplands.[79] In the lordship of Denbigh, for example, most of the bond or partly bond townships were located either on the coast or along the river valleys.[80] This geographical pattern of the distribution of bond tenants was in its turn determined in good part by the location of seignorial residences and demesne lands within each lordship. The Welsh law-texts make it abundantly clear that between the seignorial or princely court (*llys*) and the demesne land (*tir bwrdd*) on the one hand and bond settlements (*maerdrefi*) and bond land (*tir cyfrif*) on the other there was a direct relationship both in terms of labour services and more substantially in terms of the provision of food supplies. This close relationship between the distribution of major bond vills and old Welsh courts or their Anglo-Norman successors is evident time and again in the March. It is naturally most obvious in the recently conquered Marcher lordships of the north-east: in the lordship of Denbigh the main concentrations of bond tenants were to be found near to the four demesne centres of Dinorben, Denbigh, Ystradowen and Cilcennis; in Dyffryn Clwyd the three major demesne centres (all of which were almost certainly native in origin) at Ruthin, Llysfasi and Maesmynan were served by neighbouring bond settlements at Maerdref, Derwen and Aberwheeler respectively; and in Bromfield and Yale the bond population was centred around the lord's demesnes at Marford, Wrexham and Llanarmon. In the older Marcher lordships of the south, likewise, the link between seignorial demesne and the distribution of bond land was close.

---

[78] Llinos Smith, 'The Lordships of Chirk and Oswestry', Ph.D thesis (Univ. of London, 1971), 324 ff.

[79] G. R. J. Jones, 'The Distribution of Bond Settlements in North-West Wales', *W.H.R.* 2 (1964), 19–37; C. Thomas, 'Social Organisation and Rural Settlement in Medieval North Wales', *Journal of the Merioneth Historical and Record Society* 6 (1970), 121–31.

[80] H. Owen in *W.H.R.* 6 (1972), 118–19.

In the lordship of Glamorgan, for example, customary tenants were concentrated around seignorial manors in the uplands, such as Merthyr or Gelligaer, or in the lowlands, such as Whitchurch or Rudri; while in the mesne lordship of Ogmore most of the bond land was situated around the demesne centres at Broughton and Wick.[81] Most, but not all. For while many bond settlements, particularly those burdened with heavy labour services, were functionally and geographically closely related to seignorial demesne centres, this was not true of all bond land. Bond men often lived cheek by jowl with free men; bond land lay intermingled with free land. In Ogmore, for example, most of the bond land lay around Broughton and Wick but a further 400 acres was scattered in seven townships; in the lordship of Denbigh many bond settlements were far distant from the lord's demesne centres and in at least twenty-one vills (out of a total of 81 lay vills) bond men and freemen lived together.[82] Such a distribution pattern meant that in terms of agricultural activity and economic co-operation the links between free and unfree would be close; it also meant that the contrasts between the two groups in terms of personal status and tenurial obligations would be brought more sharply into focus.

These contrasts were reinforced administratively and institutionally. Welsh legal theory, in common with that of most of medieval Europe, drew a sharp line of distinction between free and unfree; and Marcher lords and administrators saw to it that this distinction was, in so far as possible, strictly upheld. The lands of free and unfree, though often intermingled,[83] might be listed in separate rentals;[84] their affairs were often controlled by different officers, a bailiff for the free and a reeve for the unfree; their contributions towards a subsidy or an aid were not infrequently separately assessed.[85] It was to freemen alone that the Marcher lords normally granted their charters of liberties. In respect of these charters and of the legal franchises appurtenant to their status, freemen often claimed privileges

---

[81] *Glam. C.H.*, iii, 312–15, 634, n. 90.

[82] D.L. 42/107; H. Owen, op. cit. 118 ff.

[83] Thus a man in Dyffryn Clwyd was said to hold land 'inter Anglicos et liberos Wallenses et custumarios': S.C. 2/218/8, m. 21ᵛ (1360).

[84] As in Dyffryn Clwyd: S.C. 2/217/7, m. 12ᵛ (1342).

[85] As in Chirkland in 1379 (N.L.W. Chirk Castle Accounts, D.35) or Dyffryn Clwyd in 1369 (S.C. 2/219/6, m. 23).

denied to their unfree neighbours.[86] It was indeed at law that the status distinction between free and unfree was often most sharply defined—in the existence of separate courts for freemen[87] or at least of exclusively free juries to hear cases relating to freemen;[88] in the way that cases might be deferred 'for lack of freemen'[89] or that judgements given by a bond jury might be reviewed by a free jury;[90] in the constitution of juries of serfs to decide issues relating to bond land and the obligations of customary tenants,[91] and of mixed juries for cases which affected free and unfree alike.[92] The parallel between the racial and the status distinction is here obviously very close: just as English and Welsh were to be kept apart, in so far as it was feasible, so also were free and unfree tenants.

Yet within the ranks of the unfree themsevles there were wide differences in status and obligations as well as in wealth and territorial endowment. In the manors of the lordship of Usk, for example, villeins (*villani*) were distinguished from customary tenants (*custumarii*); in the mesne lordship of Caldicot the bond population was divided into three categories (gafolmen, semi-virgaters and quarter-virgaters), scaled according to the size of their tenements and the consequent number of labour services exacted.[93] Likewise in a thoroughly Welsh lordship such as Denbigh the differences between various unfree tenants were fully recognized by the contemporary surveyor: the 'bond villeins' (*nativi cayth*) of Denbigh were distinguished from the 'free villeins' (*nativi reth*) because their services were more demanding and degrading (*de vilioribus et de pluris servitutibus*), while elsewhere in the lordship were tenants who were neither

---

[86] Thus in Llannerch (Dyffryn Clwyd), the lord had conceded that free men should have the right to be mainperned without making a payment to him: S.C. 2/217/10, m. 15ᵛ (1345).

[87] For a *curia francorum* at Kidwelly, see N. L. W. Muddlescombe 2143 (1317).

[88] For example, see S.C. 2/218/5, m. 2ᵛ (1356); 219/2, m. 15ᵛ (1365). Cf. B.L. Add. Charter 20414 for a deed of 1250 witnessed by the freemen of the court of Grosmont.

[89] S.C. 2/215/75, m. 7 (1315—'pro defectu liberorum').

[90] D.L. 42/16, fol. 55ᵛ (Monmouth, 1411–12).

[91] Bond juries figure very prominently in the court rolls of Overgorddwr (Caus): Staffs. R.O. D. 641/1/4T/1 (1401).

[92] For an example, see S.C. 2/218/7, m. 11 (Dyffryn Clwyd, 1359).

[93] *C.I.P.M.*, IV, no. 435, p. 335 (Usk, 1307); C. 133/10, no. 9; 92, no. 8 (Caldicot, 1275–99).

'pure free' nor yet 'pure unfree'.[94] If such gradations of unfreedom existed within a single lordship, we might expect them to be even more sharply defined as between one part of the March and another. So indeed we find it. One example may serve. The customary tenants of Caldicot on the Severn estuary and those of the manor of Brecon in the Usk valley were both legally unfree and as such they shared most of the obligations and restrictions of personal servitude. Yet in respect of their labour rent there was a difference between them in quantitative obligation which was sufficient to be qualitative in character: the men of Caldicot owed two or three days' work a week on their lord's demesne, those of Brecon no more than ten days a year.[95]

Marcher unfreedom was a very hybrid institution. In parts of the south-east it was hardly to be differentiated from the classical unfreedom of central and southern England; indeed it is from Tidenham on the edge of the Welsh March that one of the earliest surveys of the obligations of customary tenure survives.[96] Elsewhere the unfreedom of the March—with its emphasis on food renders and on building and carrying services —is much more reminiscent of customary tenure in some upland districts of northern England.[97] The unfree themselves were likewise a hybrid group, drawn from the descendants of enfranchised slaves, from the victims of warfare, expropriation and oppression in a frontier district, from freemen who had fallen on evil days, from immigrants who accepted the obligations of customary tenure and from native Welsh serfs, *taeogion*.[98] Racially they were a mixed group: in the older Marcher lordships such as Chepstow, Usk, Brecon and Hay a distinction was drawn between English manorial villeins and Welsh customary tenants, while in the more recently-conquered lordships of north-east Wales it was assumed that the *nativi* were by defini-

[94] D.L. 29/1/2, m. 3 (1305); *S.D.*, 53, 305, 312.

[95] D.L. 29/680/10999; S.C. 6/1156/15 (1362, 1372).

[96] *English Historical Documents*, ii, ed. D. C. Douglas and G. W. Greenaway, 817–18.

[97] For Northumbrian unfreedom, see J. E. A. Jolliffe in *E.H.R.* 41 (1926), 1–42 and G. W. S. Barrow in *Northern History* 4 (1969), 1–28.

[98] Even in the depressed economic conditions of the late-fourteenth century, eight men in Dyffryn Clwyd in the period 1350–70 became serfs with their families in perpetuity for the sake of good land. For a comparable example from Clun in 1372, see S.R.O. 552/1/16, m. 4.

tion Welshmen and that the nature of their obligations ought therefore to be defined in native Welsh terms. It is on this specifically Welsh element in Marcher unfreedom that we will concentrate in the present discussion.

In some respects what is most striking about the unfree Welsh tenants of the March is how many features they shared with their free colleagues.[99] For free and unfree tenants alike the major obligation to the lord was the payment of renders in kind or of their commuted equivalent in money. Indeed in the assessment of some of these renders in Denbigh the crucial division was not so much between free and unfree as between men who had tenants and those who had not, or even between men who had land and their landless colleagues.[100] In terms of inheritance-customs, likewise, there was little to distinguish free from unfree in many parts of the March. Most of the unfree tenants like their colleagues held their land in respect of membership of descent-groups (*gwelyau, gafaelion*); they were even termed 'unfree proprietors' (*priodarii nativi*),[101] with all the indefeasability of title that the term proprietor (*priodor*) implied in Welsh legal parlance; the basic rules of Welsh free tenure— partibility among male coheirs up to the third degree and the acknowledgement of the claim of sons born out of wedlock to a share in the inheritance—applied also to most bond land in the northern March.[102] With the passage of time, free and unfree grew closer to each other in the March, in terms both of their tenures and of their obligations.

Closer, maybe; yet the distinction between them remained unbridgeable, for it was a distinction rooted neither in land nor in the renders due for that land but in the person. Whereas the Welsh freeman was nobly born and nobly descended, the unfree man was strictly speaking a man without an ancestry. His status was described not in terms of his relation to his kindred but in terms of his dependence on his lord. He was a *nativus domini*; he was 'humble and obedient' towards his lord 'in his body and

---

[99] The rest of this section is largely based on the Dyffryn Clwyd court rolls. They are much the best source for the study of 'Welsh' Marcher unfreedom in the fourteenth century, for unlike the surveys and extents they show the actual character of that unfreedom in operation. The study is based on cumulative impressions as well as on individual examples; references, therefore, have been kept to a minimum.

[100] *S.D.*, xcii–xciii, 47, 149. [101] Ibid. 150, 223. [102] *Extent of Chirkland*, 61.

in his chattels'.[103] He was his lord's personal possession to be bought, sold or left by will as his lord pleased.[104] This truly degrading aspect of serfdom, that of treating a man as vendible property, was more brutally to the fore in the March than it was in contemporary England. Since the bond was a personal one it could not be undone by distance: not only did the lord control the serf's right to travel, he also claimed from him wherever he might be an annual recognition of his dependence.[105] Furthermore servile status was inherited and transmitted by blood. Such a stigma was neither lightly overlooked nor easily removed. The lord and his officers were zealous in their search for unfree tenants who were attempting to conceal their naïfty or to flee to neighbouring lordships to escape its consequences. Equally they seized on every opportunity for interpreting the holding of bond land as a pretext for claiming that its tenant was personally unfree and of converting temporary unfreedom into perpetual serfdom.[106] The taint of serfdom could only be removed by death or by manumission. Manumission was an act of generosity that was rarely displayed in the March and even then it might be limited to the life of the serf and denied to his descendants.[107] For the serf himself, proof of illegitimacy was one of the few routes of escape from his unfree status.[108]

It was not only the lord who was anxious to ensure that bondmen did not conceal their naïfty; so also was the bond community itself. The serf's unfree blood made him automatically a member of the *communitas nativorum*, just as the freeman's blood made him a member of a free descent-group. It was upon that community as a whole, rather than on its individual members, that many of the bond dues and renders were assessed. Since

---

[103] S.C. 2/218/2, m. 16ᵛ (1351).

[104] For examples, see D.L. 42/1, fol. 17ᵛ (a Welsh freeholder in Grosmont gives six of his *nativi* and their land to Edmund, earl of Lancaster); Monmouth R.O., Llanarth Collection, D.2.27 (three sons of a Welsh freeholder grant four of their *nativi* to a local knight); U.C.N.W. Penrhyn Collection 5, 217, 407 (Gwilym ap Gruffudd ap Tudur buying *nativi* and leaving twenty of them in his will in 1376).

[105] For examples of chevage in the March, see *S.D.*, 12; D.L. 29/1/2, m. 3 (Denbigh, 1305); N.L.W. Chirk Castle Accounts D.28 (Chirkland, 1366).

[106] For an attempt to convert a *nativus pro tempore* into a *nativus pro perpetuo*, see S.C. 2/218/4, m. 15ᵛ (1354) and cf. S.C. 2/218/5, m. 2ᵛ (1356).

[107] For an interesting example of manumission for life only see S.C. 2/216/14, m. 12ᵛ (1334).

[108] S.C. 2/215/69, m. 11; 217/1, m. 8ᵛ; 218/4, m. 24ᵛ (1307–54). For the attitude of English lawyers see Pollock and Maitland, op. cit. I, 423.

they were communal dues they were exacted regardless of the
number of bondmen in the community, 'even indeed if only one
bondman were left'.[109] Here was one of the most distinctive and
most oppressive features of Welsh bond tenure. It comes as no
surprise that bondmen were anxious that such communal dues
should be as broadly distributed as possible and that they should
be particularly resentful of fellow-bondmen who concealed
their naifty and thereby their obligation to pay. It was the
bond community itself which often hunted out defaulting serfs
or which brought a charge of naifty against one of its members.

Bondmen were united by a community of obligations to their
lord; they were further united by the restrictions arising out of
their bond personal status. It was these restrictions, rather than
any differences in tenure, rent or labour services, which most
clearly distinguished the bondman from the freeman in the
medieval March. 'Nativus domini humilis et justiciabilis de
corpore et catallis': this contemporary phrase sums up the legal
and social disadvantages of Marcher unfreedom. In a strict
legal sense the serf's chattels were not his own but those of his
lord.[110] They could not be sold without the lord's licence nor
could they be given as a marriage portion to his daughter; they
could most certainly not be removed from the lordship. The
lord's claim to the chattels was generally dormant during the
serf's life but death served to activate it: he would claim a
proportion of the chattels as his own and should the serf be
unfortunate enough to die intestate or without an heir of his
body, then all his goods would revert to the lord, less possibly a
share to the church and to his widow.[111] His goods were not his
own to do as he wished with them; neither was his person. He
had to procure a seignorial licence, and that at a price, if he
wished to give his daughter in marriage, especially if her prospective husband were a freeman; his son could not be tonsured
(and thereby lost to the community of bondmen) without the
lord's authority. He was not allowed to lease land from whom
he wished, particularly if it were free land; nor was he allowed
to sell his labour freely, for the lord claimed the right of first

[109] *S.D.*, 275.
[110] 'Bona eorundem sunt bona domini ut bona in manus nativorum domini':
S.C.2/218/6, m. 12 (1358).
[111] For a good example, see Staffs. R.O., D. 641/1/4T/1, m. 2 (Caus, 1401).

option on it. Physically, likewise, his freedom was limited, for he was not allowed 'to come and to go' as he wished. In the difficult years of the late-fourteenth century Marcher lords pursued an active policy of compelling serfs to find pledges to stay in the lordship; those who fled had their lands and chattels confiscated. To this extent the Marcher serf was in a very special way *adscriptus glebae*; he was bound to the soil of the lordship.

He was bound to the soil in other ways, for the lord's authority extended not only to the serf's chattels and person but also to his land. Bond land, it is true, was protected by local custom, the *consuetudo bondagiorum* as it is called. Such a custom upheld the serf's claim to a share in the land of the bond vill; it assured his heirs up to the third degree a claim to succeed to his tenement on his death; it even extended to his widow, particularly if she were pregnant, the right to hold her husband's lands during her lifetime. In this latter respect it was noticeably more liberal than the law regarding free-women, who were allowed neither to inherit land nor to claim a dower-share on their husbands' death. It is one of the paradoxes of unfreedom that whereas the serf was almost rightless *vis à vis* his lord in respect of his person and his chattels, he nevertheless had a claim on his lord for land.[112]

Custom may have assured the serf a claim to land and to certain rights in that land; but it also extended to the lord considerable power over the landed fortunes of unfreemen, as the court rolls make amply clear. It was in part a power of prohibition and control: the lord could prohibit his serfs from holding free land while bond land was available; he insisted that all sales and exchanges of customary land were recorded in his court and a fine or heriot paid to him by way of recognition; his licence was necessary not only for the sale of a customary tenement but also for mortgaging or leasing part of it. It was also a power of compulsion: he could direct his villeins to live on bond land; he could issue ordinances prohibiting them from acquiring free land either by lease or by Welsh mortgage; he could and frequently did compel them to take vacant bond land, whether or not it was theirs by hereditary right; he could

---

[112] This is clearly shown in a case of 1329 where the lord surrenders any claim of naifty against one of his serfs; the serf in exchange surrenders his claim to land in the lordship: S.C. 2/216/9, m. 12–12ᵛ.

command them to take more land and often did so in the years of land glut in the late fourteenth century. Nor were such commands idle threats: he distrained and imprisoned serfs who disobeyed him and instituted thorough inquries into those capable of holding bond land. Furthermore, since bond land was eventually the lord's land, it was the lord who decided whether his serfs were competent to hold their tenements or to add vacant ones to them.

It was in respect of their persons, their chattels and their lands that the position of Marcher serfs *vis à vis* their lords differed radically from that of free tenants; in respect of labour services there was very little to distinguish them. It is here that the difference between Marcher and English unfreedom is most marked, for in England by the thirteenth century 'the principal hallmark of servility was . . . the performance of heavy labour services'.[113] Not so in the March: there labour services were negligible and not very different as between free and unfree. To such a generalization there are, of course, exceptions but these are to be found mainly in the lowland Anglicized manors of the south and east—such as Caldicot, Chepstow and Minsterley (Caus)[114]—where heavy week work was not an unusual obligation. Elsewhere in the March, however, the pattern is remarkably consistent: light labour services largely confined to the peak period of the agricultural year. In Denbigh the Welsh villeins owed only three days' work in the autumn to the lord; in Bromfield and Yale the obligatory labour of the *nativi* was restricted to three days of hoeing and three days of reaping a year.[115] The labour services recorded on the manors of South Wales were rarely more onerous: ten days was the maximum service demanded of customary tenants in Brecon lordship, fourteen days in Whitecastle (Monmouth) and Ogmore (Glamorgan).[116] Furthermore, such boon works, when they were exacted, were often paid for in cash or in food and were occasionally only exactable, in the case of ploughing services, if the bond tenant owned a plough or a plough beast. Such minimal labour services were neither onerous to the tenant nor very useful to the lord.

[113] R. H. Hilton, *The Decline of Serfdom in Medieval England* (1969), 18.
[114] See respectively, above p. 383; Rees, op. cit. 169; *V.C.H. Salop*, viii, 318.
[115] *S.D.*, 59 ; *First Extent of Bromfield and Yale*, 48.
[116] S.C. 6/1156/13–15; D.L. 43/13/8, m. 7; D.L. 42/107.

It is, therefore, not surprising to find that they had often been commuted at an early date and amalgamated into the money rents of the unfree.[117]

Labour services in the March were light not only compared with those common on many English manors but also with the burden of other services demanded of the unfree tenant of the March, most notably building and carrying services. Such services, it should be noted, were not exclusively the obligation of the unfree. In Denbigh, for example, both the free and unfree tenants of the commote of Rhufoniog Isaled were expected to build and maintain at their own expense a hall, a chamber and other buildings for the lord; in Chirkland, likewise, the carriage of timber for the repair of the castle was an obligation on free and unfree alike; in Brecon all Welshmen regardless of status were obliged to carry timber for the repair of the lord's mills.[118] Yet proportionately these building and carrying services fell most heavily on the unfree. Heavy they certainly were. Thus whereas the labour services of the bondmen of Whitecastle were insignificant, they were expected to find an ox or an affer once a week for most of the year to carry timber for the repair of the mill or of the castle. In Sesswick (Bromfield and Yale) the *nativi* performed no agricultural services but they were expected to build, thatch and maintain the manorial buildings, to carry millstones, to clean the millpond and generally to maintain the mill in good repair. In Dyffryn Clwyd the obligations of the unfree tenants included the carriage of the lord's timber from his forest and of salt for him from Northwich in Cheshire. On the estates of the bishop of St. David's, to give a final example, there existed a class of tenants whose sole service was that of providing carts to help in the lord's rebuilding operations, while an elaborate system of carriage obligations ensured that the produce of the bishop's far-flung manors could be conveyed to the episcopal centres at St. David's and Llawhaden.[119]

Duties such as these were not merely formal obligations; they continued to be performed often long after the agricultural labour services had been commuted. The fifty-five customary

---

[117] As at Wigmore by 1324: S.C. 12/8/18. For commutation of labour services in the March generally see Rees, op. cit. 176–8.

[118] *S.D.*, 149; *Extent of Chirkland*, 61; D.L. 42/16, fol. 252ᵛ.

[119] D.L. 43/13/8, m. 7–m. 8; *First Extent of Bromfield and Yale*, 65; S.C. 2/217/10, m. 11; 217/11, m. 1; *The Black Book of St. David's, passim.*

tenants of Ogmore, for example, were required to clean out the mill pond in 1363; in 1384 the customary tenants of Radnor had to carry two millstones to the lord's mill at Knucklas; while in 1408 a strict order was issued commanding the Welshmen of Brecon to carry timber for the repair of the mill of Defynnog 'as was provided by ancient custom'.[120] A further indication of the importance of these services is the measure of resistance they elicited and the size of the fines that local communities paid either for evading them or in order to commute them. Some of the men of the bishop of St. David's in 1338 paid £20 to be exonerated from the duty of carrying timber; one of the concessions that the men of Kidwelly secured from the duke of Lancaster in 1356 was that their carriage services should henceforth be fixed in quantity; in 1391 the free and unfree tenants of Nanheudwy (Chirkland) were fined the enormous sum of £135 for resisting their obligation to carry timber for the repair of the castle; while in 1401 an equally harsh individual fine of £1 was imposed on a tenant of Overgorddwr (Caus) who dared to deny that he was obliged to carry timber to the lord's mill.[121] These building and carrying services were to remain a feature of Marcher unfreedom until its final decline.

That decline was to be long delayed, often far more so than in England. The explanation of this contrasting chronology of the decline of English and Marcher unfreedom is twofold. Marcher unfreedom, we have insisted, was not characterized by heavy labour services geared to demesne exploitation. Demesne farming had never been very extensive in the March with the exception of the south-east and had never been heavily dependent on villein labour services. The decline of demesne farming in the March did not, therefore, remove much of the economic rationale of unfreedom as it did in many English manors. Marcher unfreedom was firmly based on personal status and tenurial control; these proved a more resilient base for the survival of unfreedom than did labour services. The contrast with the serfdom of the south-east March is particularly instructive in this respect. There the decline of demesne exploitation

---

[120] D.L. 29/592/9444; N.L.W., Radnor account; D.L. 42/16, fol. 252ᵛ.
[121] B.L. Harleian 1249, fol. 88; D.L. 42/16, fol. 42ᵛ; N.L.W. Chirk Castle Accounts, D.51; Staffs. R.O. D. 641/1/4T/1.

and the collapse of the pattern of heavy labour services brought about an early decline of personal servitude and a movement to copyhold and leasehold tenure by the late fourteenth century.[122] In other parts of the March, however, bond vills and personal servitude were to survive until the early sixteenth century and were then only removed by royal or seignorial fiat. A second reason for the resilience of Marcher unfreedom lay in the fact that it was native unfreedom and as with so many native institutions in the March in the later Middle Ages it was artificially maintained for reasons of administrative convenience and social conservatism.[123] It was only in the early sixteenth century, particularly in the years 1504–7, that the attempt to bolster the status distinction between free and unfree was finally abandoned. With it was abandoned one of the most long-standing and profound status distinctions of Welsh and Marcher society. To the bondmen of Wales the claim of Tudor historians that Henry VII was a second Moses who had delivered his nation from bondage was no extravagant panegyric; it was the literal truth.[124]

[122] Below pp. 442–3.
[123] See in particular T. Jones Pierce, *Medieval Welsh Society*, 39–61 and J. B. Smith, 'Crown and Community in the Principality of North Wales in the Reign of Henry Tudor', *W.H.R.* 3 (2) (1966–7), 145–7.
[124] *Penbrokshire*, III, 36–7, 56–7; cf. David Powel, *The Historie of Cambria* (1584), ed. W. Wynne (1784), 390–1.

The Economic Structure of Marcher Society

THIS analysis of Marcher society has hitherto concentrated on two contemporary social classifications, those of race and of status. Both classifications were meaningful and important; both drew attention to some of the more important lines of division within Marcher society in terms of privilege and economic opportunity. Yet as guides to the structure of that society neither classification is adequate. In the first place they are, like all classifications, static; from being static they soon become fossilized and anachronistic and thereby serve to distort rather than to illuminate the evolution of Marcher society. Secondly, even at a descriptive level these contemporary classifications are patently inadequate in themselves as a basis for historical analysis. As with most medieval classifications they were essentially legal in character and in effect. In terms of economic realities and social structure these boundaries were far less significant than contemporary definitions and terminology might suggest. It is, therefore, to an analysis of Marcher society in terms of the distribution—and the redistribution—of wealth, and with it in large measure of social power, that we will turn in this chapter.

THE DISTRIBUTION OF WEALTH

Marcher society in the fourteenth century was predominantly a society of peasant farmers, living on individual family holdings and mainly preoccupied with the problems of producing food for the subsistence needs of their own households. Such a bald statement immediately cries out for qualification. In the first place we need to make full allowance for the role of cottagers, landless labourers and craftsmen in Marcher society, none of whom lived entirely, or even mainly, from the produce of their own holdings. Likewise we need to recognize the distinctive position of townsmen in an overwhelmingly rural society. Above all the impression of a predominantly peasant society needs to be qualified by reference to those men who had more land than was necessary for family subsistence and who lived in greater or lesser degree by the exploitation of their authority over the land and persons of other men. This group ranged from the wealthy peasants who could draw on the rents and services of a few sub-tenants to the great Marcher lords themselves; it also included a wide range of men, lay and ecclesiastical, whose social and economic power lay between these two poles of wealth. The members of this group not only produced for households far greater than the normal family-unit and for market consumption; they also claimed a substantial share of the peasant's surplus production in rents and services, in amercements and in communal dues and by means of their control of key items of the economy such as mills, forests and pasture. Yet, these qualifications apart, the overwhelmingly peasant character of Marcher society hardly admits of doubt.

The majority of peasants had to be content with an arable holding of ten acres or less. Such at least is the conclusion suggested by the rentals and surveys of the March. It is true that some surveys, notably those of Denbigh in 1334 and of Bromfield and Yale in 1315 and 1391, do not specify the acreage of peasant holdings; it is also true that rentals and surveys generally attend only to the land-holding, rent-paying tenant population and thereby doubtless underestimate the total number of men who lived partly or wholly off the land. Nevertheless they do provide us with a broad indication of the distribution of territorial wealth in Marcher society. The impression they leave very forcibly is that of the small size of most peasant holdings. In the uplands of the lordship of Hay in 1340, 90 per cent of the tenants held less than ten acres each, two-thirds of them held less than five acres of arable. In the fertile lowlands of nearby Bronllys the story is very similar, two-thirds of the tenants having holdings of five acres or less. It is a story which appears to be repeated throughout the March: more than half of the Welsh freeholders of Gwestfa Oerentlyn (Kidwelly) had less than five acres each; so also did almost half of the tenant population of the eastern lordship of Whitecastle in 1386; the size of peasant holdings appears to be markedly higher in the north, but even in Coelion (Dyffryn Clwyd) most tenants held less than twenty acres of land each.[1] It is true that some of these tenants may have held land elsewhere in their lordships and also have held land of other lords; they may also have supplemented their incomes and output from the extensive tracts of pasture, forest and upland grazing land that were to be found in much of the March. It is also obvious that in any characterization of the distribution of rural landed wealth, we must allow for regional and chronological variations. Nevertheless, the overall impression remains that of a peasant society where the average arable holding was less than ten acres in area.

Peasant society, however, has never been a society of equals. The meagre territorial endowment of most peasants only served to highlight the relative wealth of a minority of their richer neighbours. In Gwestfa Oerentlyn (Kidwelly) three men with more than sixty acres each towered above their fellow peasants; in Whitecastle six men with more than forty acres each stood apart from their neighbours; in Llanfaenor (Monmouth) a third of the tenant land was in the hands of two wealthy farmers and much the same was true of neighbouring Rockfield. Such disparities of territorial wealth may well have been a long-standing feature of Marcher society; they were also no doubt exaggerated by the accidents of inheritance and by the variations of individual initiative. Yet it can hardly be doubted that these disparities were further exaggerated by the glut of vacant holdings in the late fourteenth century and the opportunity thereby afforded for the accumulation of tenements.[2] The social stratification of the Marcher peasantry may be expressed in ways other than the acreage of arable land they held. One such alternative measuring rod is that of the number of sub-tenants who held land of the peasants themselves. It is not a measuring rod that is easily applied for the obvious reason that seignorial documents are by definition not directly concerned with sub-tenants. Yet the lords of the March themselves recognized that one of the distinctions within their own tenantry was between those tenants who had and those tenants who did not have sub-tenants. In the lordships of Denbigh and of

[1] Cardiff Central Library, Brecon Documents, 2 (Hay); C. 133/91, no. 2, m. 13 (Bronllys, 1298) D.L. 43/13/14 (Kidwelly, fourteenth century); D.L. 43/13/8 (Whitecastle); 'The Lordship of Dyffryn Clwyd in 1324', *T.D.H.S.* 17 (1968), 7–53.

[2] For Whitecastle and Kidwelly see previous footnote; for Llanfaenor, Rockfield and Hadnock see D.L. 43/13/7 (late fourteenth century).

Bromfield and Yale this distinction was one of the criteria for the assessment of renders to the lord. It was a distinction which cut across the status division between free and unfree, for while in Carnwyllion (Kidwelly) the survey refers to the dues of the villeins of freemen, in Denbigh it was envisaged that a freeman might be the sub-tenant of a villein.[3] Evidence from many parts of the March suggests that the number of sub-tenants might be very considerable and that the authority of the lord over them was often minimal. In Clun, for example, it was asserted that any land-holding tenant could accept another into his protection to become his tenant or servant and it was even claimed that the goods of a sub-tenant who died without an heir should be forfeit to the tenant who was his immediate superior, not to the lord of the lordship. In Chirkland in 1334 the lord went so far as to concede that freemen should have the death-duties (*ebediwau*) of their undertenants provided they were not in the lord's authority.[4] What our documents fail to provide is any precise information on the numbers and distribution of these undertenants and thereby of their role in the social stratification of peasant society. Madoc Hen of Monmouth, we know, had six villeins holding fifty acres of land and owing 23*s.* 2*d.* in rent; the sons of another Welsh freeman of Monmouth had four villeins. They were small fry compared with the Cardiganshire man, Ieuan ap Madoc, who had over a hundred tenants. The only overall figures of undertenants come from the commote of Isaled in Denbigh where in 1334 thirteen freemen had seventy-four undertenants, whereas the remaining one hundred and thirteen freemen had none.[5] It is a numerical proportion which corresponds fairly closely to that we have already suggested for the distribution of tenant land. It suggests clearly that peasant society in the March was not so much a pyramid in terms of wealth, but rather a broad plateau above which rose a few peaks.

[3] *S.D.*, 47, 148; S.B.Y., fol. 18ᵛ (Bromfield and Yale, 1391); D.L. 43/13/14, m. 3.

[4] S.R.O. 552/1/7, m. 7 (1337); 10, m. 14 (1344); 45, m. 2 (1424); Llinos Smith, 'The Arundel Charters to the Lordship of Chirk in the Fourteenth Century', *B.B.C.S.* 23 (1969), 161.

[5] D.L. 42/1, f. 17ᵛ; Monmouth R.O., Llanarth Collection, D. 2.27 (Monmouth); W. Rees, *South Wales and the March 1284–1415*, 244, n. 6; R. A. Griffiths, *The Principality of Wales*, i, 473 (Ieuan ap Madoc); *S.D.*, 148.

The social stratification of the peasantry was also reflected in the distribution of moveable property and stock. In an arable agrarian society no line of division was more obvious than that between peasants who had and those who did not have a ploughbeast, that is the means for the individual or co-operative cultivation of their land by animal traction. It was the distinction between the *manouvriers* and the *laboureurs* which French historians have recognized as central in the history of peasant societies.[6] The distinction was one which was certainly recognized in medieval Wales. It was only the possession of an ox or of the plough or possibly of technical skill which entitled a man to enlist in the co-operative ploughing arrangements (*cyfar*) of his vill, according to the Welsh law-texts. In Bromfield and Yale the contribution towards the *rhaglaw*'s fee varied according to whether the tenant owned a plough-beast or not; in Denbigh a special render assessed at eight pence per annum was levied from plough-owning villeins; while in the March generally the ploughing services of the unfree were dependent on the possession of an ox or a horse.[7] Such formal distinctions were only a recognition of the vast disparities in personal wealth in peasant society. Thirty-one customary tenants and advowry men died without heirs in Dyffryn Clwyd in 1349; between them their stock only amounted to twenty-six and a half cows, twenty and a half sheep, sixteen calves, seven and a half affers, seven oxen and five heifers (the half units representing the shares of neighbours or other family members in the stock). The gap in wealth between them and another villein whose stock in 1362 included twelve cows, eight calves, three steers, twenty-four sheep and ten lambs was great; between them and Iorwerth ap Bleddyn, a rich farmer with 200 sheep, forty lambs, six oxen and corn in the fields worth ten marks, the gap was truly enormous.[8]

Yet great as were these disparities in territorial wealth, few of the peasants of the March were so rich that they could not be overwhelmed by a sudden or a recurring financial demand. The frequent entries on the court rolls of the surrender of land on account of poverty (*propter inopiam, propter paupertatem*) need

[6] M. Bloch, *French Rural Society*, 193–6.
[7] S.B.Y., fol. 18ᵛ; *S.D.*, 149–50; D.L. 43/13/8, m. 7 (Whitecastle).
[8] S.C. 2/217/14 (1349); 218/10, m. 28 (1362); 216/13, m. 1ᵛ (Iorwerth ap Bleddyn, 1331).

not always be dismissed as special pleading. Iorwerth ab Ieuan ab Ednyfed of Dyffryn Clwyd was no pauper: he was the sergeant (*rhingyll*) of his commote and his stock included two cows, two steers, two horses and fourteen sheep; but even the lord had to admit that his rents and services at £3 per annum exceeded his income and so discharged him from part of his lands. For such men a sudden financial demand—a contribution towards a communal subsidy or fine, a heavy amercement in court, a virginity payment of 7s. 6d. for an errant daughter, a succession due (ranging from 7s. 6d. to £1 according to status and relationship), the expense of a wedding or a funeral and of the accompanying dues to the church—could easily overwhelm them. It was so, for example, with the sons of Iorwerth ap Gwrgenau who found themselves faced with succession dues of £4 7s. 2d. as the heirs of an uncle and three cousins who died of the plague in 1349. Such debts could be met in part by borrowing; there is indeed ample evidence of mutual lending, of sales by credit, of the mortgaging of land, and of the activities of local usurers (lending money often at 30 per cent interest or more). Yet where margins were so small and the claims of the lord and of the church on the peasant's surplus so large, the boundary between solvency and indebtedness was a very narrow one. Dafydd ap Madoc, a villein of Caus lordship, was not a poor man for his corn, stock, goods and debts owed to him were valued at over £3; but the expenses of his funeral (16s. 8d.), a heriot (8s. 10d.) and the payment of outstanding debts (2s. 6d.) meant that his resources as they were transferred to his heir were immediately halved.[9]

It is the stratification of peasant society that we have discussed so far; but in terms of land and of stock there came a point on the economic scale when a family was unable to be self-sustaining in terms of its tenement and relied on alternative sources of income for its livelihood or at least as a supplement to the produce of its land. Here we cross the line from peasant society into an area where the documents fail us almost completely. Many men in this group were classed as cottagers, living from the produce of the curtilages appurtenant to their

---

[9] S.C. 2/218/4, m. 11 (Iorwerth ap Ieuan ab Ednyfed, 1354); 217/14, m. 13[v] (Iorwerth ap Gwrgenau, 1349); Staffs. R.O. D. 641/1/4T/1, m. 2 (Dafydd ap Madoc 1400).

cottages and no doubt also from the produce of the woodland and commons. Thus on the episcopal manor of Llanddew (Brecon) in 1326, the majority of the tenant population were officially classified as cottagers and such indeed they were in terms of their minute holdings. Other members of this group doubtless helped to swell the numbers of the advowry tenants and undertenants who figure prominently in the records of some lordships. Some of them supplemented their income by taking up local crafts and becoming carpenters, smiths, masons, fullers and millers. The great majority must have found employment, on a casual or permanent basis, as agricultural labourers. Some did so in the service of local lords, squires and wealthier peasants; many formed part of a large pool of migrant labourers who moved to neighbouring lordships and often to England in search of seasonal employment, especially at harvest time. In Dyffryn Clwyd, for example, eleven men were fined for going to England to work in 1351, sixteen in 1367 and twenty-two in 1384; in Cantrefselyf most of the hundred advowry tenants were said to have 'retired from the lordship' in 1372.[10] It was doubtless from this same seasonal migrant force, so often a feature of over-populated pastoral communities, that many of those Welsh archers and footmen were drawn who formed such a significant element in English armies in the late-medieval period. Such men and women lived on or below the poverty line; they figure in the seignorial records only when they were accused of begging or of collecting sheaves in the autumn or of contravening the seignorial prohibition against the native custom of community poor relief (*commortha*).[11]

Peasant society shared many features in common throughout the March and indeed throughout medieval Europe. Yet it would be misleading to emphasize such similarities without recognizing at the same time the regional variations in the

[10] *The Black Book of St. David's, 1326,* ed. J. W. Willis-Bund, 290 (Llanddew); for advowry tenants, see above pp. 138–9; for labour migraiton to England at harvest time, see *Rot. Parl.,* II, 234 (1350); the figures for labour migration from Dyffryn Clwyd are taken from the court rolls; for the advowry tenants of Cantrefselyf, see S.C. 6/1156/14.

[11] Thus in 1337 the 'whole community of Tempseter seeks permission to give sheaves to their kinsman and neighbour, Ieuan ap Meuric' (S.R.O. 552/1/7, m. 2), while in Llannerch (Dyffryn Clwyd) in 1391 eighteen persons, of whom twelve were women, were accused of seeking *commortha* in the countryside contrary to the lord's prohibition (S.C. 2/220/12, m. 2ᵛ).

social structure of Marcher society. In this respect the returns for the 1292 subsidy are invaluable for they are one of the few non-seignorial sources of information on Marcher society and one that permits comparison to be made between different lordships. The surviving tax-returns, it is true, are restricted to a few lordships, but those lordships are sufficiently different from each other and representative of the March as a whole to allow certain broad conclusions to be drawn. The information is best set out in tabular form (as in Table 2).

The basic contrast, both in the regional and social distribution of wealth, is clearly that between the lowland eastern lordships and the upland and largely Welsh lordships. In Abergavenny and Monmouth there is a clear élite (groups *A* and *B*) composed of only 4 to 6 per cent of the tax-paying population but accounting for over 40 per cent of moveable taxable wealth. In Radnor and Powys, both of them lordships with substantial areas of good lowland arable, such an élite is by no means so prominent; in Chirkland and Cilgerran, both largely upland lordships, it is markedly smaller; in Iscennen it is non-existent. The contrast in the social and economic contours is most evident in the lordships of Monmouth and Chirkland. Here we have two lordships with fairly comparable taxable populations (794:697); but where the contrast in taxable wealth (£161:£67) is considerable. Even more marked is the distribution of that wealth within the two lordships, for whereas those with goods assessed at over 75s. in value account for 63·8 per cent of the subsidy payable in Monmouth, the proportion is only twenty-one per cent in Chirkland and there not a single person was estimated to have goods worth more than £15. Whatever margin we allow for tax-evasion and for different methods of assessment, the importance of the contrast remains. It is furthermore reinforced by similar contrasts between the two Hastings lordships of Abergavenny and Cilgerran and less markedly between the two Giffard lordships of Bronllys and Iscennen. These contrasts are no doubt to be explained in part in terms of geographical differences, in part in terms of the varying historical development of the respective districts (Iscennen, Cilgerran and Chirkland only finally succumbing to English rule after 1282) and in part perhaps in terms of the contrast between districts where opportunities for market pro-

TABLE 2

The Distribution of Taxable Wealth in the March, 1292

Lordship	POWYS	ABERGAVENNY	MONMOUTH	RADNOR	BRONLLYS	ISCENNEN	CILGERRAN	CHIRKLAND
A Number of persons taxed over £1	4 (0·2)	10 (1·6)	14 (1·7)	5 (0·6)	5 (2·1)	—	—	—
B Number of persons taxed over 10s.	14 (0·9)	13 (2·2)	30 (3·7)	9 (1·0)	1 (0·4)	—	1 (0·7)	3 (0·4)
C Number of persons taxed over 5s.	131 (8·7)	23 (4·0)	97 (12·2)	59 (7·4)	13 (5·4)	2 (1·5)	12 (8·8)	40 (6·2)
D Number of persons taxed under 5s.	1350 (90·0)	546 (92·3)	653 (82·4)	732 (90·9)	219 (92·0)	128 (98·5)	122 (90·4)	654 (93·4)
Total number of taxpayers	c. 1500	592	794	805	238	130	135	697
Amount contributed by Group A	£7 (3·5)	£31 (33·0)	£38 (23·6)	£7 (6·2)	£20 (44·4)	—	—	—
Amount contributed by Group B	£9 (4·5)	£8 (8·6)	£22 (16·6)	£5 (3·4)	£1 (2·2)	—	£1 (5·5)	£2 (3·0)
Amount contributed by Group C	£41 (20·5)	£7 (7·5)	£38 (23·6)	£17 (15·0)	£5 (11·1)	£0·1 (9·0)	£4 (22·2)	£12 (18·0)
Amount contributed by Group D	£143 (71·5)	£47 (50·5)	£63 (36·2)	£84 (74·3)	£19 (42·2)	£10 (91·0)	£13 (72·2)	£53 (79·0)
Total amount of tax (to nearest £)	c. £200	£93	£161	£113	£45	£10	£18	£67

NOTES: 1. The figures for Radnor also incorporate those for Knighton, Norton, Presteigne, Winforton and Stapleton.
2. The figures for Bronllys also incorporate those for Clifford and Glasbury.
3. The subsidy rolls for Powys and Iscennen are damaged and the figures, especially in the case of Powys, may therefore not be complete.
4. The figures in brackets represent the percentages of the totals.

SOURCES: E. 179/242/54–57, 59–60.

duction and capital accumulation were more advanced on the one hand and economically underdeveloped communities on the other.

There is little that we can add in terms of the distribution of wealth within the individual Marcher lordships beyond the truism that wealth in moveables was concentrated in certain obvious social categories. The Marcher lords themselves obviously stand out, with assessed goods ranging from £30 in the case of the de la Pole lord of Powys to £205 in that of Earl Edmund of Lancaster, lord of Monmouth and Threecastles. Yet they do not tower in the tax-returns to the same extent as they did in the social and territorial landscape of the March generally, for their wealth and authority lay in land and lordship rather than in stock and moveables. They were occasionally outstripped in tax valuations by religious houses, especially by the Cistercian houses rich in moveable wealth. Notable among these was Dore Abbey, which accounted on its own for almost a third of the tax from the Bronllys group of estates (£14:£45) and whose moveables in Bronllys, Abergavenny and Monmouth were assessed at almost £260, or, on a smaller scale, the abbey of Ystrad Marchell which was far and away the largest single taxpayer in Powys. Another category of wealthy taxpayers in the lowland March consisted of well to do squires, such as Richard Seymour or Walter Huntley in Monmouth (taxable wealth £23 and £99 respectively); it is a group to which we must return later. All that needs to be emphasized here is that such men are almost totally wanting in the Welsh upland lordships of Iscennen, Cilgerran and Chirkland. Two further groups from which the wealthier taxpayers were drawn deserve to be mentioned, namely the secular clergy and the burgesses. Among the former we may note, by way of example, Richard Clerk of Welshpool (taxable wealth £12) or Geoffrey the Clerk of Abergavenny (£30); we will encounter some of their colleagues as active land-speculators in the March. That burgesses should be relatively wealthy in taxable chattels is not surprising; but the figure that some of them cut in Marcher society is a revelation. Henry Skinner of Abergavenny with goods assessed at £100 was truly outstanding; but others such as Thomas Mercer of Monmouth or Thomas Taylor of Abergavenny or some of the burgesses of Welshpool figure prominently in the higher ranks of Marcher taxpayers. Their stature was the more impressive in a society where over ninety-two per cent of the taxpayers—and that, of course, excludes the poorest stratum of the population—were assessed at less than five shillings for tax. It is a figure which reinforces our initial claim that this was an overwhelmingly peasant society.

THE MARCHER LAND MARKET

A deep sense of family property rights in the peasant holding is one of the most widely acknowledged features of peasant society. In medieval Wales this sense of the family's property rights was greatly reinforced by the firm rules against the outright alienation of hereditary holdings and by rigid succession customs which decreed that family lands (*tir gwelyawg*) were divisible among male coheirs up to the third degree of blood relationship. *Ex hypothesi* such rules and customs should have ensured the continuity of family holdings within the same kin-group from one generation to the next and should also have militated against the development, or at least the further development, of marked economic differentiation in the ranks of the Marcher peasantry. Such a hypothesis is substantially supported by the evidence of the tax-returns of 1292, notably and significantly from lordships such as Chirkland and Iscennen. Yet we have also insisted on the evidence for some measure of economic stratification within the Marcher peasantry, a stratification which becomes more marked geographically as we descend into the eastern lowlands and more obvious chronologically from the fourteenth century onwards. Where lies the explanation? It obviously rests in some measure in a distant past, for the discrepancies in the size of peasant holdings seem to be as old in Western Europe as the records themselves.[12] It may also rest in good part in the varying geographical and agrarian features of different areas and in the economic opportunities for market production and capital accumulation. It also certainly rests in some measure in the vagaries of peasant demography, for (as we have suggested above) no feature was

---

[12] M. Bloch, *French Rural Society*, 152 ff., G. Duby, *The Early Growth of the European Economy* (1974), 79–80; R. H. Hilton, *Bond Men Made Free*, 32–4.

more significant in terms of the distribution of landed wealth in the Welshries than the calculus of mortality.

One further explanation offers itself and one which seems to become more important with the passage of time, namely the peasant land market. Our starting point in any discussion of the land market must be the distinction, which Marcher custom shared with most medieval customary laws, between hereditary land (*terra de hereditate*) and acquired land (*terra de perquisito*).[13] The former was carefully protected by age-old rules on the rights of the kin-group and the practice of partibility; the latter was regarded as being much more firmly within the individual proprietor's authority and thereby more freely his to devise and to alienate. One major category of acquired land, both in economic and in legal terms, was the land assarted from forest and waste. In the March, as elsewhere in Europe, the Middle Ages witnessed a vigorous campaign to extend the map of human settlement and the area of arable agriculture. The lordship of Brecon is a case in point: much of its terrain was mountainous and the predominantly pastoral character of its agriculture was reflected in the biennial tribute of 136 cows from the Welsh community and in the long lists of animals sent to graze in the Upper Forest district of the Epynt range. On the other hand, the documents suggest that the area of arable cultivation in the upland districts of the lordship may have been more extensive in the fourteenth century than at any subsequent stage in the history of the region: six of the seignorial mills of Brecon were located in the Great Forest and yielded 300 *summe* of oats to the lord annually, while in 1353 the community of the lordship was fined the colossal sum of £400 for land that it had acquired in the forest without the lord's licence.[14] This process of assarting was proceeding apace throughout the March. In two of the vills of Usk lordship there was half as much 'new land' as there was customary land (342 acres out of 675); in the vill of Ogmore (Glamorgan) more than a quarter of the tenant land (47 acres out of 170) was land recently assarted from the chalk downlands; in Denbigh 560 acres of land

---

[13] Note, for example, the contrast in a Builth inquisition of 1299: 'nullas terras habuit de perquisito nisi de hereditate antecessorum suorum', *Arch. Camb., Supplement Volume of Original Documents*, 1877, cxlviii.

[14] S.C. 6/1156/16–17 (1371–2); D.L. 29/671/10810, m. 21 (1353).

were assarted in Brynbagl and Cernenyfed alone in the early-fourteenth century; in Carnwyllion (Kidwelly) the area of assarts (*terra affirmata de vasto, terra assarta*) was equal to about a fifth of the area of primary settlement (588 acres out of 3,155) and a further 150 acres were recovered in the late fourteenth century.[15] This assarting movement is obviously important in the making of the Welsh landscape; it is also important in the development of landlordship in the March. Here, however, what needs to be emphasized is the opportunities it afforded for individual enterprise and for further differentiation in the economic structure of the peasantry. Assarted land was exempt from the rigid rules on alienation and partibility that applied to hereditary land; it was held directly of the lord for a fixed money rent per acre; it was, as in England, one of 'the most volatile elements in the land market'.[16] In Llanedi (Kidwelly), for example, Ieuan ap Gwlhanedd shared forty acres of hereditary land with his three brothers and in respect of his share contributed towards the communal renders of the district; as an individual he also held fifty acres of land leased from the waste at two pence per acre. It was in this latter capacity that he stood apart from his brothers and ranked well above his fellow peasants in terms of landed wealth.[17]

He could have done so also in terms of leasing escheated lands. The Marcher lords applied the law of escheat ruthlessly, especially in the new lordships of the north-eastern March. In much of the lordship of Denbigh, for example, up to half of the tenant land was declared to have escheated to the lord.[18] Such an application of the law of escheat had momentous results in terms of the authority and profits of lordship; it had equally momentous results in terms of the land market. Escheated land was withdrawn from the control of descent-groups and from the restrictions of Welsh law; it was leased by the lord at an economic rent and at his will. From the peasant's point of view, it brought a substantial amount of land onto the market, to be leased by individuals and normally to be held by English rules of inheritance. As a result many Welsh peasants in the March

---

[15] *C.I.P.M.*, IV, no. 435 (p. 325); *Glam. C.H.*, III, 296; *S.D.*, 21–5, 109–16; D.L. 43/13/14; D.L. 29/573/9063. Cf. also *The Lordship of Oswestry 1393–1607*, ed. W. J. Slack, 154, 157.

[16] E. J. King, *Peterborough Abbey 1086–1310. A Study in the Land Market* (Cambridge, 1973), 62.   [17] D.L. 43/13/14.   [18] See above pp. 104–5.

came to hold both hereditary land and leased land (*terra ad acras*). Thus of the eighteen Welsh free tenants who died in the commote of Llannerch (Dyffryn Clwyd) during the period 1342–8, ten held escheated lands in addition to their hereditary estates; for the former they paid a relief on succession and an annual rent thereafter, for the latter a fixed death duty on succession and a contribution to communal renders thereafter. Likewise, to cite an individual example, Cynfrig ap Bleddyn of Denbigh was a fairly wealthy man in respect of his membership of various descent-groups with lands extending into at least eight vills; but his economic standing was considerably enhanced by the forty-two acres of escheated and arrented lands he held in five vills. For him the lease of such lands was the path to economic success.[19]

The economic differentiation in the ranks of the peasantry could be further accentuated by the lease of demesne resources, including manors, arable, pasture, meadow, forests and mills. Occasionally the demesne resources were leased in a piecemeal fashion; elsewhere they were farmed *en bloc*, the lord reserving to himself only his judicial and franchisal rights. The men who leased those demesne resources were normally already much richer than their neighbours. They included wealthy local burgesses, such as John Yonge of Brecon; well placed local officials, such as Richard Mogholom bailiff of Hay, who leased two mills, the rich fisheries of the Wye and a share of 150 acres of demesne arable in 1374; enterprising local Welshmen such as Meurig ab Adam of Whitecastle (Monmouth), already well placed in respect of his forty acres of family land but now also one of the lessees of the demesne arable, two watermills and the pannage of the lordship. From the ranks of such men would often emerge the gentry families of the next generation: it is indicative that Meurig ab Adam was not only an enterprising farmer but also supervisor of the repairs to the castle and one of the men appointed to defend the castle during the invasion scare of 1369–70. For such men—and they are to be found in most parts of the March—the later fourteenth century was an age of opportunity.[20]

[19] S.C. 2/217/7–13 (Llannerch); *S.D.*, 157, 164, 168, 183, 193, 207 (Cynfrig ap Bleddyn).
[20] For John Yonge, see D.L. 29/671/10810, m. 22 (bailiff of Brecon town, 1354);

So far we have mentioned only what may be called the casual items of the Marcher land market—assarts, escheats and demesne resources. In acreage these items probably accounted for the greater part of the land, particularly of compact parcels of fertile land, that came on the market. We must now turn to what we may regard as the staple items of the peasant land market, the annual turnover in tenant land ranging from whole tenements to the individual messuage or a fraction of an acre, whether by sale, lease, mortgage or exchange. The extent of this land market is difficult to gauge, for two reasons. Too often estimates of the activity and range of the land market have been based on collections of deeds. Valuable as these are for documenting the history of the landed fortunes of a particular family, they are not necessarily representative of the scope or character of the land market in general. Secondly, even in the court rolls, which form a more representative guide to the peasant land market, it is difficult to know what allowances we should make for fictional sales and for unlicensed and thereby unrecorded leases and purchases.

Nor even there do our problems end, for land was conveyed in the March in at least three major ways—by the conveyancing methods of English common law (notably charter of enfeoffment and fine and recovery), by the surrender of customary land to the lord in court to the use (*ad opus*) of another tenant, and by Welsh mortgage arrangements (*prid*). Both the geography and chronology of these conveyancing methods within the March remain to be studied in detail. English common law methods of conveyancing were certainly widespread, not only in lowland districts such as Glamorgan and Pembroke but also in relatively Welsh districts such as upland Brecon where Welshmen conveyed land by charter in fee simple or leased it for a number of years with arrangements for reversion. Even in lordships such as Dyffryn Clwyd, where Welsh land law was to prove particularly resilient, English conveyancing methods were certainly employed by Welshmen. Thus in 1341 Goronwy ap Cynfrig acquired fourteen acres of free land in Faenol 'by

E. 101/32/20 (squire in retinue of earl of Hereford); S.C. 6/1156/18; *C.F.R.*, VIII, 230 (receiver of lordship of Brecon, *c.* 1366, 1374); S.C. 6/1156/15 (leases forty-three acres of the demesne of Brecon manor). For Richard Mogholom, see S.C. 6/1156/21 (1374–5); for Meurig ab Adam, see D.L. 43/13/8 (1386); D.L. 29/615/9837 (1370); D.L. 29/594/9506–07 (1370, 1378).

free charter'; while in 1365 the land alienated by one Welshman to another 'by charter' was taken into the lord's hand.[21]

In most parts of the March land held by English or customary tenure was normally transferred by surrender to the lord in court to the use (*ad opus*) of the prospective tenant. Not all such surrenders were in fact sales of land. In the commote of Llannerch (Dyffryn Clwyd) in the period 1342–7, more than 300 acres were so conveyed according to the court rolls. Some of the transfers so affected were certainly outright sales: when Master John ap David surrendered seven and a half acres to the use of Dafydd ap Hywel ab Iorwerth in 1345 there can be little doubt that the transaction was a sale, for the transfer was accompanied by the acknowledgement of a debt of £8 10s. Equally, however, some of the land so transferred was the subject of inter-family gifts and exchanges and of marriage endowments; in other cases what was envisaged was a lease for a short term of years. This method of land alienation was practised in respect of English and Welsh customary land alike; it was not unknown for land so conveyed to be held subsequently by the terms of Welsh free tenure.[22] It was also the normal method of conveyance for all categories of acquired land and for land to be held by lease- or copy-hold. Above all, it was a method of land transfer which ensured the lord a firm oversight of the land market of his tenants and an opportunity to profit by it. The Welsh terminology made this seignorial control particularly obvious: it required a tenant who wished to convey a part of his land to surrender a rod to the steward in court and to pay a fixed sum to the lord as a 'fee of investiture' (*gobrestyn*).[23]

In those parts of the March where Welsh law was vigorously upheld outright alienation of Welsh hereditary land was strictly prohibited. This prohibition was firmly maintained by English kings and Marcher lords alike in spite of the persistent demands of the native Welsh communities to give and to sell their lands

[21] For Brecon examples of the use of English common law methods, see D.L. 25/918, 920 (1312, 1337); N.L.W. Quaritch Deeds, 1–2 (1361, 1371); *Cat. MSS. Wales in B.M.*, III, 595–6 (1362, 1388). All parties to these deeds bear Welsh names. The Dyffryn Clwyd examples are taken from S.C. 2/217/6, m. 25ᵛ, 219/2, m. 20.

[22] See, for example, S.C. 2/217/7, m. 17 (marriage endowment); 271/11, m. 22 (short lease); 219/11, m. 16 (land alienated to be held by Welsh tenure).

[23] *A Survey of the Duchy of Lancaster Lordships in Wales, 1609–13*, ed. W. Rees, xxv, 177.

freely.[24] The instrument of seignorial control of the market in Welsh land was the licence required for *prid* transactions. In brief, *prid* (or Welsh mortgage as it came to be known to English lawyers) was a method whereby the hereditary proprietor of Welsh land (*priodor*) could convey that land or part of it to another party (*pridwr*) for a term of years in return for an agreed sum of money (*prid*).[25] On repayment of this sum of money, the proprietor or his heirs could recover the land in question. The amount paid as *prid* clearly varied according to the extent and quality of the land in question; the duration of the *prid* or mortgage arrangement might also vary from one year to a hundred years, but in the great majority of cases the normal term of a *prid* transaction was four years, renewable for further four-year periods until the mortgage was redeemed. It was a method of conveyance which could be, and was, employed to transmit all sorts of property, moveable and immoveable. During the fourteenth century, the technical terms of *prid* transactions were gradually refined and clauses were introduced regarding such issues as the breach of the terms of the contract, improvements to buildings and to land carried out during the period of the *prid*, rights to cut timber, and the liability of mortgagor and mortgagee for the payment of succession dues, virginity payments, debts and arrears. Much work remains to be undertaken on the geography and chronology of *prid* in late-medieval Wales. That it was extensively used in the March is clear; the evidence is most ample for the north-east March but *prid* conveyances are also to be found in areas as far apart as Clun, Brecon and Kidwelly.

The importance of *prid* in terms of the Welsh land market was undoubted; it gave Welsh land customs the measure of flexibility necessary to adjust to the fast-changing economic conditions of the fourteenth century. Its functions were various: it was used to iron out some of the problems caused by Welsh inheritance-customs, particularly with regard to the fragmentation of holdings; it could be employed as a means to consolidate holdings by securing adjacent strips of land; it was often in

---

[24] See above pp. 143–5.

[25] The institution of *prid* urgently requires a careful study. The next three paragraphs are based on a review of the Marcher evidence on *prid*; I hope to give detailed attention to the issues and to the evidence in a forthcoming article.

effect a short- or long-term lease, for the clause with regard to the right of redemption was not merely a form of words. It was extensively used as a means of side-stepping the prohibitions of Welsh law on the alienation of hereditary land to persons who were not male members of the agnatic kin-group: *prid*-lands were given to daughters as a marriage-portion, to sons-in-law as part of a marriage settlement, and to widows as dower, all of them transactions forbidden in respect of Welsh hereditary lands; they were also conveyed to third parties and, as with moveables, they could be disposed of by will. From the point of view of the needy Welsh freeholder, *prid* proved an attractive way of raising ready cash, especially to face a sudden financial emergency. There can be little doubt that *prid*-transactions were often the occasion for usurious loans, with a rate of interest of as high as thirty-three per cent concealed in the repayment sum; indeed the role of *prid* in rural credit in medieval Wales is confirmed by the instances in which the original *prid* was used as a means to raise further cash on top of the first mortgage.

In many cases a conveyance of land in *prid* was or came to be equivalent to virtual outright alienation. It could hardly be otherwise in those cases where the term of the mortgage was a hundred years, and redemption became even more difficult when the *pridwr* conveyed the land to a third party or, as was often the case, paid the dues, including the succession dues, arising from the land. In many parts of Wales *prid* in fact served as a successful device for the gradual accumulation of estates such as those of Ithel Fychan of Helygain (co. Flints.) and his descendants in the fourteenth century or of Gruffudd ap Aaron and his son Rhys around Peniarth (co. Merioneth) in the fifteenth century.[26] In Dyffryn Clwyd in the 1360s and 1370s, the most active estate-builder and land-speculator was one Ieuan ap Dafydd Fychan. He was a fairly substantial landowner in respect of his hereditary estates in Ceidio; but it was in the unusually active land market of the area that he made his fortune. In just over twenty years he invested more than £64 in twenty-two land transactions and no doubt the total sum would be nearer £100 if the records were complete. Furthermore, fourteen of these transactions were *prid* conveyances.

[26] For the growth of these two estates see respectively U.C.N.W. Mostyn Collection *passim* and N.L.W. Peniarth Collection, no. 496.

Prid was clearly attractive to the small rural capitalist intent on building a landed estate for himself.[27]

Ieuan ap Dafydd Fychan was rector of Ceidio. He thereby belonged to one of the most distinctive groups active in the Marcher land market in the fourteenth century, the rural clergy. They were often drawn from the wealthier stratum of Marcher society and in addition to their hereditary estates they also often held glebe-lands as well as the not inconsiderable profits from tithes, fees and altar offerings. If to this we add the role that some of them seem to have played as moneylenders, we begin to appreciate how well-placed they were to take advantage of the active land market in the fourteenth century. Ieuan ap Dafydd Fychan certainly had a way with money and with land: in 1365 he paid £20 for the estate of another Welsh cleric and subsequently sold a third of it for £11 13*s.* 4*d.*, realizing a handsome profit for himself; in 1380 he arranged that all his landed acquisitions (including those secured by *prid* conveyances) should henceforth be held by English tenure and then enfeoffed his lands on his elder son and his heirs with reversion to his younger son. Ieuan ap Dafydd Fychan was clearly wise in the ways of the world, particularly of Marcher land law and the land market. It was a wisdom which he shared with many of his fellow clergymen such as Master John ap David, rector of Llanfair (Dyffryn Clwyd) who paid £36 for a handsome estate in 1344, or Master Hywel Cyffin who became one of the most important landowners in Chirkland, or Master Lewis ap Gruffudd ap Llywelyn who occupied a similar role in Bromfield and Maelor Saesneg.[28] The southern March likewise had its share of such clerics—men such as Master Rees ap Hywel who built a formidable estate for himself in south-eastern Wales and passed it to his son or John Stackpole, chaplain of Pembroke, who agreed to pay £400 in rent in 1337. It comes as no surprise that among the leading patrons of the Welsh poets in the later Middle Ages were well-endowed local

---

[27] For his family estates see *T.D.H.S.* 17 (1968), 18; for his ecclesiastical position see S.C. 2/218/3, m. 14; for his landed acquisitions see S.C. 2/218/10–220/4 *passim*.

[28] S.C. 2/217/9, m. 4 (Master John ap David); Llinos Smith, 'The Lordships of Chirk and Oswestry, 1282–1415', Ph.D. thesis (Univ. of London, 1971), 320, n. 1 (Master Hywel Cyffin) B.L. Harleian 1977, fol. 111ᵛ (1340); *Cat. MSS. Wales in B.M.*, II, 434 (1340); N.L.W. Bettisfield Collection, no. 438 (1341) (Master Lewis ap Gruffudd ap Llywelyn).

clergymen such as Ithel ap Robert of Llaneurgain (co. Flints.), 'Sir' Benet parson of Corwen (co. Merioneth) or Sion Mechain parson of Llandrinio (Powys).[29]

Another group which figures prominently in the land market were the burgesses of the Marcher boroughs. They were well placed in the scramble for the leases of demesne lands and mills, which often lay close to the boroughs. In terms of available capital and of a ready market for surplus production, they were likewise well placed. As the fourteenth century progressed they also ventured increasingly into the market in vacant Welsh tenements in the countryside, even to the extent of becoming dab hands in *prid* conveyances. It was in such a fashion that the Boldes of Conway laid the base for the future Bulkeley estate in the Conway valley, that the Hollands of Abergele rose to such prominence as landowners in the lordship of Denbigh, that Richard Ireland and some of his fellow burgesses of Oswestry bought up vacant Welsh land or that the Forts of Llanstephan accumulated an estate of over 300 acres in the hinterland of the town.[30] Rich peasants and up-and-coming squires were also prominent in the ranks of the estate-builders. Some of them bequeathed the archives of their success to posterity: such were the prolific and ambitious sons of Iorwerth Foel of Chirkland or the equally remarkable sons of Ithel Fychan of Helygain (co. Flints) who were busily establishing the basis of the future Mostyn estates in the fourteenth century[31] or, on a more modest scale, Iorwerth Fychan ab Iorwerth ap Llywelyn who was assiduously piecing together an estate in the Dee valley.[32] For every such pushing freeholder who established the territorial fortunes of his descendants there must have been many others

---

[29] R. A. Griffiths, *The Principality of Wales*, i, 97–8 (Master Rees ap Hywel); *Penbrokshire*, 1, 183–4 (John Stackpole); Glanmor Williams, *The Welsh Church from Conquest to Reformation*, 127, 261–4 (clerical patrons of Welsh poets).

[30] T. Jones Pierce, *Medieval Welsh Society*, 195 ff. (Bolde); G. R. J. Jones in *Studies of Field Systems in the British Isles*, ed. A. R. H. Baker and R. A. Butlin, 468–71 (Holland); *The Lordship of Oswestry 1393–1607*, ed. W. J. Slack, 142–3, 158, 165; Llinos Smith, Ph.D. thesis, 313–15 (Richard Ireland and other Oswestry burgesses); R. A. Griffiths, 'The Cartulary and Muniments of the Fort Family of Llanstephan', *B.B.C.S.* 24 (1971), 311–84 (Fort).

[31] The growth of the estates of these two families is admirably documented, notably in U.C.N.W. Mostyn Collection and N.L.W. Chirk Castle, Bettisfield, Puleston and Plas Iolyn Collections.

[32] See above pp. 375–6.

whose ambitions and success were more modest or whose lands were dispersed at their deaths. What cannot be in doubt is the activity in the land market in the fourteenth-century March or the amount of money that was involved in some of these transactions. Sums ranging from £10 to £100 are mentioned in some of the deeds, both in outright purchases and in substantial *prid* transactions.[33] Men who had such sums of money to spare or who had the means to raise such capital clearly stood apart from their fellow-peasants; some of them were indeed no longer peasants but men with the means and the style of country squires.

Yet we must keep a sense of proportion. Collections of deeds are by their very nature the archives of success. To rely too heavily on them is to people society exclusively with up-and-coming squires and with impoverished peasants from whose misfortunes the new estates were created. That would be a distortion both of the social structure and of the character of the land market. The peasant land market by definition was not in existence merely as a pathway to creating gentry estates. Its main purpose was to give a measure of flexibility to the distribution of territorial wealth. That fact will be borne in upon us if we analyse, in so far as is possible, the territorial conveyances on a Marcher court roll, taking as our example the transactions in land in the commote of Llannerch (Dyffryn Clwyd) in the years 1340–8. What is immediately obvious is that many, even most, of the conveyances are essentially short-term leases or family arrangements. Out of sixty-five transactions, at least eleven are gifts by father to son or brother to brother, six are endowments at marriage, a further six are short-term leases, two are exchanges, seven represent leases of assarted or escheated land and in some of the other cases it is obvious that more than an outright sale was involved. In only two cases, which can certainly be classified as sales, was the total of land involved more than twenty acres. Two figures stand out in the transactions, Master John ap David a local cleric and Ieuan Kerry, land-jobber and rural usurer; but the impression is

---

[33] The following examples may serve as illustrations: £100 for lands in Chirkland in 1305; £10 for 100-year *prid* of half an inheritance in Bromfield in 1303; £80 for an eighty-year lease of lands in Clun in 1337 (U.C.N.W. Mostyn, 1627 (i); Flints. R.O., Trevor-Roper Collection, 1; S.R.O. 552/1/7, m. 8).

overwhelmingly one of a peasant society making small adjustments in its territorial fortunes but not in a major fashion changing the distribution of landed wealth. In other parts of the March the story may have been different; even in Dyffryn Clwyd by the late fourteenth century, as we shall see, it was beginning to be different.

THE MARCHER SQUIREARCHY

At several points in our discussion of the Marcher land-market we have strayed from peasant circles into those of the squirearchy. At what point we cross the line it is difficult to know, for as in England the boundary between the rich free peasant and the small landowner was far from clearly defined.[34] We may perhaps adopt as an economic denominator for this group an annual landed income of £10 or more. That is but half the income required for obligatory knighthood in late-thirteenth century England; but not only is our group deliberately broader than the 'knightly families' of English county society, its property qualification needs also to be adjusted downwards to cater for the relative poverty of Marcher society. The definition of the group likewise presents a problem. To follow the example of English historians by referring to 'the knightly class' would only cloud judgement, as knights were few in Marcher society other than in the south; to refer to them as *uchelwyr* is to appropriate for a racially-mixed group a Welsh legal term which had as yet no precise social or economic connotations. Instead we have chosen, reluctantly, to call them squires. The term 'esquire' was in current usage in both English and Welsh; it can be applied to native and settler 'gentry' alike; and in two contemporary hierarchies of status—those of military pay and sumptuary legislation—it was a recognized classification (albeit a more precise one than that which we have in mind).

That contemporaries recognized the existence of such a group seems evident enough from the documents. In Brecon, for example, the royal tax commissioners of 1292 acknowledged the existence of the group, and throughout the fourteenth century the 'mesne lords', the 'major tenants', the 'holders of

[34] See especially E. A. Kosminsky, *Studies in the Agrarian History of England in the Thirteenth Century* (Oxford, 1956), ch. v; R. H. Hilton, *A Medieval Society*, 49–61.

knights fees', as they were variously called, paid subsidies as a distinct group to the lord of Brecon.[35] In the neighbouring lordship of Blaenllyfni a separate officer, the 'beadle of the knights' (*bedellus militum*), was administratively and fiscally responsible for this group.[36] These were the men whom the Cardiff charter of 1340 described as the 'gentiles homines' of Glamorgan, a term which is echoed in a reference to the gentlemen (*gentils*) of Brecon who levied aids (*commortha*) from the poor men of the lordship.[37] In contemporary charters these men were frequently addressed as lords, *domini*; and so indeed they must have appeared, both in wealth and in eminence, within peasant society.[38] That eminence is reflected, albeit in stylized and extravagant form, in the odes addressed to them individually by the Welsh poets. It is expressed in a more precise and prosaic form in the valuations of the wardship of their heirs and the custody of their estates: in Brecon, for example, the wardship of the heir of Rhys ab Ieuan realized £40 in 1338, those of John son of John ap Rees and Walter son of Roger Vaughan 100 marks and £80 respectively in 1419.[39]

Information about individual Marcher squires and their families is not difficult to come by; it is much more difficult to gain a general picture of the geographical distribution and economic significance of the group as a whole in Marcher society. Our assessment can at best be no more than a general impression; but that impression may be less misleading if we ground it in the facts about a particular lordship, Brecon, reinforced by evidence from other parts of the March.[40] We may, for convenience's sake, classify the squires into two broad groups, the settler and the native squire families. In Brecon at

[35] D.L. 29/671/10810, m. 5, m. 8 (1341–43); S.C. 6/1156/18, m. 3 (1372); S.C. 6/1157/4 (1399).

[36] W. Rees, *South Wales and the March 1284–1415*, 103.

[37] *Cartae*, iv, no. 982; J.I. 1/1153, m. 9ᵛ (1413).

[38] See above pp. 92-3.

[39] D.L. 29/671/10810, m. 17; D.L. 42/17, fol. 44ᵛ, fol. 60ᵛ.

[40] The evidence for the Brecon squirearchy is considered in greater detail in R. R. Davies, D.Phil. thesis (Univ. of Oxford, 1965), esp. 79–80, 88–103, 115–30. References given here are kept to a bare minimum. For the early history of the settler families of the lordship see especially D. G. Walker, 'The "Honours" of the Earls of Hereford in the Twelfth Century', *Transactions of the Bristol and Gloucestershire Archaeological Society* 79 (1960), 174–211 and *idem*, 'Charters of the Earldom of Hereford, 1095–1201', *Camden Miscellany* 22 (Camden Society, 4th ser. vol. i, 1964), 1–75.

the beginning of the fourteenth century the majority of those who held by knight service were drawn from long-established settler families. Several of these families—such as the Pichards, Baskervilles, Waldeboefs and Devereux—had been associated with the lordship from at least the mid-twelfth century. Their ancestors may well have been in the original invading force of Bernard of Neufmarché, the first Norman conqueror of Brecon, and have received their original territorial endowments from him. In the lordship of Glamorgan we can trace the history of such a family, the Somerys of Dinas Powys. Roger Somery was one of the companions of Robert Fitzhamon, the conqueror of Glamorgan. From him no doubt he received the land of Dinas Powys and there built a castle on the site of an Iron Age fort and wielded his lordship over the surrounding fertile plains. He and his descendants ruled over this rich demesne lordship for over two centuries until the family failed in the male line in 1322.[41] Along the southern and eastern March there were many families of similar antiquity, real or asserted; the families of the March were as anxious to fabricate genealogies to show their descent from the original Norman invaders as were English gentry families to prove that they were descended from the companions of the Conqueror. For with age came not only the prestige of antiquity but also a measure of practical power: the Gower charter of 1306, for example, assigned a special position in the county court to the holders of the fourteen most ancient knights' fees.[42] The conquest of the March, however, had taken over two hundred years to achieve and so the list of the 'original' settler squire families of the March included relative newcomers, such as the Pulestons of Maelor Saesneg and Yale or the Crevequers of Flintshire and Dyffryn Clwyd, who only arrived in the March in the wake of the Edwardian conquest of 1282, as well as the much older families of the southern March.

The squirearchy, of course, was never a closed caste. Families died out or failed in the male line or became reduced in circumstances through economic mismanagement or political miscalculation. In Brecon, several of the most distinguished families fell on evil days in the fourteenth century: the Giffards of

[41] L. Alcock, *Dinas Powys* (Cardiff, 1963); *Glam. C.H.*, III, esp. 17–18; *Cartae*, esp. I, no. 35; II, nos. 539, 615, 632; III, no. 703; *C.I.P.M.*, II, no. 16; VI, no. 428.
[42] *Cartae*, III, no. 851 (p. 995).

Bronllys were wiped out by the events of 1322; the Mortimers of Pencelli were humiliated and largely disinherited; the Burghills of Llanfilo sold out their estate; the Earl of Hereford seized a share of the ancestral lands of the Waldeboefs and the Pichards.[43] Other families took their place. Seignorial reward was one quick route to territorial fortune: it was in that fashion that Roger Clifford, Reginald Grey and Richard Talbot, all of them friends and followers of the Lord Edward, became leading landowners in the lordship of Monmouth in the mid-thirteenth century;[44] it was in the same fashion, though in different circumstances, that John Iweyn battened on the debt-ridden lord of Gower and waxed rich at his expense.[45] Military service and marriage were the other well-established twin routes to fortune and to a place in the ranks of the squirearchy. It was by a series of remarkably fortunate marriages that the Stradlings, an immigré family of the later thirteenth century, rose to become one of the wealthiest families of Glamorgan by the early fifteenth century; it was by military service in the retinue of John of Gaunt and by a succession of wise marriages that the Greyndours of Monmouth in two generations rose to prominence in Marcher and English county society.[46] Compared with marriage and seignorial or royal patronage, territorial consolidation was a painfully slow and unspectacular way of building a family's fortune; indeed territorial consolidation served to confirm and to enhance a family's standing, but rarely could it by itself raise a family from the ranks of the peasantry into those of the squirearchy.

Many, probably most, of the settler squire families of the March continued to hold estates in England and turned easily in English county society. In Brecon, for example, the Baskervilles held estates in Herefordshire and Shropshire as well as in Pencelli; the Waldeboefs of Llanhamlach, the Burghills of Llanfilo, the Devereux of Pipton and the Pichards of Ystradyw

---

[43] See above pp. 94-5. For the sale of the Burghill estates, see D.L. 25/1594, 1607 (1315-21).

[44] *C.Ch.R.*, II, 246-7; *C.P.R.* 1272-81, 422; *1307-13*, 273, 408. The Cliffords eventually quitclaimed their lands in Monmouth; but the Talbots and the Greys (of Dingestow) remained as powerful families in the district.

[45] For his official career, see R. A. Griffiths, *The Principality of Wales*, I, 258; for his lands, see Hereford Cathedral Archives, esp. nos. 1311-13, 1529, 1761, 2661.

[46] See respectively R. A. Griffiths, 'The Rise of the Stradlings of St. Donat's, *Morgannwg* 7 (1963), 15-47 and R. R. Davies, D.Phil. thesis, 206-9.

were also all of them leading Herefordshire families. The same was true in Glamorgan: the Somerys of Dinas Powys were also barons of Dudley (co. Worcs.) and owners of other widely-scattered estates in England; the Stradlings and the Sullys held lands in Somerset, the Umfravilles in Devon. Furthermore, several Marcher families, especially those of Pembroke, had a considerable territorial stake in Ireland. The consequences of this dispersal of estates are obvious. It meant that the Marcher squirearchy was not merely an ingrown localized group; it recruited from without and its members often moved easily in English as well as in Marcher society. It also meant that the settler squirearchy of the March was less likely to go 'native' in its habits and attitudes than the Anglo-Norman families in Ireland. Neither socially nor geographically was the settler squirearchy of the March an isolated group.

The same was less true of the native Welsh squirearchy. The status definitions of Welsh law barely admitted of the existence of a noble class other than the 'innate gentlemen' of untainted Welsh blood and the bond between such 'gentlemen' was one of descent and status rather than one of wealth. Furthermore the ubiquity of the custom of partibility meant that the route to poverty was on the whole more frequently and more speedily descended by Welsh freemen than by their English colleagues. Yet in every part of the March, in greater or lesser measure, a recognizable group of native squires may be detected in the later Middle Ages. Some of them were descendants of the numerous dynasties of native Welsh princes: Llywelyn Bren, the leader of the revolt in Glamorgan in 1316 and undoubtedly 'a great and powerful man in his own country' (as the *Vita Edwardi Secundi* terms him) was almost certainly the son of the last native lord of Senghennydd (dispossessed 1266);[47] Philip ap Morgan, one of the foremost agents of the Mortimers in the later fourteenth century was likewise descended from another dispossessed princely house, that of Gwynllwg and Caerleon;[48] another leading Marcher family, that of Afan (or de Avene as it now preferred to call itself) could claim unimpeachable

[47] *Glam. C.H.*, III, 72–86.
[48] For his official career, see above pp. 205–6. He was the great-grandson of Morgan ap Maredudd, the rebel leader of 1294 and through him of the native lords of Gwynllwg; he was the ancestor of the family of Morgan of Llantarnam.

descent from Iestyn ap Gwrgant, the last native king of the land of Morgannwg.[49] Others of these native Marcher squires were men who had grown rich in the service of the native Welsh princes: native society in Dyffryn Clwyd in the early-fourteenth century was dominated by Hywel and Llywelyn ap Madoc, the descendants of a family which had been handsomely endowed by the princes of Gwynedd in the thirteenth century and whose territorial fortunes included over 800 acres of land and two mills.[50] In the March the Anglo-Norman lords were the source of patronage: in Brecon, for example, Hywel ab Einion and his descendants prospered in the service of the Bohuns; so likewise did the family of Hywel ap Meuric, faithful servants of Mortimer and Bohun since at least the mid-thirteenth century.[51] In other cases seignorial support is not so evident in the making or at least the expanding of the family fortune. All Welsh freemen claimed to be of good stock; but it was by dint of their own enterprise and ruthlessness in a buoyant land market that a few of them came to tower over their fellows. Such were the numerous descendants of Iorwerth Foel of Chirkland whose activities dominate the land-market of north-east Wales or Iorwerth Fychan ab Iorwerth ap Llywelyn of Bromfield whose estates eventually served to enhance the territorial power of the Trevors of Trefalun; such also in the southern March were the family of Gwilym ap Jenkin, ancestor of the Herberts, in Abergavenny, Monmouth and Usk or the forebears of Edward Lewis of Y Fan in Glamorgan.[52]

Between the settler and native squirearchy in the March the bonds were often close. Wealth was an efficient solvent of racial differences. Some of the great settler families, it is true, turned almost exclusively in English county society circles, and some of

---

49 *Glam. C.H.*, III, esp. 49–50, 251; for the 'maison d'Avene' see *Cartae*, IV, no. 983.

50 For grants to their father, Madoc (1260), and to their grandfather, Einion ap Maredudd (1243), see *N.L.W.J.* 3 (1943–4), 29–31, 158–62; for their lands in Dyffryn Clwyd, held by military service, see *T.D.H.S.* 17 (1968), 40. Hywel was *rhaglaw* of Dyffryn Clwyd in 1316 and his brother levied forces there in 1322. I hope to discuss their careers elsewhere.

51 For Hywel ab Einion and his descendants see above pp. 225–6; for Hywel ap Meuric and his family see briefly J. B. Smith in *B.B.C.S.* 24 (1970), 87–8; *The Welsh Assize Roll 1277–84*, ed. J. C. Davies, 117–20 and R. R. Davies, D.Phil. thesis, 88–91.

52 For collections of deeds relating to these families see respectively U.C.N.W., Mostyn Collection; Flints. R.O., Trevor-Roper Collection; N.L.W. Badminton Collection and *Glam. C.H.*, III, 330–1.

the smaller Welsh squireens had little to offer to their English neighbours. But on the whole the Marcher squirearchy was one. In Caerleon and Usk, for example, Welsh and English alike held of the lord by knight service; the only difference in tenure between them related to a few fees where the Welsh law of partibility among co-parceners applied.[53] Identity of style, manners and means was reinforced by ties of marriage. Sir Philip ap Rees of Talgarth married his daughters and heirs into the families of Peshale of Shropshire and Wrottesley of Staffordshire; Sir John ab Adam of Chepstow, notwithstanding his Welsh name (occasionally Anglicized as de Badeham!) had an English mother, took an English heiress to wife and was summoned to parliament; Owain Glyn Dŵr, impeccable as was his Welsh agnatic lineage, had a Lestrange as a grandmother and a Hanmer as wife.[54] The settler squirearchy likewise soon adapted itself to its Welsh habitat. The Hanmers of Maelor Saesneg (Flintshire) settled in Wales in the late-thirteenth century, yet within a century they were fully integrated with the native squirearchy and distinguished as patrons of Welsh culture. Much the same was true of other families such as the Pulestons of Emral (Bromfield and Yale), the Salisburys of Lleweni (Denbigh), the Havards of Pontwilym (Brecon) or the Stradlings of St. Donats (Glamorgan). This pattern of cultural assimilation in the ranks of the squirearchy has its own local geography and chronology in different parts of the March. Its character also varied from the ultimate Anglicization of many native families to the total identification of some settler families with their Welsh neighbours. In general, however, it can hardly be doubted that by the end of the fourteenth century the distinction between English and Welsh was less marked among the squirearchy than at any other level of Marcher society. It was among the 'meaner sorte of people', not among his own social peers, that George Owen of Henllys found the racial divide most profound in the sixteenth century.[55]

Landed income was obviously the main source of wealth and power of these men. To say so is to utter a truism, but not one

---

[53] *C.I.P.M.*, v, no. 538.
[54] *C.I.P.M.*, xii, no. 313; G.E.C., *The Complete Peerage*, i, 179–81; J. E. Lloyd *Owen Glendower*, 12, 16, 24–5.
[55] *Penbrokshire*, i, 39–40.

into which we can introduce many subtleties. Some of them were clearly far more powerful than others. The difference might be expressed in feudal terminology by distinguishing baronies—such as Pencelli (Brecon), Carew and Walwynscastle (Pembroke) and Coety (Glamorgan)—from knights' fees. The difference may occasionally be grasped in more clearly economic terms: Gilbert Turberville of Coety (Glamorgan), whose estates in the March were valued, modestly, at over £90 a year,[56] or Sir John Carew, the dower lands of whose widow were alone valued at £88 in 1362,[57] were obviously in a different economic category from small squires such as Robert Bruht, 'lord' of Dixton (Monmouth), whose landed fortune at his death was no more than 100 acres of arable, two acres of meadow, three acres of forest, half a water-mill and 42s. 3d. of rent.[58] In the lowland March the wealth of the squires was often founded on manors scarcely to be distinguished from those of the Marcher lords themselves. Bryndu (Brecon), the home farm of John fitz William ap Rees included a hall, chapel, grange, cowshed and two sheep-folds while its demesne resources in 1352 were itemized as four carucates of land, twenty acres of meadow, ten acres of pasture, twelve acres of wood and thirty shillings of rent.[59] In upland districts, the wealth of the squires was more obviously dependent on income from rent and mills rather than from home farms: such, for example, was almost certainly the case with Iorwerth ap Llywarch of Denbigh whose assets in 1330 included over 1,200 acres of land and several watermills or Llywelyn Fwya of Senghennydd with 600 acres of land to his name.[60]

The power of these men and the scene of their activities and ambitions were largely local; rarely did they extend beyond the boundaries of a single lordship. Yet on that stage their social superiority was obvious enough. It was manifested in the wealth

[56] D.L. 7/1, no. 27; *Cartae*, IV, no. 1, 116 (valuation of Coety in 1411 on the death of Sir Lawrence Berkerolles, the grandson of Sir Payn Turberville). Cf. also C. 47/9/32 for a survey of the lordship on the same occasion.

[57] *C.I.P.M.*, XI, no. 300; *Penbrokshire*, II, 325–34.

[58] D.L. 42/1, fol. 21ᵛ (1327). Cf. Monmouth R.O., Llanarth Court Collection, 25.

[59] D.L. 25/1624; S.C. 6/1156/13.

[60] For Iorwerth ap Llywarch, see above p. 224 and for his lands *S.D.*, 62, 135; *C. Inq. Misc. 1307–49*, no. 507; G. A. Holmes, *The Estates of the Higher Nobility*, 135, 137, 140; for Llywelyn Fwya, see *Glam. C.H.*, III, 318.

of their houses and in the splendour of their household goods. It was not mere bardic extravagance which prompted Iolo Goch to describe in detail Owain Glyn Dŵr's moated mansion of Sycharth with its tiled and chimneyed roofs, surrounded with deerpark, fishpond and mill.[61] It is a description which may be paralleled from a later period by the detailed descriptions of the new mansion of Ieuan ap Phylip at Cefnllys (Maelienydd) or of the whitewashed walls of Gwilym ap Gruffudd's new residence at Penrhyn (co. Caerns); it is briefly supported by the evidence of contemporary inquisitions such as that which describes the house of Rhys ap Robert of Rhydorddwy (co. Flints); it is also sustained by the archaeological evidence from such houses as Ty Draw, Llanarmon Myndd Mawr or Hen Gwrt near Llandeilo Gresynni.[62] By later and even by contemporary English standards these houses were modest enough; but in a Marcher and Welsh context they all suggest a considerable investment in new building and a higher standard of domestic luxury among the native squirearchy. To contemporaries the social eminence of these men was also displayed in an open-handed largesse and in an ever-open door for neighbours, kinsmen and friends. 'He was of gentle birth and bountiful', was the compliment paid by Adam of Usk to one of the native squires, 'who yearly used sixteen tuns of wine in his household'. Even in death the squires stood apart; not only in the magnificence of their funeral processions or in the munificence of their pious donations but also in their tombs, which both in their expense and their stylized forms proclaimed their social eminence.[63]

The measure of that eminence in their lifetime is not easy to gauge. They wielded authority over men as well as over estates.

---

[61] *Cywyddau Iolo Goch ac Eraill*, ed. H. Lewis, T. Roberts and I. Williams (Cardiff, 1937), 36–8. For an excellent discussion of the ode see Enid Roberts, 'Tŷ Pren Glân mewn top Bryn Glas', *T.D.H.S.* 22 (1973), 12–48.

[62] E. D. Jones, 'The Cefnllys Poems of Lewis Glyn Cothi', *Transactions of the Radnorshire Society* 6 (1936), 15–27; *Cywyddau Iolo Goch ac Eraill*, 310–13. (Gwilym ap Gruffudd's hall at Penrhyn); *History of Flintshire*, I ed. C. R. Williams (Denbigh, 1961), 99–100 (Rhys ap Robert); P. Smith and D. B. Hague, 'Tŷ Draw, Llanarmon Mynydd Mawr', *Arch. Camb.* 107 (1958), 109–26; O. E. Craster and J. M. Lewis, 'Hen Gwrt Moated Site, Llantilio Crossenny, Mon', ibid. 112 (1963), 159–83. For these sites and others, reference may now be made to P. Smith's outstanding volume, *Houses of the Welsh Countryside* (1975).

[63] *Chronicon Adae de Usk*, ed. E. M. Thompson, 70; G. A. Gresham, *Medieval Stone Carving in North Wales. Sepulchral Slabs and Effigies of the Thirteenth and Fourteenth Centuries* (Cardiff, 1968).

The mesne lords of Bronllys (Brecon), for example, had 173 villein tenants on their estates; Walter Devereux, mesne lord of the manor of Pipton, had 15 such tenants.[64] As lords of men and land these squires enjoyed the power of justice, ranging from the manorial justice which the lord of every manor claimed to the virtually royal jurisdiction of great lords such as the mesne lords of Coety and Bronllys. Nor can social power be merely measured in jurisdiction and authority over tenants. In their localities many of these lords dominated the social horizon. Llywelyn Bren, it was said, had such influence in his district that even the abbey of Llantarnam did not dare deny him the lands he wanted;[65] a century later the activities of Henry Don in the Kidwelly area likewise revealed the power of these men. Henry Don's standing in local society was obvious: when his estates were confiscated in 1389 they were said to be worth £252; his military experience embraced service in the retinue of John of Gaunt in France in 1371–2 and of Richard II in Ireland in 1393–4. Such a man was well placed to dominate his local *pays*, to secure favourable leases and to bully his weaker neighbours. Neither heavy fines nor a spell in prison for his active support of the Glyn Dŵr revolt could break the spirit or undo the power of Henry Don; in 1413, on his release from prison, he and his retinue terrorized the local community— seizing lands, demanding protection money from 200 men, and even plotting the murder of the local steward.[66] Exaggerated the charges against him almost certainly are; but even if we reduce them to more modest proportions, it still leaves us with the impression of a man of overweening power in his locality, a worthy prototype of Sion Cent's penetrating description of the oppressing and ruthless squire.[67]

Henry Don was also, albeit briefly, steward of the Lancaster lordship of Kidwelly. In the case of many of these men office holding is one of the few indications we have of their social

---

[64] S.C. 6/1156/14, m. 1ᵛ (1372); D.L. 7/1, Appendix volume, no. 22 (1419).

[65] J. A. Bradney, *A History of Monmouthshire*, III, ii, 225.

[66] The main sources for his biography are to be found in *John of Gaunt's Register, 1372–76*, ed. S. Armitage Smith (Camden Society, 1911), ii, no. 922; *1379–83*, ed. E. C. Lodge and R. Somerville (Camden Society, 1937), i, no. 621, ii, no. 827; D.L. 43/15/2, m. 2; S.C. 6/1165/8, m. 4; *C.P.R. 1391–5*, 483; *1413–16*, 29, 44; J.I. 1/1153, m. 16–m. 17ᵛ. His career is considered in some detail in R. R. Davies, D.Phil. thesis, 278–82.

[67] *Cywyddau Iolo Goch ac Eraill*, 288–92.

prestige and local power. We could hardly have guessed at the importance of the descendants of Einion Sais in the lordship of Brecon were it not for the long list of important local offices they held. As it happens, our estimate is in this case sustained by the knowledge that one of his descendants, Hywel Fychan ap Hywel ab Einion, contributed £6 to a communal fine of £50 and was able with his second cousin to pay a hundred marks annually for the lease of valuable lands in the lordship. For him the post of sheriff which he held from 1332 to 1348 was in part but a recognition of his standing in the local community.[68] So it was no doubt in many other cases. Office in the March was not so much a route to wealth and power as a confirmation of the economic power and social standing of the office-holder. It was a case of giving to those who had and thereby of affording them the means to yet further power and prestige. Most of them seized the opportunity with both hands.

Our understanding of the role of the squirearchy in Marcher society, it should now be evident, is uncomfortably dependent on examples and general impressions. The 'gentry' of the medieval March are an even more elusive group than their English equivalents. Much may yet be achieved by studies of individual families and by closer attention to a few areas (such as the county of Pembroke); but even then the material for a reliable assessment of the distribution, power and wealth of the squirearchy as a group would appear to be lacking. Our conclusions are therefore of necessity cautious and largely negative. The first is a truism: the story of the Marcher squirearchy in the fourteenth century cannot be comprehended within a single simpliste formula such as 'the rise of the gentry'. Even from the inadequate evidence to hand such a formula is belied by the ancient origins of many gentry families (especially the native Welsh ones), by the decline of others through economic or political miscalculation, and above all by the extinction of many notable families, both new and old, through the failure of direct male heirs. Nevertheless the truism bears repetition as the history of late-medieval Welsh society is often studied through the distorting mirror of successful Tudor and post-Tudor families. The second conclusion is a corollary to the first: the Welsh laws of inheritance (if strictly applied) meant that it was

[68] See above pp. 225–6.

far easier to fade from the ranks of the squirearchy, more difficult to rise into them. Partibility was a pre-eminently just principle but one which often 'mangled' an inheritance, leaving its multiple owners with a proud pedigree but little wealth.[69] That in its turn reminds us that in the study of the Marcher squirearchy we must make ample allowance for the differences of local typology, notably (as the tax returns of 1292 show) between the eastern lowland districts where the contours of a well-defined and well-endowed gentry group are unmistakeable and the upland Welsh lordships of the west where a social and economic élite had barely emerged and where social distinctions were still founded (as Welsh law provided) pre-eminently on status and birth.

Cautious and negative we should certainly be in our conclusions; but it may not be amiss to suggest that in terms of the distribution of wealth and power the late Middle Ages occupies a prominent role in the development of the squirearchy. The economic conditions of the period introduced new opportunities for enhancing their position. Furthermore, the withdrawal of the Marcher lords from many aspects of the direct economic exploitation and governance of their lordships afforded these same squires the opportunity to dominate their neighbourhoods more firmly and completely than before. This shift in power and lordship progressed at a different pace in different parts of the March; but everywhere the signs of a major transformation in the structure of Marcher society were becoming evident by 1400. It is to that transformation that we must now turn.

[69] A case in point is that of Gwilym ap Gruffudd ap Tudur, one of the wealthiest Welshmen in north Wales. On his death in 1376 his estates in Dyffryn Clwyd were divided between his five male heirs, two first cousins and three first cousins once removed: S.C. 2/219/11, m. 14; 12, m. 13ᵛ.

THE ECONOMIC BACKGROUND

THE later fourteenth century was a period of momentous change in the economic and social landscape of Europe generally. The March of Wales was no exception. In this transformation, the role of population was clearly basic. On that score all historians are agreed, even if agreement ceases once the chronology of the population movement and the precise role to be assigned to it in the economic changes of the period are discussed. In the March we can do no better in our approach to the problem than begin with the observations of the jurors of Bromfield and Yale in 1620. They explained the economic malaise of the lordship and in particular the decline in rent 'by reason of the great mortalitie and plagues which in former tymes had beene in the Reigne of Edward the Third and also of the Rebellion of Owen Glindor and troubles that thereupon ensued'.[1]

In one respect at least the jurors' emphasis can hardly be challenged: the epidemic diseases of the second half of the fourteenth century had a profound impact on the society and economy of the March. Of that we can be fairly certain even though the study of the population of medieval Wales remains largely an untouched subject. Direct evidence is scanty but unanimous in its conclusion. In the lowland Anglicized mesne lordship of Caldicot on the Severn estuary, thirty-six out of forty customary tenants were recorded as recently dead in 1362; not all their deaths need be ascribed to the plague but it must take most of the credit for such massive mortality. In the lordship of Dyffryn Clwyd we have the added advantage of being able to place the plague-mortality figures in a longer demographic perspective. In Llannerch and Coelion commotes average

[1] Quoted in A. N. Palmer and E. Owen, *A History of Ancient Tenures of Land in North Wales and the Marches*, 207.

annual tenant mortality in the years 1340–8 stood at 12·12; that figure rocketed to 173 in 1349, falling away to thirty-four in 1350 but rising sharply again to sixty-three in the second major visitation of plague in 1362.[2] Elsewhere in the March, the indirect evidence is all we have; but it also speaks with fair unanimity: in Bromfield and Yale there are frequent references to the 'first plague' as an explanation of vacant holdings or of catastrophic falls in rents in kind; in Abergavenny the guardians of the lordship claimed a reduction in the farm from £340 to £200 because of the plague; in Monmouth seignorial revenue had fallen by twenty per cent, in Ogmore by thirty per cent. And so the figures could be multiplied. No doubt the impact of pestilence, in terms both of seignorial revenue and the Marcher economy, varied from area to area; but in overall terms the more the period is studied the more devastating appears to be the impact of the plague.[3]

With plague the jurors of Bromfield in 1620 coupled the impact of the revolt of Owain Glyn Dŵr. They thereby confirmed an already well-established historical tradition, for the writers of Tudor Wales had been unanimous in ascribing the economic malaise of the country in the fifteenth century to the aftermath of the Glyn Dŵr's revolt and they had supported their explanations by graphic references to the scars of the revolt that were still to be seen in the towns and countryside of Wales.[4] We may suspect that their historical explanations were in good measure prompted by their wish to cast the Tudor sovereigns in the role of the deliverers of the Welsh from bondage and from economic misery and backwardness. We should certainly regard with distrust any economic explanation which is so simpliste and monocausal and which runs contrary to much

[2] D.L. 29/680/10999–11000 (Caldicot, 1362, 1366); S.C. 2/217/6–218/1; 218/10 (Dyffryn Clwyd, 1340–50, 1362).

[3] See, in general W. Rees, 'The Black Death in Wales', *T.R.H.S.*, 4th ser. 3 (1920), 115–35 and *idem, South Wales and the March 1284–1415*, 241–56. For Bromfield and Yale, see S.B.Y., fol. 24ᵛ; S.C. 6/1305/7 (1383). The calculations for Monmouth and Ogmore are based on figures in R. R. Davies, 'The Bohun and Lancaster Lordships in Wales in the Fourteenth and Early Fifteenth Centuries', D.Phil. thesis (Univ. of Oxford, 1965), 203–4, 233–4.

[4] Among the most famous early exponents of this historical orthodoxy were Rice Merrick, *A Booke of Glamorganshire Antiquities*, ed. J. A. Corbett (1887), 75–6 and Sir John Wynn, *The History of the Gwydir Family*, 52. Cf. also the role attributed to the revolt by Bishop Richard Davies in his Introduction to the New Testament (1567): *Rhagymadroddion 1547–1659*, ed. G. H. Hughes (Cardiff, 1951), 24.

that we know of the resilience of medieval rural society, and especially of pastoral communities, in the face of such disaster. Furthermore, the confident explanations of Tudor historians have in some measure been contradicted by recent detailed demonstrations of the remarkable recovery of seignorial income in parts of the March in the decade or so after the revolt.[5] Yet it would be idle to deny that the shadow of the Glyn Dŵr revolt falls heavily over the economic and social history of Wales and the March in the fifteenth century. Perhaps the most dramatic and certainly some of the best-documented evidence comes from the mesne lordship of Ogmore (Glamorgan) where in 1428 more than half of the land of the customary and cottager tenants still lay vacant and where seignorial revenue from such land had fallen by more than a half since 1400. Ogmore belonged to the Anglicized lowland zone of the March and may thereby be considered unrepresentative; but detailed studies of thoroughly Welsh districts such as Dyffryn Clwyd, Denbigh and Kidwelly suggest that the pattern was not radically different there.[6] Seignorial records, it is true, may exaggerate both the extent of economic upheaval and also paradoxically the speed of economic recovery, for at no stage, and least of all in the aftermath of a rebellion, are seignorial accounts of necessity an accurate barometer of the economic well-being of peasant society. Nevertheless, the unanimity of the evidence in this case suggests that it was not only the 'lords' hold' over the March which was 'permanently weakened'[7] by the revolt but also the tenurial and economic structure of medieval Welsh society as a whole.

Plague and rebellion certainly deserve a prominent place in analysis of the transformation of Marcher society in the late medieval period. We used the word 'transformation' deliberately; others would prefer to describe the economic changes that took place in more evocative and cataclysmic terminology such

[5] R. R. Davies, 'Baronial Accounts, Incomes and Arrears in the Later Middle Ages', *Econ. H.R.*, 2nd ser. 21 (1968), 211–29, esp. 225–7.

[6] *Glam. C.H.*, III, 300–2 (Ogmore); G. A. Holmes, *The Estates of the Higher Nobility in Fourteenth Century England*, 101, 160; H. D. Owen, 'The Lordship of Denbigh 1282–1425', Ph.D. thesis, (Univ. of Wales, 1967) 202–6 (Denbigh); R. R. Davies, D.Phil. thesis, 324–5 (Kidwelly). I hope to discuss the Dyffryn Clwyd evidence more fully later.

[7] G. A. Holmes. op. cit. 101.

as 'decline', 'decay' or 'crisis'. The evidence for such a cataclysmic interpretation of events is close to hand and has been
closely studied. It is particularly obvious in the drastic fall in
population, in a parallel decline in land values, in the cumula-
tively impressive evidence of vacant tenements, abandoned
mills and broken weirs, in the tediously lengthy lists of 'decayed
rents', and in the leasing of good arable land as pasture.[8]
Seignorial records from the mid-fourteenth century speak with
unwonted unanimity of a crisis of lordship which flowed from
this economic malaise—of the abandonment of demesne farming in most of the March by 1400, of the collapse of the system
of villein labour-services especially in the heavily-manorialized
lordships of the south-east, of desperate and increasingly unsuccessful attempts to retain the lord's direct authority over the
persons and land of his bond tenants, of equally desperate
efforts to bolster seignorial revenue and to keep control of an
ever-lengthening list of arrears and 'respited' dues. Nowhere
was this crisis of Marcher lordship to be more vividly revealed
than in the sharp decline in seignorial income which characterized so many Marcher lordships in the late-fourteenth century
and even more so in the fifteenth century.[9] It is little wonder
that a harassed Marcher official should utter a sigh of hope for
better times—*quousque saeculum emendetur*—in one of his
accounts.[10]

Such a pattern of economic 'crisis' and 'decay' is familiar
enough. It is true that the typology and chronology of this
process of decay varied from one part of the March to another
and that refinements can and should be introduced into the
general picture; but neither the overall direction of economic
and social change nor its tempo seem open to doubt. Yet
seignorial considerations, prompted of course by the overwhelmingly seignorial character of the documentation, have
been allowed to dominate the picture too completely and too
negatively. The elements of 'decay' and of 'dissolution' have
been emphasized to the exclusion of those features of economic
and social reorganization which also characterized this period.
Students of the late-medieval economy in recent years have

---

[8] W. Rees, *South Wales and the March 1284–1415*, 241–69.
[9] Above pp. 193–5.
[10] D.L. 29/594/9516 (Skenfrith account, 1423).

come to recognize that this was a period of reorientation, of new beginnings as well as of crisis and decay; they have characterized it more positively as a period of 'the rearrangement of rural scene and society'.[11] It is to these features of rearrangement in the society and economy of the March that we must now turn.

It is with the land that we must begin. One obvious result of the demographic collapse of the late fourteenth century was a sharp acceleration in the tempo of the land market and with it in all probability even a qualitative change in the character of the land market itself. The dimensions of the movement, at least in terms of vacant holdings, may be suggested by evidence from two contrasting regions of the March. In the mesne lordship of Caldicot not only was the plague mortality exceptionally heavy but the amount of customary land that escheated to the lord, either through failure of heirs or their unwillingness to succeed to family holdings on customary terms, was very considerable. Between 1350 and 1362 at least 600 acres of land (both demesne and customary land) came on the market in Caldicot to be leased (*terra arrentata*) to the highest bidder on the most favourable terms that the lord could command.[12] In Dyffryn Clwyd an inquiry in 1356 found thirty holdings vacant of which the heirs were alive; but in at least twenty-three cases the heir either failed to appear or abandoned his claim to the land in question. In 1360 the lord of Dyffryn Clwyd realized over £61 from the lease of vacant land.[13] Such evidence has usually been quoted to reveal the disastrous impact of plague on economic life and seignorial revenue. That is not to be doubted; but from another angle it also provides evidence of the large amount of land that came on the market, to be offered often on favourable terms and at least initially for low rents. Furthermore in Dyffryn Clwyd

[11] The phrase is that of P. J. Jones in his seminal study 'From Manor to Mezzadria: A Tuscan Case-Study in the Medieval Origins of Modern Agrarian Society', *Florentine Studies*, ed. N. Rubinstein (1968), 193–241 at p. 201. The change in emphasis in recent historiography on the late medieval economy can be most briefly and clearly grasped by comparing the first (1963) and second (1973) editions of J. Heers, *L'Occident au XIVe et XVe siècles: Aspects économiques et sociaux* (Paris). For England the case for revision is extravagantly advanced in A. R. Bridbury, *Economic Growth. England in the Later Middle Ages* (1962).

[12] D.L. 29/680/10999–11000. For the introduction of 'terra arrentata' in England after 1349 as an inducement to tenants see F. W. Maitland, *Selected Historical Essays*, ed. H. M. Cam (Cambridge, 1957), 23 ff. and J. A. Raftis, *The Estates of Ramsey Abbey* (Toronto, 1957), 251.

[13] S.C. 2/218/5, m. 10ᵛ; 218/8, m. 36.

the abundance of the evidence enables us to examine how far this activity was a short-term response to plague and how far the land-market contrasted with that of the pre-plague period. We have chosen as our sample the land transactions in the commote of Llannerch in the decade 1390–9 in order to compare them with those for the years 1340–8 discussed above.[14] The continuing glut of land on the market and thereby the depression of land prices are reflected in the fact that in the decade in question sixteen whole tenements escheated to the lord, eleven of them abandoned by their holders 'because of poverty' (*pro paupertate*) and the remainder for want of heirs or claimants. This impression is further confirmed by the fact that in all the leases of vacant land only once was the new rent higher than the old. Land prices, especially for abandoned land, may have been low; but the peasant land market was strikingly active compared with that of the 1340s. Eleven *prid* deeds are recorded involving mortgages of £21 and more than 450 acres of land changed hands in another thirty-two transactions. Even allowing for fictitious exchanges, short-term leases and family arrangements, the contrast between the land market of the 1340s and that of the 1390s is obvious, both in the number of land transactions and in the fact that whole tenements as well as fractional strips and detached quillets were now a prominent element in that market.

By the early fifteenth century the contrast stands out even more clearly. In the commote of Llannerch in the period 1410–22 at least 117 separate leases of vacant land are recorded on the court rolls.[15] The figure is in itself revealing; but what is even more striking is that the total figure includes at least 67 whole holdings which had reverted into the lord's hand to be leased by him as best he could. Nor do such figures stand alone: they could be paralleled from the Flintshire records and indirectly from those of Ogmore in Glamorgan.[16] But perhaps the best supporting evidence comes from the lordship of Kidwelly: in the commote of Carnwyllion in 1411–12 alone the land of at least thirty-six tenants who had died *contra pacem* was offered on

---

[14] S.C. 2/220/10; see above p. 412.

[15] S.C. 2/221/8.

[16] For Flintshire the records in Chester 3/20–24 are an invaluable source of information; for Ogmore see below pp. 431–4.

lease by the lord; in only eleven cases was the lessee the heir of the deceased tenant.[17] In the March, as indeed elsewhere, we have entered into a period of unusual activity on the land market and of discontinuity in the peasant inheritance customs of earlier generations.

In Carnwyllion several former holdings were now amalgamated in the hands of a single tenant. For example, Ieuan ap Jankyn, himself an erstwhile rebel, bought out the rights of three former tenants in five virgates, three acres and two houses and later acquired another substantial holding for an entry fine of £8 13s. 4d. His case directs us to another noticeable feature of this period of economic rearrangement, namely the polarization of rural wealth. Disparities there always had been in the distribution of territorial wealth in the peasant society of the March; and in most periods the accumulation of a larger share of land in fewer hands, whether by design or by accident, is a recurring feature of peasant history. Nevertheless, the circumstances of the late-fourteenth century meant that the opportunities for such territorial enrichment were far more abundant than usual and open to more men. In this respect it is the general dimensions of the movement rather than the individual example which are difficult to document. Such a movement was already well under way in the late fourteenth century. That is suggested by the evidence from Whitecastle (Monmouth) where in 1386 fifty-five out of the 190 tenants held more than one holding and from Hadnock (Monmouth) where at much the same period thirty-eight per cent of the tenants held multiple tenements.[18] Such a movement was no doubt greatly accelerated by the Glyn Dŵr revolt. The example of the township of Ogmore (Glamorgan) is perhaps the most telling: there in the mid fourteenth century twenty-two tenants occupied twenty-seven cottages and 133 acres of arable; by 1428 the tenant population was a mere six men, one of whom (Thomas Aythan) held 100 acres and twenty cottages. Such a pattern was repeated elsewhere in the lordship and it was a pattern that grew ever more distinct as the fifteenth century progressed.[19] In Ogmore one

---

[17] D.L. 28/27/4. The evidence is considered in detail in R. R. Davies, D.Phil. thesis, 312–14.
[18] D.L. 43/13/7–8.
[19] *Glam. C.H.*, III, 302.

can be fairly confident in asserting that the period from 1350 to
1450 witnessed a major transformation in the distribution of
rural wealth and with it the emergence of a class of yeomen
comparable to that which emerged in parts of England at the
same time.[20] Such examples are perhaps sufficient to suggest
that we are indeed dealing with 'a significant transformation
of the tenurial scene'.[21]

The same period, we suspect, will occupy an equally important role in the history of the making of the modern Welsh landscape. Here one can but speak in very tentative terms. The rural
scenery had, of course, never been uniform throughout the
March; its aspect was obviously determined in considerable
measure by geographical factors. Nevertheless the late Middle
Ages certainly saw the beginnings of the retreat from one of the
characteristic features of the countryside of the medieval March,
the quillets of the open fields. The process almost certainly began
earliest on meadow land, the most expensive variety of agricultural land in the medieval countryside, and to a lesser extent
on pasture.[22] How soon it began to be adopted as a practice
with regard to open-field arable is by no means so clear; but as
in England the pre-history of the enclosure movement seems to
begin in this period.[23] In Glamorgan Rice Merricke in 1578
remarked that enclosures were made by 'forefathers of old men
living now', which suggests that we may well trace the movement to the mid-fifteenth century, if not earlier. That was
certainly the case in Monmouth. There some of the arable so
enclosed was specifically to be used as pasture.[24] Pastoral husbandry had always of necessity been a prominent feature
of Marcher agriculture; but it was with the land glut of the
late fourteenth century that land hitherto cultivated as arable

---

[20] R. H. Hilton in *Studies in Leicestershire Agrarian History*, ed. W. G. Hoskins
(Leicester, 1948), 17–40; and in *V.C.H. Leicestershire*, II, ed. W. G. Hoskins (Oxford,
1954), 185–7; M. M. Postan in *The Cambridge Economic History of Europe*, I ed. M. M.
Postan, 2nd edn. (Cambridge, 1966), 630–2.

[21] G. R. J. Jones, 'The Field Systems of North Wales', *Studies of Field Systems in
the British Isles*, ed. A. R. H. Baker and R. A. Butlin, 469.

[22] W. Rees, op. cit. 263; G. R. J. Jones, op. cit. 455.

[23] Cf. R. H. Hilton, 'Old Enclosures in the West Midlands: a Hypothesis about
their Late Medieval Development', *Géographie et histoire agraires* (Nancy, 1959),
272–83; *idem*, *The English Peasantry in the Later Middle Ages* (1975), 161–73.

[24] Rice Merrick, *A Booke of Glamorganshire Antiquities*, ed. J. A. Corbett, 10;
D.L. 42/95, fol. 137.

was specifically leased for pasture. In Dyffryn Clwyd in 1360 much of the escheated and vacant land was specifically leased as pasture (*ad herbagium*), thereby indicating a clear, if temporary, change in land usage; in parts of the southern March, likewise, some of the demesne land, including probably some of the better arable land, was expressly let as pasture.[25] Such suggestions indicate that in the March as elsewhere a new balance was being struck between grain lands and grass lands[26] and that the agricultural economy of the March was becoming more overwhelmingly pastoral in character than hitherto.

The contraction of the population may also well have brought in its wake a movement for the redistribution of human settlement. The March on the whole was not a land of deserted villages, but depopulation inevitably left its impact on the countryside.[27] Several villages, if not entirely abandoned, contracted to a shadow of their former selves. In part, as along the coast of Gwent and Glamorgan, the encroachment of sea and sand must take a good measure of the blame;[28] but inland the explanation rests more obviously in the abandonment of poor agricultural land in the wake of the fall in population. It is in this fashion that we may explain why small settlements such as Sutton and Ogmore in lowland Glamorgan contracted sharply in size in this period while alternative centres such as Broughton and Wick expanded. The corollary of the contraction of old villages was very often the appearance of large consolidated farms in the countryside. We have already quoted the case of Thomas Aythan of Ogmore who, starting with a family holding of twenty-four acres, added to it the lease of a water mill, the pasture of Flemingsdown, eleven cottages and seventy-eight acres of arable. His was not a unique case for in Northdown (Glamorgan) John Hyott took the lease of sixty-seven acres of vacant land while in Sutton and Southerndown (Glamorgan) Thomas Hyott in 1433 secured a sixteen-year old lease on almost 200 acres of vacant land. Such leases did not

[25] S.C. 2/218/8, m. 36; W. Rees, op. cit. 262, n. 3.

[26] Cf. A. R. H. Baker in *A New Historical Geography of England*, ed. H. C. Darby (Cambridge, 1973), 207–10.

[27] For a recent survey, see L. A. S. Butler in *Deserted Medieval Villages*, ed. M. W. Beresford and J. G. Hurst (1971), 249–76.

[28] Beresford and Hurst, op. cit. 254; *Glam. C.H.*, III, 634, n. 101, for further references.

necessarily lead to the creation of consolidated farms and of isolated farmhouses; but they could easily do so.[29] This is a movement which has been traced in convincing detail in parts of north Wales in the fifteenth and sixteenth centuries, as at Llysdulas in Anglesey, Llwydfaen in the Conway valley and Dinorben in the lordship of Denbigh.[30] The chronology of the movement was determined in good part by the density of population and the extent of depopulation, by the existing pattern of land usage and by the tenurial structure of each district; it was also determined in part by the enterprise of local land entrepreneurs. It was often a painfully slow and hesitating movement which took many centuries to complete in some districts; but there seems to be little doubt that in parts of the March the later Middle Ages was the key period in initiating the transformation.

Not only did population decline sharply with consequent social and economic repercussions; it also became markedly more mobile. Mobility, of course, was no new feature of the Marcher population, particularly of the landless population. Nevertheless, the assumptions of Marcher lordship had included a fairly rigid control of movement in and out of each lordship, a largely hostile attitude towards aliens (*extranei*), and an attempt to treat each lordship as a self-contained economic unit within which the lord would regulate wages and trade.[31] Furthermore the pattern of inheritance customs for free and unfree alike had posited a largely self-sustaining and self-recruiting framework of succession to land, riveted by the central role assigned to blood-descent through patrilineages as the basis of title to land in Welsh law. That is, Marcher society, at least ideally, was a series of closed communities, closed by seignorial policy and community custom alike. Such a pattern was largely shattered in the late fourteenth century and was never effectively pieced together again.

Seignorial regulation of mobility of labour and wages gradually collapsed. Workers left the March in far greater

---

[29] *Glam. C.H.*, III, 302, 308.

[30] G. R. J. Jones, op. cit. 446–8, 452–7, 465–71; T. Jones Pierce, *Medieval Welsh Society*, chs. IV and VII. Cf. also C. Thomas, 'Enclosure and the Rural Landscape of Merioneth in the Sixteenth century', *Transactions of the Institute of British Geographers* 42 (1967), 153–62.

[31] See above pp. 231–7.

numbers than before: figures on the court rolls of Dyffryn Clwyd—twenty-six in 1363, eighteen in 1380, twenty-two in 1384—can hardly do more than represent the tip of an iceberg. Nor was it merely labourers who emigrated, for one strikingly novel feature of the late fourteenth century is the large number of tenants who migrated 'on account of poverty'. In the year 1384–5 alone sixteen tenants left Dyffryn Clwyd for that reason; in the decade 1390–9 a further 11 holdings were abandoned in the commote of Llannerch for the same reason. If to these figures we add the frequent references to the flight of serfs, often with their families and moveable goods, we are witnessing a population movement of no mean dimensions. Within the lordship the lord's authority over wages was likewise undermined. In Dyffryn Clwyd alone in 1373 217 men were fined £8 15s. 2d. for asking for excessive wages: we may regard the figure as a tribute to the zeal of seignorial officers, but it is also an admission of the effective collapse of statutory wage-control in the lordship.

The impact of population mobility does not end there. One of the well-recognized features of the late-medieval period was the tendency for inheritance-customs to be abandoned as peasant families, stimulated by unusual land abundance, moved from their native villages in search of better land at cheaper and more favourable terms.[32] A cursory review of the evidence suggests that the same was true in parts of the March. In Caldicot, where the impact of plague was exceptionally severe, ten out of thirty-six tenants who took vacant customary land on lease bore names hitherto not recorded in the lordship. The evidence from Dyffryn Clwyd is as usual more abundant and precise. In the commote of Dogfeilyn in the year 1365 alone at least eight aliens (specifically called *extranei*), mainly drawn from the neighbouring lordships of Denbigh and Englefield, took up at least sixty-five acres of land in the commote. The incomers were attracted by the prospect of good land, often at a reduced rent and on favourable terms and occasionally by the offer of timber for the repair of buildings. This process of population migration was accelerated by the consequences of the Glyn Dŵr revolt: of eighty-eight men who leased vacant land in

[32] See in particular R. J. Faith, 'Peasant Families and Inheritance Customs in Medieval England', *Agricultural History Review* 14 (1966), 77–95 esp. 86–92.

Llannerch commote in the period 1410–22 at least thirteen were specifically described as *extranei* and much the same proportion (10:88) applied in the commote of Coelion.[33]

The significance of such figures rests in part in the fact that they represent an entirely new departure in respect of inherited land in the March, for in Dyffryn Clwyd at least no such aliens are recorded *eo nomine* as ever acquiring hereditary tenements before 1349. More significant is the fact that no inheritance system, least of all that of medieval Wales, could withstand such transfer of land to outsiders on a substantial scale without serious consequences. Welsh land tenure, as we have already seen, was based on the proprietor's (*priodor*) membership of a descent-group (*gwely*). A good measure of population growth and an irregular pattern of population replacement could be accommodated within such an inheritance system, especially given the rule regarding the reversion of territorial claims to male relatives within the third degree of agnatic kinship. Provision was even made in Welsh law for the prolonged absence of a *priodor* and his descendants before their claim to a share of the descent-group's land was extinguished. Nevertheless, Welsh law and custom posited a closed society, entrance to which could only be secured by male blood relationship. Such a sensitive social equilibrium in respect of kinship-groups and land inheritance had already been rudely buffeted by the application of the law of escheat, particularly in the wake of the Edwardian conquest. The high mortality and population mobility which followed the plagues of the fourteenth century and the revolt of the early-fifteenth century served to undermine the whole rationale of the inheritance framework of medieval Wales.[34] The terminology of descent-groups and the practice of levying communal dues would continue for generations to come; but in reality the kindred structure and inheritance customs of medieval Wales effectively received their *coup de grâce* in the period 1350–1420. It was only the conservatism of a colonial administration and of its documentation which would serve to conceal that fact for another century.

[33] All references to the Dyffryn Clwyd evidence in this chapter are based on the appropriate court roll.
[34] Cf. E. A. Lewis, 'The Decay of Tribalism in North Wales', *T.C.S.* (1902–3), 1–76.

THE DECLINE OF SERFDOM AND CUSTOMARY TENURE

We would be the first to admit that the outline we have provided of some of the basic features of the transformation of the Marcher economic landscape in the later Middle Ages is inadmissibly schematic and provisional. Much research needs to be undertaken to discover the extent and the local typology and chronology of the movements suggested in the preceding section. Yet the exercise will have been worthwhile if it has drawn attention to the fact that in the March, as elsewhere, the later Middle Ages was not merely a period of decline and contraction but also of extensive social and economic rearrangement. That this was so becomes even clearer if we consider the impact of economic change on those socio-legal distinctions upon which the contemporary division of Marcher society was based.

Neither at the personal nor at the tenurial level was the distinction between the free and the unfree a complete or rigid one. At the personal level, marriages between free and unfree, with or without the lord's licence, were frequent and posed endless problems of personal status and inheritance rights for Marcher officials. At the tenurial level any attempt to insist that bond land should be held by bond men and free land by free tenants was more pious theory than actual practice. Bond men not infrequently leased free land,[35] acquired burgages,[36] and even became burgesses, at least for life.[37] Free men likewise often acquired bond land, in spite of the danger that their personal status might be infected by that of their land. The 1355 Chirkland charter of liberties confirmed freemen in all the bond lands they had acquired from the lord's unfree tenants, while in Whitecastle (Monmouth) in 1386 the surveyor introduced a category of 'freemen holding bond land' into his classifications.[38] In such a situation there was obviously a considerable measure of overlap between the tenants of free and bond land: in Chirkland free and unfree shared *gafaelion*

---

[35] S.C. 2/217/8, m. 13–m. 14 (Dyffryn Clwyd, 1343): commission of inquiry into serfs holding free land.

[36] S.C. 2/217/12, m. 22: *Nativus* acquires quarter of a burgage in Ruthin town, 1347.

[37] D.L. 29/594/9507: four Welsh *nativi* allowed to be free men of Monmouth town for life, 1372.

[38] *B.B.C.S.* 23 (1969), 165; D.L. 43/13/8.

together; in Ogmore (Glamorgan) most of the customary tenants also held free land and cottages according to the rental of 1428; in Whitecastle 55 tenants out of a total of 200 in 1386 held both customary and free land.[39]

The problems of upholding the distinction between bond and free in such a situation were difficult enough; they were greatly compounded by the sharp fall in the number of land-holding bondmen in the second half of the fourteenth century. Once more the most dramatic and complete evidence comes from Dyffryn Clwyd. In Clocaenog, Aberwheeler and Coelion, the major centres of bond population in the lordship, it was claimed that the number of bond tenants had fallen by 1381 from 212 to forty-seven: this catastrophic fall was explained in terms both of plague mortality and of the growing phenomenon of the flight of serfs and their families from the lordship.[40] Such figures no doubt need to be treated with a measure of suspicion; but they are supported by comparable evidence from Denbigh (where in one vill the number of bondmen had fallen from forty to five) or from Caldicot (where, as we have seen, thirty-six out of forty of the customary tenants were removed by the plague).[41] Furthermore in Wales the damage caused by such depopulation was exacerbated by a further decline in the number of customary tenants during and after the Glyn Dŵr revolt.[42] Indeed the problems of fugitive bond tenants and of the economic and social consequences of the collapse of the bond population were to be among the major administrative headaches of fifteenth-century Wales.[43]

From the lord's point of view the loss of villein tenants was particularly damaging. It undermined his revenue proportionately more than did the loss of free tenants; it also undermined his authority, for his lordship over the persons and lands of the *nativi* was notably more ample. It is not surprising, therefore, that the reaction of the Marcher lords, like that of many of

[39] *Extent of Chirkland*, 13, 14 and *passim*; D.L. 42/107; D.L. 43/13/8.

[40] S.C. 2/219/13, m. 13, m. 28; 220/1, m. 26.

[41] G. A. Holmes, *Estates of the Higher Nobility*, 98–9; S.C. 6/1184/22 (1397) (Denbigh); for Caldicot see above p. 425.

[42] For example in Cantrefselyf in 1426 only eight customary tenants accounted for their ploughing services, 'propter paucitatem custumariorum destructorum per rebellionem Wallicorum': S.C. 6/1157/5.

[43] See especially T. Jones Pierce, *Welsh Medieval Society*, ch. II and J. B. Smith in *W.H.R.* III (1966), 152–7, 162–71.

their English colleagues, to such a situation was a desperate attempt to bolster the *status quo*. It was in part a policy of threats and of the rigid enforcement of rules: heavy penalties were imposed on villeins, both as individuals and as members of the bond community, who tried to deny or to conceal their obligation to perform labour services; they were commanded not to work for freemen under pain of penalty; they were compelled to find pledges to stay on their holdings and not to leave the lordship. Villeins were ordered to take vacant bond tenements; sons of villeins were instructed to succeed to their parental holdings even when they had been abandoned for years; inquiries were frequently instituted to find whether bond tenants were holding free land or whether they were capable of holding more bond land; bondmen were given preferential treatment in the succession to bond land even at the expense of a reduction in rent. The lord pursued a policy of persuasion as well as one of threats: a bondman returning home to the lordship after sixteen years was treated as a prodigal son, reinstated in his father's holding, and the previous free tenant summarily evicted; serfs were offered timber for rebuilding their dilapidated holdings; others were offered a pardon for all offences other than felonies in return for a promise to stay in the lordship. It was a comprehensive policy, applied with persistence and flexibility.[44]

In the short term, it had a fair measure of success, at least in financial terms. Here again the Marcher evidence tallies with that of England where the short-term recovery of seignorial revenue and the considerable success of the statutory labour and wages policy have often been commented upon. In Ogmore (Glamorgan) seignorial income showed an astonishing degree of recovery by the 1380s; even by 1366 in plague-devastated Caldicot the income from the leasing of vacant land exceeded the loss occasioned by the escheat of bond tenements.[45] Yet not only do such figures conceal the fact that seignorial income could only be maintained or increased at a period of sharply-falling population by a potentially dangerous degree of pressure

---

[44] All the above examples are taken from the Dyffryn Clwyd court rolls for the period 1350–1400; many of them appear as almost annual features of seignorial policy towards the unfree tenantry.

[45] D.L. 29/592/9445 (Ogmore, 1381); D.L. 29/680/11000 (Caldicot, 1366).

on peasant resources, they also take too short-term a view of the impact of plague on the distinction between bond and free. A longer-term view suggests different conclusions. In the first place unremitting seignorial pressure to maintain the *status quo* financially and legally could produce a backlash from peasants, especially from the unfree. Such in part at least is the explanation of the Peasants' Revolt in England in 1381. In spite of fears to the contrary, the Revolt did not extend to the March.[46] In 1401, however, the serfs of Abergavenny revolted and killed Sir William Lucy;[47] and it is not fanciful to suggest that the disaffection of serfs may have played no small part in the revolt of Owain Glyn Dŵr. Short of armed rebellion, the opposition of villeins to seignorial pressure often took the form of a refusal to perform their customary services. An element of such passive opposition was an inbuilt feature of the lord-villein relationship; but there can be little doubt that, where bond services continued to be exacted, such opposition became more extensive and effective from the later fourteenth century. The lord of Dyffryn Clwyd, for example, remarked in 1398 that all the *nativi* of his lordship had constantly failed to perform their harvesting obligations and their mill dues and he threatened to fine them £5 unless they performed all their customary works (*omnia opera custumaria*).[48]

Such injunctions proved largely futile, for now the serfs held the whip hand. The eventual failure of seignorial policy became progressively clear. It is already evident, for example, in the entries relating to the serfs of Clocaenog (Dyffryn Clwyd) on the court roll of 1359: four tenants had to find pledges to stay in the lordship; orders were issued to arrest two men who had left the lordship to work during the harvest season; two more were fined for refusing to perform their labour services when summoned to do so: one was accused of holding free land instead of a bond tenement; several of them were commanded to explain why they did not hold bond land or why they gave so few services. We may construe the list as a tribute to the zeal of seignorial officials; it is even more patently a catalogue of the

[46] John of Gaunt ordered his Marcher castles to be placed in a state of defence on 19 June 1381: *John of Gaunt's Register, 1379–83*, I, no. 530–no. 532. Cf. *C.P.R. 1381–5*, 17.

[47] *Chronicon Adae de Usk A.D. 1377–1421*, ed. E. M. Thompson, 63.

[48] S.C. 2/220/12, m. 34–m. 34ᵛ.

collapse of the lord's authority. That collapse was eventually recognized by the concessions made to bond tenants. Rents were reduced: those of the *nativi* of Bromfield and Yale were cut by a third on condition that they promised to stay on their lands; likewise in Walwynscastle (Pembroke) the bondmen only agreed to stay in the lordship in return for a reduction of rent.[49] Other concessions were likewise made: multiple holdings were granted for single services; bond tenements were granted on customary terms but with exemption from the major labour services; bond communal dues were substantially reduced.[50]

Even concessions such as these proved inadequate. Bond land could now frequently only be let on non-customary terms. The tone was clearly set in Caldicot in 1368 when a villein's son refused to take his father's bond tenement unless it were freed from servile obligations and let to him for a money rent. The lord agreed, adding that 'it is permitted this year because no one wishes to hold that tenement by services and customs'.[51] It was an admission of failure that was repeated throughout the March. In Dyffryn Clwyd the movement from bond tenure to various forms of free tenure, a movement which had hitherto been carefully regulated by the lord, gathered momentum dramatically after 1349. Only eight such cases of tenurial conversion are recorded on the court rolls in the thirty years before the plague; at least fifty are entered for the following thirty years. The movement gathered greater speed after 1400: all vacant bond tenements in the commotes of Coelion and Llannerch in the period 1410–20 were now leased on non-customary terms. Furthermore, whereas conversion from bond tenure had hitherto largely appeared as a concession to new tenants (often freemen, burgesses or aliens) on taking vacant bond land,[52] it was now increasingly a privilege extended to sitting villein tenants. In 1413, for example, the bond tenants of at least 200 acres in Dyffryn Clwyd successfully petitioned to hold their lands hence-

<hr>

[49] S.C. 6/1305/7 (Bromfield and Yale, 1383); S.C. 6/1305/11 (Walwynscastle, 1406).

[50] See respectively S.C. 2/220/4, m. 16–16ᵛ (1384); 219/2, m. 16ᵛ (1365); 219/13, m. 13 (1379). These Dyffryn Clwyd examples could be multiplied many times.

[51] D.L. 29/680/11003.

[52] On occasion land passed through the whole gamut of tenures. A tenement in Penbedw (Dyffryn Clwyd), originally held on bond terms for a rent of 12s. 10d.,

forth by English tenure. The only conditions that the lord stipulated were that rents should be promptly paid and that the tenants should reside in person. The lord, it is true, also often added a clause allowing (*quousque*) for the reversion of the land in question to bond tenure if a villein could be found willing to take it on those terms; but, with one or two rare exceptions,[53] the clause was no more than a pious aspiration.

This movement away from customary tenure—and with it sooner or later from the meaningfulness of bond personal status —can be traced throughout the March. In Monmouth the status of at least 415 acres was changed from that of customary tenure to tenure at will in the years 1352–7 alone; there the final act in the decline of customary tenure was being enacted almost a century later when commissions were issued to let demesne, customary and bond land freely.[54] In Caldicot the process of transformation was even more dramatic: from being in 1340 a mesne lordship characterized by a larger proportion of unfree tenants and heavier labour services than virtually any other in the March its tenantry by the 1390s had been divided into freeholders and tenants at will.[55] The story was much the same in Brecon: by 1387 most of the customary land in Bronllys had been leased for a fixed money rent while a late fourteenth century rental of Hay divided the tenantry, not as of old into free and customary, but into free tenants and copyholders.[56] In Narberth the tenants were assured a greater measure of security of tenure by a commission authorized to convert free tenements held at will into tenements held in fee (to legitimate heirs of the body) or into life tenures.[57] Clearly the extent and the pace of this process of tenurial conversion varied greatly from one part of the March to another. Sometimes it was

was granted on free Welsh terms for a rent of 17*s*. 8*d*.; but when it escheated again it was leased to an alien from the county of Flint to be held for the original rent of 12*s*. 10*d*. 'without any customary or Welsh service but as English land and on the same terms as those of English tenants': S.C. 2/220/5, m. 7 ᵛ (1398).

[53] For two such exceptions see S.C. 2/219/5, m. 14, m. 17 (1368). In both cases the rent was substantially reduced for the tenant assuming the land on bond terms.

[54] D.L. 29/594/9506–7 (1370, 1378); N.L.W. Badminton Ms. 883, fol. 3 ff. (1447); B.L. Lansdowne 1, fol. 83 (1448, copy).

[55] The rental does not exist; but its nature can be gathered from the account for 1397–8, D.L. 29/680/11012.

[56] S.C. 6/1157/3 (Bronllys, 1387); D.L. 29/633/10317 (Hay, 1398).

[57] B.L. Egerton Roll 8718 (1395–7).

achieved with dramatic suddenness as in the lordship of Cydewain where a charter of 1447 manumitted all serfs and thereby
effectively terminated bond tenure;[58] more often it was a long-
drawn-out process extending over several generations. But
differences of pace apart, it was already becoming clear in many
parts of the March by the early fifteenth century that one of the
basic socio-legal divisions of Marcher society—that between
free and unfree and with it between free tenure and bond
tenure—was increasingly becoming anachronistic.

THE RELATIONS OF ENGLISH AND WELSH

The other socio-legal distinction in Marcher society—that
between English and Welsh—was being transformed at much
the same time. In this case the transformation for obvious
reasons was not so complete nor was it so closely related either
causally or chronologically to the impact of plague and rebellion. Rather was it a process of social and cultural adjustment
between the settler and the native population. The chronology
of this process of adjustment obviously varied greatly from one
part of the March to another, largely in relation to the density
of alien settlement and to the date of foreign colonization. The
contrast in this respect between parts of the southern March,
where alien immigration had largely been achieved by the end
of the twelfth century, and the new Marcher lordships of the
north-east where the colonists were introduced after 1282, is most
immediately evident.

This story of racial adjustment has many facets to it. It is
witnessed graphically in the intermixture of English and Welsh
placenames, including farm- and field-names, in many parts of
the March; it is also witnessed in the coexistence of Welsh and
English forms of individual placenames.[59] The social adjust-

---

[58] *C.P.R. 1494–1509*, 323–4.
[59] For this theme, see briefly A. H. Dodd, 'Welsh and English in East Denbighshire: A Historical Retrospect', *T.C.S.* (1940), 34–65; M. Richards, 'The Population of the Welsh Border', ibid. (1970), i, 77–100; B. G. Charles, 'The Welsh, their
Language and Place-names in Archenfield and Oswestry', *Angles and Britons*
(Cardiff, 1963), 85–110. For a general review of English place-names in Wales see
B. G. Charles, *Non Celtic Place-names in Wales* (1938). For a few examples of alternative Welsh and English place-name forms for the late medieval period see R. R.
Davies in *T.C.S.* (1974–5), 52–3.

ments of a frontier district are also manifested in personal
nomenclature: on the part of the natives they are seen in the
adoption of alien names (such as Almaric)[60] and in the gradual
movement towards English surname styles, as happened at an
early stage in the case of the de la Poles of Powys (the sons of
Gruffudd ap Gwenwynwyn) or the Avenes of Glamorgan; on
the part of the settler population they are seen in the adoption
of Welsh names for their children—as happened to Tangwystl
daughter of William of Pulford, Ieuan son of Hugh Staleworthman or Llywelyn son of Almaric de Marreys, to cite but three
examples from Dyffryn Clwyd—and even in the adoption of
the Welsh patronymic forms, as in the case of Gruffudd ap
David Holland, 'an Englishman and an English tenant' of
Denbigh.[61] This mutual borrowing of names and nameforms,
and with them no doubt of language and social customs, was
greatly promoted by intermarriage between settler and native
families. Some settler families no doubt kept themselves to
themselves and were proudly and exclusively English in their
attitudes.[62] But marriage into native families had been a feature
and indeed a deliberate policy of immigré families in the March
from early Norman days.[63] It remained so in the fourteenth
century as two examples from the northern and southern
March may serve to illustrate. Among the families who migrated
into the north-eastern March in the wake of Edward I's
military victories were the Pulestons of Shropshire who settled
at Emral (Bromfield and Yale) and the Hanmers of Maccles-
field who moved into Maelor Saesneg (the detached portion
of the new county of Flintshire). Initially both retained the
aloofness of the immigrant; but by the late-fourteenth century
both families were joined in marriage to some of the oldest and
noblest Welsh families of the north-eastern March (including

---

[60] One of the men who died of plague in Dyffryn Clwyd in 1349 was Almaric ab
Ithel ab Einion; his father had been in the service of Almaric Weedon (S.C.
2/217/14, m. 18). Children of the same parents were often given linguistically
mixed names e.g. *Cartae*, II, no. 491.

[61] S.C. 2/216/12, m. 24 (1332); 217/12, m. 16 (1347); 218/11, m. 20 (1363);
N.L.W. Wynnstay, 100/202, no. 4 (1447).

[62] John Wynn (*History of the Gwydir Family*, 18) remarks on the first Welsh
woman to be married into the settler family of Conway of Rhuddlan, almost a
century and a half after the first settlement of the family in Wales.

[63] Cf. A. J. Roderick, 'Marriage and Politics in Wales, 1066–1282', *W.H.R.* 4
(1968), 1–20.

that of Owain Glyn Dŵr).[64] In the southern March, one of Owain Glyn Dŵr's contemporaries and opponents was John ap Harry of Poston (co. Heref.). His lineage was impeccably Welsh, for he was of an old Welsh family of Elfael. Yet he moved easily in Marcher and English society alike: he was a leading Marcher administrator, but also a man of note in Herefordshire society and knight of the shire in more than one parliament. He took to wife Elizabeth Waterton of Eaton Tregose (co. Heref.), daughter of one of Henry of Bolingbroke's leading confidants. His son followed suit, marrying Gwenllian Hakeluyt (her name is significant) of Eaton Pyon (co. Heref.); he also began to adopt the English habit of using surnames.[65] So the examples could be easily multiplied, especially in the higher ranks of the social scale. Marriage was one of the most powerful agents of cultural integration and diffusion.

It is in the higher echelons of Marcher society likewise that we can see most clearly the cultural assimilation which is a frequent feature of frontier districts. It was in the March quite probably that Arthurian tales first captivated a Norman audience; it was there likewise that Geoffrey of Monmouth may have stocked his fertile imagination with an incomparable repertoire of stories; it was there again that two of the liveliest raconteurs of the twelfth century, Gerald of Wales and Walter Map ('a dweller on the Marches' as he called himself), were reared. Nor was the cultural traffic by any means a one-way affair. The Norman lords of the March were themselves patrons of literature and it was quite possibly *via* their courts that French tales and terminology entered the native Welsh literary tradition.[66] This dual character of Marcher literary culture continued into the later Middle Ages and beyond. It is

[64] For the careers of these two families, see briefly *Dictionary of Welsh Biography* (1959) *sub nomine*. For the early attitude of the Pulestons note esp. *The Twenty-Seventh Annual Report of the Deputy Keeper of the Public Records* (1866), Appendix, 98. For the marriage connections of the two families, see J. E. Lloyd, *Owen Glendower*, 24–5 and N.L.W. Peniarth 404 D., fol. 97.

[65] J.I. 1/1152, m. 15ᵛ; B.L. Harleian 5058, fol. 4–fol. 5ᵛ, fol. 11ᵛ–fol. 12; R. A. Griffiths, *The Principality of Wales*, I, 234–5.

[66] For an extreme statement of the impact of French literature and fashions on Wales see Morgan Watkin, *La Civilisation française dans les Mabinogion* (Paris, 1962). For literary exchanges between the Welsh and the Normans see, most recently, C. Bullock-Davies, *Professional Interpreters and the Matter of Britain* (Cardiff, 1966) and a valuable review of it by Rachel Bromwich in *Llên Cymru* 9 (1967), 249–51 which brings out well the literary significance of the south-eastern March.

vividly exemplified in the literary associations of Hergest in the lordship of Huntington. The lords of Hergest in the fourteenth century, in spite of their Welsh lineage, bore or assumed the surname of Clanvow; they turned increasingly in English court and literary circles; and it was one of their number, Sir John Clanvow (d. 1391), who was possibly the author of *The Cuckoo and the Nightingale*, one of the classics of middle English literature.[67] Hergest's literary fame in the fifteenth century, however, is linked with Wales, for the squire of Hergest, Thomas ap Roger Vaughan, was the owner of one of the most distinguished of all Welsh literary manuscripts, *Llyfr Coch Hergest*. The poet's reference to his house as a city where two languages were acceptable was an apt comment on the role of the March as a frontier area in literary culture.[68]

This process of the cultural assimilation of English and Welsh in the March of Wales is a theme that needs to be studied in depth and with great care over a long time-span. Such a survey needs to consider social institutions in the round and to assess the measure of conscious decision and unconscious evolution which characterized the process of cultural adjustment (in the broadest sense of the word 'culture'); it needs to study the very wide regional and chronological diversities in that process and to assess the nature of the adjustment from one social milieu to another. Such an ambitious enterprise is not within our competence. Our brief is a more modest one: to study the relations of English and Welsh in the March in the field of land tenure and land law and to see how far the general process of social and cultural adjustment is reflected there. The limitations of such an approach are self-evident; but at least it presents the advantage of enabling us to plot the process of adjustment in one area of Marcher life with a fair measure of documentary support and thereby of chronological certainty. Even so we must enter a caveat: our evidence is drawn largely from the north-eastern March. The experience of that area in respect of

[67] For the Clanvow family see K. B. McFarlane, *Lancastrian Kings and Lollard Knights* (Oxford, 1972) esp. 165–6, 183–4, 210–6, 230–2 and R. A. Griffiths, *The Principality of Wales*, i, 103. The family seems to have taken its name from a manor it held of the lordship of Hay: Cardiff Free Library, Brecon Documents 2 (Extent of Hay, 1339).

[68] This passage from the poet Bedo Brwynllys is quoted in F. Payne, *Crwydro Sir Faesyfed*, i (Llandybie, 1966), 33.

changes in land tenure and land law was probably not basically different from that of the rest of the March; but the chronology of the changes may well have been different.

The distinction between English and Welsh land tenure was, perhaps, the most resilient of the 'racial' distinctions of the medieval March; it related to an area where social and legal conservatism is notorious. Nevertheless, it was no more immune than were the other 'racial' distinctions from the influence of social and economic change, especially when that change accelerated out of the lord's control in the aftermath of plague and rebellion. It is not surprising, therefore, that the late medieval period witnessed the gradual collapse of the distinction between English and Welsh land tenure, inheritance, laws and customs. It was a collapse that was in part brought about by the movement of peoples. In Denbigh, for example, several of the vills, which had been designated from the late thirteenth century onwards for the exclusive use of English settlers, had been extensively penetrated by Welshmen by the early fifteenth century.[69] Much the same was true of Glamorgan: there the late medieval period witnessed the recolonization of parts of the Vale, including districts officially designated as Englishries, by native Welsh farmers.[70] Even the towns, once the bastions of colonial exclusiveness and English privileges, were not immune from the movement. By 1400 Welshmen formed a substantial proportion of the urban population both in the older Marcher boroughs such as Oswestry, Brecon and Monmouth and in the newer Edwardian foundations such as Chirk, Holt and Ruthin.[71] Sometimes they came as the husbands of the daughters or widows of English burgesses; occasionally they acquired a temporary foothold as traders or chensers; more rarely they were formally created free burgesses of the town; and no doubt many of them entered the boroughs

[69] H. D. Owen, Ph.D. thesis, 255–67.

[70] *Glam. C.H.*, III, 310. Cf. also the survey of Coety Englishry and Welshry in 1411: C. 47/9/32.

[71] B. G. Charles in *Angles and Britons*, 105–6 (Oswestry); R. R. Davies, D.Phil. thesis, 254–5; D.L. 7/1, no. 60 (Kidwelly, Monmouth); D. Pratt in *T.D.H.S.* 14 (1965), 48 (Holt); *Extent of Chirkland 1391–3*, ed. G. P. Jones, 2 ff. (Chirk); R. I. Jack in *T.D.H.S.* 18 (1969), 38 ff. (Ruthin). For Welshmen in Principality boroughs see I. J. Sanders, 'The Boroughs of Aberystwyth and Cardigan in the Early Fourteenth Century', *B.B.C.S.* 15 (1952–4), 282–93.

furtively without seignorial licence and settled there.[72] Neither vigorous protests from English burgesses nor occasional official clampdowns and evictions effectively served to stem the movement. This movement of peoples was most markedly one of Welshmen into English areas; but it was not exclusively so. So it is that we find Englishmen securing Welsh land on lease by Welsh mortgage procedure,[73] holding such land by Welsh services and dues [74] and even enrolling as members of the *gwely*, the Welsh patrilineage group.[75]

The Anglo-Norman settlers certainly borrowed some of the habits of their Welsh neighbours. Some of them, for example, adopted the Welsh practice of using verbal contracts testified by witnesses in preference to the more normal English method of written deeds of contract;[76] others, including the receiver of the lordship of Dyffryn Clwyd,[77] devised their lands by Welsh mortgage (*prid*). It was not unknown for lands held by English tenure to be divided between male heirs in the Welsh fashion;[78] such a hybrid system, known under the revealing name of

---

[72] For examples from Ruthin see S.C. 2/218/8, m. 3ᵛ–m. 4 (inquiry of 1360 into right of eight Welshmen to enjoy liberties of the town finds that several of them had acquired a claim through marriage); 219/5, m. 8 (a Welshman pays £5 for acquiring land in the town and for the right to brew and sell his wares, 1368); 221/4, m. 11 (John ab Ithel ap Dafydd created a free burgess of the town, 1410); 219/1, m. 5 (forty-three Welshmen challenged to explain how they claimed the right to trade and to enjoy the town's privileges when they were 'meer' Welshmen', 1364).

[73] For example, Roger le Hopere's estate in 1344 included lands he had acquired in *prid* from three Welshmen, whilst two Englishmen of Ruthin town conveyed a burgage to each other by the *prid* method in 1352. S.C. 2/217/9, m. 20; 218/3, m. 22ᵛ.

[74] When John Page took Welsh land in 1344 he agreed to pay all the Welsh dues and likewise Gruffudd ap David Holland, 'an Englishman and an English tenant', on acquiring land 'in the Welshry' (infra Galescheriam) in 1447 agreed to dispose of such land henceforth by *prid*: S.C. 2/217/9, m. 20ᵛ (Dyffryn Clwyd); N.L.W. Wynnstay 100/202, no. 4 (Denbigh).

[75] *S.D.*, 317, 321; *The Lordship of Oswestry 1393–1607*, ed. W. J. Slack, 158, 165.

[76] In an interesting plea of 1315 between two Englishmen of Ruthin town the plaintiff introduced the following significant argument: 'contractus inter eos factus fuit per testimonium plegiorum et aliorum proborum hominum quod tantum valet in partibus istis sicud unum scriptum in Anglia', S.C. 2/215/74, m. 16.

[77] Almaric Weedon, 1356 (S.C. 2/218/5 m fol. 1ᵛ).

[78] Thus Dafydd ab Einion, the parson of Llandyrnog (Dyffryn Clwyd), who held forty acres of land 'per liberam cartam more Anglicorum' arranged that they should be divided after his death between his six nephews: S.C. 2/216/12, m. 22ᵛ (1332). Likewise a son who succeeded to an estate of seventy-eight acres as his father's 'English' heir promptly proceeded to share it in the Welsh fashion with his six brothers: S.C. 2/220/5, m. 16 (1385).

'English law and Welsh division', survived in Pembrokeshire into the sixteenth century and beyond.[79] Another institution which admirably expressed the compromises of a frontier district was the Welsh fee. The Welsh fee owed the obligations normally associated with feudal tenure with the exception of wardship and marriage; but whereas primogeniture was the keystone of Anglo-Norman feudalism, the Welsh fee (like Welsh land generally) was divisible among co-heirs. The fact that both orthodox English and Welsh fees coexisted in the same vill and certainly in the same lordship (as in Chepstow, Usk and Cemais) is as vivid a reminder as any of how alien institutions adapted to their new Marcher environment.[80]

In social and economic terms, however, the more momentous development of the later Middle Ages was not so much that whereby settler families adjusted themselves to their Welsh habitat even to the point of becoming thoroughly native in language, sympathies and social customs but rather that whereby Welshmen themselves increasingly adopted the tenurial and inheritance customs of their English neighbours. The attractions of English tenure, and therewith the drawbacks of Welsh tenure, are adequately articulated in the contemporary evidence. In the first place Welshmen were attracted to English tenure by the prospect of freedom of alienation *inter vivos* and the right of enfeoffment that it allowed. Such freedom of alienation would liberate Welshmen from the restrictions of native land law with its firm prohibition on outright alienation of land and its insistence on the priority of the rights of the expectant heirs of the patrilineage over those of the individual proprietor. It was a liberation which English kings and Marcher lords were reluctant to concede, not so much out of deference to Welsh law but rather because of the measure of control over the land market that native custom afforded them. For the same reason several Marcher lords emerged as the champions of another key feature of Welsh land law, namely the principle that there should be no succession to land by or through females. The lords could and certainly did profit by such a total prohibition on female succession, for in the event of the failure of male heirs within the third or fourth degree of kinship the land in question

---

[79] *Penbrokshire*, III, 148 ('cyfraith Seisnig a rhan Gymreig').
[80] See above p. 76.

would escheat to them.[81] Welshmen on the other hand, became increasingly aware of the advantages of accepting that women as well as men could inherit and transmit land. Broadly speaking they were advantages which would favour the conjugal family at the expense of the patrilineal descent-group. In particular they would enable land to pass, for lack of direct male heirs, to daughters and their offspring or to female grandchildren rather than to collateral male heirs. They would also allow Welsh proprietors the opportunity to bestow land on their daughters as marriage portions and on their wives as dower gifts. English common law had the further advantage that it sanctioned primogeniture as against male partibility as the law of descent: such a practice had clear attractions for families anxious to preserve and to consolidate the integrity of the family holding. Finally, land held by English tenure was exempt from the irksome communal dues and the derogatory personal obligations (such as liability of *amobr*) that attached to Welsh land.

All in all the advantages of English land tenure to the Welsh peasant farmer were very considerable. So it is that the late medieval March is characterized by one of the most momentous movements in the history of land tenure in Wales, that whereby Welsh land tenure was increasingly replaced by English tenure, land law and inheritance practices. One major avenue of change was that presented by the market in vacant or escheated land, for the Dyffryn Clwyd evidence makes it clear enough that in the great majority of cases the new tenant was to hold such land to himself 'and his English heirs', that is his heirs as designated by English law, and often specifically by English services.[82] Furthermore the English settlers in Wales served as obvious agents for the diffusion of English tenure and land law: when they appropriated land, whether a vacant tenement or an escheated Welsh holding, they held it henceforth by English tenure; they called upon their Welsh neighbours to witness their

[81] How much profit the principle of escheat could yield may be shown by the case of Meredydd ap Llywelyn ap Rhirid. On his death in 1367 without male heirs within the fourth degree his lands were granted to six tenants for an entry fine of £30 and an increase in rent of 18s. 1½d. per annum: S.C. 2/219/5, m. 30ᵛ.

[82] For example, Hywel ap Gwilym ab Ednyfed conveyed to Dafydd Llwyd ab Iorwerth ab Ednyfed *and his English heirs* six acres in Llannerch in 1376: S.C. 22/19/11, m. 17.

charters of enfeoffment or impleaded them in cases of dower and thereby familiarized them with English land law; they not infrequently sold 'English' land to Welshmen to be held by English tenure and to the 'English heirs' of those Welshmen. Even the Marcher lords themselves, in spite of their generally conservative attitude, on occasion gave the movement towards English tenure a further fillip. A statute of 1345 issued by the lord of Dyffryn Clwyd decreed that henceforth all acquisitions of land in the lordship were legally to be made to a man 'and his English heirs' and in the search for tenants to occupy vacant holdings in the late-fourteenth century the lord conceded that aliens (*extranei*) might hold their lands by English tenure.[83] Yet increasingly the initiative in the movement towards English tenure lay neither with the lord nor with his English tenants but rather with ordinary Welsh peasants. On this score the Dyffryn Clwyd evidence speaks loud and clear. It shows how Welsh tenants from about 1370 began to surrender their holdings in order to receive them back to be held by English services and tenure; how other Welsh tenants paid substantial fines in order to enjoy English status; how sisters and daughters increasingly and with varying degrees of success petitioned the lord to succeed to Welsh land where direct male heirs were lacking.

The movement to English tenure marked a sharp break with the past and it was a break that many Welshmen were reluctant to make, at least at a stroke. Many of them kept a foothold in both tenurial camps. Such a one was Llywelyn ap Llywelyn of Chirkland. In 1348 he arranged for the enfeoffment of some of his lands to himself, his wife and his right heirs 'according to the law and custom of England' and of the rest of his lands to himself, his wife and his heirs 'according to the law and custom of Wales' (with a proviso that his heirs under the first enfeoffment were not to inherit under the second and vice-versa).[84] His compromising posture was one that was adopted by many of his fellow-Welshmen. In the field of land law Welsh and English practices were firmly intertwined: Welshmen enfeoffed some of their lands by English common law methods and devised

[83] For the 1345 statute, see S.C. 2/217/11, m. 5; for examples of the offer of English tenurial status to aliens, see S.C. 2/220/12, m. 32ᵛ (1398); 221/4, m. 1 (1399).

[84] B.L. Add. Charter 74399, briefly calendared in *Arch. Camb.*, 4th ser. 11 (1880), 140.

others by Welsh mortgage (*prid*);[85] Welsh land was often surrendered in court to the use (*ad opus*) of another tenant but to be
held by Welsh tenure;[86] final concords, that most English of
conveyancing methods, could be used to effect a partible
division of estates between male heirs in the Welsh fashion.[87]
In such a transitional situation it was not surprising that many
families and individuals held by both English and Welsh tenure,
thereby highlighting the distinction between the two tenurial
systems and that overlapping of peoples and cultures which is
such a feature of the Marcher situation.[88] Nor is it surprising
that such ambivalence of tenures should occasionally lead to
great family quarrels. That happened in Dyffryn Clwyd in 1343
on the death of a leading Welsh freeholder, Llywelyn ap
Madoc, without a male heir of his body. His agnatic relatives
inevitably emerged as the staunch upholders of Welsh law for
thereby they stood to gain by the division of his extensive
estates; the husbands and sons of his daughters, on the other
hand, were equally passionate defenders of the English law
principle of succession through and by females. It was appropriate that one of them was called Llywelyn Sais (the Englishman).[89]

In the case of the inheritance of Llywelyn ap Madoc Welsh law
was triumphant; but in the struggle as a whole English tenure
emerged supreme. That this represented a conscious movement
away from Welsh tenure is not in doubt. So much is made clear
by the evidence from Bromfield and Yale. There an enfeoffment
of land to a daughter and her first-born heir male was to be
undertaken 'so that the lands shall not be divided between male
heirs according to the law and custom of Wales'; another
enfeoffment which allowed for the reversionary claims of a

[85] David of Bachgern is a case in point, enfeoffing some of his lands and conveying
others by *prid* in 1365: S.C. 2/219/2 m. 15, m. 18ᵛ.

[86] For example, four and a half acres conveyed to the use of Einion ab Ieuan ab
Iorwerth to be held by *uchelwr* (i.e. free Welshman) terms: S.C. 2/219/11, m. 16
(1376).

[87] For a good example of a Welshman dividing his lands, unequally, between
four sons by final concord see *Penbrokshire*, III, 469–72 (1342).

[88] See, for example, *Cal. Public Records re. Pembs.*, III, 97 (man holds both by
military tenure and by Welsh law, 1353); S.C. 2/220/10, m. 1, m. 2 (English land
of a tenant in Dyffryn Clwyd is divided between his daughters and their English
heirs; his Welsh land descends to his nearest male kinsman, 1390).

[89] S.C. 2/217/8, m. 25–m. 27ᵛ.

daughter was specifically said 'to be contrary to Welsh custom
as practised from ancient time'.[90] This was also the case in
Dyffryn Clwyd: in the commote of Llannerch alone between
1410 and 1420 at least five Welshmen agreed to succeed to
their fathers' holdings only on condition that they were to be
held henceforth by free English services (*per servicia libera
anglicana*). The initiative for change certainly came from the
tenants, for the lord wished to preserve the status quo and had
no wish to encourage the abandonment of Welsh tenure. In a
lease of 1411, for example, the lord of Dyffryn Clwyd allowed
a new tenant to hold land on English terms, but only until
another tenant appeared who was willing to take the land *in
tenura wallicana*.[91]

It was no more than a pious hope, for the tide was now
running strongly in favour of English tenure. Here again the
Dyffryn Clwyd evidence enables us to pinpoint the chronology
of the movement in one area of the March; and what above
all it reveals is the significance of the late fourteenth and early
fifteenth centuries in the movement. Whereas vacant and
escheated land had already been let on English terms and
whereas an occasional wealthy freeholder had already grasped
the advantages of English inheritance and conveyance methods,
it was only from around 1370 that one can detect clearly a
movement for the conversion of land held by Welsh tenure into
land held by English tenure. The movement was given a further
massive impulse by the Glyn Dŵr revolt, both by the considerable amount of vacant and escheated land that came on the
market and by the further-strengthened bargaining position of
the tenants in a period of economic depression. They pressed
their advantage skilfully and successfully. Rents were substantially reduced, either temporarily or permanently;[92] sons were
allowed to succeed to their fathers' Welsh lands on English
terms, quit of all Welsh services;[93] daughters and sisters were
permitted to inherit Welsh holdings where there were no direct

[90] N.L.W. Peniarth MS. 404, fol. 97–fol. 98 (1425), f. 125 (1455).
[91] S.C. 2/221/8, m. 3.
[92] In Llannerch in the period 1410–22 rents of escheated land were reduced from
£29 to £23, in Coelion from £19 to £13. In one case a son only agreed to succeed
to his father's land provided the rent was reduced from 25s. 5d. to 15s.; S.C. 2/221/8,
m. 12.
[93] S.C. 2/221/8, m. 15 for one of several examples (1415).

male heirs.[94] One figure suggests dramatically the dimension of the movement to English tenure: of one hundred and eighteen parcels of vacant land (including many complete tenements) that were leased in Llannerch commote in the period 1410–22 only one was specifically let on Welsh terms and at least eighty-one were leased specifically on English terms. It is one of the paradoxes of the period that the native revolt of Owain Glyn Dŵr had accelerated the pace of the movement towards English tenure.

Elsewhere in the March the chronology of the movement may well have been different, particularly so in the lowland districts of the eastern March. Thus small collections of deeds from Brecon in the fourteenth century show how completely the Welshmen of the district had mastered the principles and practices of English land conveyance.[95] In many lordships, both in the eastern and western March, the principle of succession through and by females, in the event of the failure of direct male heirs, was already fully accepted.[96] The adoption of English tenure may have varied not only according to a regional pattern but also from one social group to another. There can be little doubt that it was the richer Welsh landowners, men who frequently intermarried with their English neighbours and moved easily in border county society, who were the first to adopt English tenurial and inheritance practices. Thus the forebears of Owain Glyn Dŵr had entailed their estates in 1328 and had thereby assured the integrity of their inheritance; another distinguished family in north Wales and the March, that represented by Gwilym ap Gruffudd ap Tudur (d. 1376), as early as 1308 had deliberately abandoned the Welsh law of partibility in favour of the effective concentration of lands in the hands of the eldest son.[97] Another group who may well have been in the van of those adopting English tenure were those estate-building and land-speculating clerics whose activities

---

[94] S.C. 2/221/8, m. 10 (daughter allowed to succeed to her father's Welsh lands for her lifetime; thereafter her heirs were to hold it by the old services); 221/9, m. 7ᵛ (sister allowed to succeed to her brother's Welsh and English lands).

[95] See above, p. 406.

[96] W. Rees, *South Wales and the March 1284–1415*, 210–11.

[97] *C.P.R. 1327–30*, 314; U.C.N.W. Penrhyn Collection, 405 (cf. J. R. Jones, 'The Development of the Penrhyn Estate to 1431', M.A. thesis (Univ. of Wales, 1955), 38–9).

have already drawn our attention. None was more successful in Dyffryn Clwyd than Ieuan ap Dafydd Fychan of Ceidio. His success was achieved in good measure by use of the Welsh device of *prid*; but once his investments in the land market were complete he paid the lord £12 to convert all his acquisitions into land held by English tenure, to extinguish all Welsh services due from them and to secure permission to enfeoff all his lands on his elder son, with reversionary rights for his younger son.[98] He and his like were showing the possibilities inherent in the adoption of English tenure and land-law; it was an example which was not lost on smaller peasant farmers. English tenure percolated down the social and economic scale of Welsh society.

We have dwelt on the movement at some length, partly because it reveals the processes of cultural diffusion precisely and clearly and partly because it had the most far-reaching implications for the social and economic configuration of the Marcher landscape. To opt for English land tenure and inheritance customs was in effect to make a crucial choice with regard to the descent and movement of landed wealth. It was to choose between a society where the movement of land was largely restricted within an agnatic descent-group and a society in which land could be freely devised by the individual owner during his lifetime and transmitted after his death through female as well as male descendants. Furthermore, the movement towards English tenure was to undermine the rationale of the distinction between English and Welsh upon which so much of Marcher governance had been founded. Lands held by English and Welsh tenure became hopelessly intermingled as they were in Welsh Gower by the sixteenth century.[99] With the gradual collapse of this tenurial distinction, the other distinctions between the races grew patently unreal. English and Welsh officers trod on each other's toes in an attempt to collect English and Welsh dues from one and the same tenant. The absurdity of the situation was already grasped in Dyffryn Clwyd by 1400 and the Welsh sergeant (*rhingyll*) was placed in authority over English and Welsh tenants alike.[100] The attempt to preserve Englishries and Welshries as separate administrative districts foundered on

[98] See above p. 409; S.C. 2/219/13, m. 25ᵛ (1379).   [99] *Glam. C.H.*, III, 215.
[100] S.C. 2/221/2, m.2ᵛ (Coelion, 1400); 221/8, m. 4 (Llannerch, 1412).

the fact that 'diverse lands of the Welshry are intermyngled among the lands of the fforenry (i.e. Englishry)'.[101] The fact that such a remark should appear in an early Stuart rental is a reminder to us that we should not expect the social and economic transformations we have outlined to be completed in a generation. It may also remind us how reluctant Marcher lords and their officials were to abandon the categories they had adopted for the classification and administration of Marcher society. Those categories had, of course, never been adequate; but their inadequacy only became glaring with the transformation of Marcher society in the period from 1350 to 1420.

[101] *A Survey of the Duchy of Lancaster Lordships in Wales, 1609–13*, ed. W. Rees, 210.

Epilogue

LORDSHIP and society in the March of Wales in the fourteenth century have been the twin themes of this book. They have of necessity been studied largely independently of each other. Between lordship and society, however, the interplay was constant and it therefore behoves us by way of conclusion at least to attempt to characterize the nature of their relationship. It is in terms of the impact of lordship on society that the documentation serves us best. We have studied that impact in a variety of ways—in the military authority which enabled the lord to impose his rule on a native population and to import settlers to people the fertile and strategically-important districts of his lordship; in the assertion of his power, his *dominium*, over the men and the land of his lordship; in his control of its economic life through monopolies and privileges, through the regulation of trade, of wages and of the movement of labour, through his claim to forests, pasture and escheated land; in a precise and ample judicial authority whereby the lord controlled the lives of his dependants; in a wide range of financial demands whereby a considerable share of the wealth of the lordship was channelled into the coffers of the lord; and in the repercussions that the lord's political fortunes had for good or ill on the lives of his tenants and dependants. The demands of lordship served to shape and to accelerate social developments. So likewise did the benefits, the favours of 'good lordship'; the lord's protection and patronage were among the major determinants of economic success and social standing in Marcher society. It was within the crucible of lordship that Marcher society in a considerable measure was moulded in the fourteenth century.[1]

To say so is to utter a truism; it is also to utter a half truth. Lordship was undoubtedly powerful; arguably it was more effectively powerful in the March in the fourteenth century than at any earlier or later stage of history. Yet neither the character

---

[1] See above Part II.

of our documentation nor our modern presuppositions should delude us into supposing that medieval lordship at its most powerful had the same capacity to shape society that is possessed by a sovereign corporate state in modern industrialized societies. In terms of social development, it is the apparent feebleness of lordship which is often most striking. At a practical level the authority of lordship extended no further than the reach of its sword. Furthermore, the lordship of the March was a lordship of foreign lords over a largely native society. Foreign lordship was by no means necessarily less effective lordship; the experience of England after 1066 and of Wales after 1282 might suggest the contrary to be the case. Yet all lordship had to adjust itself to its local context and in good measure to accept it. It could certainly introduce new dimensions of relationships and novel notions of authority over men and land into the theory and practice of lordship; but it had neither the means nor the manpower to undertake a reordering of society. Nor indeed did it have the wish to change the social order; to exploit it, maybe, but not to change it. In the March this meant that lordship operated within the context of native custom; indeed, as we have often remarked, it became the jealous guardian of that custom. Such unaccommodating conservatism meant that for the most part, at least after the initial establishment of alien lordship, the momentum for social change came not from seignorial direction or policy. More often than not seignorial policy and governance adjusted only belatedly and partially to social reordering that it was loath to recognise.

We have spoken of lordship and society where contemporaries would have talked of lordship and community. The distinction is not without significance, for whereas the preoccupations of modern historiography have been with social and economic analysis (hence the choice of the word 'society'), contemporaries saw the relationship between lordship and its dependants more in institutional or quasi-institutional terms (hence the choice of the word 'community'). This contemporary notion of community has not on the whole, with a few notable exceptions, found much favour in modern English historical writing.

Yet in the March of Wales the concept of community, 'slippery' and 'nebulous' as it is,[2] might prove of service to us in

[2] F. W. Maitland, *Township and Borough* (Cambridge, 1898), 84. See also in

analysing the fabric of power and authority. In the typology
of lordship and community the contrast between England and
the March of Wales is highly instructive. It is the contrast
between an unitary kingdom and multiple lordships; between a
kingdom where eventually in theory all land and jurisdiction
were held of the king and all lordship was mediate, and a region
where lordship was autogenous and where dominion was dispersed in a confederacy of independent lordships; between a kingdom whose unity was reflected in a single community of the realm
and a congeries of lordships where communities were as multiple
as were the lords. At a negative level the concept of community
reminds us that between—or rather alongside—lordship and
the individual in medieval society lay a broad spectrum of
associations, communities, orders or whatever we may care to
call them, more or less permanent, more or less coherent.
Positively the concept helps us to articulate the relationship
between lordship and society in contemporary terms. It was a
dualistic relationship: 'every lordship had a particular communal element associated with it',[3] and between the two there
was a permanent interaction, ranging from close co-operation
to open conflict.

What then was the community? To attempt to answer that
question is to realize the hopeless imprecision of the concept.
The community, it has been well said, 'has never been and can
never be.'[4] Like the general will of the philosopher, it was never
more than an imperfectly realized intellectual concept. It was
based on a community of interest; but the identity of aspiration
which was the cement of the community was generally restricted
in character, limited in point of time and negative in its aim.
It had to compete with the alternative aspirations and ambitions of individual members of the community; it had to resolve
the conflicting interests between members of the community
itself. The community had few or none of the juristic features of

general his introduction to his translation of Otto Gierke, *Political Theories of the
Middle Ages* (Cambridge, 1900) and his essays in *The Collected Papers of F. W.
Maitland*, III.

[3] W. Schlesinger in *Lordship and Community in Medieval Europe*, ed. F. L. Cheyette,
65.

[4] J. C. Holt on the community of the realm in 'Rights and Liberties in Magna
Carta', *Album Helen Maud Cam* (Studies presented to the International Commission
for the History of Representative and Parliamentary Institutions 23, Louvain
1960), 57–69 at p. 66.

the corporation.[5] Moreover we would do better to speak of community than of *the* community, for community was multiple not singular in its form. Each individual was at one and the same time a member of a number of overlapping communities: those of kin, race, status, neighbourhood, economic interest and lordship, to name but some of the communities which have figured in previous chapters. Furthermore behind the language of 'community' aspiration it is only too easy to detect on occasion the handiwork and ambitions of individuals, more especially of the leaders of the community. It was such men alone who were capable of standing up to the lord, of articulating their grievances in generalized terms and of presenting those grievances as the demands of community. The opposition to the lord of Gower in the opening years of the fourteenth century was led by some of the most prominent men of the county; in Chirkland in 1330 the petition against Mortimer misrule came from the community as a whole but it was clearly prompted by men of note in the community such as Ednyfed Gam, Madoc Llwyd and Master Gruffudd Trefor; in Chepstow in 1415 the opposition to the size of the general fine to be granted to the lord was led by the local prior.[6] Such men were the leaders of the community in more senses than one. It was from 'the more honest, more noble and more trustworthy' men of the community that the lord would choose his pledges for the good behaviour of the community;[7] it was from their number that men would be chosen to act as proctors in the community's negotiations with the lord and his council or to witness charters on behalf of and to the community.[8] In such circumstances, community could be and no doubt often was no more than a synonym for the ambitions of its more powerful numbers.

That may be so; but we must not construe the role of com-

[5] See in general F. Pollock and F. W. Maitland, *The History of English Law*, I, 617–34

[6] *Glam. C.H.*, III, 232–41 (Gower); J.Y.W. Lloyd, *A History of Powys Fadog*, IV, 17ff. (Chirkland); *The Marcher Lordships of South Wales, 1415–1536*, ed. T. B. Pugh, 63–4 (Chepstow).

[7] 'probiores et nobiliores et fideidigniores': D.L. 42/1, fol. 28–28ᵛ (Denbigh, 1283).

[8] For example of proctors chosen by the community see D.L. 25/1661 (Kidwelly, 1415: 'procuratour et poursuour pour les communes et tenauntz'); D.L. 42/18 fol. 264ᵛ (Ogmore, 1426); for representatives sealing an indenture on behalf of the community see *B.B.C.S.* 23 (ii) (1969), 166 (Chirkland, 1355).

munity in too narrow or cynical a fashion. Community involved the pursuit of common interest, albeit on a restricted front. So it is that the community of the vill could hold land in common, lease vacant land, take over the land previously held in the name of the kin-group or arrange for the repair of the parish church.[9] The community in one of its many forms was often the supervisor of the affairs of its members and the guardian of the communal well-being. The community could prosecute an individual for not doing his share of a communal duty;[10] it could assess individual contributions towards communal renders;[11] it could determine whether a member of the community ought to hold more land or not, whether another was too poor to pay rent or ought to be exempted from the payment of entry fines;[12] it could petition as a body for the right to distribute sheaves to a neighbour and kinsman;[13] it could even depose one of its members from what was grandly termed the *collegia communitatis* when he contracted leprosy.[14] Above all it was in its relationship with lordship that the role of community appeared at its most crucial; for in the regulation of the life of the *patria*, community was the obvious and essential counterweight to lordship.

The relationship between lord and community was established at the first entry of the lord into his lordship. 'And the said William (de Warenne) on the same day received the homage individually of [twenty-nine named Welshmen] as their true lord (*verus dominus*) and afterwards the whole community made their homage with hands joined and raised unanimously (*tota communitas patrie manibus iunctis et levatis unanimiter homagia sua fecerunt*)'.[15] So was forged in the most solemn and symbolic fashion the bond of lordship and community. It was a mutual bond: the community was expected to show 'good will', and

[9] For examples see respectively *T.D.H.S.* 17 (1968), 45 (Dyffryn Clwyd, 1324); *S.D.*, xxvii–xxviii (Denbigh, 1334); *Extent of Chirkland 1391–3*, 10; S.C. 2/216/5, m. 26 (community of vill and parish of Cyffylliog, Dyffryn Clwyd, 1325).

[10] S.C. 2/218/2, m. 18: Community of Coelion *v.* three of its members concerning their contribution to the puture of foresters, 1351.

[11] See above, p. 357.

[12] For examples see respectively S.C. 2/218/7, m. 19 (Dyffryn Clwyd, 1359); S.R.O. 552/1/27, m. 4–m.4ᵛ (*bis*) (Clun, 1397).

[13] S.R.O. 552/1/7, m. 2 (Clun, 1336).

[14] S.C. 2/217/14, m. 10 (Dyffryn Clwyd, 1349).

[15] C. 133/47, no. 13. The ceremony took place at Wrexham on 3 August 1284.

'humble obedience' to the lord, while the qualities expected of lordship were 'goodness' and favour. The interplay of community and lordship was a constant feature of governance. The officers of the lordship were the lord's servants but most of them were also members of the community and could be prosecuted by it.[16] Any extraordinary financial demand that the lord made required, in some form or other, a measure of negotiation and probably of consent by the community through its proctors. In judicial matters, likewise, whereas the courts were primarily agencies of lordship, the law itself was declared by the suitors of the court; while the jury-system ensured that guilt or innocence lay within the competence of the community (*veredictum patrie*), not of the lord.[17] The power of lordship in the March, as elsewhere, operated within a context of community liberties and conventions.

Ideally lord and community should be at one; 'good lordship' was the best guarantee of a contented community. Where that was not so, it might be due to the defiance of the community as well as to the wilfulness of lordship. The community might refuse to meet the lord's financial demands: the community of Hay Welshry, for example, claimed that the lord could not commute their cow tribute (*commorth*) at a higher rate than seven shillings a cow.[18] In such circumstances there was little the lord could do, for there was a limit to the effectiveness of distraint or to the impact of threatening letters to officials. Unacceptable seignorial demands not infrequently went unpaid; they formed part of that list of arrears and of dues respited or atterminated with which each seignorial financial account closes. The community likewise challenged the lord's interpretation of his rights on such issues as mills, forests, waste and escheats. The community of Ceri, for example, claimed that escheated land belonged to the community (*patria*) not to the lord, when such land was held by Welsh tenure.[19]

A measure of friction was a permanent feature of lordship-community relationship. It was the essence of 'good lordship'

[16] Thus in 1346 the community of bondmen of Aberwheeler laid petitions against their sergeant in the exchequer at Ruthin and he was fined £20: S.C. 2/217/11, m. 1ᵛ.

[17] See above pp. 158–63.

[18] S.C. 6/1156/21, m. 1ᵛ (1374).

[19] S.C. 6/1209/6 (1336).

that it did not allow such friction to escalate into open conflict. That might be achieved by a timely and graceful concession to the community: in 1341 the earl of Hereford was told that his tenants of Brecon could not pay a massive backlog of arrears and he magnanimously cancelled debts totalling £663.[20] Sensitive lordship was also displayed by wooing the community to grant a subsidy to the lord rather than bludgeoning it with an arbitrary demand.[21] Above all the relationship between lordship and community was improved by the grant or the confirmation of a charter of liberties. Such charters of liberties survive for many of the major Marcher lordships.[22] They correspond closely in form and in intention to the charters of

[20] D.L. 29/671/10810, m.5–m.5ᵛ. For detailed analysis of seignorial policy on arrears in one district see R. R. Davies in *Ec.H.R.*, 2nd ser. 21 (1968), 211–29, esp. 223–5.

[21] Such negotiations were not mere formalities. In 1417 a deputation of two leading Duchy of Lancaster officials escorted by thirty men, spent six days at Kidwelly, four at Brecon and three at Monmouth during negotiations for a subsidy: D.L. 42/17, fol. 126; D.L. 29/615/9845; D.L. 29/731/12026. There is a revealing eye-witness account of the conduct of such negotiations in a letter of 1377 in *Anglo-Norman Letters and Petitions*, ed. M. D. Legge, 163–4.

[22] Among charters of liberties which are either extant or referred to are the following (sums in bracket indicate the gift given by the community for the charters):

Brecon: confirmed 1297: *Cal. Anc. Corr. conc. Wales*, ed. J. G. Edwards, 101.

Cemais: to all free men, both English and Welsh 1278: *Baronia de Kemeys. From Original Documents at Bronwydd* (Cambrian Archaeological Association, 1861), 57–60.

Chirkland: to freemen, 1324 (1,600 marks); confirmed and augmented 1334 (1,600 marks); temporarily suspended; confirmed and augmented 1355 (1,200 marks). For texts of originals and of later translations see Llinos Smith, 'The Arundel Charters to the Lordship of Chirk in the Fourteenth Century', *B.B.C.S.* 23 (ii) (1969), 153–66.

Clun: to Welshmen of Tempseter 1292 (£200); brief charter on number of officers to be appointed 1317: T. Salt, 'Ancient Documents relating to the Honor, Forest and Borough of Clun', *Transactions of the Shropshire Archaeological and Natural History Society* 11 (1887–8), 244–72.

Denbigh: reference to 'the many benefits, concessions, favours and liberties' granted to the men of the lordship 1310 (£800): D.L. 42/1, fol. 29–fol. 29ᵛ.

Dyffryn Clwyd: reference to 'common charter' granted to 'all his English tenants' by Reginald Grey (i.e. pre-1308): S.C. 2/217/10, fol. 23ᵛ; reference to a charter 'to all free Welsh tenants' granted by the same Reginald Grey: S.C. 2/219/3, m. 25.

Gower: 'to all . . . tenants and their tenants and their men, both Welsh and English, within the bounds of our English county of Gower' 1306: *Cartae*, III, no. 851; to Welsh tenants of Gower Iscoed, 1348: *Sir Christopher Hatton's Book of Seals*, ed. L. C. Loyd and D. M. Stenton (Oxford, 1950), no. 398.

Kidwelly, Iscennen and Carnwyllion: 'to all our Welsh tenants', 1356 (£300): D.L. 42/16, fol. 43ᵛ–fol. 45ᵛ.

franchises to French rural communities.[23] They involved a deliberate self-limiting act on the part of the lord for henceforth his authority would be specifically limited by the liberties he had granted to the community. In juridical terms their interest lies in the fact that they recognized that the community as a body could negotiate with the lord and extract concessions from him. In substantive terms they allow us to glimpse briefly the anxieties and aspirations of the community and to identify those areas—such as law, rights of bail, forests, escheats, the numbers of officers and the administration of justice—where the claims of lordship and community overlapped and conflicted. They were granted under a variety of circumstances—sometimes under the pressure of a political crisis, sometimes in response to royal intervention, sometimes as an act of seignorial magnanimity, often in return for a massive gift to the lord, and always in response to community instigation. This latter fact serves to remind us that in its relationship with lordship the community by no means necessarily occupied a passive role or even a weaker bargaining position.

Charters of liberties acted as safety-valves in the relationship of lordship and community; where those safety-valves failed to operate rebellion was the outcome. In the context of the social relationships of the March in the later Middle Ages, rebellion represented the rejection of lordship by the community or at least by a community, the severance of the bond on which obligations and authority were based. When the men of Gwynllwg and Machen refused to do homage and fealty to the younger Despenser in 1317, they were in effect refusing to accept his lordship; when the tenants of Powys refused to obey John Charlton in 1323 the community was rejecting the

Maelienydd: Granted 1297 (£500): *C.P.R. 1292–1301*, 290. Confirmed 1314: B.L. Harleian 1240, fol. 58.

Pembroke: referred to in B.L. Harleian 433, fol. 300. See *Cat. MSS. Wales in B.M.*, II, 151.

Talgarth, Ystradyw, Crickhowell: granted 1299 (a hundred marks): E. 326/B.8812; *Descriptive Catalogue of the Charters and Muniments at Berkeley Castle*, ed. I. H. Jeayes (Bristol, 1892), no. 462.

Tidenham: granted 1305; confirmed 1415 (£20): *The Marcher Lordships of South Wales 1415–1536*, ed. T. B. Pugh, 73–4.

[23] See C. E. Perrin, 'Les Chartes des franchises de la France', *Revue Historique* 231 (1964), 27–54. Also *Les Libertés urbaines et rurales du XIe au XIVe siècle* (Brussels, 1968) and the review of it in *Annales. Économies, sociétés, civilisations* 26 (ii) (1971), 1308–14.

dominium of its lord.[24] Nowhere perhaps do we recapture more clearly this contemporary concept and terminology of rebellion than in the agreements which Henry Lacy, earl of Lincoln, concluded with his tenants of Denbigh after the Welsh wars of 1282–3 and 1294–5. On both occasions it was to the 'community' that the Earl granted his peace and remitted his indignation and rancour; on both occasions the community for its part pledged itself in massive recognizances that it would firmly observe the peace towards the lord; on both occasions what effectively happened was the renewal of the contract between lordship and community, temporarily severed by rebellion.[25] That contract was severely strained on several occasions in the fourteenth century but it was not again formally broken until the rebellion of Owain Glyn Dŵr. That rebellion has been interpreted in many ways—as a noble conspiracy, as a peasants' revolt, as an anti-colonial uprising, and as a national rebellion; but in contemporary terms it may and should be explained structurally as the collapse of the relationship between lordship and community.

To say so is not merely to restate the obvious in different words. The nature of any rebellion can only be properly understood in terms of the pattern of authority against which it is in revolt; and in the March of Wales in the fourteenth century that pattern was determined by the character of the relationship between lordship and community in the broadest possible sense. In parts of the March by 1400 the demands of lordship, especially its financial demands, had put unbearable strains on the native community while the aspirations of that community and of its leaders remained unsatisfied. Lordship was demanding rather than good; thereby the alienation of lordship and community was completed.

In terms of lordship and society in the March and of the relationship between the two the revolt of Glyn Dŵr and its aftermath proved to be a watershed.[26] Within Marcher society, as we have indicated above, the revolt precipitated profound

[24] *C.P.R. 1317–21*, 60; *1321–4*, 307, 340.

[25] D.L. 25/2063–64, partly published in F. Jones, 'Welsh Bonds for Keeping the Peace, 1283 and 1295', *B.B.C.S.* 13 (1948–50), 142–4.

[26] I hope to develop the ideas suggested in the remainder of this paragraph at greater length elsewhere and with more supporting evidence.

social transformations which were already afoot and undermined the relevance of the social and legal distinctions upon which Marcher governance in the fourteenth century had been based. In terms of Marcher lordship its impact was equally far-reaching. Militarily it presented a challenge which the Marcher lords were quite incapable of meeting individually; it thereby compelled the king of England to devise a common military policy for March and Principality alike. Constitutionally, the revolt highlighted the worst aspects of Marcher *morcellement* and thereby called forth from the English parliament one of the first fundamental questionings of the liberties of the March. Financially, both in the short run and in the longer perspective, it undermined the structure of Marcher finances; never was Marcher lordship again so profitable as it had been before 1400. More profoundly the revolt and its consequences coincided with and contributed towards a change in the character of lordship in the March of Wales. Lordship had ceased to be 'good'; it had also ceased to be effective. It failed to provide that protection which is of the essence and justification of lordship. In that situation the community looked elsewhere for protection. On the one hand the king of England came to serve as an alternative or at least an additional focus of lordship for Marcher communities and an increasingly attractive one in terms of authority, protection and patronage. On the other hand, the local squirearchy steadily emerged as a focus of command and of worship in the local community and that often to the detriment and at the expense of the lords of the March. Never again would the Marcher lords exercise so powerful and so effective a lordship in the March of Wales as they had done so in the fourteenth century.

Bibliography

THIS list is intended to include only such manuscripts, books and articles as are mentioned in the text or footnotes. The main manuscripts outside the Public Record Office have been briefly described and where no description is given it may be assumed that the manuscript consists of a collection of deeds or other miscellaneous material. Full bibliographies of relevant printed material (both primary and secondary sources) relating to the March of Wales are available in *A Bibliography of the History of Wales*, 2nd edn. (Cardiff, 1962), with supplements in subsequent volumes of *The Bulletin of the Board of Celtic Studies*, and in E. B. Graves, *A Bibliography of English History to 1485* (Oxford, 1975).

A. MANUSCRIPT SOURCES

i. *Public Record Office*

Chancery

C. 47	Miscellanea
C. 133–139	Inquisitions Post Mortem Edward I–Henry VI

Duchy of Lancaster

D.L. 7	Inquisitions Post Mortem
D.L. 10	Royal Charters
D.L. 25	Deeds, series L
D.L. 27	Deeds, series LS
D.L. 28	Accounts Various
D.L. 29	Ministers' Accounts
D.L. 30	Court Rolls
D.L. 36	Cartae Miscellaneae
D.L. 37	Chancery Rolls
D.L. 40	Return of Knights' Fees
D.L. 41	Miscellanea
D.L. 42	Miscellaneous Books
D.L. 43	Rentals and Surveys

Exchequer

E. 42	Ancient Deeds, series A. 5
E. 101	King's Remembrancer, Accounts Various
E. 159	K.R. Memoranda Rolls
E. 163	K.R. Miscellanea

E. 179   K.R. Subsidy Rolls
E. 326   Augmentations, Ancient Deeds, series B
Judicial Records
C.P. 25 (1)   Common Pleas, Feet of Fines
J.I. 1   Justices Itinerant, Assize Rolls
K.B. 27   King's Bench, Plea Rolls
Land Revenue Office
L.R. 2   Officers of the Auditors of Land Revenue, Miscellaneous Books
Palatinate of Chester
Chester 2   Recognizance Rolls
Chester 3   Inquisitions Post Mortem
Chester 25   Plea Rolls
Chester 30   Indictment Rolls
Special Collections
S.C. 2   Court Rolls
S.C. 6   Ministers' Accounts
S.C. 8   Ancient Petitions
S.C. 11   Rentals and Surveys, Rolls
S.C. 12   Rentals and Surveys, Portfolios

ii. *British Library*
Additional Charters
    8636; 20403; 20435–40; 28645; 74399.
Additional Manuscripts
    6041 (List of Mortimer muniments)
    10013 (Survey of Bromfield and Yale, 1391. Later copies of parts of this survey are to be found in N.L.W. Peniarth 404D. and N.L.W. Wynnstay L.1307)
    46846 (a late-fifteenth-century commonplace book from north-east Wales)
Cotton Charters, XI, 61
Cotton Nero A IV (*Chronicon Laudanenses*)
Egerton Rolls and Charters 8704–72 (Thoresby Park Collection, relating mainly to the Mortimer estates)
Harleian Manuscripts
    1240 (Cartulary of the Mortimer family)
    1970 (Miscellaneous transcripts including Oswestry court roll of 1382–3)
    1977 (A collection of Welsh pedigrees)
    1981 (Transcripts relating to Oswestry)
    3325 (Transcripts relating to Brecon collected by the antiquary, Hugh Thomas)
    4843 (Kniveton's History of the Earls of Arundel)

5058 (A seventeenth-century genealogical collection)
Lansdowne Collection I (a volume of sixteenth-century transcripts)
Royal Manuscripts 11 A. XI (a formulary book).

iii. *National Library of Wales, Aberystwyth*
Aston Hall Collection
Badminton Deeds and Documents
Badminton Manorial Records
Bettisfield Collection
Chirk Castle Muniments
Kentchurch Court Papers and Documents
Muddlescombe Deeds
Peniarth Manuscripts
Plas Iolyn Collection
Plas yn Cefn Collection
Puleston Collection
Quaritch Collection
Radnor Account Roll
Roger Lloyd Deeds
Slebech Deeds and Accounts
Wynnstay Collection

iv. *Cardiff Free Library*
Brecon Documents, 2 (Rental of Hay, 1340)

v. *East Sussex Record Office, Lewes*
Glynde Place Collection

vi. *Flintshire Record Office, Mold*
Trevor-Roper Collection

vii. *Hereford Cathedral Archives, Hereford*
Miscellaneous Deeds

viii. *Monmouth Record Office, Newport*
Capel Hanbury Collection
Llanarth Court Collection

ix. *Northumberland Record Office*
Swinburne (Capheaton) Collection

x. *Nottinghamshire Record Office, Nottingham*
The Miss B. E. Chambers Donation (D.D. 325. Includes account rolls of Earl Thomas of Lancaster's estates, 1317).

xi. *Shropshire Record Office, Shrewsbury*
Acton of Aldenham Collection 1093 (Valuation of Arundel estates, 1349).
Powis Collection (552/1. Accounts and court rolls of Arundel estates in the March of Wales).

xii. *Shrewsbury Public Library*
Craven Collection (including accounts relating to lordship of Oswestry).
xiii. *Staffordshire Record Office, Stafford*
Lord Stafford Collection (D. 641. Accounts and court rolls of the Stafford estates in the March).
xiv. *University College of North Wales, Bangor*
Kinmel Collection
Mostyn Collection
Penrhyn Collection
Whitney Collection

B. PRINTED SOURCES
(Place of publication is London unless otherwise stated.)
Abbreviatio Placitorum, ed. G. Rose and W. Illingworth (Record Commission, 1811).
Ancient Laws and Institutes of Wales, ed. Aneurin Owen, 2 vols. (Record Commission, 1841).
Anglo-Norman Letters and Petitions from All Souls MS. 182, ed. M. D. Legge (Anglo-Norman Text Society, No. 3, Oxford, 1941).
Anglo-Norman Political Songs, ed. Isabel S. T. Aspin (Anglo-Norman Text Society, No. 11, Oxford, 1953).
Annales sex regum Angliae, 1135–1307, ed. T. Hog (English Historical Society, 1845).
Annales Cambriae, ed. J. Williams ab Ithel (Rolls Series, 1860).
Annales Monastici, ed. H. R. Luard, 5 vols. (Rolls Series, 1864–9).
Archaeologia Cambrensis. Supplement Volume of Original Documents (1877).

Baronia de Kemeys, ed. T. D. Lloyd (Cambrian Archaeological Society, 1861).
Black Book of St. David's, ed. J. W. Willis-Bund (Cymmrodorion Record Series, No. 5, 1902).
Brenhinedd y Saesson or The Kings of the Saxons, ed. T. Jones (Cardiff, 1971).
Brut y Tywysogyon (Peniarth MS. 20), ed. T. Jones (Cardiff, 1941).
Brut y Tywysogyon or The Chronicle of the Princes (Red Book of Hergest Version), ed. T. Jones (Cardiff, 1955).

Calendar of Ancient Correspondence concerning Wales, ed. J. G. Edwards (Cardiff, 1935).
Calendar of Chancery Rolls Various, 1277–1326 (1912).
Calendar of Chancery Warrants, 1244–1326 (1927).
Calendar of Charter Rolls (1903–)

Calendar of Close Rolls (1892–)

Calendar of Fine Rolls (1911–)

Calendar of Inquisitions Miscellaneous (1916–)

Calendar of Inquisitions Post Mortem (1904–)

Calendar of Patent Rolls (1891–)

Calendar of the Gormanston Register c. *1175–1397*, ed. J. Mills and M. J. McEnery (Dublin, 1916).

Calendar of the Public Records relating to Pembrokeshire, ed. H. Owen, 3 vols. (Cymmrodorion Record Series, No. 7, 1911–18).

Cartae et alia munimenta quae ad dominium de Glamorgancia pertinent, ed. G. T. Clark, 6 vols. (Cardiff, 1910).

Catalogue of Ancient Deeds, 6 vols. (1890–1915).

Catalogue of Charters and Muniments at Berkeley Castle, ed. I. H. Jeayes (1892).

Catalogue of Manuscripts relating to Wales in the British Museum, ed. E. Owen, 4 vols. (Cymmrodorion Record Series, No. 4, 1900–22).

Charters granted to the Chief Borough of Swansea, ed. G. G. Francis (1867).

Chronicles of the Reigns of Edward I and Edward II, ed. W. Stubbs, 2 vols. (Rolls Series, 1882–3).

Chronicles of the Reigns of Stephen, Henry II and Richard I, ed. R. Howlett, 4 vols. (Rolls Series, 1884–9).

Chronicon Adae de Usk, ed. E. Maunde Thompson (1904).

Chronicon Anglicanum Radulphi de Coggeshall, ed. J. Stevenson (Rolls Series, 1875).

COLE, E. J., 'Account of the Keeper of Radnor Castle, 9–10 Edward III', *Trans. Radnorshire Society*, 33 (1963), 36–43; 'Maelienydd, 30–31 Edward III', ibid. 34 (1964), 31–9.

Collection of all the Wills of the Kings and Queens of England, ed. J. Nichols (1780).

Court Rolls of the Lordship of Ruthin or Dyffryn-Clwyd of the Reign of Edward I, ed. R. A. Roberts (Cymmrodorion Record Series, No. 2, 1893).

Crecy and Calais (1346–7) From the Public Records, ed. G. Wrottesley (William Salt Archaeological Collections, 18, part 2, 1897).

Cywyddau Dafydd ap Gwilym a'i Gyfoeswyr, ed. I. Williams and T. Roberts (Cardiff, 1935).

Cywyddau Iolo Goch ac Eraill, ed. H. Lewis, T. Roberts and I. Williams, 2nd edn. (Cardiff, 1937).

Documents Illustrative of English History in the Thirteenth and Fourteenth Century, ed. H. Cole (1844).

Domesday Book, ed. A. Farley, 2 vols. (1783).

DWNN, Lewys, *Heraldic Visitations of Wales*, ed. S. R. Meyrick, 2 vols. (Llandovery, 1846).

Early Chancery Proceedings concerning Wales, ed. E. A. Lewis (Cardiff, 1937).
Early Welsh Genealogical Tracts, ed. P. C. Bartrum (Cardiff, 1966).
English Historical Documents, vol. 2, 1042–1189, ed. D. C. Douglas and G. W. Greenaway (1953).
Episcopal Acts Relating to the Welsh Dioceses, 1066–1272, 2 vols. ed. J. Conway Davies (Historical Society of the Church in Wales, Cardiff, 1946–8).
Estate Book of Henry de Bray, ed. Dorothy Willis (Camden Society, 3rd series, No. 27, 1916).
Exchequer Proceedings (Equity) concerning Wales, Henry VIII–Elizabeth, ed. E. G. Jones (Cardiff, 1939).
Extent of Chirkland, 1391–93, ed. G. P. Jones (Liverpool, 1933).

First Extent of Bromfield and Yale A.D. 1315, ed. T. P. Ellis (Cymmrodorion Record Series, No. 11, 1924).
Fitzalan Surveys. Two Estate Surveys of the Fitzalan Earls of Arundel, ed. M. Clough (Sussex Record Society, No. 67, 1969).
Foedera, Conventiones, Litterae etc., ed. T. Rymer. Third edition, 10 vols. (The Hague, 1739–45). Revised edition by A. Clarke, F. Holbrooke and J. Coley, 4 vols. in 7 parts (Record Commission, 1816–69).

GIRALDUS CAMBRENSIS, *Opera*, ed. J. S. Brewer, J. F. Dimock and G. F. Warner, 8 vols. (Rolls Series, 1861–91).
Gwaith Guto'r Glyn, ed. I. Williams and J. Ll. Williams (Cardiff, 1939).
Gwaith Lewis Glyn Cothi, vol. 1, ed. E. D. Jones (Cardiff and Aberystwyth, 1953).
Gwaith Tudur Penllyn ac Ieuan ap Tudur Penllyn, ed. T. Roberts (Cardiff, 1958).

Herefordshire Domesday, c. 1160–70, ed. V. H. Galbraith and J. Tait (Pipe Roll Society, new ser. No. 25, 1950).

Issues of the Exchequer, Henry III–Henry IV, ed. F. Devon (Record Commission, 1847).

John of Gaunt's Register, 1372–6, ed. S. Armitage-Smith, 2 vols. (Camden Society, 3rd ser. vols. 20–2, 1911).

John of Gaunt's Register, 1379–83, ed. E. C. Lodge and R. Somerville, 2 vols. (Camden Society, 3rd ser. vols. 56–7, 1937).

LELAND, John, *The Itinerary in Wales in or about the years 1536–9*, ed. L. Toulmin Smith (1966).
LE STRANGE, Hamo, *Le Strange Records A.D. 1100–1310* (1916).
LIEBERMANN, F., *Die Gesetze der Angelsachsen*, 3 vols. (Halle, 1903–16).
Littere Wallie, ed. J. G. Edwards (Cardiff, 1940).
Llyfr Colan, ed. D. Jenkins (Cardiff, 1963).
Llyfr Iorwerth, ed. A. R. Wiliam (Cardiff, 1960).
Lordship of Oswestry, 1393–1607, ed. W. J. Slack (Shrewsbury, 1951).

Memoranda de Parliamento, 1305, ed. F. W. Maitland (Rolls Series, 1893).
MERRICK, Rice, *A Booke of Glamorganshire Antiquities*, ed. J. A. Corbett (1887).
'Ministers' Accounts for the lordships of Abergavenny, Grosmont, Skenfrith and White Castle, 1256–7', ed. A. J. Roderick and W. Rees, *South Wales and Monmouth Record Society*, vols. 2–4 (Cardiff, 1950–7).
Monasticon Anglicanum, ed. W. Dugdale. Revised edn. by J Caley, H. Ellis and B. Bandinel, 6 vols. (1830).

Oeuvre poétique de Gutun Owain, ed. E. Bachélery, 2 vols. (Paris, 1950–1).
OSCHINSKY, D., *Walter of Henley and Other Treatises on Estate Management and Accounting* (Oxford, 1971).
OWEN, George, *The Description of Penbrokeshire*, ed. H. Owen, 4 vols. (Cymmrodorion Record Series, No. 1, 1902–36).

PARIS, Matthew, *Chronica Majora*, ed. H. R. Luard, 7 vols. (Rolls Series, 1872–83).
Pipe Roll, 31 Henry II (Pipe Roll Society, No. 34, 1913).
Placito de Quo Warranto, Edward I–Edward III, ed. W. Illingworth (Record Commission, 1818).
POWEL, David, *The Historie of Cambria* (1584), ed. W. Wynne (1784).

Record of Caernarvon. Registrum vulgariter nuncupatum 'The Record of Caernarvon', ed. H. Ellis (Record Commission, 1838).
Records of the Court of Augmentations relating to Wales and Monmouthshire, ed. E. A. Lewis and J. Conway Davies (Cardiff, 1954).
Register of Edward, the Black Prince, 4 vols. (1930–3).

Registrum Epistolarum fratris Johannis Peckham, ed. C. T. Martin. 3 vols. (Rolls Series, 1882–5).

Registrum Johannis de Trilleck (Hereford), *1344–61*, ed. J. H. Parry (Canterbury and York Society, No. 8, 1912).

Rhagymadroddion 1547–1659, ed. G. H. Hughes (Cardiff, 1951).

Rotuli Hundredorum, 2 vols. (Record Commission, 1812–18).

Rotuli Parliamentorum, 7 vols. (Record Commission, 1783–1832).

SALT, T., 'Ancient Documents relating to the Honor, Forest and Borough of Clun', *Shropshire Archaeological and Natural History Society*, 11 (1887–8), 244–72.

Select Cases concerning the Law Merchant, ed. C. Gross and H. Hall, 3 vols. (Selden Society, 1908–32).

Select Cases in the Court of the King's Bench, ed. G. O. Sayles, 7 vols. (Selden Society, 1936–71).

Select Pleas in Manorial and Other Seignorial Courts, ed. F. W. Maitland (Selden Society, 1888).

Sir Christopher Hatton's Book of Seals, ed. L. C. Loyd and D. M. Stenton (1950).

Survey of the Duchy of Lancaster Lordships in Wales, 1609–13, ed. W. Rees (Cardiff, 1953).

Survey of the Honour of Denbigh 1334, ed. P. Vinogradoff and F. Morgan (British Academy Records of Social and Economic History, No. 1, 1914).

Valor Ecclesiasticus, ed. J. Caley, 6 vols. (Record Commission, 1810–1834).

Vita Edwardi Secundi: The Life of Edward the Second by the So-called Monk of Malmesbury, ed. N. Denholm-Young (1957).

The Welsh Assize Roll 1277–84, ed. J. Conway Davies (Cardiff, 1940).

WYNN, John, *History of the Gwydir Family*, ed. J. Ballinger (Cardiff, 1927).

Year Book, 12 Edward II, ed. J. P. Collas (Selden Society, 1964).

Year Book, 11 Richard II, ed. I. D. Thornley (Ames Foundation, 1937).

C. SECONDARY WORKS

ALCOCK, L., *Dinas Powys* (Cardiff, 1963).

ALTSCHUL, M., *A Baronial Family in Medieval England. The Clares 1217–1314* (Baltimore, 1965).

Angles and Britons. O'Donnell Lectures by J. R. R. Tolkien, T. H. Parry-Williams, Kenneth Jackson, B. G. Charles, N. K. Chadwick and William Rees (Cardiff, 1963).

BAKER, A. R. H. and BUTLIN, R. A. (ed.), *Studies of Field Systems in the British Isles* (Cambridge, 1973).

BALLARD, A. TAIT, J. and WEINBAUM, M. (ed.), *British Borough Charters, 1042–1660*, 3 vols. (Cambridge, 1913–43).

BARRACLOUGH, G., *The Earldom and County Palatine of Chester* (Oxford, 1953).

BARROW, G. W. S., 'Northern English Society in the Twelfth and Thirteenth Centuries', *Northern History* 4 (1969), 1–28.

— 'The Pattern of Lordship and Feudal Settlement in Cumbria', *Journal of Medieval History* 1 (1975), 117–38.

BATESON, M., 'The Laws of Breteuil', *E.H.R.* 15 (1900), 73–8, 302–18, 496–523, 754–7; 16 (1901), 82–110, 332–45.

BEAN, J. M. W., *The Estates of the Percy Family 1416–1537* (1958).

— *The Decline of English Feudalism 1215–1540* (Manchester, 1968).

BERESFORD, M. W., *New Towns of the Middle Ages* (1967).

BERESFORD, M. W. and HURST, J. G. (eds.), *Deserted Medieval Villages* (1971).

BLOCH, M., *French Rural Society* (1966).

— 'The Rise of Dependent Cultivation and Seignorial Institutions', *Cambridge Economic History of Europe*, vol. I, 2nd edn. (Cambridge, 1966), pp. 235–90.

— *Land and Work in Medieval Europe* (1967).

BOUTRUCHE, R., *Seigneurie et féodalité*, 2 vols. (Paris, 1959–70).

BRADNEY, J. A., *A History of Monmouthshire*, 4 vols. (1904–33).

BRIDBURY, A. R., *Economic Growth. England in the Later Middle Ages* (1962).

BROWN, R. A., COLVIN, H. M., and TAYLOR, A. J. (eds.), *The History of the King's Works. The Middle Ages*, 2 vols. (1963).

CAM, H. M., 'The Medieval English Franchise', *Speculum*, 32 (1957), 427–44.

CARR, A. D., 'The Barons of Edeyrnion, 1282–1485', *Journal of the Merionethshire Historical and Record Society*, 4 (1963–4), 187–93, 289–301.

— 'Medieval Dinmael', *T.D.H.S.* 13 (1964), 9–21.

— 'Welshmen and the Hundred Years' War', *W.H.R.* 4 (1968–9), 21–46.

CARTER, H., *The Towns of Wales. A Study in Urban Geography* (Cardiff, 1965).

CARUS-WILSON, E. M., *Medieval Merchant Venturers*, 2nd edn. (1967).

CHARLES, B. G., *Non-Celtic Place-Names in Wales* (1938).

— 'The Records of the Borough of Newport in Pembrokeshire', *N.L.W.J.*, 7 (1951–2), 33–45, 120–37.

— 'The Welsh, their Language and Placenames in Archenfield and Oswestry', *Angles and Britons* (Cardiff, 1963).

— 'The Early Ancestors of the Owen of Henllys Family', *N.L.W.J.* 17 (1971–2), 115–19.

— *George Owen of Henllys: A Welsh Elizabethan* (Aberystwyth, 1973).

CHARLES-EDWARDS, T. M., 'Some Celtic Kinship Terms', *B.B.C.S.* 24 (1970–2), 107–12.

— 'Kinship, Status and the Origins of the Hide', *Past and Present*, 56 (1972), 3–33.

COKAYNE, G. E., *Complete Peerage of England, Scotland, Ireland, Great Britain and the United Kingdom*. New edn. by V. Gibbs and others, 12 vols. (1910–59).

CRASTER, O. E. and LEWIS, J. M., 'Hen Gwrt Moated Site, Llantilio Crossenny, Mon.', *Arch. Camb.* 112 (1969), 159–83.

DARBY, H. C. (ed.), *A New Historical Geography of England* (Cambridge, 1973).

DAVIES, J. Conway, 'The Despenser War in Glamorgan', *T.R.H.S.* 3rd ser. 9 (1915), 21–64.

— *The Baronial Opposition to Edward II, its Character and Policy* (Cambridge, 1918).

— 'Some unpublished documents', *N.L.W.J.* 3 (1942–3), 29–32, 158–62.

— 'Lordships and Manors in the County of Montgomery', *Mont. Colls.* 49 (1946), 74–151.

DAVIES, R. R., 'The Bohun and Lancaster Lordships in Wales in the Fourteenth and Early Fifteenth Centuries' (University of Oxford D.Phil. Thesis, 1965).

'The Twilight of Welsh Law, 1284–1536', *History* 51 (1966), 143–64.

— 'Owain Glyn Dŵr and the Welsh Squirearchy', *T.C.S.* (1968) (ii), 150–69.

— 'Baronial Accounts, Incomes and Arrears in the Later Middle Ages', *Econ. H.R.* 2nd ser. 21 (1968), 211–29.

— 'The Survival of the Bloodfeud in Medieval Wales', *History* 54 (1969), 338–57.

— 'The Law of the March' *W.H.R.* 5 (1970–1), 1–30.

— 'Colonial Wales', *Past and Present* 65 (1974), 3–23.

— 'Race Relations in Post-Conquest Wales: Confrontation and Compromise', *T.C.S.* (1974–5), 32–56.

DENHOLM-YOUNG, N., *Seignorial Administration in England* (Oxford, 1937).

The Dictionary of Welsh Biography down to 1940 (1959).

DODD, A. H., 'Welsh and English in East Denbighshire: A Historical Retrospect', *T.C.S.* (1940), 34–65.

DU BOULAY, F. R. H. and BARRON, C. M. (eds.), *The Reign of Richard II. Essays in Honour of May McKisack* (1971).

DUBY, G., *L'Économie rurale et la vie des campagnes dans l'occident médieval* (Paris, 1962. English translation by Cynthia Postan, 1968).

DUGDALE, W., *The Baronage of England*, 2 vols. (1674–5).

EDWARDS, J. G., 'Taxation and Consent in the Court of Common Pleas, 1338', *E.H.R.* 57 (1942), 473–82.

— 'The Normans and the Welsh March', *Proceedings of the British Academy*, 42 (1956), 155–77.

— *The Principality of Wales 1267–1967. A Study in Constitutional History* (Caernarvon, 1969).

ELTON, G. R., *England under the Tudors* (1955).

EMDEN, A. B., *A Biographical Register of the University of Oxford to A.D. 1500*, 3 vols. (Oxford, 1957–9).

EMERY, F. V., 'West Glamorgan Farming circa 1580–1620', *N.L.W.J.* 9 (1955–6), 392–400; 10 (1956–7), 17–32.

EVANS, B., 'A Grant of Privileges to Wrexham (1380)', *B.B.C.S.* 19 (1960–2), 42–7.

— 'The Medieval Liberty of Wrexham', *T.D.H.S.* 10 (1961), 236–8.

EVANS, B. P., 'The Family of Mortimer' (University of Wales Ph.D. thesis, 1934).

EVANS, D. L., 'Some Notes on the History of the Principality of Wales in the Time of the Black Prince, 1343–76', *T.C.S.* (1925–6), 25–110.

EYTON, R. W., *Antiquities of Shropshire*, 12 vols. (1853–60).

FAIRBANK, E. R., 'The Last Earl of Warenne and Surrey and the Distribution of his Possessions', *Yorkshire Archaeological Journal*, 19 (1907), 193–267.

FAITH, R. J., 'Peasant Families and Inheritance Customs in Medieval England', *Agricultural History Review*, 14 (1966), 77–93.

FINBERG, H. P. R., 'An Early Reference to the Welsh Cattle Trade', *Agricultural History Review*, 2 (1954), 12–14.

FOSTER, I. Ll. and DANIEL, G. (eds.), *Prehistoric and Early Wales* (1965).

FOWLER, K. A., *The King's Lieutenant. Henry of Grosmont, First Duke of Lancaster 1310–61* (1969).

FOX, R., *Kinship and Marriage* (Harmondsworth, 1967).

FRANCIS, E. A. (ed.), *Studies in Medieval French Presented to Alfred Ewert in Honour of his Seventieth Birthday* (Oxford, 1961).

FRASER, C. M., *A History of Antony Bek* (Oxford, 1957).

— 'Prerogative and the Bishops of Durham, 1267–1376', *E.H.R.* 74 (1959), 467–76.

GENICOT, L., 'La Noblesse au moyen-âge dans l'ancienne Francie', *Annales économies, societés, civilisations,* 17 (1961), 1–22.

GIERKE, O., *The Political Theories of the Middle Age.* Translated and introduced by F. W. Maitland (Cambridge, 1900).

GOODY, J. (ed.), *Kinship* (1972).

GOODMAN, A., *The Loyal Conspiracy. The Lords Appellant under Richard II* (1971).

GRESHAM, C. A., 'The Bolde Rental (Bangor MS., 1939)', *Transactions of the Caernarvonshire Historical Society,* 26 (1965), 31–49.

— *Medieval Stone Carving in North Wales* (Cardiff, 1968).

GRIFFITHS, R. A., 'Royal Government in the Southern Counties of the Principality of Wales 1422–85' (University of Bristol Ph.D. thesis, 1962).

— 'The Rise of the Stradlings of St. Donat's', *Morgannwg,* 7 (1963), 15–47.

— 'The Cartulary and Muniments of the Fort Family of Llanstephan', *B.B.C.S.* 24 (1970–2), 311–84.

— *The Principality of Wales in the Later Middle Ages. The Structure and Personnel of Government: South Wales, 1277–1536* (Cardiff, 1972).

HARDING, A., *The Law Courts of Medieval England* (1973).

HEERS, J., *L'Occident au quatorzième et quinzième siècles. Aspects économiques et sociaux.* 1st and 2nd edns. (Paris, 1963, 1973).

HEWITT, H. J., *Medieval Cheshire: An Economic and Social History of Cheshire in the Reigns of the Three Edwards* (Manchester, 1929).

HILTON, R. H., 'Old Enclosures in the West Midlands', *Géographie et histoire agraires* (Nancy, 1959).

— 'Rent and Capital Formation in Feudal Society', *Proceedings of the Second International Conference of Economic History, Aix-en-Provence,* 2 (1962), 33–68.

— 'Freedom and Villeinage in England', *Past and Present,* 31 (1965), 3–19.

— *A Medieval Society: the West Midlands at the End of the Thirteenth century* (1967).

— *The Decline of Serfdom in Medieval England* (Studies in Economic History, 1969).
— *Bond Men Made Free. Medieval Peasant Movements and the English Rising of 1381* (1973).
HOGG, A. H. A. and KING, D. J. C., 'Early Castles in Wales and the Marches', *Arch. Camb.* 112 (1963), 77–124.
— 'Masonry Castles in Wales and the March', ibid. 116 (1967), 71–132.
— 'Castles in Wales and the Marches: Additions and Corrections', ibid. 119 (1970), 119–24.
HOLLISTER, C. W., *The Military Organisation of Norman England* (Oxford, 1965).
HOLMES, G. A., 'A Protest against the Despensers, 1326', *Speculum* 30 (1955), 207–12.
— *The Estates of the Higher Nobility in Fourteenth-Century England* (Cambridge, 1957).
HOLT, J. C., 'Rights and Liberties in Magna Carta', *Album Helen Maud Cam. Studies Presented to the International Commission for the History of Representative and Parliamentary Institutions*, 23 (Louvain, 1960), 57–69.
— *The Northerners* (Oxford, 1961).
HOMANS, G. C., *English Villagers of the Thirteenth Century* (New York, 1941).
HOSKINS, W. G. (ed.), *Studies in Leicestershire Agrarian History* (Leicester Archaeological Society, 1948).
HOWELL, Margaret, 'Regalian Right in Wales and the March: The Relation of Theory to Practice, *W.H.R.* 7 (1974–5), 269–88.
HOWELLS, B. E., 'Pembrokeshire Farming, circa 1580–1620', *N.L.W.J.* 9 (1955–6), 239–50, 313–33, 413–39.
— 'The Distribution of Customary Acres in South Wales', ibid. 15 (1967–8), 226–33.
HURNARD, N. D., *The King's Pardon for Homicide before A.D. 1307* (Oxford, 1969).

JACK, R. I., 'Entail and Descent: The Hastings Inheritance, 1370–1436', *Bulletin of the Institute of Historical Research* 38 (1965), 1–19.
— 'The Lordship of Dyffryn Clwyd in 1324', *T.D.H.S.* 17 (1968), 7–53.
— 'Welsh and English in the Medieval Lordship of Ruthin', *T.D.H.S.* 18 (1969), 23–49.
JENKINS, D., 'A Lawyer Looks at Welsh Land Law', *T.C.S.* (1967) (ii), 220–48.
Cyfraith Hywel (Llandysul, 1970).

JOLLIFFE, J. E. A., 'Northumbrian Institutions', *E.H.R.* 41 (1926), 1–43.

JONES, E. D., 'The Cefnllys Poems of Lewis Glyn Cothi', *Transactions of the Radnorshire Society* 6 (1936), 15–27.

JONES, F., 'An Approach to Welsh Genealogy', *T.C.S.* (1948), 303–466.

— 'Welsh Bonds for Keeping the Peace, 1283 and 1295', *B.B.C.S.* 13 (1948–50), 142–4.

JONES, G. R. J., 'The Tribal System in Wales: A Re-assessment in the Light of Settlement Studies', *W.H.R.* 1 (1960–2), 111–32.

— 'The Llanynys Quillets: A Measure of Landscape Transformation in North Wales', *T.D.H.S.* 13 (1964), 133–58.

— 'The Distribution of Bond Settlements in North Wales', *W.H.R.* 2 (1964–5), 19–37.

JONES, J. R., The Development of the Penrhyn Estate up to 1431 (University of Wales M.A. thesis, 1955).

JONES, P. J., 'From Manor to Mezzadria: A Tuscan Case-Study in the Medieval Origins of Modern Agrarian Society', *Florentine Studies*, ed. N. Rubinstein (1968), 193–241.

KEEN, M. H., *The Laws of War in the Late Middle Ages* (1965).

KING, E. J., *Peterborough Abbey 1086–1310. A Study in the Land Market* (Cambridge, 1973).

KOSMINSKY, E. A., *Studies in the Agrarian History of England in the Thirteenth Century* (Oxford, 1956).

LAPSLEY, G. T., *The County Palatine of Durham* (New York, 1900).

LENNARD, R., *Rural England 1086–1135* (Oxford, 1959).

LEWIS, E. A., 'The Decay of Tribalism in North Wales', *T.C.S.* (1902–3) 1–75.

— 'The Development of Industry and Commerce in Wales during the Middle Ages', *T.R.H.S.*, new ser. 17 (1903), 121–75.

— *The Medieval Boroughs of Snowdonia* (1912).

— 'A Contribution to the Commerical History of Medieval Wales', *Y Cymmrodor*, 24 (1913), 86–188.

LEWIS, I. M., 'Force and Fission in North Somali Lineage Structure', *American Anthropologist*, 63 (1961), 94–112.

— *Les Libertés urbaines et rurales du XIe au XIVe siècles* (Brussels, 1968).

LLOYD, J., *The Great Forest of Brecknock* (1905).

LLOYD, J. E., *A History of Wales from the Earliest Times to the Edwardian Conquest*, 2 vols. (1911).

— *Owen Glendower. Owain Glyn Dŵr* (Oxford, 1931).

LLOYD, E. J. (ed.), *A History of Carmarthenshire*, I (Cardiff, 1935).

LLOYD, J. Y. W., *History of the Princes, the Lords Marcher and the Ancient Nobility of Powys Fadog*, 6 vols. (1881–7).

LLOYD, T. H., *The Movement of Wool Prices in Medieval England* (Economic History Review Supplement, 6, 1973).

MCFARLANE, K. B., 'The Wars of the Roses', *Proceedings of the British Academy* 50 (1964), 87–119.

— *Lancastrian Kings and Lollard Knights* (Oxford, 1972).

— *The Nobility of Later Medieval England* (Oxford, 1973).

MADDICOTT, J. R., *Thomas of Lancaster 1307–1322. A Study in the Reign of Edward II* (Oxford, 1970).

MADOX, T., *Baronia Anglica: An History of Land-Honors and Baronies and of Tenure in Capite* (1736).

MAITLAND, F. W., *Township and Borough* (Cambridge, 1898).

— *Collected Papers*, H. A. L. Fisher, 3 vols. (Cambridge, 1911).

— *Selected Historical Essays*, ed. H. M. Cam (Cambridge, 1957).

— *Domesday Book and Beyond*, with an introduction by E. Miller (1960).

MATTHEW, G., *The Court of Richard II* (1968).

MILLWARD, R. and ROBINSON, A., *The Welsh Marches* (1971).

MORRIS, J. E., *The Welsh Wars of Edward I* (Oxford, 1901).

MUSGRAVE, C. A., 'Household Administration in the Fourteenth Century, with Special Reference to the Household of Elizabeth de Burgh, Lady of Clare' (University London M.A. thesis, 1923).

NICHOLLS, K., *Gaelic and Gaelicised Ireland in the Middle Ages* (Dublin, 1972).

OTWAY-RUTHVEN, A. J., 'The Constitutional Position of the Great Lordships of South Wales', *T.R.H.S.*, 5th ser. 8 (1958), 1–20.

OWEN, D. H., 'The Lordship of Denbigh 1282–1425' (University of Wales Ph.D. thesis, 1967).

— 'Tenurial and Economic Developments in North Wales in the Twelfth and Thirteenth Centuries', *W.H.R.* 6 (1972–3), 117–44.

— 'The Englishry of Denbigh: An English Colony in Medieval Wales', *T.C.S.* (1974–5), 57–76.

OWEN, H. and BLAKEWAY, J. B., *History of Shrewsbury*, 2 vols. (1825).

PAINTER, S., *Studies in the History of the English Feudal Barony* (Baltimore, 1943).

PALMER, A. N. and OWEN, E., *A History of Ancient Tenures of Land in the Marches of Wales*, 2nd edn. (Wrexham, 1910).

PATTERSON, D. R., 'Scandinavian Influence in the Place-Names and Early Personal Names of Glamorgan', *Arch. Camb.*, 6th ser. 20 (1920), 31–9.
— 'The Scandinavian Settlement of Cardiff', ibid. 7th ser. 1 (1921), 53–83.
— 'The Pre-Norman Settlement of Glamorgan', ibid. 7th ser. 2 (1922), 37–60.
PERRIN, C. E., 'Les Chartes des franchises de la France', *Revue Historique* 231 (1964), 27–54.
PEVSNER, N., *The Buildings of England. Herefordshire* (1963).
PHILLIPS, J. R. S., *Aymer de Valence, Earl of Pembroke 1307–24* (Oxford, 1972).
PIERCE, T. JONES, *Medieval Welsh Society*, ed. J. B. Smith (Cardiff, 1973).
PLUCKNETT, T. F. T., *The Legislation of Edward I* (Oxford, 1949).
— *The Medieval Bailiff* (Creighton Lecture in History, 1953).
POLLOCK, F. and MAITLAND, F. W., *The History of English Law Before the Time of Edward I*, 2 vols. 2nd edn. with introduction by S. F. C. Milsom (Cambridge, 1968).
POSTAN, M. M. (ed.), *Cambridge Economic History of Europe, I. The Agrarian Life of the Middle Ages*, 2nd edn. (Cambridge, 1966).
POSTAN, M. M., RICH, E. E., and MILLER, E. (eds.), *Cambridge Economic History of Europe, III. Economic Organisation and Policies in the Middle Ages* (Cambridge, 1963).
POWICKE, F. M., *King Henry III and the Lord Edward*, 2 vols. (Oxford, 1947).
— *The Thirteenth Century 1216–1307* (Oxford, 1953).
PRATT, D., 'The Medieval Water Mills of Wrexham', *T.D.H.S.* 13 (1964), 22–37.
PRESTWICH, M. C., *War, Politics and Finance under Edward I* (1972).
PUGH, T. B., 'The "Indenture for the Marches", between Henry VII and Edward Stafford (1477–1521), Duke of Buckingham', *E.H.R.* 71 (1956), 436–41.
— *The Marcher Lordships of South Wales, 1415–1536. Select Documents* (Cardiff, 1963).
— (ed.), *Glamorgan County History, III. The Middle Ages* (Cardiff, 1971).

RAFTIS, J. A., *The Estates of Ramsey Abbey* (Toronto, 1957).
REES, W., 'The Medieval Lordship of Brecon', *T.C.S.* (1915–16), 165–244.
— 'The Black Death in Wales', *T.R.H.S.* 4th ser. 3 (1920), 115–35.

— *South Wales and the March, 1284–1415. A Social and Agrarian Study* (Oxford, 1924).
— 'The Charters of the Boroughs of Brecon and Llandovery', *B.B.C.S.* 2 (1923–5), 243–61.
— 'A Bibliography of Published Work on the Municipal History of Wales and the Border', ibid. 321–82.
— *A Map of South Wales and the Border in the Fourteenth Century.* 4 sheets (Ordnance Survey, 1932).
— *The Union of England and Wales* (Cardiff, 1948).
— *An Historical Atlas of Wales* (Cardiff, 1951).
— 'Gower and the March of Wales', *Arch. Camb.* 110 (1961), 1–30.
RENNELL, LORD OF RODD, *Valley on the March. A History of a Group of Manors on the Herefordshire March of Wales* (Oxford, 1958).
RICHARDS, M., 'The Population of the Welsh Border', *T.C.S.* (1970) (i), 77–100.
ROBERTS, Glyn, *Aspects of Welsh History* (Cardiff, 1969).
ROBERTS, Enid P., 'Teulu Plas Iolyn', *T.D.H.S.* 13 (1964), 39–110.
    'Tŷ Pren Glân mewn top Bryn Glas', ibid. 22 (1973), 24 48.
RODERICK, A. J., 'Marriage and Politics in Wales, 1066–1282', *W.H.R.* 4 (1968–9), 1–20.
ROUND, J. H., *Family Origins and Other Studies* (1930).

SALZMAN, L. F., 'The Property of the Earl of Arundel, 1397', *Sussex Archaeological Collections* 91 (1953), 32–53.
SANDERS, I. J., 'The Boroughs of Aberystwyth and Cardigan in the Early Fourteenth Century', *B.B.C.S.* 15 (1952–4), 282–93.
— *English Baronies. A Study of their Origin and Descent 1086–1327* (Oxford, 1960).
SCAMMELL, J., 'The Origins and Limitations of the Liberty of Durham', *E.H.R.* 81 (1966), 449–73.
SEYLER, C. A., 'The Early Charters of Swansea and Gower', *Arch. Camb.*, 7th ser. 4 (1924), 59–79, 299–325; 5 (1925), 157–76.
SMITH, J. B., 'The Lordship of Glamorgan' (University of Wales M.A. thesis, 1958).
— 'The Lordship of Glamorgan', *Morgannwg*, 2 (1958), 9–38.
— 'Crown and Community in the Principality of North Wales in the Reign of Henry Tudor', *W.H.R.* 3 (1966–7), 145–71.
— 'Cydfodau o'r Bymthegfed Ganrif', *B.B.C.S.* 21 (1966), 309–24.
— 'The Middle March in the Thirteenth Century', ibid. 24 (1970–2), 77–93.
— 'Cydfodau o'r Bymthegfed Ganrif, Testunau Ychwanegol', ibid. 25 (1973), 128–34.
SMITH, Llinos, 'The Arundel Charters to the Lordship of Chirk in the

Fourteenth Century', *B.B.C.S.* 23 (1968–70), 153–66.
— 'The Lordship of Chirk and Oswestry, 1282–1415' (University of London Ph.D. thesis, 1971).
SMITH, P., *Houses of the Welsh Countryside. A Study in Historical Geography* (1975).
SMITH, P. and HAGUE, D. B., 'Tŷ Draw, Llanarmon Mynydd Mawr', *Arch. Camb.* 107 (1958), 109–26.
SOMERVILLE, R., *History of the Duchy of Lancaster, I: 1265–1603* (1953).
SPURGEON, C. J., 'Gwyddgrug Castle, Forden and the Gorddwr Dispute', *Mont. Colls.* 57 (1961–2), 125–37.
— 'The Castles of Montgomeryshire', ibid. 59 (1965–6), 1–60.
STENTON, F. M., *The First Century of English Feudalism*, 2nd edn. (Oxford, 1961).
— *Anglo-Saxon England*, 3rd edn. (Oxford, 1971).
STRAYER, J. R. and RUDISILL, G., jnr., 'Taxation and Community in Wales and Ireland 1272–1307', *Speculum*, 29 (1954), 410–16.
SYLVESTER, D., *The Rural Landscape of the Welsh Borderland. A Study in Historical Geography* (1969).

TAYLOR, J., 'A Wigmore Chronicle, 1355–77', *Proceedings of the Leeds Philosophical and Literary Society* (*Literary and Historical Section*), 11 (1964–6), 84–6.
THIRSK, J. (ed.), *The Agrarian History of England and Wales, IV, 1500–1640* (Cambridge, 1967).
THOMAS, C., 'Enclosure and the Rural Landscape of Merioneth in the Sixteenth Century', *Transactions of the Institute of British Geographers*, 42 (1967), 153–62.
— 'Social Organisation and Rural Settlement in Medieval North Wales', *Journal of the Merioneth Historical and Record Society* 6 (1970), 121–31.
TOUT, T. F., *Collected Papers of Thomas Frederick Tout*, 3 vols. (Manchester, 1932–4).

Victoria County History of Leicestershire I, ed. W. G. Hoskins (Oxford, 1954).
Victoria County History of Shropshire I, ed. A. T. Gaydon (Oxford, 1973).

WALKER, D. G., 'The "Honours" of the Earls of Hereford in the Twelfth Century', *Transactions of the Bristol and Gloucestershire Archaeological Society*, 79 (1960), 174–211.
— 'Ralph Son of Pichard', *Bulletin of the Institute of Historical Research*, 33 (1960), 195–202.

— 'Charters of the Earldom of Hereford, 1095–1201', *Camden Miscellany*, 22 (Camden Society, 4th ser. 1964), 1–75.

WALKER, R. F., 'Hubert de Burgh and Wales, 1218–32', *E.H.R.* 87 (1972), 465–94.

WARD, J. C., 'The Estates of the Clare Family, 1066–1317' (University of London Ph.D. thesis, 1962).

WILLARD, J. F., MORRIS, W. A., STRAYER, J. R. and DUNHAM, W. H., jnr., *The English Government at Work*, 3 vols. (Cambridge, Mass., 1940–50).

WILLIAMS, C. R. (ed.), *History of Flintshire, I* (Denbigh, 1961).

WILLIAMS, Glanmor, *The Welsh Church from Conquest to Reformation* (Cardiff, 1962).

WILLIAMS, J., *Records of Denbigh and its Lordship* (Wrexham, 1860).

SUPPLEMENTARY ITEMS

Since this volume was originally submitted for publication, the following important items bearing on topics discussed in it have been published.

REES, W. (ed.), *Calendar of Ancient Petitions Relating to Wales* (Cardiff, 1975). Calendars most of the Ancient Petitions (S.C.8) referred to in this book.

SMITH, Llinos Beverley, 'The Gage and the Land Market in Late Medieval Wales', *Econ.H.R.* 2nd. ser. 29 (1976), 537–50. Provides an admirable introduction to the legal and economic aspects of *prid*.

WILLIAMS-JONES, K., *The Merioneth Lay Subsidy Roll 1292–3* (Cardiff, 1976). An outstanding study of the economy and society of Gwynedd in the late thirteenth-fourteenth centuries.

Index

(The entries in capitals, e.g. BRECON, refer to the major lordships referred to in this book. Place names are identified by referring in brackets to the lordships in which they were located, e.g. Swansea (Gower)).